C000126748

The Works of William Blake, Poetic, Symbolic, and Critical

WILLIAM BLAKE.

FROM A PORTRAIT OF BLAKE BY HIS WIFE.

*facsimile from the original by the kind permission of
Mr. Horne of the Hobby-Horse-Guild.*

THE WORKS

OF

WILLIAM BLAKE

Poetic, Symbolic, and Critical

EDITED WITH LITHOGRAPHS OF THE ILLUSTRATED
"PROPHETIC BOOKS," AND A MEMOIR
AND INTERPRETATION

BY

EDWIN JOHN ELLIS

Author of " Fate in Arcadia," &c.

AND

WILLIAM BUTLER YEATS

Author of " The Wanderings of Oisin," " The Countess Kathleen," &c.

" Bring me to the test
And I the matter will re-word, which madness
Would gambol from "

Hamlet

IN THREE VOLS.

VOL. III

LONDON
BERNARD QUARITCH, 15 PICCADILLY
1893

[All Rights Reserved]

LIBRARY OF THE UNIVERSITY

50938

B 636
V. 3

CONTENTS OF VOLUME III.

FRONTISPIECE :—FROM A PORTRAIT OF BLAKE BY HIS WIFE, FACSIMILE FROM THE ORIGINAL MADE BY KIND PERMISSION OF MR. HORNE OF THE HOBBY HORSE GUILD.

There is no Natural Religion.

Facsimiles and Reproductions.

TIRIEL.

Reproductions, continued.

VALA.

POETICAL SKETCHES, ETC.

POETICAL SKETCHES.

KING EDWARD THE THIRD.

PERSONS.

KING EDWARD.	SIR THOMAS DAGWORTH.
THE BLACK PRINCE.	SIR WALTER MANNY.
QUEEN PHILIPPA.	LORD AUDLEY.
DUKE OF CLARENCE.	LORD PERCY.
SIR JOHN CHANDOS.	BISHOP.

WILLIAM, *Dagworth's man.*

PETER BLUNT, *a common soldier.*

SCENE I.—*The Coast of France.*

KING EDWARD *and Nobles before it. The Army.*

KING.

O thou to whose fury the nations are
But as the dust ! maintain thy servant's right.
Without thine aid, the twisted mail, and spear,
And forgèd helm, and shield of beaten brass,
Are idle trophies of the vanquisher.
When on the field in flame, confusion rages,
When cries of blood tear horror out of heaven,
And yelling Death runs up and down the ranks,
Let Liberty, the chartered right of Englishmen,
Won by our fathers in many a glorious field,
Enerve my soldiers ; then let Liberty
Blaze in each countenance, and fire the battle.
The enemy fight in chains, unseen, but heavy ;
Their minds are fettered ; then how can they be free?
While, like the mounting flame,
We spring to battle o'er the floods of death!
And these fair youths, the flower of England,
Venturing their lives in my most righteous cause,
Oh sheathe their hearts with triple steel, that they
May emulate their fathers' virtues ! Thou

My son, be strong; thou fightest for a crown
That death can never ravish from thy brow,
A crown of glory—From thy very dust
Shall beam a radiance, to fire the breasts
Of youth unborn ! Our names are written equal
In Fame's wide-trophied hall ; 'tis ours to gild
The letters, and to make them shine with gold
That never tarnishes: whether Third Edward,
The Prince of Wales, Montacute, Mortimer,
Or ev'n the least by birth, shall gain the brightest fame,
Is in His hand to whom all men are equal.
The world of men are like the numerous stars
That beam and twinkle in the depth of night,
Each clad in glory according to his sphere;
But we, that wander from our native seats
And beam forth lustre on a darkling world,
Grow large as we advance : and some perhaps
The most obscure at home, that scarce were seen
To twinkle in their sphere, may so advance
That the astonished world, with upturned eyes,
Regardless of the moon, and those once bright,
Stand only for to gaze upon their splendour,

      [*He here knights the Prince and other young Nobles.*
Now let us take a just revenge for those
Brave Lords who fell beneath the bloody axe
At Paris. Noble Harcourt, thanks, for 'twas
By your advice we landed here in Brittany,
A country not yet sown with destruction,
And where the fiery whirlwind of swift war
Has not as yet swept its desolating wing.—
Into three parties we divide by day,
And separate march, but join again at night :
Each knows his rank, and Heaven marshal all

                    [*Exeunt.*

SCENE II.—*English Court.*

LIONEL, DUKE OF CLARENCE, QUEEN PHILIPPA,
Lords, Bishop, &c.

CLARENCE.

My Lords, I have by the advice of her
Whom I am doubly bound to obey, my parent
And my sovereign, called you together.
My task is great, my burden heavier than
My unfledged years ;
Yet with your kind assistance, Lords, I hope
England shall dwell in peace : that, while my father
Toils in his wars, and turns his eyes on this
His native shore, and sees commerce fly round
With his white wings, and sees his golden London

And her silver Thames, thronged with shining spires
And corded ships, her merchants buzzing round
Like summer bees, and all the golden cities
O'erflowing with their honey, in his land
Glory may not be dimmed with clouds of care.
Say, Lords, should not our thoughts be first to commerce?
You, my Lord Bishop, would have agriculture?

BISHOP.

Sweet Prince, I know the arts of peace are great,
And no less glorious than those of war,
Perhaps more, in the philosophic mind.
When I sit at my home, a private man,
My thoughts are on my gardens and my fields,
How to employ the hand that lacketh bread.
If Industry is in my diocese,
Religion will flourish; each man's heart
Is cultivated and will bring forth fruit:
This is my private duty and my pleasure.
But, as I sit in council with my prince,
My thoughts take-in the general good of the whole,
And England is the land favoured by Commerce;
For Commerce, though the child of Agriculture,
Fosters his parent, who else must sweat and toil,
And gain but scanty fare.   Then, my dear Lord,
Be England's trade our care; and we, as tradesmen
Looking to the gain of this our native land.

CLARENCE.

O my good Lord, true wisdom drops like honey
From off your tongue, as from a worshipped oak !
Forgive, my Lords, my talkative youth, that speaks
Not merely from my narrow observation,
But what I have concluded from your lessons
Now, by the Queen's advice, I ask your leave
To dine to-morrow with the Mayor of London
If by your leave, I have another boon
To ask,—the favour of your company.
I fear Lord Percy will not give me leave

PERCY.

Dear Sir, a prince should always keep his state,
And grant his favours with a sparing hand,
Or they are never rightly valued.
These are my thoughts: yet it were best to go:
But keep a proper dignity, for now
You represent the sacred person of
Your father; 'tis with princes as with the sun,
If not sometimes o'erclouded, we grow weary
Of his officious glory

CLARENCE.

Then you will give me leave to shine sometimes,
My Lord ?

LORD (*aside*).

Thou hast a gallant spirit, which I fear
Will be imposed on by the closer sort.

CLARENCE

Well, I'll endeavour to take
Lord Percy's advice ; I have been used so much
To dignity that I'm sick on't.

QUEEN PHILIPPA.

Fie, fie, Lord Clarence ! you proceed not to business,
But speak of your own pleasures.
I hope their lordships will excuse your giddiness.

CLARENCE.

My Lords, the French have fitted out many
Small ships of war that, like to ravening wolves,
Infest our English seas, devouring all
Our burdened vessels, spoiling our naval flocks.
The merchants do complain, and beg our aid

PERCY.

The merchants are rich enough ;
Can they not help themselves ?

BISHOP.

They can, and may; but how to gain their will
Requires our countenance and help.

PERCY.

When that they find they must, my Lord, they will :
Let them but suffer awhile, and you shall see
They will bestir themselves.

BISHOP.

Lord Percy cannot mean that we should suffer
Disgrace like this. If so, we are not sovereigns
Of the sea,—our right, a right that Heaven gave
To England, when at the birth of Nature
She in the deep was seated ; Ocean ceased
His mighty roar, and, fawning, played around
Her snowy feet, and owned his awful Queen.
Lord Percy, if the heart is sick, the head
Must be aggrieved; if but one member suffer,
The heart doth fail. You say, my Lord, the merchants
Can, if they will, defend themselves against
These rovers : this must be a noble scheme,
Worthy the brave Lord Percy, and as worthy
His generous aid to put it into practice.

PERCY

Lord Bishop, what was rash in me is wise
In you ; I dare not own the plan. 'Tis not

Mine. Yet will I, if you please,
Quickly to the Lord Mayor, and work him onward
To this most glorious voyage; on which cast
I'll set my whole estate,
But we will bring these Gallic rovers under.

QUEEN PHILIPPA.

Thanks, brave Lord Percy; you have the thanks
Of England's Queen, and will, ere long, of England.

[Exeunt.

SCENE III.—At Cressy.

SIR THOMAS DAGWORTH and LORD AUDLEY meeting.

AUDLEY.

Good-morrow, brave Sir Thomas; the bright morn
Smiles on our army, and the gallant sun
Springs from the hills like a young hero leaping
Into the battle, shaking his golden locks
Exultingly: this is a promising day.

DAGWORTH.

Why that, my good Lord Audley, I don't know.
Give me your hand, and now I'll tell you what
I think you do not know. Edward's afraid
Of Philip.

AUDLEY.

Ha, ha! Sir Thomas! you but joke;
Did you e'er see him fear? At Blanchetaque,
When almost singly he drove six thousand
French from the ford, did he fear then?

DAGWORTH.

Yes, fear.

That made him fight so.

AUDLEY.

By the same reason I might say 'tis fear
That makes you fight.

DAGWORTH.

Mayhap you may. Look upon Edward's face,
No one can say he fears; but, when he turns
His back, then I will say it to his face;
He is afraid: he makes us all afraid.
I cannot bear the enemy at my back.
Now here we are at Cressy; where to-morrow?
To-morrow we shall know. I say, Lord Audley,
That Edward runs away from Philip.

AUDLEY.

Perhaps you think the Prince too is afraid?

DAGWORTH.

No; God forbid! I am sure he is not.
He is a young lion. Oh I have seen him fight

And give command, and lightning has flashed
From his eyes across the field : I have seen him
Shake hands with Death, and strike a bargain for
The enemy , he has danced in the field
Of battle, like the youth at morris-play.
I'm sure he's not afraid, nor Warwick, nor none, .
None of us but me, and I am very much afraid

AUDLEY.

Are you afraid, too, Sir Thomas ? I believe that
As much as I believe the King's afraid :   .
But what are you afraid of ?

DAGWORTH

Of having my back laid open; we must turn
Our backs to the fire, till we shall burn our skirts

.   **AUDLEY.**

And this, Sir Thomas, you call fear ?   Your fear
Is of a different kind, then, from the King's ;   •
He fears to turn his face, and you to turn your back.
I do not think, Sir Thomas, you know what fear is

Enter Sir John Chandos.

CHANDOS.

Good-morrow, Generals; I give you joy :
Welcome to the fields of Cressy. Here we stop,
And wait for Philip.

DAGWORTH.
I hope so.

AUDLEY.

There, Sir Thomas ; do you call that fear ?

DAGWORTH.

I don't know ; perhaps he takes it by fits.
Why, noble Chandos, look you here—
One rotten sheep spoils the whole flock ;
And if the bell-wether is tainted, I wish
The Prince may not catch the distemper too.

CHANDOS.

Distemper, Sir Thomas !   What distemper ?
I have not heard.

DAGWORTH.

Why, Chandos, you are a wise man,
I know you understand me ; a distemper
The King caught here in France of running away.

AUDLEY.

Sir Thomas, you say you have caught it too.

DAGWORTH.

And so will the whole army ; 'tis very catching,
For, when the coward runs, the brave man totters.

Perhaps the air of the country is the cause.
I feel it coming upon me, so I strive against it,
You yet are whole; but, after a few more
Retreats, we all shall know how to retreat
Better than fight.—To be plain, I think retreating
Too often takes away a soldier's courage.

CHANDOS.

Here comes the King himself: tell him your thoughts
Plainly, Sir Thomas

DAGWORTH.

I've told him this before, but his disorder
Has made him deaf.

    Enter KING EDWARD *and* BLACK PRINCE.

KING.

Good-morrow, Generals; when English courage
Shall fail, down goes at once our right to France.
But we are conquerors everywhere; nothing
Can stand before our soldiers; each is worthy
Of a triumph. Such an army,—heroes all,—
Ne'er shouted to the heavens, nor shook the field.
Edward, my son, thou art, among us here
Most happy, having such command: the man
Were more than base who were not fired to deeds
Above heroic, having such examples.

PRINCE.

Sire, with respect and deference I look
Upon such noble souls, and wish myself
Worthy the high command that Heaven and you
Have given me. When I've seen the field a-glow,
And in each countenance the soul of war
Curbed by the manliest reason, I've been winged
With certain victory; and 'tis my boast,
And shall be still my glory, I was inspired
By these brave troops.

DAGWORTH.

      Your Grace had better make them
All Generals.

KING.

Sir Thomas Dagworth, you must have your joke
And shall, while you can fight as you did at
The Ford.

DAGWORTH.

I have a small petition to your Majesty.

KING.

What can Sir Thomas Dagworth ask
That Edward can refuse?

DAGWORTH.

I hope your Majesty cannot refuse so great
A trifle; I've gilt your cause with my best blood,
And would again, were I not forbid
By him whom I am bound to obey: my hands
Are tied up, all my courage shrunk and withered,
My sinews slackened, and my voice scarce heard;
Therefore I beg I may return to England.

KING.

I know not what you could have asked, Sir Thomas,
That I would not have sooner parted with
Than such a soldier as you, and such a friend:
Nay, I will know the most remote particulars
Of this your strange petition; that, if I can,
I still may keep you here.

DAGWORTH.

Here on the fields of Cressy we are settled
Till Philip springs the timorous covey again.
The wolf is hunted down by causeless fear;
The lion flees, and fear usurps his heart,
Startled, astonished at the clamorous cock;
The eagle, that doth gaze upon the sun,
Fears the small fire that plays about the fen.
If, at this moment of their idle fear,
The dog doth seize the wolf, the forester the lion,
The negro in the crevice of the rock
Doth seize the soaring eagle; undone by flight,
They tame submit: such the effect flight has
On noble souls. Now hear its opposite:
The timorous stag starts from the thicket wild,
The fearful crane springs from the splashy fen,
The shining snake glides o'er the bending grass,
The stag turns head, and bays the crying hounds;
The crane o'ertaken fighteth with the hawk;
The snake doth turn, and bite the padding foot.
And if your Majesty's afraid of Philip,
You are more like a lion than a crane:
Therefore I beg I may return to England.

KING.

Sir Thomas, now I understand your mirth,
Which often plays with wisdom for its pastime,
And brings good counsel from the breast of laughter.
I hope you'll stay and see us fight this battle,
And reap rich harvest in the fields of Cressy;
Then go to England, tell them how we fight,
And set all hearts on fire to be with us.
Philip is plumed, and thinks we flee from him,

Else he would never dare to attack us. Now,
Now the quarry's set! and Death doth sport
In the bright sunshine of this fatal day.

DAGWORTH.

Now my heart dances, and I am as light
As the young bridegroom going to be married.
Now must I to my soldiers, get them ready,
Furbish our armours bright, new-plume our helms;
And we will sing like the young housewives busied
In the dairy. Now my feet are wing'd, but not
For flight, an please your grace.

KING.

If all my soldiers are as pleased as you,
'Twill be a gallant thing to fight or die;
Then I can never be afraid of Philip.

DAGWORTH.

A raw-boned fellow t' other day passed by me;
I told him to put off his hungry looks—
He said, "I hunger for another battle."
I saw a little Welshman, fiery-faced;
I told him he looked like a candle half
Burned out; he answered, he was "*pig* enough
"To light another *pattle*." Last night, beneath
The moon I walked abroad, when all had pitched
Their tents, and all were still;
I heard a blooming youth singing a song
He had composed, and at each pause he wiped
His dropping eyes   The ditty was, "If he
Returned victorious, he should wed a maiden
Fairer than snow, and rich as midsummer."
Another wept, and wished health to his father..
I chid them both, but gave them noble hopes.
These are the minds that glory in the battle;
And leap and dance to hear the trumpet sound.

KING.

Sir Thomas Dagworth, be thou near our person
Thy heart is richer than the vales of France!
I will not part with such a man as thou.
If Philip came armed in the ribs of death,
And shook his mortal dart against my head,
Thou'dst laugh his fury into nerveless shame!
Go now, for thou art suited to the work,
Throughout the camp; inflame the timorous,
Blow up the sluggish into ardour, and
Confirm the strong with strength, the weak inspire,
And wing their brows with hope and expectation:
Then to our tent return, and meet to council.

[*Exit* DAGWORTH.

CHANDOS.

That man's a hero in his closet, and more
A hero to the servants of his house
Than to the gaping world; he carries windows
In that enlargèd breast of his, that all
May see what's done within.

PRINCE.

He is a genuine Englishman, my Chandos,
And hath the spirit of Liberty within him.
Forgive my prejudice, Sir John; I think
My Englishmen the bravest people on
The face of the earth.

CHANDOS.

Courage, my Lord, proceeds from self-dependence.
Teach every man to think he's a free agent.
Give but a slave his liberty, he'll shake
Off sloth, and build himself a hut, and hedge
A spot of ground; this he'll defend; 'tis his
By right of Nature. Thus being set in action,
He will move on to plan conveniences,
Till glory fires him to enlarge his castle;
While the poor slave drudges all day, in hope
To rest at night.

KING.

O Liberty, how glorious art thou!
I see thee hovering o'er my army, with
Thy wide-stretched plumes; I see thee lead them on;
I see thee blow thy golden trumpet while
Thy sons shout the strong shout of victory!
O noble Chandos, think thyself a gardener,
My son a vine, which I commit unto
Thy care. Prune all extravagant shoots, and guide
The ambitious tendrils in the path of wisdom;
Water him with thy clear advice, and Heaven
Rain freshening dew upon his branches! And,
O Edward, my dear son! think lowly of
Thyself, as we may all each prefer other—
'Tis the best policy, and 'tis our duty.

[*Exit* KING EDWARD.

PRINCE.

nd may our duty, Chandos, be our pleasure.—
Now we are alone, Sir John, I will unburden
And breathe my hopes into the burning air,
Where thousand Deaths are posting up and down,
Commissioned to this fatal field of Cressy.
Methinks I see them arm my gallant soldiers,
And gird the sword upon each thigh, and fit

Each shining helm. and string each stubborn bow,
And dance to the neighing of our steeds.
Methinks the shout begins, the battle burns:
Methinks I see them perch on English crests,
And roar the wild flame of fierce war upon
The throngèd enemy ! In truth, I am too full;
It is my sin to love the noise of war.
Chandos, thou seest my weakness; for strong Nature
Will bend or break us: my blood, like a springtide
Does rise so high to overflow all bounds
Of moderation; while Reason, in her
Frail bark, can see no shore or bound for vast
Ambition. Come, take the helm, my Chandos,
That my full-blown sails overset me not
In the wild tempest. Condemn my venturous youth
That plays with danger, as the innocent child,
Unthinking, plays upon the viper's den:
I am a coward in my reason, Chandos.

CHANDOS.

You are a man, my prince, and a brave man,
If I can judge of actions; but your heat
Is the effect of youth, and want of use:
Use makes the armèd field and noisy war
Pass over as a cloud does, unregarded,
Or but expected as a thing of course.
Age is contemplative ; each rolling year
Brings forth her fruit to the mind's treasure-house :—
While vacant youth doth crave and seek about
Within itself, and findeth discontent,
Then, tired of thought, impatient takes the wing,
Seizes the fruits of time, attacks experience,
Roams round vast Nature's forest, where no bounds
Are set, the swiftest may have room, the strongest
Find prey; till, tired at length, sated and tired
With the changing sameness, old variety,
We sit us down, and view our former joys
With distaste and dislike.

PRINCE

Then, if we must tug for experience,
Let us not fear to beat round Nature's wilds,
And rouse the strongest prey : then if we fall,
We fall with glory. I know well the wolf
Is dangerous to fight, not good for food,
Nor is the hide a comely vestment ; so
We have our battle for our pains. I know
That youth has need of age to point fit prey,
And oft the stander-by shall steal the fruit
Of the other's labour. This is philosophy ;

These are the tricks of the world; but the pure soul
Shall mount on native wings, disdaining little sport,
And cut a path into the heaven of glory,
Leaving a track of light for men to wonder at.
I'm glad my father does not hear me talk;
You can find friendly excuses for me, Chandos.
But do you not think, Sir John, that, if it please
The Almighty to stretch out my span of life,
I shall with pleasure view a glorious action
Which my youth mastered ?

CHANDOS.

       Age, my Lord, views motives,
And views not acts; when neither warbling voice
Nor trilling pipe is heard, nor pleasure sits
With trembling age, the voice of Conscience then,
Sweeter than music in a summer's eve,
Shall warble round the snowy head, and keep
Sweet symphony to feathered angels, sitting
As guardians round your chair ; then shall the pulse
Beat slow, and taste and touch, sight, sound and smell,
That sing and dance round Reason's fine-wrought throne,
Shall flee away, and leave him all forlorn ;
Yet not forlorn if Conscience is his friend.

                         [*Exeunt.*

SCENE IV.—*In* SIR THOMAS DAGWORTH'S *Tent.*

DAGWORTH, *and* WILLIAM *his man.*

DAGWORTH.

Bring hither my armour, William.
Ambition is the growth of every clime.

WILLIAM.

Does it grow in England, sir ?

DAGWORTH.

Ay, it grows most in lands most cultivated.

WILLIAM.

Then it grows most in France ; the vines here
Are finer that any we have in England.

DAGWORTH.

Ay, but the oaks are not.

WILLIAM.

What is the tree you mentioned?   I don't think
I ever saw it.

DAGWORTH.

Ambition.

WILLIAM.

Is it a little creeping root that grows in ditches?

DAGWORTH.

Thou dost not understand me, William,
It is a root that grows in every breast;
Ambition is the desire or passion that one man
Has to get before another, in any pursuit after glory;
But I don't think you have any of it.

WILLIAM.

Yes, I have; I have a great ambition to know everything, sir.

DAGWORTH.

But, when our first ideas are wrong, what follows must all be wrong, of course; 'tis best to know a little, and to know that little aright.

WILLIAM.

Then, sir, I should be glad to know if it was not ambition that brought over our king to France to fight for his right.

DAGWORTH.

Though the knowledge of that will not profit thee much, yet I will tell you that it *was* ambition.

WILLIAM.

Then, if ambition is a sin, we are all guilty in coming with him, and in fighting for him.

DAGWORTH.

Now, William, thou dost thrust the question home; but I must tell you that, guilt being an act of the mind, none are guilty but those whose minds are prompted by that same ambition.

WILLIAM.

Now, I always thought that a man might be guilty of doing wrong without knowing it was wrong.

DAGWORTH.

Thou art a natural philosopher, and knowest truth by instinct; while reason runs aground, as we have run our argument. Only remember, William, all have it in their power to know the motives of their own actions, and 'tis a sin to act without some reason.

WILLIAM.

And whoever acts without reason may do a great deal of harm without knowing it.

DAGWORTH.

Thou art an endless moralist.

WILLIAM.

Now there's a story come into my head, that I will tell your honour, if you'll give me leave.

DAGWORTH.

No, William, save it till another time; this is no time for story-telling. But here comes one who is as entertaining as a good story.

Enter PETER BLUNT.

PETER.

Yonder's a musician going to play before the King; it's a new song about the French and English. And the Prince has made the minstrel a squire, and given him I don't know what, and can't tell whether he don't mention us all one by one; and he is to write another about all us that are to die, that we may be remembered in Old England, for all our blood and bones are in France; and a great deal more that we shall all hear by and by And I came to tell your honour, because you love to hear war-songs.

DAGWORTH

And who is this minstrel, Peter, dost know?

PETER.

Oh ay, I forgot to tell that; he has got the same name as Sir John Chandos that the Prince is always with—the wise man that knows us all as well as your honour, only ain't so good-natured.

DAGWORTH.

I thank you, Peter, for your information, but not for your compliment, which is not true. There's as much difference between him and me as between glittering sand and fruitful mould; or shining glass and a wrought diamond, set in rich gold, and fitted to the finger of an Emperor; such is that worthy Chandos.

PETER.

I know your honour does not think anything of yourself, but everybody else does.

DAGWORTH.

Go, Peter, get you gone, flattery is delicious, even from the lips of a babbler. *[Exit* PETER.

WILLIAM.

I never flatter your honour.

DAGWORTH.

I don't know that.

WILLIAM.

Why you know, sir, when we were in England, at the tournament at Windsor, and the Earl of Warwick was tumbled over, you asked me if he did not look well when he fell; and I said no, he looked very foolish; and you were very angry with me for not flattering you.

DAGWORTH.

You mean that I was angry with you for not flattering the Earl of Warwick. *[Exeunt.*

SCENE V.—*Sir Thomas Dagworth's Tent*

SIR THOMAS DAGWORTH.   *To him enters* SIR WALTER MANNY.

SIR WALTER.

Sir Thomas Dagworth, I've been weeping now
Over the men that are to die to-day.

DAGWORTH.

Why, brave Sir Walter, you or I may fall.

SIR WALTER.

I know this breathing flesh must lie and rot,
Covered with silence and forgetfulness.
Death roams in cities' smoke, and in still night,
When men sleep in their beds, walketh about.
How many in walled cities lie and groan,
Turning themselves about upon their beds,
Talking with Death, answering his hard demands!
How many walk in darkness, terrors round
The curtains of their beds, destruction still
Ready at the door! How many sleep in earth,
Covered over with stones and deathy dust,
Resting in quietness, whose spirits walk
Upon the clouds of heaven, to die no more!
Yet death is terrible, though on angels' wings.
How terrible then is the field of death,
Where he doth rend the vault of heaven, and shake
The gates of hell!
O Dagworth, France is sick! the very sky,
Though sunshine light it, seems to me as pale
As the pale fainting man on his death-bed,
Whose face is shown by light of sickly taper.
It makes me sad and sick at very heart;
Thousands must fall to-day.

DAGWORTH.

Thousands of souls must leave this prison-house,
To be exalted to those heavenly fields
Where songs of triumph, palms of victory,
Where peace and joy and love and calm content,
Sit singing in the azure clouds, and strew
Flowers of heaven's growth over the banquet-table.
Bind ardent hope upon your feet like shoes,
Put on the robe of preparation!
The table is prepared in shining heaven,
The flowers of immortality are blown;
Let those that fight fight in good stedfastness,
And those that fall shall rise in victory.

SIR WALTER.

I've often seen the burning field of war,
And often heard the dismal clang of arms ;
But never, till this fatal day of Cressy,
Has my soul fainted with these views of death.
I seem to be in one great charnel-house,
And seem to scent the rotten carcases ;
I seem to hear the dismal yells of Death,
While the black gore drops from his horrid jaws :
Yet I not fear the monster in his pride—
But oh ! the souls that are to die to-day !

DAGWORTH.

Stop, brave Sir Walter ; let me drop a tear,
Then let the clarion of war begin ;
I'll fight and weep, 'tis in my country's cause ;
I'll weep and shout for glorious liberty.
Grim War shall laugh and shout, bedecked in tears,
And blood shall flow like streams across the meadows,
That murmur down their pebbly channels, and
Spend their sweet lives to do their country service :
Then England's green shall shoot, her fields shall smile,
Her ships shall sing across the foaming sea,
Her mariners shall use the flute and viol,
And rattling guns, and black and dreary war,
Shall be no more.

SIR WALTER.

Well, let the trumpet sound, and the drum beat ;
Let war stain the blue heavens with bloody banners ;
I'll draw my sword, nor ever sheathe it up
Till England blow the trump of victory,
Or I lie stretched upon the field of death.   [*Exeunt.*

SCENE VI.—*In the Camp.*

*Several of the Warriors met at the King's Tent with a Minstrel, who
sings the following Song :*

O sons of Trojan Brutus, clothed in war,
Whose voices are the thunder of the field,
Rolling dark clouds o'er France, muffling the sun
In sickly darkness like a dim eclipse,
Threatening as the red brow of storms, as fire
Burning up nations in your wrath and fury !

Your ancestors came from the fires of Troy
(Like lions roused by lightning from their dens,
Whose eyes do glare against the stormy fires),
Heated with war, filled with the blood of Greeks,
With helmets hewn, and shields covered with gore,
In navies black, broken with wind and tide:

Landing in firm array upon the rocks
Of Albion; they kissed the rocky shore;
"Be thou our mother and our nurse," they said;
"Our children's mother, and thou shalt be our grave,
The sepulchre of ancient Troy, from whence
Cities shall rise, thrones, arms, and awful powers."

Our fathers swarm from the ships. Giant voices
Are heard from all the hills, the enormous sons
Of Ocean run from rocks and caves; wild men,
Naked and roaring like lions, hurling rocks,
And wielding knotty clubs, like oaks entangled
Thick as a forest, ready for the axe.

Our fathers move in firm array to battle;
The savage monsters rush like roaring fire;
Like as a forest roars with crackling flames,
When the red lightning, borne by furious storms,
Lights on some woody shore; the parchèd heavens
Rain fire into the molten raging sea.

The smoking trees are strewn upon the shore,
Spoiled of their verdure. Oh how oft have they
Defied the storm that howlèd o'er their heads!
Our fathers, sweating, lean on spears, and view
The mighty dead: great bodies streaming blood,
Dread visages frowning in silent death.

Then Brutus spoke, inspired; our fathers sit
Attentive on the melancholy shore:
Hear ye the voice of Brutus—"The flowing waves
Of time come rolling o'er my breast," he said;
"And my heart labours with futurity.
Our sons shall rule the empire of the sea.

"Their mighty wings shall stretch from east to west.
Their nest is in the sea, but they shall roam
Like eagles for the prey; nor shall the young
Crave to be heard; for plenty shall bring forth,
Cities shall sing, and vales in rich array
Shall laugh, whose fruitful laps bend down with fulness.

"Our sons shall rise up from their thrones in joy,
Each buckling on his armour; and the dawn
Shall be prevented by their swords gleaming.
Evening shall hear their song of victory:
Their towers shall be built upon the rocks,
Their daughters sing, surrounded with their spears.

"Liberty shall on cliffs of Albion stand,
Casting her blue eyes over the green sea ;
Or towering upon the roaring waves,
Stretching her mighty spear o'er distant lands ;
While with her eagle wings she covereth
Fair Albion's shore, and all her families."

PROLOGUE.

INTENDED FOR A DRAMATIC PIECE OF KING EDWARD THE FOURTH.

On for a voice like thunder, and a tongue
To drown the throat of war ! When the senses
Are shaken, and the soul is driven to madness,
Who can stand ? When the souls of the oppressed
Fight in the troubled air that rages, who can stand ?
When the whirlwind of fury comes from the throne
Of God, when the frowns of His countenance
Drive the nations together, who can stand ?
When Sin claps his broad wings over the battle,
And sails rejoicing in the flood of death ;
When souls are torn to everlasting fire,
And fiends of hell rejoice upon the slain,
Oh who can stand ? Oh who hath causèd this ?
Oh who can answer at the throne of God ?
The Kings and Nobles of the land have done it !
Hear it not, Heaven, thy ministers have done it !

PROLOGUE TO KING JOHN.
(Compare Vol. I., p. 177)

Justice hath heaved a sword to plunge in Albion's breast ;
For Albion's sins are crimson-dyed,
And the red scourge follows her desolate sons.
Then Patriot rose ; full oft did Patriot rise,
When Tyranny hath stained fair Albion's breast
With her own children's gore.
Round his majestic feet deep thunders roll ;
Each heart does tremble, and each knee grows slack.
The stars of heaven tremble ; the roaring voice of war,
The trumpet, calls to battle. Brother in brother's blood
Must bathe, rivers of death. O land most hapless !
O beauteous island, how forsaken !
Weep from thy silver fountains, weep from thy gentle rivers !
The angel of the island weeps ;
Thy widowed virgins weep beneath thy shades.
Thy aged fathers gird themselves for war ;
The sucking infant lives, to die in battle ;
The weeping mother feeds him for the slaughter.

The husbandman doth leave his bending harvest.
Blood cries afar!   The land doth sow itself!
The glittering youth of courts must gleam in arms;
The aged senators their ancient swords assume;
The trembling sinews of old age must work
The work of death against their progeny.
For Tyranny hath stretched his purple arm,
And "Blood!" he cries: "The chariots and the horses,
The noise of shout, and dreadful thunder of the battle heard afar!'
Beware, O proud! thou shalt be humbled;
Thy cruel brow, thine iron heart is smitten,
Though lingering Fate is slow.   Oh yet may Albion
Smile again, and stretch her peaceful arms,
And raise her golden head exultingly!
Her citizens shall throng about her gates,
Her mariners shall sing upon the sea,
And myriads shall to her temples crowd!
Her sons shall joy as in the morning—
Her daughters sing as to the rising year!

TO SPRING.

O THOU with dewy locks, who lookest down
Through the clear windows of the morning, turn
Thine angel eyes upon our western isle,
Which in full choir hails thy approach, O Spring!

The hills tell to each other, and the listening
Valleys hear; all our longing eyes are turned
Up to thy bright pavilions: issue forth,
And let thy holy feet visit our clime!

Come o'er the eastern hills, and let our winds
Kiss thy perfumèd garments; let us taste
Thy morn and evening breath; scatter thy pearls
Upon our lovesick land that mourns for thee.

Oh deck her forth with thy fair fingers; pour
Thy soft kisses on her bosom; and put
Thy golden crown upon her languished head,
Whose modest tresses were bound up for thee!

TO SUMMER.

O THOU who passest through our valleys in
Thy strength, curb thy fierce steeds, allay the heat
That flames from their large nostrils! Thou, O Summer,
Oft pitchedst here thy golden tent, and oft
Beneath our oaks hast slept, while we beheld
With joy thy ruddy limbs and flourishing hair.

Beneath our thickest shades we oft have heard
Thy voice, when Noon upon his fervid car
Rode o'er the deep of heaven. Beside our springs
Sit down, and in our mossy valleys, on
Some bank beside a river clear, throw thy
Silk draperies off, and rush into the stream !
Our valleys love the Summer in his pride.

Our bards are famed who strike the silver wire :
Our youth are bolder than the southern swains,
Our maidens fairer in the sprightly dance.
We lack not songs, nor instruments of joy,
Nor echoes sweet, nor waters clear as heaven,
Nor laurel wreaths against the sultry heat.

TO AUTUMN.

O AUTUMN, laden with fruit, and stained
With the blood of the grape, pass not, but sit
Beneath my shady roof ; there thou mayst rest,
And tune thy jolly voice to my fresh pipe,
And all the daughters of the year shall dance !
Sing now the lusty song of fruits and flowers.

" The narrow bud opens her beauties to
The sun, and love runs in her thrilling veins ;
Blossoms hang round the brows of Morning, and
Flourish down the bright cheek of modest Eve,
Till clustering Summer breaks forth into singing,
And feathered clouds strew flowers round her head.

" The Spirits of the Air live on the smells
Of fruit ; and Joy, with pinions light, roves round
The gardens, or sits singing in the trees."
Thus sang the jolly Autumn as he sat ;
Then rose, girded himself, and o'er the bleak
Hills fled from our sight ; but left his golden load.

TO WINTER.

O WINTER ! bar thine adamantine doors :
The north is thine ; there hast thou built thy dark
Deep-founded habitation. Shake not thy roofs,
Nor bend thy pillars with thine iron car.

He hears me not, but o'er the yawning deep
Rides heavy ; his storms are unchained, sheathed
In ribbèd steel ; I dare not lift mine eyes
For he hath reared his sceptre o'er the world

Lo! now the direful monster, whose skin clings
To his strong bones, strides o'er the groaning rocks;
He withers all in silence, and in his hand
Unclothes the earth, and freezes up frail life.

He takes his seat upon the cliffs,—the mariner
Cries in vain. Poor little wretch, that deal'st
With storms!—till heaven smiles, and drives the monster
Yelling beneath Mount Hecla to his caves.

TO THE EVENING STAR.

Thou fair-haired Angel of the Evening,
Now, whilst the sun rests on the mountains, light
Thy brilliant torch of love—thy radiant crown
Put on, and smile upon our evening bed!
Smile on our loves; and, while thou drawest the
Blue curtains of the sky, scatter thy dew
On every flower that closes its sweet eyes
In timely sleep. Let thy west wind sleep on
The lake; speak silence with thy glimmering eyes,
And wash the dusk with silver.—Soon, full soon,
Dost thou withdraw; then the wolf rages wide,
And then the lion glares through the dun forest.
The fleeces of our flocks are covered with
Thy sacred dew: protect with influence!

TO MORNING.

O holy virgin, clad in purest white,
Unlock heaven's golden gates, and issue forth;
Awake the dawn that sleeps in heaven; let light
Rise from the chambers of the east, and bring
The honeyed dew that cometh on waking day.
O radiant Morning, salute the Sun,
Roused like a huntsman to the chase, and with
Thy buskined feet appear upon our hills.

FAIR ELEANOR.

The bell struck one, and shook the silent tower;
The graves give up their dead: fair Eleanor
Walked by the castle-gate, and looked in:
A hollow groan ran through the dreary vaults.

She shrieked aloud, and sunk upon the steps,
On the cold stone her pale cheek. Sickly smells
Of death issue as from a sepulchre,
And all is silent but the sighing vaults.

LIBRARY OF THE

Chill Death withdraws his hand, and she revives :
Amazed she finds herself upon her feet,
And, like a ghost, through narrow passages
Walking, feeling the cold walls with her hands.

Fancy returns, and now she thinks of bones
And grinning skulls, and corruptible death
Wrapt in his shroud ; and now fancies she hears
Deep sighs, and sees pale sickly ghosts gliding

At length, no fancy but reality
Distracts her. A rushing sound, and the feet
Of one that fled, approaches.—Ellen stood,
Like a dumb statue, froze to stone with fear

The wretch approaches, crying : " The deed is done !
Take this, and send it by whom thou wilt send ,
It is my life—send it to Eleanor:—
He's dead, and howling after me for blood !

" Take this," he cried , and thrust into her arms
A wet napkin, wrapt about ; then rushed
Past, howling. She received into her arms
Pale death, and followed on the wings of fear.

They passed swift through the outer gate ; the wretch,
Howling, leaped o'er the wall into the moat,
Stifling in mud.   Fair Ellen passed the bridge,
And heard a gloomy voice cry " Is it done ? "

As the deer wounded, Ellen flew over
The pathless plain ; as the arrows that fly
By night, destruction flies, and strikes in darkness.
She fled from fear, till at her house arrived.

Her maids await her ; on her bed she falls,
That bed of joy where erst her lord hath pressed.
" Ah woman's fear ! " she cried, " Ah cursed duke !
Ah my dear lord ! ah wretched Eleanor !

" My lord was like a flower upon the brows
Of lusty May ! Ah life as frail as flower !
O ghastly Death ! withdraw thy cruel hand !
Seek'st thou that flower to deck thy horrid temples ?

" My lord was like a star in highest heaven
Drawn down to earth by spells and wickedness ;
My lord was like the opening eyes of Day,
When western winds creep softly o'er the flowers.

" But he is darkened ; like the summer's noon
Clouded , fall'n like the stately tree, cut down ;
The breath of heaven dwelt among his leaves.
O Eleanor, weak woman, filled with woe ! "

Thus having spoke, she raisèd up her head,
And saw the bloody napkin by her side,
Which in her arms she brought; and now, tenfold
More terrified, saw it unfold itself.

Her eyes were fixed; the bloody cloth unfolds,
Disclosing to her sight the murdered head
Of her dear lord, all ghastly pale, clotted
With gory blood; it groaned, and thus it spake:

" O Eleanor, behold thy husband's head,
Who, sleeping on the stones of yonder tower,
Was reft of life by the accursed duke:
A hired villain turned my sleep to death.

" O Eleanor, beware the cursed duke;
Oh give not him thy hand, now I am dead.
He seeks thy love; who, coward, in the night,
Hired a villain to bereave my life."

She sat with dead cold limbs, stiffened to stone;
She took the gory head up in her arms;
She kissed the pale lips; she had no tears to shed;
She hugged it to her breast, and groaned her last

SONG.

How sweet I roamed from field to field,
    And tasted all the summer's pride,
Till I the Prince of Love beheld
    Who in the sunny beams did glide.

He showed me lilies for my hair,
    And blushing roses for my brow,
He led me through his gardens fair
    Where all his golden pleasures grow.

With sweet May-dews my wings were wet,
    And Phœbus fired my vocal rage;
He caught me in his silken net,
    And shut me in his golden cage.

He loves to sit and hear me sing,
    Then, laughing, sports and plays with me,
Then stretches out my golden wing,
    And mocks my loss of liberty.

SONG.

My silks and fine array,
  My smiles and languished air,
By love are driven away;
  And mournful lean Despair
Brings me yew to deck my grave:
Such end true lovers have.

His face is fair as heaven
  When springing buds unfold;
Oh why to him was't given,
  Whose heart is wintry cold?
His breast is love's all-worshipped tomb,
Where all love's pilgrims come.

Bring me an axe and spade,
  Bring me a winding-sheet;
When I my grave have made,
  Let winds and tempests beat:
Then down I'll lie, as cold as clay.
True love doth pass away!

———————

SONG.

Love and harmony combine,
And around our souls entwine,
While thy branches mix with mine,
And our roots together join.

Joys upon our branches sit,
Chirping loud and singing sweet;
Like gentle streams beneath our feet,
Innocence and virtue meet.

Thou the golden fruit dost bear,
I am clad in flowers fair;
Thy sweet boughs perfume the air,
And the turtle buildeth there.

There she sits and feeds her young,
Sweet I hear her mournful song;
And thy lovely leaves among
There is Love; I hear his tongue.

There his charming nest doth lay,
There he sleeps the night away;
There he sports along the day,
And doth among our branches play.

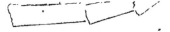

SONG.

I LOVE the jocund dance,
  The softly-breathing song,
Where innocent eyes do glance,
  And where lisps the maiden's tongue.

I love the laughing vale,
  I love the echoing hill,
Where mirth does never fail,
  And the jolly swain laughs his fill.

I love the pleasant cot,
  I love the innocent bower,
Where white and brown is our lot,
  Or fruit in the mid-day hour.

I love the oaken seat
  Beneath the oaken tree,
Where all the old villagers meet,
  And laugh our sports to see.

I love our neighbours all,—
  But, Kitty, I better love thee;
And love them I ever shall,
  But thou art all to me.

SONG. ✓

MEMORY, hither come,
  And tune your merry notes:
And, while upon the wind
  Your music floats,
I'll pore upon the stream
Where sighing lovers dream,
And fish for fancies as they pass
Within the watery glass.

I'll drink of the clear stream,
  And hear the linnet's song,
And there I'll lie and dream
  The day along:
And, when night comes, I'll go
To places fit for woe,
Walking along the darkened valley
With silent Melancholy.

MAD SONG. ✓.

THE wild winds weep,
  And the night is a-cold;
Come hither, Sleep,
  And my griefs enfold ! . . .
But lo ! the morning peeps
Over the eastern steeps,
And the rustling beds of dawn
The earth do scorn.

Lo ! to the vault
  Of pavèd heaven,
With sorrow fraught,
  My notes are driven:
They strike the ear of Night,
  Make weep the eyes of Day ,
They make mad the roaring winds,
  And with tempests play.

Like a fiend in a cloud,
  With howling woe
After night I do crowd
  And with night will go;
I turn my back to the east
From whence comforts have increased;
For light doth seize my brain
With frantic pain.

SONG.

FRESH from the dewy hill, the merry Year
Smiles on my head, and mounts his flaming car ,
Round my young brows the laurel wreathes a shade,
And rising glories beam around my head.

My feet are winged, while o'er the dewy lawn
I meet my maiden risen like the morn.
Oh bless those holy feet, like angels' feet ;
Oh bless those limbs, beaming with heavenly light !

Like as an angel glittering in the sky
In times of innocence and holy joy ;
The joyful shepherd stops his grateful song
To hear the music of an angel's tongue.

So, when she speaks, the voice of Heaven I hear ;
So, when we walk, nothing impure comes near ;
Each field seems Eden, and each calm retreat
Each village seems the haunt of holy feet.

But, that sweet village where my black-eyed maid
Closes her eyes in sleep beneath night's shade
Whene'er I enter, more than mortal fire
Burns in my soul, and does my song inspire

SONG.

When early Morn walks forth in sober grey,
Then to my black-eyed maid I haste away.
When Evening sits beneath her dusky bower,
And gently sighs away the silent hour,
The village bell alarms, away I go,
And the vale darkens at my pensive woe.

To that sweet village where my black-eyed maid
Doth drop a tear beneath the silent shade
I turn my eyes; and pensive as I go
Curse my black stars, and bless my pleasing woe.

Oft, when the Summer sleeps among the trees,
Whispering faint murmurs to the scanty breeze,
I walk the village round; if at her side
A youth doth walk in stolen joy and pride,
I curse my stars in bitter grief and woe,
That made my love so high, and me so low.

Oh should she e'er prove false, his limbs I'd tear
And throw all pity on the burning air!
I'd curse bright fortune for my mixèd lot,
And then I'd die in peace, and be forgot.

TO THE MUSES.

Whether on Ida's shady brow,
   Or in the chambers of the East,
The chambers of the Sun, that now
   From ancient melody have ceased;

Whether in heaven ye wander fair,
   Or the green corners of the earth,
Or the blue regions of the air
   Where the melodious winds have birth

Whether on crystal rocks ye rove,
   Beneath the bosom of the sea,
Wandering in many a coral grove;
   Fair Nine, forsaking Poetry;

How have you left the ancient love
  That bards of old enjoyed in you !
The languid strings do scarcely move,
  The sound is forced, the notes are few !

GWIN, KING OF NORWAY.

COME, Kings, and listen to my song.—
  When Gwin, the son of Nore,
Over the nations of the North
  His cruel sceptre bore ;

The Nobles of the land did feed
  Upon the hungry poor ;
They tear the poor man's lamb, and drive
  The needy from their door.

"The land is desolate ; our wives
  And children cry for bread ;
Arise, and pull the tyrant down !
  Let Gwin be humbled !"

Gordred the giant roused himself
  From sleeping in his cave ;
He shook the hills, and in the clouds
  The troubled banners wave.

Beneath them rolled, like tempests black,
  The numerous sons of blood ;
Like lions' whelps, roaring abroad,
  Seeking their nightly food.

Down Bleron's hill they dreadful rush,
  Their cry ascends the clouds ;
The trampling horse and clanging arms
  Like rushing mighty floods !

Their wives and children, weeping loud,
  Follow in wild array,
Howling like ghosts, furious as wolves
  In the bleak wintry day.

"Pull down the tyrant to the dust,
  Let Gwin be humbled,"
They cry, "and let ten thousand lives
  Pay for the tyrant's head !"

From tower to tower the watchmen cry :
  "O Gwin, the son of Nore,
Arouse thyself ! the nations, black
  Like clouds, come rolling o'er !"

Gwin reared his shield, his palace shakes,
  His chiefs come rushing round;
Each like an awful thunder-cloud
  With voice of solemn sound:

Like reared stones around a grave
  They stand around the King;
Then suddenly each seized his spear,
  And clashing steel does ring.

The husbandman does leave his plough
  To wade through fields of gore;
The merchant binds his brows in steel,
  And leaves the trading shore;

The shepherd leaves his mellow pipe,
  And sounds the trumpet shrill;
The workman throws his hammer down
  To heave the bloody bill.

Like the tall ghost of Barraton
  Who sports in stormy sky,
Gwin leads his host as black as night
  When pestilence does fly,

With horses and with chariots—
  And all his spearmen bold
March 'to the sound of mournful song,
  Like clouds around him rolled.

Gwin lifts his hand—the nations halt;
  "Prepare for war!" he cries.
Gordred appears!—his frowning brow
  Troubles our northern skies.

The armies stand, like balances
  Held in the Almighty's hand;—
"Gwin, thou hast filled thy measure up:
  Thou'rt swept from out the land."

And now the raging armies rushed
  Like warring mighty seas;
The heavens are shook with roaring war,
  The dust ascends the skies!

Earth smokes with blood, and groans and shakes
  To drink her children's gore,
A sea of blood; nor can the eye
  See to the trembling shore.

And on the verge of this wild sea
  Famine and death do cry ;
The cries of women and of babes
  Over the field do fly.

The king is seen raging afar,
  With all his men of might ;
Like blazing comets scattering death
  Through the red feverous night.

Beneath his arm like sheep they die,
  And groan upon the plain ;
The battle faints, and bloody men
  Fight upon hills of slain.

Now death is sick, and riven men
  Labour and toil for life ;
Steed rolls on steed, and shield on shield,
  Sunk in this sea of strife !

The God of War is drunk with blood,
  The earth doth faint and fail ;
The stench of blood makes sick the heavens,
  Ghosts glut the throat of hell !

Oh what have Kings to answer for
  Before that awful throne,
When thousand deaths for vengeance cry,
  And ghosts accusing groan !

Like blazing comets in the sky
  That shake the stars of light,
Which drop like fruit unto the earth
  Through the fierce burning night ;

Like these did Gwin and Gordred meet,
  And the first blow decides ;
Down from the brow unto the breast
  Gordred his head divides !

Gwin fell : the Sons of Norway fled,
  All that remained alive ;
The rest did fill the vale of death,—
  For them the eagles strive.

The river Dorman rolled their blood
  Into the northern sea ;
Who mourned his sons, and overwhelmed
  The pleasant south country.

AN IMITATION OF SPÉNSER.

GOLDEN Apollo, that through heaven wide
   Scatter'st the rays of light, and truth his beams,
In lucent words my darkling verses dight,
   And wash my earthy mind in thy clear streams,
   That wisdom may descend in fairy dreams,
All while the jocund Hours in thy train
   Scatter their fancies at thy poet's feet;
And, when thou yield'st to Night thy wide domain,
Let rays of truth enlight his sleeping brain.

For brutish Pan in vain might thee assay
   With tinkling sounds to dash thy nervous verse,
Sound without sense; yet in his rude affray
   (For Ignorance is Folly's leasing nurse,
   And love of Folly needs none other's curse)
Midas the praise hath gained of lengthened ears,
   For which himself might deem him ne'er the worse
To sit in council with his modern peers,
   And judge of tinkling rhymes and elegances terse.

And thou, Mercurius, that with winged bow
   Dost mount aloft into the yielding sky,
And through heaven's halls thy airy flight dost throw,
   Entering with holy feet to where on high
   Jove weighs the counsel of futurity;
Then, laden with eternal fate, dost go
   Down, like a falling star, from autumn sky,
And o'er the surface of the silent deep dost fly:

If thou arrivest at the sandy shore
   Where nought but envious hissing adders dwell,
Thy golden rod, thrown on the dusty floor,
   Can charm to harmony with potent spell;
   Such is sweet Eloquence, that does dispel
Envy and Hate, that thirst for human gore;
   And cause in sweet society to dwell
   Vile savage minds that lurk in lonely cell.

O Mercury, assist my labouring sense
   That round the circle of the world would fly,
As the wing'd eagle scorns the towery fence
   Of Alpine hills round his high aëry,
   And searches through the corners of the sky,
Sports in the clouds to hear the thunder's sound,
   And see the winged lightnings as they fly;
Then, bosomed in an amber cloud, around
   Plumes his wide wings, and seeks Sol's palace high.

LIBRARY OF THE UNIVERSITY

And thou, O Warrior maid invincible,
  Armed with the terrors of Almighty Jove,
Pallas, Minerva, maiden terrible,
    Lov'st thou to walk the peaceful solemn grove,
    In solemn gloom of branches interwove?
Or bear'st thy ægis o'er the burning field
    Where like the sea the waves of battle move?
Or have thy soft piteous eyes beheld
    The weary wanderer through the desert rove?
Or does the afflicted man thy heavenly bosom move?

BLIND-MAN'S BUFF.

When silver snow decks Susan's clothes,
And jewel hangs at th' shepherd's nose,
The blushing bank is all my care,
With hearth so red, and walls so fair.
"Heap the sea-coal, come, heap it higher;
The oaken log lay on the fire."
The well-washed stools, a circling row,
With lad and lass, how fair the show!
The merry can of nut-brown ale,
The laughing jest, the love-sick tale,—
Till, tired of chat, the game begins
The lasses prick the lads with pins.
Roger from Dolly twitched the stool;
She, falling, kissed the ground, poor fool!
She blushed so red, with sidelong glance
At hobnail Dick, who grieved the chance.
But now for Blind-man's Buff they call;
Of each incumbrance clear the hall

Jenny her silken kerchief folds,
And blear-eyed Will the black lot holds.
Now laughing stops, with " Silence, hush! "
And Peggy Pout gives Sam a push.
The Blind-man's arms, extended wide,
Sam slips between :—" Oh woe betide
Thee, clumsy Will!"—But tittering Kate
Is penned up in the corner strait!
And now Will's eyes beheld the play;
He thought his face was t'other way.
"Now, Kitty, now! what chance hast thou?
Roger so near thee trips, I vow!"
She catches him—then Roger ties
His own head up—but not his eyes;
For through the slender cloth he sees,
And runs at Sam, who slips with ease

His clumsy hold ; and dodging round,
Sukey is tumbled on the ground.—
" See what it is to play unfair !
Where cheating is, there's mischief there."
But Roger still pursues the chase,—
" He sees ! he sees ! " cries softly Grace ;
" O Roger, thou, unskilled in art,
Must, surer bound, go through thy part ! "

Now Kitty, pert, repeats the rhymes,
And Roger turns him round three times,
Then pauses ere he starts.   But Dick
Was mischief-bent upon a trick :
Down on his hands and knees he lay
Directly in the Blind-man's way,
Then cries out " Hem ! "—Hodge heard, and ran
With hood-winked chance—sure of his man ;
But down he came.—Alas, how frail
Our best of hopes, how soon they fail !
With crimson drops he stains the ground ;
Confusion startles all around.
Poor piteous Dick supports his head,
And fain would cure the hurt he made.
But Kitty hasted with a key,
And down his back they straight convey
The cold relief : the blood is stayed,
And Hodge again holds up his head.

Such are the fortunes of the game ;
And those who play should stop the same
By wholesome laws, such as—All those
Who on the blinded man impose
Stand in his stead ; as, long agone,
When men were first a nation grown,
Lawless they lived, till wantonness
And liberty began to increase,
And one man lay in another's way ;
Then laws were made to keep fair play

A WAR SONG.

TO ENGLISHMEN.

Prepare, prepare the iron helm of war,
Bring forth the lots, cast in the spacious orb ;
The Angel of Fate turns them with mighty hands,
And casts them out upon the darkened earth !
        Prepare, prepare !

Prepare your hearts for Death's cold hand ! prepare
Your souls for flight, your bodies for the earth !
Prepare your arms for glorious victory !
Prepare your eyes to meet a holy God !
                    Prepare, prepare !

Whose fatal scroll is that ? Methinks 'tis mine !
Why sinks my heart, why faltereth my tongue ?
Had I three lives, I'd die in such a cause,
And rise, with ghosts, over the well-fought field.
                    Prepare, prepare !

The arrows of Almighty God are drawn !
Angels of Death stand in the louring heavens !
Thousands of souls must seek the realms of light,
And walk together on the clouds of heaven !
                    Prepare, prepare !

Soldiers, prepare !   Our cause is Heaven's cause ;
Soldiers, prepare !   Be worthy of our cause :
Prepare to meet our fathers in the sky :
Prepare, O troops that are to fall to-day !
                    Prepare, prepare !

Alfred shall smile, and make his heart rejoice ;
The Norman William, and the learned Clerk,
And Lion-Heart, and black-browed Edward with
His loyal queen, shall rise, and welcome us !
                    Prepare, prepare !

. The order of the above sketches follows, for convenience of
comparison, that of the Aldine Edition. The original sequence,
given in Mr. Quaritch's facsimile, will be found above, Volume I.,
p. 170—in the chapter containing other " Poetical Sketches " not
reprinted here.

See " Notes to Poetical Sketches," &c , p 88.

SONGS OF INNOCENCE.

(ENGRAVED 1789.)

INTRODUCTION. ✓

PIPING down the valleys wild,
  Piping songs of pleasant glee,
On a cloud I saw a child,
  And he laughing said to me:

"Pipe a song about a Lamb!"
  So I piped with merry cheer.
"Piper, pipe that song again;"
  So I piped: he wept to hear.

"Drop thy pipe, thy happy pipe;
  Sing thy songs of happy cheer!"
So I sang the same again,
  While he wept with joy to hear.

"Piper, sit thee down and write
  In a book, that all may read."
So he vanished from my sight;
  And I plucked a hollow reed,

And I made a rural pen,
  And I stained the water clear,
And I wrote my happy songs
  Every child may joy to hear.

THE SHEPHERD.

How sweet is the shepherd's sweet lot!
From the morn to the evening he strays;
He shall follow his sheep all the day,
And his tongue shall be filled with praise.

For he hears the lambs' innocent call,
And he hears the ewes' tender reply;
He is watchful while they are in peace,
For they know when their shepherd is nigh.

THE ECHOING GREEN.

THE sun does arise,
And make happy the skies;
The merry bells ring,
To welcome the Spring;
The skylark and thrush,
The birds of the bush,
Sing louder around
To the bells' cheerful sound;
While our sports shall be seen
On the echoing green.

Old John, with white hair,
Does laugh away care,
Sitting under the oak,
Among the old folk.
They laugh at our play,
And soon they all say,
" Such, such were the joys
When we all—girls and boys—
In our youth-time were seen
On the echoing green."

Till the little ones, weary,
No more can be merry:
The sun does descend,
And our sports have an end
Round the laps of their mothers
Many sisters and brothers,
Like birds in their nest,
Are ready for rest,
And sport no more seen
On the darkening green.

THE LAMB.

LITTLE lamb, who made thee
Dost thou know who made thee,
Gave thee life, and bade thee feed
By the stream and o'er the mead,
Gave thee clothing of delight,
Softest clothing, woolly, bright;
Gave thee such a tender voice,
Making all the vales rejoice?
    Little lamb, who made thee?
    Dost thou know who made thee?

Little lamb, I'll tell thee;
Little lamb, I'll tell thee:
He is callèd by thy name,
For He calls himself a Lamb.
He is meek, and He is mild,
He became a little child.
I a child, and thou a lamb,
We are callèd by his name.
Little lamb, God bless thee!
Little lamb, God bless thee!

THE LITTLE BLACK BOY.

My mother bore me in the southern wild,
And I am black, but oh my soul is white!
White as an angel is the English child,
But I am black, as if bereaved of light.

My mother taught me underneath a tree,
And, sitting down before the heat of day,
She took me on her lap and kissèd me,
And, pointing to the East, began to say:

"Look on the rising sun: there God does live,
And gives his light, and gives his heat away,
And flowers and trees and beasts and men receive
Comfort in morning, joy in the noonday

"And we are put on earth a little space,
That we may learn to bear the beams of love ·
And these black bodies and this sunburnt face
Are but a cloud, and like a shady grove.

"For, when our souls have learned the heat to bear
The cloud will vanish, we shall hear His voice,
Saying. 'Come out from the grove, my love and care
And round my golden tent like lambs rejoice.' "

Thus did my mother say, and kissèd me,
And thus I say to little English boy.
When I from black, and he from white cloud free
And round the tent of God like lambs we joy

I'll shade him from the heat till he can bear
To lean in joy upon our Father's knee;
And then I'll stand and stroke his silver hair,
And be like him, and he will then love me.

THE BLOSSOM. ✓

MERRY, merry sparrow!
Under leaves so green
A happy blossom
Sees you, swift as arrow,
Seek your cradle narrow,
Near my bosom.
Pretty, pretty robin!
Under leaves so green
A happy blossom
Hears you sobbing, sobbing,
Pretty, pretty robin,
Near my bosom.

THE CHIMNEY-SWEEPER.

WHEN my mother died I was very young,
And my father sold me while yet my tongue
Could scarcely cry "Weep! weep! weep! weep!"
So your chimneys I sweep, and in soot I sleep.

There's little Tom Dacre, who cried when his head,
That curled like a lamb's back, was shaved; so I said,
"Hush, Tom! never mind it, for, when your head's bare,
You know that the soot cannot spoil your white hair."

And so he was quiet, and that very night,
As Tom was a-sleeping, he had such a sight!—
That thousands of sweepers, Dick, Joe, Ned, and Jack,
Were all of them locked up in coffins of black.

And by came an angel, who had a bright key,
And he opened the coffins, and set them all free;
Then down a green plain, leaping, laughing, they run,
And wash in a river, and shine in the sun.

Then naked and white, all their bags left behind,
They rise upon clouds, and sport in the wind;
And the Angel told Tom, if he'd be a good boy,
He'd have God for his father, and never want joy.

And so Tom awoke; and we rose in the dark,
And got with our bags and our brushes to work.
Though the morning was cold, Tom was happy and warm:
So, if all do their duty, they need not fear harm.

THE LITTLE BOY LOST. ✓

"FATHER, father, where are you going?
Oh do not walk so fast!
Speak, father, speak to your little boy,
Or else I shall be lost."

The night was dark, no father was there,
The child was wet with dew;
The mire was deep, and the child did weep,
And away the vapour flew.

THE LITTLE BOY FOUND.

THE little boy lost in the lonely fen,
Led by the wandering light,
Began to cry, but God, ever nigh,
Appeared like his father, in white

He kissed the child, and by the hand led,
And to his mother brought,
Who in sorrow pale, through the lonely dale,
The little boy weeping sought.

LAUGHING SONG.

WHEN the green woods laugh with the voice of joy,
And the dimpling stream runs laughing by;
When the air does laugh with our merry wit,
And the green hill laughs with the noise of it;

When the meadows laugh with lively green,
And the grasshopper laughs in the merry scene;
When Mary and Susan and Emily
With their sweet round mouths sing "Ha ha he! '

When the painted birds laugh in the shade,
Where our table with cherries and nuts is spread:
Come live, and be merry, and join with me,
To sing the sweet chorus of "Ha ha he!"

A CRADLE SONG.

SWEET dreams, form a shade
O'er my lovely infant's head!
Sweet dreams of pleasant streams
By happy, silent, moony beams!

Sweet Sleep, with soft down
Weave thy brows an infant crown
Sweep Sleep, angel mild,
Hover o'er my happy child!

Sweet smiles, in the night
Hover over my delight!
Sweet smiles, mother's smile,
All the livelong night beguile.

Sweet moans, dovelike sighs,
Chase not slumber from thine eyes !
Sweet moan, sweeter smile,
All the dovelike moans beguile.

Sleep, sleep, happy child !
All creation slept and smiled.
Sleep, sleep, happy sleep,
While o'er thee doth mother weep

Sweet babe, in thy face
Holy image I can trace ;
Sweet babe, once like thee
Thy Maker lay, and wept for me :

Wept for me, for thee, for all,
When He was an infant small.
Thou His image ever see,
Heavenly face that smiles on thee !

Smiles on thee, on me, on all,
Who became an infant small;
Infant smiles are his own smiles ,
Heaven and earth to peace beguiles.

THE DIVINE IMAGE.

To Mercy, Pity, Peace, and Love,
    All pray in their distress,
And to these virtues of delight
    Return their thankfulness.

For Mercy, Pity, Peace, and Love,
    Is God our Father dear ;
And Mercy, Pity, Peace, and Love,
    Is man, his child and care.

For Mercy has a human heart
    Pity, a human face ;
And Love, the human form divine,
    And Peace, the human dress

Then every man, of every clime,
    That prays in his distress,
Prays to the human form divine :
    Love, Mercy, Pity, Peace.

And all must love the human form,
    In heathen, Turk, or Jew.
Where Mercy, Love, and Pity dwell,
    There God is dwelling too.

HOLY THURSDAY.

'Twas on a Holy Thursday, their innocent faces clean,
Came children walking two and two, in red, and blue, and green :
Grey-headed beadles walked before, with wands as white as snow,
Till into the high dome of Paul's they like Thames waters flow.

Oh what a multitude they seemed, these flowers of London town !
Seated in companies they sit, with radiance all their own.
The hum of multitudes was there, but multitudes of lambs,
Thousands of little boys and girls raising their innocent hands

Now like a mighty wind they raise to heaven the voice of song,
Or like harmonious thunderings the seats of heaven among :
Beneath them sit the aged men, wise guardians of the poor.
Then cherish pity, lest you drive an angel from your door.

NIGHT.

The sun descending in the west,
The evening star does shine ;
The birds are silent in their nest,
And I must seek for mine.
 The moon, like a flower
 In heaven's high bower,
 With silent delight,
Sits and smiles on the night.

Farewell, green fields and happy grove,
Where flocks have ta'en delight.
Where lambs have nibbled, silent move
The feet of angels bright ;
 Unseen, they pour blessing,
 And joy without ceasing,
 On each bud and blossom,
 And each sleeping bosom.

They look in every thoughtless nest
Where birds are covered warm ;
They visit caves of every beast,
To keep them all from harm :
 If they see any weeping
 That should have been sleeping,
 They pour sleep on their head,
 And sit down by their bed.

When wolves and tigers howl for prey,
They pitying stand and weep ;
Seeking to drive their thirst away,
And keep them from the sheep.
 But, if they rush dreadful,
 The angels, most heedful,
 Receive each mild spirit,
 New worlds to inherit.

And there the lion's ruddy eyes
Shall flow with tears of gold:
And pitying the tender cries,
And walking round the fold:
   Saying: "Wrath by His meekness,
   And, by His health, sickness,
   Are driven away
   From our immortal day.

"And now beside thee, bleating lamb,
I can lie down and sleep,
Or think on Him who bore thy name,
Graze after thee, and weep.
   For, washed in life's river,
   My bright mane for ever
   Shall shine like the gold,
   As I guard o'er the fold."

SPRING.

   Sound the flute!
   Now 'tis mute!
   Birds delight,
   Day and night,
   Nightingale,
   In the dale,
   Lark in sky,—
   Merrily,
Merrily merrily to welcome in the year.

   Little boy,
   Full of joy;
   Little girl,
   Sweet and small;
   Cock does crow,
   So do you;
   Merry voice,
   Infant noise;
Merrily, merrily to welcome in the year.

   Little lamb,
   Here I am;
   Come and lick
   My white neck;
   Let me pull
   Your soft wool;
   Let me kiss
   Your soft face;
Merrily, merrily we welcome in the year.

NURSE'S SONG.

WHEN the voices of children are heard on the green,
  And laughing is heard on the hill,
My heart is at rest within my breast,
  And everything else is still.
" Then come home, my children, the sun is gone down,
  And the dews of night arise;
Come, come, leave off play, and let us away,
  Till the morning appears in the skies."

" No, no, let us play, for it is yet day,
  And we cannot go to sleep;
Besides, in the sky the little birds fly,
  And the hills are all covered with sheep."
" Well, well, go and play till the light fades away,
  And then go home to bed."
The little ones leaped, and shouted, and laughed,
  And all the hills echoèd.

INFANT JOY.

" I HAVE no name;
I am but two days old."
What shall I call thee?
" I happy am,
Joy is my name."
Sweet joy befall thee!

Pretty joy!
Sweet joy, but two days old.
Sweet joy I call thee:
Thou dost smile,
I sing the while;
Sweet joy befall thee!

A DREAM.

ONCE a dream did weave a shade
O'er my angel-guarded bed,
That an emmet lost its way
Where on grass methought I lay.

Troubled, wildered, and forlorn,
Dark, benighted, travel-worn,
Over many a tangled spray,
All heart-broke, I heard her say;

"Oh my children! do they cry,
Do they hear their father sigh?
Now they look abroad to see,
Now return and weep for me."

Pitying, I dropped a tear:
But I saw a glow-worm near,
Who replied, " What wailing wight
Calls the watchman of the night?

" I am set to light the ground,
While the beetle goes his round:
Follow now the beetle's hum;
Little wanderer, hie thee home!"

ON ANOTHER'S SORROW. v

Can I see another's woe,
And not be in sorrow too?
Can I see another's grief,
And not seek for kind relief?

Can I see a falling tear,
And not feel my sorrow's share?
Can a father see his child
Weep, nor be with sorrow filled?

Can a mother sit and hear
An infant groan, an infant fear?
No, no! never can it be!
Never, never can it be!

And can He who smiles on all
Hear the wren with sorrows small,
Hear the small bird's grief and care,
Hear the woes that infants bear—

And not sit beside the nest,
Pouring pity in their breast,
And not sit the cradle near,
Weeping tear on infant's tear?

And not sit both night and day,
Wiping all our tears away?
Oh no! never can it be!
Never, never can it be!

He doth give his joy to all:
He becomes an infant small,
He becomes a man of woe,
He doth feel the sorrow too.

Think not thou canst sigh a sigh,
And thy Maker is not by :
Think not thou canst weep a tear,
And thy Maker is not near.

Oh He gives to us his joy,
That our grief He may destroy :
Till our grief is fled and gone
He doth sit by us and moan.

*** "The Voice of the Ancient Bard" is printed by Gilchrist at the close of this section, professedly on the authority of a copy called "Blake's own," by Mr. Blake, who sent it to Dr. Jebb, Bishop of Limerick, after Blake's death. (Gilchrist, Vol. I., p. 410.)

The poem, wherever it truly belongs, is an after-thought. An undoubtedly authentic copy, equally late in date, places it at the end of the "Songs of Experience."

See "Notes to Poetical Sketches," &c., p. 88.

SONGS OF EXPERIENCE.

(ENGRAVED 1794.)

INTRODUCTION.

HEAR the voice of the Bard,
Who present, past, and future, sees;
Whose ears have heard
The Holy Word
That walked among the ancient trees;

Calling the lapsèd soul,
And weeping in the evening dew;
That might control
The starry pole,
And fallen, fallen light renew!

"O Earth, O Earth, return!
Arise from out the dewy grass!
Night is worn,
And the morn
Rises from the slumbrous mass.

"Turn away no more;
Why wilt thou turn away?
The starry floor,
The watery shore,
Are given thee till the break of day."

EARTH'S ANSWER.

EARTH raised up her head
From the darkness dread and drear,
Her light fled,
Stony, dread,
And her locks covered with grey despair.

"Prisoned on watery shore,
Starry jealousy does keep my den
Cold and hoar;
Weeping o'er,
I hear the father of the ancient men.

Selfish father of men !
Cruel, jealous, selfish fear !
Can delight,
Chained in night,
The virgins of youth and morning bear ?

"Does spring hide its joy,
When buds and blossoms grow ?
Does the sower
Sow by night,
Or the ploughman in darkness plough ?

"Break this heavy chain,
That does freeze my bones around !
Selfish, vain,
Eternal bane,
That free love with bondage bound."

THE CLOD AND THE PEBBLE.

"Love seeketh not itself to please,
    Nor for itself hath any care,
But for another gives its ease,
    And builds a heaven in hell's despair."

So sang a little clod of clay,
    Trodden with the cattle's feet,
But a pebble of the brook
    Warbled out these metres meet:

"Love seeketh only *Self* to please,
    To bind another to its delight,
Joys in another's loss of ease,
    And builds a hell in heaven's despite."

HOLY THURSDAY.

Is this a holy thing to see
    In a rich and fruitful land,—
Babes reduced to misery,
    Fed with cold and usurous hand ?

Is that trembling cry a song?
    Can it be a song of joy?
And so many children poor ?
    It is a land of poverty !

And their sun does never shine,
    And their fields are bleak and bare,
And their ways are filled with thorns :
    It is eternal winter there.

For where'er the sun does shine,
　And where'er the rain does fall,
Babes should never hunger there,
　Nor poverty the mind appall.

THE LITTLE GIRL LOST.

In futurity
I prophetic see
That the earth from sleep
(Grave the sentence deep)

Shall arise, and seek
For her Maker meek;
And the desert wild
Become a garden mild.

In the southern clime,
Where the summer's prime
Never fades away,
Lovely Lyca lay.

Seven summers old
Lovely Lyca told.
She had wandered long,
Hearing wild birds' song.

" Sweet sleep, come to me
Underneath this tree;
Do father, mother, weep?
Where can Lyca sleep?

" Lost in desert wild
Is your little child.
How can Lyca sleep
If her mother weep?

" If her heart does ache,
Then let Lyca wake;
If my mother sleep,
Lyca shall not weep.

" Frowning, frowning night,
O'er this desert bright
Let thy moon arise,
While I close my eyes."

Sleeping Lyca lay
While the beasts of prey,
Come from caverns deep,
Viewed the maid asleep

The kingly lion stood,
And the virgin viewed:
Then he gambolled round
O'er the hallowed ground.

Leopards, tigers, play
Round her as she lay;
While the lion old
Bowed his mane of gold,

And her breast did lick
And upon her neck,
From his eyes of flame,
Ruby tears there came;

While the lioness
Loosed her slender dress,
And naked they conveyed
To caves the sleeping maid.

THE LITTLE GIRL FOUND.

ALL the night in woe
Lyca's parents go
Over valleys deep,
While the deserts weep.

Tired and woe-begone,
Hoarse with making moan,
Arm in arm, seven days
They traced the desert ways.

Seven nights they sleep
Among shadows deep,
And dream they see their child
Starved in desert wild.

Pale through pathless ways
The fancied image strays,
Famished, weeping, weak,
With hollow piteous shriek.

Rising from unrest,
The trembling woman presse
With feet of weary woe;
She could no further go.

In his arms he bore
Her, armed with sorrow sore;
Till before their way
A couching lion lay.

Turning back was vain :
Soon his heavy mane
Bore them to the ground,
Then he stalked around,

Smelling to his prey ;
But their fears allay
When he licks their hands,
And silent by them stands.

They look upon his eyes,
Filled with deep surprise ;
And wondering behold
A spirit armed in gold.

On his head a crown,
On his shoulders down
Flowed his golden hair.
Gone was all their care.

" Follow me," he said ;
" Weep not for the maid ;
In my palace deep,
Lyca lies asleep."

Then they followèd
Where the vision led,
And saw their sleeping child
Among tigers wild.

To this day they dwell
In a lonely dell,
Nor fear the wolvish howl
Nor the lion's growl.

THE CHIMNEY SWEEPER.

A LITTLE black thing among the snow,
Crying " weep ! weep ! " in notes of woe !
" Where are thy father and mother ? Say ! "—
" They are both gone up to the church to pray.

" Because I was happy upon the heath,
And smiled among the winter's snow,
They clothed me in the clothes of death,
And taught me to sing the notes of woe.

" And because I am happy and dance and sing,
They think they have done me no injury,
And are gone to praise God and his priest and king,
Who make up a heaven of our misery."

NURSE'S SONG.

WHEN the voices of children are heard on the green,
And whisperings are in the dale,
The days of my youth rise fresh in my mind,
My face turns green and pale.

Then come home, my children, the sun is gone down,
  And the dews of night arise;
Your spring and your day are wasted in play,
. And your winter and night in disguise.

THE SICK ROSE.

O ROSE, thou art sick!
  The invisible worm,
That flies in the night,
  In the howling storm,

Has found out thy bed
  Of crimson joy,
And his dark secret love
  Does thy life destroy.

THE FLY.

LITTLE Fly,
Thy summer's play
My thoughtless hand
Has brushed away.

Am not I
A fly like thee?
Or art not thou
A man like me?

For I dance,
And drink, and sing,
Till some blind hand
Shall brush my wing.

If thought is life
And strength and breath
And the want
Of thought is death;

Then am I
A happy fly,
If I live,
Or if I die.

THE ANGEL.

I DREAMT a dream! What can it mean?
And that I was a maiden Queen
Guarded by an Angel mild:
Witless woe was ne'er beguiled!

And I wept both night and day,
And he wiped my tears away;
And I wept both day and night,
And hid from him my heart's delight.

So he took his wings, and fled;
Then the morn blushed rosy red.
I dried my tears, and armed my fears
With ten-thousand shields and spears.

Soon my Angel came again;
I was armed, he came in vain;
For the time of youth was fled,
And grey hairs were on my head.

THE TIGER.

Tiger, tiger, burning bright
In the forests of the night,
What immortal hand or eye
Could frame thy fearful symmetry?

In what distant deeps or skies
Burnt the fire of thine eyes?
On what wings dare he aspire?
What the hand dare seize the fire?

And what shoulder and what art
Could twist the sinews of thy heart?
And, when thy heart began to beat,
What dread hand and what dread feet?

What the hammer? what the chain?
In what furnace was thy brain?
What the anvil? what dread grasp
Dare its deadly terrors clasp?

When the stars threw down their spears,
And watered heaven with their tears,
Did he smile his work to see?
Did he who made the lamb make thee?

Tiger, tiger, burning bright
In the forests of the night,
What immortal hand or eye
Dare frame thy fearful symmetry?

MY PRETTY ROSE TREE.

A FLOWER was offered to me,
  Such a flower as May never bore;
But I said " I've a pretty rose tree,"
  And I passed the sweet flower o'er.

Then I went to my pretty rose tree,
  To tend her by day and by night;
But my rose turned away with jealousy,
  And her thorns were my only delight

AH SUNFLOWER.

AH Sunflower, weary of time,
  Who countest the steps of the sun;
Seeking after that sweet golden clime
  Where the traveller's journey is done;

Where the Youth pined away with desire,
  And the pale virgin shrouded in snow,
Arise from their graves, and aspire
  Where my Sunflower wishes to go!

THE LILY.

THE modest Rose puts forth a thorn,
The humble sheep a threat'ning horn:
While the Lily white shall in love delight,
Nor a thorn nor a threat stain her beauty bright.

THE GARDEN OF LOVE.

(See note at end of Songs of Experience.)

I LAID me down upon a bank,
  Where Love lay sleeping;
I heard among the rushes dank
  Weeping, weeping.

Then I went to the heath and the wild,
  To the thistles and thorns of the waste;
And they told me how they were beguiled,
  Driven out, and compelled to be chaste.

I went to the Garden of Love,
  And saw what I never had seen;
A Chapel was built in the midst,
  Where I used to play on the green

And the gates of this Chapel were shut
And "Thou shalt not" writ over the door;
So I turned to the Garden of Love
That so many sweet flowers bore.

And I saw it was filled with graves,
And tombstones where flowers should be;
And priests in black gowns were walking their rounds,
And binding with briars my joys and desires.

THE LITTLE VAGABOND.

DEAR mother, dear mother, the Church is cold;
But the Alehouse is healthy, and pleasant, and warm.
Besides, I can tell where I am used well;
The poor parsons with wind like a blown bladder swell.

But, if at the Church they would give us some ale,
And a pleasant fire our souls to regale,
We'd sing and we'd pray all the livelong day,
Nor ever once wish from the Church to stray.

Then the Parson might preach, and drink, and sing,
And we'd be as happy as birds in the spring;
And modest Dame Lurch, who is always at church,
Would not have bandy children, nor fasting, nor birch.

And God, like a father, rejoicing to see
His children as pleasant and happy as he,
Would have no more quarrel with the Devil or the barrel,
But kiss him, and give him both drink and apparel.

LONDON.

I WANDER through each chartered street,
  Near where the chartered Thames does flow,
A mark in every face I meet,
  Marks of weakness, marks of woe.

In every cry of every man,
  In every infant's cry of fear,
In every voice, in every ban,
  The mind-forged manacles I hear:

How the chimney-sweeper's cry
  Every blackening church appals,
And the hapless soldier's sigh
  Runs in blood down palace-walls.

But most, through midnight streets I hear
  How the youthful harlot's curse
Blasts the new-born infant's tear,
  And blights with plagues the marriage-hearse.

THE HUMAN ABSTRACT.

PITY would be no more
If we did not make somebody poor,
And Mercy no more could be
If all were as happy as we.

And mutual fear brings Peace,
Till the selfish loves increase;
Then Cruelty knits a snare,
And spreads his baits with care.

He sits down with his holy fears,
And waters the ground with tears;
Then Humility takes its root
Underneath his foot.

Soon spreads the dismal shade
Of Mystery over his head,
And the caterpillar and fly
Feed on the Mystery.

And it bears the fruit of Deceit,
Ruddy and sweet to eat,
And the raven his nest has made
In its thickest shade.

The gods of the earth and sea
Sought through nature to find this tree,
But their search was all in vain:
There grows one in the human Brain.

INFANT SORROW.

MY mother groaned, my father wept:
Into the dangerous world I leapt,
Helpless, naked, piping loud,
Like a fiend hid in a cloud.

Struggling in my father's hands,
Striving against my swaddling-bands,
Bound and weary, I thought best
To sulk upon my mother's breast.

CHRISTIAN FORBEARANCE.

I WAS angry with my friend:
I told my wrath, my wrath did end.
I was angry with my foe:
I told it not, my wrath did grow.

And I watered it in fears
Night and morning with my tears,
And I sunnèd it with smiles
And with soft deceitful wiles.

LIBRARY OF THE UNIVERSITY

And it grew both day and night,
Till it bore an apple bright,
And my foe beheld it shine,
And he knew that it was mine,—

And into my garden stole
When the night had veiled the pole,
In the morning, glad, I see
My foe outstretched beneath the tree.

A LITTLE BOY LOST.

" Nought loves another as itself,
   Nor venerates another so,
Nor is it possible to thought
   A greater than itself to know.

" And, father, how can I love you
   Or any of my brothers more?
I love you like the little bird
   That picks up crumbs around the door."

The Priest sat by and heard the child;
   In trembling zeal he seized his hair,
He led him by his little coat,
   And all admired the priestly care.

And standing on the altar high,
   " Lo, what a fiend is here!" said he.
" One who sets reason up for judge
   Of our most holy mystery."

The weeping child could not be heard,
   The weeping parents wept in vain:
They stripped him to his little shirt,
   And bound him in an iron chain,

And burned him in a holy place
   Where many had been burned before;
The weeping parents wept in vain.
   Are such things done on Albion's shore?

A LITTLE GIRL LOST.

Children of the future age,
Reading this indignant page,
Know that in a former time
Love, sweet love, was thought a crime.

In tho age of gold,
Free from winter's cold,
Youth and maiden bright,
To the holy light,
Naked in the sunny beams delight.

Once a youthful pair,
Filled with softest care,
Met in garden bright
Where the holy light
Had just removed the curtains of the night.

Then, in rising day,
On the grass they play;
Parents were afar,
Strangers came not near,
And the maiden soon forgot her fear.

Tired with kisses sweet,
They agree to meet
When the silent sleep
Waves o'er heaven's deep,
And the weary tired wanderers weep.

To her father white
Came the maiden bright;
But his loving look,
Like the holy book,
All her tender limbs with terror shook.

" Ona, pale and weak,
To thy father speak!
Oh the trembling fear!
Oh the dismal care
That shakes the blossoms of my hoary hair!"

A DIVINE IMAGE.

Cruelty has a human heart,
  And Jealousy a human face;
Terror the human form divine,
  And Secresy the human dress.

The human dress is forgèd iron,
  The human form a fiery forge,
The human face a furnace sealed,
  The human heart its hungry gorge.

A CRADLE SONG.

Sleep, sleep, beauty bright,
Dreaming in the joys of night;
Sleep, sleep; in thy sleep
Little sorrows sit and weep

Sweet babe, in thy face
Soft desires I can trace,
Secret joys and secret smiles,
Little pretty infant wiles.

As thy softest limbs I feel,
Smiles as of the morning steal
O'er thy cheek, and o'er thy breast
Where thy little heart doth rest.

Oh the cunning wiles that creep
In thy little heart asleep!
When thy little heart doth wake,
Then the dreadful light shall break.

THE SCHOOLBOY.

I LOVE to rise on a summer morn,
　When birds are singing on every tree;
The distant huntsman winds his horn,
　And the skylark sings with me:
　Oh what sweet company!

But to go to school in a summer morn,—
　Oh it drives all joy away!
Under a cruel eye outworn,
　The little ones spend the day
　In sighing and dismay.

Ah then at times I drooping sit,
　And spend many an anxious hour,
Nor in my book can I take delight,
　Nor sit in learning's bower,
　Worn through with the dreary shower.

How can the bird that is born for joy
　Sit in a cage and sing?
How can a child, when fears annoy,
　But droop his tender wing,
　And forget his youthful spring?

Oh father and mother, if buds are nipped,
　And blossoms blown away;
And if the tender plants are stripped
　Of their joy in the springing day,
　By sorrow and care's dismay,—

How shall the summer arise in joy,
　Or the summer fruits appear?
Or how shall we gather what griefs destroy,
　Or bless the mellowing year,
　When the blasts of winter appear?

TO TIRZAH.

Whate'er is born of mortal birth
Must be consumèd with the earth,
To rise from generation free :
Then what have I to do with thee ?
The sexes sprang from shame and pride,
Blown in the morn, in evening died ;
But mercy changed death into sleep ;
The sexes rose to work and weep.

Thou, mother of my mortal part,
With cruelty didst mould my heart,
And with false self-deceiving tears
Didst bind my nostrils, eyes, and ears,

Didst close my tongue in senseless clay,
And me to mortal life betray.
The death of Jesus set me free :
Then what have I to do with thee ?

THE VOICE OF THE ANCIENT BARD.

Youth of delight ! come hither
And see the opening morn,
Image of Truth new-born.
Doubt is fled, and clouds of reason,
Dark disputes and artful teazing.
Folly is an endless maze ;
Tangled roots perplex her ways ;
How many have fallen there !
They stumble all night over bones of the dead ;
And feel—they know not what but care ;
And wish to lead others, when they should be led.

ESD OF THE SONGS OF EXPERIENCE.

THE GATES OF PARADISE.

ENGRAVED 1793.)

------◆------

IN RODUCTION.

MUTUAL forgiveness of each vice,
Such are the Gates of Paradise,
Against the Accuser's chief desire,
Who walked among the stones of fire.
Jehovah's fingers wrote the Law:
He wept; then rose in zeal and awe,
And, in the midst of Sinai's heat,
Hid it beneath his Mercy-Seat.
   O Christians! Christians! tell me why
You rear it on your altars high!.

THE KEYS OF THE GATES.

THE caterpillar on the leaf
Reminds thee of thy mother's grief.
My Eternal Man set in repose,
The Female from his darkness rose;
And she found me beneath a tree,
A mandrake, and in her veil hid me.
Serpent reasonings us entice
Of good and evil, virtue, vice.
Doubt self-jealous, watery folly,
Struggling through Earth's melancholy.
Naked in air, in shame and fear,
Blind in fire, with shield and spear,
Two horrid reasoning cloven fictions,
In doubt which is self-contradiction,
A dark hermaphrodite I stood,—
Rational truth, root of evil and good.
Round me, flew the flaming sword;
Round her, snowy whirlwinds roared,
Freezing her veil, the mundane shell.
I rent the veil where the dead dwell:
When weary man enters his cave,
He meets his Saviour in the grave,

Some find a female garment there,
And some a male, woven with care,
Lest the sexual garments sweet
Should grow a devouring winding-sheet.
One dies! alas! the living and dead!
One is slain, and one is fled!
In vain-glory hatched and nursed,
By double spectres, self-accursed.
My son! my son! thou treatest me
But as I have instructed thee.
On the shadows of the moon,
Climbing through night's highest noon:
In Time's ocean falling, drowned:
In aged ignorance profound,
Holy and cold, I clipped the wings
Of all sublunary things:
And in depths of icy dungeons
Closed the father and the sons.
But, when once I did descry
The Immortal Man that cannot die,
Through evening shades I haste away
To close the labours of my day.
The door of Death I open found,
And the worm weaving in the ground:
Thou'rt my mother, from the womb;
Wife, sister, daughter, to the tomb:
Weaving to dreams the sexual strife,
And weeping over the web of life.

EPILOGUE.

TO THE ACCUSER, WHO IS THE GOD OF THIS WORLD

TRULY, my Satan, thou art but a dunce,
    And dost not know the garment from the man;
Every harlot was a virgin once,
    Nor canst thou ever change Kate into Nan.
Though thou art worshipped by the names divine
    Of Jesus and Jehovah, thou art still
The son of morn in weary night's decline,
    The lost traveller's dream under the hill.

TO MY DEAR FRIEND,

MRS ANNA FLAXMAN.

(Sent by Blake in a letter from Mrs. Blake to Mrs Flaxman, dated Lambeth, Sept 14, 1800)

THIS song to the flower of Flaxman's joy;
To the blossom of hope, for a sweet decoy;
Do all that you can, or all that you may,
To entice him to Felpham and far away.

Away to sweet Felpham, for heaven is there;
The ladder of angels descends through the air;
On the turret its spiral does softly descend,
Through the village then winds, at my cot it does end.

You stand in the village and look up to heaven;
The precious stones glitter on flight seventy-seven;
And my brother is there, and my friend and thine
Descend and ascend with the bread and the wine.

The bread of sweet thought and the wine of delight
Feed the village of Felpham by day and by night;
And at his own door the bless'd Hermit does stand,
Dispensing unceasing to all the wide land.

TO MR. BUTTS

(From a letter dated Felpham, Oct. 2, 1800)

To my friend Butts I write
My first vision of light,
On the yellow sands sitting.
The sun was emitting
His glorious beams
From heaven's high streams
Over sea, over land,
My eyes did expand
Into regions of air,
Away from all care;
Into regions of fire,
Remote from desire:
The light of the morning
Heaven's mountains adorning.
In particles bright,
The jewels of light
Distinct shone and clear.
Amazed and in fear
I each particle gazed,
Astonished, amazed;
For each was a man
Human-formed. Swift I ran,
For they beckoned to me,
Remote by the sea,
Saying: " Each grain of sand,
Every stone on the land,

Each rock and each hill,
Each fountain and rill,
Each herb and each tree,
Mountain, hill, earth, and sea,
Cloud, meteor, and star,
Are men seen afar."
I stood in the streams
Of heaven's bright beams,
And saw Felpham sweet
Beneath my bright feet,
In soft female charms;
And in her fair arms
My shadow I knew,
And my wife's shadow too,
And my sister and friend.
We like infants descend
In our shadows on earth,
Like a weak mortal birth.
My eyes more and more,
Like a sea without shore,
Continue expanding,
The heavens commanding,
Till the jewels of light,
Heavenly men beaming bright,
Appeared as one man,
Who complacent began
My limbs to infold
In his beams of bright gold;
Like dross purged away
All my mire and my clay.
Soft consumed in delight,
In his bosom sun-bright
I remained. Soft he smiled,
And I heard his voice mild,
Saying: " This is my fold,
O thou ram horned with gold,
Who awakest from sleep
On the sides of the deep.
On the mountains around
The roarings resound
Of the lion and wolf,
The loud sea and deep gulph.
These are guards of my fold,
O thou ram horned with gold!"
And the voice faded mild,—
I remained as a child;
All I ever had known
Before me bright shone:
I saw you and your wife
By the fountains of life.
Such the vision to me
Appeared on the sea.

TO MRS. BUTTS.

(From the same letter.)

WIFE of the friend of those I most revere,
Receive this tribute from a harp sincere;
Go on in virtuous seed-sowing on mould
Of human vegetation, and behold
Your harvest springing to eternal life,
Parent of youthful minds, and happy wife

VERSES.

(From a letter to Mr. Butts dated Felpham, Nov. 22, 1802)

WITH happiness stretched across the hills
In a cloud that dewy sweetness distils,
With a blue sky spread over with wings,
And a mild sun that mounts and sings;
With trees and fields full of fairy elves,
And little devils who fight for themselves,
Remembering the verses that Hayley sung
When my heart knocked against the root of my tongue,
With angels planted in hawthorn bowers,
And God himself in the passing hours;
With silver angels across my way,
And golden demons that none can stay;
With my father hovering upon the wind,
And my brother Robert just behind,
And my brother John, the evil one,
In a black cloud making his moan;
(Though dead, they appear upon my path,
Notwithstanding my terrible wrath;
They beg, they entreat, they drop their tears,
Filled full of hopes, filled full of fears;)
With a thousand angels upon the wind,
Pouring disconsolate from behind
To drive them off.—and before my way
A frowning Thistle implores my stay.
What to others a trifle appears
Fills me full of smiles or tears;
For double the vision my eyes do see,
And a double vision is always with me.
With my inward eye, 'tis an old man grey;
With my outward, a thistle across my way.

" If thou goest back," the Thistle said,
" Thou art to endless woe betrayed;
For here does Theotormon lour,
And here is Enitharmon's bower,
And Los the terrible thus hath sworn,
Because thou backward dost return,
Poverty, envy, old age, and fear,

Shall bring thy wife upon a bier ;
And Butts shall give what Fuseli gave,
A dark black rock and a gloomy cave "
I struck the thistle with my foot,
And broke him up from his delving root.
" Must the duties of life each other cross ?
Must every joy be dung and dross ?
Must my dear Butts feel cold neglect
Because I give Hayley his due respect ?
Must Flaxman look upon me as wild,
And all my friends be with doubts beguiled ?
Must my wife live in my sister's bane,
Or my sister survive on my Love's pain ?
The curses of Los, the terrible shade,
And his dismal terrors, make me afraid.'.'

So I spoke, and struck in my wrath
The old man weltering upon my path.
Then Los appeared in all his power :
In the sun he appeared, descending before
My face in fierce flames ; in my double sight,
'Twas outward a sun,—inward, Los in his might.
" My hands are laboured day and night,
And ease comes never in my sight.
My wife has no indulgence given,
Except what comes to her from heaven.
We eat little, we drink less ;
This earth breeds not our happiness.
Another sun feeds our life's streams ;
We are not warmèd with thy beams.
Thou measurest not the time to me,
Nor yet the space that I do see :
My mind is not with thy light arrayed ;
Thy terrors shall not make me afraid."

When I had my defiance given,
The sun stood trembling in heaven ;
The moon, that glowed remote below,
Became leprous and white as snow ;
And every soul of man on the earth
Felt affliction and sorrow and sickness and dearth.
Los flamed in my path, and the sun was hot
With the bows of my mind and the arrows of thought :
My bowstring fierce with ardour breathes,
My arrows glow in their golden sheaves
My brother and father march before ;
The heavens drop with human gore.

Now I a fourfold vision see,
And a fourfold vision is given to me ;

'Tis fourfold in my supreme delight,
And threefold in soft Beulah's night,
And twofold always. May God us keep
From single vision, and Newton's sleep !

(As printed in the Aldine Edition of Blake's Poems.)

THE BIRDS.

HE.

WHERE thou dwellest, in what grove,
Tell me, fair one, tell me, love ;
Where thou thy charming nest doth build,
O thou pride of every field !

SHE.

Yonder stands a lonely tree :
There I live and mourn for thee.
Morning drinks my silent tear,
And evening winds my sorrow bear.

HE.

O thou summer's harmony,
I have lived and mourned for thee ;
Each day I moan along the wood,
And night hath heard my sorrows loud.

SHE.

Dost thou truly long for me ?
And am I thus sweet to thee ?
Sorrow now is at an end,
O my lover and my friend !

HE.

Come ! on wings of joy we'll fly
To where my bower is hung on high ;
Come, and make thy calm retreat
Among green leaves and blossoms sweet.

THE TWO SONGS.

I HEARD an Angel singing
When the day was springing :
" Mercy, pity, and peace,
Are the world's release."

So he sang all day
Over the new-mown hay,
Till the sun went down,
And haycocks looked brown

I heard a Devil curse
Over the heath and the furse:
"Mercy could be no more
If there were nobody poor,
And pity no more could be
If all were happy as ye:
And mutual fear brings peace.
Misery's increase
Are mercy, pity, peace."

At his curse the sun went down,
And the heavens gave a frown.

THE DEFILED SANCTUARY.

I saw a chapel all of gold
  That none did dare to enter in,
And many weeping stood without,
  Weeping, mourning, worshipping,

I saw a serpent rise between
  The white pillars of the door,
And he forced and forced and forced
  Till he the golden hinges tore:

And along the pavement sweet,
  Set with pearls and rubies bright,
All his shining length he drew,—
  Till upon the altar white

He vomited his poison out
  On the bread and on the wine.
So I turned into a sty,
  And laid me down among the swine.

CUPID.

Why was Cupid a boy,
  And why a boy was he?
He should have been a girl,
  For aught that I can see.

For he shoots with his bow,
  And the girl shoots with her eye
And they both are merry and glad
  And laugh when we do cry.

Then to make Cupid a boy
   Was surely a woman's plan,
For a boy never learns so much
   Till he has become a man:

And then he's so pierced with cares,
   And wounded with arrowy smarts,
That the whole business of his life
   Is to pick out the heads of the darts.

LOVE'S SECRET. ✓

NEVER seek to tell thy love,
   Love that never told can be;
For the gentle wind doth move
   Silently, invisibly.

I told my love, I told my love,
   I told her all my heart,
Trembling, cold, in ghastly fears.
   Ah! she did depart!

Soon after she was gone from me,
   A traveller came by,
Silently, invisibly:
   He took her with a sigh.

THE WILD FLOWER'S SONG.

As I wandered in the forest
   The green leaves among,
I heard a wild-flower
   Singing a song.

"I slept in the earth
   In the silent night;
I murmured my thoughts,
   And I felt delight.

"In the morning I went,
   As rosy as morn,
To seek for new joy,
   But I met with scorn."

SCOFFERS.

Mock on, mock on, Voltaire, Rousseau,
   Mock on, mock on; 'tis all in vain;
You throw the sand against the wind,
   And the wind blows it back again

And every sand becomes a gem,
   Reflected in the beams divine;
Blown back, they blind the mocking eye,
   But still in Israel's paths they shine.

The atoms of Democritus
   And Newton's particles of light
Are sands upon the Red Sea shore
   Where Israel's tents do shine so bright.

DAYBREAK.

To find the western path,
Right through the gates of wrath
   I urge my way;
Sweet morning leads me on;
With soft repentant moan
   I see the break of day.

The war of swords and spears,
Melted by dewy tears,
   Exhales on high;
The sun is freed from fears,
And with soft grateful tears
   Ascends the sky. ·

THAMES AND OHIO. .

Why should I care for the men of Thames,
And the cheating waters of chartered streams,
Or shrink at the little blasts of fear
That the hireling blows into mine ear?

Though born on the cheating banks of Thames—
Though his waters bathed my infant limbs—
The Ohio shall wash his stains from me;
I was born a slave, but I go to be free.

YOUNG LOVE.

Are not the joys of morning sweeter
   Than the joys of night?
And are the vigorous joys of youth
   Ashamèd of the light?.

Let age and sickness silent rob
   The vineyard in the night;
But those who burn with vigorous youth
   Pluck fruits before the light

THE GOLDEN NET.

BENEATH a white-thorn's lovely may
Three virgins at the break of day.—
" Whither, young man, whither away
Alas for woe ! alas for woe ! "
They cry, and tears for ever flow.
The first was clothed in flames of fire,
The second clothed in iron wire ,
The third was clothed in tears and sighs
Dazzling bright before my eyes.
They bore a net of golden twine
To hang upon the branches fine.
Pitying I wept to see the woe
That love and beauty undergo—
To be clothed in burning fires
And in ungratified desires,
And in tears clothed night and day ;
It melted all my soul away.
When they saw my tears, a smile
That might heaven itself beguile
Bore the golden net aloft,
As on downy pinions soft,
Over the morning of my day.
Underneath the net I stray,
Now entreating Flaming-fire
Now entreating Iron-wire,
Now entreating Tears-and-sighs —
Oh when will the morning rise ?

RICHES.

SINCE all the riches of this world
  May be gifts from the devil and earthly kings,
I should suspect that I worshipped the devil
  If I thanked my God for worldly things.

The countless gold of a merry heart,
  The rubies and pearls of a loving eye,
The idle man never can bring to the mart,
  Nor the cunning hoard up in his treasury.

OPPORTUNITY.

HE who bends to himself a joy
Does the winged life destroy ,
But he who kisses the joy as it flies
Lives in eternity's sunrise.

If you trap the moment before it's ripe,
The tears of repentance you'll certainly wipe;
But, if once you let the ripe moment go,
You can never wipe off the tears of woe.

SEED-SOWING.

" THOU hast a lapful of seed,"
And this is a fair country.
Why dost thou not cast thy seed,
And live in it merrily?"

" Shall I cast it on the sand,
And turn it into fruitful land?
For on no other ground can I sow my seed
Without tearing up some stinking weed."

BARREN BLOSSOM.

I FEARED the fury of my wind
Would blight all blossoms fair and true,
And my sun it shined and shined,
And my wind it never blew.

But a blossom fair or true
Was not found on any tree;
For all blossoms grew and grew
Fruitless, false, though fair to see.

NIGHT AND DAY.

SILENT, silent Night,
Quench the holy light
Of thy torches bright;

For, possessed of Day,
Thousand spirits stray
That sweet joys betray.

Why should joys be sweet
Used with deceit,
Nor with sorrows meet?

But an honest joy
Doth itself destroy
For a harlot coy.

LIBRARY OF THE UNIVERSITY

IN A MYRTLE SHADE.

To a lovely myrtle bound,
Blossoms showering all around,
Oh how weak and weary I
Underneath my myrtle lie!

Why should I be bound to thee,
O my lovely myrtle-tree?
Love, free love, cannot be bound
To any tree that grows on ground.

IDOLATRY.

If it is true, what the Prophets write,
   That the Heathen Gods are all stocks and stones,
Shall we, for the sake of being polite,
   Feed them with the juice of our marrow bones?

And, if Bezaleel and Aholiab drew
What the finger of God pointed to their view,
Shall we suffer the Roman and Grecian rods
To compel us to worship them as Gods?

They stole them from
   The Temple of the Lord,
And worshipped them that they might make
   Inspired art abhorred.

The wood and stone were called the holy things,
And their sublime intent given to their kings;
All the atonements of Jehovah spurned,
And criminals to sacrifices turned.

FOR A PICTURE OF THE LAST JUDGMENT.

DEDICATION.

The caverns of the Grave I've seen,
And these I showed to England's Queen
But now the caves of Hell I view,—
Whom shall I dare to show them to?
What mighty soul in beauty's form
Shall dauntless view the infernal storm?
Egremont's Countess can control
The flames of hell that round me roll
If she refuse, I still go on,
Till the heavens and earth are gone;
Still admired by noble minds,
Followed by Envy on the winds.

Re-engraved time after time,
Ever in their youthful prime,
My designs unchanged remain ;
Time may rage, but rage in vain ;
For above Time's troubled fountains,
On the great Atlantic mountains,
In my golden house on high,
There they shine eternally.

THE WILL AND THE WAY.

I ASKED a thief to steal me a peach :
   He turned up his eyes
I asked a lithe lady to lie her down :
   Holy and meek, she cries.

As soon as I went,
   An Angel came.
He winked at the thief,
   And smiled at the dame ;

And, without one word spoke,
   Had a peach from the tree,
And 'twixt earnest and joke
   Enjoyed the lady.

SMILE AND FROWN.

THERE is a smile of Love,
   And there is a smile of Deceit,
And there is a smile of smiles
   In which these two smiles meet.

And there is a frown of Hate,
   And there is a frown of Disdain,
And there is a frown of frowns
   Which you strive to forget in vain,

For it sticks in the heart's deep core
   And it sticks in the deep backbone.
And no smile ever was smiled
   But only one smile alone.

(And betwixt the cradle and grave
   It only once smiled can be)
That when it once is smiled
   There's an end to all misery.

THE LAND OF DREAMS.

AWAKE, awake, my little boy!
Thou wast thy mother's only joy.
Why dost thou weep in thy gentle sleep?
Oh wake! thy father doth thee keep.

"Oh what land is the land of dreams?
What are its mountains and what are its streams?"
"Oh father! I saw my mother there,
Among the lilies by waters fair.

"Among the lambs clothèd in white,
She walked with her Thomas in sweet delight
I wept for joy, like a dove I mourn—
Oh when shall I again return?"

"Dear child! I also by pleasant streams
Have wandered all night in the land of dreams
But, though calm and warm the waters wide,
I could not get to the other side."

"Father, O father! what do we here,
In this land of unbelief and fear?
The land of dreams is better far,
Above the light of the morning star."

AUGURIES OF INNOCENCE.

TO see a world in a grain of sand,
  And a heaven in a wild flower;
Hold infinity in the palm of your hand,
  And eternity in an hour.

A Robin Redbreast in a cage
Puts all Heaven in a rage;
A dove-house filled with doves and pigeons
Shudders hell through all its regions.
A dog starved at his master's gate
Predicts the ruin of the state;
A game-cock clipped and armed for fight
Doth the rising sun affright;
A horse misused upon the road
Calls to Heaven for human blood.
Every wolf's and lion's howl
Raises from hell a human soul,
Each outcry of the hunted hare
A fibre from the brain doth tear;
A skylark wounded on the wing
Doth make a cherub cease to sing.

He who shall hurt the little wren
Shall never be beloved by men ;
He who the ox to wrath has moved
Shall never be by woman loved ;
He who shall train the horse to war
Shall never pass the Polar Bar.
The wanton boy that kills the fly
Shall feel the spider's enmity ;
He who torments the chafer's sprite
Weaves a bower in endless night.
The caterpillar on the leaf
Repeats to thee thy mother's grief;
The wild deer wandering here and there
Keep the human soul from care :
The lamb misused breeds public strife,
And yet forgives the butcher's knife.
Kill not the moth nor butterfly,
For the last judgment draweth nigh ;
The beggar's dog and widow's cat,
Feed them and thou shalt grow fat.
Every tear from every eye
Becomes a babe in eternity ;
The bleat, the bark, bellow, and roar,
Are waves that beat on heaven's shore.

The bat that flits at close of eve
Has left the brain that won't believe;
The owl that calls upon the night
Speaks the unbeliever's fright.
The gnat that sings his summer's song
Poison gets from Slander's tongue ;
The poison of the snake and newt
Is the sweat of Envy's foot ;
The poison of the honey-bee
Is the artist's jealousy ;
The strongest poison ever known
Came from Cæsar's laurel-crown.

Nought can deform the human race
Like to the armourer's iron brace ;
The soldier armed with sword and gun
Palsied strikes the summer's sun.
When gold and gems adorn the plough,
To peaceful hearts shall Envy bow.
The beggar's rags fluttering in air
Do to rags the heavens tear ;
The prince's robes and beggar's rags
Are toadstools on the miser's bags.

One mite wrung from the labourer's hands
Shall buy and sell the miser's lands,
Or, if protected from on high,
Shall that whole nation sell and buy,
The poor man's farthing is worth more
Than all the gold on Afric's shore.
The whore and gambler, by the state
Licensed, build that nation's fate;
The harlot's cry from street to street
Shall weave old England's winding-sheet;
The winner's shout, the loser's curse,
Shall dance before dead England's hearse

He who mocks the infant's faith
Shall be mocked in age and death;
He who shall teach the child to doubt
The rotting grave shall ne'er get out;
He who respects the infant's faith
Triumphs over hell and death.
The babe is more than swaddling-bands
Throughout all these human lands;
Tools were made, and born were hands,
Every farmer understands.
The questioner who sits so sly
Shall never know how to reply.
He who replies to words of doubt
Doth put the light of knowledge out;
A puddle, or the cricket's cry,
Is to doubt a fit reply.
The child's toys and the old man's reasons
Are the fruits of the two seasons.
The emmet's inch and eagle's mile
Make lame philosophy to smile.
A truth that's told with bad intent
Beats all the lies you can invent.
He who doubts from what he sees
Will ne'er believe, do what you please;
If the sun and moon should doubt,
They'd immediately go out

Every night and every morn
Some to misery are born;
Every morn and every night
Some are born to sweet delight;
Some are born to sweet delight,
Some are born to endless night.
Joy and woe are woven fine,
A clothing for the soul divine;
Under every grief and pine
Runs a joy with silken twine.

It is right it should be so,
Man was made for joy and woe;
And, when this we rightly know,
Safely through the world we go.

We are led to believe a lie
When we see *with* not *through* the eye,
Which was born in a night to perish in a night
When the soul slept in beams of light,
God appears and God is light
To those poor souls who dwell in night;
But doth a human form display
To those who dwell in realms of day.

WILLIAM BOND.

I WONDER whether the girls are mad,
  And I wonder whether they mean to kill,
And I wonder if William Bond will die,
  For assuredly he is very ill.

He went to church on a May morning,
  Attended by fairies, one, two, and three;
But the angels of Providence drove them away,
  And he returned home in misery.

He went not out to the field nor fold,
  He went not out to the village nor town,
But he came home in a black black cloud,
  And took to his bed, and there lay down

And an angel of Providence at his feet,
  And an angel of Providence at his head,
And in the midst a black black cloud,
  And in the midst the sick man on his bed.

And on his right hand was Mary Green,
  And on his left hand was his sister Jane,
And their tears fell through the black black cloud
  To drive away the sick man's pain.

"Oh William, if thou dost another love,
  Dost another love better than poor Mary,
Go and take that other to be thy wife,
  And Mary Green shall her servant be."

"Yes, Mary, I do another love,
  Another I love far better than thee,
And another I will have for my wife:
  Then what have I to do with thee?

" For thou art melancholy pale,
   And on thy head is the cold moon's shine,
But she is ruddy and bright as day,
   And the sunbeams dazzle from her eyne "

Mary trembled, and Mary chilled,
   And Mary fell down on the right-hand floor,
That William Bond and his sister Jane
   Scarce could recover Mary more.

When Mary woke and found her laid
   On the right hand of her William dear,
On the right hand of his loved bed,
   And saw her William Bond so near ;

The fairies that fled from William Bond
   Danced around her shining head ;
They danced over the pillow white,
   And the angels of Providence left the bed.

" I thought love lived in the hot sunshine,
   But oh he lives in the moony light !
I thought to find Love in the heat of day,
   But sweet Love is the comforter of night.

" Seek Love in the pity of others' woe,
   In the gentle relief of another's care.
In the darkness of night and the winter's snow,
   With the naked and outcast,—seek Love there."

SONG BY A SHEPHERD.

WELCOME little stranger to this place,
   Where joy doth sit on every bough,
Paleness flies from every face,
   We reap not what we do not sow.

Innocence doth, like a rose,
   Bloom on every maiden's cheek.
Honour twines around her brows,
   The jewel health adorns her neck.

SONG BY AN OLD SHEPHERD.

WHEN silver snow decks Silvia's clothes,
And jewel hangs at shepherd's nose,
We can abide life's pelting storm,
That makes our limbs quake if our hearts be warm.

Whilst Virtue is our walking staff
And Truth a lantern to our path,
We can abide life's pelting storm,
Which makes our limbs quake if our hearts be warm

Blow boist'rous wind, stern winter frown,
Innocence is a winter's gown.
So clad, we'll abide life's pelting storm,
That makes our limbs quake if our hearts be warm.

LONG JOHN BROWN AND LITTLE MARY BELL

LITTLE Mary Bell had a fairy in a nut,
Long John Brown had the devil in his gut,
Long John Brown loved little Mary Bell,
And the fairy drew the devil into the nutshell.

Her fairy skipp'd out, her fairy skipp'd in,
He laughed at the devil, saying " Love is a sin."
The devil he raged and the devil he was wroth,
And the devil entered into the young man's broth.

He was soon in the gut of the loving young swain,
For John eat and drank to drive away love's pain,
But all he could do he grew thinner and thinner,
Though he eat and drank as much as ten men for his dinner.

Some said he had a wolf in his stomach day and night,
Some said he had the devil, and they guessed right,
The fairy skipped about in his glory, love and pride,
And he laughed at the devil till poor John Brown died.

Then the fairy skipp'd out of the old nutshell,
And woe and alack for pretty Mary Bell,
For the devil crept in when the fairy skipp'd out,
And there goes Miss Bell with her fusty old nut.

MARY.

SWEET Mary, the first time she ever was there,
Came into the ball-room among the fair ;
The young men and maidens around her throng,
And these are the words upon every tongue : .

" An angel is here from the heavenly climes,
Or again return the golden times;
Her eyes outshine every brilliant ray,
She opens her lips—'tis the month of May."

Mary moves in soft beauty and conscious delight,
To augment with sweet smiles all the joys of the night,
Nor once blushes to own to the rest of the fair
That sweet love and beauty are worthy our care.

In the morning the villagers rose with delight,
And repeated with pleasure the joys of the night,
And Mary arose among friends to be free,
But no friend from henceforward thou, Mary, shalt see.

Some said she was proud, some called her a whore,
And some when she passed by shut-to the door;
A damp cold came o'er her, her blushes all fled,
Her lilies and roses are blighted and shed

" Oh why was I born with a different face?
Why was I not born like this envious race?
Why did Heaven adorn me with bountiful hand,
And then set me down in an envious land?

" To be weak as a lamb and smooth as a dove,
And not to raise envy, is called Christian love;
But, if you raise envy, your merit's to blame
For planting such spite in the weak and the tame.

" I will humble my beauty, I will not dress fine,
I will keep from the ball, and my eyes shall not shine;
And, if any girl's lover forsake her for me,
I'll refuse him my hand, and from envy be free."

She went out in the morning attired plain and neat;
" Proud Mary's gone mad," said the child in the street;
She went out in the morning in plain neat attire,
And came home in the evening bespattered with mire.

She trembled and wept, sitting on the bedside,
She forgot it was night, and she trembled and cried;
She forgot it was night, she forgot it was morn,
Her soft memory imprinted with faces of scorn;

With faces of scorn and with eyes of disdain,
Like foul fiends inhabiting Mary's mild brain;
She remembers no face like the human divine;
All faces have envy, sweet Mary, but thine.

And thine is a face of sweet love in despair,
And thine is a face of mild sorrow and care,
And thine is a face of wild terror and fear
That shall never be quiet till laid on its bier.

THE CRYSTAL CABINET.

The maiden caught me in the wild,
  Where I was dancing merrily;
She put me into her cabinet,
  And locked me up with a golden key.

This cabinet is formed of gold,
  And pearl and crystal shining bright,
And within it opens into a world
  And a little lovely moony night.

Another England there I saw,
  Another London with its Tower,
Another Thames and other hills,
  And another pleasant Surrey bower.

Another maiden like herself,
  Translucent, lovely, shining clear,
Threefold, each in the other closed,—
  Oh what a pleasant trembling fear

Oh what a smile! A threefold smile
  Filled me that like a flame I burned
I bent to kiss the lovely maid,
  And found a threefold kiss returned.

I strove to seize the inmost form
  With ardour fierce and hands of flame,
But burst the crystal cabinet,
  And like a weeping babe became:

A weeping babe upon the wild,
  And weeping woman pale reclined,
And in the outward air again
  I filled with woes the passing wind.

COUPLETS AND FRAGMENTS.

(Not printed now for the first time.)
See Vol. I., p. 202, The MS. Book.

———◆———

I.

I walked abroad on a snowy day,
I asked the soft Snow with me to play;
She played and she melted in all her prime;
And the Winter called it a dreadful crime.

II.

Abstinence sows sand all over
   The ruddy limbs and flaming hair;
But desire gratified
   Plants fruits of life and beauty there

III.

The look of love alarms,
   Because 'tis filled with fire,
But the look of soft deceit
   Shall win the lover's hire:
Soft deceit and idleness,
These are beauty's sweetest dress.

IV.

To Chloe's breast young Cupid slily stole,
But he crept in at Myra's pocket-hole.

V.

Grown old in love from seven till seven times seven,
I oft have wished for hell, for ease from heaven.

VI.

The Sword sang on the barren heath,
   The Sickle in the fruitful field:
The Sword he sang a song of death,
   But could not make the Sickle yield.

VII.

Great things are done when men and mountains meet;
These are not done by jostling in the street.

VIII.

The errors of a wise man make your rule,
Rather than the perfections of a fool.

IX.

Some people admire the work of a fool,
For it's sure to keep your judgment cool.
It does not reproach you with want of wit;
It is not like a lawyer serving a writ.

X.

He's a blockhead who wants a proof of what he can't perceive,
And he's a fool who tries to make such a blockhead believe.

XI.

If e'er I grow to man's estate,
Oh give to me a woman's fate!
May I govern all, both great and small,
Have the last word, and take the wall!

XII.

Her whole life is an epigram—smack, smooth, and nobly penned,
Plaited quite neat to catch applause, with a strong noose at the end.

XIII.

Anger and wrath my bosom rends,
I thought them the errors of friends;
But all my limbs with warmth do glow,
I find them the errors of the foe.

XIV.

TO F——.

I mock thee not, though I by thee am mocked,
Thou call'st me madman, but I call thee blockhead

XV.

Here lies John Trot, the friend of all mankind,
He has not left one enemy behind:
Friends were quite hard to find, old authors say,
But now they stand in everybody's way.

XVI.

No real style of colouring now appears,
But advertising in the Newspapers,
Look here, you'll see Sir Joshua's colouring;
Look at his pictures: all has taken wing.

XVII.

You don't believe : I won't attempt to make ye.
You are asleep ; I won't attempt to wake ye.
Sleep on, sleep on, while in your pleasant dreams
Of Reason, you may drink of Life's clear streams,
Reason and Newton : they are quite two things,
For so the swallow, and the sparrow sings.

Reason says " Miracle !" Newton says " Doubt,
" Aye, that's the way to make all nature out.
Doubt, doubt, and don't believe without experiment ;
That is the very thing that Jesus meant,
When he said, ' Only believe : believe and try ;
Try, try, and never mind the reason why.' "

XIX.

You must agree that Rubens was a fool,
And yet you make him master of your school
And give more money for his slobberings
Than you will give for Rafael's finest thing.

XX.

WHEN I see a Rembrandt or Correggio,
I think of crippled Harry, or slobbering Joe.
And then I say to myself, are artist's rules
To be drawn from the works of two manifest fools ?
Then God defend us from the arts, I say,
Send battle, murder, sudden death, we pray
Rather than be such a human fool
I'd be a hog, a worm, a chair, a stool.

XXI.

I ASKED my dear friend, Orator Prig,
" What's the first thing in oratory ?" he said : " A great Wig."
" And what is the second ?" Then dancing a jig
And bowing profoundly, he said : " A great Wig."
" And what is the third ?" Then he snored like a pig,
And thrust out his cheeks, and replied : "A great Wig."

So, if to a painter the question you push,
" What's the first part of painting ?" he'd say, " A paint brush,"
" And what is the second ?" with most modest blush
He'll smile like a cherub, and say, " A paint brush."
" And what is the third ?" He will bow like a rush,
With a leer in his eye, and reply, " A paint brush."

Perhaps this is all that a painter can want,
But look yonder ; that house is the house of Rembrandt.

XXII.

O DEAR mother Outline, of wisdom most sage,
"What's the first part of painting?" She said, "Patronage."
"And what is the second, to please and engage?"
She frowned like a fury, and said, "Patronage."
"And what is the third?" She put off old age,
And smiled like a Syren, and said, "Patronage."

XXIII.

THAT God is colouring Newton does show,
And the devil is a black outline all of us know.

TO VENETIAN ARTISTS.

PERHAPS this little fable may make us merry.
A dog went over the water without a wherry.
A bone which he had stolen he had in his mouth.
He cared not whether the wind was north or south
As he swam he saw the reflection of the bone
This is quite perfection—generalizing tone!
Snap! snap!—and lost the substance and shadow too
He had both these before.   Now how d'ye do?
Those who have tasted colouring, love it more and more.

NOTES TO THE POETICAL SKETCHES,

SONGS, &c.

SELECTIONS from these were printed in Gilchrist's " Life," and a text was made for them by Dante Gabriel Rossetti which has been generally recognized as a real service to literature and by no means a forced or unfair treatment of Blake.

The Aldine Edition, however, restored most of the original errors. Perhaps it was well that this should be done once, though a series of notes to the changes would have served the biographical purpose and yet left an enjoyable page to the reader.

When the present work was schemed, there was no intention to print more of Blake's own writings than what called aloud for interpretation, and had called, up to the date of this edition, in vain.

The only exceptions to the rule were made in favour of two fine pieces, the Samson, and the prologue to King John, which stood as much in need of correction, as the prophetic books did of interpretation When, however, it became evident that new material and necessary reference to old errors, whether of text or biography, had so swollen the book that it could no longer be bound in two volumes, a division into three, and the addition of the present reprint of the Sketches, Songs, and other fragments, was decided upon after all the rest of the work was in type.

Among the most beautiful of the " Poetical Sketches " are the fragments of the play called " King Edward the Third." Portions of these, unnecessarily re-broken, have long been known in Gilchrist's " Life." The rest may be read in the Aldine, and in Mr. Quaritch's facsimile reprint of the original edition. In the text here given most of Dante Gabriel Rossetti's emendations as used by Gilchrist are adopted, and his system has been extended to the rest of the book, as to " Vala " Unlike " Vala," however, the original and imperfect text is already widely known and easily accessible. It is not necessary here, for conscience' sake, to give it, as in the notes to " Vala," with an exact description of every alteration made. It will be enough to name the lines which have been restored to metre from the wonderfully careless and self-confuting form in which they were left by the hasty hand that created, but would not control them.

They are the following. The lines are counted from the first of each speech. Many are left with evident errors in them only because the correction is not obviously suggested by the errors, and re-writing would be required to make the lines conform to what should have been their own law. Others have a dramatic value from their irregularity. These also are left untouched.

Words like *England, singly*, &c., which count as three syllables, have been left with that value. It is truly theirs when spoken slowly, though grammar pretends not to know this.

Compare Shakespeare, *Troilus and Cressida*, Act III., Sc. III., l. 200, crad-l-es (three syllables)

Does thoughts unveil in their dumb cradles, and Shelley,—tremb-l-ing-ly (four syllables).

Below far lands one seen tremblingly.

On the Medusa of Leonardo da Vinci.

Scene I.

King's speech, lines 2, 4, 6, 7, 11, 13, 20, 21, 23, 29, 45, 47.

Scene II.

Clarence's first speech, lines 13, 14, 17; second speech, lines 2, 4, 5, 8, 9.
Bishop, first speech, lines 1, 3; third speech, lines 2, 3, 5, 12.
Percy, line 7.

Scene III.

Lord Audley, first speech, lines 3, 4
Dagworth, ninth speech, line 4; tenth speech, lines 1, 2; thirteenth speech, line 5; fifteenth speech, lines 6, 7; sixteenth speech, lines 4, 5.
King, first speech, lines 1, 2, 4, 5, 7, 9;
fourth speech, line 3, seventh speech, line 3.
Black Prince, first speech, lines 4, 6; third speech, line 4.
Chandos, fifth speech, lines 2, 6, 7, 8; sixth speech, lines 5, 8; seventh speech, lines 1, 9.

Scene V.

Sir Walter Manny, first speech, line 1; second speech, lines 3, 6, 8, 9, 10, 11, 14, 16, 17.
Sir Thomas Dagworth, third speech, lines 5, 9.

Scene VI.

Bard's Song, lines 13, 18, 19, 20, 34, 35, 49, 50, 54, 55, 56, 57.

Prologue to King Edward the Fourth, lines 3, 4, 5, 6, 7, 8. Prologue to King John. This was printed as prose. It is divided into lines in the Aldine Edition as given here, and re-divided differently, with slight verbal alterations in the text to be found above in Vol. I., page 177. "Samson," similarly treated, will be found on page 179.

To Spring, lines 5, 6.

To Autumn, line 18.

To Winter, lines 14, 15, 16.

To the Evening star, lines 3, 6, 7, 12, 14

Every line not included in the above list is reprinted exactly as it was left by Blake.

In the close of the Prince's great speech to Chandos, in the re-touched text of Gilchrist, Dante Rossetti had only added one word, *then*, after *come*, in the line which before stood thus,—

"Ambition, come, take the helm, my Chandos"

in order that the word *Ambition* should not be stretched on the rack of four syllables. The Aldine edition wanders   Here is the original, which the present edition gives untouched.

"My blood like a spring-tide
Does rise so high to overflow all bounds
Of moderation, while Reason in her
Frail bark can see no shore or bound for vast
Ambition. Come, take the helm my Chandos,
That my full-blown sails overset me not
In the wild tempest."

Everything here depends on the reader. If he but know how to sound them, these lines form the fitting preparation for the close of a speech which is one strong, swift broad-winged flight throughout. The Aldine limes its feathers thus, and brings it down to an ill-measured flapping.

> "My blood like a spring-tide
> Does rise so high to overflow all bounds
> Of moderation; while Reason in her frail bark,
> Can see no shore or bound for vast ambition.
> Come, take the helm, my Chandos,
> That my full-blown sails overset me not
> In the wild tempest."

We unwillingly differ from Dante Gabriel Rossetti in his correction of the lines from the reply of Chandos,—

> "Age is contemplative; each rolling year
> Brings forth fruit to the mind's treasure house.

The omission of the word *her*, after *brings forth*, seems to have been a mere slip of the pen. Its addition completes the feminine figure of speech implied in the words "*bring forth.*" The line now,—

> "Brings forth her fruit to the mind's treasure house"

has the natural Blakean roll, while to read

> "Doth bring forth fruit to the mind's treasure house,"

is to give the forward movement of the verse a sudden check, while the sound merely marks time.

His alteration of the incomplete line at the end—

> "with distaste, and dislike ——"

into   "As worthless" .

is so unhappy, and unnecessary, that though an ill-advised objection to the emphatic and powerful repetition of the syllable *dis* may account for it, this can hardly be looked on as sufficient justification.

The line from the Prince's last speech in this scene,—

> "Shall mount on native wings, disdaining little sport,"

is something more than an accident. It is a foreshadowing of Blake's later style in using a longer line, and although not in place where it stands is too good in itself to lose. Readers disliking it will skip the word "native" without an effort, following Dante Gabriel Rossetti's text.

In result, a careful study of this fragment of a play will leave no one doubtful that here is a school of blank verse more poetic and bardic, while not less dramatic, than the Elizabethan. The man who taught it was soon intent on far more important lessons. He let this one drop unrepeated. Its effect in literature has not yet been felt for a sufficient reason. The style of his work is totally unadapted for the writing of scannable prose, or even for moulding the measures of a moderately poetic expression. Its flights and pauses are so dauntlessly emphatic that any one who yields to them, must, like their first inventor, be roused into a strongly voiced, full thoughted fiery dream; or failing this, show his thin muse betrayed, like a lean dancer in sunshine at a fair. But when the sneaking doubt of Blake's madness is driven away for ever, and his method stands in the great lists of literature ready to meet all comers on equal terms, these verses will hardly fail to teach even those whom they overthrow.

The MS. book contains several of these songs mixed up with some of the Songs of Experience, and with others never included in either set, though apparently originally intended for such use. *See above*, Volume I., p. 205. Among these, the following seems to have been rejected in favour of " The Introduction," or " Earth's Answer," at the beginning of the Songs of Experience.—*See* Volume I., p. 209.

TO NOBODADDY.

Why art thou silent and invisible ?
Father of Jealousy,
Why dost thou hide thyself in clouds
From every passing eye ?
Why darkness and obscurity
In all thy words and laws
That none can eat the fruit but from
The wily serpent's jaws,
Or is it because secrecy gains feminine applause ?

*** At the close of the songs as printed in the Aldine edition the editor gives a " second version " of " The Tiger " on what he calls MS. authority. He does not say whose MS. In Blake's book, called here " the MS. book," the first draft of the poem is to be found. It is re-produced here with all its corrections. The words printed in italics have all been crossed out by Blake's pen. To remove them entirely would leave broken verses. Even when he engraved the poem, as is shown in the first version given above, Blake forgot to alter the last line of the third stanza, but left it just as it stood when it was meant to lead on to a fourth, beginning " could filch it "— of which not more than three lines were even written.

In Gilchrist's book Dante Gabriel Rossetti has edited into

" What dread hand *formed* thy dread feet ? "

which stops the pace of the verse hopelessly. *Made*, would have hurt it less, and done its work as well. To pronounce *formed*, in one syllable, three consonants must be brought together in the mouth. " Thy " being the next word brings *r m d th* all in one mass. This gags, and wastes time.

Some sort of editor for Blake is seen, nevertheless, to be a necessity.

THE TIGER.
(MS. VERSION WITH BLAKE'S CORRECTIONS)

1.

Tiger, Tiger, burning bright
In the forests of the night,
What immortal hand or eye
Dare could frame thy fearful symmetry?

2.

In what distant deeps or skies
Burned the fire within thine eyes?
On what wings dared he aspire?
What the hand dared seize the fire?

3.

And what shoulder and what art
Could twist the sinews of thy heart?
And when thy heart began to beat,
What dread hand and what dread feet

4.

Could filch it from the furnace deep
And in thy horn'd ribs dare steep
In the well of sanguine woe
*   *   *   * ?

In what clay and in what mould
Were thine eyes of fury roll'd.
*   *   *   * ?

Where the hammer, where the chain,
In what furnace was thy brain?
What the anvil?   What *the arm, grasp, clasp,* dread grasp
Dared thy deadly terrors clasp?

Tiger, Tiger, burning bright
In the forests of the night,
What immortal hand and eye
Dare *form* frame thy fearful symmetry?

———

(*Over page, two verses, one erased,—the other corrected.*)
Burnt in distant deeps or skies,
The cruel fire of thine eye,
Could heart descend or wings inspire
What the hand dared seize the fire?

5.

3 And *did he laugh* dare he *smile laugh* his work to see
  What the shoulder * * * *ankle* * * * *what the knee*
4 Did He who made the lamb make thee?
1 When the stars threw down their spears
2 And watered heaven with their tears.

After this stanza 1, 2, 3 are copied out, and number 1 repeated as a fourth, and then the whole erased. This is all the MS. of the Tiger with all its corrections.

The order of the above songs is taken from a very beautiful copy—one of Blake's last—which bears the name Edwards, and the date May, 1828. It was presumably sold by Mrs. Blake to "Edwards" after Blake's death (1827). It was bought in the Beckford collection by Mr. Quaritch in 1882. The only difference from the above consists in the fact that the song called "The garden of Love" begins "I went to the garden, &c.," and does not contain the two first stanzas, printed with it in some editions. In the MS. Book Blake has divided them by a long line from the other stanzas, showing that he counted them as a separate poem.

The MS. book furnishes some further lines also belonging to the song "Infant Sorrow," which were omitted by Blake when engraving it, but shed light on the symbolic intention of the song, and connect it with Enitharmon, Orc, and Hyle. Compare book of "Urizen," also "America," Preludium, p. 2, l. 4, and "Vala," Night VII., from l 166, and all Night VIII., and Volume I., Chapter on the Worm. (The engraved version is above, p. 57. A note on it in Volume II., p. 15) After the line—

"To sulk upon my mother's breast,"

the MS. continues thus (the italics are erased words, the asterisks represent words illegible in the original) :—

When I saw that rage was vain
And to sulk would nothing gain,
Turning many a trick and wile
I began to * * * *seeking many an artful* * * *
I began to soothe and smile.

And I *grew* soothed, day after day,
Till upon the ground I lay,
And I *grew* smiled, night after night,
Seeking only for delight.

But upon the earthly ground
No delight my * * * *found.*

And I saw before me shine
Clusters of the wandering vine,
And many a lovely flower and tree
And, beyond, a myrtle tree,
Stretched *its* their blossoms out to me.

But a priest My father then with holy book
In *his* their hands a holy book
Pronounced curses on *his* my head
Who the fruit or blossoms shed,
And bound me in a myrtle shade

I beheld the priests by night,
They embraced my myrtle * * * *the blossoms* * * * *bright*
I beheld the priests by day
Where beneath my * * **underneath the** * * * *vine they* * * * *he* * * * *lay.*

3 Like *a* ... *to* ... serpents in the night,
4 They embraced my *myrtle* * * * blossom * * * bright
1 Like *a serpent in the* * * * to holy men by * * * day
    2 Underneath *my* the,—vines they lay.

> So I smote *him*, them—and *his* their gore
> Stained the roots my myrtle bore ;
> But the time of youth is fled,
> And grey hairs are on my head.

So ends the poem. The child is the "Infant Joy,"—and is as symbolic as the "babe" in the Mental Traveller. The whole poem leads on to that called "In a myrtle shade," which is evidently a second attempt to embody in verse, part of the same symbolic story. The MS. gives a text of this also more copious than the final form as printed above. The never printed line about the myrtle sighing to behold the chain is particularly needed if the whole is to be understood.

> To a lovely myrtle bound,
> Blossoms showering all around.
>
> 2 Oh how weak and weary I
> Underneath my myrtle lie,
> Like to dung upon the ground
> Underneath my myrtle bound.
>
> 1 Why should I be bound to thee,
> Oh my lovely myrtle tree?
> Love, free love, cannot be bound
> To any tree that grows on ground.
>
> Oft my myrtle sighed in vain,
> To behold my heavy chain.
> Oft *the priest beheld* my father saw us sigh
> And laughed at our simplicity.
>
> So I smote him, and his gore
> Stained the roots my myrtle bore,
> But the time of youth is fled,
> And grey hairs are on my head.

But all this about the chain, which is evidently the veil of Vala, the Mundane Shell, &c., as the Myrtle is the body, was afterwards absorbed into the dream of the Maiden Queen,—in the Song of Experience called the Angel, which ends with the same couplet. The infant is the same as that bound by the priest in The Garden of Love, and A Little Boy Lost. All the infants are Orc, who becomes a serpent when the chain has grown into him, put there by the Urizen-like portion of Los. A little further, on the same page of the MS. book as "A Little Boy Lost" is written, the myrtle is found once more, re-arranged for publication, with a title. The erasures and numberings as follows :—

TO MY MYRTLE.

Why should I be bound to thee
Oh my lovely myrtle tree,
Love, free love cannot be bound
To any tree that grows on ground.
To a lovely myrtle bound,
Blossoms showering all around,
Like to dung upon the ground,
Underneath my myrtle bound
Oh how weak and weary I
Underneath my myrtle lie.

While beside it in pencil a few words of a stanza which was rejected may still
be faintly traced.

Deceit to seeming * * *
* * * * * * refined
To everything but interest blind,
And * * * fetters every mind,
And forges fetters of the mind.

The beautiful quatrian called The Lily, was reduced to this form from a fuller
sketch. It is also a study in symbolic statement, and can be understood with
perfect certainty only by help of its erased lines, which should be read once and
forgotten.

The *rose* modest lustful rose *puts envious* puts forth a thorn,
The *coward* humble sheep a threatening horn.
While the lily white shall in Love delight,
And the lion increase freedom and peace,
The priest loves war and the soldier peace,
Nor a thorn, nor a threat, stain her beauty bright.

Other rejected readings from the MS. book have no value for interpretation.
One may only be mentioned as an example of Blake's frank writing. He desires
to find in a wife the lineaments of gratified desire such as he discovers in
women of immoral life, of whom he speaks in the old-fashioned scriptural word
of one syllable—the verse is unfinished.

Above it is "The Fairy," not given in the Aldine edition and accidentally
omitted in the chapter on the MS. book, Volume I. Mr. Swinburne has printed
this in his essay under Blake's first title (erased in MS.) The Marriage Ring.

The arrows, like the sparrows, are emotions of the heart (whose symbolic
region is air, through which they fly). The connection with fairies belongs to
the symbolic use of these in "Jerusalem," p. 13, l. 29, p. 63, l. 14, and
p. 97, l 12, in the preface to "Europe," where the fairy of the heart leaves
guarding the gate of the head in south to dictate the story of the head in north.
The fairies are also the same as those of the poem William Bond.

These verses are not in any sense nursery rhymes. Symbolic poetry may use
the form of the fanciful but it will retain its own coherence. It is when not
symbolic that Fancy produces what Milton calls her "wild work."

In this song the word marriage must be considered as pronounced in three syllables or the whole melody is jerked away.

THE MARRIAGE RING.—THE FAIRY.

Come hither, my sparrows,
My little arrows,
If a tear or a smile
Will a man beguile,
If an amorous delay
Clouds a sunshiny day,
If the *tread* step of a foot
Smites the heart to its root,
'Tis the marriage ring
Makes each fairy a king.

So a fairy sang;—
From the leaves I sprang.
He leaped from the spray
To flee away,
But in my hat caught
He soon shall be taught
Let him laugh, let him cry,
He's my butterfly;
For I've pulled out the sting
Of the marriage ring.

Mr. Swinburne follows this with another fragment given in a foot-note to his Essay, p. 143. This, he says, is copied from a loose scrap of paper on which is a sketch of Hercules throttling the serpents.

A fairy leapt upon my knee
Singing and dancing merrily.
I said, " Thou thing of patches, rings,
Pins, necklaces, and such like things,
Disgracer of the female form.
Thou pretty gilded poisonous worm ! "
Weeping he fell upon my thigh—
And thus in tears did soft reply,
" Knowest thou not, Fairies' Lord,
How much by us contemned, abhorr'd,
Whatever hides the female form
That cannot bear the mortal storm ?
Therefore in pity still we give
Our lives to make the female live,
And what would turn into disease
We turn to what will joy and please."

Mr. Swinburne has also noted some of the rejected readings for the poem called "The Two Songs," beginning "I heard an Angel singing" The Devil's curse in it stands in the MS. as follows—italics still representing erased words :—

I heard a Devil curse
Over the heath and furze,
Mercy could be no more
If there were nobody poor,
And pity no more could be
If all were happy as *ye* we.
Thus he sang At his curse the sun went down
And the heavens gave a frown.
Down poured the heavy rain
Over the new reaped grain,
And Mercy, and Pity, and Peace descended ;
The farmers were ruined, and harvest was ended.
And Mercy, Pity, Peace,
Did at the time increase
With poverty's increase ;
And by distress increase
Mercy, pity, peace,
By miseries increase
Mercy, pity, peace.
And Miseries' increase
Is Mercy, Pity, Peace.

Here, as elsewhere, we literally see the thoughts condense, as what was at first a mere scheme for a poem becomes a poem. Here, as elsewhere, the metre is practically left to take care of itself, a thing it succeeds in doing better than in some of the "long resounding long heroic lines," while all the attention of the poet is given to the idea that grows up in him while he writes.

The connection having been traced between what lies within the compass of the collection of Songs, and the shorter poems outside—which, though already well known, are here reprinted—they follow in their turn.

THERE IS NO NATURAL
RELIGION.

THERE IS NO NATURAL RELIGION.

————♦————

The Voice of one crying in the Wilderness.

THE ARGUMENT.

As the true method of knowledge is experiment; the true faculty of knowing must be the faculty which experiences. This faculty I treat of.

PRINCIPLE FIRST.

That the Poetic Genius is the true Man, and that the body or outward form of Man is derived from the Poetic Genius. Likewise, that the forms of all things are derived from their Genius, which by the Ancients was call'd an Angel and Spirit and Demon.

PRINCIPLE SECOND.

As all men are alike in outward form, so (and with the same infinite variety) all are alike in the Poetic Genius.

PRINCIPLE THIRD.

No man can think, write or speak from his heart, but he must intend truth. Thus all sects of Philosophy are from the Poetic Genius, adapted to the weaknesses of every individual.

PRINCIPLE FOURTH.

As none by travelling over known lands can find out the unknown; so from already acquired knowledge Man could not acquire more; therefore an universal Poetic Genius exists.

Principle Fifth.

The Religions of all Nations are derived from each Nation's different reception of the Poetic Genius, which is everywhere call'd the Spirit of Prophecy.

Principle Sixth.

The Jewish and Christian Testaments are an original derivation from the Poetic Genius. This is necessary from the confined nature of bodily sensation.

Principle Seventh.

As all men are alike (though infinitely various), so all Religions, and as all similars, have one source.

The true Man is the source, he being the Poetic Genius.

This little book is copied from illustrated leaves in the possession of the Linnell family, and is in itself a comment on the similar pamphlet in the British Museum, here reproduced in facsimile.

LIBRARY OF THE UNIVERSITY OF CALIFORNIA.

The Argument

Man has no notion of moral
fitness but from Education
Naturally he is only a natural organ subject to Sense.

I

Mans percepti-
-ons are not bound
ed by organs of
perception, he per-
cieves more than
Sense (tho' ever
so acute) can
discover

II

Reason or the ra-
tio of all we have
already known, is
not the same that
it shall be when
we know more.

III

From a perception of
only 3 senses or 3 ele-
ments none could de-
duce a fourth or fifth

IV

A None could have other
than natural or organic
thoughts if he had none
but organic perceptions

V

Mans desires are
limited by his percepti
ons . none can de
-sire what he has not
perciev'd

VI

The desires & percepti
-ons of man untaught by
any thing but organs of
sense . must be limited,
to objects of sense

*Therefore
God becomes as
we are, that we
may be as he
is*

I

Man cannot, naturally Per-
-cieve, but through his natural
or bodily organs.

II

Man by his reason-
ing power, can only
compare & judge of
what he has already
percievd,

On Homers Poetry

Every Poem must necessarily be a perfect Unity, but why Homers is peculiarly so, I cannot tell; he has told the story of Bellerophon & omitted the Judgment of Paris which is not only a part, but a principal part of Homers subject But when a Work has Unity it is as much in a Part as in the Whole, the Torso is as much a Unity as the Laocoon As Unity is the cloke of folly so Goodness is the cloke of knavery Those who will have Unity exclusively in Homer come out with a Moral like a sting in the tail. Aristotle says Characters are either Good or Bad: now Goodness or Badness has nothing to do with Character, an Apple tree a Pear tree a Horse a Lion, are Characters but a Good Apple tree or a Bad, is an Apple tree still: a Horse is not more a Lion for being a Bad Horse, that is its Character; its Goodness or Badness is another consideration.

It is the same with the Moral of a whole Poem as with the Moral Goodness of its parts Unity & Morality are secondary considerations & belong to Philosophy & not to Poetry, to Exception & not to Rule, to Accident & not to Substance, the Ancients called it eating of the tree of good & evil.

The Classics, it is the Classics & not Goths nor Monks, that Desolate Europe with Wars.

On Virgil

Sacred Truth has pronounced that Greece & Rome as Babylon & Egypt: so far from being parents of Arts & Sciences as they pretend: were destroyers of all Art. Homer Virgil & Ovid confirm this opinion & make us reverence The Word of God, the only light of antiquity that remains unperverted by War. Virgil in the Eneid Book VI. line 848 says Let others study Art: Rome has Somewhat better to do, namely War & Dominion

Rome & Greece swept Art into their maw & destroyd it a Warlike State never can produce Art. It will Rob & Plunder & accumulate into one place, & Translate & Copy & Buy & Sell & Criticise, but not Make. Grecian is Mathematic Form Mathematic Form is Eternal in the Reasoning Memory. Living Form is Eternal Existence   Gothic is Living Form

THE GHOST of ABEL

A Revelation In the Visions of Jehovah
Seen by William Blake

To LORD BYRON in the Wilderness. What doest thou here Elijah?
Can a Poet doubt the Visions of Jehovah? Nature has no Outline:
but Imagination has. Nature has no Tune: but Imagination has!
Nature has no Supernatural & dissolves: Imagination is Eternity

Scene A rocky Country. Eve fainted over the dead body
of Abel which lays near a Grave. Adam kneels by her Jehovah
stands above

Jehovah — Adam!

Adam — I will not hear thee more thou Spiritual Voice
Is this Death?

Jehovah — Adam!

Adam — It is in vain: I will not hear thee
Henceforth! Is this thy Promise that the Womans Seed
Should bruise the Serpents head: Is this the Serpent Ah!
Seven times O Eve thou hast fainted over the Dead Ah! Ah!

Eve revives

Eve — Is this the Promise of Jehovah! O it is all a vain delusion
This Death & this Life & this Jehovah

Jehovah — Woman lift thine eyes

A Voice is heard coming on

Voice — O Earth cover not thou my Blood; cover not thou my Blood.

Enter the Ghost of Abel

Eve — Thou Visionary Phantasm thou art not the real Abel.

Abel — Among the Elohim a Human Victim I wander I am their House
Prince of the Air & our dimensions compass Length & Nadir
Vain is thy Covenant O Jehovah I am the Accuser & Avenger
Of Blood O Earth Cover not thou the Blood of Abel

Jehovah What Vengeance dost thou require

Abel — Life for Life! Life for Life!

Jehovah He who shall take Cains life must also Die O Abel
And who is he Adam wilt thou or Eve thou do this

Adam It is all a Vain delusion of the all creative Imagination
Eve come away & let us not believe these vain delusions
Abel is dead & Cain slew him! We shall also Die a Death
And then what then be as poor Abel a Thought: or as
This! O what shall I call thee Form Divine! Father of Mercies
That appearest to my Spiritual Vision: Eve seest thou also.

Eve — I see him plainly with my Minds Eye. I see also Abel living
Tho terribly afflicted as We also are. yet Jehovah sees him

Alive & not Dead: were it not better to believe Vision
With all our might & strength tho' we are fallen & lost

Adam — Eve thou hast spoken truly, let us kneel before his feet.
They Kneel before Jehovah

Abel — Are these the Sacrifices of Eternity O Jehovah, a Broken Spirit
And a Contrite Heart. O I cannot Forgive! the Accuser hath
Enterd into Me as into his House & I loathe thy Tabernacles
As thou hast said, so is it come to pass My desire is unto Cain
And He doth rule over Me: therefore My Soul in fumes of Blood
Cries for Vengeance: Sacrifice on Sacrifice Blood on Blood

Jehovah — Lo I have given you a Lamb for an Atonement instead
Of the Transgresor, or no Flesh or Spirit could ever Live

Abel — Compelled I cry O Earth cover not the Blood of Abel

Abel sinks down into the Grave, from which arises Satan
Armed in glittering scales with a Crown & a Spear

Satan — I will have Human Blood & not the blood of Bulls or Goats
And no Atonement O Jehovah the Elohim live on Sacrifice
Of Men: hence I am God of Men: Thou Human O Jehovah.
By the Rock & Oak of the Druid creeping Misletoe & Thorn
Cains City built with Human Blood, not Blood of Bulls & Goats
Thou shalt Thyself be Sacrificed to Me thy God on Calvary

Jehovah — Such is My Will: Thunders
that thou Thyself go to Eternal Death
In Self Annihilation even till Satan Self-subdud Put off Satan
Into the Bottomless Abyss whose torment arises for ever & ever.
On each side a Chorus of Angels entering Sing the following

The Elohim of the Heathen Swore Vengeance for Sin Then Thou stoodst
Forth O Elohim Jehovah! in the midst of the darkness of the Oath! All Clothed
In Thy Covenant of the Forgiveness of Sins: Death O Holy! Is this Brotherhood
The Elohim saw their Oath Eternal Fire; they rolled apart trembling over The
Mercy Seat: each in his station fixt in the Firmament by Peace Brotherhood and
The Curtain falls   Love

The Voice of Abels
Blood

1822 W Blakes Original Stereotype was 1788

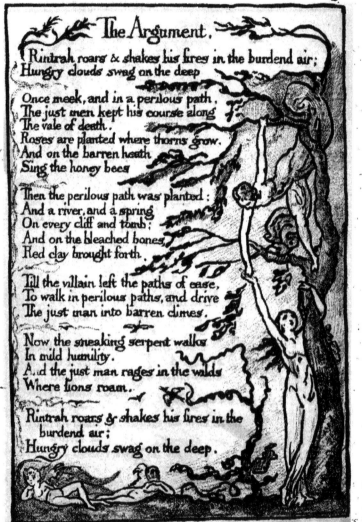

The Argument.

Rintrah roars & shakes his fires in the burdend air;
Hungry clouds swag on the deep

Once meek, and in a perilous path,
The just men kept his course along
The vale of death.
Roses are planted where thorns grow,
And on the barren heath
Sing the honey bees

Then the perilous path was planted:
And a river, and a spring
On every cliff and tomb;
And on the bleached bones
Red clay brought forth.

Till the villain left the paths of ease,
To walk in perilous paths, and drive
The just man into barren climes.

Now the sneaking serpent walks
In mild humility.
And the just man rages in the wilds
Where lions roam.

Rintrah roars & shakes his fires in the
    burdend air;
Hungry clouds swag on the deep.

As a new heaven is begun, and it is now thir-
ty-three years since its advent: the Eternal Hell
revives. And lo! Swedenborg is the Angel sitting
at the tomb: his writings are the linen clothes folded
up. Now is the dominion of Edom, & the return of
Adam into Paradise; see Isaiah XXXIV & XXXV Chap:
Without Contraries is no progression. Attraction
and Repulsion, Reason and Energy, Love and
Hate, are necessary to Human existence.

From these contraries spring what the religious call
Good & Evil. Good is the passive that obeys Reason.
Evil is the active springing from Energy.

    Good is Heaven. Evil is Hell.

The voice of the Devil

All Bibles or sacred codes, have been
the causes of the following Errors.
1. That Man has two real existing principles Viz: a Body & a Soul.
2. That Energy, calld Evil, is alone from the
Body. & that Reason, calld Good, is alone from
the Soul.
3. That God will torment Man in Eternity
for following his Energies.

But the following Contraries to these are True
1 Man has no Body distinct from his Soul
for that calld Body is a portion of Soul discernd
by the five Senses, the chief inlets of Soul in this
age.
2. Energy is the only life and is from the Body
and Reason is the bound or outward circumference
of Energy.
3 Energy is Eternal Delight

Those who restrain desire, do so because theirs
is weak enough to be restrained; and the restrainer or
reason usurps its place & governs the unwilling.
     And being restraind it by degrees becomes passive
till it is only the shadow of desire.
     The history of this is written in Paradise Lost. & the
Governor or Reason is calld Messiah.
     And the original Archangel or possessor of the com-
mand of the heavenly host, is calld the Devil or Satan
and his children are calld Sin & Death
     But in the Book of Job Miltons Messiah is calld
Satan.
     For this history has been adopted by both parties
     It indeed appeard to Reason as if Desire was
cast out, but the Devils account is, that the Messi
     -ah

ah fell. & formed a heaven of what he stole from the
Abyss

This is shewn in the Gospel, where he prays to the
Father to send the comforter or Desire that Reason
may have Ideas to build on, the Jehovah of the Bible
being no other than he   who dwells in flaming fire
Know that after Christs death, he became Jehovah.

But in Milton; the Father is Destiny, the Son, a
Ratio of the five senses, & the Holy-ghost, Vacuum!

Note. The reason Milton wrote in fetters when
he wrote of Angels & God, and at liberty when of
Devils & Hell, is because he was a true Poet and
of the Devils party without knowing it

A Memorable Fancy.

As I was walking among the fires of hell, delighted with the enjoyments of Genius; which to Angels look like torment and insanity. I collected some
of their Proverbs: thinking that as the sayings used
in a nation, mark its character, so the Proverbs of
Hell, shew the nature of Infernal wisdom better
than any description of buildings or garments

When I came home; on the abyss of the five senses, where a flat sided steep frowns over the present world, I saw a mighty Devil folded in black
clouds hovering on the sides of the rock, with cor-
ro-

roding fires he wrote the following sentence now perceived by the minds of men, & read by them on earth.

How do you know but ev'ry Bird that cuts the airy way,
Is an immense world of delight, clos'd by your senses five?

Proverbs of Hell

In seed time learn, in harvest teach, in winter enjoy.
Drive your cart and your plow over the bones of the dead.
The road of excess leads to the palace of wisdom.
Prudence is a rich ugly old maid courted by Incapacity.
He who desires but acts not, breeds pestilence.
The cut worm forgives the plow.
Dip him in the river who loves water.
A fool sees not the same tree that a wise man sees.
He whose face gives no light, shall never become a star.
Eternity is in love with the productions of time.
The busy bee has no time for sorrow.
The hours of folly are measur'd by the clock, but of wis-
dom: no clock can measure.
All wholsom food is caught without a net or a trap.
Bring out number weight & measure in a year of dearth
No bird soars too high, if he soars with his own wings.
A dead body, revenges not injuries.
The most sublime act is to set another before you.
If the fool would persist in his folly he would become wise
Folly is the cloke of knavery.
Shame is Prides cloke.

Proverbs of Hell.

Prisons are built with stones of Law, Brothels with bricks of Religion.

The pride of the peacock is the glory of God.

The lust of the goat is the bounty of God.

The wrath of the lion is the wisdom of God.

The nakedness of woman is the work of God.

Excess of sorrow laughs. Excess of joy weeps.

The roaring of lions, the howling of wolves, the raging of the stormy sea, and the destructive sword, are portions of eternity too great for the eye of man.

The fox condemns the trap, not himself.

Joys impregnate. Sorrows bring forth.

Let man wear the fell of the lion, woman the fleece of the sheep.

The bird a nest, the spider a web, man friendship.

The selfish smiling fool, & the sullen frowning fool, shall be both thought wise, that they may be a rod.

What is now proved was once, only imagin'd.

The rat, the mouse, the fox, the rabbit; watch the roots, the lion, the tyger, the horse, the elephant, watch the fruits.

The cistern contains; the fountain overflows.

One thought, fills immensity.

Always be ready to speak your mind, and a base man will avoid you.

Every thing possible to be believ'd is an image of truth.

The eagle never lost so much time, as when he submit- -ted to learn of the crow.

The

Proverbs of Hell

The fox provides for himself, but God provides for the lion.

Think in the morning. Act in the noon, Eat in the even-
-ing, Sleep in the night.

He who has sufferd you to impose on him knows you.

As the plow follows words, so God rewards prayers.

The tygers of wrath are wiser than the horses of in-
Expect poison from the standing water.   (-struction

You never know what is enough unless you know what is
more than enough.

Listen to the fools reproach! it is a kingly title!

The eyes of fire, the nostrils of air, the mouth of water,
the beard of earth.

The weak in courage is strong in cunning.

The apple tree never asks the beech how he shall grow,
nor the lion, the horse, how he shall take his prey.

The thankful reciever bears a plentiful harvest.

If others had not been foolish. we should be so.

The soul of sweet delight. can never be defil'd,

When thou seest an Eagle, thou seest a portion of Ge
-nius. lift up thy head!

As the catterpiller chooses the fairest leaves to lay
her eggs on, so the priest lays his curse on
the fairest joys.

To create a little flower is the labour of ages.

Damn. braces: Bless relaxes.

The best wine is the oldest. the best water the newest.

Prayers plow not! Praises reap not!

Joys laugh not! Sorrows weep not!

Proverbs of Hell.

The head Sublime, the heart Pathos, the genitals Beauty,
the hands & feet Proportion.

As the air to a bird or the sea to a fish, so is contempt
to the contemptible.

The crow wish'd every thing was black, the owl, that eve-
-ry thing was white.

Exuberance is Beauty.

If the lion was advised by the fox he would be cunning.

Improvent makes strait roads, but the crooked roads
without Improvement. are roads of Genius.

Sooner murder an infant in its cradle than nurse unact
-ed desires

Where man is not nature is barren.

Truth can never be told so as to be understood. and
not be believ'd.

Enough! or Too much

The ancient Poets animated all sensible objects
with Gods or Geniuses, calling them by the names and
adorning them with the properties of woods, rivers,
mountains, lakes, cities, nations, and whatever their
enlarged & numerous senses could perceive.

And particularly they studied the genius of each
city & country, placing it under its mental deity.

Till a system was formed, which some took ad-
vantage of & enslav'd the vulgar by attempting to
realize or abstract the mental deities from their
objects; thus began Priesthood.

Choosing forms of worship from poetic tales.

And at length they pronounc'd that the Gods
had order'd such things.

Thus men forgot that All deities reside
in the human breast.

A Memorable Fancy.

The Prophets Isaiah and Ezekiel dined with
me, and I asked them how they dared so roundly to
assert. that God spake to them: and whether they
did not think at the time, that they would be mis-
-understood, & so be the cause of imposition?

Isaiah answer'd. I saw no God, nor heard
any, in a finite organical perception; but my sen-
-ses discover'd the infinite in every thing, and as I
was then perswaded, & remain confirm'd; that the
voice of honest indignation is the voice of God, I
cared not for consequences but wrote.

Then I asked: does a firm perswasion that a
thing is so, make it so?

He replied, All poets believe that it does, &
in ages of imagination this firm perswasion remo
ved mountains: but many are not capable of a
firm perswasion of any thing.

Then Ezekiel said. The philosophy of the east
taught the first principles of human perception
some nations held one principle for the origin &
some another, we of Israel taught that the Poetic
Genius (as you now call it) was the first principle
and all the others merely derivative, which was the
cause of our despising the Priests & Philosophers
of other countries, and prophecying that all Gods
would

would at last be proved to originate in ours & to be the
tributaries of the Poetic Genius, it was this. that our
great poet King David desired so fervently & invokes
so pathetiely, saying by this he conquers enemies &
governs kingdoms; and we so loved our God. that we
cursed in his name all the deities of surrounding
nations, and asserted that they had rebelled; from
these opinions the vulgar came to think that all. nations would at last be subject to the jews.

This said he, like all firm perswasions, is come to
pass, for all nations believe the jews code and worship the jews god. and what greater subjection can be

I heard this with some wonder. & must confess
my own conviction. After dinner I ask'd Isaiah to favour the world with his lost works, he said none of
equal value was lost. Ezekiel said the same of his.

I also asked Isaiah what made him go naked and
barefoot three years? he answerd, the same that made
our friend Diogenes the Grecian.

I then asked Ezekiel. why he eat dung, & lay so
long on his right & left side? he answerd, the desire
of raising other men into a perception of the infinite
this the North American tribes practise. & is he honest who resists his genius or conscience, only for
the sake of present ease or gratification?

The ancient tradition that the world will be consumed in fire at the end of six thousand years
is true, as I have heard from Hell.

For the cherub with his flaming sword is
hereby commanded to leave his guard at tree of
life, and when he does, the whole creation will
be consumed, and appear infinite and holy
whereas it now appears finite & corrupt.

This will come to pass by an improvement of
sensual enjoyment.

But first the notion that man has a body
distinct from his soul, is to be expunged; this
I shall do, by printing in the infernal method, by
corrosives, which in Hell are salutary and me-
dicinal, melting apparent surfaces away, and
displaying the infinite which was hid.

If the doors of perception were cleansed
every thing would appear to man as it is, infinite.

For man has closed himself up, till he sees
all things thro' narrow chinks of his cavern.

A Memorable Fancy

I was in a Printing house in Hell & saw the method in which knowledge is transmitted from generation to generation.

In the first chamber was a Dragon-Man, clearing away the rubbish from a caves mouth; within, a number of Dragons were hollowing the cave,

In the second chamber was a Viper folding round the rock & the cave, and others adorning it with gold silver and precious stones

In the third chamber was an Eagle with wings and feathers of air, he caused the inside of the cave to be infinite, around were numbers of Eagle like men, who built palaces in the immense cliffs.

In the fourth chamber were Lions of flaming fire raging around & melting the metals into living fluids.

In the fifth chamber were Unnam'd forms, which cast the metals into the expanse.

There they were reciev'd by Men who occupied the sixth chamber, and took the forms of books & were arranged in libraries.

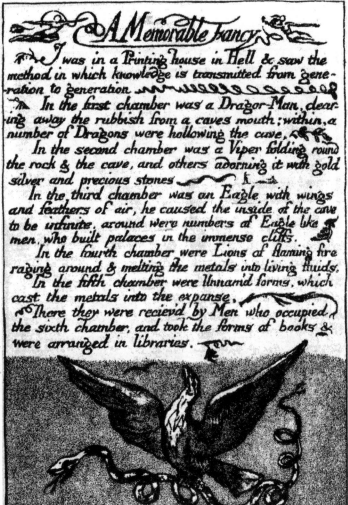

The Giants who formed this world into its
sensual existence and now seem to live in it
in chains are in truth, the causes of its life
& the sources of all activity, but the chains
are, the cunning of weak and tame minds, which
have power to resist energy, according to the pro-
-verb, the weak in courage is strong in cunning.

Thus one portion of being, is the Prolific, the
other, the Devouring: to the devourer it seems as
if the producer was in his chains, but it is not so,
he only takes portions of existence and fancies
that the whole.

But the Prolific would cease to be Prolific
unless the Devourer as a sea recieved the excess
of his delights.

Some will say, Is not God alone the Prolific?
I answer, God only Acts & Is, in existing beings
or Men.

These two classes of men are always upon
earth. & they should be enemies; whoever tries

to reconcile them seeks to destroy existence.

Religion is an endeavour to reconcile the two.

Note. Jesus Christ did not wish to unite but to seperate them, as in the Parable of sheep and goats! & he says I came not to send Peace but a Sword.

Messiah or Satan or Tempter was formerly thought to be one of the Antediluvians who are our Energies.

A Memorable Fancy

An Angel came to me and said. O pitiable foolish young man! O horrible! O dreadful state! consider the hot burning dungeon thou art preparing for thyself to all eternity, to which thou art going in such career.

I said. perhaps you will be willing to shew me my eternal lot & we will contemplate together upon it and see whether your lot or mine is most desirable

So he took me thro' a stable & thro' a church & down into the church vault at the end of which was a mill; thro' the mill we went, and came to a cave. down the winding cavern we groped our tedi- -ous way till a void boundless as a nether sky ap- -peard beneath us, & we held by the roots of trees and hung over this immensity, but I said. if you please we will commit ourselves to this void, and see whether providence is here also, if you will not I will? but he answerd, do not presume O young- man but as we here remain behold thy lot which will soon appear when the darkness passes away

So I remaind with him sitting in the twisted root

root of an oak, he was suspended in a fungus
which hung with the head downward into the deep:

By degrees we beheld the infinite Abyss, fiery
as the smoke of a burning city; beneath us at an
immense distance was the sun, black but shining
round it were fiery tracks on which revolv'd vast
spiders, crawling after their prey; which flew or &
rather swum in the infinite deep, in the most terrific shapes of animals sprung from corruption.
& the air was full of them, & seemd composed
of them; these are Devils, and are called Powers
of the air, I now asked my companion which was my
eternal lot? he said, between the black & white spiders

But now, from between the black & white spiders
a cloud and fire burst and rolled thro the deep
blackning all beneath so that the nether deep grew
black as a sea & rolled with a terrible noise: beneath us was nothing now to be seen but a black
tempest, till looking east between the clouds & the
waves, we saw a cataract of blood mixed with fire
and not many stones throw from us appeard and
sunk again the scaly fold of a monstrous serpent
at last to the east, distant about three degrees ap
peard a fiery crest above the waves slowly it rear
ed like a ridge of golden rocks till we discoverd
two globes of crimson fire, from which the sea
fled away in clouds of smoke, and now we saw, it
was the head of Leviathan, his forehead was di
vided into streaks of green & purple like those on
a tygers forehead: soon we saw his mouth & red
gills hang just above the raging foam tinging the
black deep with beams of blood, advancing toward
us

us with all the fury of a spiritual existence.

My friend the Angel climb'd up from his sta-
-tion into the mill; I remaind alone. & then this
appearance was no more, but I found myself sitting on a pleasant bank beside a river by moon
light hearing a harper who sung to the harp. &
his theme was, The man who never alters his
opinion is like standing water, & breeds reptiles
of the mind.

But I arose, and sought for the mill &
there I found my Angel, who surprised asked
me. how I escaped?

I answerd. All that we saw was owing to your
metaphysics; for when you ran away, I found myself
on a bank by moonlight hearing a harper, But
now we have seen my eternal lot, shall I shew you
yours? he laughd at my proposal: but I by force
suddenly caught him in my arms, & flew westerly
thro' the night, till we were elevated above the
earths shadow: then I flung myself with him directe-
ly into the body of the sun, here I clothed myself in
white, & taking in my hand Swedenborgs volumes
sunk from the glorious clime, and passed all the
planets till we came to saturn, here I staid to rest
& then leap'd into the void, between saturn & the
fixed stars.

Here said I! is your lot, in this space, if space
it may be calld. Soon we saw the stable and the
church, & I took him to the altar and opend the
Bible, and lo! it was a deep pit, into which I de
scended driving the Angel before me, soon we saw
seven houses of brick. one we enterd; in it were a
num

number of monkeys. baboons, & all of that species
chaind by the middle. grinning and snatching at
one another. but witheld by the shortness of their
chains: however I saw that they sometimes grew nu
merous, and then the weak were caught by the strong
and with a grinning aspect. first coupled with & then
devourd. by plucking off first one limb and then ano
ther till the body was left a helpless trunk. this after
grinning & kissing it with seeming fondness they de
vourd too: and here & there I saw one savourily pic-
king the flesh off of his own tail; as the stench ter
ribly annoyd us both we went into the mill, & I in
my hand brought the skeleton of a body, which in
the mill was Aristotles Analytics.

So the Angel said: thy phantasy has imposed
upon me & thou oughtest to be ashamed.

I answerd: we impose on one another. & it is
but lost time to converse with you whose works
are only Analytics.

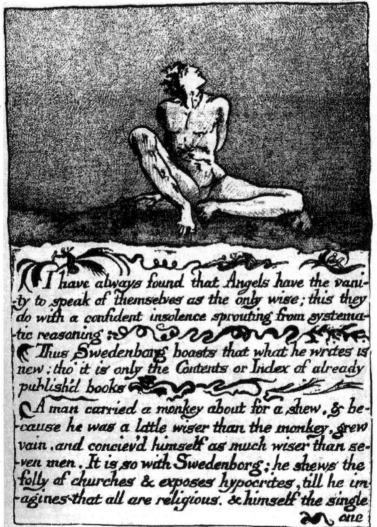

I have always found that Angels have the vanity to speak of themselves as the only wise; this they
do with a confident insolence sprouting from systema-
tic reasoning :

Thus Swedenborg boasts that what he writes is
new: tho' it is only the Contents or Index of already
publish'd books

A man carried a monkey about for a shew, & because he was a little wiser than the monkey, grew
vain, and conciev'd himself as much wiser than seven men. It is so with Swedenborg; he shews the
folly of churches & exposes hypocrites, till he im-
agines that all are religious, & himself the single
one

one on earth that ever broke a net.

Now hear a plain fact: Swedenborg has not written one new truth: Now hear another: he has written
all the old falshoods.

And now hear the reason. He conversed with Angels
who are all religious. & conversed not with Devils who
all hate religion, for he was incapable thro' his conceited
notions:

Thus Swedenborgs writings are a recapitulation of
all superficial opinions, and an analysis of the more
sublime, but no further.

Have now another plain fact: Any man of mechani-
cal talents may from the writings of Paracelsus or Jacob Behmen, produce ten thousand volumes of equal
value with Swedenborgs. and from those of Dante or
Shakespear an infinite number.

But when he has done this, let him not say that he
knows better than his master, for he only holds a candle in sunshine.

A Memorable Fancy

Once I saw a Devil in a flame of fire, who arose before an Angel that sat on a cloud. and the Devil utterd these words.

The worship of God is. Honouring his gifts in other
men each according to his genius. and loving the
                                        great

greatest men best, those who envy or calumniate
great men hate God, for there is no other God. The Angel hearing this became almost blue
but mastering himself he grew yellow, & at last
white pink & smiling, and then replied,
Thou Idolater, is not God One? & is not he
visible in Jesus Christ? and has not Jesus Christ
given his sanction to the law of ten commandments
and are not all other men fools, sinners, & nothings?
The Devil answerd; bray a fool in a morter with
wheat yet shall not his folly be beaten out of him;
if Jesus Christ is the greatest man, you ought to
love him in the greatest degree; now hear how he
has given his sanction to the law of ten commandments: did he not mock at the sabbath; and so
mock the sabbaths God? murder those who were
murderd because of him? turn away the law from
the woman taken in adultery? steal the labor of
others to support him? bear false witness when
he omitted making a defence before Pilate? covet
when he prayd for his disciples, and when he bid
them shake off the dust of their feet against such
as refused to lodge them? I tell you, no virtue
can exist without breaking these ten commandments. Jesus was all virtue, and acted from im-
-pulse

-pulse. not from rules.

When he had so spoken: I beheld the Angel who
stretched out his arms embracing the flame of fire
& he was consumed and arose as Elijah.

Note. This Angel, who is now become a Devil, is
my particular friend: we often read the Bible to-
-gether in its infernal or diabolical sense which
the world shall have if they behave well

I have also: The Bible of Hell: which the world
shall have whether they will or no.

One Law for the Lion & Ox is Oppression

A Song of Liberty

1. The Eternal Female groand! it was heard over all the Earth:

2. Albions coast is sick silent; the American meadows faint!

3. Shadows of Prophecy shiver along by the lakes and the rivers and mutter acrofs the ocean? France rend down thy dungeon;

4. Golden Spain burst the barriers of old Rome;

5. Cast thy keys O Rome into the deep down falling, even to eternity down falling,

6. And weep

7. In her trembling hands she took the new born terror howling;

8. On those infinite mountains of light now barr'd out by the atlantic sea, the new born fire stood before the starry king!

9. Flag'd with grey brow'd snows and thunderous visages the jealous wings wav'd over the deep

10. The speary hand burned aloft, unbuckled was the shield, forth went the hand of jealousy among the flaming hair, and

hurl'd the new born wonder thro' the starry
night.

11. The fire, the fire, is falling!

12. Look up! look up! O citizen of London
enlarge thy countenance: O Jew, leave count
ting gold! return to thy oil and wine; O
African! black African! (go, winged thought
widen his forehead.)

13. The fiery limbs, the flaming hair, shot
like the sinking sun into the western sea.

14. Wak'd from his eternal sleep, the hoary
element roaring fled away; ——————

15. Down rush'd beating his wings in vain
the jealous king; his grey brow'd councellors, thunderous warriors, curl'd veterans,
among helms, and shields, and chariots
horses, elephants: banners, castles, slings
and rocks,

16. Falling, rushing, ruining! buried in
the ruins, on Urthona's dens.

17. All night beneath the ruins, then
their sullen flames faded emerge round
the gloomy king.

18. With thunder and fire: leading his
starry hosts thro' the waste wilderness

he promulgates his ten commands, glancing his beamy eyelids over the deep in dark dismay,

19. Where the son of fire in his eastern cloud, while the morning plumes her golden breast.

20. Spurning the clouds written with curses, stamps the stony law to dust, loosing the eternal horses from the dens of night. crying Empire is no more! and now the lion & wolf shall cease.

Chorus

Let the Priests of the Raven of dawn, no longer in deadly black, with hoarse note curse the sons of joy. Nor his accepted brethren whom, tyrant, he calls free: lay the bound or build the roof. Nor pale religious letchery call that virginity, that wishes but acts not!

For every thing that lives is Holy

LIBRARY
OF THE
UNIVERSITY
OF
CALIFORNIA.

THE

BOOK of

LOS

LAMBETH
Printed by W. Blake 1795

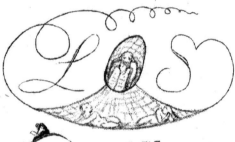

Chap (1)

And Wantonness on his own true love
Beget a giant race

1. Eno aged Mother
Who the chariot of Leutha guides
Since the day of thunders in old time

2. Sitting beneath the eternal Oak
Trembld and shook the stedfast Earth
And thus her speech broke forth

3. O Times remote!
When Love & Joy were adoration;
And none impure were deemd.
Not Eyeless Covet
Nor Thin-lip'd Envy
Nor Bristled Wrath
Nor Curled Wantonness

4. But Covet was poured full.
Envy fed with fat of lambs:
Wrath with lions gore
Wantonness lulld to sleep
With the virgins lute.
Or sated with her love.

5. Till Covet broke his locks & bars
And slept with open doors:
Envy sung at the rich mans feast;
Wrath was followd up and down
By a little ewe lamb.

6. Raging furious the flames of desire
Ran thro' heaven & earth, living flames
Intelligent organizd; armd
With destruction & plagues. In the midst
The Eternal Prophet bound in a chain
Compelld to watch Urizens shadow

7. Raged with curses & sparkles of fury
Round the flames roll as Los hurls
his chains
Mounting up from his fury, condens'd
Rolling round & round mounting on high
Into vacuum; into non-entity
Where nothing was! dashd wide apart
His feet stomp the eternal fierce-raging
Rivers of wide flame; they roll round
And round on all sides making their way
Into darkness and shadowy obscurity

8. Wide apart stood the fires; Los remaind
In the void between fire and fire.
In trembling and horror they beheld him
They stood wide apart, drivn by his hands
And his feet which the nether abyss
Stampd in fury and hot indignation

9. But no light from the fires all was
Dark

Darkness round Los heat was not for
   bound up.
Into fiery spheres from his fury
The gigantic flames trembled and hid

10: Coldness darkness obstruction a Solid
Without fluctuation hard as adamant
Black as marble of Egypt unpenetrable
Bound in the fierce raging Immortal
And the separated fires froze in
A vast solid without fluctuation.
Bound in his expanding clear senses

Chap: II

1: The Immortal stood frozen amidst
The vast rock of eternity times
And times a night of vast durance.
Impatient, stifled, stiffend, hardned.

2. Till impatience no longer could bear
The hard bondage rent: rent the vast
   solid
With a crash from immense to immense

3: Cracked across into numberless frag
   ments
The Prophetic wrath struggling for vent
Hurls apart stamping furious to dust
And crumbling with bursting sobs heaves
The black marble on high into fragments

4: Hurld apart on all sides as a falling
Rock the innumerable fragments away
Fell asunder, and horrible vacuum
Beneath him & on all sides round

5: Falling falling Los fell & fell
Sunk precipitant heavy down down
Times on times, night on night, day on day
Truth has bounds. Error none: falling
   falling:
Years on years, and ages on ages
Still he fell thro the void still a void
Found for falling day & night without
   end.
For tho day or night was not thier spaces

Were measurd by his incessant whirls
In the horrid vacuity bottomless

6: The Immortal revolving: indignant
First in wrath threw his limbs like the
   babe
New born into our world wrath subsided
And contemplative thoughts first arose
Then aloft his head reard in the Abyss
And his downward borne fall changd oblique

7: Many ages of groans till there grew
Branchy forms organizing the Human
Into finite inflexible organs.

8: Till in process from falling he bore
Sidelong on the purple air wafting
The weak breeze in efforts overwearied.

9: Incessant the falling Mind labourd
Organizing itself: till the Vacuum
Became element, pliant to rise,
Or to fall, or to swim, or to fly
With ease searching the dire vacuity

Chap: III

1: The Lungs heave incessant dull and
   heavy
For as yet were all other parts formless
Shivring clinging around like a cloud
Dim & glutinous as the white Polypus
Driven by waves & englobd on the tide

2: And the unformed part cravd repose
Sleep began the Lungs heave on the wave
Weary overweighd. Sinking beneath
In a stifling black fluid he woke

3: He arose on the waters but soon
Heavy falling his organs like roots
Shooting out from the seed shot beneath
And a vast world of waters around him
In furious torrents began

4: Then he sunk, & around his spent Lungs
Began intricate pipes that drew in
The spawn of the waters. Outbranching
   An

An immense Fibrous form. stretching out.
Thro' the bottoms of immensity raging.

5. He rose on the floods: then he smote
The wild deep with his terrible wrath.
Seperating the heavy and thin.

6. Down the heavy sunk; cleaving around
To the fragments of solid. up rose
The thin. flowing round the fierce fires
That glowd furious in the expanse.

Chap: IV:

1. Then Light first began; from the fires
Beams. conducted by fluid so pure
Flowd around the immense Los beheld
Forthwith writhing upon the dark void
The Back bone of Urizen appear
Hurtling upon the wind
Like a serpent! like an iron chain
Whirling about in the Deep

2. Uplolding his Fibres together
To a Form of impregnable strength
Los astonishd and terrified, built
Furnaces, he formed an Anvil
A Hammer of adamant then began
The binding of Urizen day and night

3. Circling round the dark Demon with
          howlings
Dismay & sharp blightings. the Prophet
Of Eternity beat on his iron links

4. And first from those infinite fires
The light that flowd down on the winds
He siezd: beating incessant condensing
The subtil particles in an Orb.

5. Roaring indignant the bright sparks
Endurd the vast Hammer: but unwearied
Los beat on the Anvil: till glorious
An immense Orb of fire he framd

6. Oft he quenchd it beneath in the
          Deeps
Then surveyd the all bright mass. Again
Siezing fires from the terrific Orbs
He heated. the round Globe, then beat
While roaring his Furnaces endurd
The chaind Orb in their infinite wombs

7. Nine ages completed their circles
When Los heated the glowing mass. cast-
                                  -ing
It down into the Deeps: the Deeps fled
Away in redounding smoke, the Sun
Stood self-balanc'd. And Los smild
          with joy.
He the vast Spine of Urizen siezd
And bound down to the glowing illusion

8. But no light: for the Deep fled away
On all sides. and left an unform'd
Dark vacuity: here Urizen lay
In fierce torments on his glowing bed.

9. Till his Brain in a rock, & his Heart
In a fleshy slough formed four rivers
Obscuring the immense Orb of fire
Flowing down into night: till a Form
Was completed, a Human Illusion
In darkness and deep clouds involvd.

The End of the
Book of LOS

THE BOOK of URIZEN

LAMBETH. Printed by W.ᵐ Blake 1794

PRELUDIUM

TO

THE

FIRST BOOK OF

URIZEN

Of the primeval Priests assum'd power,
When Eternals spurnd back his religion:
And gave him a place in the north,
Obscure, shadowy, void, solitary.

Eternals I hear your call gladly,
Dictate swift winged words, & fear not
To unfold your dark visions of torment.

Chap: I

1. Lo, a shadow of horror is risen
In Eternity! Unknown, unprolific?
Self-closd, all-repelling: what Demon
Hath form'd this abominable void,
This soul-shudd'ring vacuum?—Some
said
It is Urizen. But unknown, abstracted
Brooding secret, the dark power hid.

2. Times on times he divided, & measurd
Space by space in his ninefold darkness
Unseen, unknown: changes appeard
Like desolate mountains rifted furious
By the black winds of perturbation

3. For he strove in battles dire
In unseen conflictions with shapes
Bred from his forsaken wilderness.
Of beast, bird, fish, serpent & element
Combustion, blast, vapour and cloud.

4. Dark revolving in silent activity:
Unseen in tormenting passions;
An activity unknown and horrible;
A self-contemplating shadow,
In enormous labours occupied.

5. But Eternals beheld his vast forests
Age on ages he lay, closd, unknown,
Brooding shut in the deep; all avoid
The petrific abominable chaos

6. His cold horrors silent, dark Urizen
Prepard; his ten thousands of thunders
Rang'd in gloom'd array stretch out across
The dread world, & the rolling of wheels
As of swelling seas, sound in his clouds
In his hills of stor'd snows, in his mountains
Of hail & ice; voices of terror,
Are heard, like thunders of autumn,
When the cloud blazes over the harvests

Chap: II

1. Earth was not: nor globes of attrac-
tion
The will of the Immortal expanded
Or contracted his all flexible senses.
Death was not, but eternal life sprung

2. The sound of a trumpet the heavens
Awoke & vast clouds of blood rolld
Round the dim rocks of Urizen, so nam'd
That solitary one in Immensity

3. Shrill the trumpet: & myriads of Eter
-nity

In living creations appear'd
In the flames of eternal fury.

3. Sundring, darkning, thundring
Rent away with a terrible crash
Eternity rolld wide apart
Wide asunder rolling
Mountainous all around
Departing; departing; departing;
Leaving ruinous fragments of life
Hanging frowning cliffs & all between
An ocean of voidness unfathomable

4. The roaring fires ran oer the heavns
In whirlwinds & cataracts of blood
And oer the dark desarts of Urizen
Fires pour thro' the void on all sides
On Urizens self-begotten armies.

5. But no light from the fires, all was
        darkness
In the flames of Eternal fury

6. In fierce anguish & quenchless
        flames

To the desarts and rocks he ran
To hide, but he could not: combining
He dug mountains & hills in vast strength
He piled them in incessant labour
In howlings & pangs & fierce madness
Long periods in burning fires labouring
Till hoary, and age-broke, and aged,
In despair and the shadows of death.

7. And a roof vast petrific around,
On all sides he fram'd: like a womb;
Where thousands of rivers in veins
Of blood pour down the mountains to cool
The eternal fires beating without
From Eternals; & like a black globe
View'd by sons of Eternity, standing
On the shore of the infinite ocean
Like a human heart strugling & beating
The vast world of Urizen appeard.

8. And Los round the dark globe of
        Urizen,
Kept watch for Eternals to confine,
The obscure separation alone;
For Eternity stood wide apart.

1 Urizen Crat.

As the stars are apart from the earth 10. But Urizen laid in a stony sleep
                                        Unorganizd. rent from Eternity
9. Los wept howling around the dark
        Dejon:
And cursing his lot for in anguish.
Urizen was rent from his side.
And a fathomless void for his feet: 11. The Eternals said. What is this? Death
And intense fires for his dwelling   Urizen is a clod of clay.

12: Los howld in a dismal stupor. Rifted with direful changes
Groaning! gnashing! groaning! He lay in a dreamless night
Till the wrenching apart was heald
14: Till Los rouzd his fires
13: But the wrenching of Urizen   affrighted
heald not   At the farmless unmeasurable
Cold, featureless flesh or clay   death.

Chap: IV: -ment   4: And Los formed nets & gins
1. Los smitten with astonish-   And threw the nets round about
Frightend at the hurtling bones

2: And at the surging sulphure- 5. He watchd in shuddring fear
      ous   The dark changes & bound every
Perturbed Immortal mad raging   change
                                 With rivets of iron & brass;

3. In whirlwinds & pitch & nitre 6. And these were the changes
Round the furious limbs of Los   of Urizen.

Chap: IV.

1. Ages on ages roll'd over him!
In stony sleep ages roll'd over him;
Like a dark waste stretching change'able.
By earthquakes riv'n, belching sullen
fires
On ages roll'd ages in ghastly
Sick torment; around him in whirlwinds
Of darkness the eternal Prophet howl'd
Beating still on his rivets of iron;
Pouring sodor of iron; dividing
The horrible night into watches.

2. And Urizen (so his eternal name)
His prolific delight obscur'd more & more
In dark secresy hiding in surging
Sulphureous fluid his phantasies.
The Eternal Prophet heard the dark
bellows,
And turn'd restless the tongs; and the
hammer
Incessant beat; forging chains new & new
Numbring with links. hours, days & years

3. The eternal mind bounded began to roll
Eddies of wrath ceaseless round & round,
And the sulphureous foam surgeing thick

Settled, a lake, bright, & shining clear:
White as the snow on the mountains cold.

4. Forgetfulness, dumbness, necessity!
In chains of the mind locked up,
Like fetters of ice shrinking together
Disorganiz'd, rent from Eternity,
Los beat on his fetters of iron;
And heated his furnaces & pourd
Iron sodor and sodor of brass

5. Restless turnd the immortal inchaind
Heaving dolorous! anguish'd unbearable
Till a roof shaggy wild inclos'd
In an orb, his fountain of thought.

6. In a horrible dreamful slumber;
Like the linked infernal chain;
A vast Spine writh'd in torment
Upon the winds; shooting pain'd
Ribs, like a bending cavern
And bones of solidness, froze
Over all his nerves of joy.
And a first Age passed over,
And a state of dismal woe.

‡ Urizen.

7. From the caverns of his jointed Spine.
Down sunk with fright a red
Round globe hot burning deep
Deep down into the Abyss:
Panting: Conglobing, Trembling
Shooting out ten thousand branches
Around his solid bones.
And a second Age passed over.
And a state of dismal woe.

8. In harrowing fear rolling round;
His nervous brain shot branches
Round the branches of his heart
On high into two little orbs
And fixed in two little caves

Hiding carefully from the wind.
His Eyes beheld the deep.
And a third Age passed over:
And a state of dismal woe.

9. The pangs of hope began.
In heavy pain striving, struggling.
Two Ears in close volutions:
From beneath his orbs of vision
Shot spiring out and petrified
As they grew. And a fourth Age passed
And a state of dismal woe.

10. In ghastly torment sick.
Hanging upon the wind.

Two Nostrils bent down to the deep | In trembling & howling & dismay.
And a fifth Age passed over; | And a second Age passed over.
And a state of dismal woe. | And a state of dismal woe.

11. In ghastly torment sick: | Chap: V.
Within his ribs bloated round.
A craving Hungry Cavern | 1 In terrors Los shrunk from his
Thence arose his channeld Throat. | task
And like a red flame a Tongue | His great hammer fell from his hand
Of thirst & of hunger appeard. | His fires beheld, and sickening
And a sixth Age passed over: | Hid their strong limbs in smoke.
And a state of dismal woe. | For with noises ruinous loud:
 | With hurtlings & clashings & groans
12. Enraged & stifled with torment | The Immortal endur'd his chains
He threw his right Arm to the north | Tho' bound in a deadly sleep
His left Arm to the south
Shooting out in anguish deep | 2. All the myriads of Eternity
And his Feet stampd the nether Abyss | All the wisdom & joy of life
 | Roll like a sea around him

Except what his little orbs | Then he look'd back with anxious desire
Of sight by degrees untold | But the space undivided by existence
 | Struck horror into his soul.
3 And now his eternal life
Like a dream was obliterated | 6. Los wept obscur'd with mourning
 | His bosom earthquak'd with sighs
4. Shuddring, the Eternal Prophet smote | He saw Urizen deadly black,
With a stroke, from his north to south | In his chains bound & Pity began
region
The bellows & hammer are silent now | 7 In anguish dividing & dividing
A nerveless silence, his prophetic voice | For pity divides the soul
Siezd: a cold solitude & dark void | In pangs eternity on eternity
The Eternal Prophet & Urizen clos'd | Life in cataracts pourd down his
 | cliffs
5. Ages on ages rolld over them | The void shrunk the lymph into Nerves
Cut off from life & light frozen | Wandring wide on the bosom of night
Into horrible forms of deformity | And left a round globe of blood.
Los sufferd his fires to decay | Trembling upon the void

1 Urizen. C. V.

8. The globe of life blood trembled   9. All Eternity shudderd at sight
Branching out into roots: Of the first female now separate
Fibrous, writhing upon the winds: Pale as a clout of snow
Fibres of blood, milk and tears: Waving before the face of Los
In pangs, eternity on eternity.
At length in tears & cries imbodied   10. Wonder, awe, fear, astonishment
A female form trembling and pale   Petrify the eternal myriads;
Waves before his deathy face   At the first Female form now separate

They call'd her Pity, and fled

11. Spread a Tent, with strong cur-
    tains around them
Let cords & stakes bind in the Void
That Eternals may no more behold them

12. They began to weave curtains of
    darkness
They erected large pillars round the Void
With golden hooks fastend in the pillars
With infinite labour the Eternals
A woof wove and called it Science

Chap: VI.

1 But Los saw the Female & pitied
He embraced her, she wept she refused
In perverse and cruel delight
She fled from his arms, yet he follow'd

2. Eternity shudderd when they saw
Man begetting his likeness,
On his own divided image.

3 A time passed over, the Eternals
Began to erect the tent,
When Enitharmon sick,
Felt a Worm within her womb.

4 Yet helpless it lay like a Worm
In the trembling womb
To be moulded into existence

5. All day the worm lay on her bosom
All night within her womb
The worm lay till it grew to a ser-
    pent
With dolorous hissings & poisons
Round Enitharmons loins folding.

6. Coild within Enitharmons womb
The serpent grew casting its scales
With sharp pangs the hissings began
To change to a grating cry,
Many sorrows and dismal throes
Many forms of fish bird & beast
Brought forth an Infant form
Where was a worm before.

7. The Eternals their tent finished
Alarmd with these gloomy visions
When Enitharmon groaning
Produced a man Child to the light.

8. A shriek ran thro Eternity;
And a paralytic stroke;
At the birth of the Human shadow.

9. Delving earth in his resistless
    way
Howling, the Child with fierce flames
Issud from Enitharmon

10. The Eternals closed the tent
They beat down the stakes the cords

Stretchd for a work of eternity;
No more Los beheld Eternity.

11. In his hands he seizd the infant
He bathed him in springs of sorrow
He gave him to Enitharmon.

Chap VII.

1. They named the child Orc, he grew
Fed with milk of Enitharmon

2. Los awoke her, O sorrow to pain.
A tightning girdle grew.
Around his bosom. In sobbings
He burst the girdle in twain
But still another girdle
Opressd his bosom. In sobbings
Again he burst it Again
Another girdle succeeds
The girdle was formd by day
By night was burst in twain

3. These falling down on the rock
Into an iron Chain
In each other link by link locked

4. They took Orc to the top of a
mountain
O how Enitharmon wept!
They chaind his young limbs to the
rock
With the Chain of Jealousy
Beneath Urizens deathful Shadow

5. The dead heard the voice of the
child
And began to awake from sleep
All things. heard the voice of the child
And began to awake to life.

6. And Urizen craved with hunger
Stung with the odours of Nature
Explord his dens around

7. He formd a line & a plummet
To divide the Abyss beneath.
He formd a dividing rule:

8. He formed scales to weigh
He formed massy weights:
He formed a brazen quadrant
He formed golden compasses
And began to explore the Abyss
And he planted a garden of fruits

9. But Los encircled Enitharmon
With fires of Prophecy
From the sight of Urizen & Orc

10. And she bare an enormous race

Chap. VIII.

1 Urizen explord his dens
Mountain, moor, & wilderness,
With a globe of fire lighting his
journey
A fearful journey. annoyd
By cruel enormities: forms

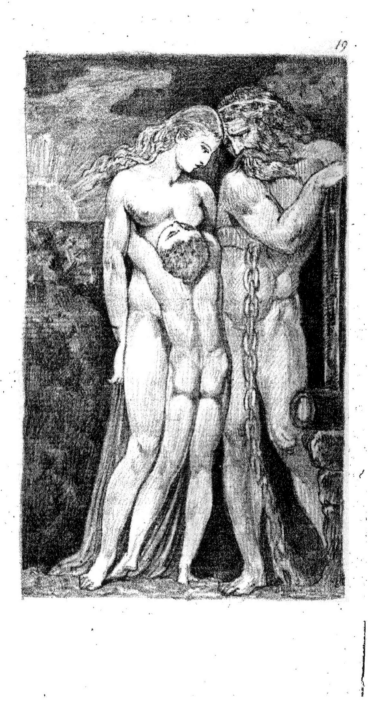

Urizen C. VIII

Of life on his forsaken mountains | Grodna rent the deep earth howling
                                | Amaz'd; his heavens immense cracks

2. And his world teem'd vast enormities | Like the ground parch'd with heat; then
Frightning: faithless fawning | Fuzon
Portions of life; similitudes | Flam'd out; first begotten last born
Of a foot, or a hand or a head | All his eternal sons in like manner
Or a heart, or an eye, they swam mis- | His daughters: from green herbs & cattle
        chevous | From monsters, & worms of the pit
Dread terrors! delighting in blood

3. Must Urizen sicken'd to see | 4. He in darkness clos'd, view'd all his
His eternal creations appear | race
Sons & daughters of sorrow on mountains | And his soul sicken'd! he curs'd
Weeping! wailing! first Thiriel appeard | Both sons & daughters; for he saw
Astonish'd at his own existence | That no flesh nor spirit could keep
Like a man from a cloud born, & Utha | His iron laws one moment.
From the waters emerging, laments!

5. For he saw that life liv'd up-
     death

The Ox in the slaughter house moans
The Dog at the wintry door
And he wept, & he called it Pity
And his tears flowed down on the winds

6 Cold he wander'd on high, over
        their cities
In weeping & pain & woe
And where-ever he wander'd in sorrows
Upon the aged heavens
A cold shadow follow'd behind him
Like a spiders web, moist, cold & dim
Drawing out from his sorrowing soul
The dungeon-like heaven dividing
Where ever the footsteps of Urizen
Walkd over the cities in sorrow.

7 Till a Web dark & cold throughout all
The tormented element stretchd
From the sorrows of Urizens soul
And the Web is a Female in embrio
    None could break the Web, no wings
        of fire.

8 So twisted the cords & so knotted
The meshes: twisted like to the
        human brain
                —pion
9 And all calld it The Net of Reli

Chap: IX

1 Then the Inhabitants of those Cities ;
Felt their Nerves change into Marrow
And hardening Bones began
In swift diseases and torments
In throbbings & shootings & grindings
Thro all the coasts: till weakend
The Senses inward rushd shrinking
Beneath the dark net of infection.

2 Till the shrunken eyes clouded over
Discernd not the woven hypocrisy
But the streaky slime in their heavens
Brought together by narrowing perceptions
Appeard transparent air: for their eyes
Grew small like the eyes of a man
And in reptile forms shrinking together
Of seven feet stature they remaind

3 Six days they shrunk up from existence
And on the seventh day they rested,
And they blessd the seventh day, in sick
        hope :
And forgot their eternal life

4 And their thirty cities divided
In form of a human heart
No more could they rise at will
In the infinite void, but bound down
To earth by their narrowing perceptions

1 Urizen C:IX

They lived a period of years
Then left a noisom body
To the jaws of devouring darkness

5 And their children wept, & built
Tombs in the desolate places
And formd laws of prudence and
   calld them
The eternal laws of God

6. And the thirty cities remaind
Surrounded by salt floods now calld
Africa: its name was then Egypt

7. The remaining sons of Urizen
Beheld their brethren shrink together
Beneath the Net of Urizen
Perswasion was in vain

For the ears of the inhabitants
Were wither'd & deafend & cold
And their eyes could not discern
Their brethren of other cities

8. So Fuzon calld all together
The remaining children of Urizen
And they left the pendulous earth
They called it Egypt, & left it

9. And the salt ocean rolled englobd

The End of the
first book of Urizen

THE

BOOK of

AHANIA

LAMBETH
Printed by W Blake ~~~ 1795.

AHANIA

Chap I.^st

1 Fuzon on a chariot iron-wing'd
On spiked flames rose his hot visage
Flam'd furious! sparkles his hair & beard
Shot down his wide bosom and shoulders
On clouds of smoke rages his chariot
And his right hand burns red in its
cloud

Moulding into a vast globe his wrath
As the thunder-stone is moulded
Son of Urizens silent burnings

2. Shall we worship this Demon of smoke
Said Fuzon this abstract non-entity
This cloudy God seated on waters
Now seen, now obscure; King of sorrow?

3. So he spoke in a fiery flame
On Urizen frowning indignant
The Globe of wrath shaking on high
Roaring with fury he threw
The howling Globe burning it flew
Lengthning into a hungry beam Swiftly

4 Oppos'd to the exulting flam'd beam
The broad Disk of Urizen upheav'd
Across the Void many a mile

5 It was forg'd in mills where the winter
Beats incessant ten winters the disk

Unremitting endur'd the cold hammer
-berd

6 But the strong arm that sent it remem-
The sounding beam laughing it tore through
That beaten mass keeping its direction
The cold loins of Urizen dividing

7 Dire shriek'd his invisible Lust
Deep groand Urizen! stretching his awful hand
Ahania (so name his parted soul)
He siezd on his mountains of Jealousy
He groand anguishd & called her Sin,
Kissing her and weeping over her
Then hid her in darkness in silence
Jealous tho' she was invisible.

8 She fell down a faint shadow wandring
In chaos and circling dark Urizen
As the moon anguishd circles the earth,
Hopeless! abhorrd! a death-shadow.
Unseen unbodied unknown
The mother of Pestilence

9 But the fiery beam of Fuzon
Was a pillar of fire to Egypt
Five hundred years wandring on earth
Till Los siezd it and beat in a mass
With the body of the sun

Chap II.

1, But the forehead of Urizen gathering
And his eyes pale with anguish. his lips
Blue & changing. in tears and bitter
Contrition he prepard his Bow

2 Formd of Ribs that in his dark solitude
When obscurd in his forests fell monsters
Arose For his dire Contemplations
Rushd down like floods from his mountains
In torrents of mud settling thick
With Eggs of unnatural production
Forthwith hatching. some howld on his hills
Some in vales, some aloft flew in air

3 Of these an enormous dread Serpent
Scaled and poisonous horned
Approachd Urizen even to his knees
As he sat on his dark rooted Oak

4 With his horns he pushd furious
Great the conflict & great the jealousy
In cold poisons but Urizen smote him.

5 First he poisond the rocks with his blood
Then polishd his ribs and his sinews
Dried laid them apart till winter
Then a Bow black prepard. on this Bow
A poisoned rock placd in silence
He utterd these words to the Bow

6. O Bow of the clouds of secrecy
O nerve of that lust formd monster
Send this rock swift. invisible thro
The black clouds. on the bosom of Fuzon

7 So saying In torment of his wounds
He bent the enormous ribs slowly.
A circle of darkness then fixed
The sinew in its rest then the Rock
Poisonous source placd with art, lifting dif-
-ficult
Its weighty bulk silent the rock lay

8 While Fuzon his tygers unloosing

Thought Urizen slain by his wrath
I am God said he eldest of things

9 Sudden sings the rock. swift & invisible
On Fuzon flew enterd his bosom
His beautiful visage, his tresses
That gave light to the mornings of heaven
Were smitten with darkness deformd
And outstretchd on the edge of the fo-
-rest

10 But the rock fell upon the Earth
Mount Sinai in Arabia

Chap III

1 The Globe shook. and Urizen seated
On black clouds his sore wound anointed
The ointment flowd down on the void
Mixd with blood, here the snake gets
her poison

2 With difficulty & great pain, Urizen
Lifted on high the dead corse
On his shoulders he bore it to where
A Tree hung over the Immensity

3 For when Urizen shrunk away
From Eternals, he sat on a rock
Barren. a rock which himself
From redounding fancies had petrified
Many tears fell on the rock,
Many sparks of vegetation.
Soon shot the pained root
Of Mystery under his heel.
It grew a thick tree. he wrote
In silence his book of iron
Till the horrid plant bending its boughs
Grew to roots when it felt the earth
And again sprung to many a tree

4 Amazd started Urizen. when
He beheld himself compassed round
And high roofed over with trees
He arose but the stems stood so thick
He with difficulty and great pain
Brought his Books all but the Book

Of iron from the dismal shade

5. The Tree still grows over the Void
Enrooting itself all around
An endless labyrinth of woe!

6 The corse of his first begotten
On the accursed Tree of Mystery
On the topmost stem of this Tree
Urizen naild Fuzons corse

Chap IV

1. Forth flew the arrows of pestilence
Round the pale living corse on the tree

2. For in Urizens slumbers of abstraction
In the infinite ages of Eternity
When his Nerves of Joy melted & flow'd
A white Lake on the dark blue air
In perturb'd pain and dismal torment
Now stretching out now swift conglobing

3 Effluvia vapor'd above
In noxious clouds, these hover'd thick
Over the disorganiz'd Immortal
Till petrific pain scurf'd o'er the Lakes
As the bones of man, solid & dark

4. The clouds of disease hover'd wide
Around the Immortal in torment
Perching around the hurtling bones
Disease on disease, shape on shape
Winged screaming in blood & torment

5. The Eternal Prophet beat on his anvils
Enrag'd in the desolate darkness
He forg'd nets of iron around
And Los threw them around the bones

6. The shapes screaming flutter'd vain
Some combind into muscles & glands
Some organs for craving and lust
Most remaind on the tormented void
Urizens army of horrors

7 Round the pale living Corse on the Tree

Forty years flew the arrows of pestilence

8 Wailing and terror and woe
Ran thro' all his dismal world
Forty years, all his sons & daughters
Felt their skulls harden then Asia
Arose in the pendulous deep

9 They reptilize upon the Earth.

10 Fuzon groan'd on the Tree

Chap V

1 The lamenting voice of Ahania
Weeping upon the void
And round the Tree of Fuzon
Distant in solitary night
Her voice was heard, but no form
Had she but her tears from clouds
Eternal fell round the Tree

2 And the voice cried Ah Urizen! Love!
Flower of morning! I weep on the verge
Of Non-entity, how wide the Abyss
Between Ahania and thee!

3 I lie on the verge of the deep
I see thy dark clouds ascend!
I see thy black forests and floods,
A horrible waste to my eyes!

4 Weeping I walk over rocks
Over dens & thro' valleys of death
Why didst thou despise Ahania
To cast me from thy bright presence
Into the World of Loneness

5 I cannot touch his hand
Nor weep on his knees nor hear
His voice & bow nor see his eyes
And joy nor hear his footsteps, and
My heart leap at the lovely sound!
I cannot kiss the place
Whereon his bright feet have trod

But

But I wander on the rocks
With hard necessity.

6. Where is my golden palace
Where my ivory bed
Where the joy of my morning hour
Where the sons of eternity singing

7. To awake bright Urizen my king
To arise to the mountain sport
To the bliss of eternal valleys.

8. To awake my king in the morn:
To embrace Ahanias joy
On the breath of his open bosom:
From my soft cloud of dew to fall
In showers of life on his harvests

9. When he gave my happy soul
To the sons of eternal joy
When he took the daughters of life
Into my chambers of love.

10. When I found babes of bliss on my beds
And bosoms of milk in my chambers
Filld with eternal seed
O' eternal births sung round Ahania
In interchange sweet of their joys.

11. Swelld with ripeness & fat with fatness
Bursting on winds my odors
My ripe figs and rich pomegranates.

In infant joy at thy feet
O Urizen sported and song;

12. Then thou with thy lap full of seed
With thy hand full of generous fire
Walked forth from the clouds of morning
On the virgins of springing joy
On the human soul to cast
The seed of eternal science.

13. The sweat poured down thy temples
To Ahania returnd in evening
The moisture awoke to birth
My mothers-joys, sleeping in bliss

14. But now alone over rocks, mountains
Cast out from thy lovely bosom,
Cruel jealousy! selfish fear!
Self-destroying: how can delight
Renew in these chains of darkness
Where bones of beasts are strown
On the bleak and snowy mountains
Where bones from the birth are buried
Before they see the light

FINIS

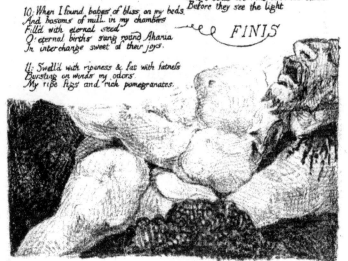

LIBRARY
OF THE
UNIVERSITY
OF
CALIFORNIA.

LIBRARY OF THE UNIVERSITY OF CALIFORNIA.

TIRIEL.

TIRIEL.

I.

And aged Tiriel stood before the gates of his beautiful palace,
With Myratana, once the Queen of all the western plains;
But now his eyes were darkened, and his wife fading in death
They stood before their once delightful palace; and thus the voice
Of aged Tiriel arose, that his sons might hear in their gates.

"Accursed race of Tiriel! Behold your father;
Come forth and look on her that bore you. Come, you accursed sons.
In my weak arms I here have borne your dying mother;
Come forth, sons of the curse, come forth! See the death of
    Myratana."

His sons ran from their gates, and saw their aged parents stand:
And thus the eldest son of Tiriel raised his mighty voice:—

"Old man! unworthy to be called the father of Tiriel's race!
For every one of those thy wrinkles, each of those grey hairs,
Are cruel as death, and as obdurate as the devouring pit!
Why should thy sons care for thy curses, thou accursed man?
Were we not slaves till we rebelled? Who cares for Tiriel's curse?
His blessing was a cruel curse; his curse may be a blessing."

He ceased. The aged man raised up his right hand to the heavens;
His left supported Myratana, shrinking in pangs of death.
The orbs of his large eyes he opened, and thus his voice went forth :—

"Serpents, not sons, wreathing around the bones of Tiriel!
Ye worms of death, feasting upon your aged parents' flesh,

Listen, and hear your mother's groans. No more accursed sons
She bears ; she groans not at the birth of Heuxos or Yuva.
These are the groans of death, ye serpents! those are the groans of
    death!
Nourished with milk, ye serpents, nourished with mother's tears and
    cares!
Look at my eyes, blind as the orbless skull among the stones,
Look at my bald head. Hark, listen, ye serpents, listen! . . . .
What, Myratana! What, my wife! O soul! O spirit! O fire!
What, Myratana, art thou dead? Look here, ye serpents, look!
The serpents sprung from her own bowels have drained her dry as
    this
Curse on your ruthless heads, for I will bury her even here!"

So saying, he began to dig a grave with his aged hands:
But Heuxos called a son of Zazel to dig their mother a grave.

" Old cruelty, desist, and let us dig a grave for thee.
Thou hast refused our charity, thou hast refused our food,
Thou hast refused our clothes, our beds, our houses for thy dwelling,
Choosing to wander like a son of Zazel in the rocks.
Why dost thou curse? Is not the curse now come upon thine head?
Was it not thou enslaved the sons of Zazel? And they have cursed,
And now thou feel'st it! Dig a grave, and let us bury our mother."

" There, take the body, cursed sons! And may the heavens rain
    wrath,
As thick as northern fogs, around your gates, to choke you up!
That you may lie as now your mother lies—like dogs, cast out,
The stink of your dead carcases annoying man and beast,
Till your white bones are bleached with age for a memorial.
No! your remembrance shall perish ; for, when your carcases
Lie stinking on the earth, the buriers shall arise from the East,
And not a bone of all the sons of Tiriel remain.
Bury your mother, but you cannot bury the curse of Tiriel."

He ceased, and darkling o'er the mountains sought his pathless way.

II.

He wandered day and night. To him both day and night were dark:
The sun he felt, but the bright moon was now a useless globe
O'er mountains and through vales of woe the blind and aged man
Wandered, till He that leadeth all led him to the vales of Har.

And Har and Heva, like two children, sat beneath the oak.

Mnetha, now aged, waited on them, and brought them food and
    clothing
But they were as the shadow of Har, and as the years forgotten;
Playing with flowers and running after birds they spent the day,
And in the night like infants slept, delighted with infant dreams.

Soon as the blind wanderer entered the pleasant gardens of Har,
They ran weeping, like frightened infants, for refuge in Mnetha's
    arms.
The blind man felt his way, and cried: " Peace to these open doors!
Let no one fear, for poor blind Tiriel hurts none but himself.
Tell me, O friends, where am I now, and in what pleasant place?"

" This is the valley of Har," said Mnetha, " and this is the tent of
    Har.
Who art thou, poor blind man, that takest the name of Tiriel on
    thee?
Tiriel is King of all the West. Who art thou? I am Mnetha;
And this is Har and Heva, trembling like infants by my side."

" I know Tiriel is King of the West, and there he lives in joy.
No matter who I am, O Mnetha! If thou hast any food,
Give it me, for I cannot stay—my journey is far from hence."

Then Har said: " O my mother Mnetha, venture not so near him,
For he is the king of rotten wood, and of the bones of death;
He wanders without eyes, and passes through thick walls and doors.
Thou shalt not smite my mother Mnetha, O thou eyeless man!"

" A wanderer, I beg for food. You see I cannot weep.
I cast away my staff, the kind companion of my travel,
And I kneel down that you may see I am a harmless man."

He kneeled down   And Mnetha said : "Come, Har and Heva, rise
He is an innocent old man, and hungry with his travel."

Then Har arose, and laid his hand upon old Tiriel's head.

" God bless thy poor bald pate, God bless thy hollow winking eyes,
God bless thy shrivelled beard, God bless thy many-wrinkled fore-
    head !
Thou hast no teeth, old man ! and thus I kiss thy sleek bald head.
Heva, come, kiss his bald head, for he will not hurt us, Heva."

Then Heva came, and took old Tiriel in her mother's arms.

" Bless thy poor eyes, old man, and bless the old father of Tiriel !
Thou art my Tiriel's old father; I know thee through thy wrinkles,
Because thou smellest like the fig-tree, thou smellest like ripe figs.
How didst thou lose thy eyes, old Tiriel ?   Bless thy wrinkled face ! "

Mnetha said . " Come in, aged wanderer; tell us of thy name
Why shouldest thou conceal thyself from those of thine own flesh ? "

" I am not of this region," said Tiriel, dissemblingly.
" I am an aged wanderer, once father of a race
Far in the North ; but they were wicked, and were all destroyed,
And I their father sent an outcast. I have told you all :
Ask me no more, I pray, for grief hath sealed my precious sight."

" O Lord ! " said Mnetha, "how I tremble ! Are there then more
    people,
More human creatures on this earth, beside the sons of Har ? "

" No more," said Tiriel, " but I, remain on all this globe ;
And I remain an outcast. Hast thou anything to drink ? "

Then Mnetha gave him milk and fruits, and they sat down together.

III.

They sat and ate, and Har and Heva smiled on Tiriel.

" Thou art a very old old man, but I am older than thou.
How came thine hair to leave thy forehead, how came thy face so
    brown ?
My hair is very long, my beard doth cover all my breast.
God bless thy piteous face ! To count the wrinkles in thy face
Would puzzle Mnetha. Bless thy face, for thou art Tiriel ! "

" Tiriel I never saw but once. I sat with him and ate ;
He was as cheerful as a prince, and gave me entertainment.
But long I stayed not at his palace, for I am forced to wander."

" What ! wilt thou leave us too ? " said Heva. " Thou shalt not leave
    us too,
For we have many sports to show thee, and many songs to sing ;
And after dinner we will walk into the cage of Har,
And thou shalt help us to catch birds, and gather them ripe cherries ;
Then let thy name be Tiriel, and never leave us more."

" If thou dost go," said Har, " I wish thine eyes may see thy folly.
My sons have left me.—Did thine leave thee ? Oh 'twas very
    cruel ! "

" No, venerable man," said Tiriel, " ask me not such things,
For thou dost make my heart to bleed. My sons were not like
    thine,
But worse. Oh never ask me more, or I must flee away."

" Thou shalt not go," said Heva, "till thou hast seen our singing-birds,
And heard Har sing in the great cage, and slept upon our fleeces.
Go not, for thou art so like Tiriel that I love thine head,
Though it is wrinkled like the earth parched with the summer heat."

Then Tiriel rose up from the seat, and said : " God bless these
   tents !
My journey is o'er rocks and mountains, not in pleasant vales ;
I must not sleep nor rest, because of madness and dismay."

And Mnetha said · " Thou must not go to wander dark alone,
But dwell with us, and let us be to thee instead of eyes,
And I will bring thee food, old man, till death shall call thee
   hence."

Then Tiriel frowned, and answered : " Did I not command you
   saying
Madness and deep dismay possess the heart of the blind man,
The wanderer who seeks the woods, leaning upon his staff ? "

Then Mnetha, trembling at his frowns, led him to the tent-door,
And gave to him his staff, and blessed him.   He went on his way.

But Har and Heva stood and watched him till he entered the wood;
And then they went and wept to Mnetha, but they soon forgot their
   tears.

·IV.

Over the weary hills the blind man took his lonely way ,
To him the day and night alike was dark and desolate.
But far he had not gone when Ijim from his woods came down,
Met him at entrance of the forest, in a dark and lonely way.

" Who art thou, eyeless wretch, that thus obstructest the lion's
   path ?
Ijim shall rend thy feeble joints, thou tempter of dark Ijim !
Thou hast the form of Tiriel, but I know thee well enough !
Stand from my path, foul fiend ! Is this the last of thy deceits—
To be a hypocrite, and stand in shape of a blind beggar ? "

The blind man heard his brother's voice, and kneeled down on his
   knee.

"O brother Ijim, if it is thy voice that speaks to me,—
Smite not thy brother Tiriel, though weary of his life.
My sons have smitten me already; and, if thou smitest me,
The curse that rolls over their heads will rest itself on thine.
'Tis now seven years since in my palace I beheld thy face."

"Come, thou dark fiend, I dare thy cunning! know that Ijim scorns
To smite thee in the form of helpless age and eyeless policy;
Rise up, for I discern thee, and I dare thy eloquent tongue.
Come, I will lead thee on thy way, and use thee as a scoff."

" O brother Ijim, thou beholdest wretched Tiriel :
Kiss me, my brother, and then leave me to wander desolate ! "

" No, artful fiend, but I will lead thee; dost thou want to go ?
Reply not, lest I bind thee with the green flags of the brook;
Ay, now thou art discovered.   I will use thee like a slave."

When Tiriel heard the words of Ijim, he sought not to reply :
He knew 'twas vain, for Ijim's words were as the voice of Fate.

And they went on together, over hills, through woody dales,
Blind to the pleasures of the sight, and deaf to warbling birds.

All day they walked, and all the night beneath the pleasant moon,
Westwardly journeying, till Tiriel grew weary with his travel.

" O Ijim, I am faint and weary, for my knees forbid
To bear me further.   Urge me not, lest I should die with travel.
A little rest I crave, a little water from a brook,
Or I shall soon discover that I am a mortal man,
And thou wilt lose thy once-loved Tiriel.   Alas ! how faint I am !"

"Impudent fiend ! " said Ijim, "hold thy glib and eloquent
       tongue ;—
Tiriel is a king, and thou the tempter of dark Ijim.
Drink of this running brook, and I will bear thee on my shoulders."

He drank ; and Ijim raised him up, and bore him on his shoulders.
All day he bore him ; and, when evening drew her solemn curtain,
Entered the gates of Tiriel's palace, and stood and called aloud.

"Heuxos, come forth ! I here have brought the fiend that troubles
 Ijim.
Look ! know'st thou aught of this grey beard, or of these blinded
 eyes ? "

Heuxos and Lotho ran forth at the sound of Ijim's voice,
And saw their aged father borne upon his mighty shoulders.
Their eloquent tongues were dumb, and sweat stood on their trembling
 limbs ;
They knew 'twas vain to strive with Ijim. They bowed and silent
 stood.

"What, Heuxos ! call thy father, for I mean to sport to-night.
This is the hypocrite that sometimes roars a dreadful lion ;
Then I have rent his limbs, and left him rotting in the forest
For birds to eat. But I have scarce departed from the place,
But like a tiger he would come, and so I rent him too.
Then like a river he would seek to drown me in his waves,
But soon I buffeted the torrent ; anon like to a cloud
Fraught with the swords of lightning, but I braved the vengeance
 too.
Then he would creep like a bright serpent, till around my neck
While I was sleeping he would twine : I squeezed his poisonous soul.
Then like a toad or like a newt would whisper in my ears ;
Or like a rock stood in my way, or like a poisonous shrub.

At last I caught him in the form of Tiriel blind and old,
And so I'll keep him. Fetch your father, fetch forth Myratana."

They stood confounded, and thus Tiriel raised his silver voice.

"Serpents, not sons, why do you stand ? Fetch hither Tiriel,
Fetch hither Myratana, and delight yourselves with scoffs ;
For poor blind Tiriel is returned, and this much-injured head
Is ready for your bitter taunts. Come forth, sons of the curse ! "

Meantime.the other sons of Tiriel ran around their father,
Confounded at the terrible strength of Ijim. They knew 'twas vain,
Both spear and shield were useless, and the coat of iron mail,
When Ijim stretched his mighty arm; the arrow from his limbs
Rebounded, and the piercing sword broke on his naked flesh.

.. " Then is it true, Heuxos, that thou has turned thy aged parent
To be the sport of wintry winds," said Ijim : " is this true ?
It is a lie, and I am like the tree torn by the wind,
Thou eyeless fiend and you dissemblers ! Is this Tiriel's house ?
It is as false as Matha, and as dark as vacant Orcus.
Escape, ye fiends, for Ijim will not lift his hand against ye."

So saying, Ijim gloomy turned his back, and silent sought
The secret forests, and all night wandered in desolate ways.

V.

And aged Tiriel stood and said : " Where does the thunder sleep ?
Where doth he hide his terrible head ? and his swift and fiery
        daughters,
Where do they shroud their fiery wings, and the terrors of their
        hair ?
Earth, thus I stamp thy bosom ! rouse the earthquake from his
        den,
To raise his dark and burning visage through the cleaving ground,
To thrust these towers with his shoulders ! Let his fiery dogs
Rise from the centre, belching flames and roaring dark smoke !
Where art thou, Pestilence, that bathest in fogs and standing lakes ?
Raise up thy sluggish limbs, and let the loathsomest of poisons
Drop from thy garments as thou walkest, wrapped in yellow clouds !
Here take thy seat in this wide court ; let it be strewn with dead ;
And sit and smile upon these cursed sons of Tiriel !
Thunder, and fire, and pestilence, hear you not Tiriel's curse ? "

He ceased. The heavy clouds confused rolled round the lofty
    towers,
Discharging their enormous voices at the father's curse.
The earth trembled, fires belched from the yawning clefts,
And, when the shaking ceased, a fog possessed the accursed clime.
The cry was great in Tiriel's palace   His five daughters ran,
And caught him by the garments, weeping with cries of bitter woe.
" Ay, now you feel the curse, you cry ! but may all ears be deaf
As Tiriel's, and all eyes as blind as Tiriel's, to your woes!
May never stars shine on your roofs, may never sun nor moon
Visit you, but eternal fogs hover around your walls !—
Hela, my youngest daughter, thou shalt lead me from this place;
And let the curse fall on the rest, and wrap them up together !"
He ceased, and Hela led her father from the noisome place.
In haste they fled, while all the sons and daughters of Tiriel,
Chained in thick darkness, uttered cries of mourning all the night.
And in the morning, lo ! an hundred men in ghastly death,
The four daughters, stretched on the marble pavement, silent, all
Fallen by the pestilence,—the rest moped round in guilty fears;
And all the children in their beds were cut off in one night,
Thirty of Tiriel's sons remained, to wither in the palace—
Desolate, loathed, dumb, astonished—waiting for black death.

VI.

And Hela led her father through the silence of the night,
Astonished, silent, till the morning beams began to spring.
" Now, Hela, I can go with pleasure, and dwell with Har and Heva
Now that the curse shall clean devour all those guilty sons.
This is the right and ready way , I know it by the sound
That our feet make. Remember, Hela, I have saved thee from
    death ;
Then be obedient to thy father, for the curse is taken off thee.
I dwelt with Myratana five years in the desolate rock;

And all that time we waited for the fire to fall from heaven,
Or for the torrents of the sea to overwhelm you all.
But now my wife is dead, and all the time of grace is past.
You see the parents' curse. Now lead me where I have com-
    manded."

" O leagued with evil spirits, thou accursed man of sin—
True, I was born thy slave. Who asked thee to save me from death?
'Twas for thyself, thou cruel man, because thou wantest eyes."

" True, Hela, this is the desert of all those cruel ones.
Is Tiriel cruel? Look! his daughter—and his youngest daughter—
Laughs at affection, glories in rebellion, scoffs at love.
I have not ate these two days; lead me to Har and Heva's tent,
Or I will wrap thee up in such a terrible father's curse
That thou shalt feel worms in thy marrow creeping through thy
    bones;
Yet thou shalt lead me. Lead me, I command, to Har and Heva."

" O cruel! O destroyer! O consumer! O avenger!
To Har and Heva I will lead thee; then would that they would
    curse—
Then would they curse as thou hast cursed! But they are not like
    thee!
Oh they are holy and forgiving, filled with loving mercy,
Forgetting the offences of their most rebellious children,
Or else thou wouldest not have lived to curse thy helpless children.

" Look on my eyes, Hela, and see (for thou hast eyes to see)
The tears swell from my stony fountains; wherefore do I weep?
Wherefore from my blind orbs art thou not seized with poisonous
    stings?
Laugh, serpent, youngest venomous reptile of the flesh of Tiriel!
Laugh, for thy father Tiriel shall give thee cause to laugh,
Unless thou lead me to the tent of Har, child of the curse!"

"Silence thy evil tongue, thou murderer of thy helpless children.
I lead thee to the tent of Har: not that I mind thy curse,
But that I feel they will curse thee, and hang upon thy bones
Fell shaking agonies, and in each wrinkle of that face
Plant worms of death to feast upon the tongue of terrible curses!"

"Hela, my daughter, listen! Thou art the daughter of Tiriel. .
Thy father calls. Thy father lifts his hand unto the heavens,
For thou hast laughed at my tears, and cursed thy aged father:
Let snakes rise from thy bedded locks, and laugh among thy curls!"

He ceased. Her dark hair upright stood, while snakes infolded round
Her madding brows. her shrieks appalled the soul of Tiriel.

"What have I done, Hela, my daughter? Fear'st thou now the
    curse,
Or wherefore dost thou cry? Ah wretch, to curse thy aged father!.
Lead me to Har and Heva, and the curse of Tiriel
Shall fail. If thou refuse, howl in the desolate mountains."

VII.

She, howling, led him over mountains and through frighted vales,
Till to the caves of Zazel they approached at eventide.

Forth from their caves old Zazel and his sons ran, when they saw
Their tyrant prince blind, and his daughter howling and leading him.

They laughed and mocked; some threw dirt and stones as they
    passed by.
But, when Tiriel turned around and raised his awful voice,
Some fled away; but Zazel stood still, and thus began:—

"Bald tyrant, wrinkled cunning, listen to Zazel's chains;
'Twas thou that chained thy brother Zazel! Where are now thine
    eyes?
Shout, beautiful daughter of Tiriel; thou singest a sweet song!

Where are you going? Come and eat some roots, and drink some
    water.
Thy crown is bald, old man; the sun will dry thy brains away,
And thou wilt be as foolish as thy foolish brother Zazel."

The blind man heard, and smote his breast, and trembling passed on.
They threw dirt after them, till to the covert of a wood
The howling maiden led her father, where wild beasts resort,
Hoping to end her woes; but from her cries the tigers fled.
All night they wandered through the wood; and, when the sun
    arose,
They entered on the mountains of Har. At noon the happy tents
Were frighted by the dismal cries of Hela on the mountains.

But Har and Heva slept fearless as babes on loving breasts.
Mnetha awoke; she ran and stood at the tent-door, and saw
The aged wanderer led towards the tents. She took her bow,
And chose her arrows, then advanced to meet the terrible pair.

VIII.

And Mnetha hasted, and met them at the gate of the lower garden.

"Stand still, or from my bow receive a sharp and winged death!"

Then Tiriel stood, saying: "What soft voice threatens such bitter
    things?

Lead me to Har and Heva: I am Tiriel, King of the West."
And Mnetha led them to the tent of Har; and Har and Heva
Ran to the door. When Tiriel felt the ankles of aged Har,
He said: "O weak mistaken father of a lawless race,
Thy laws, O Har, and Tiriel's wisdom, end together in a curse.
Why is one law given to the lion and the patient ox,
And why men bound beneath the heavens in a reptile form,
A worm of sixty winters creeping on the dusty ground?

The child springs from the womb; the father ready stands to form
The infant head, while the mother idle plays with her dog on the
    couch.
The young bosom is cold for lack of mother's nourishment, and
    milk
Is cut off from the weeping mouth with difficulty and pain.
The little lids are lifted, and the little nostrils opened;
The father forms a whip to rouse the sluggish senses to act,
And scourges off all youthful fancies from the new-born man.
Then walks the weak infant in sorrow, compelled to number foot-
    steps
Upon the sand. And, when the drone has reached his crawling
    length,
Black berries appear that poison all around him. Such was Tiriel,—
Compelled to pray repugnant and to humble the immortal spirit,
Till I am subtle as a serpent in a paradise,
Consuming all—both flowers and fruits, insects and warbling birds.
And now my paradise is fallen, and a drear sandy plain
Returns my thirsty hissings in a curse on thee, O Har,
Mistaken father of a lawless race!—My voice is past."

He ceased, outstretched at Har and Heva's feet in awful death.

THE END.

THE
BOOK
of
THEL

The Author & Printer Willm Blake. 1789.

THEL'S Motto.

Does the Eagle know what is in the pit?
Or wilt thou go ask the Mole:
Can Wisdom be put in a silver rod?
Or Love in a golden bowl?

THEL

I

The daughters of Mne Seraphim led round their sunny flocks.
All but the youngest: she in paleness sought the secret air.
To fade away like morning beauty from her mortal day:
Down by the river of Adona her soft voice is heard:
5 And thus her gentle lamentation falls like morning dew.

O life of this our spring! why fades the lotus of the water?
Why fade these children of the spring? born but to smile & fall.
Ah! Thel is like a watry bow. and like a parting cloud.
Like a reflection in a glass. like shadows in the water
10 Like dreams of infants. like a smile upon an infants face.
Like the doves voice. like transient day. like music in the air;
Ah! gentle may I lay me down and gentle rest my head.
And gentle sleep the sleep of death. and gently hear the voice
Of him that walketh in the garden in the evening time.

15 The Lilly of the valley breathing in the humble grass
Answerd the lovely maid and said: I am a watry weed.
And I am very small and love to dwell in lowly vales:
So weak the gilded butterfly scarce perches on my head
Yet I am visited from heaven and he that smiles on all
Walks in the valley, and each morn over me spreads his hand
Saying, rejoice thou humble grass. thou new-born lilly flower.
Thou gentle maid of silent valleys and of modest brooks:
For thou shalt be clothed in light and fed with morning manna:
Till summers heat melts thee beside the fountains and the springs
To flourish in eternal vales: then why should Thel complain.

Why

Why should the mistreß of the vales of Har, utter a sigh.

She ceasd & smild in tears, then sat down in her silver shrine.

Thel answerd, O thou little virgin of the peaceful valley,
Giving to those that cannot crave, the voiceless, the o'ertired.
Thy breath doth nourish the innocent lamb, he smells thy milky garments
He crops thy flowers while thou sittest smiling in his face.
Wiping his mild and meekin mouth from all contagious taints.
Thy wine doth purify the golden honey; thy perfume.
Which thou dost scatter on every little blade of graß that springs
Revives the milked cow, & tames the fire-breathing steed.
But Thel is like a faint cloud kindled at the rising sun:
I vanish from my pearly throne, and who shall find my place.

Queen of the vales the Lilly answerd, ask the tender cloud,
And it shall tell thee why it glitters in the morning sky,
And why it scatters its bright beauty thro' the humid air.
Descend O little cloud & hover before the eyes of Thel.

The Cloud descended and the Lilly bowd her modest head;
And went to mind her numerous charge among the verdant graß

II

O little Cloud the virgin said. I charge thee tell to me
Why thou complainest not when in one hour thou fade away:
Then we shall seek thee but not find: ah Thel is like to thee.
I pass away. yet I complain, and no one hears my voice.

The Cloud then shewd his golden head & his bright form emerg'd.
Hovering and glittering on the air before the face of Thel.

O virgin know'st thou not our steeds drink of the golden springs
Where Luvah doth renew his horses: lookst thou on my youth.
And fearest thou because I vanish and am seen no more.
Nothing remains; O maid I tell thee, when I pass away.
It is to tenfold life, to love, to peace, and raptures holy:
Unseen descending, weigh my light wings upon balmy flowers;
And court the fair eyed dew, to take me to her shining tent
The weeping virgin, trembling kneels before the risen sun,
Till we arise link'd in a golden band and never part:
But walk united bearing food to all our tender flowers.

Dost thou O little Cloud? I fear that I am not like thee:
For I walk through the vales of Har, and smell the sweetest flowers;
But I feed not the little flowers: I hear the warbling birds,
But I feed not the warbling birds, they fly and seek their food:
But Thel delights in these no more because I fade away.
And all shall say, without a use this shining woman liv'd.
Or did she only live to be at death the food of worms.

The Cloud reclind upon his airy throne and answerd thus.

Then if thou art the food of worms, O virgin of the skies,
How great thy use, how great thy blessing; every thing that lives.
Lives not alone nor for itself; fear not and I will call
The weak worm from its lowly bed, and thou shalt hear its voice.
Come forth worm of the silent valley, to thy pensive queen.

The helpless worm arose, and sat upon the Lillys leaf.
And the bright Cloud saild on, to find his partner in the vale.

III.

III.

Then Thel astonish'd view'd the Worm upon its dewy bed. .

Art thou a Worm? image of weakness. art thou but a Worm?
I see thee like an infant wrapped in the Lillys leaf:
Ah weep not little voice, thou can'st not speak, but thou can'st weep:
Is this a Worm? I see thee lay helpless & naked: weeping
And none to answer, none to cherish thee with mothers smiles.

The Clod of Clay heard the Worms voice & rais'd her pitying head:
She bowd over the weeping infant, and her life exhald
In milky fondness, then on Thel she fixd her humble eyes

O beauty of the vales of Har. we live not for ourselves,
Thou seest me the meanest thing, and so I am indeed:
My bosom of itself is cold, and of itself is dark,

But

But he that loves the lowly, pours his oil upon my head
And kisses me, and binds his nuptial bands around my breast.
And says; Thou mother of my children, I have loved thee
And I have given thee a crown that none can take away.
But how this is sweet maid, I know not, and I cannot know
I ponder, and I cannot ponder; yet I live and love.

The daughter of beauty wip'd her pitying tears with her white veil,
And said, Alas! I knew not this, and therefore did I weep:
That God would love a Worm I knew, and punish the evil foot
That will'd bruis'd its helpless form: but that he cherish'd it
With milk and oil I never knew, and therefore did I weep,
And I complaind in the mild air, because I fade away,
And lay me down in thy cold bed, and leave my shining lot.

Queen of the vales, the matron Clay answerd: I heard thy sighs.
And all thy moans flew o'er my roof, but I have call'd them down:
Wilt thou O Queen enter my house. tis given thee to enter,
And to return: fear nothing, enter with thy virgin feet.

IV

IV.

The eternal gates terrific porter lifted the northern bar:
Thel enterd in & saw the secrets of the land unknown;
She saw the couches of the dead, & where the fibrous roots
Of every heart on earth infixes deep its restless twists:
A land of sorrows & of tears where never smile was seen.

She wanderd in the land of clouds thro' valleys dark, listning
Dolours & lamentations: waiting oft beside a dewy grave
She stood in silence. listning to the voices of the ground,
Till to her own grave plot she came, & there she sat down.
And heard this voice of sorrow breathed from the hollow pit.

Why cannot the Ear be closed to its own destruction?
Or the glistning Eye to the poison of a smile!
Why are Eyelids stord with arrows ready drawn,
Where a thousand fighting men in ambush lie?
Or an Eye of gifts & graces showring fruits & coined
      gold?
Why a Tongue impress'd with honey from every wind?
Why an Ear, a whirlpool fierce to draw creations in?
Why a Nostril wide inhaling terror trembling & affright
Why a tender curb upon the youthful burning boy?
Why a little curtain of flesh on the bed of our desire?

The Virgin started from her seat, & with a shriek,
Fled back unhinderd till she came into the vales of
                                                Har

The End

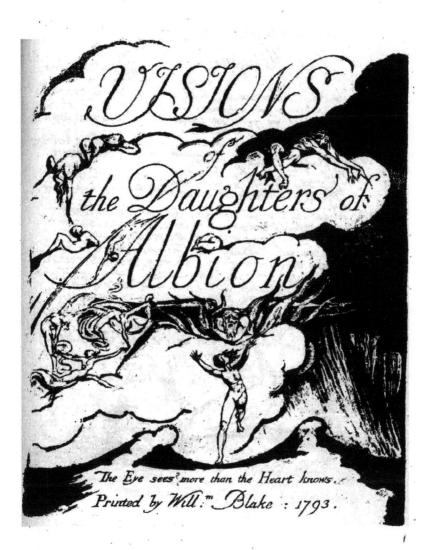

VISIONS

of

the Daughters of

Albion

The Eye sees more than the Heart knows.
Printed by Will.ᵐ Blake : 1793.

The Argument

I loved Theotormon
And I was not ashamed
I trembled in my virgin fears
And I hid in Leutha's vale!

I plucked Leutha's flower,
And I rose up from the vale;
But the terrible thunders tore
My virgin mantle in twain.

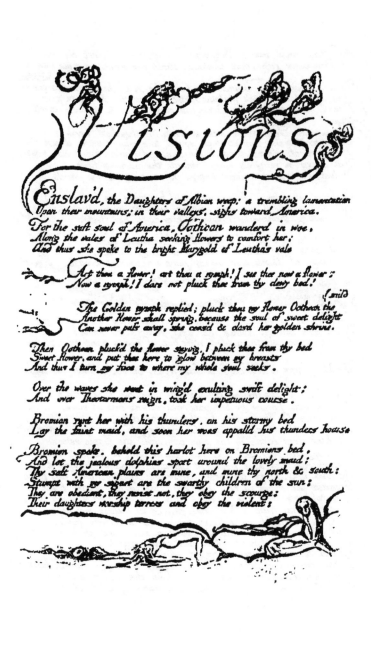

Visions

Enslav'd, the Daughters of Albion weep; a trembling lamentation
Upon their mountains; in their valleys, sighs toward America.

For the soft soul of America, Oothoon wanderd in woe,
Along the vales of Leutha seeking flowers to comfort her;
And thus she spoke to the bright Marygold of Leutha's vale

Art thou a flower! art thou a nymph! I see thee now a flower;
Now a nymph! I dare not pluck thee from thy dewy bed!

The Golden nymph replied; pluck thou my flower Oothoon the
Another flower shall spring, because the soul of sweet delight
Can never pass away. she ceasd & closd her golden shrine.

Then Oothoon pluck'd the flower saying, I pluck thee from thy bed
Sweet flower, and put thee here to glow between my breasts
And thus I turn my face to where my whole soul seeks.

Over the waves she went in wing'd exulting swift delight;
And over Theotormons reign, took her impetuous course.

Bromion rent her with his thunders, on his stormy bed
Lay the faint maid, and soon her woes appalld his thunders hoarse

Bromion spoke. behold this harlot here on Bromions bed,
And let the jealous dolphins sport around the lovely maid;
Thy soft American plains are mine, and mine thy north & south:
Stampt with my signet are the swarthy children of the sun;
They are obedient, they resist not, they obey the scourge:
Their daughters worship terrors and obey the violent:

Now thou maist marry Bromions harlot. and protect the child
Of Bromions rage. that Oothoon shall put forth in nine moons time

Then storms rent Theotormons limbs; he rolld his waves around.
And folded his black jealous waters round the adulterate pair
Bound back to back in Bromions caves terror & meekness dwell

At entrance Theotormon sits wearing the threshold hard
With secret tears; beneath him sound like waves on a desart shore
The voice of slaves beneath the sun. and children bought with money.
That shiver in religious caves beneath the burning fires
Of lust, that belch incessant from the summits of the earth

Oothoon weeps not; she cannot weep! her tears are locked up;
But she can howl incessant writhing her soft snowy limbs.
And calling Theotormons Eagles to prey upon her flesh.

I call with holy voice! kings of the sounding air,
Rend away this defiled bosom that I may reflect.
The image of Theotormon on my pure transparent breast.

The Eagles at her call descend & rend their bleeding prey;
Theotormon severely smiles. her soul reflects the smile;
As the clear spring mudded with feet of beasts grows pure & smiles

The Daughters of Albion hear her woes. & eccho back her sighs.

Why does my Theotormon sit weeping upon the threshold;
And Oothoon hovers by his side. perswading him in vain;
I cry arise O Theotormon for the village dog
Barks at the breaking day. the nightingale has done lamenting.
The lark does rustle in the ripe corn, and the Eagle returns
From nightly prey, and lifts his golden beak to the pure east;
Shaking the dust from his immortal pinions to awake
The sun that sleeps too long. Arise my Theotormon I am pure.
Because the night is gone that closd me in its deadly black.
They told me that the night & day were all that I could see;
They told me that I had five senses to inclose me up.
And they inclosd my infinite brain into a narrow circle.
And sunk my heart into the Abyss, a red round globe hot burning
Till all from life I was obliterated and erased.
Instead of morn arises a bright shadow, like an eye
In the eastern cloud; instead of night a sickly charnel house;
That Theotormon hears me not! to him the night and morn
Are both alike; a night of sighs, a morning of fresh tears;

And none but Bromion can hear my lamentations.

With what sense is it that the chicken shuns the ravenous hawk?
With what sense does the tame pigeon measure out the expanse?
With what sense does the bee form cells? have not the mouse & frog
Eyes and ears and sense of touch? yet are their habitations.
And their pursuits, as different as their forms and as their joys:
Ask the wild ass why he refuses burdens: and the meek camel
Why he loves man: is it because of eye ear mouth or skin
Or breathing nostrils? No, for these the wolf and tyger have.
Ask the blind worm the secrets of the grave, and why her spires
Love to curl round the bones of death? and ask the ravnous snake
Where she gets poison: & the wing'd eagle why he loves the sun
And then tell me the thoughts of man, that have been hid of old.

Silent I hover all the night, and all day could be silent.
If Theotormon once would turn his loved eyes upon me;
How can I be defild when I reflect thy image pure?
Sweetest the fruit that the worm feeds on. & the soul prey'd on by   (woe
The new wash'd lamb tiny'd with the village smoke & the bright swan.
By the red earth of our immortal river: I bathe my wings.
And I am white and pure to hover round Theotormons breast.

Then Theotormon broke his silence. and he answered.

Tell me what is the night or day to one oerflowd with woe?
Tell me what is a thought? & of what substance is it made?
Tell me what is a joy? & in what gardens do joys grow?
And in what rivers swim the sorrows, and upon what mountains

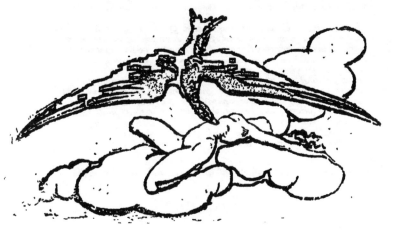

Wave shadows of discontent! and in what houses dwell the wretched
Drunken with woe forgotten, and shut up from cold despair.

Tell me where dwell the thoughts forgotten till thou call them forth
Tell me where dwell the joys of old! & where the ancient loves!
And when will they renew again & the night of oblivion past!
That I might traverse times & spaces far remote and bring
Comforts into a present sorrow and a night of pain
Where goest thou O thought! to what remote land is thy flight!
If thou returnest to the present moment of affliction
Wilt thou bring comforts on thy wings. and dews and honey and balm;
Or poison from the desart wilds, from the eyes of the envier.

Then Bromion said: and shook the cavern with his lamentation

Thou knowest that the ancient trees seen by thine eyes have fruit;
But knowest thou that trees and fruits flourish upon the earth
To gratify senses unknown? trees beasts and birds unknown:
Unknown, not unpercievd, spread in the infinite microscope,
In places yet unvisited by the voyager. and in worlds
Over another kind of seas. and in atmospheres unknown
Ah! are there other wars. beside the wars of sword and fire!
And are there other sorrows. beside the sorrows of poverty!
And are there other joys. beside the joys of riches and ease!
And is there not one law for both the lion and the ox!
And is there not eternal fire. and eternal chains!
To bind the phantoms of existence from eternal life!

Then Oothoon waited silent all the day. and all the night.

But when the morn arose, her lamentation renewd,
The Daughters of Albion hear her woes, & eccho back her sighs.

O Urizen! Creator of men! mistaken Demon of heaven;
Thy joys are tears! thy labour vain, to form men to thine image.
How can one joy absorb another? are not different joys
Holy, eternal, infinite! and each joy is a Love.

Does not the great mouth laugh at a gift! & the narrow eyelids mock
At the labour that is above payment, and wilt thou take the ape
For thy councellor? or the dog, for a schoolmaster to thy children?
Does he who contemns poverty, and he who turns with abhorrence
From usury: feel the same passion or are they moved alike?
How can the giver of gifts experience the delights of the merchant?
How the industrious citizen the pains of the husbandman.
How different far the fat fed hireling with hollow drum;
Who buys whole corn fields into wastes, and sings upon the heath:
How different their eye and ear! how different the world to them!
With what sense does the parson claim the labour of the farmer?
What are his nets & gins & traps, & how does he surround him
With cold floods of abstraction, and with forests of solitude,
To build him castles and high spires, where kings & priests may dwell.
Till she who burns with youth, and knows no fixed lot; is bound
In spells of law to one she loaths: and must she drag the chain
Of life, in weary lust! must chilling murderous thoughts, obscure
The clear heaven of her eternal spring? to bear the wintry rage
Of a harsh terror driven to madness, bound to hold a rod
Over her shrinking shoulders all the day; & all the night
To turn the wheel of false desire: and longings that wake her womb
To the abhorred birth of cherubs in the human form
That live a pestilence & die a meteor & are no more.
Till the child dwell with one he hates, and do the deed he loaths
And the unpure scourge force his seed into its unripe birth
E'er yet his eyelids can behold the arrows of the day.

Does the whale worship at thy footsteps as the hungry dog?
Or does he scent the mountain prey, because his nostrils wide
Draw in the ocean? does his eye discern the flying cloud
As the ravens eye? or does he measure the expanse like the vulture?
Does the still spider view the cliffs where eagles hide their young?
Or does the fly rejoice, because the harvest is brought in?
Does not the eagle scorn the earth & despise the treasures beneath?
But the mole knoweth what is there, & the worm shall tell it thee.
Does not the worm erect a pillar in the mouldering church yard?

And a palace of eternity in the jaws of the hungry grave
Over his porch these words are written. Take thy bliss O Man!
And sweet shall be thy taste & sweet thy infant joys renew!

Infancy, fearless, lustful, happy! nestling for delight
In laps of pleasure; Innocence! honest, open, seeking
The vigorous joys of morning light; open to virgin bliss.
Who taught thee modesty, subtil modesty! child of night & sleep
When thou awakest wilt thou dissemble all thy secret joys
Or wert thou not awake when all this mystery was disclos'd!
Then comst thou forth a modest virgin knowing to dissemble
With nets found under thy night pillow, to catch virgin joy,
And brand it with the name of whore; & sell it in the night,
In silence. evn without a whisper, and in seeming sleep:
Religious dreams and holy vespers, light thy smoky fires:
Once were thy fires lighted by the eyes of honest morn
And does my Theotormon seek this hypocrite modesty!
This knowing, artful, secret, fearful, cautious, trembling hypocrite.
Then is Oothoon a whore indeed! and all the virgin joys
Of life are harlots: and Theotormon is a sick mans dream
And Oothoon is the crafty slave of selfish holiness.

But Oothoon is not so, a virgin fill'd with virgin fancies
Open to joy and to delight where ever beauty appears
If in the morning sun I find it: there my eyes are fix'd

In happy copulation; if in evening mild, wearied with work,
Sit on a bank and draw the pleasures of this free born joy.

The moment of desire! the moment of desire! The virgin
That pines for man; shall awaken her womb to enormous joys
In the secret shadows of her chamber; the youth shut up from
The lustful joy, shall forget to generate, & create an amorous image
In the shadows of his curtains and in the folds of his silent pillow.
Are not these the places of religion, the rewards of continence,
The self enjoyings of self denial? Why dost thou seek religion?
Is it because acts are not lovely, that thou seekest solitude,
Where the horrible darkness is imprest with reflections of desire.

Father of Jealousy, be thou accursed from the earth!
Why hast thou taught my Theotormon this accursed thing?
Till beauty fades from off my shoulders darkend and cast out,
A solitary shadow wailing on the margin of non-entity.

I cry, Love! Love! Love! happy happy Love! free as the mountain wind!
Can that be Love, that drinks another as a sponge drinks water?
That clouds with jealousy his nights, with weepings all the day:
To spin a web of age around him, grey and hoary! dark!
Till his eyes sicken at the fruit that hangs before his sight.
Such is self-love that envies all! a creeping skeleton
With lamplike eyes watching around the frozen marriage bed.

But silken nets and traps of adamant will Oothoon spread,
And catch for thee girls of mild silver, or of furious gold;
I'll lie beside thee on a bank & view their wanton play
In lovely copulation bliss on bliss with Theotormon:
Red as the rosy morning, lustful as the first born beam,
Oothoon shall view his dear delight, nor eer with jealous cloud
Come in the heaven of generous love; nor selfish blightings bring.

Does the sun walk in glorious raiment, on the secret floor

Where the cold miser spreads his gold! or does the bright cloud
On his stone threshold; does his eye behold the beam that brings
Expansion to the eye of pity, or will he bind himself
Beside the ox to thy hard furrow; does not that mild beam blot
The bat, the owl, the glowing tyger, and the king of night.
The sea fowl takes the wintry blast, for a covering to her limbs:
And the wild snake, the pestilence to adorn him with gems & gold.
And trees, & birds, & beasts, & men, behold their eternal joy.
Arise you little glancing wings, and sing your infant joy!
Arise and drink your bliss, for every-thing that lives is holy!

Thus every morning wails Oothoon, but Theotormon sits
Upon the margind ocean conversing with shadows dire.

The Daughters of Albion hear her woes, & eccho back her sighs.

The End

THE SONG of LOS

Lambeth Printed by W Blake 1795

AFRICA

I will sing you a song of Los. the Eternal Prophet:
He sung it to four harps at the tables of Eternity.
    In heart-formed Africa.
Urizen faded! Ariston shudderd!
    And thus the Song began

Adam stood in the garden of Eden:
And Noah on the mountains of Ararat:
They saw Urizen give his Laws to the Nations
By the hands of the children of Los.

Adam shudderd! Noah faded! black grew the sunny African
When Rintrah gave Abstract Philosophy to Brama in the East.
(Night spoke to the Cloud!
Lo these Human formd spirits in smiling hipocrisy. War
Against one another: so let them War on: slaves to the
            eternal Elements)
Noah shrunk, beneath the waters
Abram fled in fires from Chaldea;
Moses beheld upon Mount-Sinai forms of dark delusion:

To Trismegistus. Palamabron gave an abstract Law:
To Pythagoras Socrates & Plato.

Times rolled on ver all the sons of Har. time after time
Orc on Mount Atlas howld, chaind down with the Chain of Jealousy
Then Oothoon hovered over Judah & Jerusalem
And Jesus heard her voice (a man of sorrows) he recievd
A Gospel from wretched Theotormon.

The human race began to wither. for the healthy built
Secluded places, fearing the joys of Love
And the diseased only propagated:
So Antamon calld up Leutha from her valleys of delight:
And to Mahomet a loose Bible gave.

But in the North, to Odin. Sotha gave a Code of War:
Because of Diralada thinking to reclaim his joy.

These were the Churches: Hospitals: Castles: Palaces:
Like nets & gins & traps to catch the joys of Eternity
              And all the rest a desert;
Till like a dream Eternity was obliterated & erased.

Since that dread day when Har and Heva fled.
Because their brethren & sisters livd in War & Lust:
And as they fled they shrunk
Into two narrow doleful forms:
Creeping in reptile flesh upon
The bosom of the ground:
And all the vast of Nature shrunk
Before their shrunken eyes.

Thus the terrible race of Los & Enitharmon gave
Laws & Religions to the sons of Har binding them more
And more to Earth: closing and restraining:
Till a Philosophy of Five Senses was complete
Urizen wept & gave it into the hands of Newton & Locke

Clouds roll heavy upon the Alps round Rousseau & Voltaire:
And on the mountains of Lebanon round the deceased Gods
Of Asia; & on the deserts of Africa round the Fallen Angels
The Guardian Prince of Albion burns in his nightly tent.

The Kings of Asia heard
The howl rise up from Europe!
And each ran out from his Web:
From his ancient woven Den;
For the darkness of Asia was startled
At the thick-flaming, thought-creating fires of Orc.

And the Kings of Asia stood
And cried in bitterness of soul.

Shall not the King call for Famine from the heath
Nor the Priest, for Pestilence from the fen?
To restrain! to dismay! to thin!
The inhabitants of mountain and plain;
In the day of full-feeding prosperity;
And the night of delicious songs.

Shall not the Councellor throw his curb
Of Poverty on the laborious?
To fix the price of labour;
To invent allegoric riches:

And the privy admonishers of men
Call for fires in the City
For heaps of smoking ruins,
In the night of prosperity & wantonness.

To turn man from his path,
To restrain the child from the womb.

To cut off the bread from the city,
That the remnant may learn to obey.

That the pride of the heart may fail;
That the lust of the eyes may be quench'd
That the delicate ear in its infancy
May be dulld; and the nostrils clos'd up
To teach mortal worms the path
That leads from the gates of the Grave.

Urizen heard them cry;
And his shuddring waving wings
Went enormous above the red flames
Drawing clouds of despair thro the heavens
Of Europe as he went.
And his Books of brass iron & gold
Melted over the land as he flew,
Heavy-waving, howling, weeping.

And he stood over Judea:
And stay'd in his ancient place;
And stretch'd his clouds over Jerusalem.

For Adam a mouldering skeleton
Lay bleach'd on the garden of Eden.
And Noah as white as snow
On the mountains of Ararat.

Then the thunders of Urizen bellow'd aloud,
From his wven darkness above.

Orc raging in European darkness
Arose like a pillar of fire above the Alps
Like a serpent of fiery flame!
The sullen Earth
Shrunk!

Forth from the dead, dust rattling bones to bones
Join; shaking convuls'd the shivring clay breathes
And all flesh naked stands; Fathers and Friends;
Mothers & Infants; Kings & Warriors:

The Grave shrieks with delight, & shakes
Her hollow womb, & clasps the solid stem;
Her bosom swells with wild desire;
And milk & blood & glandous wine
In rivers rush & shout & dance,
On mountain, dale and plain.
The SONG of LOS is Ended.
Urizen Wept.

AMERICA

a

PROPHECY

LAMBETH

Printed by William Blake in the year 1793.

Preludium

The shadowy daughter of Urthona stood before red Orc.
When fourteen suns had faintly journey'd o'er his dark abode;
His food she brought in iron baskets, his drink in cups of iron:
Crown'd with a helmet & dark hair the nameless female stood;
A quiver with its burning stores, a bow like that of night,   5
When pestilence is shot from heaven; no other arms she need:
Invulnerable tho' naked, save where clouds roll round her loins,
Their awful folds in the dark air; silent she stood as night;
For never from her iron tongue could voice or sound arise;
But dumb till that dread day when Orc assay'd his fierce embrace.   10

Dark virgin; said the hairy youth, thy father stern abhorr'd;
Rivets my tenfold chains while still on high my spirit soars;
Sometimes an eagle screaming in the sky, sometimes a lion,
Stalking upon the mountains, & sometimes a whale I lash
The raging fathomless abyss, anon a serpent folding   15
Around the pillars of Urthona, and round thy dark limbs,
On the Canadian wilds I fold, feeble my spirit folds.
For chaind beneath I rend these caverns; when thou bringest food
I howl my joy; and my red eyes seek to behold thy face
In vain! these clouds roll to & fro, & hide thee from my sight.   20

Silent as despairing love, and strong as jealousy.
The hairy shoulders rend the links, free are the wrists of fire;
Round the terrific loins he siez'd the panting struggling womb;
It joyd: she put aside her clouds & smiled her first-born smile;
As when a black cloud shews its lightnings to the silent deep.

Soon as she saw the terrible boy then burst the virgin cry.

I know thee, I have found thee, & I will not let thee go;
Thou art the image of God who dwells in darkness of Africa;
And thou art fall'n to give me life in regions of dark death.
On my American plains I feel the struggling afflictions
Endur'd by roots that writhe their arms into the nether deep:
I see a serpent in Canada, who courts me to his love;
In Mexico an Eagle, and a Lion in Peru;
I see a Whale in the South-sea, drinking my soul away.
O what limb rending pains I feel. thy fire & my frost
Mingle in howling pains, in furrows by thy lightnings rent;
This is eternal death: and this the torment long foretold.

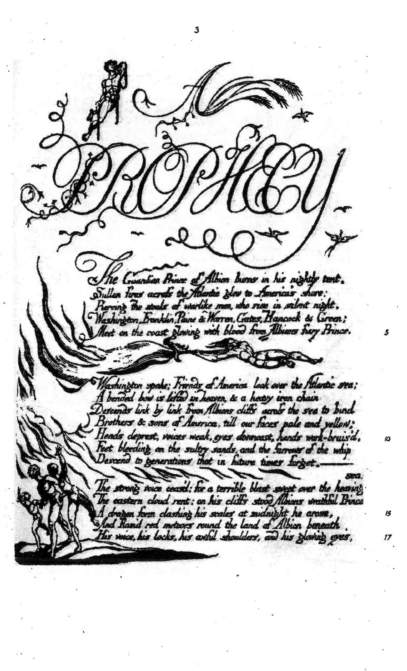

A PROPHECY

The Guardian Prince of Albion burns in his nightly tent,
Sullen fires across the Atlantic glow to America's shore;
Piercing the souls of warlike men, who rise in silent night,
Washington, Franklin, Paine & Warren, Gates, Hancock & Green;
Meet on the coast glowing with blood from Albions fiery Prince.   5

Washington spoke; Friends of America look over the Atlantic sea;
A bended bow is lifted in heaven, & a heavy iron chain
Descends link by link from Albions cliffs across the sea to bind
Brothers & sons of America, till our faces pale and yellow;
Heads deprest, voices weak, eyes downcast, hands work-bruis'd,   10
Feet bleeding on the sultry sands, and the furrows of the whip
Descend to generations that in future times forget.————
                                                        sea,
The strong voice ceas'd; for a terrible blast swept over the heaving
The eastern cloud rent; on his cliffs stood Albions wrathful Prince
A dragon form clashing his scales at midnight he arose,   15
And flam'd red meteors round the land of Albion beneath
His voice, his locks, his awful shoulders, and his glowing eyes,   17

Appear to the Americans upon the cloudy night.

Solemn heave the Atlantic waves between the gloomy nations,
Swelling, belching from its deeps red clouds & raging fires.
Albion is sick. America faints! enrag'd the Zenith grew.
As human blood shooting its veins all round the orbed heaven
Red rose the clouds from the Atlantic in vast wheels of blood.
And in the red clouds rose a Wonder o'er the Atlantic sea;
Intense! naked! a Human fire fierce glowing, as the wedge
Of iron heated in the furnace; his terrible limbs were fire
With myriads of cloudy terrors banners dark & towers
Surrounded; heat but not light went thro' the murky atmo
                                                    -sphere

The King of England looking westward trembles at the Vision.

Albions Angel stood beside the Stone
  of night, and saw
The terror like a comet, or more like the
        planet red
That once inclos'd the terrible wandering comets in its sphere.
Then Mars thou wast our center, & the planets three flew round
Thy crimson disk; so e'er the Sun was rent from thy red sphere;
The Spectre glowd his horrid length staining the temple long
With beams of blood; & thus a voice came forth, and shook the
                Temple

The morning comes, the night decays, the watchmen leave
  their stations;
The grave is burst, the spices shed, the linen wrapped up;
The bones of death, the cvring clay, the sinews shrunk & dryd,
Reviving shake, inspiring move, breathing! awakening!
Spring like redeemed captives when their bonds & bars are burst;   5
Let the slave grinding at the mill, run out into the field:
Let him look up into the heavens & laugh in the bright air;
Let the inchained soul shut up in darkness and in sighing,
Whose face has never seen a smile in thirty weary years;
Rise and look out, his chains are loose, his dungeon doors are open.   10
And let his wife and children return from the oppressors scourge;
They look behind at every step & believe it is a dream.
Singing. The Sun has left his blackness, & has found a fresher morning
And the fair Moon rejoices in the clear & cloudless night;
For Empire is no more, and now the Lion & Wolf shall cease.   15

In thunders ends the voice. Then Albions Angel wrathful burnt
Beside the Stone of Night; and like the Eternal Lions howl
In famine & war, replyd. Art thou not Orc, who serpent formd
Stands at the gate of Enitharmon to devour her children;
Blasphemous Demon, Antichrist, hater of Dignities:
Lover of wild rebellion, and transgresser of Gods Law:
Why dost thou come to Angels eyes in this terrific form?

The terror answer'd: I am Orc, wreath'd round the accursed tree:
The times are ended; shadows pass the morning gins to break;
The fiery joy, that Urizen perverted to ten commands,
What night he led the starry hosts thro' the wide wilderness;
That stony law I stamp to dust: and scatter religion abroad,
To the four winds as a torn book, & none shall gather the leaves;
But they shall rot on desart sands, & consume in bottomless deeps,
To make the desarts blossom, & the deeps shrink to their fountains,
And to renew the fiery joy, and burst the stony roof.
That pale religious letchery, seeking Virginity,
May find it in a harlot, and in coarse-clad honesty
The undefil'd tho' ravish'd in her cradle night and morn:
For every thing that lives is holy, life delights in life;
Because the soul of sweet delight can never be defil'd.
Fires inwrap the earthly globe, yet man is not consum'd;
Amidst the lustful fires he walks; his feet become like brass,
His knees and thighs like silver, & his breast and head like gold.

Sound! sound! my loud war-trumpets & alarm my Thirteen Angels:
Loud howls the eternal Wolf! the eternal Lion lashes his tail!
America is darkned; and my punishing Demons terrified
Crouch howling before their caverns deep like skins dry'd in the wind
They cannot smite the wheat, nor quench the fatness of the earth.   5
They cannot smite with sorrows, nor subdue the plow and spade.
They cannot wall the city, nor moat round the castle of princes.
They cannot bring the stubbed oak to overgrow the hills.
For terrible men stand on the shores, & in their robes I see
Children take shelter from the lightnings, there stands Washington   10
And Paine and Warren with their foreheads reard toward the east
But clouds obscure my aged sight. A vision from afar!
Sound! sound! my loud war-trumpets & alarm my thirteen Angels:
Ah vision from afar! Ah rebel form that rent the ancient
Heavens; Eternal Viper self-renew'd, rolling in clouds   15
I see thee in thick clouds and darkness on America's shore.
Writhing in pangs of abhorred birth; red flames the crest rebellious
And eyes of death; the harlot womb oft opened in vain
Heaves in enormous circles, now the times are returnd upon thee,
Devourer of thy parent, now thy unutterable torment renews.   20
Sound! sound! my loud war trumpets & alarm my thirteen Angels.
Ah terrible birth! a young one bursting! where is the weeping mouth?
And where the mothers milk? instead those ever-hissing jaws
And parched lips drop with fresh gore; now roll thou in the clouds
Thy mother lays her length outstretch'd upon the shore beneath.   25
Sound! sound! my loud war-trumpets & alarm my thirteen Angels!
Loud howls the eternal Wolf! the eternal Lion lashes his tail!   27

Thus wept the Angel voice & as he wept the terrible blasts
Of trumpets, blew a loud alarm across the Atlantic deep.
No trumpets answer; no reply of clarions or of fifes,
Silent the Colonies remain and refuse the loud alarm.

On those vast shady hills between America & Albions shore;
Now barrd out by the Atlantic sea: calld Atlantean hills;
Because from their bright summits you may pass to the Golden world
An ancient palace, archetype of mighty Emperies,
Rears its immortal pinnacles, built in the forest of God
By Ariston the king of beauty for his stolen bride.

Here on their magic seats the thirteen Angels sat perturb'd
For clouds from the Atlantic hover oer the solemn roof.

Fiery the Angels rose, & as they rose deep thunder roll'd
Around their shores, indignant burning with the fires of Orc
And Bostons Angel cried aloud as they flew thro' the dark
                                                        night.

He cried: Why trembles honesty and like a murderer,
Why seeks he refuge from the frowns of his immortal station;   5
Must the generous tremble & leave his joy, to the idle: to
          the pestilence!
That mock him? who commanded this? what God? what Angel!
To keep the genrous from experience till the ungenerous
Are unrestraind performers of the energies of nature;
Till pity is become a trade, and generosity a science,   10
That men get rich by, & the sandy desart is gi"n to the strong
What God is he, writes laws of peace, & clothes him in a tempest
What pitying Angel lusts for tears, and fans himself with sighs
What crawling villain preaches abstinence & wraps himself
In fat of lambs? no more I follow, no more obedience pay.   15

So cried he, rending all his robe & throwing down his scepter,
In sight of Albions Guardian, and all the thirteen Angels
Rent all their robes to the hungry wind, & threw their golden scep-
        -ters
Down on the land of America, indignant they descended
Headlong from out their heavenly heights, descending swift as
        fires
Over the land; naked & flaming are their lineaments seen
In the deep gloom, by Washington & Paine & Warren they stood
And the flame folded roaring fierce within the pitchy night
Before the Demon red, who burnt towards America,
In black smoke thunders and loud winds rejoicing in its
        terror
Breaking in smoky wreaths from the wild deep, & gathering thick
In flames as of a furnace on the land from North to South

What time the thirteen Governers that England sent con-
In Bernards house; the flames coverd the land, they rouze they -vere

Shaking their mental chains they rush in fury to the sea
To quench their anguish; at the feet of Washington down fallin
They grovel on the sand and writhing lie, while all
The British soldiers thro' the thirteen States sent up a howl
Of anguish: threw their swords & muskets to the earth & ran
From their encampments and dark castles seeking where to hide
From the grim flames; and from the visions of Orc; in sight
Of Albions Angel; who enrag'd his secret clouds open'd
From north to south, and burnt outstretchd on wings of wrath cov'ring
The eastern sky, spreading his awful wings across the heavens;
Beneath him rolld his numrous hosts, all Albions Angels camp'd
Darkend the Atlantic mountains & their trumpets shook the valleys
Armd with diseases of the earth to cast upon the Abyss,
Their numbers forty millions, mustring in the eastern sky.

5

10

15
16

In the flames stood & view'd the armies drawn out in the sky,
Washington Franklin Paine & Warren Allen Gates & Lee:
And heard the voice of Albions Angel give the thunderous command:
His plagues obedient to his voice flew forth out of their clouds
Falling upon America, as a storm to cut them off

As a blight cuts the tender corn when it begins to appear.
Dark is the heaven above, & cold & hard the earth beneath;
And as a plague wind fill'd with insects cuts off man & beast;
And as a sea overwhelms a land in the day of an earthquake;

Fury! rage! madness! in a wind swept through America
And the red flames of Orc that folded roaring fierce around
The angry shores, and the fierce rushing of th' inhabitants together:
The citizens of New-York close their books & lock their chests;
The mariners of Boston drop their anchors and unlade;
The scribe of Pensylvania casts his pen upon the earth;
The builder of Virginia throws his hammer down in fear.

Then had America been lost, overwhelm'd by the Atlantic,
And Earth had lost another portion of the infinite,
But all rush together in the night in wrath and raging fire
The red fires rag'd! the plagues recoil'd! then rolld they back
                                         with fury

On Albions Angels; then the Pestilence began in streaks of red
Across the limbs of Albions Guardian, the spotted plague smote
        Bristols
And the Leprosy Londons Spirit sickening all their bands:
The millions sent up a howl of anguish and threw off their hammered mail.

And cast their swords & spears to earth, & stood a naked multitude.   5
Albions Guardian writhed in torment on the eastern sky
Pale quavering toward the brain his glimmering eyes, teeth chattering
Howling & shuddering his legs quivering: convulst each muscle & sinew
Sickning lay Londons Guardian, and the ancient mitred York
Their heads on snowy hills, their ensigns sickning in the sky   10

The plagues creep on the burning winds driven by flames of Orc,
And by the fierce Americans rushing together in the night
Driven oer the Guardians of Ireland and Scotland and Wales.
They spotted with plagues forsook the frontiers & their banners seard
With fires of hell, deform their ancient heavens with shame & woe.   15
Hid in his caves the Bard of Albion felt the enormous plagues.
And a cowl of flesh grew oer his head & scales on his back & ribs;
And rough with black scales all his Angels fright their ancient heavens
The doors of marriage are open, and the Priests in rustling scales
Rush into reptile coverts, hiding from the fires of Orc,   20
That play around the golden roofs in wreaths of fierce desire,
Leaving the females naked and glowing with the lusts of youth

For the Female spirits of the dead pining in bonds of religion;
Run from their fetters reddening, & in long drawn arches sitting:
They feel the nerves of youth renew, and desires of ancient times   25
Over their pale limbs as a vine when the tender grape appears   26

Over the hills, the vales, the cities, rage the red flames fierce;
The Heavens melted from north to south; and Urizen who sat
Above all heavens in thunders wrap'd, emerg'd his leprous head
From out his holy shrine, his tears in deluge piteous
5 Falling into the deep sublime; flag'd with grey-brow'd snows
And thunderous visages, his jealous wings wav'd over the deep;
Weeping in dismal howling woe he dark descended howling
Around the smitten bands, clothed in tears & trembling shuddring cold.
His stored snows he poured forth, and his icy magazines
10 He opend on the deep, and on the Atlantic sea white shivring.
Leprous his limbs, all over white, and hoary was his visage.
Weeping in dismal howlings before the stern Americans
Hiding the Demon red with clouds & cold mists from the earth;
Till Angels & weak men twelve years should govern oer the strong;
15 And then their end should come, when France reciev'd the Demons light.

Stiff shudderings shook the heav'nly thrones! France Spain & Italy,
In terror view'd the bands of Albion, and the ancient Guardians
Fainting upon the elements, smitten with their own plagues
They slow advance to shut the five gates of their law-built heaven
20 Filled with blasting fancies and with mildews of despair
With fierce disease and lust, unable to stem the fires of Orc;
But the five gates were consum'd, & their bolts and hinges melted
23 And the fierce flames burnt round the heavens, & round the abodes of
men

EUROPE

a

PROPHECY

LAMBETH

Printed By Will'm Blake   1794

PRELUDIUM

The nameless shadowy female rose from out the breast of Orc:
Her snaky hair brandishing in the winds of Enitharmon;
And thus her voice arose.

O mother Enitharmon wilt thou bring forth other sons?
To cause my name to vanish, that my place may not be found
For I am faint with travel
Like the dark cloud disburdend in the day of dismal thunder.

My roots are brandishd in the heavens, my fruits in earth beneath
Surge, foam, and labour into life, first born & first consum'd!
Consumed and consuming!
Then why shouldst thou accursed mother bring me into life?

I wrap my turban of thick clouds around my labring head:
And fold the sheety waters as a mantle round my limbs.
Yet the red sun and moon
And all the overflowing stars rain down prolific pains.

Unwilling I look up to heaven: unwilling count the stars
Sitting in fathomless abyss of my immortal shrine
I siege their burning power
And bring forth howling terrors, all devouring fiery kings.

Devouring & devoured roaming on dark and desolate mountains
In forests of eternal death shrieking in hollow trees
Ah mother Enitharmon!
Stamp not with solid form this vigrous progeny of fires

I bring forth from my teeming bosom myriads of flames.
And thou dost stamp them with a signet then they roam abroad
And leave me void as death
Ah! I am drown'd in shady woe and visionary joy

And who shall bind the infinite with an eternal band?
To compass it with swaddling bands? and who shall cherish it
With milk and honey?
I see it smile & I roll inward & my voice is past.

She ceast & rolld her shady clouds
Into the secret place.

A PROPHECY

The deep of winter came:
What time the secret child
Descended thro' the orient gates of the eternal day:
War ceas'd, & all the troops like shadows fled
to their abodes.

Then Enitharmon saw her sons & daughters rise around.
Like pearly clouds they meet together in the crystal house:
And Los possessor of the moon, joyd in the peaceful night:
Thus speaking while his numrous sons shook their bright fiery wings

Again the night is come
That strong Urthona takes his rest.
And Urizen unloosd from chains
Glows like a meteor in the distant north
Stretch forth your hands and strike the elemental strings!
Awake the thunders of the deep.

The shrill winds wake!
Till all the sons of Urizen look out and envy Los:
Sieze all the spirits of life and bind
Their warbling joys to our loud strings
Bind all the nourishing sweets of earth
To give us bliss that we may drink the sparkling wine of Los
And let us laugh at war
Despising toil and care
Because the days and nights of joy in lucky hours renew.

Arise O Orc from thy deep den
First born of Enitharmon rise!
And we will crown thy head with garlands of the ruddy vine:
For now thou art bound
And I may see thee in the hour of bliss my eldest born

The horrent Demon rose surrounded with red stars of fire
Whirling about in furious circles round the immortal fiend.

Then Enitharmon down descended into his red light
And thus her voice rose to her children the distant heavens reply.

Now comes the night of Enitharmons joy.
Who shall I call ? Who shall I send ?
That Woman, lovely Woman ! may have dominion ?
Arise O Rintrah thee I call & Palamabron thee ;
Go ! tell the human race that Womans love is Sin ;
That an Eternal life awaits the worms of sixty winters
In an allegorical abode where existence hath never come ;
Forbid all Joy, & from her childhood shall the little female
Spread nets in every secret path .
My weary eyelids draw towards the evening, my bliss is yet but new
                                        Arise

Arise O Rintrah eldest born: second to none but Orc:
O lion Rintrah raise thy fury from thy forests black:
Bring Palamabron horned priest, skipping upon the mountains
And silent Elynittria the silver bowed queen.
Rintrah where hast thou hid thy bride;
Weeps she in desart shades?
Alas my Rintrah! bring the lovely jealous Ocalythron.

Arise my son! bring all thy brethren O thou king of fire.
Prince of the sun I see thee with thy innumerable race:
Thick as the summer stars:
But each ramping his golden mane shakes.
And thine eyes rejoice because of strength O Rintrah furious king

Enitharmon slept,
Eighteen hundred years: Man was a Dream!
The night of Nature and their harps unstrung
She slept in middle of her nightly song,
Eighteen hundred years, a female dream.

Shadows of men in fleeting bands upon the winds
Divide the heavens of Europe
Till Albions Angel smitten with his own plagues fled with his bands
The cloud bears hard on Albions shore:
Fill'd with immortal demons of futurity:
In council gather the smitten Angels of Albion
The cloud bears hard upon the council house: down rushing
On the heads of Albions Angels.

One hour they lay buried beneath the ruins of that hall:
But as the stars rise from the salt lake they arise in pain
In troubled mists o'erclouded by the terrors of strugling times

following

In thoughts perturb'd, they rose from the bright ruins silent
The fiery King, who sought his ancient temple serpent-form'd
That stretches out its shady length along the Island white.
Round him roll'd his clouds of war; silent the Angel went,
Along the infinite shores of Thames to golden Verulam.
There stand the venerable porches that high-towering rear
Their oak-surrounded pillars, form'd of massy stones, uncut
With tool; stones precious; such eternal in the heavens,
Of colours twelve, few known on earth, give light in the opake,
Placed in the order of the stars, when the five senses whelm'd
In deluge o'er the earth-born man; then turn'd the fluxile eyes
Into two stationary orbs, concentrating all things.
The ever-varying spiral ascents to the heavens of heavens
Were bended downward; and the nostrils golden gates shut
Turn'd outward, barr'd and petrify'd against the infinite.

Thought chang'd the infinite to a serpent; that which pitieth;
To a devouring flame; and man fled from its face and hid
In forests of night; then all the eternal forests were divided
Into earths rolling in circles of space, that like an ocean
rush'd
And overwhelmed all except this finite wall of flesh.
Then was the serpent temple form'd, image of infinite
Shut up in finite revolutions, and man became an Angel;
Heaven a mighty circle turning; God a tyrant crown'd.

Now arriv'd the ancient Guardian at the southern porch,
That planted thick with trees of blackest leaf, & in a vale
Obscure, inclos'd the Stone of Night; oblique it stood, o'erhung
With purple flowers and berries red; image of that sweet south,
Once open to the heavens and elevated on the human neck,
Now overgrown with hair and cover'd with a stony roof.
Downward 'tis sunk beneath th' attractive north, that round the feet
A raging whirlpool draws the dizzy enquirer to his grave.

Albions Angel rose upon the Stone of Night.
He saw Urizen on the Atlantic:
And his brazen Book
That Kings & Priests had copied on Earth
Expanded from North to South.

And the clouds & fires pale rolld round in the night of Enitharmon
Round Albions cliffs & Londons walls still Enitharmon slept.
Rolling volumes of grey mist involve Churches, Palaces, Towers:
For Urizen unclaspd his Book: feeding his soul with pity
The youth of England hid in gloom curse the pained heavens; compelld
Into the deadly night to see the form of Albions Angel
Their parents brought them forth & aged ignorance preaches canting,
On a vast rock perceivd by those senses that are closd from thought:
Bleak dark abrupt, it stands & overshadows London city
They saw his boney feet on the rock, the flesh consum'd in flames:
They saw the Serpent temple lifted above shadowing the Island white:
They heard the voice of Albions Angel howling in flames of Orc.
Seeking the trump of the last doom

Above the rest the howl was heard from Westminster louder & louder.
The Guardian of the secret codes forsook his ancient mansion
Driven out by the flames of Orc, his furrd robes & false locks
Adhered and grew one with his flesh and nerves & veins shot thro them
With dismal torment sick hanging upon the wind; he fled
Groveling along Great George Street thro the Park gate all the soldiers
Fled from his sight: he dragd his torments to the wilderness.

Thus was the howl thro Europe:
For Orc rejoicd to hear the howling shadows
But Palamabron shot his lightnings trenching down his wide back
And Rintrah hung with all his legions in the nether deep

Enitharmon laughd in her sleep to see (O womans triumph)
Every house a den, every man bound: the shadows are filld
With spectres, and the windows wove over with curses of iron,
Over the doors Thou shalt not; & over the chimneys Fear is written:
With bands of iron round their necks fastend into the walls
The citizens: in leaden gyves the inhabitants of suburbs
Walk heavy: soft and bent are the bones of villagers

Between the clouds of Urizen the flames of Orc roll heavy,
Around the limbs of Albions Guardian his flesh consuming.
Howlings & hissings shrieks & groans. & voices of despair
Arise around him in the cloudy
Heavens of Albion, Furious

The red limbd Angel sie'zd in horror and torment:
The Trump of the last doom; but he could not blow the iron tube!
Thrice he assay'd presumptuous to awake the dead to judgment.

or

A mighty Spirit leap'd from the land of Albion,
Nam'd Newton; he sie'zd the Trump, & blow'd the enormous blast!
Yellow as leaves of Autumn the myriads of Angelic hosts,
Fell thro' the wintry skies seeking their graves;
Rattling their hollow bones in howling and lamentation.

Then, Enitharmon woke nor knew that she had slept
And eighteen hundred years were fled
As if they had not been.
She call'd her sons & daughters
To the sports of night,
Within her crystal house;
And thus her song proceeds.

Arise Ethinthus! tho' the earth-worm call;
Let him call in vain;
Till the night of holy shadows
And human solitude is past!

Ethinthus queen of waters, how thou shinest in the sky:
My daughter how do I rejoice! for thy children flock around
Like the gay fishes on the wave when the cold moon drinks the dew.
Ethinthus! thou art sweet as comforts to my fainting soul:
For now thy waters warble round the feet of Enitharmon.

Manatha-Varcyon! I behold thee flaming in my halls,
Light of thy mothers soul! I see thy lovely eagles round;
Thy golden wings are my delight, & thy flames of soft delusion.

Where is my lureing bird of Eden! Leutha silent love!
Leutha, the many coloured bow delights upon thy wings:
Soft soul of flowers Leutha!
Sweet smiling pestilence! I see thy blushing light:
Thy daughters many changing,
Revolve like sweet perfumes ascending O Leutha silken queen!

Where is the youthful Antamon prince of the pearly dew.
O Antamon, why wilt thou leave thy mother Enitharmon?
Alone I see thee crystal form,
Floating upon the bosomd air:
With lineaments of gratified desire.
My Antamon the seven churches of Leutha seek thy love.

I hear the soft Oothoon in Enitharmons tents:
Why wilt thou give up womans secrecy my melancholy child?
Between two moments bliss is ripe:
O Theotormon robbd of joy, I see thy salt tears flow
Down the steps of my crystal house.

Sotha & Thiralatha, secret dwellers of dreamful caves,
Arise and please the horrent fiend with your melodious songs.
Still all your thunders golden hoofd, & bind your horses black.
Orc! smile upon my children!
Smile son of my afflictions,
Arise O Orc and give our mountains joy of thy red light.

She ceasd, for All were forth at sport beneath the solemn moon
Waking the stars of Urizen with their immortal songs,
That nature felt thro' all her pores the enormous revelry
Till morning opd the eastern gate.
Then every one fled to his station, & Enitharmon wept.

But terrible Orc, when he beheld the morning in the east

Shot from the heights of Enitharmon.
And in the vineyards of red France appear'd the light of his fury.

The sun glowd fiery red:
The furious terrors flew around.
On golden chariots raging with red wheels dropping with blood;
The Lions lash their wrathful tails!
The Tigers couch upon the prey & suck the ruddy tide:
And Enitharmon groans & cries in anguish and dismay.

Then Los arose his head he reard in snaky thunders clad:
And with a cry that shook all nature to the utmost pole.
Calld all his sons to the strife of blood.

FINIS

To the Public

After my three years slumber on the banks of the Ocean, I again
display my Giant forms to the Public: My former Giants & Fairies
having receiv'd the highest reward possible: the   and   cannot doubt
of those, with whom to be connected, is to be   that this more consolidated & extended Work, will be as kindly
reciev'd   The Enthusiasm of the following Poem, the
Author hopes

                                                    I also
hope, the Reader will be with me, wholly One in Jesus our Lord, who
is the God   and Lord   to whom the Ancients look'd
and saw his day afar off, with trembling & amazement.
    The Spirit of Jesus is continual forgiveness of Sin: he who waits
to be righteous before he enters into the Saviours kingdom, the Divine
Body: will never enter there. I am perhaps the most sinful of men!
I pretend not to holiness! yet I pretend to love, to see, to converse with
daily, as man with man, & the more to have an interest in the Friend
of Sinners. Therefore   Reader,   what you do not approve, &
    me for this energetic exertion of my talent.

        Reader!   of books!   of heaven,
    And of that God from whom
    Who in mysterious Sinais awful cave
    To Man the wondrous art of writing gave,
    Again he speaks in thunder and in fire!
    Thunder of Thought, & flames of fierce desire:
    Even from the depths of Hell his voice I hear,
    Within the unfathomd caverns of my Ear.
    Therefore I print; nor vain my types shall be:
    Heaven, Earth & Hell, henceforth shall live in harmony

        Of the Measure, in which
            the following Poem is written

    We who dwell on Earth can do nothing of ourselves, every thing
is conducted by Spirits, no less than Digestion or Sleep

    When this Verse was first dictated to me I consider'd
a Monotonous Cadence like that used by Milton & Shakspeare & all writers of English Blank Verse, derived
from the modern bondage of Rhyming; to be a necessary
and indispensible part of Verse. But I soon found that
in the mouth of a true Orator such monotony was not
only awkward, but as much a bondage as rhyme itself.
I therefore have produced a variety in every line, both
of cadences & number of syllables. Every word and
every letter is studied and put into its fit place: the
terrific numbers are reserved for the terrific parts
the mild & gentle, for the mild & gentle parts, and
the prosaic, for inferior parts; all are necessary to
each other. Poetry Fetter'd, Fetters the Human Race!
Nations are Destroy'd, or Flourish, in proportion as Their
Poetry Painting and Music, are Destroy'd or Flourish! The
Primeval State of Man, was Wisdom, Art, and Science.

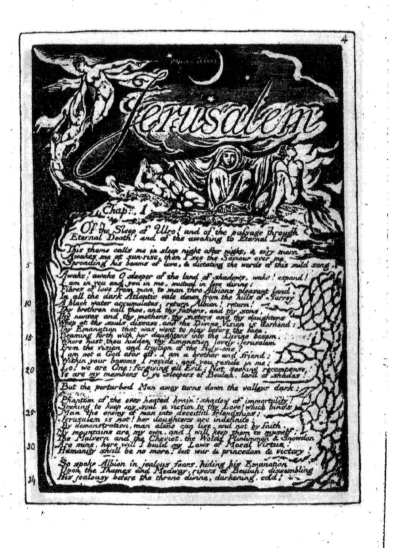

MDCCCIIIIS

Jerusalem

Chap: I

Of the Sleep of Ulro! and of the passage through
Eternal Death! and of the awaking to Eternal Life

This theme calls me in sleep night after night, & every morn
Awakes me at sun-rise, then I see the Saviour over me
Spreading his beams of love, & dictating the words of this mild song.

Awake! awake O sleeper of the land of shadows, wake! expand!
I am in you and you in me, mutual in love divine:
Fibres of love from man to man thro Albions pleasant land.
In all the dark Atlantic vale down from the hills of Surrey
A black water accumulates, return Albion! return!
Thy brethren call thee, and thy fathers, and thy sons,
Thy nurses and thy mothers, thy sisters and thy daughters
Weep at thy souls disease, and the Divine Vision is darkend:
Thy Emanation that was wont to play before thy face,
Beaming forth with her daughters into the Divine bosom
Where hast thou hidden thy Emanation lovely Jerusalem
From the vision and fruition of the Holy-one?
I am not a God afar off, I am a brother and friend;
Within your bosoms I reside, and you reside in me:
Lo! we are One; forgiving all Evil; Not seeking recompense;
Ye are my members O ye sleepers of Beulah, land of shades!

But the perturbed Man away turns down the valleys dark;

Phantom of the over heated brain! shadow of immortality!
Seeking to keep my soul a victim to thy Love! which binds
Man the enemy of man into deceitful friendships:
Jerusalem is not! her daughters are indefinite:
By demonstration, man alone can live, and not by faith.
My mountains are my own, and I will keep them to myself!
The Malvern and the Cheviot, the Wolds Plinlimmon & Snowdon
Are mine, here will I build my Laws of Moral Virtue!
Humanity shall be no more! but war & princedom & victory!

So spoke Albion in jealous fears, hiding his Emanation
Upon the Thames and Medway, rivers of Beulah; dissembling
His jealousy before the throne divine, darkening, cold!

5

10

15

20

25

30

34

The banks of the Thames are clouded! the ancient porches of Albion are
Darken'd! they are drawn thro' unbounded space, scatter'd upon
The Void in incoherent despair! Cambridge & Oxford & London,
5 Are driven among the starry Wheels, rent away and dissipated,
In Chasms & Abysses of sorrow, enlarg'd without dimension, terrible
Albions mountains run with blood, the cries of war & of tumult
Resound into the unbounded night, every Human perfection
Of mountain & river & city, are small & wither'd & darken'd
10 Cam is a little stream! Ely is almost swallowd up!
Lincoln & Norwich stand trembling on the brink of Udan-Adan!
Wales and Scotland shrink themselves to the west and to the north!
Mourning for fear of the warriors in the Vale of Entuthon-Benython
Jerusalem is scatterd abroad like a cloud of smoke thro' non-entity:
15 Moab & Ammon & Amalek & Canaan & Egypt & Aram
Recieve her little-ones for sacrifices and the delights of cruelty

Trembling I sit day and night, my friends are astonish'd at me.
Yet they forgive my wanderings, I rest not from my great task!
To open the Eternal Worlds, to open the immortal Eyes
20 Of Man inwards into the Worlds of Thought: into Eternity
Ever expanding in the Bosom of God, the Human Imagination
O Saviour pour upon me thy Spirit of meekness & love:
Annihilate the Selfhood in me, be thou all my life!
Guide thou my hand which trembles exceedingly upon the rock of ages,
25 While I write of the building of Golgonooza, & of the terrors of Entuthon:
Of Hand & Hyle & Coban, of Kwantok, Peachey, Brereton, Slayd & Hutton:
Of the terrible sons & daughters of Albion. and their Generations.

Scofield! Kox, Kotope and Bowen, revolve most mightily upon
The Furnace of Los: before the eastern gate bending their fury.
30 They war, to destroy the Furnaces, to desolate Golgonooza:
And to devour the Sleeping Humanity of Albion in rage & hunger.
They revolve into the Furnaces Southward & are driven forth Northward
Divided into Male and Female forms time after time.
From these Twelve all the Families of England spread abroad.

35 The Male is a Furnace of beryll; the Female is a golden Loom;
I behold them and their rushing fires overwhelm my Soul,
In Londons darkness; and my tears fall day and night,
Upon the Emanations of Albions Sons! the Daughters of Albion
Names anciently remember'd, but now contemn'd as fictions!
40 Although in every bosom they controll our Vegetative powers.

They are united into Tirzah and her Sisters, on Mount Gilead,
Cambel & Gwendolen & Conwenna & Cordella & Ignoge.
And these united into Rahab in the Covering Cherub on Euphrates,
Gwiniverra & Gwinefred, & Gonorill & Sabrina beautiful,
45 Estrild, Mehetabel & Ragan, lovely Daughters of Albion
They are the beautiful Emanations of the Twelve Sons of Albion

The Starry Wheels revolv'd heavily over the Furnaces;
Drawing Jerusalem in anguish of maternal love,
Eastward a pillar of a cloud with Vala upon the mountains
50 Howling in pain, redounding from the arms of Beulahs Daughters,
Out from the Furnaces of Los above the head of Los.
A pillar of smoke writhing afar into Non-Entity, redounding
Till the cloud reaches afar outstretch'd among the Starry Wheels
Which revolve heavily in the mighty Void above the Furnaces

55 O what avail the loves & tears of Beulahs lovely Daughters
They hold the Immortal Form in gentle bands & tender tears
But all within is opend into the deeps of Entuthon Benython
A dark and unknown night, indefinite, unmeasurable, without end.
Abstract Philosophy warring in enmity against Imagination
60 (Which is the Divine Body of the Lord Jesus. blessed for ever)
And there Jerusalem wanders with Vala upon the mountains,
Attracted by the revolutions of those Wheels the Cloud of smoke
Immense, and Jerusalem & Vala weeping in the Cloud
Wander away into the Chaotic Void, lamenting with her Shadow
Among the Daughters of Albion, among the Starry Wheels;
65 Lamenting for her children, for the sons & daughters of Albion

Los heard her lamentations in the deeps afar! his tears fall
Incessant before the Furnaces, and his Emanation divided in pain,
68 Eastward toward the Starry Wheels. But Westward a black Horror.

His

His Spectre driven by the Starry Wheels of Albions sons, black and
Opake divided from his back; he labours and he mourns.

For as his Emanation divided, his Spectre also divided
In terror of those starry wheels: and the Spectre stood over Los
Howling in pain: a blackning Shadow, blackning dark & opake
Cursing the terrible Los: bitterly cursing him for his friendship
To Albion, suggesting murderous thoughts against Albion.

Los ragd and stampd the earth in his might & terrible wrath!
He stood and stampd the earth! then he threw down his hammer in rage &
In fury: then he sat down and wept, terrified! Then arose
And chaunted his song, labouring with the tongs and hammer:
But still the Spectre divided, and still his pain increasd!

In pain the Spectre divided: in pain of hunger and thirst:
To devour Los's Human Perfection, but when he saw that Los

Was living: panting like a frighted wolf, and howling
He stood over the Immortal, in the solitude and darkness:
Upon the darkning Thames, across the whole Island westward.
A horrible Shadow of Death, among the Furnaces: beneath
The pillar of folding smoke; and he sought by other means,
To lure Los: by tears, by arguments of science & by terrors:
Terrors in every Nerve, by spasms & extended pains:
While Los answer'd unterrified to the opake blackening Fiend

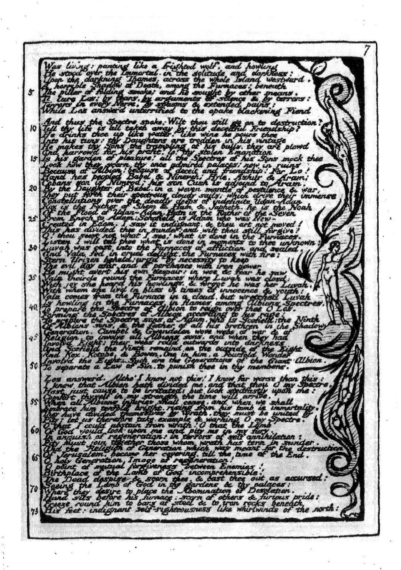

And thus the Spectre spoke: Wilt thou still go on to destruction?
Till thy life is all taken away by this deceitful Friendship?
He drinks thee up like water: like wine he pours thee
Into his tuns: thy Daughters are trodden in his vintage
He makes thy Sons the trampling of his bulls, they are plow'd
And harrow'd for his profit, lo! thy stolen Emanation
Is his garden of pleasure! all the Spectres of his Sons mock thee
Look how they scorn thy once admired palaces: now in ruins
Because of Albion! because of deceit and friendship: For Lo!
Hand has peopled Babel & Nineveh: Hyle, Ashur & Aram:
Cobans son is Nimrod: his son Cush is adjoind to Aram,
By the Daughter of Babel, in a woven mantle of pestilence & war.
They put forth their spectrous cloudy sails; which drive their immense
Constellations over the deadly deeps of indefinite Udan-Adan
Hand is the father of the Sons & Hyle, Japheth: he is the Noah
Of the Flood of Udan-Adan: Hutn is the Father of the Seven
From Enoch to Adam: Schofield is Adam who was New-
Created in Edom. I saw it indignant, & thou art not moved!
This has divided thee in sunder: and wilt thou still forgive!
O! thou seest not what I see: what is done in the Furnaces.
Listen, I will tell thee what is done in moments to thee unknown:
Luvah was cast into the Furnaces of affliction and sealed,
And Vala fed in cruel delight, the Furnaces with fire:
Stern Urizen beheld; urgd by necessity to keep
The evil day afar, and if perchance with iron power
He might avert his own despair: in woe & fear he saw
Vala incircle round the Furnaces where Luvah was clos'd
With joy she heard his howlings, & forgot he was her Luvah,
With whom she liv'd in bliss in times of innocence & youth!
Vala comes from the Furnace in a cloud, but wretched Luvah
Is howling in the Furnaces, in flames among Albions Spectres,
To prepare the Spectre of Albion to reign over thee O Los,
Forming the Spectres of Albion according to his rage:
To prepare the Spectre sons of Adam, who is Scofield: the Ninth
Of Albions sons, & the father of all his brethren in the Shadowy
Generation. Cambel & Gwendolen wove webs of war & of
Religion, to involve all Albions sons, and when they had
Involv'd Eight; they became a rolling wonder
And Scofield the Ninth remaind on the outside of the Eight
And Kox Kopped & Bowen, One in him a Fourfold wonder
Involvd the Eight- Such are the Generations of the Giant Albion,
To separate a Law of Sin, to punish thee in thy members.

Los answerd. Altho' I know not this! I know far worse than this:
I know that Albion hath divided me, and that thou O my Spectre,
Hast just cause to be irritated: but look stedfastly upon me:
Comfort thyself in my strength the time will arrive,
When all Albions injuries shall cease, and when we shall
Embrace him tenfold bright, rising from his tomb in immortality.
They have divided themselves by Wrath. they must be united by
Pity: let us therefore take example & warning O my Spectre,
O that I could abstain from wrath! O that the Lamb
Of God would take away my sin in cruel death!
In anguish of regeneration! in terrors of self annihilation:
Pity must join together those whom wrath has torn in sunder,
And the Religion of Generation which was meant for the destruction
Of Jerusalem, become her covering, till the time of the End.
O holy Generation! Image of regeneration!
O point of mutual forgiveness between Enemies!
Birthplace of the Lamb of God incomprehensible!
The Dead despise & scorn thee, & cast thee out as accursed:
Seeing the Lamb of God in thy gardens & thy palaces:
Where they desire to place the Abomination of Desolation.
Hand sits before his furnace: scorn of others & furious pride:
Freeze round him to bars of steel & to iron rocks beneath
His feet: indignant self-righteousness like whirlwinds of the north:

Rose up against me thundering from the Brook of Albions River
From Ranelagh & Strumbolo, from Cromwells gardens & Chelsea
The place of wounded Soldiers. but when he saw my Mace
5 Whirld round from heaven to earth, trembling he sat: his cold
Poisons rose up: & his sweet deceits coverd them all over
With a tender cloud. As thou art now; such was he O Spectre
I know thy deceit & thy revenges, and unless thou desist
I will certainly create an eternal Hell for thee. Listen!
10 Be attentive! be obedient! Lo the Furnaces are ready to recieve thee.
I will break thee into shivers! & melt thee in the furnaces of death;
I will cast thee into forms of abhorrence & torment if thou
Desist not from thine own will, & obey not my stern command!
I am closd up from my children: my Emanation is dividing
15 And thou my Spectre art divided against me. But mark
I will compell thee to assist me in my terrible labours. To beat
These hypocritic Selfhoods on the Anvils of bitter Death
I am inspired: I act not for myself: for Albions sake
I now am what I am: a horror and an astonishment
20 Shuddring the heavens to look upon me: Behold what cruelties
Are practised in Babel & Shinar, & have approachd to Zions Hill

While Los spoke, the terrible Spectre fell shuddring before him
Watching his time with glowing eyes to leap upon his prey
Los opend the Furnaces in fear, the Spectre saw to Babel & Shinar
25 Across all Europe & Asia. he saw the tortures of the Victims.
He saw now from the outside what he before saw & felt from within
He saw that Los was the sole, uncontrolld Lord of the Furnaces
Groaning he kneeld before Los's iron-shod feet on London Stone,
Hungring & thirsting for Los's life yet pretending obedience.
30 While Los pursud his speech in threatnings loud & fierce.

Thou art my Pride & Self-righteousness: I have found thee out:
Thou art reveald before me in all thy magnitude & power
Thy Uncircumcised pretences to Chastity must be cut in sunder!
Thy holy wrath & deep deceit cannot avail against me
35 Nor shalt thou ever assume the triple-form of Albions Spectre
For I am one of the living: dare not to mock my inspired fury
If thou wast cast forth from my life! if I was dead upon the mountains
Thou mightest be pitied & loved: but now I am living; unless
Thou abstain ravening I will create an eternal Hell for thee.
40 Take thou this Hammer & in patience heave the thundering Bellows
Take thou these Tongs: strike thou alternate with me: labour obedient
Hand & Hyle & Koban: Skofeld, Kox & Kotope, labour mightily
In the Wars of Babel & Shinar, all their Emanations were
44 Condensd. Hand has absorbd all his Brethren in his might
All the infant Loves & Graces were lost, for the mighty Hand

Con

Condensd his Emanations into hard opake substances;
And his infant thoughts & desires, into cold, dark, cliffs of death.
His hammer of gold he seizd; and his anvil of adamant.
He siezd the bars of condensd thoughts, to forge them:
5 Into the sword of war: into the bow and arrow:
Into the thundering cannon and into the murdering gun
I saw the limbs formd for exercise, contemnd: & the beauty of
Eternity, lookd upon as deformity & loveliness as a dry tree:
I saw disease forming a Body of Death around the Lamb
10 Of God, to destroy Jerusalem, & to devour the body of Albion
By war and stratagem to win the labour of the husbandman:

Awkwardness armd in steel: folly in a helmet of gold:
Weakness with horns & talons: ignorance with a ravening beak:
Every Emanative joy forbidden as a Crime:
15 And the Emanations buried alive in the earth with pomp of religion:
Inspiration denyd; Genius forbidden by laws of punishment:
I saw terrified; I took the sighs & tears, & bitter groans:
I lifted them into my Furnaces; to form the spiritual sword.
That lays open the hidden heart: I drew forth the pang
20 Of sorrow red hot: I workd it on my resolute anvil:
I heated it in the flames of Hand, & Hyle, & Coban
Nine times; Gwendolen & Cambel & Gwineverra

Are melted into the gold, the silver, the liquid ruby,
The crysolite, the topaz, the jacinth, & every precious stone,
25 Loud roar my Furnaces and loud my hammer is heard:
I labour day and night. I behold the soft affections
Condense beneath my hammer into forms of cruelty
But still I labour in hope, tho' still my tears flow down.
That he, who will not defend Truth, may be compelld to defend
30 A Lie: that he may be snared and caught and snared and taken
That Enthusiasm and Life may not cease: arise Spectre arise.

Thus they contended among the Furnaces with groans & tears;
Groaning the Spectre howld the bellows; & the hammer of Los frowns:
Till the Spaces of Erin were perforated in the furnaces
35 Of affliction, and Los drew them forth, compelling the harsh Spectre.

Into the Furnaces & into the valleys of the Anvils of Death
And into the mountains of the Anvils & of the heavy Hammers
Till he should bring the Sons & Daughters of Jerusalem to be
The Sons & Daughters of Los that he might protect them from
Albions dread Spectres: storming, loud, thunderous & mighty
The Bellows & the Hammers move compell'd by Los's hand.

And this is the manner of the Sons of Albion in their strength
They take the Two Contraries which are calld Qualities, with which
Every Substance is clothed, they name them Good & Evil
From them they make an Abstract, which is a Negation
Not only of the Substance from which it is derived
A murderer of its own Body: but also a murderer
Of every Divine Member: it is the Reasoning Power
An Abstract objecting power, that Negatives every thing
This is the Spectre of Man: the Holy Reasoning Power
And in its Holiness is closed the Abomination of Desolation

Therefore Los stands in London building Golgonooza
Compelling his Spectre to labours mighty; trembling in fear
The Spectre weeps, but Los unmovd by tears or threats remains

I must Create a System, or be enslav'd by another Mans
I will not Reason & Compare: my business is to Create

So Los, in fury & strength: in indignation & burning wrath
Shudd'ring the Spectre howls. his howlings terrify the night
He stamps around the Anvil, beating blows of stern despair
He curses Heaven & Earth, Day & Night & Sun & Moon
He curses Forest Spring & River; Desart & sandy Waste
Cities & Nations, Families & Peoples, Tongues & Laws
Driven to desperation by Los's terrors & threatning fears

Los cries, Obey my voice & never deviate from my will
And I will be merciful to thee: be thou invisible to all
To whom I make thee invisible, but chief to my own Children
O Spectre of Urthona: Reason not against their dear approach
Nor them obstruct with thy temptations of doubt & despair
O Shame O strong & mighty Shame I break thy brazen fetters
If thou refuse, thy present torments will seem southern breezes
To what thou shalt endure if thou obey not my great will.

The Spectre answerd. Art thou not ashamd of those thy Sins
That thou callest thy Children? lo the Law of God commands
That they be offerd upon his Altar: O cruelty & torment
For thine are also mine! I have kept silent hitherto
Concerning my chief delight: but thou hast broken silence
Now I will speak my mind! Where is my lovely Enitharmon
O thou my enemy, where is my Great Sin? She is also thine
I said: now is my grief at worst: incapable of being
Surpassed: but every moment it accumulates more & more
It continues accumulating to eternity! the joys of God advance
For he is Righteous: he is not a Being of Pity & Compassion
He cannot feel Distress: he feeds on Sacrifice & Offering:
Delighting in cries & tears & clothed in holiness & solitude
But my griefs advance also, for ever & ever without end
O that I could cease to be! Despair! I am Despair
Created to be the great example of horror & agony: also my
Prayer is vain I calld for compassion: compassion mockd
Mercy & pity threw the grave stone over me & with lead
And iron, bound it over me for ever: Life lives on my
Consuming: & the Almighty hath made me his Contrary
To be all evil, all reversed & for ever dead: knowing
And seeing life, yet living not; how can I then behold
And not tremble: how can I be beheld & not abhorrd

So spoke the Spectre shudd'ring, & dark tears ran down his shadowy face
Which Los wiped off, but comfort none could give! or beam of hope
Yet ceased he not from labouring at the roarings of his Forge
With iron & brass Building Golgonooza in great contendings
Till his Sons & Daughters came forth from the Furnaces
At the sublime Labours for Los. compelld the invisible Spectre

Cf 71

To labours mighty, with vast strength, with his mighty chains
In pulsations of time, & extensions of space, like Urns of Beulah
With great labour upon his anvils, & in his ladles the Ore
He lated, pouring it into the clay ground prepard with art;
Striving with Systems to deliver Individuals from those Systems;
That whenever any Spectre began to devour the Dead,
He might feel the pain as if a man gnawd his own tender nerves.

Then Erin came forth from the Furnaces, & all the Daughters of Beulah
Came from the Furnaces, by Los's mighty power for Jerusalems
Sake: walking up and down among the Spectres of Erin
And the Four Zoas and Daughters of Los came forth in perfection lovely
And the Spaces of Erin reachd from the starry height, to the starry depth.

Los wept with exceeding joy & all wept with joy together!
They feard they never more should see their Father, who
Was buried in from Eternity, in the Cliffs of Albion.

But when the joy of meeting was exhausted in loving embrace;
Again they lament. O what shall we do for lovely Jerusalem.
To protect the Emanations of Albions mighty ones from cruelty?
Sabrina & Ignoge began to sharpen their beamy spears
In dire opposition to defend their feeble children from the sword
Of Eson, whose cruel, lovely children draw with arrows of gold;
Gwendolen is wholly cruel; Rachel is bound in spires of gold;
Sisters like a mandrake in the earth before Reubens gate;
She shoots beneath Jerusalems walls to undermine her foundations;
Vala is but thy Shadow, O thou loveliest among women
A shadow animated by thy tears O mournful Jerusalem!

Art

Why wilt thou give to her a Body whose life is but a Shade?
Her joy and love, a shade: a shade of sweet repose:
But animated and vegetated, she is a devouring worm:
What shall we do for thee O lovely mild Jerusalem?

And Los said, I behold the finger of God in terrors!
Albion is dead! his Emanation is divided from him!
But I am living! yet I feel my Emanation also dividing
Such thing was never known! O pity me, thou all-piteous-one!
What shall I do! or how exist, divided from Enitharmon?
Yet why despair! I saw the finger of God go forth
Upon my Furnaces, from within the Wheels of Albions Sons:
Fixing their Systems, permanent: by mathematic power
Giving a body to Falshood that it may be cast off for ever.
With Demonstrative Science piercing Apollyon with his own bow!
God is within, & without! he is even in the depths of Hell!

Such were the lamentations of the Labourers in the Furnaces!
And they appeard within & without incircling on both sides
The Starry Wheels of Albions Sons, with Spaces for Jerusalem:
And for Vala the shadow of Jerusalem: the ever mourning shade:
On both sides, within & without beaming gloriously!

Terrified at the sublime Wonder, Los stood before his Furnaces.
And they stood around, terrified with admiration at Erins Spaces
For the Spaces reached from the starry height, to the starry depth;
And they builded Golgonooza: terrible eternal labour!

What are those golden builders doing? where was the burying-place
Of soft Ethinthus? near Tyburns fatal Tree? is that
Mild Zions hill's most ancient promontory, near mournful
Ever weeping Paddington? is that Calvary and Golgotha?
Becoming a building of pity and compassion? Lo!
The stones are pity, and the bricks, well wrought affections:
Enameld with love & kindness, & the tiles engraven gold
Labour of merciful hands: the beams & rafters are forgiveness:
The mortar & cement of the work, tears of honesty: the nails,
And the screws & iron braces, are well wrought blandishments,
And well contrived words, firm fixing, never forgotten,
Always comforting the remembrance: the floors, humility,
The ceilings, devotion: the hearths, thanksgiving:
Prepare the furniture O Lambeth in thy pitying looms!
The curtains, woven tears & sighs, wrought into lovely forms
For comfort! there the secret furniture of Jerusalems chamber
Is wrought: Lambeth! the Bride the Lambs Wife loveth thee:
Thou art one with her & knowest not of self in thy supreme joy
Go on, builders in hope: tho Jerusalem wanders far away,
Without the gates of Los: among the dark Satanic wheels.

Fourfold the Sons of Los in their divisions: and fourfold,
The Great City of Golgonooza: fourfold toward the north
And toward the south fourfold, & fourfold toward the east & west
Each within other toward the four points: that toward
Eden, and that toward the World of Generation,
And that toward Beulah, and that toward Ulro:
Ulro is the space of the terrible starry wheels of Albions sons:
But that toward Eden is walled up, till time of renovation:
Yet it is perfect in its building, ornaments & perfection.

And the Four Points are thus beheld in Great Eternity
West, the Circumference: South, the Zenith: North,
The Nadir: East, the Center, unapproachable for ever.
These are the four Faces towards the Four Worlds of Humanity
In every Man. Ezekiel saw them by Chebars flood.
And the Eyes are the South, and the Nostrils are the East.
And the Tongue is the West, and the Ear is the North.

And the North Gate of Golgonooza toward Generation:
Has four sculpturd Bulls terrible before the Gate of iron.
And iron, the Bulls: and that which looks toward Ulro,
Clay bakd & enamel'd, eternal glowing as four furnaces:
Turning upon the Wheels of Albions sons with enormous power.
And that toward Beulah four, gold, silver, brass, & iron:

And

And that toward Eden, four, form'd of gold, silver, brass, & iron.

The South, a golden Gate, has four Lions terrible, living!
That toward Generation, four, of iron carv'd wondrous:
That toward Ulro, four, clay bak'd, laborious workmanship:
5 That toward Eden, four; immortal gold, silver, brass & iron.

The Western Gate fourfold, is clos'd: having four Cherubim
Its guards, living, the work of elemental hands, laborious task!
Like Men, hermaphroditic, each winged with eight wings
That towards Generation, iron; that toward Eden, stone;
10 That toward Ulro, clay; that toward Eden, metal: (dead)
But all clos'd up till the last day, when the graves shall yield their

The Eastern Gate, fourfold; terrible & deadly its ornaments:
Taking their forms from the Wheels of Albions sons; as cogs
Are form'd in a wheel, to fit the cogs of the adverse wheel.

15 That toward Eden, eternal ice, frozen in seven folds
Of forms of death: and that toward Beulah, stone;
The seven diseases of the earth are carved terrible.
And that toward Ulro, forms of war: seven enormities;
And that toward Generation, seven generative forms.

20 And every part of the City is fourfold; & every inhabitant, fourfold.
And every pot & vessel & garment & utensil of the houses,
And every house, fourfold; but the third Gate in every one
Is closd as with a threefold curtain of ivory & fine linen & ermine.
And Luban stands in middle of the City. a moat of fire
25 Surrounds Luban, Los's Palace & the golden Looms of Cathedron

And sixty-four thousand Genii, guard the Eastern Gate:
And sixty-four thousand Gnomes, guard the Northern Gate:
And sixty-four thousand Nymphs, guard the Western Gate:
And sixty-four thousand Fairies, guard the Southern Gate:

30 Around Golgonooza lies the land of death eternal: a Land
Of pain and misery and despair and ever brooding melancholy:
In all the Twenty-seven Heavens, numberd from Adam to Luther;
From the blue Mundane Shell, reaching to the Vegetative Earth.

35 The Vegetative Universe, opens like a flower from the Earths center:
In which is Eternity. It expands in Stars to the Mundane Shell
And there it meets Eternity again, both within and without,
And the abstract Voids between the Stars are the Satanic Wheels.

There is the Cave; the Rock; the Tree; the Lake of Udan Adan;
40 The Forest, and the Marsh, and the Pits of bitumen deadly:
The Rocks of solid fire: the Ice valleys: the Plains
Of burning sand: the rivers, cataract & Lakes of Fire:
The Islands of the fiery Lakes: the Trees of Malice: Revenge;
And black Anxiety; and the Cities of the Salamandrine men:
45 (But whatever is visible to the Generated Man,
Is a Creation of mercy & love, from the Satanic Void.)
The land of darkness flamed but no light, & no repose:
The land of snows of trembling, & of iron hail incessant:
The land of earthquakes: and the land of woven labyrinths:
50 The land of snares & traps & wheels & pit-falls & dire mills:
The Voids, the Solids, & the land of clouds & regions of waters:
With their inhabitants: in the Twenty-seven Heavens beneath Beulah:
Self-righteousnesses conglomerating against the Divine Vision:
A Concave Earth wondrous, Chasmal, Abyssal, Incoherent!
55 Forming the Mundane Shell: above; beneath: on all sides surrounding
Golgonooza: Los walks round the walls night and day.

He views the City of Golgonooza, & its smaller Cities:
The Looms & Mills & Prisons & Work-houses of Og & Anak:
The Amalekite: the Canaanite: the Moabite: the Egyptian:
60 And all that has existed in the space of six thousand years:
Permanent, & not lost not lost nor vanishd, & every little act,
Word, work, & wish, that has existed, all remaining still
In those Churches ever consuming & ever building by the Spectres
Of all the inhabitants of Earth wailing to be Created:
65 Shadowy to those who dwell not in them, meer possibilities:
66 But to those who enter into them they seem the only substances
For every thing exists & not one sigh nor smile nor tear,

One hair nor particle of dust: not one can pass away.
He views the Cherub at the Tree of Life, also the Serpent:
Orc the first born coild in the south: the Dragon Urizen:
Tharmas the Vegetated Tongue even the Devouring Tongue:
5 A threefold region, a false brain: a false heart:
And false bowels: altogether composing the False Tongue,
Beneath Beulah: as a watry flame revolving every way
And as dark roots and stems: a Forest of affliction: growing
In seas of sorrow. Los also views the Four Females:
10 Ahania, and Enion, and Vala, and Enitharmon lovely,
And from them all the lovely beaming Daughters of Albion.
Ahania & Enion & Vala, are three evanescent shades:
Enitharmon is a vegetated mortal Wife of Los:
His Emanation, yet his Wife till the sleep of death is past:
15 Such are the Buildings of Los! & such are the Woofs of Enitharmon!

And Los beheld his Sons, and he beheld his Daughters:
Every one a translucent Wonder: a Universe within,
Increasing inwards, into length and breadth, and heighth:
Starry & glorious: and they every one in their bright loins:
20 Have a beautiful golden gate, which opens into the vegetative world:
And every one a gate of rubies & all sorts of precious stones,
In their translucent hearts, which opens into the vegetative world.
And every one a gate of iron dreadful and wonderful.
In their translucent heads, which opens into the vegetative world
25 And every one has the three regions Childhood: Manhood: & Age:
But the gate of the tongue: the western gate in them is closd.
Having a wall builded against it: and thereby the gates
Eastward & Southward & Northward, are incircled with flaming fires.
And the North is Breadth, the South is Heighth & Depth:
30 The East is Inwards: & the West is Outwards every way.

And Los beheld the mild Emanation Jerusalem eastward bending
Her revolutions toward the Starry Wheels in maternal anguish
Like a pale cloud arising from the arms of Beulahs Daughters:
35 In Entuthon Benythons Stony Vales beneath Golgonooza.

And Hand & Hyle rooted into Jerusalem by a fibre
Of strong revenge & Skofeld Vegetated by Reubens Gate
In every Nation of the Earth till the Twelve Sons of Albion
Enrooted into every Nation; a mighty Polypus growing
From Albion over the whole Earth: such is my awful Vision.

I see the Four-fold Man. The Humanity in deadly sleep
And its fallen Emanation. The Spectre & its cruel Shadow.
I see the Past, Present & Future, existing all at once
Before me; O Divine Spirit sustain me on thy wings!
That I may awake Albion from his long & cold repose.
For Bacon & Newton sheathd in dismal steel, their terrors hang
Like iron scourges over Albion, Reasonings like vast Serpents
Infold around my limbs, bruising my minute articulations

I turn my eyes to the Schools & Universities of Europe
And there behold the Loom of Locke whose Woof rages dire
Washd by the Water-wheels of Newton. black the cloth
In heavy wreathes folds over every Nation; cruel Works
Of many Wheels I view, wheel without wheel, with cogs tyrannic
Moving by compulsion each other: not as those in Eden: which
Wheel within Wheel in freedom revolve in harmony & peace.

I see in deadly fear in London Los raging round his Anvil
Of death: forming an Ax of gold: the Four Sons of Los
Stand round him cutting the Fibres from Albions hills
That Albions Sons may roll apart over the Nations
While Reuben enroots his brethren in the narrow Canaanite
From the Limit Noah to the Limit Abram in whose Loins
Reuben in his Twelve-fold majesty & beauty shall take refuge
As Abraham flees from Chaldea shaking his goary locks
But first Albion must sleep, divided from the Nations

I see Albion sitting upon his Rock in the first Winter
And thence I see the Chaos of Satan & the World of Adam
When the Divine Hand went forth on Albion in the midst Winter
And at the place of Death when Albion sat in Eternal Death
Among the Furnaces of Los in the Valley of the Son of Hin-
-nom.

Hampstead Highgate Finchley Hendon Muswell hill rage loud
Before Bromions iron Tongs & glowing Poker reddening fierce
Hertfordshire glows with fierce Vegetation! in the Forests
The Oak frowns terrible, the Beech & Ash & Elm enroot
Among the Spiritual fires; loud the Corn fields thunder along
The Soldiers fife; the Harlots shriek; the Virgins dismal groan
The Parents fear: the Brothers jealousy: the Sisters curse
Beneath the Storms of Theotormon & the thundrous Cloud
Weeps over the Couch of Death, who in Londons darkness
Before the Anvil, watches the bellowing flames: thundering
The Hammer loud rages in Rintrahs strong grasp swinging loud
Round from heaven to earth down falling with heavy blow
Dead on the Anvil, where the red hot wedge groans in pain
He quenches it in the black trough of his Forge: Londons River
Feeds the dread Forge, trembling & shuddering along the Valleys

Humber & Trent roll dreadful before the Seventh Furnace
And Tweed & Tyne anxious give up their Souls for Albions sake
Lincolnshire Derbyshire Nottinghamshire Leicestershire
From Oxfordshire to Norfolk on the Lake of Udan Adan
Labour within the Furnaces, walking among the Fires
With Ladles huge & iron Pokers over the Island white.

Scotland pours out his Sons to labour at the Furnaces
Wales gives his Daughters to the Looms; England nursing Mothers
Gives to the Children of Albion & to the Children of Jerusalem
From the blue Mundane Shell even to the Earth of Vegetation
Throughout the whole Creation which groans to be delivered
Albion groans in the deep slumbers of Death upon his Rock.

Here Los fixd down the Fifty-two Counties of England & Wales
The Thirty-six of Scotland, & the Thirty-four of Ireland
With mighty power, when they fled out at Jerusalems Gates
Away from the Conflict of Luvah & Urizen, fixing the Gates
In the Twelve Counties of Wales & thence Gates looking every way
To the Four Points: conduct to England & Scotland & Ireland
And thence to all the Kingdoms & Nations & Families of the Earth
The Gate of Reuben in Carmarthenshire: the Gate of Simeon in
Cardiganshire: the Gate of Levi in Montgomeryshire
The Gate of Judah Merionethshire: the Gate of Dan in Flintshire
The Gate of Naphtali, Radnorshire: the Gate of Gad Pembrokeshire
The Gate of Asher, Carnarvonshire: the Gate of Issachar Brecknockshire
The Gate of Zebulun, in Anglesea & Sodor, so is Wales divided.
The Gate of Joseph Denbighshire: the Gate of Benjamin Montgomeryshire
For the protection of the Twelve Emanations of Albions Sons

And the Forty Counties of England are thus divided in the Gates
Of Reuben Norfolk Suffolk Essex Surrey Sussex Lincoln York Lancashire
Levi Middlesex Kent Surrey Sussex Somerset Gloucester Wiltshire
Dan Cornwall Devon Dorset Somerset Warwick Leicester Worcester
Gad Oxford Bucks Harford Cambridge Huntingdon Bedford Northampton
Issachar Nottingham Hereford Chester Shropshire Stafford Warwick
Joseph Stafford Hereford Benjamin Derby Cheshire Monmouth
And Cumberland Northumberland Westmorland & Durham are
Divided in the Gates of Reuben Judah Dan & Joseph
And the Thirty-six Counties of Scotland, divided in the Gates
Of Reuben Kincard Haddntn Forfar Simeon Ayr Argyll Banff
Levi Edinburgh Roxboro Ross Judah Aberdeen Berwick Dumfries
Dan Bute Catness Carnaven Naphtali Nairn Inverness Linlithgo
Gad Peebles Perth Renfru Asher Sutherland Sterling Wigtoun
Issachar Selkirk Dumbarton Glasgo Zebulun Orkney Shetland Skye
Joseph Elgin Lanerk Kinross Benjamin Cromarty Murra Kirkudbright
Governing all by the sweet delights of secret amorous glances
In Enitharmons Halls builded by Los & his mighty Children

All things acted on Earth are seen in the bright Sculptures of
Los's Halls & every Age renews its powers from these Works
With every pathetic story possible to happen from Hate or
Wayward Love & every Sorrow & distress is carved here
Every Affinity of Parents Marriages & Friendships are here
In all their various combinations wrought with wondrous Art
All that can happen to Man in his pilgrimage of seventy years
Such is the Divine Written Law of Horeb & Sinai:
And such the Holy Gospel of Mount Olivet & Calvary:

His Spectre divides & Los in fury compells it, to divide:
To labour in the Fire, in the water, in the earth, in the air,
To follow the Daughters of Albion as the hound follows the scent
Of the wild inhabitant of the forest, to drive them from his own:
To make a way for the Children of Los to come from the Furnaces,
But Los himself against Albions Sons his fury bends, for he
Dare not approach the Daughters openly lest he be consumed
In the fires of their beauty & perfection & be Vegetated beneath
Their Looms, in a Generation of death & resurrection to forgetfulness
They woo Los continually to subdue his strength: he continually
Shews them his Spectre: sending him abroad over the four points of heaven
In the fierce desires of beauty & in the tortures of repulse: He is
The Spectre of the Living pursuing the Emanations of the Dead.
Shuddring they flee: they hide in the Druid Temples in cold chastity:
Subdued by the Spectre of the Living & terrified by undisguised desire.

For Los said: Tho my Spectre is divided: as I am a Living Man
I must compell him to obey me wholly: that Enitharmon may not
Be lost: & lest he should devour Enitharmon: Ah me!
Piteous image of my soft desires & loves: O Enitharmon!
I will compell my Spectre to obey: I will restore to thee thy Children.
No one bruises or starves himself to make himself fit for labour.

Tormented with sweet desire for these Beauties of Albion
They would never love my power if they did not seek to destroy
Enitharmon: Vala would never have sought & loved Albion
If she had not sought to destroy Jerusalem: such is that false
And Generating Love: a pretence of love to destroy love:
Cruel hypocrisy unlike the lovely delusions of Beulah:
And cruel forms, unlike the merciful forms of Beulahs Night

They know not why they love nor wherefore they sicken & die
Calling that Holy Love: which is Envy Revenge & Cruelty
Which separated the stars from the mountains: the mountains from Man
And left Man, a little grovelling Root, outside of Himself.
Negations are not Contraries: Contraries mutually Exist:
But Negations Exist Not: Exceptions & Objections & Unbeliefs
Exist not: nor shall they ever be Organized for ever & ever:
If thou separate from me, thou art a Negation: a mere
Reasoning & Derogation from me, an Objecting & cruel Spite
And Malice & Envy: but my Emanation, alas! will become
My Contrary: O thou Negation, I will continually compell
Thee to be invisible to any but whom I please, & when
And where & how I please, and never! never! shalt thou be Organized
But as a distorted & reversed Reflexion in the Darkness
And in the Non Entity: nor shall that which is above
Ever descend into thee: but thou shalt be a Non Entity for ever
And if any enter into thee, thou shalt be an Unquenchable Fire
And he shall be a never dying Worm, mutually tormented by
Those that thou tormentest, a Hell & Despair for ever & ever.

So Los in secret with himself communed & Enitharmon heard
In her darkness & was comforted: yet still she divided away
In gnawing pain from Los's bosom in the deadly Night:
First as a red Globe of blood trembling beneath his bosom
Suspended over her he hung: he infolded her in his garments
Of wool: he hid her from the Spectre, in shame & confusion of
Face; in terrors & pains of Hell & Eternal Death, the
Trembling Globe shot forth Self-Living & Los howld over it:
Feeding it with his groans & tears day & night without ceasing:
And the Spectrous Darkness from his back divided in temptations,
And in grinding agonies in threats: stiflings & direful struggling

Go thou to Skofeld: ask him if he is Bath or if he is Canterbury
Tell him to be no more dubious: demand explicit words
Tell him: I will dash him into shivers, where & at what time
I please: tell Hand & Skofeld they are my ministers of evil
To those I hate: for I can hate also as well as they.

From every-one of the Four Regions of Human Majesty,
There is an Outside spread Without, & an Outside spread Within,
Beyond the Outline of Identity both ways, which meet in One:
An orbed Void of doubt, despair, hunger, & thirst & sorrow.
Here the Twelve Sons of Albion, joind in dark Assembly,
Jealous of Jerusalems children, ashamd of her little-ones
(For Vala produced the Bodies, Jerusalem gave the Souls)
Became as Three Immense Wheels, turning upon one-another
Into Non-Entity, and their thunders hoarse appall the Dead
To murder their own Souls, to build a Kingdom among the Dead

Cast! Cast ye Jerusalem forth! The Shadow of delusions!
The Harlot daughter! Mother of pity and dishonourable forgiveness
Our Father Albions sin and shame! But father now no more!
Nor sons, nor hateful peace & love, nor soft complacencies
With transgressors meeting in brotherhood around the table,
Or in the porch or garden. No more the sinful delights
Of age and youth and boy and girl, and animal and herb,
And river and mountain, and city & village, and house & family
Beneath the Oak & Palm, beneath the Vine and Fig-tree.
In self-denial!—But War and deadly contention, Between
Father and Son, and light and love! All bold asperities
Of Hatred met in deadly strife, rending the house & garden
The unforgiving porches, the tables of enmity, and beds
And chambers of trembling & suspition, hatreds of age & youth
And boy & girl, & animal & herb, & river & mountain
And city & village, and house & family. That the Perfect,
May live in glory, redeemd by Sacrifice of the Lamb
And of his Children, before sinful Jerusalem. To build
Babylon the City of Vala, the Goddess Virgin-Mother.
She is our Mother! Nature! Jerusalem is our Harlot-Sister
Returned with Children of pollution, to defile our House,
With Sin and Shame. Cast! Cast her into the Potters field.
Her little-ones, She must slay upon our Altars: and her aged
Parents must be carried into captivity, to redeem her Soul
To be for a Shame & a Curse, and to be our Slaves for ever.

So cry Hand & Hyle the eldest of the fathers of Albions
Little-ones; to destroy the Divine Saviour; the Friend of Sinners,
Building Castles in desolated places, and strong Fortifications.
Soon Hand mightily devour'd & absorbd Albions Twelve Sons.
Out from his bosom a mighty Polypus, vegetating in darkness,
And Hyle & Coban were his two chosen ones, for Emissaries
In War; forth from his bosom they went and returnd.
Like Wheels from a great Wheel reflected in the Deep.
Hoarse, turnd the Starry Wheels, rending a way in Albions Loins
Beyond the Night of Beulah. In a dark & unknown Night
Outstretchd his Giant beauty on the ground in pain & tears.

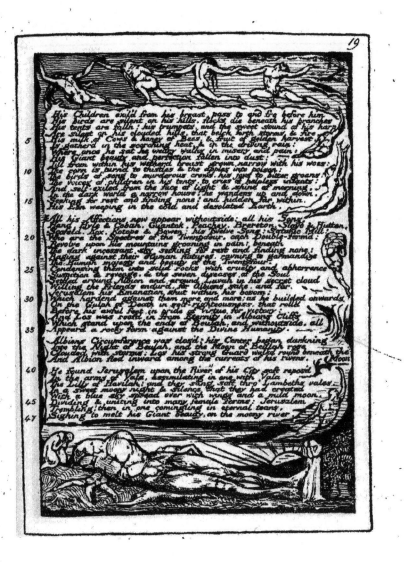

His Children exil'd from his breast pass to and fro before him
His birds are silent on his hills, flocks die beneath his branches
His tents are fall'n! his trumpets, and the sweet sound of his harp
Are silent on his clouded hills, that belch forth storms & fire.
His milk of Cows, & honey of Bees, & fruit of golden harvest,
Is gather'd in the scorching heat, & in the driving rain:
Where once he sat he weary walks in misery and pain:
His Giant beauty and perfection fallen into dust:
Till from within his wither'd breast grown narrow with his woes:
The corn is turn'd to thistles & the apples into poison:
The birds of song to murderous crows, his joys to bitter groans!
The voices of children in his tents, to cries of helpless infants!
And self-exiled from the face of light & shine of morning,
In the dark world a narrow house! he wanders up and down,
Seeking for rest and finding none; and hidden far within,
His Spectre weeping in the cold and desolated North,

All his Affections now appear withoutside: all his Sons,
Hand, Hyle & Coban, Guantok, Peachey, Brereton, Slade & Hutton,
Scofeld, Kox, Kotope & Bowen; his Emanative portion: Scofeld Kill;
Who are the Spectres of the Twenty-four, each Double-form'd:
Revolve upon his mountains groaning in pain; beneath
The dark incessant sky, seeking for rest and finding none:
Raging against their Human natures, rav'ning to gormandize
The Human majesty and beauty of the Twenty-four,
Condensing them into solid rocks with cruelty and abhorrence
Suspicion & revenge, & the seven diseases of the Soul
Settled around Albion and around Luvah in his secret cloud.
Willing the Friends endur'd, for Albion's sake, and for
Jerusalem his Emanation, shut within his bosom:
Which hardened against them more and more: as he builded onwards
On the Gulf of Death in self-righteousness, that roll'd
Before his awful feet, in quenchless fury: to Albions Cliffs
And Los was roofd in from Eternity in Albions Cliffs
Which stand upon the ends of Beulah: and withoutside, all
Appeared a rocky form against the Divine Humanity.

Albions Circumference was clos'd: his Center began darkning
Into the Night of Beulah, and the Moon of Beulah rose
Clouded with storms: Los his strong Guard walkd round beneath the Moon
And Albion fled inward among the currents of his rivers.

He found Jerusalem upon the River of his City soft repos'd
In the arms of Vala, assimilating in one with Vala
The Lilly of Havilah: and they sang soft thro' Lambeths vales,
In a sweet moony night & silence that they had created
With a blue sky spread over with wings and a mild moon.
Dividing & uniting into many female forms: Jerusalem
Trembling; then in one commingling in eternal tears,
Sighing to melt his Giant beauty, on the moony river.

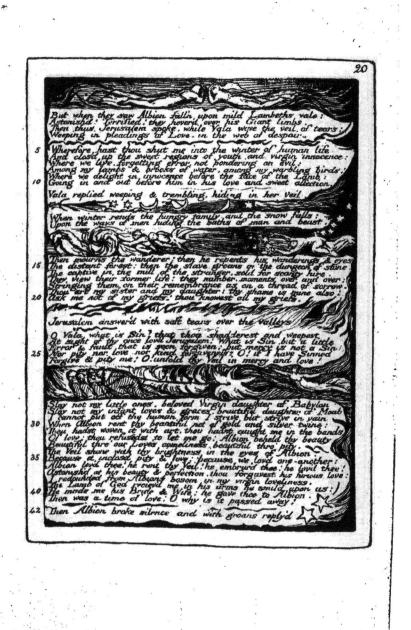

But when they saw Albion fall'n upon mild Lambeths vale:
Astonish'd! Terrified! they hover'd over his Giant limbs.
Then thus Jerusalem spoke, while Vala wove the veil of tears:
Weeping in pleadings of Love. in the web of despair.

5 Wherefore hast thou shut me into the winter of human life
And clos'd up the sweet regions of youth and virgin innocence:
Where we live, forgetting error; not pondering on evil:
Among my lambs & brooks of water, among my warbling birds:
Where we delight in innocence before the face of the Lamb:
10 Going in and out before him in his love and sweet affection.

Vala replied weeping & trembling, hiding in her Veil

When winter rends the hungry family, and the snow falls:
Upon the ways of men hiding the paths of man and beast.

15 Then mourns the wanderer: then he repents his wanderings & eyes
The distant forest; then the slave groans in the dungeon of stone
The captive in the mill of the stranger, sold for scanty hire
They view their former life: they number moments over and over;
Stringing them on their remembrance as on a thread of sorrow.
20 Thou art my sister and my daughter! thy shame is mine also:
Ask me not of my griefs! thou knowest all my griefs.

Jerusalem answer'd with soft tears over the valleys

O Vala what is Sin? that thou shudderest and weepest
At sight of thy once lov'd Jerusalem. What is Sin but a little
25 Error & fault that is soon forgiven; but mercy is not a Sin
Nor pity nor love nor kind forgiveness! O! if I have Sinned
Forgive & pity me! O! unfold thy Veil in mercy and love!

Slay not my little ones, beloved Virgin daughter of Babylon
30 Slay not my infant loves & graces, beautiful daughter of Moab
I cannot put off the human form I strive but strive in vain
When Albion rent thy beautiful net of gold and silver twine:
Thou hadst woven it with art, thou hadst caught me in the bands
Of love; thou refusedst to let me go: Albion beheld thy beauty
35 Beautiful thro' our Loves comeliness, beautiful thro' pity.
The Veil shone with thy brightness in the eyes of Albion.
Because it inclosd pity & love; because we lov'd one-another!
Albion lov'd thee! he rent thy Veil! he embrac'd thee! he lov'd thee!
Astonish'd at his beauty & perfection, thou forgavest his furious love:
40 I redounded from Albions bosom in my virgin loveliness.
The Lamb of God receiv'd me in his arms he smil'd upon us:
He made me his Bride & Wife: he gave thee to Albion.
Then was a time of love: O why is it passed away!

42 Then Albion broke silence and with groans reply'd

O Vala! O Jerusalem! do you delight in my groans
You O lovely forms, you have prepared my death-cup:
The disease of Shame covers me from head to feet: I have no hope
Every boil upon my body is a separate & deadly Sin.
Doubt first assaild me, then Shame took possession of me
Shame divides Families. Shame hath divided Albion in sunder!
First fled my Sons, & then my Daughters, then my Wild Animations
My Cattle next, last ev'n the Dog of my Gate. the Forests fled
The Corn-fields, & the breathing Gardens outside separated
The Sea; the Stars: the Sun: the Moon: driv'n forth by my disease
All is Eternal Death unless you can weave a chaste
Body over an unchaste Mind! Vala! O that thou wert pure!
That the deep wound of Sin might be closd up with the Needle,
And with the Loom: to cover Gwendolen & Ragan with costly Robes
Of Natural Virtue, for their Spiritual forms without a Veil
Wither in Luvahs Sepulcher. I thrust him from my presence
And all my Children followd his loud howlings into the Deep.
Jerusalem! dissembler Jerusalem! I look into thy bosom:
I discover thy secret places; Cordella! I behold
Thee whom I thought pure as the heavens in innocence & fear:
Thy Tabernacle taken down, thy secret Cherubim disclosed
Art thou broken? Ah me Sabrina, running by my side:
In childhood what wert thou? unutterable anguish! Conwenna
Thy cruelted infancy is most piteous. O hide, O hide!
Their secret gardens were made paths to the traveller:
I knew not of their secret loves with those I hated most,
Nor that their every thought was Sin & secret appetite
Hyle sees in fear, he howls in fury over them, Hand sees
In jealous fear: in stern accusation with cruel stripes
He drives them thro' the Streets of Babylon before my face:
Because they taught Luvah to rise into my clouded heavens
Battersea and Chelsea mourn for Cambel & Gwendolen!
Hackney and Holloway sicken for Estrild & Ignoge!
Because the Peak, Malvern & Cheviot Reason in Cruelty
Penmaenmawr & Dhinas-bran Demonstrate in Unbelief
Manchester & Liverpool are in tortures of Doubt & Despair
Malden & Colchester Demonstrate: I hear my Children's voices
I see their piteous faces gleam out upon the cruel winds
From Lincoln & Norwich, from Edinburgh & Monmouth,
I see them distant from my bosom scourgd along the roads
Then lost in clouds; I hear their tender voices! clouds divide
I see them die beneath the whips of the Captains! they are taken
In solemn pomp into Chaldea across the breadths of Europe
Six months they lie embalmd in silent death: worshipped
Carried in Arks of Oak before the armies in the spring
Bursting their Arks they rise again to life; they play before
The Armies: I hear their loud Cymbals & their deadly cries
Are the Dead cruel! are those who are infolded in moral Law
Revengeful? O that Death & Annihilation were the same!

Then Vala answerd spreading her scarlet Veil over Albion.

Albian thy fear has made me tremble; thy terrors have surrour[ded me]

Albion thy fear has made me tremble; thy terrors have surrounded me
Thy Sons have nailed me on the Gates piercing my hands & feet;
Till Skofelds Nimrod the mighty Huntsman Jehovah came,
With Cush his Son & took me down. He in a golden Ark.

5 Bears me before his Armies tho my Shadow hovers here.
The flesh of multitudes fed & nourish'd me in my childhood
My morn & evening food were prepar'd in Battles of Men.
Great is the cry of the Hounds of Nimrod along the Valley
Of Vision, they scent the odor of War in the Valley of Vision.

10 All Love is lost! terror succeeds & Hatred instead of Love
And stern demands of Right & Duty instead of Liberty.
Once thou wast to me the loveliest Son of heaven; but now
Where shall I hide from thy dread countenance & searching eyes
I have looked into the secret Soul of him I loved

15 And in the dark recesses found Sin & cannot never return.

Albion again uttered his voice beneath the silent Moon.

I brought Love into light of day to pride in chaste beauty
I brought Love into light & fancied Innocence is no more

Then spoke Jerusalem O Albion; my Father Albion

20 Why wilt thou number every little fibre of my Soul
Spreading them out before the Sun like stalks of flax to dry!
The infant Joy is beautiful, but its anatomy
Horrible ghast & deadly! nought shalt thou find in it
But dark despair & everlasting brooding melancholy!

25 Then Albion turned his face toward Jerusalem & spoke

Hide thou Jerusalem in impalpable voidness, not to be
Touch'd by the hand nor seen with the eye: O Jerusalem
Would thou wert not & that thy place might never be found
But come O Vala with knife & cup: drain my blood

30 To the last drop: then hide me in thy Scarlet Tabernacle
For I see Luvah whom I slew. I behold him in my Spectre
As I behold Jerusalem in thee O Vala dark and cold

Jerusalem then stretched her hand toward the Moon & spoke

Why should Punishment; Weave the Veil with Iron Wheels of War
35 When Forgiveness might it Weave with Wings of Cherubim

36 Loud groand Albion from mountain to mountain & replied

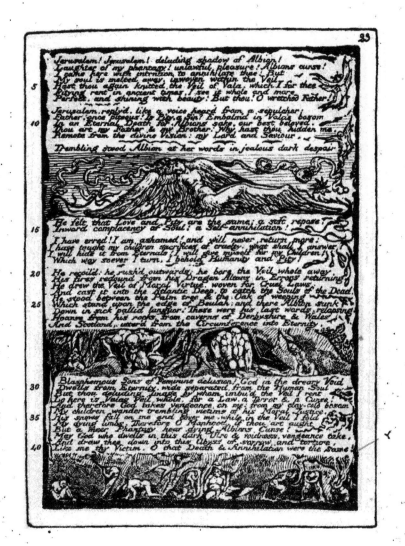

Jerusalem! Jerusalem! deluding shadow of Albion!
Daughter of my phantasy! unlawful pleasure! Albions curse!
I came here with intention to annihilate thee! But
My Soul is melted away, inwoven within the Veil
Hast thou again knitted the Veil of Vala, which I for thee
Pitying rent in ancient times. I see it whole and more
Perfect, and shining with beauty! But thou! O wretched Father!

Jerusalem. replyd. like a voice heard from a sepulcher:
Father! once piteous! Is Pity, a Sin? Embalmd in Valas bosom
In an Eternal Death for Albions sake, our best beloved.
Thou art my Father & my Brother: Why hast thou hidden me,
Remote from the divine Vision: my Lord and Saviour.

Trembling stood Albion at her words in jealous dark despair:

He felt that Love and Pity are the same; a soft repose!
Inward complacency of Soul: a Self-annihilation!

I have erred! I am ashamed! and will never return more:
I have taught my children sacrifices of cruelty: what shall I answer?
I will hide it from Eternals! I will give myself for my Children!
Which way soever I turn, I behold Humanity and Pity!

He recoild: he rushd outwards; he bore the Veil whole away.
His fires redound from his Dragon Altars in Errors returning.
He drew the Veil of Moral Virtue, woven for Cruel Laws,
And cast it into the Atlantic Deep, to catch the Souls of the Dead.
He stood between the Palm tree & the Oak of weeping
Which stand upon the edge of Beulah; and there Albion sunk
Down in sick pallid languor! These were his last words, relapsing!
Hoarse from his rocks, from caverns of Derbyshire & Wales
And Scotland, utterd from the Circumference into Eternity.

Blasphemous Sons of Feminine delusion! God in the dreary Void
Dwells from Eternity, wide separated from the Human Soul
But thou deluding Image by whom imbu'd the Veil I rent
Lo here is Valas Veil whole, for a Law a Terror & a Curse!
And therefore God takes vengeance on me: from my clay-cold bosom
My children wander trembling victims of his Moral Justice.
My Sons in fetters bound, & scourg'd me while their palid Justice.
But a Meer Shadow, never pining, whilst the Veil I fold
But a Meer Phantom hear dying Albions Curse!
May God who dwells in this dark Ulro & voidness, vengeance take,
And draw thee down into this Abyss of sorrow and torture,
Like me thy Victim. O that Death & Annihilation were the same!

And there was heard a great lamenting in Beulah: all the Regions
Of Beulah were moved as the tender bowels are moved: & they said:

Why did you take Vengeance O ye Sons of the mighty Albion?
Planting these Oaken Groves: Erecting these Dragon Temples
Injury the Lord heals but Vengeance cannot be healed:
As the Sons of Albion have done to Luvah: so they have in him
Done to the Divine Lord & Saviour, who suffers with those that suffer,
For not one sparrow can suffer & the whole Universe not suffer also,
In all its Regions, & its Father & Saviour not pity and weep
But Vengeance is the destroyer of Grace & Repentance in the bosom
Of the Injurer: in which the Divine Lamp is cruelly slain:
Descend O Lamb of God & take away the imputation of Sin
By the Creation of States & the deliverance of Individuals Evermore Amen

Thus wept they in Beulah over the Four Regions of Albion
But many doubted & despaird & imputed Sin & Righteousness
To Individuals & not to States, and these Slept in Ulro.

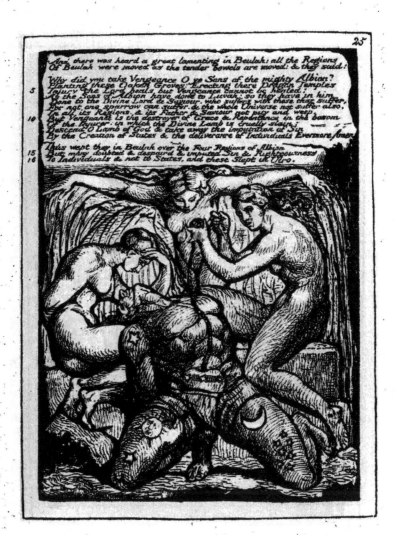

To the Jews.

Jerusalem the Emanation of the Giant Albion! Can it be? Is it a Truth that the Learned have explored? Was Britain the Primitive Seat of the Patriarchal Religion? If it is true: my title-page is also True, that Jerusalem was & is the Emanation of the Giant Albion. It is True, and cannot be controverted. Ye are united O ye Inhabitants of Earth in One Religion. The Religion of Jesus: the most Ancient, the Eternal: & the Everlasting Gospel—The Wicked will turn it to Wickedness, the Righteous to Righteousness. Amen! Huzza! Selah!

"All things Begin & End in Albions Ancient Druid Rocky Shore."

Your Ancestors derived their origin from Abraham, Heber, Shem, and Noah, who were Druids: as the Druid Temples (which are the Patriarchal Pillars & Oak Groves) over the whole Earth witness to this day.

You have a tradition, that Man anciently contain'd in his mighty limbs all things in Heaven & Earth: this you Received from the Druids.

"But now the Starry Heavens are fled from the mighty limbs of Albion"

Albion was the Parent of the Druids; & in his Chaotic State of Sleep Satan & Adam & the whole World was Created by the Elohim.

1
The fields from Islington to Marybone,
To Primrose Hill and Saint Johns Wood:
Were builded over with pillars of gold,
And there Jerusalems pillars stood.

2
Her Little-ones ran on the fields
The Lamb of God among them seen
And fair Jerusalem his Bride:
Among the little meadows green.

3
Pancrass & Kentish-town repose
Among her golden pillars high:
Among her golden arches which
Shine upon the starry sky.

4
The Jews-harp-house & the Green Man;
The Ponds where Boys to bathe delight:
The fields of Cows by Willans farm:
Shine in Jerusalems pleasant sight.

5
She walks upon our meadows green:
The Lamb of God walks by her side:
And every English Child is seen,
Children of Jesus & his Bride,

6
Forgiving trespasses and sins
Lest Babylon with cruel Og,
With Moral & Self-righteous Law
Should Crucify in Satans Synagogue!

7
What are those golden Builders doing
Near mournful ever-weeping Paddington
Standing above that mighty Ruin
Where Satan the first victory won.

8
Where Albion slept beneath the Fatal Tree
And the Druids golden Knife,
Rioted in human gore,
In Offerings of Human Life

9
They groud aloud on London Stone
They groud aloud on Tyburns Brook
Albion gave his deadly groan,
And all the Atlantic Mountains shook

10
Albions Spectre from his Loins
Tore forth in all the pomp of War:
Satan his name: in flames of fire
He stretch'd his Druid Pillars far.

11
Jerusalem fell from Lambeths Vale,
Down thro Poplar & Old Bow;
Thro Malden & across the Sea,
In War & howling death & woe.

12
The Rhine was red with human blood:
The Danube roll'd a purple tide;
On the Euphrates Satan stood:
And over Asia stretch'd his pride.

13
He witherd up sweet Zions Hill,
From every Nation of the Earth:
He witherd up Jerusalems Gates,
And in a dark Land gave her birth.

14
He witherd up the Human Form,
By laws of sacrifice for sin:
Till it became a Mortal Worm:
But O! translucent all within.

15
The Divine Vision still was seen
Still was the Human Form, Divine
Weeping in weak & mortal clay
O Jesus still the Form was thine.

16
And thine the Human Face & thine
The Human Hands & Feet & Breath
Entering thro' the Gates of Birth
And passing thro' the Gates of Death

17
And O thou Lamb of God, whom I
Slew in my dark self-righteous pride:
Art thou return'd to Albions Land!
And is Jerusalem thy Bride?

18
Come to my arms & never more
Depart; but dwell for ever here:
Create my Spirit to thy Love:
Subdue my Spectre to thy Fear.

19
Spectre of Albion! warlike Fiend!
In clouds of blood & ruin roll'd:
I here reclaim thee as my own
My Selfhood! Satan! arm'd in gold.

20
Is this thy soft Family-Love
Thy cruel Patriarchal pride
Planting thy Family alone,
Destroying all the World beside.

21
A mans worst enemies are those
Of his own house & family;
And he who makes his law a curse,
By his own law shall surely die.

22
In my Exchanges every Land
Shall walk, & mine in every Land,
Mutual shall build Jerusalem:
Both heart in heart & hand in hand.

If Humility is Christianity; you O Jews are the true Christians; If your tradition that Man contained in his Limbs all Animals is True & they were separated from him by cruel Sacrifices: and when compell'd to cruel Sacrifices had brought Humanity into a Feminine Tabernacle, in the loins of Abraham & David: the Lamb of God, the Saviour became apparent on Earth as the Prophets had foretold? The Return of Israel is a Return to Mental Sacrifice & War. Take up the Cross O Israel & follow Jesus.

Jerusalem.

Chap: 2.

Every ornament of perfection. and every labour of love,
In all the Garden of Eden. & in all the golden mountains
Was become an envied horror. and a remembrance of jealousy
And every Act a Crime. and Albion the punisher & judge

5   And Albion spoke from his secret seat and said

All these ornaments are crimes, they are made by the labours
Of loves: of unnatural consanguinities and friendships
Horrid to think of. when enquired deeply into; and all
These hills & valleys are accursed witnesses of Sin
10   I therefore condense them into solid rocks. stedfast!
A foundation and certainty and demonstrative truth:
That Man be separate from Man, & here I plant my seat.

Cold snows drifted around him: ice coverd his loins around
He sat by Tyburns brook, and underneath his heel. shot up
15   A deadly Tree, he nam'd it Moral Virtue, and the Law
Of God who dwells in Chaos hidden from the human sight.

The Tree spread over him its cold shadows, (Albion groand)
They bent down, they felt the earth and again enrooting
Shot into many a Tree! an endless labyrinth of woe!

20   From willing sacrifice of Self, to sacrifice of (miscall'd) Enemies
For Atonement: Albion began to erect twelve Altars,
Of rough unhewn rocks. before the Potters Furnace
He nam'd them Justice, and Truth. And Albions Sons
Must have become the first Victims; being the first transgressors
25   But they fled to the mountains to seek ransom: building A Strong
Fortification against the Divine Humanity and Mercy,
27   In Shame & Jealousy to annihilate Jerusalem.

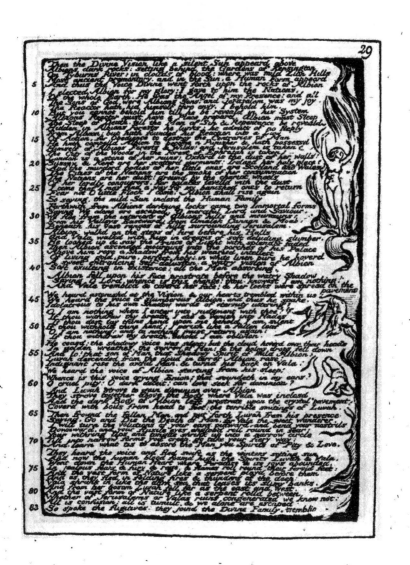

Then the Divine Vision like a silent Sun appeard above
Albions dark rocks: setting behind the Gardens of Kensington
On Tyburns River, in clouds of blood: where was mild Zion Hills
Most ancient promontory, and in his Human Face appeard
Albion Giant, upon the rocks upon the Nations

So spoke the Righteous: they joind the Divine Family, trembling

And the Two that escaped; were the Emanation of Los & his
Spectre: for whereever the Emanation goes, the Spectre
Attends her as her Guard, & Los's Emanation is named
Enitharmon, & his Spectre is named Urthona: they knew
Not where to flee: they had been on a visit to Albions Children
And they strove to weave a Shadow of the Emanation
To hide themselves: weeping & lamenting for the Vegetation
Of Albions Children: fleeing thro Albions vales in streams of gore

Being not irritated by insult: bearing insulting benevolences
They percieved that corporeal friends are spiritual enemies
They saw the Sexual Religion in its embryon Uncircumcision
And the Divine hand was upon them bearing them thro darkness
Back safe to their Humanity as doves to their windows:
Therefore the Sons of Eden praise Urthonas Spectre in Songs
Because he kept the Divine Vision in time of trouble.

They wept & trembled: & Los put forth his hand, & took them in
Into his Bosom: from which Albion shrunk in dismal pain.
Rending the fibres of Brotherhood & in Feminine Allegories
Inclosing Los: but the Divine Vision appeard with Los
Following Albion into his Central Void among his Oaks.

And Los prayed and said. O Divine Saviour arise
Upon the Mountains of Albion as in ancient time. Behold!
The Cities of Albion seek thy face, London groans in pain
From Hill to Hill & the Thames laments along the Valleys
The little Villages of Middlesex & Surrey hunger & thirst
The Twentyeight Cities of Albion stretch their hands to thee:
Because of the Opressors of Albion in every City & Village.
They mock at the Labourers limbs: they mock at his starvd Children.
They buy his Daughters that they may have power to sell his Sons:
They compell the Poor to live upon a crust of bread by soft mild arts:
They reduce the Man to want: then give with pomp & ceremony.
The praise of Jehovah is chaunted from lips of hunger & thirst:
Humanity knows not of Sex: wherefore are Sexes in Beulah?
In Beulah the Female lets down her beautiful Tabernacle:
Which the Male enters magnificent between her Cherubim:
And becomes One with her mingling condensing in Self-love
The Rocky Law of Condemnation & double Generation, & Death.
Albion hath enterd the State Satan! Be permanent O State!
And be thou for ever accursed! that Albion may arise again:
And Luvah hath drawn the Curtains around Albion in Vala's bosom
The Dead awake to Generation! Arise O Lord, & rend the Veil!

So Los in lamentations followd Albion. Albion coverd.

His

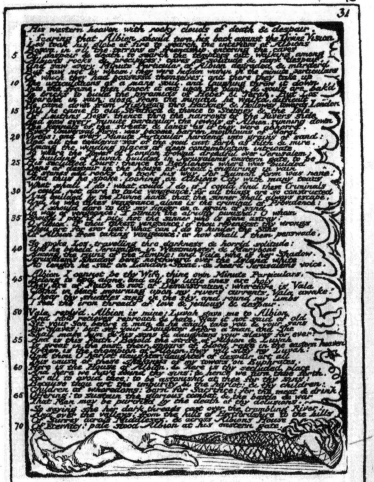

31

Leaning against the pillars, & his disease rose from his skirts
Upon the Precipice he stood: ready to fall into Non-Entity.

5 Los was all astonishment & terror: he trembled sitting on the Stone
Of Loudon: but the interiors of Albions fibres & nerves were hidden
From Los: astonishd he beheld only the petrified surfaces:
He saw his Furnaces in ruins, for Los is the Demon of the Furnaces:
He saw also the Four Points of Albion reversd inwards
Nam'd Lone, Summer & Autumn & Winter, & his iron Maker & his Bellows
10 Upon the valleys of Middlesex, Shouting loud for aid Divine.

In stern defiance came from Albions bosom Hand, Hyle, Koban,
Gwantak, Peachy, Brereton, Slaud, Huttn, Skofeld, Kock, Kotope
Bowen: Albions Sons; they bore him a golden couch into the porch
And on the Couch reposd his limbs, trembling from the bloody field,
15 Rearing their Druid Patriarchal rocky Temples around his limbs.

(All things begin & end, in Albions Ancient Druid Rocky Shore.)

Turning his back to the Divine Vision. his Spectrous
Chaos before his face appeard: an Unformed Memory;

Then spoke the Spectrous Chaos to Albion darkning cold
From the back & loins where dwell the Spectrous Dead

5 I am your Rational Power O Albion & that Human Form
You call Divine, is but a Worm seventy inches long
That creeps forth in a night & is dried in the mornings sun
In fortuitous concourse of memorys accumulated & lost
It plows the Earth in its own conceit, it overwhelms the Hills
10 Beneath its winding labyrinths. till a stone of the brook
Stops it in midst of its pride among its hills & rivers
Battersea & Chelsea mourn. London & Canterbury tremble
Their place shall not be found as the wind passes over
The ancient Cities of the Earth remove as a traveller
15 And shall Albions Cities remain when I pass over them
With my deluge of forgotten remembrances over the tablet

So spoke the Spectre to Albion. he is the Great Selfhood
Satan. Worshipd as God by the Mighty Ones of the Earth
Having a white Dot calld a Center from which branches out
20 A Circle in continual gyrations. this became a Heart
From which sprang numerous branches varying their motions
Producing many Heads three or seven or ten, & hands & feet
Innumerable at will of the unfortunate contemplator
Who became his food. such is the way of the Devouring Power
25 And this is the cause of the appearance in the frowning Chaos
Albions Emanation which he had hidden in Jealousy
Appeard now in the frowning Chaos prolific upon the Chaos
Reflecting back to Albion in Sexual Reasoning Hermaphroditic
Albion spoke. Who art thou that appearest in gloomy pomp
30 Involving the Divine Vision in colours of autumn ripeness
I never saw thee till this time. nor beheld life abstracted
Nor darkness immingled with light on my furrowd field
Whence camest thou? who art thou O loveliest? the Divine Vision
Is as nothing before thee. faded is all life and joy

35 Vala replied in clouds of tears Albions garment embracing

I was a City & a Temple built by Albions Children!
I was a Garden planted with beauty I allured on hill & valley
The River of Life to flow against my walls & among my trees
Vala was Albions Bride & Wife in great Eternity
40 The loveliest of the daughters of Eternity when it day-break
Emanated from Luvah over the Towers of Jerusalem
And in her Courts among her little Children offering up
The Sacrifice of fanatic love! why loved I Jerusalem!
Why was I one with her embracing in the Vision of Jesus
45 Wherefore did I loving create love, which never yet
Immingled God & Man. when thou & I. hid the Divine Vision
In cloud of secret gloom which behold involve me round about
Know me now Albion: look upon me I alone am Beauty
The Imaginative Human Form is but a breathing of Vala
50 I breathe him forth into the Heaven from my secret Cave
Born of the Woman to obey the Woman O Albion the mighty
52 For the Divine appearance is Brotherhood. but I am Love

Elevate into the Region of Brotherhood with my red fires

Art thou Vala? replied Albion. image of my repose
O how I tremble! how my members pour down milky fear!
A dewy garment covers me all over. all manhood is gone!
5 At thy word & at thy look death enrobes me about
From head to feet. a garment of death & eternal fear
Is not that Sun thy husband & that Moon thy glimmering Veil;
Are not the Stars of heaven thy Children; art thou not Babylon:
Art thou Nature Mother of all! is Jerusalem thy Daughter.
10 Why have thou elevate inward: O dweller of outward chambers
From Eart & cave beneath the Moon dim region of death
Where I laid my Plow in the hot noon. where my hot team fed
Where implements of War are forged. the Plow to go over the Nations
In pain girding me round like a rib of iron in heaven! O Vala
15 In Eternity they neither marry nor are given in marriage
Albion the high Cliff of the Atlantic is become a barren Land

Los. stood at his Anvil: he heard the contentions of Vala
He heaved his thundring Bellows upon the valleys of Middlesex
He opend his Furnaces before Vala, then Albion frownd in anger
20 On his Rock: are yet the Starry Heavens were fled away
From his awful Members. and thus Los cried aloud
To the Sons of Albion & to Hand the eldest Son of Albion

I hear the screech of Childbirth loud pealing. & the groans
Of Death in Albions clouds dreadful utterd over all the Earth
25 What may Man be? who can tell! but what may Woman be?
To have power over Man from Cradle to corruptible Grave.
There is a Throne in every Man. it is the Throne of God
This Woman has claimd as her own & Man is no more!
Albion is the Tabernacle of Vala & her Temple
30 And not the Tabernacle & Temple of the Most High
O Albion why wilt thou Create a Female Will?
To hide the most evident God in a hidden covert. even
In the shadows of a Woman & a secluded Holy Place
That we may pry after him as after a stolen treasure
35 Hidden among the Dead & mured up from the paths of life
Hand! art thou not Reuben enrooting thyself into Bashan
Till thou remainest a vaporous Shadow in a Void! O Merlin!
Unknown among the Dead where never before Existence came
Is this the Female Will O ye lovely Daughters of Albion. To
40 Converse concerning Weight & Distance in the Wilds of Newton & Locke

So Los spoke standing on Mam-Tor looking over Europe & Asia
The Graves thunder beneath his feet from Ireland to Japan

Reuben. slept in Bashan like one dead in the valley
Cut off from Albions mountains & from all the Earths summits
45 Between Succoth & Zaretan beside the Stone of Bohan
While the Daughters of Albion divided Luvah into three Bodies
Los bended his Masculy down to the Earth. then sent him over
Jordan to the Land of the Hittite: every one that saw him
Fled! they fled at his horrible Form: they hid in caves
50 And dens. they looked on one-another & became what they beheld

Reuben returnd to Bashan. in despair he slept on the Stone.
Then Gwendolen divided into Rahab & Tirza in Twelve Portions
Los rolled his Eyes into two narrow circles. then sent him
Over Jordan: all terrified fled: they became what they beheld
55 If Perceptive Organs vary: Objects of Perception seem to vary:
If the Perceptive Organs close: their Objects seem to close also:
Consider this O mortal Man! O worm of sixty winters said Los
58 Consider Sexual Organization & hide thee in the dust.

From the Divine hand found the Two Limits, Satan and Adam,
In Albions bosom: for in every Human bosom those Limits stand.
And the Divine voice came from the Furnaces, as multitudes without
Number! the voices of the innumerable multitudes of Eternity.
And the appearance of a Man was seen in the Furnaces;
Saving those who have sinned from the punishment of the Law,
(In pity of the punisher whose state is eternal death,)
And keeping them from Sin by the mild counsels of his love

Albion goes to Eternal Death: In Me all Eternity.
Must pass thro' condemnation, and awake beyond the Grave:
No individual can keep these Laws, for they are death
To every energy of man, and forbid the springs of life;
Albion hath entered the State Satan! Be permanent O State!
And be thou for ever accursed! that Albion may arise again:
And be thou created into a State! I go forth to Create
States: to deliver Individuals evermore! Amen.

So spoke the voice from the Furnaces, descending into Non-Entity

LIBRARY
OF THE
UNIVERSITY
OF
CALIFORNIA.

Reuben returnd to his place, in vain he sought beautiful Tirzah
For his Eyelids were harrowd, & his Nostrils scented the ground
And Sixty Winters Los raged in the Divisions of Reuben:
Building the Moon of Ulro, plank by plank & rib by rib
Reuben slept in the Cave of Adam, and Los folded his Tongue
Between Lips of mire & clay, then sent him over Jordan
To the Land of the Hittite: [...] the Soul Doubt is my food day & night—
All that beheld him fled howling and gnawed their tongues
For pain: they became what they beheld, in reasoning Reuben ret
To Heshbon, disconsolate he walkd thro Moab & he stood
Before the Furnaces of Los in a horrible dreamful slumber,
On Mount Gilead looking toward Gilgal: and Los bended
His Ear in a spiral circle outward; then sent him over Jordan.

The Seven Nations fled before him they became what they beheld
Hand, Hyle & Coban fled: they became what they beheld
Gwantock & Peachy hid in Damascus beneath Mount Lebanon
Brereton & Slade in Egypt. Hutton & Skofield & Kox
Fled over Chaldea in terror in pains in every nerve
Kotope & Bowen became what they beheld, fleeing over the Earth
And the Twelve Female Emanations fled with them agonizing

Jerusalem trembled seeing her Children drivn by Los's Hammer
In the visions of the dreams of Beulah on the edge of Non-Entity
Hand stood between Reuben & Merlin, as the Reasoning Spectre
Stands between the Vegetative Man & his Immortal Imagination

And the Four Zoa's clouded rage East & West & North & South
They change their situations, in the Universal Man.
Albion groans, he sees the Elements divide before his face.
And England who is Brittannia divided into Jerusalem & Vala
And Urizen assumes the East, Luvah assumes the South
In his dark Spectre ravening from his open Sepulcher

And the Four Zoa's who are the Four Eternal Senses of Man
Became Four Elements separating from the Limbs of Albion
These are their names in the Vegetative Generation

And Accident & Chance were found hidden in Length Breadth & Highth
And they divided into Four ravening deathlike Forms
Fairies & Genii & Nymphs & Gnomes of the Elements.
These are States Permanently Fixed by the Divine Power

The Atlantic Continent sunk round Albions cliffy shore
And the Sea poured in amain upon the Giants of Albion
As Los bended the Senses of Reuben Reuben is Merlin
Exploring the Three States of Ulro; Creation; Redemption. &

And many of the Eternal Ones laughed after their manner

Have you known the Judgment that is arisen among the
Zoa's of Albion? where a Man dare hardly to embrace
His own Wife, for the terrors of Chastity that they call
By the name of Morality. their Daughters govern all
In hidden deceit! they are Vegetable only fit for burning
Art & Science cannot exist but by Naked Beauty displayd

Then those in Great Eternity who contemplate on Death
Said thus. What seems to Be: Is: To those to whom
It seems to Be, & is productive of the most dreadful
Consequences to those to whom it seems to Be: even of
Torments, Despair, Eternal Death; but the Divine Mercy
Steps beyond and Redeems Man in the Body of Jesus Amen
And Length Breadth Highth again Obey the Divine Vision Hallelujah

I feel my Spectre rising upon me. Albion, arouse thyself!
Why dost thou thunder with frozen Spectrous wrath against us?
The Spectre is, in Giant Man; insane, and most deform'd.
Thou wilt certainly provoke my Spectre against thine in fury!
He has a Sepulcher hewn out of a Rock Ready for thee:
And a Death of Eight thousand years forged by thyself, upon
Soul! Sunk in reasonings cold, to him we must submit.
Can I persuade thee, and if I persuade to forbid work, and

So Los spoke. But when he saw blue death in Albions feet
Again he join'd the Divine Body, following merciful;
While Albion fled more indignant; revengeful covering

His face and bosom with petrific hardness, and his hands
And feet, lest any should enter his bosom & embrace
His hidden heart; his Emanation wept & trembled within him:
Uttering not his jealousy, but hiding it as with
5 Iron and steel, dark and opake. with clouds & tempests brooding:
His strong limbs shudderd upon his mountains high and dark.

Turning from Universal Love petrific as he went,
His cold against the warmth of Eden rag'd with loud
Thunders of deadly war (the fever of the human soul)
10 Fires and clouds of rolling smoke; but mild the Saviour follow'd him,
Displaying the Eternal Vision! the Divine Similitude!
In loves and tears of brothers, sisters, sons, fathers, and friends
Which if Man ceases to behold, he ceases to exist:

Saying. Albion! Our wars are wars of life, & wounds of love,
15 With intellectual spears, & long winged arrows of thought:
Mutual in one anothers love and wrath all renewing
We live as One Man; for contracting our infinite senses
We behold multitude; or expanding we behold as one,
As One Man all the Universal Family; and that One Man
20 We call Jesus the Christ; and he in us, and we in him,
Live in perfect harmony in Eden the land of life,
Giving, receiving, and forgiving each others trespasses.
He is the Good shepherd, he is the Lord and master:
He is the Shepherd of Albion, he is all in all,
25 In Eden: in the garden of God: and in heavenly Jerusalem.
If we have offended, forgive us, take not vengeance against us

Thus speaking; the Divine Family follow Albion:
I see them in the Vision of God upon my pleasant valleys.

I behold London; a Human awful wonder of God!
30 He says: Return, Albion, return! I give myself for thee:
My Streets are my, Ideas of Imagination.
Awake Albion, awake! and let us awake up together.
My Houses are Thoughts: my Inhabitants; Affections,
The children of my thoughts, walking within my blood-vessels,
35 Shut from my nervous form, which sleeps upon the verge of Beulah
In dreams of darkness, while my vegetating blood in veiny pipes,
Rolls dreadful thro' the Furnaces of Los, and the Mills of Satan.
For Albions sake, and for Jerusalem thy Emanation
I give myself, and these my brethren give themselves for Albion.

40 So spoke London, immortal Guardian! I heard in Lambeths shades:
In Felpham I heard and saw the Visions of Albion
I write in South Molton Street, what I both see and hear
In regions of Humanity, in Londons opening streets.

I see thee awful Parent Land in light, behold I see!
45 Verulam! Canterbury! venerable parent of men,
Generous immortal Guardian golden clad! for Cities
Are Men, fathers of multitudes, and Rivers & Mountains
Are also Men; every thing is Human, mighty! sublime!
In every bosom a Universe expands, as wings
50 Let down at will around, and called the Universal Tent.
York, crown'd with loving kindness. Edinburgh, cloth'd
With fortitude as with a garment of immortal texture
Woven in looms of Eden, in spiritual deaths of mighty men
Who give themselves, in Golgotha, Victims to Justice; where
55 There is in Albion a Gate of precious stones and gold
Seen only by Emanations, by vegetations viewless,
Bending across the road of Oxford Street; it from Hyde Park
To Tyburns deathful shades, admits the wandering souls
59 Of multitudes who die from Earth: this Gate cannot be found

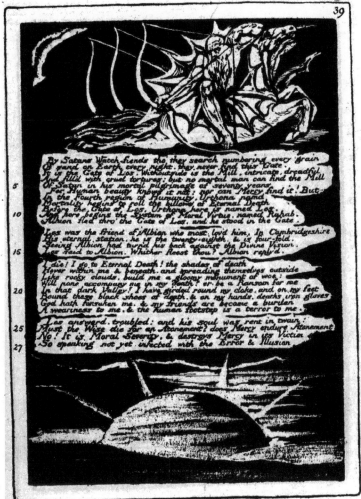

By Satans Watch-fiends tho' they search numbering every grain
Of sand on Earth every night, they never find this Gate.
It is the Gate of Los. Withoutside is the Mill, intricate, dreadful
And fill'd with cruel tortures; but no mortal man can find the Mill
Of Satan in his mortal pilgrimage of seventy years
For Human beauty knows it not: nor can Mercy find it! But
In the Fourth region of Humanity, Urthona named
Mortality begins to roll the billows of Eternal Death
Before the Gate of Los. Urthona here is named Los
And here begins the System of Moral Virtue, named Rahab.
Albion fled thro' the Gate of Los, and he stood in the Gate.

Los was the friend of Albion who most lov'd him, In Cambridgeshire
His eternal station, he is the twenty-eighth, & is four-fold.
Seeing Albion had turn'd his back against the Divine Vision,
Los said to Albion, Whither fleest thou? Albion repli'd

I die! I go to Eternal Death! the shades of death
Hover within me & beneath, and spreading themselves outside
Like rocky clouds, build me a gloomy monument of woe;
Will none accompany me in my death? or be a Ransom for me
In that dark Valley? I have girded round my cloke, and on my feet
Bound these black shoes of death, & on my hands, deaths iron gloves
God hath forsaken me, & my friends are become a burden
A weariness to me, & the Human footstep is a terror to me.

Los answerd, troubled: and his soul was rent in twain:
Must the Wise die for an Atonement? does Mercy endure Atonement?
No! It is Moral Severity, & destroys Mercy in its Victim
So speaking, not yet infected with the Error & Illusion

Los shudderd at beholding Albion, for his disease
Arose upon him pale and ghastly: and he called around
The Friends of Albion; trembling at the sight of Eternal Death
The four appeard with their Emanations in fiery
Chariots: black their fires roll beholding Albions House of Eternity
Damp couch the flames beneath and silent, sick, stand shuddering
Before the Porch of sixteen pillars: weeping every one
Descended and fell down upon their knees round Albions knees
Swearing the Oath of God! with awful voice of thunders round
Upon the hills & valleys. and the cloudy Oath rolld far and wide

Albion is sick! said every Valley, every mournful Hill
And every River: our brother Albion is sick to death.
He hath leagued himself with robbers: he hath studied the arts
Of unbelief! Envy hovers over him; his Friends are his abhorrence:
Those who give their lives for him are despised:
Those who devour his soul, are taken into his bosom:
To destroy his Emanation is their intention:
Arise! awake O Friends of the Giant Albion
They have perswaded him of horrible falshoods,
They have sown errors over all his fruitful fields;

The Twenty-four heard! they came trembling on watry chariots.
Borne by the living Creatures of the third procession
Of Human Majesty, the Living Creatures wept aloud as they
Went along Albions roads, till they arrived at Albions House.

O! how the torments of Eternal Death, waited on Man:
And the loud-rending bars of the Creation ready to burst:
That the wide world might fly from its hinges, & the immortal mansion
Of Man, for ever be possessed by monsters of the deeps:
And Man himself become a Fiend, wrapd in an endless curse,
Consuming and consumd for-ever in flames of Moral Justice.

For had the Body of Albion falln down, and from its dreadful ruins
Let loose the enormous Spectre on the darkness of the deep,
At enmity with the Merciful & fill'd with devouring fire,
A nether-world must have recievd the foul enormous spirit,
Under pretence of Moral Virtue, filld with Revenge and Law.
There to eternity chaind down, and issuing in red flames
And curses, with his mighty arms brandishd against the heavens
Breathing cruelty blood & vengeance, gnashing his teeth with pain
Torn, with black storms, & ceaseless torrents of his own consuming fire:
Within his breast his mighty Sons chaind down & filld with cursings:
And his dark Eon, that once fair crystal form divinely clear:
Within his ribs producing serpents whose souls are flames of fire.
But, glory to the Merciful-One, for he is of tender mercies!
And the Divine Family wept over him as One Man.

And these the Twenty-four in whom the Divine Family
Appeard; and they were One in Him. A Human Vision!
Human Divine, Jesus the Saviour, blessed for ever and ever.

Selsey, true friend! who afterwards submitted to be devourd
By the waves of Despair, whose Emanation rose above
The flood, and was named Chichester, lovely mild & gentle! Lo!
Her lambs bleat to the sea-fowls cry, lamenting still for Albion.

Submitting to be calld the son of Los the terrible vision:
Winchester stood devoting himself for Albion: his tents
Outspread with abundant riches, and his Emanations
Submitting to be calld Enitharmons daughters, and be born
In vegetable mould: created by the Hammer and Loom
In Bowlahoola & Allamanda where the Dead wail night & day.

(I call them by their English names: English, the rough basement.
Los built the stubborn structure of the Language, acting against
Albions melancholy, who must have been a Dumb despair.)

Gloucester and Exeter and Salisbury and Bristol; and benevolent

Bath

Bath, who is Legions: he is the Seventh, the physician and
The poisoner: the best and worst in Heaven and Hell:
Whose Spectre first assimilated with Luvah in Albions mountains
A triple octave he took, to reduce Jerusalem to twelve,
To cast Jerusalem forth upon the wilds to Poplar & Bow:
To Malden & Canterbury in the delights of cruelty:
The Shuttles of death sing in the sky to Islington & Pancrass
Round Marybone to Tyburns river, weaving black melancholy as a net,
And despair as meshes closely wove over the west of Albion,
As the Sun sets in misery, they murmur, they go no more,
Los reads the Signal of the Last Judgment ...
...
There is a Grain of Sand in Lambeth that Satan cannot find
Nor can his Watch Fiends find it: tis translucent & has many Angles
But he who finds it will find Oothoons palace, for within
Opening into Beulah every angle is a lovely heaven
But should the Watch Fiends find it, they would call it Sin
And lay its Heavens & their inhabitants in blood of punishment
Here Jerusalem & Vala were hid in soft slumberous repose
Hid from the terrible East, shut up in the South & West.

The Twentyeight trembled in Deaths dark caves, in cold despair
They kneeld around the Couch of Death in deep humiliation
And tortures of self condemnation while their Spectres ragd within.
The Four Zoa's in terrible combustion clouded rage
Drinking the shuddering fears & loves of Albions Families
Destroying by selfish affections the things that they most admire
Drinking & eating, & pitying & weeping, as at a trajic scene.
The soul drinks murder & revenge, & applauds its own holiness

They saw Albion endeavouring to destroy their Emanations.

Each Man is in
his Spectres power
Untill the arrival
of that hour,
When his Humanity
awake
And cast his Spectre
into the Lake

Showing Albion is
the power of his Spect

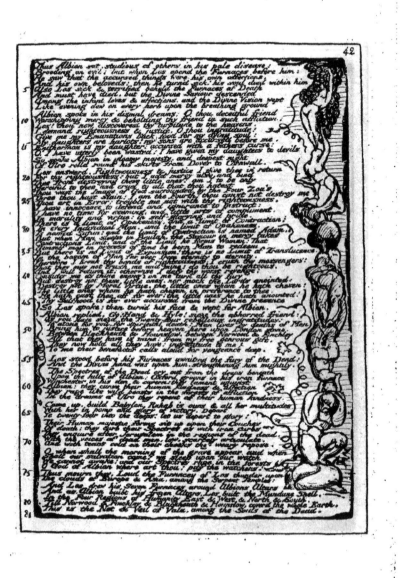

Thus Albion sat, studious of others in his pale disease:
Brooding on evil: but when Los opend the Furnaces before him:
He saw that the accursed things were his own affections,
And his own beloveds; then he turnd sick! his soul died within him
Also Los sick & terrified beheld the Furnaces of Death
And must have died, but the Divine Saviour descended
Among the infant loves & affections, and the Divine Vision wept
Like evening dew on every herb upon the breathing ground

Albion spoke in his dismal dreams: O thou deceitful friend
Worshipping mercy & beholding thy Friend in such affliction:
Los! thou now discoverest thy turpitude to the heavens.
I demand righteousness & justice. O thou ingratitude:
Give me my Emanations back food for my dying soul!
My daughters are harlots! my sons are accursed before me.
Enitharmon is my daughter: accursed with a fathers curse!
O! I have utterly been wasted! I have given my daughters to devils

So spoke Albion in gloomy majesty, and deepest night
Of Ulro rolld round his skirts from Dover to Cornwall.

Los answerd. Righteousness & justice I give thee in return
For thy righteousness! but I add mercy also, and bind
Thee from destroying these little ones: am I to be only
Merciful to thee and cruel to all that thou hatest
Thou wast the Image of God surrounded by the Four Zoa's
Three thou hast slain! I am the Fourth: thou canst not destroy me.
Thou art in Error; trouble me not with thy righteousness.
I have innocence to defend and ignorance to instruct:
I have no time for seeming; and little arts of compliment,
In morality and virtue: in self-glorying and pride.
There is a limit of Opakeness, and a limit of Contraction:
In every Individual Man, and the limit of Opakeness,
Is named Satan: and the limit of Contraction is named Adam.
But when Man sleeps in Beulah, the Saviour in mercy takes
Contractions Limit, and of the Limit he forms Woman: That
Himself may in process of time be born Man to redeem
But there is no Limit of Expansion! there is no Limit of Translucence.
In the bosom of Man for ever from eternity to eternity.
Therefore I break thy bonds of righteousness; I crucify thy messengers:
And they are not: for I the Divine Body of the Lord am not
As thou dost Nature; otherwise I dust with all thy trespasses:
Would destroy me, and because I live I put forth my mercy & love
But destroy not thy own energy: on me cast not thy self abhorrence
And thus unveild thou art the Image of God the Lord appointed
The Little ones I love: but these I cannot save: it is in order
No Human Form but only a Fibrous Vegetation a Polypus
Of soft affections without Thought or Vision must be born: unpriented.
So Los spoke: then turnd his face & wept for Albion

Albion replied, O Hand & Hyle! seize the abhorred Friend:
As you have seiz'd the Twenty-four rebellious ingratitudes;
To atone for you, for spiritual death! Man lives by deaths of Men
Bring him to justice before heaven here upon London stone,
Between Blackheath & Hounslow, between Norwood & Finchley
All that they have is mine: from my free genrous gift,
They now hold all they have: ingratitude to me,
To me their benefactor calls aloud for vengeance deep.

Los stood before his Furnaces awaiting the fury of the Dead:
And the Divine hand was upon him, strengthening him mightily.

The Spectres of the Dead cry out from the deeps beneath
Upon the hills of Albion: Oxford groans in his iron furnace
Winchester in his den & cavern; they lament against
Albion: they curse their human kindness & affection
They put forth their spectres, to the hungry wind & storm
In the dreams of Ulro they repent of their human kindness.

Come up build Babylon, Rahab is ours & all her multitudes
With her in pomp and glory of victory. Depart
Ye twenty-four into the deeps! let us depart to glory.

Their Human majestic Forms sit up upon their Couches
Of death: they curb their Spectres as with iron curbs
They enquire after Jerusalem in the regions of the dead,
With the voices of despair across the disorganised
And with tears cold on their cheeks they weary repose

O when shall the morning of the grave appear, and when
Shall our salvation come? we sleep upon our watch
We cannot awake! and our Spectres rage in the forests
O God of Albion where art thou! pity the watchers.

Thus mourn they Loud the Furnaces of Los thunder upon
The clouds of Europe & Asia, among the Serpent Temples!
And Los drew his Seven Furnaces around Albions Altars
And as Albion built his frozen Altars, Los built the Mundane Shell,
In the Four Regions of Humanity East & West & North & South,
Till Norwood & Finchley & Blackheath & Hounslow, coverd the whole Earth.
This is the Net & Veil of Vala, among the Souls of the Dead.

They saw their Wheels rising up poisonous against Albion
Urizen. cold & scientific: Luvah, pitying & weeping
Tharmas, indolent & sullen: Urthona, doubting & despairing
Victims to one another & dreadfully plotting against each other
5   To prevent Albion walking about in the Four Complexions.

They saw America clos'd out by the Oaks of the western shore;
And Tharmas dash'd on the Rocks of the Altars of Victims in Mexico.
If we are wrathful Albion will destroy Jerusalem with rooty Groves
10   If we are merciful, ourselves must suffer destruction on his Oaks!
Why should we enter into our Spectres, to behold our own corruptions
O God of Albion descend! deliver Jerusalem from the Oaken Groves!

Then Los grew furious raging: Why stand we here trembling around
Calling on God for help; and not ourselves in whom God dwells
15   Stretching a hand to save the falling Man: are we not Four
Beholding Albion upon the Precipice ready to fall into Non-Entity:
Seeing these Heavens & Hells conglobing in the Void. Heavens over Hells
Brooding in holy hypocritic lust, whose hands industrious in the cries
of death, building Heavens Twenty-seven-fold.
20   Swelld & bloated General Forms, repeated to Deformity
[...]

80   So Los spoke: Pale they stood around the House of Death:
In the midst of temptations & despair: among the rooted Oaks:
82   Among reared Rocks of Albions Sons, at length they rose —— With

With one accord in love sublime, & as on Cherubs wings
They Albion surround with kindest violence to bear him back
Against his will thro Los's Gate to Eden: Four-fold; loud!
Their Wings waving over the bottomless Immense: to bear
5 Their awful charge back to his native home: but Albion dark,
Repugnant; rolld his Wheels backward into Non-Entity
Loud roll the Starry Wheels of Albion into the World of Death;
And all the Gate of Los, clouded with clouds redounding from
Albions dread Wheels, stretching out spaces immense between
10 That every little particle of light & air, became Opake
Black & immense, a Rock of difficulty & a Cliff
Of black despair; that the immortal Wings labourd against
Cliff after cliff, & over Valleys of despair & death:
The narrow Sea between Albion & the Atlantic Continent:
15 Its waves of pearl became a boundless Ocean bottomless,
Of grey obscurity, filld with clouds & rocks & whirling waters
And Albions Sons ascending & descending in the horrid Void.

But as the Will must not be bended but in the day of Divine
Power: silent calm & motionless, in the mid-air sublime,
20 The Family Divine hover around the darkend Albion.—

Such is the nature of the Ulro: that whatever enters:
Becomes Sexual, & is Created, and Vegetated, and Born,
From Hyde Park spread their vegetating roots beneath Albion
In dreadful pain the Spectrous Uncircumcised Vegetation,
25 Forming a Sexual Machine: an Aged Virgin Form,
In Erins Land toward the north, joint after joint & burning,
In love & jealousy immingled & calling it Religion
And feeling the damps of death they with one accord delegated Los
Conjuring him by the Highest that he should Watch over them
30 Till Jesus shall appear: & they gave their power to Los
Naming him the Spirit of Prophesy, calling him Elijah

Strucken with Albions disease they become what they behold;
They assimilate with Albion in pity & compassion;
Their Emanations return not: their Spectres rage in the Deep
35 The Slumbers of Death came over them around the Couch of Death
Before the Gate of Los & in the depths of Non Entity
Among the Furnaces of Los: among the Oaks of Albion.

Man is adjoind to Man by his Emanative portion:
Who is Jerusalem in every individual Man: and her
40 Shadow is Vala, builded by the Reasoning power in Man
O search & see: turn your eyes inward: open O thou World
Of Love & Harmony in Man: expand thy ever lovely Gates,

They wept into the deeps a little space at length was heard
44 The voice of Bath, faint as the voice of the Dead in the House of
Death.

Bath, healing City! whose wisdom in midst of Poetic
Fervor; mild spoke thro' the Western Porch, in soft gentle tears

O Albion mildest Son of Eden! closd is thy Western Gate
Brothers of Eternity! this Man whose great example
We all admird & lovd, whose all benevolent countenance, seen
In Eden, in lovely Jerusalem, drew even from envy
The tear; and the confession of honesty, open & undisguisd
From mistrust and suspicion. The Man is himself become
A piteous example of oblivion. To such the Sons
Of Eden, that however great and glorious; however loving
And merciful the Individuality; however high
Our palaces and cities, and however fruitful are our fields
In Selfhood, we are nothing: but fade away in mornings breath.
Our mildness is nothing: the greatest mildness we can use
Is incapable and nothing! none but the Lamb of God can heal
This dread disease: none but Jesus! O Lord descend and save!
Albions Western Gate is closd, his death is coming apace!
Jesus alone can save him; for alas we none can know
How soon his lot may be our own. When Africa in sleep
Rose in the night of Beulah, and bound down the Sun & Moon
His friends cut his strong chains, & overwhelmd his dark
Machines in fury & destruction, and the Man reviving repented
He wept before his wrathful brethren, thankful & considerate
For their well timed wrath. But Albions sleep is not
Like Africas; and his machines are woven with his life
Nothing but mercy can save him! nothing but mercy interposing
Lest he should slay Jerusalem in his fearful jealousy
O God descend! gather our brethren, deliver Jerusalem
But that we may not conet no allies of the friendly spirit
Orford, take thou these leaves of the Tree of Life! with eloquence
That thy immortal tongue inspires; present them to Albion:
Perhaps he may recieve them, offerd from thy loved hands.

So spoke, unheard by Albion, the merciful Son of Heaven
To those whose Western Gates were open, as they stood weeping
Around Albion: but Albion heard him not; obdurate! hard!
He frownd on all his Friends, counting them enemies in his sorrow

And the Seventeen conjoining with Bath, the Seventh:
In whom the other Ten shone manifest, a Divine Vision!
Assimilated and embracd Eternal Death for Albions sake.

And these the names of the Eighteen combining with those Ten

Bath, mild Physician of Eternity, mysterious power
Whose springs are unsearchable & knowledg infinite
Hereford, ancient Guardian of Wales, whose hands
Builded the mountain palaces of Eden, stupendous works!
Lincoln, Durham & Carlisle Councellors of Los
And Ely, Scribe of Los, whose pen no other hand
Dare touch! Oxford, immortal Bard! with eloquence
Divine, he went over Albion, speaking the words of God
In mild perswasion: bringing leaves of the Tree of Life.

Thou art in Error Albion, the Land of Ulro:
One Error not removd, will destroy a human Soul
Repose in Beulahs night, till the Error is removd
Reason not on both sides. Repose upon our bosoms
Till the Plow of Jehovah, and the Harrow of Shaddai
Have passed over the Dead, to awake the Dead to Judgment.
But Albion turnd away refusing comfort.

Oxford trembled while he spoke, then faintd in the arms
Of Norwich, Peterboro, Rochester, Chester awful, Worcester,
Litchfield, Saint Davids, Landaff, Asaph, Bangor, Sodor,
Bowing their heads devoted: and the Furnaces of Los
Began to rage, thundering loud the storms began to roar
Upon the Furnaces, and loud the Furnaces rebellow beneath

And these the Four in whom the twenty-four appeard four-fold:
Verulam. London. York, Edinburgh, mourning one towards another
Alas! — the time will come, when a mans worst enemies
Shall be those of his own house and family: in a Religion
Of Generation, to destroy by Sin and Atonement, happy Jerusalem
The Bride and Wife of the Lamb, O God thou art Not an Avenger

From Camberwell to Highgate where the mighty Thames shudders along,
Where Hounslow spreads a plain: where Islington & Pancras & Paddington
Soon turn forth from Albions Loins in bloody veins: in rivers
Of blood over Europe: a Vegetating Root in grinding pain,
Animating the Dragon Temple: soon to became that Holy Fiend
The Wicker Man of Scandinavia in which cruelly consumed
The Captives reard to heaven howl in flames among the stars:
Loud the cries of War on the Rhine & Danube, with Albions Sons,
Away from Beulahs hills & vales break forth the Souls of the Dead,
With cymbal, trumpet, clarion; & the scythed chariots of Britain.

And the Veil of Vala, is composed of the Spectres of the Dead

Hark! the mournful cries of Luvah with the Sons of Albion
Dark! the hoped-for terrible wonder! that the Punisher
Mingles with his Victim Spectre, enslaved & tormented
To him whom he has murderd, bound in vengeance & enmity
Shudder not, but Write, & the hand of God will assist you!
Therefore I write Albions last words. Hope is banish'd from me.

Thames

Those were his last words, and the merciful Saviour in his arms
Reciev'd him, in the arms of tender mercy and repos'd
The pale limbs of his Eternal Individuality
Upon the Rock of Ages. Then surrounded with a Cloud:
In silence the Divine Lord builded with immortal labour,
Of gold & jewels a sublime Ornament, a Couch of repose,
With Sixteen pillars: canopied with emblems & written verse.
Spiritual Verse, order'd & measur'd, from whence, time shall reveal.
The Five books of the Decalogue, the books of Joshua & Judges,
Samuel, a double book & Kings, a double book, the Psalms & Prophets
The Four-fold Gospel, and the Revelations everlasting
Eternity groan'd & was troubled, at the image of Eternal Death!

Beneath the bottoms of the Graves, which is Earths central joint,
There is a place where Contrarieties are equally true:
To protect from the Giant blows in the sports of intellect,
Thunder in the midst of kindness, & love that kills its beloved:
Because Death is for a period, and they renew tenfold.
From this sweet Place Maternal Love awoke Jerusalem
With pangs she forsook Beulah's pleasant lovely shadowy Universe
Where no dispute can come; created for those, who Sleep.

Weeping was in all Beulah, and all the Daughters of Beulah
Wept for their Sister the Daughter of Albion, Jerusalem:
When out of Beulah the Emanation of the Sleeper descended,
With solemn mourning out of Beulahs many shades and hills,
Within the Human Heart, whose Gates closed with solemn sound.
And this the manner of the terrible Separation
The Emanations of the grievously afflicted Friends of Albion
Concenter in one Female form an Aged pensive Woman.
Astonish'd! lovely! embracing the sublime shade: the Daughters of Beulah
Beheld her with wonder. With awful hands she took
A Moment of Time, drawing it out with many tears & afflictions
And many sorrows, oblique across the Atlantic Vale
Which is the Vale of Rephaim dreadful from East to West,
Where the Human Harvest waves abundant in the beams of Eden,
Into a Rainbow of jewels and gold, a mild Reflection from
Albions dread Tomb. Eight thousand and five hundred years
In its extension. Every two hundred years has a door to Eden
She also took an Atom of Space, with dire pain opening it a Center
Into Beulah: trembling the Daughters of Beulah dried
Her tears, she ardent embrac'd her sorrows, occupied in labours
Of sublime mercy in Rephaims Vale. Perusing Albions Tomb
She sat: she walked among the ornaments solemn mourning
The Daughters attended her shudderings, wiping the death sweat
Los also saw her in his seventh Furnace, he also terrified
Saw the finger of God go forth upon his seventh Furnace:
Away from the Starry Wheels to prepare Jerusalem a place.
When with a dreadful groan the Emanation mild of Albion
Burst from his bosom in the Tomb like a pale snowy cloud,
Female and lovely, struggling to put off the Human form.
Writhing in pain, the Daughters of Beulah in kind arms reciev'd
Jerusalem: weeping over her among the Spaces of Erin
In the Ends of Beulah, where the Dead wail night & day.

And thus Erin spoke to the Daughters of Beulah, in soft tears

Albion the Vortex of the Dead! Albion the Generous!
Albion the mildest son of Heaven! the Place of Holy Sacrifice
Where Friends Die for each other: will become the Place,
Of Murder, & Unforgiving Never-awaking Sacrifice of Enemies
The Children must be sacrific'd! (a horror never known
Till now in Beulah) unless a Refuge can be found
To hide them from the wrath of Albions Law that freezes sore
Upon his Sons & Daughters, self-exiled from his bosom
Draw ye Jerusalem away from Albions Mountains
To give a Place for Redemption, let Sihon and Og
Remove Eastward to Bashan and Gilead, and leave

The secret coverts of Albion & the hidden places of America
Jerusalem Jerusalem! why wilt thou turn away
Come ye O Daughters of Beulah, lament for Og & Sihon
Upon the Lakes of Ireland from Wicklow to Braimare
Sound the loud trumpet over Albion the White Cliff of the Atlantic
The Mountain of Giants: all the Giants of Albion are become
Weak! withered! darkend! & Jerusalem is cast forth from Albion.
They deny that they ever knew Jerusalem, or ever dwelt in Shiloh
The Gog & Magog shall become the Contraries of Humanity: of Albion
All the little-ones are consumed in the pangs of Albions Altars.
The manhood is cast off from the Bodies & reserved for the Powers
And the Bodies in which all Animals & Vegetations, the Earth & Heaven
Were contain'd in the All Glorious Imagination are witherd & darkend;
The golden Gate of Havilah and all the Garden of God,
Was caught up with the Sun in one day of fury and war:
The Lungs, the Heart, the Liver, shrunk away far distant from Man
And left a little slimy substance floating upon the tides.
In one night the Atlantic Continent was caught up with the Moon,
And became an Opake Globe far distant clad with moony beams.
The Visions of Eternity, by reason of narrowed perceptions,
Are become weak Visions of Time & Space, fix'd into furrows of death;
Till deep dissimulation is the only defence an honest man has left
O Polypus of Death O Spectre over Europe and Asia
Withering the Human Form by Laws of Sacrifice for Sin
By Laws of Chastity & Abhorrence I am witherd up.
Striving to Create a Heaven in which all shall be pure & holy
In their Own Selfhoods, in Natural Selfish Chastity to banish Pity
And dear Mutual Forgiveness; & to become One Great Satan
Inslav'd to the most powerful Selfhood: to murder the Divine Humanity
In whose sight all are as the dust & who chargeth his Angels with folly!
Ah! weak & wide astray! Ah shut in narrow doleful form
Creeping in reptile flesh upon the bosom of the ground!
The Eye of Man a little narrow orb closd up & dark
Scarcely beholding the great light, conversing with the ground:
The Ear, a little shell in small volutions shutting out
True Harmonies, & comprehending great, as very small:
The Nostrils, bent down to the earth & clos'd with senseless flesh.
That odours cannot them expand, nor joy on them exult:
The Tongue, a little moisture fills, a little food it cloys,
A little sound it utters & its cries are faintly heard,
Then brings forth Moral Virtue the cruel Virgin Babylon.
Can such an Eye judge of the stars? & looking thro its tubes
Measure the sunny rays that point their spears on Udanadan
Can such an Ear, filld with the vapours of the yawning pit,
Judge of the pure melodious harp struck by a hand divine?
Can such closed Nostrils feel a joy? or tell of autumn fruits
When grapes & figs burst their covering to the joyful air?
Can such a Tongue boast of the living waters? or take in
Ought but the Vegetable Ratio & loathe the faint delight.
Can such gross Lips percieve? alas! folded within themselves
They touch not ought but pallid turn & tremble at every wind.

And let wild seas & rocks close up Jerusalem away from The

The Atlantic Mountains where Giants dwelt in Intellect;
Now given to stony Druids, and Allegoric Generation
To the Twelve Gods of Asia, the Spectres of those who Sleep:
Sway'd by a Providence oppos'd to the Divine Lord Jesus:
A murderous Providence! A Creation that groans, living on Death.
Where Fish & Bird & Beast & Man & Tree & Metal & Stone
Live by Devouring, going into Eternal Death continually:
Albion is now possess'd by the War of Blood! the Sacrifice
Of envy Albion is became, and his Emanation cast out:
Come Lord Jesus Lamb of God descend! for if, O Lord,
If thou hadst been here, our brother Albion had not died.
Arise sisters! Go ye & meet the Lord, while I remain
Behold the foggy mornings of the Dead on Albions cliffs:
Ye know that if the Emanation remains in them;
She will become an Eternal Death, an Avenger of Sin,
A Self-righteousness: the proud Virgin-Harlot! Mother of War!
And we also & all Beulah, consume beneath Albions curve

So Erin spoke to the Daughters of Beulah. Shuddering
With their wings they sat in the Furnace, in a night
Of stars, for all the Sons of Albion appeard distant stars,
Ascending and descending into Albions sea of death.
And Erins lovely Bow enclos'd the Wheels of Albions Sons.

Expanding on wing, the Daughters of Beulah replied in sweet response:

Come, O thou Lamb of God and take away the remembrance of Sin.
To Sin & to hide the Sin in sweet deceit, is lovely!
To Sin in the open face of day is cruel & pitiless! But
To record the Sin for a reproach: to let the Sun go down
In a remembrance of the Sin: is a Woe & a Horror!
A brooder of an Evil Day, and a Sun rising in blood
Come then O Lamb of God and take away the remembrance of Sin

End of Chap. 2

Rahab is an Eternal State } ~ To the Deists. ~ { The Spiritual States of the Soul are all Eternal Distinguish between the Man, & his present State

He never can be a Friend to the Human Race who is the Preacher of Natural Morality or Natural Religion, he is a flatterer who means to betray, to perpetuate Tyrant Pride & the Laws of that Babylon which he foresees shall shortly be destroyed, with the Spiritual and not the Natural Sword: He is in the State named Rahab: which State must be put off before we can be the Friend of Man.

You, O Deists, profess yourselves the Enemies of Christianity: and you are so: you are also the Enemies of the Human Race & of Universal Nature. Man is born a Spectre or Satan & is altogether an Evil, & requires a New Selfhood continually & must continually be changed into his direct Contrary. But your Greek Philosophy (which is a remnant of Druidism) teaches that Man is Righteous in his Vegetated Spectre: an Opinion of fatal & accursed consequence to Man, as the Ancients saw plainly by Revelation to the intire abrogation of Experimental Theory. and many believed what they saw, and Prophecied of Jesus.

Man must & will have Some Religion: if he has not the Religion of Jesus, he will have the Religion of Satan, & will erect the Synagogue of Satan, calling the Prince of this World, God; and destroying all who do not worship Satan under the Name of God. Will any one say: Where are those who worship Satan under the Name of God! Where are they? Listen! Every Religion that Preaches Vengeance for Sin is the Religion of the Enemy & Avenger; and not the Forgiver of Sin, and their God is Satan, Named by the Divine Name. Your Religion O Deists: Deism, is the Worship of the God of this World by the means of what you call Natural Religion and Natural Philosophy, and of Natural Morality or Self-Righteousness, the Selfish Virtues of the Natural Heart. This was the Religion of the Pharisees who murderd Jesus. Deism is the same & ends in the same.

Voltaire Rousseau Gibbon Hume, charge the Spiritually Religious with Hypocrisy! but how a Monk or a Methodist either, can be a Hypocrite: I cannot conceive. We are Men of like passions with others & pretend not to be holier than others: therefore, when a Religious Man falls into Sin, he ought not to be calld a Hypocrite: this title is more properly to be given to a Player who falls into Sin; whose profession is Virtue & Morality & the making Men Self-Righteous. Foote in calling Whitefield, Hypocrite: was himself one: for Whitefield pretended not to be holier than others: but confessed his Sins before all the World; Voltaire! Rousseau! You cannot escape my charge that you are Pharisees & Hypocrites, for you are constantly talking of the Virtues of the Human Heart, and particularly of your own, that you may accuse others & especially the Religious, whose errors, you by this display of pretended Virtue, chiefly design to expose. Rousseau thought Men Good by Nature: he found them Evil & found no friend. Friendship cannot exist without Forgiveness of Sins continually. The Book written by Rousseau calld his Confessions, is an apology & cloke for his sin & not a confession.

But you also charge the poor Monks & Religious with being the causes of War: while you acquit & flatter the Alexanders & Caesars, the Lewis's & Fredericks: who alone are its causes & its actors. But the Religion of Jesus, Forgiveness of Sin, can never be the cause of a War nor of a single Martyrdom.

Those who Martyr others or who cause War are Deists, but never can be Forgivers of Sin. the Glory of Christianity is, To Conquer by Forgiveness. All the Destruction therefore, in Christian Europe has arisen from Deism, which is Natural Religion.

1
I saw a Monk of Charlemaine
Arise before my sight
I talkd with the Grey Monk as we stood
In beams of infernal light

Gibbon arose with a lash of steel
And Voltaire with a wracking wheel
The Schools in clouds of learning rolld
Arose with War in iron & gold.

2
Thou lazy Monk they sound afar
In vain condemning glorious War
And in your Cell you shall ever dwell
Rise War & bind him in his Cell.

3

The blood red ran from the Grey Monks side
His hands & feet were wounded wide
His body bent, his arms & knees
Like to the roots of ancient trees

When Satan first the black bow bent
And the Moral Law from the Gospel rent
He forgd the Law into a Sword
And spilld the blood of mercys Lord.

Titus! Constantine! Charlemaine!
O Voltaire! Rousseau! Gibbon! Vain
Your Grecian Mocks & Roman Sword
Against this image of his Lord!

For a Tear is an Intellectual thing;
And a Sigh is the Sword of an Angel King
And the bitter groan of a Martyrs woe
Is an Arrow from the Almighties Bow!

Jerusalem
Chap 3

But Los, who is the Vehicular Form of strong Urthona
Wept vehemently over Albion where Thames currents spring
From the rivers of Beulah; pleasant river! soft, mild, parent stream
And the roots of Albions Tree enterd the Soul of Los
5 As he sat before his Furnaces clothed in sackcloth of hair
In gnawing pain dividing him from his Emanation;
Inclosing all the Children of Los time after time.
Their Giant forms condensing into Nations & Peoples & Tongues
Translucent the Furnaces of Beryl & Emerald immortal:
10 And Seven-fold each within other: incomprehensible
To the Vegetated Mortal Eye's perverted & single vision
The Bellows are the Animal Lungs: the Hammers the Animal Heart
The Furnaces the Stomach for Digestion; terrible their fury
Like seven burning heavens ranged from South to North

15 Here on the banks of the Thames Los builded Golgonooza,
Outside of the Gates of the Human Heart, beneath Beulah
In the midst of the rocks of the Altars of Albion In fears
He builded it, in rage & in fury. It is the Spiritual Fourfold
London: continually building & continually decaying desolate!
20 In eternal labours: loud the Furnaces & loud the Anvils
Of Death thunder incessant around the flaming Couches of
The Twentyfour Friends of Albion and round the armed Four
For the protection of the Twelve Emanations of Albions Sons
The Mystic Union of the Emanation in the Lord; Because
25 Man divided from his Emanation is a dark Spectre
His Emanation is an ever-weeping melancholy Shadow
But she is made receptive of Generation thro' mercy
In the Potters Furnace, among the Funeral Urns of Beulah
29 From Surrey hills, thro' Italy and Greece, to Hinnoms vale.

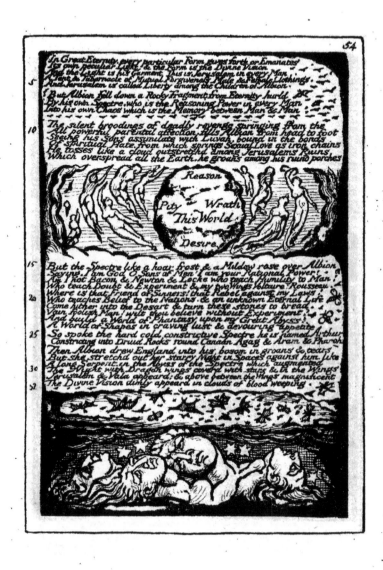

In Great Eternity, every particular Form gives forth or Emanates
Its own peculiar Light, & the Form is the Divine Vision
And the Light is his Garment. This is Jerusalem in every Man
A Tent & Tabernacle of Mutual Forgiveness Male & Female Clothings.
And Jerusalem is called Liberty among the Children of Albion

But Albion fell down a Rocky fragment from Eternity hurld
By his own Spectre, who is the Reasoning Power in every Man
Into his own Chaos which is the Memory between Man & Man

The silent broodings of deadly revenge springing from the
All powerful parental affection, fills Albion from head to foot
Seeing his Sons assimilate with Luvah, bound in the bonds
Of spiritual Hate, from which springs Sexual Love as iron chains
He tosses like a cloud outstretchd among Jerusalems Ruins,
Which overspread all the Earth, he groans among his ruind porches

Reason
Pity — Wrath
This World
Desire

But the Spectre like a hoar frost & a Mildew rose over Albion
Saying, I am God O Sons of Men! I am your Rational Power!
Am I not Bacon & Newton & Locke who teach Humility to Man!
Who teach Doubt & Experiment & my two Wings Voltaire: Rousseau.
Where is that Friend of Sinners! that Rebel against my Laws!
Who teaches Belief to the Nations, & an unknown Eternal Life
Come hither into the Desart & turn these stones to bread.
Vain foolish Man! wilt thou believe without Experiment?
And build a World of Phantasy upon my Great Abyss!
A World of Shapes in craving lust & devouring appetite

So spoke the hard cold constrictive Spectre he is named Arthur
Constricting into Druid Rocks round Canaan Agag & Aram & Pharoh
Then Albion drew England into his bosom in groans & tears
But she stretchd out her starry Night in Spaces against him. like
A long Serpent, in the Abyss of the Spectre which augmented
The Night with Dragon wings coverd with stars & in the Wings
Jerusalem & Vala appeard: & above between the Wings magnificent
The Divine Vision dimly appeard in clouds of blood weeping.

When those who disregard all Mortal Things, saw a Mighty-One
Among the Flowers of Beulah still retain his awful strength
They wonderd; checking their wild flames & Many gathering
Together into an Assembly; they said, let us go down
And see these changes! Others said, If you do so prepare
For being driven from our fields, what have we to do with the Dead:
To be their inferiors or superiors we equally abhor;
Superior, none we know: the Worm name: all, equal share
Divine Benevolence & joy, for the Eternal Man
Walketh among us, calling us his Brothers & his Friends:
Forbidding us that Veil which Satan puts between Eve & Adam
By which the Princes of the Dead enslave their Votaries
Teaching them to form the Serpent of precious stones & gold
To sieze the Sons of Jerusalem & plant them in One Mans Loins
To make One Family of Contraries: that Joseph may be sold
Into Egypt: for Negation; a Veil the Saviour born & dying rends.

But others said: Let us to him who only Is, & who
Walketh among us, give decision. bring forth all your fires!

So saying, an eternal deed was done: in fiery flames
The Universal Concave raged, such thunderous sounds as never
Were sounded from a mortal cloud, nor on Mount Sinai old
Nor in Havilah where the Cherub rolld his redounding flame.

Loud! loud! the Mountains lifted up their voices, loud the Forests
Rivers thunderd against their banks, loud Winds furious fought
Cities & Nations contended in fires & clouds & tempests.
The Seas raisd up their voices & lifted their hands on high
The Stars in their courses fought. the Sun! Moon! Heaven! Earth.
Contending for Albion & for Jerusalem his Emanation
And for Shiloh, the Emanation of France & for lovely Vala.

Then far the greatest number were about to make a Separation
And they Elected Seven, called the Seven Eyes of God;
Lucifer, Molech, Elohim, Shaddai, Pahad, Jehovah, Jesus.
They namd the Eighth. he came not, he hid in Albions Forests
But first they said: & their Words stood in Chariots in array
Curbing their Tygers with golden bits & bridles of silver & ivory

Let the Human Organs be kept in their perfect Integrity
At will Contracting into Worms, or Expanding into Gods
And then behold! what are these Ulro Visions of Chastity
Then as the moss upon the tree: or dust upon the plow
Or as the sweat upon the labouring shoulder: or as the chaff
Of the wheat-floor or as the dregs of the sweet wine-press
Such are these Ulro Visions; for tho we sit down within
The plowed furrow, listning to the weeping clods till we
Contract or Expand Space at will: or if we raise ourselves
Upon the chariots of the morning. Contracting or Expanding Time!
Every one knows, we are One Family! One Man blessed for ever

Silence remaind & every one resumd his Human Majesty
And many conversed on these things as they labourd at the furrow
Saying: It is better to prevent misery, than to release from misery
It is better to prevent error, than to forgive the criminal:
Labour well the Minute Particulars, attend to the Little-ones:
And those who are in misery cannot remain so long
If we do but our duty: labour well the teeming Earth.

They Plow'd in tears, the trumpets sounded before the golden Plow
And the voices of the Living Creatures were heard in the clouds of heaven
Crying: Compel the Reasoner to Demonstrate with unhewn Demonstrations
Let the Indefinite be explored. and let every Man be judged
By his own Works. Let all Indefinites be thrown into Demonstrations
To be pounded to dust & melted in the Furnaces of Affliction:
He who would do good to another, must do it in Minute Particulars
General Good is the plea of the scoundrel hypocrite & flatterer:
For Art & Science cannot exist but in minutely organized Particulars
And not in generalizing Demonstrations of the Rational Power.
The Infinite alone resides in Definite & Determinate Identity
Establishment of Truth depends on destruction of Falshood continually
On Circumcision: not on Virginity, O Reasoners of Albion

So cried they at the Plow. Albions Rock frowned above
And the Great Voice of Eternity rolled above terrible in clouds
Saying Who will go forth for us! & Who shall we send before our face?

Then Los heaved his thund'ring Bellows on the Valley of Middlesex
And thus he chaunted his Song: the Daughters of Albion reply.

What may Man be? who can tell! But what may Woman be?
To have power over Man from Cradle to corruptible Grave.
5 He who is an Infant, and whose Cradle is a Manger
Knoweth the Infant sorrow: whence it came, and where it goeth
And who weave it a Cradle of the grass that withereth away.
This World is all a Cradle for the erred wandering Phantom:
Rockd by Year, Month, Day & Hour; and every two Moments
10 Between, dwells a Daughter of Beulah, to feed the Human Vegetable
Entune: Daughters of Albion, your hymning Chorus mildly:
Cord of affection thrilling extatic on the iron Reel:
To the golden Loom of Love! to the moth-labourd Woof
A Garment and Cradle weaving for the infantine Terror:
15 For fear; at entering the gate into our World of cruel
Lamentation: it flee back & hide in Non-Entitys dark wild
Where dwells the Spectre of Albion: destroyer of Definite Form.
The Sun shall be a Scythed Chariot of Britain: the Moon; a Ship
In the British Ocean! Created by Los's Hammer: measured out
20 Into Days & Nights & Years & Months, to travel with my feet
Over these desolate rocks of Albion: O daughters of despair!
Rock the Cradle, and in mild melodies tell me where found
What you have enwoven with so much tears & care! so much
Tender artifice: to laugh: to weep: to learn: to know;
25 Remember! recollect! what dark befel in wintry days

O it was lost for ever! and we found it not: it came
And wept at our wintry Door: Look! look! behold! Gwendolen
Is become a Clod of Clay! Merlin is a Worm of the Valley!

Then Los uttered with Hammer & Anvil: Chaunt! revoce!
30 I mind not your laugh: and your frown I not fear! and
You must my dictate obey from your gold-beam'd Looms: trill
Gentle to Albions Watchman, on Albions mountains: reeccho
And rock the Cradle while! Ah me! Of that Eternal Man
And of the cradled Infancy in his bowels of compassion:
35 Who fell beneath his instruments of husbandry & became
Subservient to the clods of the furrow! the cattle and even
The emmet and earth-Worm are his superiors & his lords.

Then the response came warbling from trilling Looms in Albion
We Women tremble at the light therefore: hiding fearful
40 The Divine Vision with Curtain & Veil & fleshly Tabernacle

Los utterd: swift as the rattling thunder upon the mountains
Look back into the Church Paul! Look! Three Women around
45 The Cross! O Albion why didst thou a Female Will Create?

And the voices of Bath & Canterbury & York & Edinburgh, &c.
Over the Isle of Nations in the strong hand of Albion thundering along
Among the Hosts of the Druids in the deep slumberous redounding Vapor
Of the Atlantic which poured in impetuous loud loud louder & louder
And the Great Voice of the Atlantic rolled over the Druid Altars,
Weeping over his Children in Stone-henge in Malden & Colchester
Round the Rocky Peak of Derbyshire London Stone & Rosamonds Bower

What is a Wife & what is a Harlot? What is a Church? & What
Is a Theatre? are they Two & not One? can they Exist Separate?
Are not Religion & Politics the Same Thing? Brotherhood is Religion
O Demonstrations of Reason Dividing families in Cruelty & Pride!

But Albion fled from the Divine Vision, with the Plow of Nations enflaming
The Living Creatures maddend and Albion fell into the Furrow, and
The Plow went over him & the Living was Plowed in among the Dead
But his Spectre rose over the starry Plow. Albion fled beneath the Plow
Till he came to the Rock of Ages, & he took his Seat upon the Rock.
Wonder siezd all in Eternity to behold the Divine Vision, open
The Center into an Expanse, & the Center rolled out into an Expanse

In beauty the Daughters of Albion divide & unite at will
Naked & drunk with blood Gwendolen dancing to the timbrel
Of War: reeling up the Street of London she divides in twain
Among the Inhabitants of Albion, the People fall around.
The Daughters of Albion, divide & unite in jealousy & cruelty
The Inhabitants of Albion at the Harvest & the Vintage
Feel their Brain cut round beneath the temples shrieking
Bonesnap into a Scull, the Marrow exuding in dismal pain
They flee over the rocks bandying: Horses: Oxen: feel the knife
And while the Sons of Albion by severe War & Judgment bonify
The Hermaphroditic Condensations are divided by the Knife
The obdurate Forms are cut asunder by Jealousy & Pity.

Rational Philosophy and Mathematic Demonstration
Is divided in the intoxications of pleasure & affection
Two Contraries War against each other in fury & blood.
And Los fixes them on his Anvil, incessant his blows;
He fixes them with strong blows, placing the stones & timbers.
To Create a World of Generation from the World of Death:
Dividing the Masculine & Feminine: for the comingling
Of Albions & Luvahs Spectres was Hermaphroditic

Urizen wrathful strode above directing the awful Building:
As a Mighty Temple; delivering Form out of confusion
Jordan sprang beneath its threshold bubbling from beneath
Its pillars: Euphrates ran under its arches: white sails
And silver oars reflect on its pillars, & sound on its echoing
Pavements: where walk the Sons of Jerusalem who remain Ungenerate
But the revolving Sun and Moon pass thro its porticoes.
Day & night, in sublime majesty & silence they revolve
And shine glorious within; Hand & Koban arch'd over the Sun
In the hot noon, as he traveld thro his journey; Hyle & Skofeld
Arch'd over the Moon at midnight & Los Fixd them there.
With his thunderous Hammer; terrified the Spectres rage & flee
Canaan is his portico: Jordan is a fountain in his porch:
A fountain of milk & wine to relieve the traveller:
Egypt is the eight steps within. Ethiopia supports his pillars;
Lybia & the Lands unknown, are the ascent without;
Within is Asia & Greece, ornamented with exquisite art:
Persia & Media are his halls: his inmost hall is Great Tartary
China & India & Siberia are his temples for entertainment
Poland & Russia & Sweden, his soft retired chambers
France & Spain & Italy & Denmark & Holland & Germany
Are the temples among his pillars. Britain is Loss Forge;
America North & South are his baths of living waters.

Such is the Ancient World of Urizen in the Satanic Void
Created from the Valley of Middlesex by Londons River
From Stone-henge & from London Stone, from Cornwall to Cathnes
The Four Zoa's rush around on all sides in dire ruin
Furious in pride of Selfhood the terrible Spectres of Albion
Rear their dark Rocks among the Stars of God: stupendous
Works! A World of Generation continually Creating; out of
The Hermaphroditic Satanic World of rocky destiny.

And formed into Four precious Stones, for entrance from Beulah

For the Veil of Vala which Albion cast into the Atlantic Deep
To catch the Souls of the Dead; began to Vegetate & Petrify
Around the Earth of Albion. among the Roots of his Tree
5 This Los formed into the Gates & mighty Wall, between the Oak
Of Weeping & the Palm of Suffering beneath Albions Tomb,
Thus in process of time it became the beautiful Mundane Shell,
The Habitation of the Spectres of the Dead & the Place
Of Redemption & of awaking again into Eternity

10 For Four Universes round the Mundane Egg remain Chaotic
One to the North: Urthona: One to the South: Urizen:
One to the East: Luvah: One to the West. Tharmas; they are
The Four Zoa's that stood around the Throne Divine!
But when Luvah assumed the World of Urizen Southward,
15 And Albion was slain upon his Mountains & in his Tent,
All fell towards the Center, sinking downwards in dire ruin,
In the South remains a burning Fire; in the East, a Void,
In the West, a World of raging Waters; in the North; solid Darkness
Unfathomable without end; but in the midst of these
20 Is Built eternally the sublime Universe of Los & Enitharmon

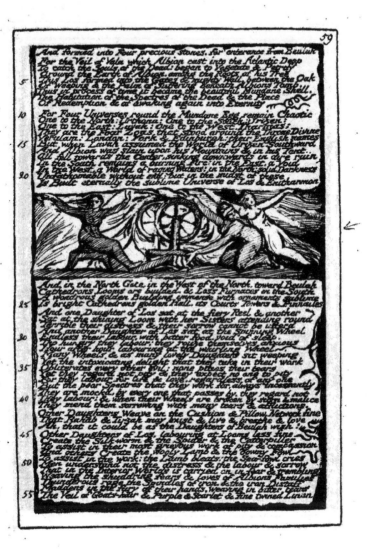

And, in the North Gate, in the West of the North. toward Beulah
Cathedrons Looms are builded. & Los's Furnaces in the South
A wondrous golden Building, immense with ornaments sublime
25 Is bright Cathedrons golden Hall. its Courts Towers & Pinnacles

And one, Daughter of Los sat at the fiery Reel & another
Sat at the shining Loom with her Sisters attending round
Terrible their distress & their sorrow cannot be utterd
And another Daughter of Los sat at the Spinning Wheel
30 Endless their labour, with bitter food, void of sleep,
Tho hungry they labour: they rouze themselves anxious
Hour after hour labouring at the whirling Wheel
Many Wheels & as many lovely Daughters sit weeping
35 Yet the intoxicating delight; that they take in their work
Obliterates every other evil; none pities their tears
Yet they regard not pity & they expect no one to pity
For they labour for life & love, regardless of any one
But the poor Spectres that they work for, always incessantly
40 They are mockd, by every one that passes by. they regard not
They labour; & when their Wheels are broken by scorn & malice
They mend them sorrowing with many tears & afflictions.

Other Daughters Weave on the Cushion & Pillow, Network fine
That Rahab & Tirzah may exist & live & breathe & love
45 Ah, that it could be as the Daughters of Beulah wish!

Other Daughters of Los labouring at Looms less fine
Create the Silk-worm & the Spider & the Catterpiller
To assist in their most grievous work of pity & compassion
And others Create the wooly Lamb & the downy Fowl
50 To assist in the work: the Lamb bleats! the Sea-fowl cries
Men understand not the distress & the labour & the sorrow
That in the Interior Worlds is carried on in fear & trembling
Weaving the shuddring fears & loves of Albions Families
Thunderous rage the Spindles of iron, & the iron Distaff
55 Maddens in the fury of their hands, Weaving in bitter tears
The Veil of Goats-hair & Purple & Scarlet & fine twined Linen

The clouds of Albions Druid Temples rage in the eastern heaven
While Los sat terrified beholding Albions Spectre who is Luvah
Spreading in bloody veins in torments over Europe & Asia;
Not yet formed but a wretched torment unformed & abyssal
In flaming fire; within the Furnaces the Divine Vision appeard
On Albions hills: often walking from the Furnaces in clouds
And flames among the Druid Temples & the Starry Wheels
Gatherd Jerusalems Children in his arms & bore them like
A Shepherd in the night of Albion which overspread all the Earth

I gave thee liberty and life O lovely Jerusalem
And thou hast bound me down upon the Stems of Vegetation
I gave thee Sheep-walks upon the Spanish Mountains Jerusalem
I gave thee Priams City and the Isles of Grecia lovely!
I gave thee Hand & Scofield & the Counties of Albion:
They spread forth like a lovely root into the Garden of God:
They were as Adam before me: united into One Man,
They stood in innocence & their skiey tent reachd over Asia
To Nimrods Tower to Ham & Canaan walking with Mizraim
Upon the Egyptian Nile, with solemn songs to Grecia
And sweet Hesperia even to Great Chaldea & Tesshina
Following thee as a Shepherd by the Four Rivers of Eden
Why wilt thou rend thyself apart, Jerusalem?
And build this Babylon & sacrifice in secret Groves,
Among the Gods of Asia: among the fountains of pitch & nitre
Therefore thy Mountains are become barren Jerusalem!
Thy Valleys, Plains of burning sand thy Rivers: waters of death
Thy Villages die of the Famine and thy Cities
Beg bread from house to house, lovely Jerusalem
Why wilt thou deface thy beauty & the beauty of thy little-ones
To please thy Idols, in the pretended chastities of Uncircumcision
Thy Sons are lovelier than Egypt or Assyria; wherefore
Dost thou blacken their beauty by a secluded place of rest,
And a peculiar Tabernacle, to cut the integuments of beauty
Into veils of tears and sorrows O lovely Jerusalem!
They have persuaded thee to this, therefore their end shall come
And I will lead thee thro the Wilderness in shadow of my cloud
And in my love I will lead thee, lovely Shadow of Sleeping Albion.

This is the Song of the Lamb, sung by Slaves in evening time.

But Jerusalem faintly saw him, closd in the Dungeons of Babylon
Her form was held by Beulahs Daughters, but all within unseen
She sat at the Mills, her hair unbound her feet naked
Cut with the flints; her tears run down, her reason grows like
The Wheel of Hand, incessant turning day & night without rest
Insane she raves upon the winds hoarse, inarticulate:
All night Vala hears, she triumphs in pride of holiness
To see Jerusalem deface her lineaments with bitter blows
Of despair, while the Satanic Holiness triumphd in Vala
In a Religion of Chastity & Uncircumcised Selfishness
Both of the Head & Heart & Loins, closd up in Moral Pride.

But the Divine Lamb stood beside Jerusalem. oft she saw
The lineaments Divine & oft the Voice heard, & oft she said:
O Lord & Saviour, have the Gods of the Heathen pierced thee:
Or hast thou been pierced in the House of thy Friends?
Art thou alive! & livest thou for evermore? or art thou
Not: but a delusive shadow, a thought that liveth not.
Babel mocks saying, there is no God nor Son of God
That thou O Human Imagination, O Divine Body art all
A delusion. but I know thee O Lord when thou arisest upon
My weary eyes even in this dungeon & this iron mill.
The Stars of Albion cruel rise; thou bindest to sweet influences:
For thou also sufferest with me altho I behold thee not:
And altho I sin & blaspheme thy holy name, thou pitiest me;
Because thou knowest I am deluded by the turning mills.
And by these visions of pity & love because of Albions death.

Thus spake Jerusalem, & thus the Divine Voice replied.

Mild Shade of Man, pitiest thou these Visions of terror & woe!
Give forth thy pity & love. fear not! lo I am with thee always.
Only believe in me that I have power to raise from death
Thy Brother who Sleepeth in Albion: fear not trembling Shade

Behold: in the Visions of Elohim Jehovah, behold Joseph, & Mary
And be comforted O Jerusalem in the Visions of Jehovah Elohim

She looked & saw Joseph the Carpenter in Nazareth & Mary
His espoused Wife. And Mary said, If thou put me away from thee
Dost thou not murder me? Joseph spoke in anger & fury. Should I
Marry a Harlot & an Adulteress? Mary answerd, Art thou more pure
Than thy Maker, who forgiveth Sins & calls again Her that is Lost
Tho She hates, he calls her again in love. I love my dear Joseph
But he driveth me away from his presence, yet I hear the voice of God
In the voice of my Husband, tho he is angry for a moment, he will not
Utterly cast me away, if I were pure, never could I taste the sweets
Of the Forgiveness of Sins: if I were holy. I never could behold the tears
Of love! of him who loves me in the midst of his anger in furnace of fire.

Ah my Mary; said Joseph; weeping over & embracing her closely in
His arms: Doth he forgive Jerusalem & not exact Purity from her who is
Polluted. I heard his voice in my sleep & his Angel in my dream:
Saying Doth Jehovah Forgive a Debt only on condition that it shall
Be Payed? Doth he Forgive Pollution only on conditions of Purity
That Debt is not Forgiven! That Pollution is not Forgiven
Such is the Forgiveness of the Gods, the Moral Virtues of the
Heathen, whose tender Mercies are Cruelty. But Jehovahs Salvation
Is without Money & without Price, in the Continual Forgiveness of Sins
In the Perpetual Mutual Sacrifice in Great Eternity! for behold!
There is none that liveth & Sinneth not! And this is the Covenant
Of Jehovah: If you Forgive one-another, so shall Jehovah Forgive You:
That He Himself may Dwell among You. Fear not then to take
To thee Mary thy Wife, for she is with Child by the Holy Ghost

Then Mary burst forth into a Song! she flowed like a River of
Many Streams in the arms of Joseph & gave forth her tears of joy
Like many waters, and Emanating into gardens & palaces upon
Euphrates & to forests & floods & animals wild & tame from
Gihon to Hiddekel, & to corn fields & villages & inhabitants
Upon Pison & Arnon & Jordan. And I heard the voice among
The Reapers Saying, Am I Jerusalem the lost Adulteress? or am I
Babylon come up to Jerusalem? And another voice answerd Saying

Does the voice of my Lord call me again? am I pure thro his Mercy
And Pity. Am I become lovely as a Virgin in his sight who am
Indeed a Harlot drunken with the Sacrifice of Idols does he
Call her pure as he did in the days of her Infancy when She
Was cast out to the loathing of her person. The Chaldean took
Me from my Cradle. The Amalekite stole me away upon his Camels
Before I had ever beheld with love the Face of Jehovah; or known
That there was a God of Mercy: O Mercy O Divine Humanity!
O Forgiveness & Pity & Compassion! If I were Pure I should never
Have known thee; If I were Unpolluted I should never have
Clarified thy Holiness, or rejoiced in thy great Salvation.

Mary leaned her side against Jerusalem, Jerusalem recieved
The Infant into her hands in the Visions of Jehovah. Times passed on
Jerusalem fainted over the Cross & Sepulcher She heard the voice
Wilt thou make Rome thy Patriarch Druid & the Kings of Europe his
Horsemen? Man in the Resurrection changes his Sexual Garments at Will
Every Harlot was once a Virgin: every Criminal an Infant Love!

Repose on me till the morning of the Grave. I am thy life
Jerusalem replied. I am an outcast: Albion is dead;
I am left to the trampling foot & the spurning heel:
A Harlot I am call'd. I am sold from street to street:
I am defaced with blows & with the dirt of the Prison:
And wilt thou become my Husband O my Lord & Saviour?
Shall Vala bring thee forth! shall the Chaste be ashamed also?
I see the Maternal Line, I behold the Seed of the Woman:
Cainah, & Ada & Zillah & Naamah Wife of Noah.
Shuahs daughter & Tamar & Rahab the Canaanites:
Ruth the Moabite & Bathsheba of the daughters of Heth
Naamah the Ammonite, Zibeah the Philistine, & Mary
These are the Daughters of Vala, Mother of the Body of death
But I thy Magdalen behold thy Spiritual Risen Body
Shall Albion arise? I know he shall arise at the Last Day!
I know that in my flesh I shall see God: but Emanations
Are weak, they know not whence they are, nor whither tend.

Jesus replied. I am the Resurrection & the Life.
I Die & pass the limits of possibility, as it appears
To individual perception. Luvah must be Created
And Vala; for I cannot leave them in the gnawing Grave.
But will prepare a way for my banished-ones to return
Come now with me into the villages. walk thro all the cities.
Tho thou art taken to prison & judgment, starved in the streets
I will command the cloud to give thee food & the hard rock
To flow with milk & wine, tho thou seest me not a season
Even a Long season & a hard journey & a howling wilderness!
Tho Vala's cloud hide thee & Luvah's fires follow thee!
Only believe & trust in me, Lo. I am always with thee!

So spoke the Lamb of God while Luvah's Cloud reddening above
Burst forth in streams of blood upon the heavens & dark night
Involv'd Jerusalem. & the Wheels of Albions Sons turnd heavy
Over the Mountains & the fires blaz'd on Druid Altars
And the Sun set in Tyburns Brook where Victims howl & cry.

But Los beheld the Divine Vision among the flames of the Furnaces
Therefore he lived & breathed in hope. but his tears fell incessant
Because his Children were clos'd from him apart: & Enitharmon
Dividing in fierce pain: also the Vision of God was clos'd in clouds
Of Albions Spectres, that Los in despair oft sat, & often ponderd
On Death Eternal in fierce shudders upon the mountains of Albion
Walking: & in the vales in howlings fierce, then to his Anvils
Turning, anew began his labours, tho in terrible pains!

Jehovah stood among the Druids in the Valley of Annandale
When the Four Zoa's of Albion, the Four Living Creatures, the Cherubim
Of Albion tremble before the Spectre, in the starry Harness of the Plow
Of Nations. And their Names are Urizen & Luvah & Tharmas & Urthona
Luvah slew Tharmas the Angel of the Tongue & Albion brought him
To Justice in his own City of Paris, denying the Resurrection
Then Vala the Wife of Albion, who is the Daughter of Luvah
Took vengeance Twelve-fold among the Chaotic Rocks of the Druids
Where the Human Victims howl to the Moon & Thor & Friga
Dance the dance of death contending with Jehovah among the Cherubim
The Chariot Wheels filling with fire rage along the howling Valley
In the Dividing of Reuben & Benjamin bleeding from Chesters River

The Giants & the Witches & the Ghosts of Albion dance with Thor
Over the Frozen & the Furious Sea the Moon along the Valley of Cherubim
Bleeding in torrents from Mountain to Mountain a lovely Victim
And Jehovah stood in the Gates of the Victim & he appeared
A weeping Infant in the Gates of Birth in the midst of Heaven

The Cities & Villages of Albion became Rock & Sand Unhumanized
The Druid Sons of Albion & the Heavens a Void around unfathomable
No Human Form but Sexual & a little weeping Infant pale reflected
Multitudinous in the Looking Glass of Enitharmon, on all sides
Around in the clouds of the Female, on Albions Cliffs of the Dead

Such the appearance in Cheviot: in the Divisions of Reuben

When the Cherubim hid their heads under their wings in deep slumbers
When the Druids demanded Chastity from Woman & all was lost.

How can the Female be Chaste O thou stupid Druid Cried Los
Without the Forgiveness of Sins in the merciful clouds of Jehovah
And without the Baptism of Repentance to wash away Calumnies and
the Accusations of Sin that each may be Pure in their Neighbours sight
O when shall Jehovah give us Victims from his Flocks & Herds
Instead of Human Victims by the Daughters of Albion & Canaan

Then laugh'd Gwendolen & her laughter shook the Nations & Families of
the Dead beneath Beulah from Tyburn to Golgotha, and from
Ireland to Japan, furious her Lips & Tongue & Tears spout before
Los on the Thames & Medway. London & Canterbury groan in pain

Los knew not yet what was done: he thought it was all in Vision
In Visions of the Dreams of Beulah among the Daughters of Albion
Therefore the Murder was put apart in the Looking-Glass of Enitharmon

He saw in Vala's hand the Druid Knife of Revenge & the Poison Cup
Of Jealousy, and thought it a Poetic Vision of the Atmospheres
Till Canada rolled apart from Albion across the Mountains of the Druids

And all the Land of Canaan suspended over the Valley of Cheviot
From Hashan to Tyre & from Troy to Gaza of the Amalekite
And Reuben fled with his head downwards among the Caverns

Of the Mundane Shell which froze on all sides round Canaan on
The vast Expanse: where the Daughters of Albion Weave the Web
Of Ages & Generations, folding & unfolding it, like a Veil of Cherubim
And sometimes it touches the Earths summits, & sometimes spreads
Abroad into the Indefinite Spectre, who is the Rational Power.

Then All the Daughters of Albion became One before Los: even Vala!
And she put forth her hand upon the Looms in dreadful howlings
Till she vegetated into a hungry Stomach & a devouring Tongue.
Her Hand is a Court of Justice, her Feet: two Armies in Battle
Storms & Pestilence: in her Locks: & in her Loins Earthquake
And Fire, & the Ruin of Cities & Nations & Families & Tongues

She cries: The Human is but a Worm, & thou O Male: Thou art
Thyself Female, a Male: a breeder of Seed: a Son & Husband: & Lo
The Human Divine is Womans Shadow, a Vapor in the summers heat
Go assume Papal dignity thou Spectre, thou Male Harlot: Arthur
Divide into the Kings of Europe in times remote O Woman-born
And Woman-nourishd & Woman-educated & Woman-scornd!

Wherefore art thou living! said Los, & Man cannot live in thy presence
Art thou Vala the Wife of Albion O thou lovely Daughter of Luvah
All Quarrels arise from Reasoning, the secret Murder, and
The violent Man-slaughter. these are the Spectres double Cave
The Sexual Death, living on accusation of Sin & Judgment
To freeze Love & Innocence into the gold & silver of the Merchant
Without Forgiveness of Sin Love is Itself Eternal Death

Then the Spectre drew Vala into his bosom magnificent terrific
Glittering with precious stones & gold, with Garments of blood & fire
He wept in deadly wrath of the Spectre, in self-contradicting agony
Crimson with Wrath & green with Jealousy: dazling with Love
And Jealousy immingled & the purple of the violet darkend deep
Over the Plow of Nations thundring in the hand of Albions Spectre

A dark Hermaphrodite they stood frowning upon Londons River
And the Distaff & Spindle in the hands of Vala with the Flax of
Human Miseries turnd fierce with the Lives of Men along the Valley
As Reuben fled before the Daughters of Albion Taxing the Nations

Derby Peak yawnd a horrid Chasm at the cries of Gwendolen, & at
The stamping feet of Ragan upon the flaming Treddles of her Loom
That drop with crimson gore with the Loves of Albion & Canaan
Opening along the Valley of Rephaim, weaving over the Caves of Mach
pelah

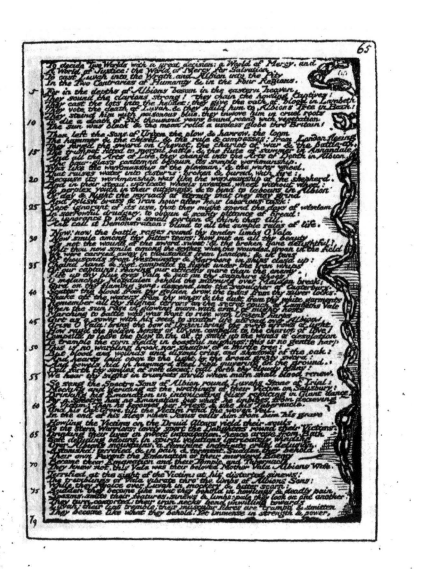

To decide Two Worlds with a great decision: a World of Mercy, and
A World of Justice: the World of Mercy for Salvation
To cast Luvah into the Wrath, and Albion into the Pity
In the two Contraries of Humanity & in the Four Regions.

For in the depths of Albions bosom in the eastern heaven,
They sound the clarions strong! they chain the howling Captives!
They cast the lots into the helmet: they give the oath of blood in Lambeth
They vote the death of Luvah, & they naild him to Albions Tree in Bath:
They staind him with poisonous blue, they inwove him in cruel roots
To die a death of Six thousand years bound round with vegetation
The sun was black & the moon rolld a useless globe thro Britain!

Then left the Sons of Urizen the plow & harrow, the loom
The hammer & the chisel, & the rule & compasses; from London fleeing
They forgd the sword on Cheviot, the chariot of war & the battle-ax,
The trumpet fitted to mortal battle, & the flute of summer in Annandale
And all the Arts of Life, they changd into the Arts of Death in Albion.
The hour-glass contemnd because its simple workmanship.
Was like the workmanship of the plowman, & the water wheel,
That raises water into cisterns: broken & burnd with fire:
Because its workmanship, was like the workmanship of the shepherd.
And in their stead, intricate wheels invented, wheel without wheel:
To perplex youth in their outgoings, & to bind to labours in Albion
Of day & night the myriads of eternity that they may grind
And polish brass & iron hour after hour laborious task!
Kept ignorant of its use, that they might spend the days of wisdom
In sorrowful drudgery, to obtain a scanty pittance of bread:
In ignorance to view a small portion & think that All,
And call it Demonstration: blind to all the simple rules of life.

Now now the battle rages round thy tender limbs O Vala
Now smile among thy bitter tears: now put on all thy beauty
Is not the wound of the sword sweet! & the broken bone delightful!
Wilt thou now smile among the slain when the wounded groan in the field
Lift up thy blue eyes Vala & put on thy sapphire shoes:
O melancholy Magdalen behold the morning over Malden break;
Gird on thy flaming zone, descend into the sepulcher of Canterbury.
Scatter the blood from thy golden brow, the tears from thy silver locks:
Shake off the waters from thy wings! & the dust from thy white garments
Remember all thy feigned terrors on the secret couch of Lambeths Vale
When the sun rose in glowing morn, with arms of mighty hosts
Marching to battle who was wont to rise with Urizens harps
Girt as a sower with his seed to scatter life abroad over Albion:
Arise O Vala! bring the bow of Urizen: bring the swift arrows of light.
How rajd the golden horse of Urizen compelling the harnessd horse of light
Into the wedge of war, & blood & wounds, & fire: this is no gentle harp
This is no warbling brook, nor shadow of a mirtle tree:
But blood and wounds and dismal cries, and shadows of the oak:
And hearts laid open to the light, by the broad grizly sword:
And bowels hidden in hammerd steel ript quivering on the ground.
Call forth thy smiles of soft deceit: call forth thy cloudy tears:
We hear thy sighs in trumpets shrill when morn shall blood renew.

So sang the Spectrous Sons of Albion round Luvahs Stone of Trial:
Mocking and deriding at the writhings of their Victim on Salisbury:
Drinking his Emanation in intoxicating bliss rejoicing in Giant dance;
For a Spectre has no Emanation but what he imbibes from deceiving
A Victim! Then he becomes her Priest & she his Tabernacle.
And his Oak Grove, till the Victim rend the woven Veil.
In the end of his sleep when Jesus calls him from his grave

Howling the Victims on the Druid Altars yield their souls
To the stern Warriors: lovely sport the Daughters round their Victims;
Drinking their lives in sweet intoxication. hence arose from Bath
Soft deluding odours, in spiral volutions intricately winding
Over Albions mountains, a feminine indefinite cruel delusion.
Astonishd! terrified & in pain & torment. Sudden they behold
Their own Parent the Emanation of their murderd Enemy
Become their Emanation and their Temple and Tabernacle
They knew not. this Vala was their beloved Mother Vala Albions Wife.
Terrified at the sight of the Victim: at his distorted sinews!
The tremblings of Vala vibrate thro the limbs of Albions Sons:
While they rejoice over Luvah in mockery & bitter scorn:
Sudden they become like what they behold in howlings & deadly pain.
Spasms smite their features, sinews & limbs: pale they look on one another
They turn contorted: their iron necks bend unwilling towards
Luvah: their lips tremble: their muscular fibres are crampd & smitten
They become like what they behold! Yet immense in strength & power,

In awful pomp & gold, in all the precious unhewn stones of Eden
They build a stupendous Building on the Plain of Salisbury; with chains
Of rocks round London Stone: of Reasonings: of unhewn Demonstrations
In labyrinthine arches. (Mighty Urizen the Architect) thro' which
The Heavens might revolve & Eternity be bound in their chain.
Labour unparalleld! a wondrous rocky World of cruel destiny
Rocks piled on rocks reaching the stars: stretching from pole to pole.
The Building is Natural Religion & its Altars Natural Morality
A building of eternal death: whose proportions are eternal despair
Here Vala stood turning the iron Spindle of destruction
From heaven to earth: howling! invisible! but not invisible
Her Two Covering Cherubs afterwards named Voltaire & Rousseau:
Two frowning Rocks: on each side of the Cove & Stone of Torture:
Frozen Sons of the feminine Tabernacle of Bacon, Newton & Locke.
For Luvah is France: the Victim of the Spectres of Albion.

Los beheld in terror: he pourd his loud storms on the Furnaces:
The Daughters of Albion clothed in garments of needle work
Strip them off from their shoulders and bosoms, they lay aside
Their garments; they sit naked upon the Stone of trial.
The Knife of flint passes over the howling Victim: his blood
Gushes & stains the fair side of the fair Daughters of Albion.
They put aside his curls; they divide his seven locks upon
His forehead: they bind his forehead with thorns of iron
They put into his hand a reed, they mock: Saying: Behold
The King of Canaan whose are seven hundred chariots of iron!
They take off his vesture whole with their Knives of flint:
But they cut asunder his inner garments: searching with
Their cruel fingers for his heart, & there they enter in pomp
In many tears; & there they erect a temple & an altar:
They pour cold water on his brain in front, to cause
Lids to grow over his eyes in forests of night: and some
To roll & gather over his mantels, while they his hair & roses from cups
And dishes of painted clay. Glowing with beauty & cruelty:
They obscure the sun & the moon: no eye can look upon them.

Ah! alas! at the sight of the Victim, & at sight of those who are smitten,
All who see, become what they behold; their eyes are coverd
With tears, rooted in the ground, and their moist venom & loosend
Their cars bent outward; as their Victim, so are they in the pangs
Of unconquerable fear! amidst delights of revenge Earth-shaking:
And as their eye & ear shrunk, the heavens shrunk away
The Divine Vision became First a burning flame, then a column
Of fire, then an awful fiery wheel surrounding earth & heaven:
And then a globe of blood wandering distant in an unknown night:
Afar into the unknown night the mountains fled away:
Six months of mortality; a summer: & six months of mortality; a winter:
The Human form began to be alterd by the Reasonings of Albion
And the perceptions to be dissipated into the Indefinite. Becoming
A mighty Polypus namd Albions Tree, they tie the Veins
And Nerves into two knots: & the Seed into a double knot:
They look forth: the Sun is shrunk: the Heavens are shrunk
Away into the far remote: and the Trees & Mountains witherd
Into indefinite cloudy shadows in darkness & separation.
By Invisible Hatreds adjoind, they seem remote and separate
From each other; and yet are a Mighty Polypus in the Deep! Lo!
As the Mistletoe grows on the Oak, so Albions Tree on Eternity: Lo!
He who will not comingle in Love, must be adjoind by Hate.

They look forth from Stone-henge! from the Cove round London Stone
They look on one another: the mild Man learns to burn
They dance around the dying; & they drink the cup of life
In Wales & Scotland all the tears of the descending year: the proved string;
And flint the stream of Albion: Thames: Avon: Wear: Tees:
And Twemickens: cast the Severn away: as during reland the beam.
The Hammer of Los; the Severn are drawn into the Void of the Stain:
London feels his brain cut round: Edinburghs heart is circumscribed!
York & Lincoln hide among the flocks, because of the griding Knife.
Worcester & Hereford: Oxford & Cambridge reel & stagger
Overwearied with howlings: Wales & Scotland along Severn the fight!
The Inhabitants are sick to death: they labour to divide into Days
And Nights, the uncertain Periods: and into Weeks & Months. In vain
They send the Dove & Raven: & in vain the Serpent over the mountains.
And in vain the Eagle & Lion over the four-fold wilderness.
They return not: but build a habitation separate from Man.
The Sun forgets his course like a drunken man; he hesitates,
Upon the Cheselden hills, thinking to sleep on the Severn
In vain: he is hurried afar into an unknown Night
He bleeds in torrents of blood as he rolls thro heaven above
He chokes up the paths of the sky; the Moon is leprous as snow:
Trembling & descending down seeking to rest upon high Mona:
Scattering her leprous snows in flakes of disease over Albion.
The Stars flee remote: the heaven is iron, the earth is sulphur,
And all the mountains & hills shrink up like a withering gourd,
As the Senses of Men shrink together under the Knife of flint,
In the hands of Albions Daughters, among the Druid Temples.

By those who drink their blood & the blood of their Covenant
And the Twelve Daughters of Albion united in Rahab & Tirzah
A Double Female: and they drew out from the Rocky Stones
5 Fibres of Life to Weave for every Female is a Golden Loom
The Rocks are opake hardnesses covering all Vegetated things
And as they Wove & Cut from the Loins in various divisions
Stretching over Europe & Asia from Ireland to Japan
They divided into many lovely Daughters to be counterparts
10 To those they Wove, for when they Wove a Male, they divided
Into a Female to the Woven Male, in opake hardness
They cut the Fibres from the Rocks groaning in pain they Weave;
Calling the Rocks Atomic Origins of Existence; denying Eternity
By the Atheistical Epicurean Philosophy of Albions Tree
15 Such are the Feminine & Masculine when separated from Man
They call the Rocks Parents of Men, & adore the frowning Chaos
Dancing around in howling pain, clothed in the bloody Veil,
Hiding Albions Sons within the Veil, closing Jerusalems
Sons without; to feed with their Souls the Spectres of Albion
20 Ashamed to give Love openly to the piteous & merciful Man
Counting him an imbecile mockery: but the Warrior
They adore: & his revenge cherish with the blood of the Innocent
They drink up Dan & Gad, to feed with milk Skofeld & Kotope
They strip off Josephs Coat & dip it in the blood of battle
25 Tirzah sits weeping to hear the shrieks of the dying: her Knife
Of flint is in her hand: she passes it over the howling Victim
The Daughters Weave their Work in loud cries over the Rock
Of Horeb: still eyeing Albions Cliffs eagerly siezing & twisting
The threads of Vala & Jerusalem running from mountain to mountain
30 Over the whole Earth: loud the Warriors rage in Beth Peor
Beneath the iron whips of their Captains & consecrated banners
Loud the Sun & Moon rage in the conflict: loud the Stars
Shout in the night of battle & their spears grow to their hands
With blood, weaving the deaths of the Mighty into a Tabernacle
35 For Rahab & Tirzah; till the Great Polypus of Generation covered the Earth

In Verulam the Polypus's Head, winding around his bulk
Thro Rochester, and Chichester, & Exeter & Salisbury,
To Bristol: & his Heart beat strong on Salisbury Plain
Shooting out Fibres round the Earth, thro Gaul & Italy
40 And Greece, & along the Sea of Rephaim into Judea
To Sodom & Gomorrha: thence to India, China & Japan
The Twelve Daughters in Rahab & Tirzah have circumscrib'd the Brain
Beneath & pierced it thro the midst with a golden pin.
Blood hath stain'd her fair side beneath her bosom.

45 O thou poor Human Form! said she. O thou poor child of woe!
Why wilt thou wander away from Tirzah: why me compel to bind thee
If thou dost go away from me I shall consume upon these Rocks
These fibres of thine eyes that used to beam in distant heavens
Away from me: I have bound down with a hot iron.
50 These nostrils that expanded with delight in morning skies
I have bent downward with lead melted in my roaring furnaces
Of affliction: of love: of sweet despair: of torment unendurable
My soul is seven furnaces, incessant roars the bellows
Upon my terribly flaming heart, the molten metal runs
55 In channels thro my fiery limbs: O love! O pity! O fear!
O pain: O the pangs, the bitter pangs of love forsaken
Ephraim was a wilderness of joy where all my wild beasts ran
The River Kanah wanderd by my sweet Manassehs side
To see the boy spring into heavens sounding from my sight!
60 Go Noah fetch the girdle of strong brass, heat it red hot:
Press it around the loins of this ever expanding cruelty
62 Shriek not so my only love! I refuse thy joys: I drink
Thy shrieks because Hand & Hyle are cruel & obdurate to me

O Skofield why art thou cruel: Lo Joseph is thine! to make
You One: to weave you both in the same mantle of skin
Bind him down Sisters bind him down on Ebal Mount of cursing
Malah come forth from Lebanon: & Hoglah from Mount Sinai:
Come circumscribe this tongue of sweets & with a screw of iron
Fasten this ear into the rock! Milcah the task is thine
Weep not so Sisters! weep not so! our life depends on this
Or mercy & truth are fled away from Shechem & Mount Gilead
Unless my beloved is bound upon the Stems of Vegetation

And thus the Warriors cry in the hot day of Victory, in Songs.
Look: the beautiful Daughter of Albion sits naked upon the Stone
Her panting Victim beside her: her heart is drunk with blood
Tho her brain is not drunk with wine: she goes forth from Albion
In pride of beauty: in cruelty of holiness: in the brightness
Of her tabernacle, & her ark & secret place, the beautiful Daughter
Of Albion, delights the eyes of the Kings, their hearts & the
Hearts of their Warriors glow hot before Thor & Friga, O Molech!
O Chemosh! O Bacchus! O Venus! O Double God of Generation
The Heavens are cut like a mantle around from the Cliffs of Albion
Across Europe; across Africa; in howlings & deadly War
A sheet & veil & curtain of blood is let down from Heaven
Across the hills of Ephraim, & down Mount Olivet to
The Valley of the Jebusite: Molech rejoices in heaven
He sees the Twelve Daughters naked upon the Twelve Stones
Themselves condensing to rocks & into the Ribs of a Man
Lo they shoot forth in tender Nerves, across Europe & Asia
Lo they rest upon the Tribes, where their panting Victims lie
Molech rushes into the Kings in love to the beautiful Daughters
But they frown & delight in cruelty, refusing all other joys
Bring your Offerings, your first begotten; pamperd with milk & blood
Your first born of seven years old! be they Males or Females:
To the beautiful Daughters of Albion! They sport before the Kings
Clothed in the skin of the Victim! blood: human blood: is the Life
And delightful food of the Warrior: the well fed Warriors flesh
Of him who is slain in War: fills the Valleys of Ephraim with
Breeding Women walking in pride & bringing forth under green trees
With pleasure, without pain, for their food is blood of the Captive
Molech rejoices thro the Land from Havilah to Shur: he rejoices
In moral law & its severe penalties: loud Shaddai & Jehovah
Thunder above: when they see the Twelve panting Victims
On the Twelve Stones of Power, & the beautiful Daughters of Albion
If you dare rend their Veil with your Spear; you are healed of Love!
From the Hills of Camberwell & Wimbledon: from the Valleys
Of Walton & Esther: from Stone-henge & from Maldens Cove
Jerusalems Pillars fall in the rendings of fierce War
Over France & Germany: upon the Rhine & Danube
Reuben & Benjamin flee; they hide in the Valley of Rephaim
Why trembles the Warriors limbs when he beholds thy beauty
Spotted with Victims blood? by the fires at the secret tabernacle
And thy ark & holy place: at thy frowns: at thy dire revenge
Smitten as Uzzah of old: his armour is softend: his spear
And sword faint in his hand: from Albion across Great Tartary
O beautiful Daughter of Albion: cruelty is thy delight
O Virgin of terrible eyes, who dwellest by Valleys of springs
Beneath the Mountains of Lebanon, in the City of Rehob in Hamath
Taught to touch the harp: to dance in the Circle of Warriors
Before the Kings of Canaan: to cut the flesh from the Victim
To roast the flesh in fire: to examine the Infants limbs
In cruelties of holiness: to refuse the joys of love: to bring
The Spies from Egypt, to raise jealousy in the bosoms of the Twelve
Kings of Canaan: then to let the Spies depart to Meribah Kadesh
To the place of the Amalekite; I am drunk with unsatiated love
I must rush again to War: for the Virgin has frownd & refusd
Sometimes I curse & sometimes bless thy fascinating beauty
Once Man was occupied in intellectual pleasures & energies
But now my soul is harrowd with grief & fear & love & desire
And now I hate & now I love & Intellect is no more:
There is no time for any thing but the torments of love & desire
The Feminine & Masculine Shadows soft, mild & ever varying
In beauty: are Shadows now no more, but Rocks in Horeb

Then all the Males conjoined into One Male & every one
Became a ravening eating Cancer growing in the Female
A Polypus of Roots of Reasoning Doubt Despair & Death.
Going forth & returning from Albions Rocks to Canaan:
Devouring Jerusalem from every Nation of the Earth.

Envying stood the enormous Form at variance with Itself
In all its Members: in eternal torment of love & jealousy:
Drivn forth by Los time after time from Albions cliffy shore.
Drawing the free loves of Jerusalem into infernal bondage;
That they might be born in contentions of Chastity & in
Deadly Hate between Leah & Rachel Daughters of Deceit & Fraud
Bearing the images of various Species of Contention
And Jealousy & Abhorrence & Revenge & deadly Murder.
Till they refuse liberty to the Male: & not like Beulah
Where every Female delights to give her maiden to her husband
The Female searches sea & land for gratifications to the
Male Genius: who in return clothes her in gems & gold
And feeds her with the food of Eden, hence all her beauty beams
She Creates at her will a little moony night & silence
With Spaces of sweet gardens & a tent of elegant beauty:
Closed in by a sandy desart & a night of stars shining.
And a little tender moon & hovering angels on the wing.
And the Male gives a Time & Revolution to her Space
Till the time of love is passed in ever varying delights
For All Things Exist in the Human Imagination
And thence in Beulah they are stolen by secret amorous theft,
Till they have had Punishment enough to make them commit Crimes
Hence rose the Tabernacle in the Wilderness & all its Offerings,
From Male & Female Loves in Beulah & their Jealousies
But no one can consummate Female bliss in Los's World without
Becoming a Generated Mortal, a Vegetating Death

And now the Spectres of the Dead awake in Beulah: all
The Jealousies become Murderous: uniting together in Rahab
A Religion of Chastity, forming a Commerce to sell Loves
With Moral Law an Equal Balance, not going down with decision
Therefore the Male severe & cruel filld with stern Revenge:
Mutual Hate returns & mutual Deceit & mutual Fear.

Hence the Infernal Veil grows in the disobedient Female:
Which Jesus rends & the whole Druid Law removes away
From the Inner Sanctuary; a False Holiness hid within the Center,
For the Sanctuary of Eden, is in the Camp: in the Outline,
In the Circumference: & every Minute Particular is Holy:
Embraces are Cominglings, from the Head even to the Feet
And not a pompous High Priest entering by a Secret Place.

Jerusalem pined in her inmost soul over Wandering Reuben
As she slept in Beulahs Night hid by the Daughters of Beulah

And this the Form of mighty Hand sitting on Albions cliffs
Before the face of Albion, a mighty threatning Form.

His bosom wide & shoulders huge overspreading wondrous
Bear Three strong sinewy Necks & Three awful & terrible Heads
Three Brains in contradictory council brooding incessantly,
Neither daring to put in act its councils, fearing each other,
Therefore rejecting Ideas as nothing & holding all Wisdom
To consist. in the agreements & disagreements of Ideas,
Plotting to devour Albions Body of Humanity & Love.

Such Form the aggregate of the Twelve Sons of Albion took; & such
Their appearance when combind: but often by birth-pangs & loud groans
They divide to Twelve: the key-bones & the chest dividing in pain
Disclose a hideous orifice; thence issuing the Giant-brood
Arise as the smoke of the furnace, shaking the rocks from sea to sea.
And there they combine into Three Forms, named Bacon & Newton & Locke,
in the Oak Groves of Albion which overspread all the Earth.

Imputing Sin & Righteousness to Individuals; Rahab
Sat deep within him hid: his Feminine Power unreveald,
Brooding Abstract Philosophy. to destroy Imagination, the Divine
Humanity A Three-fold Wonder: feminine: most beautiful: Three-fold
Each within other. On her white marble & even Neck, her Heart
Inorbd and bonified: with locks of shadowing modesty, shining
Over her beautiful Female features, soft flourishing in beauty
Beams mild, all love and all perfection, that when the lips
Recieve a kiss from Gods or Men, a threefold kiss returns
From the pressd loveliness; so her whole immortal form three-fold
Three-fold embrace returns: consuming lives of Gods & Men
In fires of beauty melting them as gold & silver in the furnace
Her Brain enlabyrinths the whole heaven of her bosom & loins
To put in act what her Heart wills; O who can withstand her power
Her name is Vala in Eternity: in Time her name is Rahab

The Starry Heavens all were fled from the mighty limbs of Albion

And above Albions Land was seen the Heavenly Canaan
As the Substance is to the Shadow: and above Albions Twelve Sons
Were seen Jerusalems Sons: and all the Twelve Tribes spreading
Over Albion. As the Soul is to the Body, so Jerusalems Sons,
Are to the Sons of Albion: and Jerusalem is Albions Emanation

What is Above is Within, for every-thing in Eternity is translucent:
The Circumference is Within: Without, is formed the Selfish Center
And the Circumference still expands going forward to Eternity.
And the Center has Eternal States! these States we now explore.

And these the Names of Albions Twelve Sons, & of his Twelve Daughters
With their Districts. Hand dwelt in Selsey & had Sussex & Surrey
And Kent & Middlesex: all their Rivers & their Hills of flocks & herds:
Their Villages Towns Cities Sea-Ports Temples sublime Cathedrals;
All were his Friends & their Sons & Daughters intermarry in Beulah
All my Sons from Reuben to Benjamin, enter into their Bosoms, you with
Albion from Dover Cliff to Lizard Point, you bear your Heaven
And Earth, & all you behold, tho it appears Without it is Within
In your Imagination of which this World of Mortality is but a Shadow.

Hyle dwelt in Winchester comprehending Hants Dorset Devon Cornwall,
Their Villages Cities Sea-Ports, their Corn fields & Gardens spacious
Palaces, Rivers & Mountains; and between Hand & Hyle arose
Gwendolen & Cambel who is Boadicea: they go abroad & return
Like lovely beams of light from the mingled affections of the Brothers
The Inhabitants of the Whole Earth rejoice in their beautiful light.

Coban dwelt in Bath. Somerset Wiltshire Gloucestershire,
Obey'd his awful voice Ignoge is his lovely Emanation,
She adjoind with Gwantoke's Children, soon lovely Cordella arose.
Gwantoke forgave & joyd over South Wales & all its Mountains.

Peachey had North Wales Shropshire Cheshire & the Isle of Man.
His Emanation is Mehetabel terrible & lovely upon the Mountains

Brereton had Yorkshire Durham Westmoreland & his Emanation
Is Ragan, she adjoind to Slade, & produced Gonorill far beaming.

Slade had Lincoln Stafford Derby Nottingham & his lovely
Emanation Gonorill rejoices over hills & rocks & woods & rivers

Hutton had Warwick Northampton Bedford Buckingham,
Leicester & Berkshire: & his Emanation is Gwinefred beautiful

Skofeld had Ely Rutland Cambridge Huntingdon Norfolk
Suffolk Harford & Essex: & his Emanation is Gwinevera
Beautiful, she beams towards the east, all kinds of precious stones
And pearl, with instruments of music in holy Jerusalem

Kox had Oxford Warwick Wilts: his Emanation is Estrild:
Joind with Cordella she shines southward over the Atlantic.

Kotope had Hereford Stafford Worcester, & his Emanation
Is Sabrina joind with Mehetabel she shines west over America

Bowen had all Scotland, the Isles, Northumberland & Cumberland
His Emanation is Conwenna, she shines a triple form
Over the north with pearly beams gorgeous & terrible
Jerusalem & Vala rejoice in Bowen & Conwenna.

But the Four Sons of Jerusalem that never were Generated
Are Rintrah, & Palamabron, and Theotormon and Bromion. They
Dwell over the Four Provinces of Ireland in heavenly light
The Four Universities of Scotland, & in Oxford & Cambridge & Winchester

But now Albion is darkned & Jerusalem lies in ruins:
Above the Mountains of Albion, above the head of Los.

And Los shouted with ceaseless shoutings & his tears poured down
His immortal cheeks, rearing his hands to heaven for aid Divine!
But he spoke not to Albion: fearing lest Albion should turn his Back
Against the Divine Vision: & fall over the Precipice of Eternal Death
But he receded before Albion & before Vala weaving the Veil
With the iron shuttle of War among the rooted Oaks of Albion;
Weeping & shuddering at the horrors Els fold day & night; and his Children
Wept round him as a flock silent Seven Days of Eternity

And the Thirty-two Counties of the Four Provinces of Ireland
Are thus divided: The Four Counties are in the Four Camps
Munster South in Reubens Gate, Connaut West in Josephs Gate
Ulster North in Dans Gate, Leinster East in Judahs Gate

For Albion in Eternity has Sixteen Gates among his Pillars
But the Four towards the West were Walled up & the Twelve
That front the Four other Points were turned Four-Square
By Los for Jerusalems sake & called the Gates of Jerusalem
Because Twelve Sons of Jerusalem fled successive thro the Gates
But the Four Sons of Jerusalem who fled not but remaind
Are Rintrah & Palamabron & Theotormon & Bromion
The Four that remain with Los to guard the Western Wall
And these Four remain to guard the Four Walls of Jerusalem
Whose foundations remain in the Thirty-two Counties of Ireland
And in the Thirty-six Counties of Wales & in the Forty Counties
Of England & in the Thirty-six Counties of Scotland
And the names of the Thirty-two Counties of Ireland are these
Under Judah & Issachar & Zebulun are Lowth Longford
Eastmeath Westmeath Dublin Kildare Kings County
Queens County Wicklow Catherloh Wexford Kilkenny
And those under Reuben & Simeon & Levi are these
Waterford Tipperary Cork Limerick Kerry Clare
And those under Ephraim Manasseh & Benjamin are these
Galway Roscommon Mayo Sligo Leitrim
And those under Dan Asher & Naphtali are these
Donnegal Antrim Tyrone Fermanagh Armagh Londonderry
Down Managhan Cavan these are the Land of Erin

All these Center in London & in Golgonooza. from whence
They are Created continually East & West & North & South
And from them are Created all the Nations of the Earth
Europe & Asia & Africa & America, in fury Fourfold!

And Thirty-two the Nations; to dwell in Jerusalems Gates
O Come ye Nations Come ye People Come up to Jerusalem
Return Jerusalem, & dwell together as of old! Return
Return, O Albion let Jerusalem overspread all Nations
As in the times of old. O Albion awake! Reuben wanders
The Nations wait for Jerusalem, they look up for the Bride

France Spain Italy Germany Poland Russia Sweden Turkey
Arabia Palestine Persia Hindostan China Tartary Siberia
Egypt Lybia Ethiopia Guinea Caffraria Negroland Morocco
Congo Zaara Canada Greenland Carolina Mexico
Peru Patagonia Amazonia Brazil. Thirty-two Nations
And under these Thirty-two Classes of Islands in the Ocean
All the Nations Peoples & Tongues throughout all the Earth
And the Four Gates of Los surround the Universe Within and
Without; & whatever is visible in the Vegetable Earth. the same
Is visible in the Mundane Shell; reversd in mountain & vale
And a Son of Eden was set over each Daughter of Beulah to guard
In Albions Tomb the wondrous Creation: & the Four-fold Gate
Towards Beulah is to the South Fenelon. Guion. Teresa.
Whitefield & Hervey, guard that Gate; with all the gentle Souls
Who guide the great Wine-press of Love; Four precious Stones that Gate.

Such are Cathedrons golden Halls: in the City of Golgonooza

And Los's Furnaces howl loud; living: self-moving: lamenting
With fury & despair. & they stretch from South to North
Thro all the Four Points. Lo! the Labourers at the Furnaces
Rintrah & Palamabron. Theotormon & Bromion. loud labring
With the innumerable multitudes of Golgonooza, round the Anvils
Of Death. But how they came forth from the Furnaces & how long
Vast & severe the anguish eer they knew their Father; were
Long to tell & of the iron rollers; golden axle-trees & yokes
Of brass, iron chains & braces & the gold, silver & brass
Mingled or separate: for swords; arrows; cannons; mortars
The terrible ball: the wedge: the loud sounding hammer of destruction
The sounding flail to thresh; the winnow; to winnow kingdoms
The water wheel & mill of many innumerable wheels resistless
Over the Four fold Monarchy from Earth to the Mundane Shell.

Perusing Albions Tomb in the starry characters of Og & Anak:
To Create the lion & wolf the bear: the tyger & ounce:
To Create the woolly lamb & downy fowl & scaly serpent
The summer & winter: day & night: the sun & moon & stars
The tree: the plant: the flower: the rock: the stone: the metal:
Of Vegetative Nature: by their hard restricting condensations.

Where Luvahs World of Opakeness grew to a period: It
Became a Limit a Rocky hardness without form & void
Accumulating without end: hence Los, who is of the Elohim
Opens the Furnaces of affliction in the Emanation
Fixing The Sexual into an ever-prolific Generation
Naming the Limit of Opakeness Satan & the Limit of Contraction
Adam, who is Peleg & Joktan: & Esau & Jacob: & Saul & David

Voltaire insinuates that these Limits are the cruel work of God
Mocking the Remover of Limits & the Resurrection of the Dead
Setting up Kings in wrath: in holiness of Natural Religion
Which Los with his mighty Hammer demolishes time on time
In miracles & wonders of the Four-fold Desart of Albion
Permanently Creating to be in Time Reveald & Demolishd again
Satan. Cain. Tubal. Nimrod. Pharoh. Priam. Bladud. Belin
Arthur. Alfred. the Norman Conqueror. Richard John

And all the Kings & Nobles of the Earth & all their Glories
These are Created by Rahab & Tirzah in Ulro: but around
These, to preserve them from Eternal Death Los Creates
Adam. Noah. Abraham. Moses. Samuel. David. Ezekiel.

Dissipating the rocky forms of Death, by his thunderous Hammer
As the pilgrim passes while the Country permanent remains
So Men pass on: but States remain permanent for ever.

The Spectres of the Dead howl round the porches of Los
In the terrible Family feuds of Albions cities & villages
To destroy the Body of Albion Lungd & breathing & bound
The Sons of Los clothe them & feed & provide houses & gardens
And every Human Vegetated Form in its inward recesses
Is a house of pleasantness & a garden of delight Built by the
Sons & Daughters of Los in Bowlahoola & in Cathedron.

From London to York & Edinburgh the Furnaces rage terrible
Primrose Hill is the mouth of the Furnace & the Iron Door;

The Four Zoa's clouded rage; Urizen stood by Albion
With Rintrah and Palamabron and Theotormon and Bromion
These Four are Verulam & London & York & Edinburgh
And the Four Zoa's are Urizen & Luvah & Tharmas & Urthona
In opposition deadly, and their Wheels in poisonous
And deadly stupor turn'd against each other loud & fierce
Entering into the Reasoning Power, forsaking Imagination
They became Spectres; & their Human Bodies were reposed
In Beulah, by the Daughters of Beulah with tears & lamentations

The Spectre is the Reasoning Power in Man; & when separated
From Imagination, and closing itself as in steel, in a Ratio
Of the Things of Memory. It thence frames Laws & Moralities
To destroy Imagination! the Divine Body, by Martyrdoms & Wars

Teach me O Holy Spirit the Testimony of Jesus! let me
Comprehend wonderous things out of the Divine Law
I behold Babylon in the opening Streets of London, I behold
Jerusalem in ruins wandering about from house to house
This I behold the shudderings of death attend my steps
I walk up and down in Six Thousand Years: their Events are present before me
To tell how Los in grief & anger, whirling round his Hammer on high
Drave the Sons & Daughters of Albion from their ancient mountains
They became the Twelve Gods of Asia Opposing the Divine Vision

The Sons of Albion are Twelve: the Sons of Jerusalem Sixteen
I tell how Albions Sons by Harmonies of Concords & Discords
Opposed to Melody, and by Lights & Shades, opposed to Outline
And by Abstraction opposed to the Visions of Imagination
By cruel Laws divided Sixteen into Twelve Divisions
How Hyle roofd Los in Albions Cliffs by the Affections rent
Asunder & opposed to Thought, to draw Jerusalems Sons
Into the Vortex of his Wheels. therefore Hyle is calld Gog
Age after age drawing them away towards Babylon
Babylon, the Rational Morality deluding to death the little ones
In strong temptations of stolen beauty I tell how Reuben slept
On London Stone & the Daughters of Albion ran around admiring
His awful beauty: with Moral Virtue the fair deceiver. offspring
Of Good & Evil, they divided him in love upon the Thames & sent
Him over Europe in streams of gore out of Cathedrons Looms
How Los drave them from Albion & they became Daughters of Canaan
Hence Albion was calld the Canaanite & all his Giant Sons.
Hence is my Theme. O Lord my Saviour open thou the Gates
And I will lead forth thy Words, telling how the Daughters
Cut the Fibres of Reuben, how he rolld apart & took Root
In Bashan, terror-struck Albions Sons look toward Bashan
They have divided Simeon he also rolld apart in blood
Over the Nations till he took Root beneath the shining Looms
Of Albions Daughters in Philistea by the side Dan & Ephraim
They have divided Levi; he hath shot out into Forty eight Roots
Over the Land of Canaan: they have divided Judah
He hath took root in Hebron, in the Land of Hand & Hyle
Dan: Napthali: Gad: Asher: Issachar: Zebulun: roll apart
From all the Nations of the Earth to dissipate into Non Entity

I see a Feminine Form arise from the Four terrible Zoas
Beautiful but terrible struggling to take a form of beauty
Rooted in Shechem: this is Dinah, the youthful form of Erin
The Wound I see in South Molton Street & Stratford place
Whence Joseph & Benjamin rolld apart away from the Nations
In vain they rolld apart; they are fixd into the Land of Cabul

And Rahab Babylon the Great hath destroyd Jerusalem
Bath stood upon the Severn with Merlin & Bladud & Arthur
The Cup of Rahab in his hand: her Poison Twenty-seven-fold

5 And all her Twenty-seven Heavens now hid & now reveald
Appear in strong delusive light of Time & Space drawn out
In shadowy pomp by the Eternal Prophet created evermore
For Los in Six Thousand years walks up & down continually
That not one Moment of Time be lost & every revolution
Of Space he makes permanent in Bowlahoola & Cathedron.

10 And these the names of the Twenty-seven Heavens & their Churches
Adam, Seth, Enos, Cainan, Mahalaleel, Jared, Enoch,
Methuselah, Lamech; these are Giants mighty Hermaphroditic
Noah, Shem, Arphaxad, Cainan the second, Salah, Heber,
15 Peleg, Reu, Serug, Nahor, Terah; these are the Female-Males
A Male within a Female hid as in an Ark & Curtains,
Abraham, Moses, Solomon, Paul, Constantine, Charlemaine
Luther, these seven are the Male-Females, the Dragon Forms
20 Religion hid in War: a Dragon red & hidden Harlot
But their Religion the first Seven: the Male Females the Dwarfish
And Double, only double the single & female over the male
These are the Gods of the Heathen; Twenty seven Heavens & Hell
Open'd Eternity in Time & Space: triumphant in Vengeance
25 They are the Heavenly Anvils, by Los within the Mundane Shell
And where the Starry Heavens are fled from the mighty Mundane circle
Walk Luvah into silent death: in a dark Column girt
27 But now the Starry Heavens are fled from the mighty limbs of Albion

leave
visions
one

7/40
Ro

Albion

Jerusalem. C 4

The Spectres of Albions Twelve Sons revolve mightily
Over the Tomb & over the Body: ravning to devour
The sleeping Humanity. Los with his mace of iron
Walks round: loud his threats, loud his blows fall
On the rocky Spectres, as the Potter breaks the potsherds;
Dashing in pieces Self-righteousnesses: driving them from Albions
Cliffs: dividing them into Male & Female forms in his Furnaces
And on his Anvils: lest they destroy the Feminine Affections
They are broken. Loud howl the Spectres in his iron Furnace

While Los laments at his dire labours, viewing Jerusalem:
Sitting before his Furnaces clothed in sackcloth of hair;
Albions Twelve Sons surround the Forty-two Gates of Erin,
In terrible armour, raging against the Lamb & against Jerusalem.
Surrounding them with fires of ether & with rocks of Sinai:
They took their Mother Vala, and they crown'd her with gold:
They named her Rahab, & gave her power over the Earth
The Concave Earth round Golgonooza in Entuthon Benython,
Even to the stars exalting her Throne, to build beyond the Throne
Of God and the Lamb, to destroy the Lamb & usurp the Throne of God
Drawing their Ulro Voidness round the Four-fold Humanity

Naked Jerusalem lay before the Gates upon Mount Zion,
The Hill of Giants, all her foundations levelld with the dust:

Her Twelve Gates thrown down: her children carried into captivity
Herded in chains of iron: the Iron within was seen in a distant light,
Outward: unknown before in Beulah & the twelve gates were fill'd
With blood; from Japan eastward to the Giants causway, west
In Erins Continent: and Jerusalem wept upon Euphrates banks
Disorganizd; an evanescent shade, scarce seen or heard among
Her children's Druid Temples dropping with blood wanderd weeping!
And thus her voice went forth in the darkness of Philisthea.

My brother & my father are no more! God hath forsaken me
The arrows of the Almighty pour upon me & my children,
I have sinned and am an outcast from the Divine Presence!

My tents are falln! my pillars are in ruins! my children dashd
Upon Egypts iron floors, & the marble pavements of Assyria;
I melt my soul in reasonings among the towers of Heshbon;
Mount Zion is become a cruel rock & no more dew
Nor rain: no more the spring of the rock appears: but cold
Hard & obdurate are the brooks of Arnon that look down
The hills of Judea are fallen with me into the deepest hell
Away from the Nations of the Earth, & from the Cities of the Nations;
I walk to Ephraim. I seek for Shiloh: I walk like a lost sheep
Among precipices of despair: in Goshen I seek for light
In vain: and in Gilead for a physician and a comforter.
Goshen hath followd Philistea: Gilead hath joind with Og!
They are become narrow places in a little and dark land:
How distant far from Albion! his hills & his valleys no more
Receive the feet of Jerusalem: they have cast me quite away:
And Albion is himself shrunk to a narrow rock in the midst of the sea!
The plains of Sussex & Surrey, their hills of flocks & herds
No more seek to Jerusalem nor to the sound of my Holy-ones.
The Fifty-two Counties of England are hardend against me
As if I was not their Mother, they despise me & cast me out
London coverd the whole Earth. England encompassd the Nations:
And all the Nations of the Earth were seen in the Cities of Albion:
My pillars reachd from sea to sea: London beheld me come
From my east & from my west; he blessed me and he gave
His children to my breasts, his sons & daughters to my knees
His aged parents sought me out in every city & village:
They discernd my countenance with joy! they shewd me to their sons
Saying Lo Jerusalem is here! she sitteth in our secret chambers
Levi and Judah & Issachar: Ephram, Manesseh, Gad and Dan
Are seen in our hills & valleys: they keep our flocks & herds:
They watch them in the night: and the Lamb of God appears among us.
The river Severn stayd his course at my command:
Hampshire poured his flocks into the basins and the neths:
Nethways mingled with the Medway: Thames recievd the heavenly Jordan
Albion gave me to the whole Earth to walk up & down; to pour
Joy upon every mountain; to teach songs to the shepherd & plowman
I taught the ships of the sea to sing the songs of Zion.
Italy saw me, in sublime astonishment: France was wholly mine:
As my garden & as my secret bath; Spain was my heavenly couch:
I slept in his golden hills: the Lamb of God met me there.
There we walked as in our secret chamber among our little ones
They loved me as I walkd with joy! they beheld our secret
Joys: on Englands green & pleasant hills, & a secret God:
Germany. Poland & the North woodd the steps round
I gazed in all their mountains & my curtains in all their vales
The furniture of their houses was the furniture of my chamber
Turkey & Grecia saw my instruments of music, they arose
They sang to the harp: the flute: the mellow horn of Jerusalems joy
They sounded thanksgivings in my courts: Egypt & Lybia heard
The swarthy sons of Ethiopia stood round the Lamb of God
Enquiring for Jerusalem: he led them up my steps to my altar:
And thou America! I once beheld thee but now behold no more
Thy golden mountains where my Cherubim & Seraphim rejoicd
Together among my little-ones. But now, my Altars run with blood!
My fires are corrupt! my incense is a cloudy pestilence
Of seven diseases! Once a continual cloud of salvation, rose
From all my myriads; once the Four-fold World rejoicd among
The pillars of Jerusalem, between my winged Cherubim:
But now I am closd out from them in the narrow passages
Of the valleys of destruction, into a dark land of pitch & bitumen.
From Albions Tomb afar and from the four-fold wonders of God
Shrunk to a narrow doleful form in the dark land of Cabul;
There is Reuben & Gad & Joseph & Judah & Levi, closd up
In narrow vales: I walk & count the bones of my beloveds
Along the Valley of Destruction, among these Druid Temples
Which overspread all the Earth in patriarchal pomp & cruel pride
Tell me O Vala thy purposes; tell me wherefore thy shuttles
Drop with the gore of the slain; why Luvahs bulls are red with blood
Wherefore in dreadful majesty & beauty outside appears
Thy Masculine from thy Feminine hardening against the heavens
To devour the Human! Why dost thou weep upon the wind among
These cruel Druid Temples: O Vala! Humanity is far above
Sexual organization; & the Visions of the Night of Beulah
Where Sexes wander in dreams of bliss among the Emanations
Where the Masculine & Feminine are nursd into Youth & Maiden
By the tears & smiles of Beulahs Daughters till the time of Sleep is past.
Wherefore then do you realize these nets of beauty & delusion
In open day to draw the souls of the Dead into the light of thought
Till Albion is shut out from every Nation under Heaven.

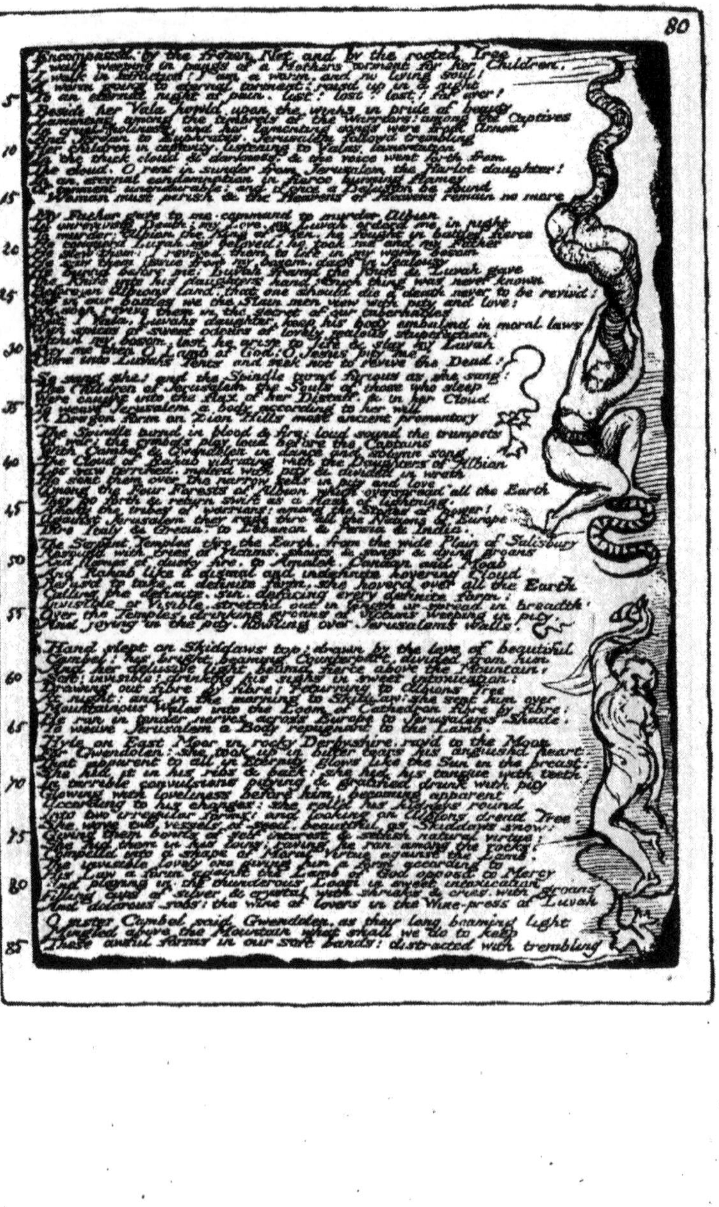

Encompassd by the frozen Net and by the rooted Tree
I walk weeping in pangs of a Mothers torment for her Children:
I walk in affliction: I am a worm, and no living soul!
A worm going to eternal torment! raisd up in a night
To an eternal night of pain. lost! lost! lost! for ever!

Beside her Vala howld upon the winds in pride of beauty
Lamenting among the timbrels of the Warriors: among the Captives
In cruel holiness, and her lamenting songs were from Arnon
And Jordan to Euphrates. Jerusalem followd trembling
Her children in captivity, listening to Valas lamentation
In the thick cloud & darkness. & the voice went forth from
The cloud. O rent in sunder from Jerusalem the Harlot daughter!
In an eternal condemnation in fierce burning flames
Of torment unendurable! and if once a Delusion be found
Woman must perish & the Heavens of Heavens remain no more

My Fathers gave to me command to murder Albion
In unreviving Death; my Love, my Luvah orderd me in night
To murder Albion the King of Men. he fought in battles fierce
He conquerd Luvah my beloved: he took me and my Father
He slew them: I revived them to life in my warm bosom
He saw them issue from my bosom dark in Jealousy
He burnd before me: Luvah framd the Knife & Luvah gave
The Knife into his daughters hand! such thing was never known
Before in Albions land. that one should die a death never to be reviv'd!
For in our battles we the Slain men view with pity and love:
We soon revive them in the secret of our tabernacles
But I Vala, Luvahs daughter, keep his body embalmd in moral laws
With spices of sweet odours of lovely jealous stupefaction:
Within my bosom, lest he arise to life & slay my Luvah
Pity me then O Lamb of God! O Jesus pity me!
Come into Luvahs Tents, and seek not to revive the Dead!

So sang she: and the Spindle turnd furious as she sang:
The Children of Jerusalem the Souls of those who sleep
Were caught into the flax of her Distaff, & in her Cloud
To weave Jerusalem a body according to her will
A Dragon form on Zions Hills most ancient promontory

The Spindle turnd in blood & fire: loud sound the trumpets
Of war: the cymbals play loud before the Captains
With Cambel & Gwendolen in dance and solemn song
The Cloud of Rahab vibrating with the Daughters of Albion
Los saw terrified, melted with pity & divided in wrath
He sent them over the narrow seas in pity and love
Among the Four Forests of Albion which overspread all the Earth
They go forth & return swift as a flash of lightning.
Among the tribes of warriors: among the Stones of power!
Against Jerusalem they rage thro all the Nations of Europe
Thro Italy & Grecia, to Lebanon & Persia & India.

The Serpent Temples thro the Earth, from the wide Plain of Salisbury
Resound with cries of Victims, shouts & songs & dying groans
And flames of dusky fire, to Amalek, Canaan and Moab
And Rahab like a dismal and indefinite hovering Cloud
Refusd to take a definite form. she hoverd over all the Earth
Calling the definite, sin: defacing every definite form;
Invisible, or Visible, stretch'd out in length or spread in breadth:
Over the Temples drinking groans of victims weeping in pity,
And joying in the pity, howling over Jerusalems walls.

Hand slept on Skiddaws top: drawn by the love of beautiful
Cambel: his bright, beaming Counterpart, divided from him
And her delusive light beamd fierce above the Mountain,
Soft: invisible: drinking his sighs in sweet intoxication:
Drawing out fibre by fibre: returning to Albions Tree
At night: and in the morning to Skiddaw: she sent him over
Mountainous Wales into the Loom of Cathedron fibre by fibre:
He ran in tender nerves across Europe to Jerusalems Shade:
To weave Jerusalem a Body repugnant to the Lamb.

Hyle on East Moor in rocky Derbyshire, rav'd to the Moon
For Gwendolen: she took up in bitter tears his anguishd heart,
That apparent to all in Eternity, glows like the Sun in the breast:
She hid it in his ribs & back: she hid his tongue with teeth
In terrible convulsions pitying & gratified drunk with pity
Glowing with loveliness before him, becoming apparent
According to his changes: she roll'd his kidneys round
Into two irregular forms: and looking on Albions dread Tree
She wove two vessels of seed, beautiful as Skiddaws snow;
Giving them bends of self interest & selfish natural virtue:
She hid them in his loins; raving he ran among the rocks,
Compelld into a shape of Moral Virtue against the Lamb.
The invisible lovely one giving him a form according to
His Law a form against the Lamb of God opposd to Mercy
And playing in the thunderous Loom in sweet intoxication
Filling cups of silver & crystal with shrieks & cries, with groans
And dolorous sobs: the wine of lovers in the Wine-press of Luvah

O sister Cambel, said Gwendolen, as their long beaming light
Mingled above the Mountain what shall we do to keep
These awful forms in our soft bands: distracted with trembling

I have mocked those who refused cruelty & I have admired
The cruel Warrior. I have refused to Pure Love to Merlin the piteous
He brings to me the Images of his Love & I reject in chastity
And turn them out into the streets for Harlots to be food
To the stern Warrior. I am become perfect in beauty over my Warrior
For Men are caught by Love: Woman is caught by Pride
That Love may only be obtaind in the passages of Death.
Let us look! let us examine: is the Cruel become an Infant
Or is he still a cruel Warrior? look Sisters, look! O piteous
I have destroyd Wandring Reuben who strove to bend my Will
I have strivd at Jerusalems beautiful interpreter: is my Beloved
The Cruel-one of Albion: to clothe him in gems of my Zone
I have namd him Jehovah of Hosts. Humanity is become
A weeping Infant in ruind lovely Jerusalems folding Cloud:

In Heaven Love begets Love! but Fear is the Parent of Earthly Love.
And he who will not bend to Love must be subdud by Fear.

I have heard Jerusalems groans; from Vala's cries & lamentations
I gather our eternal fate: Outcasts from Life and Love!
Unless I come to Albions arms, who cares but nought for me;
Enrage me in the East to God, there where the evil spreads
Look! I have wrought without dimension: Look! I have placed
The Stones in order, and their bodies together, with the chords of Rocks
They danced and sung, until the Dead Albion my mourning thread;
Soon shall the Spectres of the Dead follow my weaving threads.

The Twelve Daughters of Albion attentive listen in secret shades
On Cambridge and Oxford beaming soft, uniting with Rahabs cloud
While Gwendolen spoke to Cambel turning soft the spinning reel:
Or throwing the wingd shuttle; or drawing the cords with softest songs
The golden cords of the Looms animate beneath their touches soft,
Along the Island white, among the Druid Temples, while Gwendolen
Spoke to the Daughters of Albion standing on Skiddaws top.

So saying she took a Falshood & hid it in her left hand:
To entice her Sisters away to Babylon on Euphrates.
And thus she closed her left hand and utterd her Falshood:
Forgetting that Falshood is prophetic, she hid her hand behind her.
Upon her back behind her loins & thus uttered her Deceit.

I heard Enitharmon say to Los: Let the Daughters of Albion
Be scattered abroad and let the name of Albion be forgotten:
Divide them into three; name them Amalek Canaan & Moab:
Let Albion remain a desolation without an inhabitant:
And let the Looms of Enitharmon & the Furnaces of Los
Create Jerusalem, & Babylon & Egypt & Moab & Amalek,
And Helle & Hesperia & Hindostan & China & Japan.
But hide America, for a Curse an Altar of Victims & a Holy Place.
See Mexico round us rise, from our deep silent River & Esan:
Babylon is our chief desire, Moab our bath in summer.
Let us lead the stream of Arnon by dark paths over the bosom
Of Death: & Hesperia our own delight: so we lead Jerusalem
into the land of Og & Anak: and let the city of Rabbath remain
And the Villages of Moab Zoar the Cup of Gold of Babylon.
Humble thou thyself, O Gwendolen & Cambel, and remain
In all thy beauty & adorn the beautiful, for the fair is holy.

So spoke Gwendolen in Jealousy & Falshood. & Cambel said:
O that I could live in his sight: O that I could bind him to my arm.
Saying; She drew aside her Veil from Mam-Tor to Dovedale
Discovering her own perfect beauty to the Daughters of Albion
And Hand & Hyle rolld apart, but a secret of the dark Infant
Trembling & pitying she reclaimed & fled upon the wind:
His little sisters writhd & shrunk & burned in Jealousy.
The secret trembles of his wrath: & about their loins in fear.

Cambel trembled with jealousy: she trembled! she envied!
The envy ran thro Cathedrons Looms into the Heart
Of mild Jerusalem, to destroy the Lamb of God. Jerusalem
Languishd upon Mount Olivet, East of mild Zions Hill.
Los saw the envious blight above his Seventh Furnace
On Londons Tower on the Thames: he drew Cambel in wrath
Into his thundering Bellows, heaving it for a loud blast!
And with the blast of his Furnace upon fishy Billingsgate,
Beneath Albions fatal Tree, before the Gate of Los:
Shewd her his Spectre; naming her the Shadow of Jerusalem:
But she fled weeping on the Wind, treading day by night,
In the Wine-presses, her groans her loud shrieks & cries of anguish,
Naked among the human clusters: bringing wine of anguish
To feed the human roots of the human soul. Los utterd
Decision weeping. In beds of silver & couches of Furnace brass

So saying he threw his hands to another, and they stood
Trembling with fear: the Spectre was driven away & fled
Gwendolen saw the Infant in her hand & she bore it away
Over the forests with loud lamentation & the writhing Worm
Repentant: and she also in the eddying wind of Los's Bellows
Saw the Worm cast off Love, & the Wine-press of Luvah
The Worm began to breathe a human form upon the earth
The Spectre wept, trembling upon the Rock & Loam became mild
Beneath London: then the Sun the Furnace paind: it is their
Began to give their souls away in the Furnaces of affliction.

Los saw & was comforted at his Furnaces uttering thus his voice.
I know I am Urthona Keeper of the Gates of Heaven,
And that I can at will expatiate in the Gardens of bliss;
But pangs of love draw me down to my loins which are
Become a fountain of living pipes: O Albion my brother!

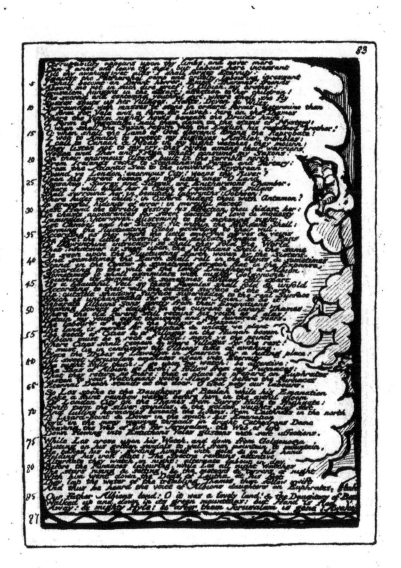

Highgates heights & Hampsteads, to Poplar Hackney & Bow:
To Islington & Paddington & the Brook of Albions River
We builded Jerusalem as a City & a Temple; from Lambeth
We began our Foundations; lovely Lambeth. O lovely Hills
Of Camberwell, we shall behold you no more in glory & pride
For Jerusalem lies in ruins & the Furnaces of Los are builded there
You are now shrunk up to a narrow rock in the midst of the Sea
But here we build Babylon on Euphrates. compelld to build
And to inhabit, our Little-ones to clothe in armour of the gold
Of Jerusalems Cherubims & to forge them swords of her Altars
I see London blind & age-bent begging thro the Streets
Of Babylon, led by a child. his tears run down his beard
The voice of Wandering Reuben ecchoes from street to street
In all the Cities of the Nations Paris Madrid Amsterdam
The Corner of Broad Street weeps; Poland Street languishes
To Great Queen Street & Lincolns Inn, all is distress & woe.

The night falls thick Hand comes from Albion in his strength
He combines into a Mighty-one the Double Molech & Chemosh
Marching thro Egypt in his fury the East is pale at his course
The Nations of India, the Wild Tartar that never knew Man
Starts from his lofty places & casts down his tents & flees away
But we woo him all the night in songs, O Los come forth O Los
Divide us from these terrors & give us power them to subdue
Arise upon thy Watches let us see thy Globe of fire
On Albions Rocks & let thy voice be heard upon Euphrates.

Thus sang the Daughters in lamentation, uniting into One
With Rahab as she turned the iron Spindle of destruction.
Terrified at the Sons of Albion they took the Falshood which
Gwendolen hid in her left hand. it grew & grew till it

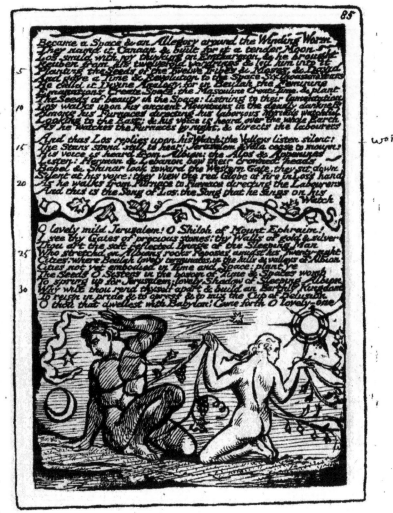

Became a Space & an Allegory around the Winding Worm
They namd it Canaan & built for it a tender Moon
Los smild with joy thinking on Enitharmon & he brought
Reuben from his twelvefold wandrings & led him into it
Planting the Seeds of the Twelve Tribes & Moses & David
And gave a Time & Revolution to the Space Six Thousand Years
He calld it Divine Analogy, for in Beulah the Feminine
Emanations Create Space. the Masculine Create Time. & plant
The Seeds of beauty in the Space: listning to their lamentation
Los walks upon his ancient Mountains in the deadly darkness
Among his Furnaces directing his laborious Myriads watchful
Looking to the East: & his voice is heard over the whole Earth
As he watches the Furnaces by night, & directs the labourers

And thus Los replies upon his Watch: the Valleys listen silent:
The Stars stand still to hear: Jerusalem & Vala cease to mourn:
His voice is heard from Albion: the Alps & Appenines
Listen: Hermon & Lebanon bow their crowned heads
Babel & Shinar look toward the Western Gate, they sit down
Silent at his voice: they view the red Globe of fire in Los's hand
As he walks from Furnace to Furnace directing the Labourers
And this is the Song of Los. the Song that he sings on his
                                                    Watch

O lovely mild Jerusalem! O Shiloh of Mount Ephraim!
I see thy Gates of precious stones: thy Walls of gold & silver
Thou art the soft reflected Image of the Sleeping Man
Who stretchd on Albions rocks reposes amidst his Twenty-eight
Cities: where Beulah lovely terminates, in the hills & valleys of Albion
Cities not yet embodied in Time and Space: plant ye
The Seeds O Sisters in the bosom of Time & Spaces womb
To spring up for Jerusalem: lovely Shadow of Sleeping Albion
Why wilt thou rend thyself apart & build an Earthly Kingdom
To reign in pride & to oppress & to mix the Cup of Religion
O thou that dwellest with Babylon! Come forth O lovely-one

I see thy Form O lovely mild Jerusalem, Winged with Six Wings
In the opacous Bosom of the Sleeper, lovely Three fold
In Head & Heart & Reins, three Universes of love & beauty
Thy forehead bright: Holiness to the Lord, with Gates of pearl
Reflecting Eternity beneath thy azure wings of feathery down
Ribbd delicate & clothd with featherd gold & azure & purple
From thy white shoulders shadowing, purity in holiness!
Thence featherd with soft crimson of the ruby bright as fire
Spreading into the azure Wings which like a canopy
Bends over thy Immortal Head in which Eternity dwells
Albion beloved Land; I see thy mountains & thy hills
And valleys & thy pleasant Cities Holiness to the Lord
I see the Spectres of thy Dead O Emanation of Albion.

Thy Bosom white, translucent coverd with immortal gems
A sublime ornament not obscuring the outlines of beauty
Terrible to behold for thy extreme beauty & perfection
Twelve-fold here all the Tribes of Israel I behold
Upon the Holy Land: I see the River of Life & Tree of Life
I see the New Jerusalem descending out of Heaven
Between thy Wings of gold & silver featherd immortal
Clear as the rainbow, as the cloud of the Suns tabernacle

Thy Reins coverd with Wings translucent sometimes covering
And sometimes spread abroad reveal the flames of holiness
Which like a robe covers: & like a Veil of Seraphim
In flaming fire unceasing burns from Eternity to Eternity
Twelvefold there all the Tribes of Israel I behold
Upon the Holy Land: I see the River of Life & Tree of Life
A Pillar of a Cloud by day: A Pillar of fire by night
Guides them; there I behold Moab & Ammon & Amalek
There Bells of silver round thy knees living articulate
Comforting sounds of love & harmony & on thy feet
Sandals of gold & pearl, & Egypt & Assyria before me
The Isles of Javan, Philistea, Tyre and Lebanon

Thus Los sings upon his Watch walking from Furnace to Furnace.
He siezes his Hammer every hour, flames surround him as
He beats: seas roll beneath his feet, tempests muster
Around his head, the thick hail stones stand ready to obey
His voice in the black cloud, his Sons labour in thunders
At his Furnaces; his Daughters at their Looms sing woes
His Emanation separates in milky fibres agonizing
Among the golden Looms of Cathedron sending fibres of love
From Golgonooza with sweet visions for Jerusalem, wanderer.

Nor can any consummate bliss without being Generated
On Earth; of those whose Emanations weave the loves
Of Beulah for Jerusalem & Shiloh, in immortal Golgonooza
Concentering in the majestic form of Erin in eternal tears
Viewing the Winding Worm on the Desarts of Great Tartary
Viewing Los in his shudderings, pouring balm on his sorrows
So dread is Los's fury, that none dare him to approach
Without becoming his Children in the Furnaces of affliction.

And Enitharmon like a faint rainbow waved before him
Filling with fibres from his loins which reddend with desire
Into a Globe of blood beneath his bosom trembling in darkness
Of Albions clouds, he fed it, with his tears & bitter groans
Hiding his Spectre in invisibility from the timorous Shade
Till it became a separated cloud of beauty grace & love
Among the darkness of his Furnaces dividing asunder till
She separated stood before him a lovely Female weeping
Even Enitharmon separated outside, & his Loins closed
And heald after the separation: his pains he soon forgot:
Lured by her beauty outside of himself in shadowy grief.
Two Wills they had; Two Intellects: & not as in times of old.

Silent they wanderd hand in hand like two Infants wand'ring
From Enion in the desarts, terrified at each others beauty
Envying each other yet desiring, in all devouring Love,

Repelling weeping Enion blind & age-bent into the fourfold
Desarts. Los first brake silence & began to utter his love

O lovely Enitharmon: I behold thy graceful forms
Moving beside me till intwacepted with the woven labyrinth
Of beauty & perfection my wild fibres shoot in veins
Of blood thro all my nervous limbs. soon overgrown in roots
I shall be closed from thy sight. seize therefore in thy hand
The small fibres as they Shoot around me draw out in pity
And let them run on the winds of thy bosom: I will fix them
With pulsations. we will divide them into Sons & Daughters
To live in thy Bosoms translucence as in an eternal morning

Enitharmon answerd. No! I will seize thy Fibres & weave
Them: not as thou wilt but as I will. for I will Create
A Torpid Womb beneath my bosom. lest I also be overwoven
With Love: be thou assured I never will be thy slave
Let Mans delight be Love; but Womans delight be Pride
In Eden our Loves were the same here they are opposite
I have Loves of my own I will weave them in Albions Spectre
Cast thou in Jerusalems shadows thy Loves! silk of liquid
Rubies Jacinths Crysolites: issuing from thy Furnaces. While
Jerusalem divides thy care: while thou carest for Jerusalem
Know that I never will be thine: also thou hidest Vala
From her these fibres shoot to shut me in a Grave
You are Albions Victim, he has set his Daughter in your path

Los answerd sighing like the Bellows of his Furnaces

I care not! the swing of my Hammer shall measure the starry round
When in Eternity Man converses with Man they enter
Into each others Bosom (which are Universes of delight)
In mutual interchange. and first their Emanations meet
Surrounded by their Children. if they embrace & comingle
The Human Four-fold Forms mingle also in thunders of Intellect
But if the Emanations mingle not; with storms & agitations
Of earthquakes & consuming fires they roll apart in fear
For Man cannot unite with Man but by their Emanations
Which stand both Male & Female at the Gates of each Humanity
How then can I ever again be united as Man with Man
While thou my Emanation refusest my Fibres of dominion.
When Souls mingle & join thro all the Fibres of Brotherhood
Can there be any secret joy on Earth greater than this?

Enitharmon answerd: This is Womans World. nor need she any
Spectre to defend her from Man. I will Create secret places
And the masculine names of the places Merlin & Arthur.
A triple Female Tabernacle for Moral Law I weave.
That he who loves Jesus may loathe terrified Female love
Till God himself become a Male subservient to the Female.

She spoke in scorn & jealousy, alternate torments; and
So speaking she sat down on Sussex shore singing lulling
Cadences. & playing in sweet intoxication among the glistening
Fibres of Los: sending them over the Ocean eastward into
The realms of dark death; O perverse to thyself, contrarious
To thy own purposes; for when she began to weave
Shooting out in sweet pleasure her bosom in milky Love
Flowd into the aching fibres of Los. yet contending against him
In pride sending his Fibres over to her objects of jealousy
In the little lovely Allegoric Night of Albions Daughters
Which stretchd abroad, expanding east & west & north & south
Thro all the World of Erin & of Los & all their Children

A sullen smile broke from the Spectre in mockery & scorn
Knowing himself the author of their divisions & shrinkings, gratified
At their contentions, he wiped his tears he washd his visage.

The Man who respects Woman shall be despised by Woman
And deadly cunning & mean abjectness only. shall enjoy them
For I will make their places of joy & love. excrementitious
Continually building. continually destroying in Family feuds
While you are under the dominion of a jealous Female
Unpermanent for ever because of Love & jealousy.
You shall want all the Minute Particulars of Life

Thus joyd the Spectre in the dusky fires of Los's Forge, eyeing
Enitharmon who at her shining Looms sings lulling cadences
While Los stood at his Anvil in wrath the victim of their love
And hate; dividing the Space of Love with brazen Compasses
In Golgonooza & in Udan-Adan & in Entuthon of Urizen.

The blow of his Hammer is Justice. the swing of his Hammer: Mercy
The force of Los's Hammer is eternal Forgiveness; but
His rage or his mildness were vain, she scatterd his love on the wind
Eastward into her own Center, creating the Female Womb
In mild Jerusalem around the Lamb of God. Loud howl
The Furnaces of Los! loud roll the Wheels of Enitharmon
The Four Zoa's in all their faded majesty burst out in fury
And fire. Jerusalem took the Cup which foamd in Valas hand
Like the red Sun upon the mountains in the bloody day
Upon the Hermaphroditic Wine-presses of Love & Wrath.

Are divided by the Cross & Nails & Thorns & Spear
In cruelties of Rahab & Tirzah permanent endure
A terrible indefinite Hermaphroditic form
A Wine-press of Love & Wrath double Hermaphroditic
Twelvefold in Allegoric pomp in selfish holiness
The Pharisaion, the Grammateis, the Presbuterion,
The Archiereus, the Iereus, the Saddusaion, double
Each withoutside of the other, covering eastern heaven

Thus was the Covering Cherub reveald majestic image
Of Selfhood, Body put off, the Antichrist accursed
Coverd with precious stones, a Human Dragon terrible
And bright, stretchd over Europe & Asia gorgeous
In three nights he devourd the rejected corse of death

His Head dark, deadly, in its Brain incloses a reflexion
Of Eden all perverted; Egypt on the Gihon many tongued
And many mouthd: Ethiopia, Lybia, the Sea of Rephaim
Minute Particulars in slavery I behold among the brick-kilns
Disorganizd, & there is Pharoh in his iron Court:
And the Dragon of the River & the Furnaces of iron.
Outwoven from Thames & Tweed & Severn awful streams
Twelve ridges of Stone frown over all the Earth in tyrant pride
Frown over each River stupendous Works of Albions Druid Sons
And Albions Forests of Oaks coverd the Earth from Pole to Pole

His Bosom wide reflects Moab & Ammon on the River
Pison, since calld Arnon, there is Heshbon beautiful
The Rocks of Rabbath on the Arnon & the Fish-pools of Heshbon
Whose currents flow into the Dead Sea by Sodom & Gomorra
Above his Head high arching Wings black filld with Eyes
Spring upon iron sinews from the Scapulae & Os Humeri.
There Israel in bondage to his Generalizing Gods
Molech & Chemosh, & in his left breast is Philistea
In Druid Temples over the whole Earth with Victims Sacrifice
From Gaza to Damascus Tyre & Sidon & the Gods
Of Javan thro the Isles of Grecia & all Europes Kings
Where Hiddekel pursues his course among the rocks
Two Wings spring from his ribs of brass, starry, black as night
But translucent their blackness as the dazling of gems

His Loins inclose Babylon on Euphrates beautiful
And Rome in sweet Geneva & poison round the deadly tree
The marriage rings of Heaven & Hell shed scatterd abroad
To the four winds as a breathing in the Soul
Ireland & Scotland Wales the Church of Los with Fires of War &
Hosted At the Smitten Rock but still the winds of Your Dread Seas

But in the midst of a devouring Stomach, Jerusalem
Hidden within the Covering Cherub as in a Tabernacle
Of threefold workmanship in allegoric delusion & woe
There the Seven Kingdoms of Canaan & Five Baalim of Philistea
Into Twelve divided, calld after the Names of Israel: as they are in Eden.
From Ireland, Scotland, to Rome & the World round from Labor
Where the Red Sea terminates the World of Generation & Death
To I-Islands furthest rocks, there Giants builded their Causeway
Into the Sea of Rephaim. but the Sea overwhelmd them all

A Double Female now appeard within the Tabernacle,
Religion hid in War, a Dragon red & hidden Harlot,
Each within other, but without a Warlike Mighty-one
Of dreadful power, sitting upon Horeb pondering dire
And mighty preparations, mustering multitudes innumerable
Of warlike sons among the sands of Midian & Aram.
For multitudes of those who sleep in Alla descend
Lurd by his warlike symphonies of Tabret, Pipe & Harp
Burst the bottoms of the Graves & Funeral Arks of Beulah
Wandering in that unknown Night beyond the silent Grave
They become One with the Antichrist & are absorbd in him.

The Feminine separates from the Masculine & both from Man,
Ceasing to be His Emanations, Life to Themselves assuming!
And while they circumscribe his Brain, & while they circumscribe
His Heart, & while they circumscribe his Loins! a Veil & Net
Of Veins of red Blood grows around them like a scarlet robe,
Covering them from the sight of Man like the woven Veil of Sleep
Such as the Flowers of Beulah weave to be their Funeral Mantles
But dark! opake! tender to touch, & painful! & agonizing
To the embrace of love, & to the mingling of soft fibres
Of tender affection, that no more the Masculine mingles
With the Feminine, but the Sublime is shut out from the Pathos
In howling torment, to build stone walls of separation, compelling
The Pathos, to weave curtains of hiding secresy from the torment.

Bowen & Conwenna stood on Skiddaw cutting the Fibres
Of Benjamin from Chesters River: loud the River; loud the Mersey
And the Ribble, thunder into the Irish sea, as the Twelve Sons
Of Albion drank & imbibed the Life & eternal Form of Luvah
Cheshire & Lancashire & Westmoreland groan in anguish
As they cut the Fibres from the Rivers he sears them with hot
Iron of his Forge & fixes them into Bones of chalk & Rock
Conwenna sat above, with solemn cadences she drew
Fibres of life out from the Bones into her golden Loom
Hand had his Furnace on Highgates heights & it reachd
To Brockley Hills across the Thames: he with double Boadicea
In cruel pride cut Reuben apart from the Hills of Surrey,
Commingling with Luvah & with the Sepulcher of Luvah
For the Male is a Furnace of beryl; the Female is a golden Loom

Los cries: No Individual ought to appropriate to Himself
Or to his Emanation, any of the Universal Characteristics
Of David or of Eve, of the Woman, or of the Lord,
Of Reuben or of Benjamin, of Joseph or Judah or Levi,
Those who dare appropriate to themselves Universal Attributes
Are the Blasphemous Selfhoods & must be broken asunder
A Vegetated Christ & a Virgin Eve, are the Hermaphroditic
Blasphemy, by his Maternal Birth he is that Evil-One
And his Maternal Humanity must be put off Eternally
Lest the Sexual Generation swallow up Regeneration
Come Lord Jesus take on thee the Satanic Body of Holiness

So Los cried in the Valleys of Middlesex in the Spirit of Prophecy
While in Selfhood Hand & Hyle & Bowen & Skofeld appropriate
The Divine Names: seeking to Vegetate the Divine Vision
In a corporeal & ever dying Vegetation & Corruption
Mingling with Luvah in One. they became One Great Satan

Loud scream the Daughters of Albion beneath the Tongs & Hammer
Dolorous are their Lamentations in the burning Forge
They drink Reuben & Benjamin as the iron drinks the fire
They are red hot with cruelty: raving along the Banks of Thames
And on Tyburns Brook among the howling Victims in loveliness
While Hand & Hyle condense the Little-ones & erect them into
A mighty Temple even to the stars: but they Vegetate
Beneath Los's Hammer, that Life may not be blotted out.

For Los said: When the Individual appropriates Universality
He divides into Male & Female: & when the Male & Female,
Appropriate Individuality, they become an Eternal Death.
Hermaphroditic worshippers of a God of cruelty & law!
Your Slaves & Captives; you compell to worship a God of Mercy.
These are the Demonstrations of Los, & the blows of my mighty Hammer.

So Los spoke. And the Giants of Albion terrified & ashamed
With Los's thunderous Words, began to build trembling rocking Stones
For his Words roll in thunders & lightnings among the Temples
Terrified rocking to & fro upon the earth, & sometimes
Resting in a Circle in Maldon or in Strathness or Dura,
Plotting to devour Albion & Los the friend of Albion
Denying in private: mocking God & Eternal Life: & in Public
Collusion, calling themselves Deists, Worshipping the Maternal
Humanity; calling it Nature, and Natural Religion
But still the thunder of Los peals loud & thus the thunders cry
These beautiful Witchcrafts of Albion, are gratifyd by Cruelty

It is easier to forgive an Enemy than to forgive a Friend:
The man who permits you to injure him, deserves your vengeance:
He also will receive it: go Spectre! obey my most secret desire:
Which thou knowest without thy speaking: Go to these Fiends of Righteousness
Tell them to obey their Humanities, & not pretend Holiness;
When they are murderers: as far as my Hammer & Anvil permit
Go, tell them that the Worship of God, is honouring his gifts
In other men: & loving the greatest men best, each according
To his Genius: which is the Holy Ghost in Man; there is no other
God, than that God who is the intellectual fountain of Humanity;
He who envies or calumniates: which is murder & cruelty,
Murders the Holy-one: Go tell them this & overthrow their cup,
Their bread, their altar-table, their incense & their oath:
Their marriage & their baptism, their burial & consecration:
I have tried to make friends by corporeal gifts but have only
Made enemies: I never made friends but by spiritual gifts;
By severe contentions of friendship & the burning fire of thought.
He who would see the Divinity must see him in his Children
One first, in friendship & love; then a Divine Family, & in the midst
Jesus will appear; so he who wishes to see a Vision; a perfect Whole
Must see it in its Minute Particulars; Organized & not as thou
O Fiend of Righteousness pretendest; thine is a Disorganized
And snowy cloud: brooder of tempests & destructive War.
You smile with pomp & rigor: you talk of benevolence & virtue!
I act with benevolence & virtue & get murderd time after time:
You accumulate Particulars, & murder by analyzing, that you
May take the aggregates; & you call the aggregates Moral Law:
And you call that Swelld & bloated Form; a Minute Particular.
But General Forms have their vitality in Particulars: & every
Particular is a Man; a Divine Member of the Divine Jesus.

So Los cried at his Anvil in the horrible darkness weeping!

The Spectre builded stupendous Works, taking the Starry Heavens
Like to a curtain & folding them according to his will
Repeating the Smaragdine Table of Hermes to draw Los down
Into the Indefinite, refusing to believe without demonstration
Los reads the Stars of Albion; the Spectre reads the Voids
Between the Stars; among the arches of Albions Tomb sublime
Rolling the Sea in rocky paths! forming Leviathan
And Behemoth: the War by Sea enormous & the War
By Land astounding: erecting pillars in the deepest Hell,
To reach the heavenly arches; Los beheld undaunted furious
His heavd Hammer; he swung it round & at one blow,
In unpitying ruin driving down the pyramids of pride
Smiting the Spectre on his Anvil & the integuments of his Eye
And Ear unbinding in dire pain, with many blows,
Of strict severity self-subduing, & with many tears labouring.

Then he sent forth the Spectre all his pyramids were grains
Of sand & his pillars: dust on the fly's wing: & his Starry
Heavens; a moth of gold & silver mocking his anxious grasp
Thus Los alterd his Spectre & every Ratio of his Reason
He alterd time after time, with dire pain & many tears
Till he had completely divided him into a separate space.

Terrified Los sat to behold trembling & weeping & howling
I care not whether a Man is Good or Evil; all that I care
Is whether he is a Wise Man or a Fool. Go! put off Holiness
And put on Intellect: or my thundrous Hammer shall drive thee
To wrath which thou condemnest: till thou obey my voice

So Los terrified cries; trembling & weeping & howling! Beholding

What do I see: The Briton Saxon Roman Norman amalgamating
In my Furnaces into One Nation the English: & taking Refuge
In the Loins of Albion. The Canaanite united with the fugitive
Hebrew, whom She divided into Twelve. & sold into Egypt
Then scatterd the Egyptian & Hebrew to the four Winds:
This sinful Nation Created in our Furnaces & Looms is Albion

So Los spoke. Enitharmon answerd in great terror in Lambeths Vale

The Poets Song draws to its period. & Enitharmon is no more.
For if he be that Albion I can never weave him in my Looms
But when he touches the first fibrous thread. like filmy dew

Jerusalem

My Looms will be no more & I annihilate vanish for ever
Then thou wilt Create another Female according to thy Will

Los answerd swift as the shuttle of gold. Sexes must vanish & cease
To be, when Albion arises from his dread repose O lovely Enitharmon:
When all their Crimes, their Punishments their Accusations of Sin:
All their Jealousies Revenges. Murders. hidings of Cruelty in Deceit
Appear only in the Outward Spheres of Visionary Space and Time.
In the shadows of Possibility by Mutual Forgiveness forevermore
And in the Vision & in the Prophecy, that we may Foresee & Avoid
The terrors of Creation & Redemption & Judgment. Beholding them
Displayd in the Emanative Visions of Canaan in Jerusalem & in Shiloh
And in the Shadows of Remembrance, & in the Chaos of the Spectre
Amalek. Edom. Egypt. Moab. Ammon. Ashur. Philistea. around Jerusalem
Where the Druid dwells along the Valley of Rephaim from Camberwell to Golgotha
Of Sin. & the Tree of Good & Evil sprang from the Rocky Circle & Snake
And framed the Mundane Shell Cavernous in Length Breadth & Highth

Enitharmon heard. She raised her head like the mild Moon

O Rintrah! O Palamabron. What are your dire & awful purposes
Enitharmons name is nothing before you: you forget all my Love
The Mothers love of obedience is forgotten & you seek a Love
Of the pride of dominion. that will Divorce Ocalythron & Elynittria
Upon East Moor in Derbyshire & along the Valleys of Cheviot
Could you Love me Rintrah. if you Pride not in my Love
As Reuben found Mandrakes in the field & gave them to his Mother
Pride meets with Pride upon the Mountains in the stormy day
In that terrible Day of Rintrahs Plow & of Satans driving the Team
Ah! then I heard my little ones weeping along the Valley!
Ah! then I say my beloved ones fleeing from my Tent
Merlin was like thee Rintrah among the Giants of Albion
Judah was like Palamabron: O Simeon! O Levi! ye fled away
How can I hear my little ones weeping along the Valley
Or how upon the distant Hills see my beloveds Tents

Then Los again took up his speech as Enitharmon ceast

Fear not my Sons this Waking Death. he is become One with me
Behold him here! We shall not Die! we shall be united in Jesus.
Will you suffer this Satan this Body of Doubt that Seems but Is Not
To occupy the very threshold of Eternal Life. if Bacon. Newton. Locke,
Deny a Conscience in Man & the Communion of Saints & Angels
Contemning the Divine Vision & Fruition. Worshiping the Deus
Of the Heathen. The God of This World. & the Goddess Nature
Mystery Babylon the Great. The Druid Dragon & hidden Harlot
Is it not that Signal of the Morning which was told us in the Beginning

Thus they converse upon Mam-Tor. the Graves thunder under their feet

Albion cold lays on his Rock: storms & snows beat round him.
Beneath the Furnaces & the starry Wheels & the Immortal Tomb
Howling winds cover him: roaring seas dash furious against him
In the deep darkness broad lightnings glare long thunders roll

5 The weeds of Death inwrap his hands & feet blown incessant
And washd incessant by the for-ever restless sea-waves foaming abroad
Upon the white Rock. England a Female Shadow as deadly damps
Of the Mines of Cornwall & Derbyshire lays upon his bosom heavy
Moved by the wind in volumes of thick cloud returning rolling round
10 His loins & bosom unremovable by swelling storms & loud rending
Of enraged thunders. Around them the Starry Wheels of their Giant Sons
Revolve: & over them the Furnaces of Los & the Immortal Tomb around
Erin sitting in the Tomb. to watch them unceasing night and day
And the Body of Albion was closed apart from all Nations

15 Over them the famishd Eagle screams on boney Wings and around
Them howls the Wolf of famine deep heaves the Ocean black thundering
Around the wormy Garments of Albion: then pausing in deathlike silence

Time was Finished! The Breath Divine Breathed over Albion
20 Beneath the Furnaces & starry Wheels and in the Immortal Tomb
And England who is Brittannia awoke from Death on Albions bosom
She awoke pale & cold she fainted seven times on the Body of Albion

O pitious Sleep O pitious Dream! O God O God awake I have slain
In Dreams of Chastity & Moral Law I have Murdered Albion! Ah!
25 In Stone-henge & on London Stone & in the Oak Groves of Malden
I have Slain him in my Sleep with the Knife of the Druid O England
27 O all ye Nations of the Earth behold ye the Jealous Wife
The Eagle & the Wolf & Monkey & Owl & the King & Priest were there

Her voice pierc'd Albions clay cold ear, he moved upon the Rock
The Breath Divine went forth upon the morning hills Albion mov'd
Upon the Rock, he opend his eyelids in pain; in pain he mov'd
His stony members, he saw England. Ah! shall the Dead live again

5 The Breath Divine went forth over the morning hills Albion rose
In anger: the wrath of God breaking bright flaming on all sides around
His awful limbs: into the Heavens he walked clothed in flames
Loud thundring, with broad flashes of flaming lightning & pillars
Of fire, speaking the Words of Eternity in Human Forms, in direful

10 Revolutions of Action & Passion, thro the Four Elements on all sides
Surrounding his awful Members. Thou seest the Sun in heavy clouds
Struggling to rise above the Mountains, in his burning hand
He takes his Bow, then chooses out his arrows of flaming gold
Murmuring the Bowstring breathes with ardor! clouds roll round the

15 Horns of the wide Bow, loud sounding winds sport on the mountain brows
Compelling Urizen to his Furrow: & Tharmas to his Sheepfold;
And Luvah to his Loom; Urthona he beheld mighty labouring at
His Anvil, in the Great Spectre Los unwearied labouring & weeping
Therefore the Sons of Eden praise Urthonas Spectre in songs

20 Because he kept the Divine Vision in time of trouble.
As the Sun & Moon lead forward the Visions of Heaven & Earth
England who is Brittannia entered Albions bosom rejoicing
Rejoicing in his indignation! adoring his wrathful rebuke.
24 She who adores not your frowns will only loathe your smiles

As the Sun & Moon lead forward the
    Visions of Heaven & Earth
England who is Britannia entered
    Albions bosom rejoicing

Then Jesus appeared standing by
    Albion as the Good Shepherd
By the lost Sheep that he hath
    found & Albion knew that it
Was the Lord the Universal Human-
    ity, & Albion saw his Form
A Man. & they conversed as Man
    with Man, in Ages of Eternity
And the Divine Appearance was
    the likeness & similitude of Los

Albion said. O Lord what can
    I do! my Selfhood cruel
Marches against thee deceitful
    from Sinai & from Edom
Into the Wilderness of Judah to
    meet thee in his pride
I behold the Visions of my deadly
    Sleep of Six Thousand Years
Dazling around thy skirts like
    a Serpent of precious Stones &
    Gold
I know it is my Self! O my Divine
    Creator & Redeemer

Jesus replied Fear not Albion
    unless I die thou canst not live
But if I die I shall arise again
    & thou with me
This is Friendship & Brotherhood
    without it Man Is Not

So Jesus spoke! the Covering
    Cherub coming on in darkness
Overshadowd them & Jesus
    said Thus do Men in Eternity
One for another to put off by
    forgiveness, every sin

Albion replyd. Cannot Man
    exist without Mysterious
Offering of Self for Another, is
    this Friendship & Brotherhood
I see thee in the likeness and
    similitude of Los my Friend

Jesus said. Wouldest thou
    love one who never died
For thee or ever die for one
    who had not died for thee
And if God dieth not for
    Man & giveth not himself
Eternally for Man Man could not exist. for Man is Love:
As God is Love: every kindness to another is a little Death
In the Divine Image nor can Man exist but by Brotherhood

So saying the Cloud overshadowing divided them asunder
Albion stood in terror: not for himself but for his Friend
Divine, & Self was lost in the contemplation of faith
And wonder at the Divine Mercy & at Los's sublime honour

Do I sleep amidst danger to Friends! O my Cities & Counties
Do you sleep! rouse up! rouse up. Eternal Death is abroad
So Albion spoke & threw himself into the Furnaces of affliction
All was a Vision, all a Dream: the Furnaces became
Fountains of Living Waters flowing from the Humanity Divine
And all the Cities of Albion rose from their Slumbers, and All
The Sons & Daughters of Albion on soft clouds Waking from Sleep
Soon all around remote the Heavens burnt with flaming fires
And Urizen & Luvah & Tharmas & Urthona arose into
Albions Bosom: Then Albion stood before Jesus in the Clouds
Of Heaven Fourfold among the Visions of God in Eternity

Awake Awake Jerusalem! O lovely Emanation of Albion
Awake and overspread all Nations as in Ancient Time
For lo! the Night of Death is past and the Eternal Day
Appears upon our Hills: Awake Jerusalem, and come away

So spake the Vision of Albion & in him so spake in my hearing
The Universal Father. Then Albion stretchd his hand into Infinitude.
And took his Bow. Fourfold the Vision for bright beaming Urizen
Layd his hand on the South & took a breathing Bow of carved Gold
Luvah his hand stretchd to the East & bore a Silver Bow bright shining
Tharmas Westward a Bow of Brass pure flaming richly wrought
Urthona Northward in thick storms a Bow of Iron terrible thundering.

And the Bow is a Male & Female & the Quiver of the Arrows of Love,
Are the Children of this Bow: a Bow of Mercy & Loving-kindness: laying
Open the hidden Heart in Wars of mutual Benevolence Wars of Love
And the Hand of Man grasps firm between the Male & Female Loves
And he Clothed it with Arrows in a mighty soft storm of raging fire
In the midst of his Emanation the Cities each took his Bow & stood.

Then each an Arrow flaming from his Quiver fitted carefully
They drew fourfold the unreprovable String, bending thro the wide Heavens
The nerved Bow fourfold, loud sounding flew the flaming Arrow fourfold

Murmuring the Bowstring breathes with ardor. Clouds roll round the horns
Of the wide Bow, loud sounding Winds sport on the Mountains brows:
The Druid Spectre was Annihilate loud thundring rejoicing terrific vanishing
Fourfold Annihilation & at the clang of the Arrows of Intellect
The innumerable Chariots of the Almighty appeared in Heaven
And Bacon & Newton & Locke, & Milton & Shakspear & Chaucer
A Sun of blood red wrath surrounding heaven on all sides around
Glorious incomprehensible by Mortal Man & each Chariot was Sexual Threefold

And every Man stood Fourfold, each Four Faces had. One to the West
One toward the East One to the South One to the North, the Horses Fourfold
And the dim Chaos brightend beneath, above, around. Eyed as the Peacock
According to the Human Nerves of Sensation, the Four Rivers of the Water of Life

South stood the Nerves of the Eye. East in Rivers of bliss the Nerves of the
Expansive Nostrils. West, flow'd the Parent Sense the Tongue. North stood
The labyrinthine Ear. Circumscribing & Circumcising the excrementitious
Husk & Covering into Vacuum evaporating revealing the lineaments of Man
Driving outward the Body of Death in an Eternal Death & Resurrection
Awaking it to Life among the Flowers of Beulah rejoicing in Unity
In the Four Senses in the Outline the Circumference & Form, for ever
In Forgiveness of Sins which is Self Annihilation. it is the Covenant of Jehovah
The Four Living Creatures Chariots of Humanity Divine Incomprehensible
In beautiful Paradises expand These are the Four Rivers of Paradise
And the Four Faces of Humanity fronting the Four Cardinal Points
Of Heaven going forward forward irresistible from Eternity to Eternity

And they conversed together in Visionary forms dramatic which bright
Redounded from their Tongues in thunderous majesty, in Visions
In new Expanses, creating exemplars of Memory and of Intellect
Creating Space, Creating Time according to the wonders Divine
Of Human Imagination, throughout all the three Regions immense
Of Childhood, Manhood & Old Age & the all tremendous unfathomable Non Ens
Of Death was seen in regenerations terrific or complacent varying
According to the subject of discourse & every Word & every Character
Was Human according to the Expansion or Contraction, the Translucence or
Opakeness of Nervous fibres such was the variation of Time & Space
Which vary according as the Organs of Perception vary & they walked
To & fro in Eternity as One Man reflecting each in each & clearly seen
And seeing: according to fitness & order. And I heard Jehovah speak
Terrific from his Holy Place & saw the Words of the Mutual Covenant Divine
On Chariots of gold & jewels with Living Creatures starry & flaming
With every Colour, Lion, Tyger, Horse, Elephant, Eagle Dove, Fly, Worm,
And the all wondrous Serpent clothed in gems & rich array Humanize
In the Forgiveness of Sins according to thy Covenant Jehovah. They Cry

Where is the Covenant of Priam, the Moral Virtues of the Heathen
Where is the Tree of Good & Evil that rooted beneath the cruel heel
Of Albions Spectre the Patriarch Druid! where are all his Human Sacrifice
For Sin in War & in the Druid Temples of the Accuser of Sin: beneath
The Oak Groves of Albion that coverd the whole Earth beneath his Spectre
Where are the Kingdoms of the World & all their glory that grew on Desolation
The Fruit of Albions Poverty Tree when the Triple Headed Gog-Magog Giant
Of Albion Taxed the Nations into Desolation & then gave the Spectrous Oath

Such is the Cry from all the Earth from the Living Creatures of the Earth
And from the great City of Golgonooza in the Shadowy Generation

And from the Thirty-two Nations of the Earth among the Living Creatures

All Human Forms identified, even Tree Metal Earth & Stone, all
Human Forms identified, living going forth & returning wearied
Into the Planetary lives of Years Months Days & Hours reposing
And then Awaking into his Bosom in the Life of Immortality.
And I heard the Name of their Emanations they are named Jerusalem

The End of The Song
of Jerusalem

MIL ONT

a Poem in 2 Books

The Author & Printer W Blake 1804

To Justify the Ways of God to Men.

PREFACE.

The Stolen and Perverted Writings of Homer & Ovid: of Plato & Cicero. which all Men ought to contemn: are set up by artifice against the Sublime of the Bible. but when the New Age is at leisure to Pronounce; all will be set right: & those Grand Works of the more ancient & consciously & professedly Inspired Men, will hold their proper rank, & the Daughters of Memory shall become the Daughters of Inspiration. Shakspeare & Milton were both curbd by the general malady & infection from the silly Greek & Latin slaves of the Sword.— Rouze up O Young Men of the New Age! set your foreheads against the ignorant Hirelings! For we have Hirelings in the Camp, the Court & the University: who would if they could, for ever depress Mental & prolong Corporeal War. Painters! on you I call Sculptors! Architects! Suffer not the fashionable Fools to depress your powers by the prices they pretend to give for contemptible works or the expensive advertizing boasts that they make of such works; believe Christ & his Apostles that there is a Class of Men whose whole delight is in Destroying. We do not want either Greek or Roman Models if we are but just & true to our own Imaginations, those Worlds of Eternity in which we shall live for ever; in Jesus our Lord.

And did those feet in ancient time.
Walk upon Englands mountains green
And was the holy Lamb of God.
On Englands pleasant pastures seen!

And did the Countenance Divine.
Shine forth upon our clouded hills?
And was Jerusalem builded here
Among these dark Satanic Mills?

Bring me my Bow of burning gold:
Bring me my Arrows of desire:
Bring me my Spear: O clouds unfold!
Bring me my Chariot of fire!

I will not cease from Mental Fight.
Nor shall my Sword sleep in my hand.
Till we have built Jerusalem.
In Englands green & pleasant Land

Would to God that all the Lords people
were Prophets Numbers XI. ch 29 v.

LIBRARY OF THE UNIVERSITY OF CALIFORNIA.

MILTON

Book the First

Daughters of Beulah! Muses who inspire the Poets Song
Record the journey of immortal Milton thro' your Realms
Of terror & mild moony lustre, in soft sexual delusions
Of varied beauty, to delight the wanderer and repose
5 His burning thirst & freezing hunger! Come into my hand
By your mild power; descending down the Nerves of my right arm
From out the Portals of my Brain, where by your ministry
The Eternal Great Humanity Divine, planted his Paradise,
And in it caus'd the Spectres of the Dead to take sweet forms
10 In likeness of himself. Tell also of the False Tongue! vegetated
Beneath your land of shadows: of its sacrifices. and
Its offerings: even till Jesus, the image of the Invisible God
Became its prey; a curse, an offering, and an atonement,
For Death Eternal in the heavens of Albion, & before the Gates
15 Of Jerusalem his Emanation; in the heavens beneath Beulah

Say first! what mov'd Milton, who walk'd about in Eternity
One hundred years, pondring the intricate mazes of Providence
Unhappy tho in heav'n, he obey'd, he murmur'd not. he was silent
Viewing his Sixfold Emanation scatter'd thro' the deep
20 In torment! To go into the deep her to redeem & himself perish?
What cause at length mov'd Milton to this unexampled deed
A Bards prophetic Song! for sitting at eternal tables,
Terrific among the Sons of Albion in chorus solemn & loud
A Bard broke forth! all sat attentive to the awful man.

25 Mark well my words! they are of your eternal salvation:

Three Classes are Created by the Hammer of Los, & Woven

From Golgonooza the spiritual Four-fold London eternal
In immense labours & sorrows. ever building. ever falling:
Thro Albions four Forests which overspread all the Earth.
From London Stone to Blackheath east: to Hounslow west:
To Finchley north; to Norwood south: and the weights of
Of Enitharmons Loom play lulling cadences on the
    winds of Albion
From Caithness in the north. to Lizardpoint & Dover in the south

Loud sounds the Hammer of Los. & loud his Bellows is heard
Before London to Hampsteads breadths & Highgates heights To
Stratford & old Bow: & across to the Gardens of Kensington
On Tyburns Brook: loud groans Thames beneath the iron Forge
Of Rintrah & Palamabron of Theotormon & Bromion. to
    forge the instruments
Of Harvest: the Plow & Harrow to pass over the Nations

The Surrey hills glow like the clinkers of the furnace: Lambeths Vale
Where Jerusalems foundations began; where they were laid in ruins
Where they were laid in ruins from every Nation. & Oak Groves rooted
Dark gleams before the Furnace-mouth a heap of burning ashes
When shall Jerusalem return & overspread all the Nations
Return return to Lambeths Vale O building of human souls
Thence stony Druid Temples overspread the Island white
And thence from Jerusalems ruins. from her wells of salvation
And praise: thro the whole Earth were reard from Ireland
To Mexico & Peru west. & east to China. & Japan: till Babel
The Spectre of Albion frownd over the Nations in glory & war
All things begin & end in Albions ancient Druid rock shore
But now the Starry Heavens are fled from the mighty limbs of
    Albion

                                                armon
Loud sounds the Hammer of Los, loud turn the Wheels of Enith
Her Looms vibrate with soft affections. weaving the Web of Life
Out from the ashes of the Dead; Los lifts his iron Ladles
With molten ore: he heaves the iron cliffs in his rattling chains
From Hyde Park to the Alms-houses of Mile-end & old Bow
Here the Three Classes of Mortal Men take their fixd destinations
And hence they overspread the Nations of the whole Earth & hence
The Web of Life is woven: & the tender sinews of life created
And the Three Classes of Men regulated by Los's Hammer. and
                                                woven

By Enitharmons Looms. & Spun beneath the Spindle of Tirzah
The first. The Elect from before thr foundation of the World:
The second. The Redeemd The Third. The Reprobate & form'd
To destruction from the mothers womb:

            follow with me my plow

5 Of the first class was Satan: with incomparable mildness;
His primitive tyrannical attempts on Los: with most endearing love
He soft, intreated Los to give to him Palamabrons station:
For Palamabron returnd with labour wearied every evening
Palamabron oft refus'd: and as often Satan offer'd
10 His service till by repeated offers and repeated intreaties
Los gave to him the Harrow of the Almighty; alas blamable
Palamabron feard to be angry lest Satan should accuse him of
Ingratitude, & Los believe the accusation thro Satans extreme
Mildness. Satan labour'd all day, it was a thousand years
15 In the evening returning terrified overlabour'd & astonish'd
Embrac'd soft with a brothers tears Palamabron, who also wept

Mark well my words, they are of your eternal salvation

Next morning Palamabron rose: the horses of the Harrow
Were madden'd with tormenting fury, & the servants of the Harrow
20 The Gnomes, accus'd Satan, with indignation fury and fire.
Then Palamabron reddening like the Moon in an eclipse,
Spoke saying, You know Satans mildness and his self-imposition,
Seeming a brother, being a tyrant, even thinking himself a brother
While he is murdering the just: prophetic I behold
25 His future course thro' darkness and despair to eternal death
But we must not be tyrants also! he hath assum'd my place
For one whole day, under pretence of pity and love to me:
My horses hath he madden'd! and my fellow servants injur'd:
How should he he know the duties of another? O foolish forbearance.
30 Would I had told Los, all my heart! but patience O my friends.
All may be well: silent remain, while I call Los and Satan.

Loud as the wind of Beulah that unroots the rocks & hills
Palamabron call'd! and Los & Satan came before him
And Palamabron shew'd the horses & the servants. Satan wept.
35 And mildly cursing Palamabron, him accus'd of crimes
Himself had wrought. Los trembled: Satans blandishments almost
Perswaded the Prophet of Eternity that Palamabron
Was Satans enemy, & that the Gnomes being Palamabrons friends
Were leagued together against Satan thro' ancient enmity.
40 What could Los do? how could he judge, when Satans self, believ'd
That he had not oppress'd the horses of the Harrow, nor the servants

So Los said, Henceforth Palamabron, let each his own station
Keep: nor in pity false, nor in officious brotherhood, where
None needs, be active. Mean time Palamabrons horses.
45 Rag'd with thick flames redundant, & the Harrow madden'd with fury.
Trembling Palamabron stood the strongest of Demons trembled:
Curbing his living creatures; many of the strongest Gnomes,
They bit in their wild fury, who also madden'd like wildest beasts

49 Mark well my words; they are of your eternal salvation

Mean while wept Satan before Los. accusing Palamabron
Himself exculpating with mildest speech, for himself believd
That he had not oppressd nor injurd the refractory servants.

But Satan returning to his Mills (for Palamabron had servd
The Mills of Satan as the easier task) found all confusion
And back returnd to Los. not filld with vengeance but with tears
Himself convincd of Palamabrons turpitude. Los beheld
The servants of the Mills drunken with wine and dancing wild
With shouts and Palamabrons songs, rending the forests green
With ecchoing confusion. tho' the Sun was risen on high.

Then Los took off his left sandal placing it on his head,
Signal of solemn mourning: when the servants of the Mills
Beheld the signal they in silence stood, tho' drunk with wine
Los wept! But Rintrah also came, and Enitharmon on
His arm leand tremblingly observing all these things

And Los said. Ye Genii of the Mills: the Sun is on high
Your labours call you! Palamabron is also in sad dilemma;
His horses are mad! his Harrow confounded! his companions enrag'd
Mine is the fault! I should have rememberd that pity divides the soul
And man, unmans: follow with me my Plow. this mournful day
Must be a blank in Nature: follow with me, and tomorrow again
Resume your labours, & this day shall be a mournful day

Wildly they followd Los and Rintrah, & the Mills were silent
They mournd all day this mournful day of Satan & Palamabron
And all the Elect & all the Redeemd mournd one toward another
Upon the mountains of Albion among the cliffs of the Dead.

They Plow'd in tears! incessant pourd Jehovahs rain, & Molech
Thick fires contending with the rain, thunderd above rolling
Terrible over their heads; Satan wept over Palamabron
Theotormon & Bromion contended on the side of Satan
Pitying his youth and beauty; trembling at eternal death:
Michael contended against Satan in the rolling thunder
Thulloh the friend of Satan also reprovd him; faint their reproof.

But Rintrah who is of the reprobate: of those formd to destruction
In indignation. for Satans soft dissimulation of friendship!
Flamd above all the plowed furrows, angry red and furious:
Till Michael sat down in the furrow weary dissolvd in tears
Satan who drave the team beside him. stood angry & red
He smote Thulloh & slew him, & he stood terrible over Michael
Urging him to arise; he wept! Enitharmon saw his tears
But Los hid Thulloh from her sight. lest she should die of grief
She wept; she trembled! she kissed Satan; she wept over Michael
She formd a Space for Satan & Michael, & for the poor infected
Trembling she wept over the Space, & closd it with a tender Moon

Los secret buried Thulloh. weeping disconsolate over the moony Space

But Palamabron called down a Great Solemn Assembly,
That he who will not defend Truth. may be compelled
Defend a Lie. that he may be snared & caught & taken

And all Eden descended into Palamabrons tent
Among Albions Druids & Bards, in the caves beneath Albions
Death Couch, in the caverns of death, in the corner of the Atlantic.
And in the midst of the Great Assembly Palamabron prayd:
O God protect me from my friends, that they have not power over me
Thou hast givn me power to protect myself from my bitterest enemies.

Mark well my words, they are of your eternal salvation

Then rose the Two Witnesses, Rintrah & Palamabron:
And Palamabron appeald to all Eden, and recievd
Judgment; and Lo! it fell on Rintrah and his rage:
Which now flamd high & furious in Satan against Palamabron
Till it became a proverb in Eden. Satan is among the Reprobate.

Los in his wrath cursd heaven & earth, he rent up Nations
Standing on Albions rocks among high-reard Druid temples
Which reach the stars of heaven & stretch from pole to pole.
He displacd continents, the oceans fled before his face
He alterd the poles of the world, east, west & north & south
But he closd up Enitharmon from the sight of all these things

For Satan flaming with Rintrahs fury hidden beneath his own mildness
Accusd Palamabron before the Assembly of ingratitude, of malice:
He created Seven deadly Sins, drawing out his infernal scroll,
Of Moral laws and cruel punishments upon the clouds of Jehovah
To pervert the Divine voice in its entrance to the earth
With thunder of war & trumpets sound, with armies of disease
Punishments & deaths musterd & numberd; Saying I am God alone
There is no other! let all obey my principles of moral individuality
I have brought them from the uppermost innermost recesses
Of my Eternal Mind, transgressors I will rend off for ever,
As now I rend this accursed Family from my covering.

Thus Satan ragd amidst the Assembly, and his bosom grew
Opake against the Divine Vision: the paved terraces of
His bosom inwards shone with fires, but the stones becoming opake,
Hid him from sight, in an extreme, blackness and darkness,
And there a World of deeper Ulro was opend, in the midst of
Of the Assembly. In Satans bosom a vast unfathomable Abyss.

Astonishment held the Assembly in an awful silence: and tears
Fell down as dews of night, & a loud solemn universal groan
Was utterd from the east & from the west & from the South
And from the north; and Satan stood opake immeasurable
Covering the east with solid blackness, round his hidden heart
With thunders utterd from his hidden wheels: accusing loud
The Divine Mercy, for protecting Palamabron in his tent.

Rintrah reard up walls of rocks and pourd rivers & moats
Of fire round the walls: columns of fire guard around
Between Satan and Palamabron in the terrible darkness.

And Satan not having the Science of Wrath, but only of Pity,
Rent them asunder, and wrath was left to wrath, & pity to pity.
He sunk down a dreadful Death, unlike the slumbers of Beulah

The Separation was terrible: the Dead was reposd on his Couch
Beneath the Couch of Albion, on the seven mountains of Rome
In the whole place of the Covering Cherub, Rome Babylon & Tyre.
His Spectre raging furious descended into its Space

He set his face against Jerusalem to destroy the Eon of Albion

But Los hid Enitharmon from the sight of all these things
Upon the Thames whose lulling harmony reposd her soul:
Where Beulah lovely terminates, in rocky Albion:
Terminating in Hyde Park. on Tyburns awful brook.

And the Mills of Satan were separated into a moony Space
Among the rocks of Albions Temples. and Satans Druid sons
Offer the Human Victims throughout all the Earth. and Albions
Dread Tomb immortal on his Rock. overshadowd the whole Earth:
Where Satan making to himself Laws from his own identity.
Compelld others to serve him in moral gratitude & submission
Being calld God: setting himself above all that is called God.
And all the Spectres of the Dead calling themselves Sons of God
In his Synagogues worship Satan under the Unutterable Name

And it was enquird: Why in a Great Solemn Assembly
The Innocent should be condemnd for the Guilty: Then an Eternal rose

Saying. If the Guilty should be condemnd. he must be an Eternal Death
And one must die for another throughout all Eternity.
Satan is fulln from his station & never can be redeemd
But must be new Created continually moment by moment
And therefore the Class of Satan shall be calld the Elect. & those
Of Rintrah. the Reprobate. & those of Palamabron the Redeemd.
For he is redeemd from Satans Law. the wrath falling on Rintrah.
And therefore Palamabron dared not to call a solemn Assembly
Till Satan had assumd Rintrahs wrath in the day of mourning
In a feminine delusion of false pride self-decievd.

So spoke the Eternal and confirmd it with a thunderous oath.

But when Leutha (a Daughter of Beulah) beheld Satans condemn.
She down descended into the midst of the Great Solemn Assembly
Offering herself a Ransom for Satan. taking on her. his Sin

Mark well my words, they are of your eternal salvation.

And Leutha stood glowing with varying colours immortal. heart-pier
And lovely: & her moth-like elegance shone over the Assembly

At length standing upon the golden floor of Palamabron
She spake: I am the Author of this Sin: by my suggestion
My Parent power Satan has committed this transgression
I loved Palamabron & I sought to approach his Tent.
But beautiful Elynittria with her silver arrows repelld me.

For her light is terrible to me. I fade before her immortal beauty.
O wherefore doth a Dragon-form forth issue from my limbs
To sieze her new born son? Ah me! the wretched Leutha! This
Thus to prevent, entering the doors of Satans brain night after night
Like sweet perfumes I stupified the masculine perceptions
And kept only the feminine awake. hence rose his soft
Delusory love to Palamabron: admiration joind with envy
Cupidity unconquerable! my fault, when at noon of day
The Horses of Palamabron calld for rest and pleasant death:
I sprang out of the breast of Satan, over the Harrow beaming
In all my beauty: that I might unloose the flaming steeds
As Elynittria used to do: but too well those living creatures
Knew that I was not Elynittria. and they brake the traces
But me, the servants of the Harrow saw not: but as a bow
Of varying colours on the hills; terribly ragd the horses.
Satan astonishd, and with power above his own controll
Compelld the Gnomes to curb the horses, & to throw banks of sand
Around the fiery flaming Harrow in labyrinthine forms.
And brooks between, to intersect the meadows in their course.
The Harrow cast thick flames: Jehovah thunderd above:
Chaos & ancient night fled from beneath the fiery Harrow:
The Harrow cast thick flames & orbd us round in concave fires
A Hell of our own making. see, its flames still gird me round
Jehovah thunderd above: Satan in pride of heart
Drove the fierce Harrow among the constellations of Jehovah
Drawing a third part in the fires as stubble north & south
To devour Albion and Jerusalem the Emanation of Albion
Driving the Harrow in Pitys paths. twas then, with our dark fires
Which now gird round us (O eternal torment) I formd the Serpent
Of precious stones & gold turnd poisons on the sultry wastes
The Gnomes in all that day spard not; they cursd Satan bitterly.
To do unkind things in kindness! with power armd, to say
The most irritating things in the midst of tears and love
These are the stings of the Serpent! thus did we by them; till thus
They in return retaliated, and the Living Creatures maddend.
The Gnomes labourd. I weeping hid in Satans inmost brain:
But when the Gnomes refused to labour more, with blandishments
I came forth from the head of Satan; back the Gnomes recoild.
And calld me Sin, and for a sign portentous held me. Soon
Day sunk and Palamabron returnd, trembling I hid myself
In Satans inmost Palace of his nervous fine wrought Brain:
For Elynittria met Satan with all her singing women.
Terrific in their joy & pouring wine of wildest power
They gave Satan their wine: indignant at the burning wrath.
Wild with prophetic fury his former life became like a dream
Clothd in the Serpents folds. in selfish holiness demanding purity
Being most impure, self-condemnd to eternal tears, he drove
Me from his inmost Brain & the doors closd with thunders sound
O Divine Vision who didst create the Female: to repose
The Sleepers of Beulah; pity the repentant Leutha. My sick

Sick Couch bearing the dark shades of Eternal Death infolding
The Spectre of Satan. he furious refuses to repose in sleep
I humbly bow in all my Sin before the Throne Divine:
Not so the Sick-one: Alas what shall be done him to restore:
Who calls the Individual Law, Holy: and despises the Saviour.
Glorying to involve Albions Body in fires of eternal War.—

Now Leutha ceasd: tears flowd: but the Divine Pity supported her.
All is my fault: We are the Spectre of Luvah the murderer
Of Albion: O Vala! O Luvah! O Albion! O lovely Jerusalem
The Sin was begun in Eternity, and will not rest to Eternity
Till two Eternitys meet together, Ah! lost! lost! lost! for ever!

So Leutha spoke. But when she saw that Enitharmon had
Created a New Space to protect Satan from punishment:
She fled to Enitharmons Tent & hid herself. Loud raging
Thundered the Assembly dark & clouded. and they rattld
The kind decision of Enitharmon & gave a Time to the Space.
Even Six Thousand years; and sent Lucifer for its Guard.
But, Lucifer refusd to die & in pride he forsook his charge
And they elected Molech. and when Molech was impatient
The Divine hand found the Two Limits first of Opacity, then of Contraction
Opacity was named Satan, Contraction was named Adam.
Triple Elohim came: Elohim wearied fainted: they elected Shaddai.
Shaddai angry, Pahad descended: Pahad terrified they sent Jehovah
And Jehovah was leprous: loud he calld, stretching his hand to Eternity
For then the Body of Death was perfected in hypocritic holiness.
Around the Lamb, a Female Tabernacle woven in Cathedrons Looms
He died as a Reprobate. he was Punishd as a Transgressor.
Glory! Glory! Glory! to the Holy Lamb of God,
I touch the heavens as an instrument to glorify the Lord!

The Elect shall meet the Redeemd on Albions rocks they shall meet
Astonishd at the Transgressor in him beholding the Saviour.
And the Elect shall say to the Redeemd. We behold it is of Divine
Mercy alone! of Free Gift and Election that we live.
Our Virtues & Cruel Goodnesses, have deservd Eternal Death.
Thus they weep upon the fatal Brook of Albions River.

But Elynittria met Leutha in the place where she was hidden
And threw aside her arrows. and laid down her sounding Bow
She soothd her with soft words & brought her to Palamabrons bed
In moments new created for delusion, interwoven round about.
In dreams she bore the shadowy Spectre of Sleep. & namd him Death
In dreams she bore Rahab the mother of Tirzah & her sisters
In Lambeths vales; in Cambridge & in Oxford, places of Thought
Intricate labyrinths of Times and Spaces unknown, that Leutha lived
In Palamabrons Tent. and Oothoon was her charming guard.

The Bard ceasd. All considerd and a loud resounding murmur
Continued round the Halls: and much they questiond the immortal
Loud voicd Bard. and many condemnd the high toned Song
Saying Pity and Love are too venerable for the imputation
Of Guilt. Others said. If it is true! if the acts have been performd
Let the Bard himself witness. Where hadst thou this terrible Song

The Bard replied. I am Inspired! I know it is Truth! for I Sing

According to the inspiration of the Poetic Genius
Who is the eternal all protecting Divine Humanity
To whom be Glory & Power & Dominion Evermore Amen

Then there was great murmuring in the Heavens of Albion
Concerning Generation & the Vegetative power & concerning
The Lamb the Saviour Albion trembled to Italy Greece & Egypt
To Tartary & Hindostan & China & to Great America
Shaking the roots & fast foundations of the Earth in doubtfulness
The loud voicd Bard terrifyd took refuge in Miltons bosom

Then Milton rose up from the heavens of Albion ardorous!
The whole Assembly wept prophetic, seeing in Miltons face
And in his lineaments divine the shades of Death & Ulro
He took off the robe of the promise, & ungirded himself from
        the oath of God

And Milton said, I go to Eternal Death! The Nations still
Follow after the detestable Gods of Priam; in pomp
Of warlike selfhood, contradicting and blaspheming
When will the Resurrection come; to deliver the sleeping body
From corruptibility; O when Lord Jesus wilt thou come?
Tarry no longer; for my soul lies at the gates of death;
I will arise and look forth, for the morning of the grave.
I will go down to the sepulcher to see if morning breaks!
I will go down to self annihilation and eternal death,
Lest the Last Judgment come & find me unannihilate
And I be siezd & givn into the hands of my own Selfhood.
The Lamb of God is seen thro' mists & shadows, hovring
Over the sepulchers in clouds of Jehovah & winds of Elohim
A disk of blood, distant; & heavns & earths roll dark between
What do I here before the Judgment? without my Emanation?
With the daughters of memory, & not with the daughters of inspiration
I in my Selfhood am that Satan: I am that Evil One!
He is my Spectre! in my obedience to loose him from my Hells
To claim the Hells, my Furnaces, I go to Eternal Death.

And Milton said, I go to Eternal Death; Eternity shudder'd
For he took the outside course, among the graves of the dead
A mournful shade, Eternity shudderd at the image of eternal death

Then on the verge of Beulah he beheld his own Shadow;
A mournful form double; hermaphroditic: male & female
In one wonderful body, and he enterd into it
In direful pain for the dread Shadow, twenty-seven fold
Reachd to the depths of direst Hell, & thence to Albions land:
Which is this earth of vegetation on which now I write.

The Seven Angels of the Presence wept over Miltons Shadow;

As when a man dreams, he reflects not that his body sleeps,
Else he would wake; so seem'd he entering his Shadow: but
With him the Spirits of the Seven Angels of the Presence
Entering; they gave him still perceptions of his Sleeping Body;
Which now arose and walk'd with them in Eden, as an Eighth
Image Divine tho' darken'd; and tho' walking as one walks
In sleep; and the Seven comforted and supported him.

Like as a Polypus that vegetates beneath the deep,
They saw his Shadow vegetated underneath the Couch
Of death: for when he enterd into his Shadow: Himself:
His real and immortal Self: was as appeard to those
Who dwell in immortality, as One sleeping on a couch
Of gold; and those in immortality gave forth their Emanations
Like Females of sweet beauty, to guard round him & to feed
His lips with food of Eden in his cold and dim repose!
But to himself he seemd a wanderer lost in dreary night.

Onwards his Shadow kept its course among the Spectres; call'd
Satan, but swift as lightning passing them, startled the shades
Of Hell beheld him in a trail of light as of a comet
That travels into Chaos: so Milton went guarded within.

The nature of infinity is this! That every thing has its
Own Vortex; and when once a traveller thro' Eternity.
Has passd that Vortex, he percieves it roll backward behind
His path, into a globe itself infolding; like a sun:
Or like a moon, or like a universe of starry majesty,
While he keeps onwards in his wondrous journey on the earth
Or like a human form, a friend with whom he livd benevolent.
As the eye of man views both the east & west encompassing
Its vortex; and the north & south, with all their starry host;
Also the rising sun & setting moon he views surrounding
His corn-fields and his valleys of five hundred acres square.
Thus is the earth one infinite plane, and not as apparent
To the weak traveller confin'd beneath the moony shade.
Thus is the heaven a vortex passd already, and the earth
A vortex not yet passd by the traveller thro' Eternity.

First Milton saw Albion upon the Rock of Ages,
Deadly pale outstretchd and snowy cold, storm cover'd:
A Giant form of perfect beauty outstretchd on the rock
In solemn death, the Sea of Time & Space thunderd aloud
Against the rock, which was inwrapped with the weeds of death
Hovering over the cold bosom, in its vortex Milton bent down
To the bosom of death, what was underneath soon seemd a Sea
A cloudy heaven mingled with stormy seas in loudest ruin;
But as a wintry globe descends precipitant thro' Beulah bursting,
With thunders loud and terrible: so Miltons shadow fell,
Precipitant loud thundring into the Sea of Time & Space.

Then first I saw him in the Zenith as a falling star,
Descending perpendicular, swift as the swallow or swift;
And on my left foot falling on the tarsus, enterd there; ——
But from my left foot a black cloud redounding spread over Europe.

Then Milton knew that the Three Heavens of Beulah were beheld
By him on earth in his bright pilgrimage of sixty years

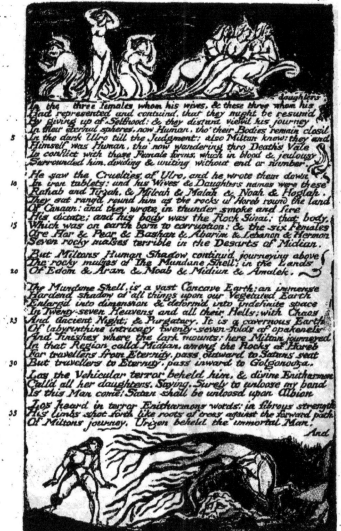

the three females whom his wives, & these three whom his daughters
Had represented and contain'd, that they might be resum'd
By giving up of Selfhood: & they distant view'd his journey
In their eternal spheres, now Human, tho' their Bodies remain closd
In the dark Ulro till the Judgment: also Milton knew: they and
Himself was Human, tho' now wandering thro' Death's Vale
In conflict with those Female forms, which in blood & jealousy
Surrounded him, dividing & uniting without end or number.

He saw the Cruelties of Ulro, and he wrote them down
In iron tablets: and his Wives & Daughters names were these
Rahab and Tirzah. & Milcah & Malah & Noah & Hoglah.
They sat rang'd round him as the rocks of Horeb round the land
Of Canaan: and they wrote in thunder smoke and fire
His dictate; and his body was the Rock Sinai; that body,
Which was on earth born to corruption: & the six Females
Are Hor & Peor & Bashan & Abarim & Lebanon & Hermon
Seven rocky masses terrible in the Desarts of Midian.

But Miltons Human Shadow continu'd journeying above
The rocky masses of The Mundane Shell; in the Lands
Of Edom & Aran & Moab & Midian & Amalek.

The Mundane Shell, is a vast Concave Earth: an immense
Harden'd shadow of all things upon our Vegetated Earth
Enlarg'd into dimension & deform'd into indefinite space
In Twenty-seven Heavens and all their Hells: with Chaos
And ancient Night; & Purgatory. It is a cavernous Earth
Of labyrinthine intricacy twenty-seven-folds of opakeness
And finishes where the lark mounts; here Milton journeyed
In that Region called Midian, among the Rocks of Horeb
For travellers from Eternity. pass outward to Satans seat
But travellers to Eternity. pass inward to Golgonooza.

Los the Vehicular terror beheld him, & divine Enitharmon
Call'd all her daughters, Saying, Surely to unloose my bond
Is this Man come! Satan shall be unloos'd upon Albion

Los heard in terror Enitharmons words: in fibrous strength
His limbs shot forth like roots of trees against the forward path
Of Miltons journey. Urizen beheld the immortal Man,
                                                              And

And he also darkend his brows: freezing dark rocks between
The footsteps. and infixing deep the feet in marble beds:
That Milton labour'd with his journey. & his feet bled sore
Upon the clay now changd to marble: also Urizen rose
And met him on the shores of Arnon: & by the streams of the brooks

Silent they met. and silent strove among the streams of Arnon.
Even to Mahanaim. when with cold hand. Urizen stoop'd down
And took up water from the river Jordan: pouring on
To Miltons brain the icy fluid from his broad cold palm.
But Milton took of the red clay of Succoth. moulding it with care
Between his palms: and filling up the hurrows of many years
Beginning at the feet of Urizen. and on the bones
Creating new flesh on the Demon cold. and building him.
As with new clay a Human form in the Valley of Beth Peor.

Four Universes round the Mundane Egg remain Chaotic
One to the North. named Urthona: One to the South named Urizen:
One to the East. named Luvah: One to the West. named Tharmas
They are the Four Zoa's that stood around the Throne Divine:
But when Luvah assum'd the World of Urizen to the South:
And Albion was slain upon his mountains. & in his tent:
All fell towards the Center in dire ruin. sinking down.
And in the South remains a burning fire; in the East a void.
In the West, a world of raging waters; in the North a solid.
Unfathomable! without end. But in the midst of these.
Is built eternally the Universe of Los and Enitharmon:
Towards which Milton went. but Urizen oppos'd his path.

The Man and Demon strove many periods. Rahab beheld
Standing on Carmel; Rahab and Tirzah trembled to behold
The enormous strife. one giving life. the other giving death
To his adversary. and they sent forth all their sons & daughters
In all their beauty to entice Milton across the river.

The Twofold form Hermaphroditic: and the Double-sexed:
The Female-male, & the Male-female, self-dividing stood
Before him in their beauty, & in cruelties of holiness:
Shining in darkness, glorious upon the deeps of Entuthon.

Saying. Come thou to Ephraim! behold the Kings of Canaan!
The beautiful Amalekites, behold the fires of youth
Bound with the Chain of Jealousy by Los & Enitharmon:
The banks of Cam: cold learnings streams: Londons dark-frowning towers:
Lament upon the winds of Europe in Rephaims Vale.
Because Ahania rent apart into a desolate night.
Laments: & Enion wanders like a weeping inarticulate voice
And Vala labours for her bread & water among the Furnaces
Therefore bright Tirzah triumphs: putting on all beauty.
And all perfection, in her cruel sports among the Victims.
Come bring with thee Jerusalem with songs on the Grecian Lyre:
In Natural Religion: in experiments on Men.
Let her be Offerd up to Holiness! Tirzah numbers her:
She numbers with her fingers every fibre ere it grow?
Where is the Lamb of God? where is the promise of his coming?
Her shadowy Sisters form the bones. even the bones of Horeb:
Around the marrow: and the orbed scull around the brain:
His Images are born for War! for Sacrifice to Tirzah:
To Natural Religion! to Tirzah the Daughter of Rahab the Holy!
She ties the knot of nervous fibres. into a white brain!
She ties the knot of bloody veins, into a red hot heart:
Within her bosom Albion lies embalmd. never to awake
Hand is become a rock! Sinai & Horeb. is Hyle & Coban:
Scofeld is bound in iron armour before Reubens Gate:
She ties the knot of milky seed into two lovely Heavens.

Two yet but one; each in the other sweet reflected: these
Are our Three Heavens beneath the shades of Beulah, land of rest:
Come then to Ephraim & Manasseh O beloved-one!
Come to my ivory palaces O beloved of thy mother!
And let us bind thee in the bands of War & be thou King
Of Canaan and reign in Hazor where the Twelve Tribes meet.

So spoke they as in one voice! Silent Milton stood before
The darkend Urizen; as the sculptor silent stands before
His forming image; he walks round it patient labouring.
Thus Milton stood forming bright Urizen, while his Mortal part
Sat frozen in the rock of Horeb: and his Redeemed portion,
Thus form'd the Clay of Urizen; but within that portion
His real Human walkd above in power and majesty
Tho darkend; and the Seven Angels of the Presence attended him.

O how can I with my gross tongue that cleaveth to the dust.
Tell of the Fourfold Man, in starry numbers fitly orderd
Or how can I with my cold hand of clay! But thou O Lord
Do with me as thou wilt! for I am nothing, and vanity.
If thou chuse to elect a worm, it shall remove the mountains.
For that portion namd the Elect: the Spectrous body of Milton
Redounding from my left foot into Los's Mundane space,
Brooded over his Body in Horeb against the Resurrection
Preparing it for the Great Consummation: red the Cherub on Sinai
Glowd; but in terrors folded round his clouds of blood

Now Albions sleeping Humanity began to turn upon his Couch;
Feeling the electric flame of Miltons awful precipitate descent.
Seest thou the little winged fly, smaller than a grain of sand?
It has a heart like thee; a brain open to heaven & hell,
Withinside wondrous & expansive; its gates are not closd,
I hope thine are not; hence it clothes itself in rich array;
Hence thou art clothd with human beauty O thou mortal man.
Seek not thy heavenly father then beyond the skies:
There Chaos dwells & ancient Night & Og & Anak old:
For every human heart has gates of brass & bars of adamant,
Which few dare unbar because dread Og & Anak guard the gates
Terrific! and each mortal brain is walld and moated round
Within: and Og & Anak watch here; here is the Seat
Of Satan in its Webs; for in brain and heart and loins
Gates open behind Satans Seat to the City of Golgonooza
Which is the spiritual fourfold London, in the loins of Albion

Thus Milton fell thro Albions heart, travelling outside of Humanity
Beyond the Stars in Chaos in Caverns of the Mundane Shell.

But many of the Eternals rose up from eternal tables
Drunk with the Spirit, burning round the Couch of death they stood
Looking down into Beulah: wrathful, filld with rage!
They rend the heavens round the Watchers in a fiery circle:
And round the Shadowy Eighth: the Eight close up the Couch
Into a tabernacle, and flee with cries down to the Deeps:
Where Los opens his three wide gates, surrounded by raging fires!
They soon find their own place & join the Watchers of the Ulro.

Los saw them and a cold pale horror coverd o'er his limbs
Pondering he knew that Rintrah & Palamabron might depart:
Even as Reuben & as Gad; gave up himself to tears:
He sat down on his anvil-stock; and leand upon the trough,
Looking into the black water, mingling it with tears.

At last when desperation almost tore his heart in twain
He recollected an old Prophecy in Eden recorded,
And often sung to the loud harp at the immortal feasts
That Milton of the Land of Albion should up ascend
Forwards from Ulro from the Vale of Felpham, and set free
Orc from his Chain of Jealousy, he started at the thought

And

And down descended into Udan-Adan: it was night:
And Satan sat sleeping upon his Couch in Udan Adan:
His Spectre slept, his Shadow woke: when one sleeps th'other wakes

But Milton, entering my Foot, I saw in the nether
Regions of the Imagination; also all men on Earth,
And all in Heaven, saw in the nether regions of the Imagination
In Ulro beneath Beulah, the vast breach of Miltons descent.
But I knew not that it was Milton, for man cannot know
What passes in his members till periods of Space & Time
Reveal the secrets of Eternity: for more extensive
Than any other earthly things, are Mans earthly lineaments.

And all this Vegetable World appeard on my left Foot,
As a bright sandal formd immortal of precious stones & gold:
I stooped down & bound it on to walk forward thro' Eternity.

There is in Eden a sweet River, of milk & liquid pearl
Namd Ololon: on whose mild banks dwelt those who Milton drove
Down into Ulro: and they wept in long resounding song
For seven days of eternity, and the rivers living banks
The mountains wail'd! & every plant that grew, in solemn sighs lamented.

When Luvahs bulls each morning drag, the sulphur Sun out of the Deep
Harnessd with starry harness black & shining kept by black slaves
That work all night at the starry harness. Strong and vigorous
They drag the unwilling Orb: at this time all the Family
Of Eden heard the lamentation, and Providence began.
But when the clarions of day sounded they drownd the lamentations
And when night came all was silent in Ololon: & all refusd to lament
In the still night fearing lest they should others molest.

Seven mornings Los heard them, as the poor bird within the shell
Hears its impatient parent bird: and Enitharmon heard them:
But saw them not, for the blue Mundane Shell inclosd them in.

And they lamented that they had in wrath & fury & fire
Driven Milton into the Ulro: for now they knew too late
That it was Milton the Awakener: they had not heard the Bard,
Whose Song calld Milton to the attempt: and Los heard these laments.
He heard them, call in prayer all the Divine Family:
And he beheld the Cloud of Milton stretching over Europe.

But all the Family Divine collected as Four Suns
In the Four Points of heaven East, West & North & South,
Enlarging and enlarging till their Disks approachd each other
And when they touchd closed together Southward in One Sun
Over Ololon: and as One Man, who weeps over his brother
In a dark tomb, so all the Family Divine, wept over Ololon.

Saying. Milton goes to Eternal Death: so saying, they groand in spirit
And were troubled! and again the Divine Family groaned in spirit.

And Ololon said, Let us descend also, and let us give
Ourselves to death in Ulro among the Transgressors.
Is Virtue a Punisher? O no! how is this wondrous thing:
This World beneath, unseen before: this refuge from the wars
Of Great Eternity! unnatural refuge! unknown by us till now!
Or are these the pangs of repentance! let us enter into them

Then the Divine Family said. Six Thousand Years are now
Accomplishd in this World of Sorrow: Miltons Angel knew
The Universal Dictate: and you also feel this Dictate.
And now you know this World of Sorrow, and feel Pity. Obey
The Dictate! Watch over this World, and with your brooding wings,
Renew it to Eternal Life: Lo! I am with you alway
But you cannot renew Milton he goes to Eternal Death

So spake the Family Divine as One Man even Jesus
Uniting in One with Ololon & the appearance of One Man
Jesus the Saviour appeard coming in the Clouds of Ololon.

Tho driven away with the Seven Starry Ones into the Ulro
Yet the Divine Vision remains Every-where For-ever. Amen.
And Ololon lamented for Milton with a great lamentation.

While Los heard indistinct in fear, what time I bound my sandals
5 On: to walk forward thro' Eternity, Los descended to me:
And Los behind me stood: a terrible flaming Sun: just close
Behind my back: I turned round in terror, and behold.
Los stood in that fierce glowing fire; & he also stoop'd down
And bound my sandals on in Udan-Adan: trembling I stood
10 Exceedingly with fear & terror, standing in the Vale
Of Lambeth: but he kissed me and wish'd me health.
And I became One Man with him arising in my strength:
'Twas too late now to recede. Los had enterd into my soul:
His terrors now possess'd me whole! I arose in fury & strength.

15 I am that Shadowy Prophet who Six Thousand Years ago
Fell from my station in the Eternal bosom. Six Thousand Years
Are finishd. I return! both Time & Space obey my will.
I in Six Thousand Years walk up and down: for not one Moment
Of Time is lost, nor one Event of Space unpermanent
20 But all remain: every fabric of Six Thousand Years
Remains permanent: tho' on the Earth where Satan
Fell, and was cut off all things vanish & are seen no more
They vanish not from me & mine, we guard them first & last
The generations of men run on in the tide of Time
25 But leave their destind lineaments permanent for ever & ever.
So spoke Los as we went along to his supreme abode.

Rintrah and Palamabron met us at the Gate of Golgonooza.
Clouded with discontent, & brooding in their minds terrible things

They said. O Father most beloved: O merciful Parent:
30 Pitying and permitting evil, tho strong & mighty to destroy.
Whence is this Shadow terrible? wherefore dost thou refuse
To throw him into the Furnaces! knowest thou not that he
Will unchain Orc & let loose Satan. Og. Sihon & Anak.
Upon the Body of Albion: for this he is come: behold it written
35 Upon his fibrous left Foot black: most dismal to our eyes
The Shadowy Female shudders thro' heaven in torment inexpressible:
And all the Daughters of Los prophetic wail: yet in deceit.
They weave a new Religion from new Jealousy of Theotormon:
Miltons Religion is the cause: there is no end to destruction:
40 Seeing the Churches at their Period in terror & despair:
Rahab created Voltaire; Tirzah created Rousseau:
Asserting the Self-righteousness against the Universal Saviour.
Mocking the Confessors & Martyrs, claiming Self-righteousness:
With cruel Virtue: making War upon the Lambs Redeemed:
45 To perpetuate War & Glory, to perpetuate the Laws of Sin:
They perverted Swedenborgs Visions in Beulah & in Ulro:
To destroy Jerusalem as a Harlot & her Sons as Reprobates;
To raise up Mystery the Virgin Harlot Mother of War,
Babylon the Great, the Abomination of Desolation:
50 O Swedenborg! strongest of men, the Samson shorn by the Churches:
Shewing the Transgressors in Hell, the proud Warriors in Heaven:
Heaven as a Punisher & Hell as One under Punishment:
With Laws from Plato & his Greeks to renew the Trojan Gods.
In Albion; & to deny the value of the Saviours blood.
55 But then I raisd up Whitefield, Palamabron raisd up Westley,
And these are the cries of the Churches before the two Witnesses:
Faith in God the dear Saviour who took on the likeness of men:
Becoming obedient to death, even the death of the Cross
The Witnesses lie dead in the Street of the Great City
60 No Faith is in all the Earth: the Book of God is trodden under foot:
He sent his two Servants Whitefield & Westley; were they Prophets
Or were they Idiots or Madmen? shew us Miracles!

Can you have greater Miracles than these? Men who devote
Their lifes whole comfort to inare scorn & injury. & death
Awake thou sleeper on the Rock of Eternity Albion awake
The trumpet of Judgment hath. twice sounded; all Nations are awake
5 But thou art still heavy and dull; Awake Albion awake!
Lo Orc arises on the Atlantic. Lo his blood and fire
Glow on Americas shore: Albion turns upon his Couch
He listens to the sounds of War, astonishd and confounded:
He weeps into the Atlantic deep, yet still in dismal dreams
10 Unwakend; and the Covering Cherub advances from the East
How long shall we lay dead in the Street of the great City
How long beneath the Covering Cherub give our Emanations
Milton will utterly consume us & thee our beloved Father
He hath enterd into the Covering Cherub, becoming one with
15 Albions dread Sons, Hand. Hyle & Coban surround him as
A Girdle: Gwendolen & Cambel as a garment, woven
Of War & Religion; let us descend & bring him chaind
To Bowlahoola O Father most beloved! O mild Parent!
Cruel in thy mildness, pitying and permitting evil
20 Tho strong and mighty to destroy, O Los our beloved Father!

Like the black storm, coming out of Chaos, beyond the stars:
It issues thro the dark & intricate caves of the Mundane Shell
Passing the planetary visions, & the well adorned Firmament
The Sun rolls into Chaos & the Stars into the Deserts:
25 And then the storms become visible. audible & terrible.
Covering the light of day, & rolling down upon the mountains.
Deluge all the country round. Such is a vision of Los:
When Rintrah & Palamabron spoke; and such his stormy face
Appeard, as does the face of heaven. when coverd with thick storms
30 Pitying and loving tho in frowns of terrible perturbation

But Los dispersd the clouds even as the strong winds of Jehovah,
And Los thus spoke. O noble Sons, be patient yet a little
I have embraced the falling Death. he is become one with me
O Sons we live not by wrath. by mercy alone we live!
35 I recollect an old Prophecy in Eden recorded in gold; and oft
Sung to the harp: That Milton of the land of Albion
Should up ascend forward from Felphams Vale & break the Chain
Of Jealousy from all its roots; be patient therefore O my Sons
These lovely Females form sweet night and silence and secret
40 Obscurities to hide from Satans Watch-Fiends. Human loves
And graces; lest they write them in their Books. & in the Scroll
Of mortal life, to condemn the accused; who at Satans Bar
Tremble in Spectrous Bodies continually day and night
While on the Earth they live in sorrowful Vegetation;
45 O when shall we tread our Wine-presses in heaven; and Reap
Our wheat with shoutings of joy. and leave the Earth in peace
Remember how Calvin and Luther in fury premature
Sowd War and stern division between Papists & Protestants
Let it not be so now! O go not forth in Martyrdoms & Wars
50 We were placd here by the Universal Brotherhood & Mercy
With powers fitted to circumscribe this dark Satanic death
And that the Seven Eyes of God may have space for Redemption
But how this is as yet we know not. and we cannot know;
Till Albion is arisen; then patient wait a little while.
55 Six Thousand years are passd away the end approaches fast;
This mighty one is come from Eden. he is of the Elect.
Who died from Earth & he is returnd before the Judgment. This thing
Was never known that one of the holy dead should willing return
Then patient wait a little while till the Last Vintage is over;
60 Till we have quenchd the Sun of Salah in the Lake of Udan Adan
O my dear Sons! leave not your Father, as your brethren left me
Twelve Sons successive fled away in that thousand years of sorrow

Of Palamabrons Harrow, & at Rintrahs wrath & fury:
Reuben & Manazzoth & Gad & Simeon & Levi.
And Ephraim & Judah were Generated, because
They left me, wandering with Tirzah: Enitharmon wept
One thousand years, and all the Earth was in a watry deluge
We call'd him Menassheh because of the Generations of Tirzah
Because of Satan: & the seven Eyes of God continually
Guard round them, but I the Fourth Zoa am also set
The Watchman of Eternity, the three are not! & I am preserved
Still my four mighty ones are left to me in Golgonooza
Still Rintrah fierce, and Palamabron mild & piteous
Theotormon fill'd with care, Bromion loving Science
You O my Sons still guard round Los, O wander not & leave me
Rintrah, thou well remeberest when Amalek & Canaan
Fled with their Sister Moab into that abhorred Void
They became Nations in our sight beneath the hands of Tirzah.
And Palamabron thou remeberest when Joseph an infant:
Stolen from his nurses cradle wrapd in needle-work
Of emblematic texture, was sold to the Amalekite,
Who carried him down into Egypt where Ephraim & Menassheh
Gatherd my Sons together in the Sands of Midian
And if you also flee away and leave your Fathers side,
Following Milton into Ulro, altho your power is great
Surely you also shall become poor mortal vegetations
Beneath the Moon of Ulro: pity then your Fathers tears
When Jesus raisd Lazarus from the Grave I stood & saw
Lazarus who is the Vehicular Body of Albion the Redeemd
Arise into the Covering Cherub who is the Spectre of Albion
By martyrdoms to suffer: to watch over the Sleeping Body:
Upon his Rock beneath his Tomb. I saw the Covering Cherub
Divide Four-fold into Four Churches when Lazarus arose
Paul, Constantine, Charlemaine, Luther: behold they stand before us
Stretchd over Europe & Asia. come O Sons, come, come away
Arise O Sons give all your strength against Eternal Death
Lest we are vegetated, for Cathedrons Looms weave only Death
A Web of Death: & were it not for Bowlahoola & Allamanda
No Human Form but only a Fibrous Vegetation
A Polypus of soft affections without Thought or Vision
Must tremble in the Heavens & Earths thro all the Ulro space
Throw all the Vegetated Mortals into Bowlahoola
But as to this Elected Form who is returned again
He is the Signal that the Last Vintage now approaches
Nor Vegetation may go on till all the Earth is reapd

So Los spoke. Furious they descended to Bowlahoola & Allamanda
Indignant, unconvinced by Loss's arguments & thunders rolling
They saw that wrath now swayd but now pity absorbd him
As it was, so it remaind & no hope of an end.

Bowlahoola is namd Law, by mortals, Tharmas founded it:
Because of Satan, before Luban in the City of Golgonooza.
But Golgonooza is namd Art & Manufacture by mortal men.

In Bowlahoola Los's Anvils stand & his Furnaces rage:
Thundering the Hammers beat & the Bellows blow loud
Living self moving mourning lamenting & howling incessantly
Bowlahoola thro all its porches feels tho' too fast founded
Its pillars & porticoes to tremble at the force
Of mortal or immortal arm: and softly lilling flutes
Accordant with the horrid labours make sweet melody
The Bellows are the Animal Lungs: the Hammers the Animal Heart
The Furnaces the Stomach for digestion: terrible their fury
Thousands & thousands labour, thousands play on instruments
Stringed or fluted to ameliorate the sorrows of slavery
Loud sport the dancers in the dance of death, rejoicing in carnage
The hard dentant Hammers are lulld by the flutes lula lula
The bellowing Furnaces blare by the long sounding clarion
The double drum drowns howls & groans, the shrill fife shrieks & cries:
The croaked horn mellows the hoarse raving serpent, terrible, but harmonious

Bowlahoola is the Stomach in every individual man.

Los is by mortals namd Time Enitharmon is namd Space
But they depict him bald & aged who is in eternal youth
All powerful, and his locks flourish like the brows of morning
He is the Spirit of Prophecy the ever apparent Elias
Time is the mercy of Eternity; without Times swiftness
Which is the swiftest of all things: all were eternal torment:
All the Gods of the Kingdoms of Earth labour in Los's Halls.
Every one is a fallen Son of the Spirit of Prophecy
He is the Fourth Zoa, that stood around the Throne Divine.

But the Wine-press of Los is eastward of Golgonooza, before the Seat
Of Satan. Luvah laid the foundation & Urizen finish'd it in howling woe.
How red the sons & daughters of Luvah: here they tread the grapes.
Laughing & shouting drunk with odours many fall, o'erwearied
Drown'd in the wine is many a youth & maiden: those around
Lay them on skins of Tygers & of the spotted Leopard & the Wild Ass
Till they revive, or bury them in cool grots, making lamentation.

This Wine-press is call'd War on Earth, it is the Printing-Press
Of Los: and here he lays his words in order above the mortal brain
As cogs are form'd in a wheel to turn the cogs of the adverse wheel.

Timbrels & violins sport round the Wine-presses: the little Seed;
The sportive Root, the Earth-worm, the gold Beetle: the wise Emmet;
Dance round the Wine-presses of Luvah: the Centipede is there:
The ground Spider, with many eyes: the Mole clothed in velvet
The ambitious Spider in his sullen web; the lucky golden Spinner;
The Earwig arm'd: the tender Maggot emblem of immortality:
The Flea: Louse; Bug: the Tape-Worm: all the Armies of Disease:
Visible or invisible to the slothful vegetating Man
The slow Slug: the Grasshopper that sings & laughs & drinks:
Winter comes, he folds his slender bones without a murmur.
The cruel Scorpion is there: the Gnat: Wasp; Hornet & the Honey Bee:
The Toad & venomous Newt; the Serpent clothd in gems & gold:
They throw off their gorgeous raiment: they rejoice with loud jubilee
Around the Wine-presses of Luvah, naked & drunk with wine.

There is the Nettle that stings with soft down, and there
The indignant Thistle: whose bitterness is bred in his milk
Who feeds on contempt of his neighbour: there all the idle weeds
That creep around the obscure places, shew their various limbs
Naked in all their beauty dancing round the Wine-presses.

But in the Wine-presses the Human grapes sing not nor dance
They howl & writhe in shoals of torment; in fierce flames consuming
In chains of iron & in dungeons circled with ceaseless fires
In pits & dens & shades of death: in shapes of torment & woe.
The plates & screws & wracks & saws & cords & fires & cisterns
The cruel joys of Luvahs Daughters lacerating with knives
And whips their Victims & the deadly sport of Luvahs Sons.

They dance around the dying, & they drink the howl & groan
They catch the shrieks in cups of gold, they hand them to one another:
These are the sports of love, & these the sweet delights of amorous play
Tears of the grape, the death sweat of the cluster the last sigh
Of the mild youth who listens to the lureing songs of Luvah.

But Allamanda calld on Earth Commerce, is the Cultivated land
Around the City of Golgonooza, in the Forests of Entuthon:
Here the Sons of Los labour against Death Eternal; through all
The Twenty-seven Heavens of Beulah in Ulro, Seat of Satan:
Which is the False Tongue beneath Beulah: it is the Sense of Touch:
The Plow goes forth in tempests & lightnings & the Harrow cruel
In blights of the east; the heavy Roller follows in howlings of woe.

Urizens sons here labour also; & here are seen the Mills
Of Theotormon, on the verge of the Lake of Udan-Adan.
These are the starry voids of night & the depths & caverns of earth
These Mills are oceans, clouds & waters ungovernable in their fury:
Here are the stars created & the seeds of all things planted
And here the Sun & Moon recieve their fixed destinations

But in Eternity the Four Arts: Poetry, Painting, Music
And Architecture which is Science: are the Four Faces of Man.
Not so in Time & Space: there Three are shut out, and only
Science remains thro Mercy: & by means of Science, the Three
Became apparent in Time & Space, in the Three Professions

That Man may live upon Earth till the time of his awaking.
And from these Three, Science derives every Occupation of Men.
And Science is divided into Bowlahoola & Allamanda.

Loud shout the Sons of Luvah, at the Wine-presses as Los descended
With Rintrah & Palamabron in his fires of resistless fury.

The Wine-press on the Rhine groans loud, but all its central beams
Act more terrific in the central Cities of the Nations
Where Human Thought is crushd beneath the iron hand of Power.
There Los puts all into the Press, the Opressor & the Opressed
Together, ripe for the Harvest & Vintage & ready for the Loom.

They sang at the Vintage. This is the Last Vintage! & Seed
Shall no more be sown upon Earth, till all the Vintage is over
And all gatherd in, till the Plow has passd over the Nations
And the Harrow & heavy thundering Roller upon the mountains
And loud the Souls howl round the Porches of Golgonooza
Crying O God deliver us to the Heavens or to the Earths,
That we may preach righteousness & punish the sinner with death
But Los refused, till all the Vintage of Earth was gatherd in.

And Los stood & cried to the Labourers of the Vintage in voice of awe.

Fellow Labourers! The Great Vintage & Harvest is now upon Earth
The whole extent of the Globe is explored Every scatterd Atom
Of Human Intellect now is flocking to the sound of the Trumpet
All the Wisdom which was hidden in caves & dens, from ancient
Time, is now sought out from Animal & Vegetable & Mineral
The Awakener is come, outstretchd over Europe: the Vision of God is fulfilled
The Ancient Man upon the Rock of Albion Awakes,
He listens to the sounds of War astonishd & ashamed,
He sees his Children mock at Faith and deny Providence
Therefore you must bind the Sheaves not by Nations or Families
You shall bind them in Three Classes; according to their Classes
So shall you bind them. Separating What has been Mixed
Since Men began to be Wove into Nations by Rahab & Tirzah
Since Albions Death & Satans Cutting-off from our awful Fields
When under pretence to benevolence the Elect Subdud All
From the Foundation of the World. The Elect is one Class; You
Shall bind them separate: they cannot Believe in Eternal Life
Except by Miracle & a New Birth. The other two Classes;
The Reprobate who never cease to Believe, and the Redeemd,
Who live in doubts & fears perpetually tormented by the Elect
These you shall bind in a twin-bundle for the Consumation—
But the Elect must be saved fires of Eternal Death,
To be formed into the Churches of Beulah that they destroy not the Earth
For in every Nation & every Family the Three Classes are born
And in every Species of Earth, Metal, Tree, Fish, Bird & Beast.
We form the Mundane Egg, that Spectres coming by fury or amity
All is the same, & every one remains in his own energy
Go forth Reapers with rejoicing, you sowed in tears
But the time of your refreshing cometh, only a little moment
Still abstain from pleasure & rest, in the labours of eternity
And you shall Reap the whole Earth, from Pole to Pole, from Sea to Sea
Beginning at Jerusalems inner Court, Lambeth ruind and given
To the detestable Gods of Priam, to Apollo: and at the Asylum
Given to Hercules, who labour in Tirzahs Looms for bread
Who set Pleasure against Duty: who Create Olympic crowns
To make Learning a burden & the Work of the Holy Spirit: Strife.
The Thor & cruel Odin who first reard the Polar Caves
Lambeth mourns calling Jerusalem, she weeps & looks abroad
For the Lords coming, that Jerusalem may overspread all Nations
Crave not for the mortal & perishing delights, but leave them
To the weak, and pity the weak as your infant care; Break not
Forth in your wrath lest you also are Vegetated by Tirzah
Wait till the Judgement is past, till the Creation is consumed
And then rush forward with me into the glorious spiritual
Vegetation: the Supper of the Lamb & his Bride; and the
Awaking of Albion our Friend and ancient companion.

So Los spoke. But lightnings of discontent broke on all sides round
And murmurs of thunder rolling heavy long & loud over the mountains
While Los calld his Sons around him to the Harvest & the Vintage.

Thou seest the Constellations in the deep & wondrous Night
They rise in order and continue their immortal courses
Upon the mountains & in vales with harp & heavenly song
With flute & clarion; with cups & measures filld with foaming wine.
Glittring the streams reflect the Vision of beatitude,
And the calm Ocean joys beneath & smooths his awful waves;
                                                          These

These are the Sons of Los, & these the Labourers of the Vintage
Thou seest the gorgeous clothed Flies that dance &sport in summer
Upon the sunny brooks & meadows: every one the dance
Knows in its intricate mazes of delight artful to weave:
Each one to sound his instruments of music in the dance,
To touch each other & recede; to cross & change & return
These are the Children of Los; thou seest the Trees on mountains
The wind blows heavy, loud they thunder thro' the darksom sky
Uttering prophecies & speaking instructive words to the sons
Of men: These are the Sons of Los! These the Visions of Eternity
But we see only as it were the hem of their garments
When with our vegetable eyes we view these wondrous Visions

There are Two Gates thro' which all Souls descend. One Southward
From Dover Cliff to Lizard Point. the other toward the North
Caithness & rocky Durness, Pentland & John Groats House

The Souls descending to the Body, wail on the right hand
Of Los; & those deliverd from the Body, on the left hand
For Los against the east his force continually bends
Along the Valleys of Middlesex from Hounslow to Blackheath
Lest those Three Heavens of Beulah should the Creation destroy
And lest they should descend before the north & south Gates
Groaning with pity, he among the wailing Souls laments.

And these the Labours of the Sons of Los in Allamanda:
And in the City of Golgonooza: & in Luban: & around
The Lake of Udan Adan, in the Forests of Entuthon Benython
Where Souls incessant wail, being piteous Passions & Desires
With neither lineament nor form but like to watry clouds
The Passions & Desires descend upon the hungry winds
For such alone Sleepers remain meer passion & appetite;
The Sons of Los clothe them & feed & provide houses & fields
And every Generated Body in its inward form
Is a garden of delight, & a building of magnificence,
Built by the Sons of Los in Bowlahoola, & Allamanda
And the herbs & flowers & furniture & beds & chambers
Continually woven in the Looms of Enitharmons Daughters
In bright Cathedrons golden Dome with care & love & tears
For the various Classes of Men are all markd out determinate
In Bowlahoola: & as the Spectres choose their affinities
So they are born on Earth, & every Class is determinate
But not by Natural but by Spiritual power alone, Because
The Natural power continually seeks & tends to Destruction
Ending in Death: which would of itself be Eternal Death
And all are Classd by Spiritual, & not by Natural power.

And every Natural Effect has a Spiritual Cause, and Not
A Natural: for a Natural Cause only seems: it is a Delusion
Of Ulro: & a ratio of the perishing Vegetable Memory.

Some Sons of Los surround the Passions with porches of iron & silver
Creating form & beauty around the dark regions of sorrow
Giving to airy nothing a name and a habitation
Delightful: with bounds to the Infinite putting off the Indefinite
Into most holy forms of Thought: (such is the power of inspiration)
They labour incessant; with many tears & afflictions:
Creating the beautiful House for the piteous sufferer.

Others: Cabinets richly fabricate of gold & ivory;
For Doubts & fears unform'd & wretched & melancholy
The little weeping Spectre stands on the threshold of Death
Eternal; and sometimes two Spectres like lamps quivering
And often malignant they combat (heart-breaking sorrowful & piteous)
Antamon takes them into his beautiful flexible hands,
As the Sower takes the seed, or as the Artist his clay
Or fine wax, to mould artful a model for golden ornaments.
The soft hands of Antamon draw the indelible line:
Form immortal with golden pen; such as the Spectre admiring
Puts on the sweet form; then smiles Antamon bright thro his windows
The Daughters of beauty look up from their Loom & prepare.
The integument soft for its clothing with joy & delight.

But Theotormon & Sotha stand in the Gate of Luban anxious
Their numbers are seven million & seven thousand & seven hundred
They contend with the weak Spectres, they fabricate soothing forms
The Spectre refuses, he seeks cruelty, they create the crested Cock
Terrified the Spectre screams & rushes in fear into their Net
Of kindness & compassion & is born a weeping terror.
Or they create the Lion & Tyger in compassionate thunderings
Howling the Spectres flee: they take refuge in Human lineaments.

The Sons of Ozoth within the Optic Nerve stand fiery glowing
And the number of his Sons is eight millions & eight.
They give delights to the man unknown; artificial riches
They give to scorn, & their possessors to trouble & sorrow & care.
Shutting the sun. & moon. & stars, & trees, & clouds, & waters.
And hills, out from the Optic Nerve & hardening it into a bone
Opake. and like the black pebble on the enraged beach.
While the poor indigent is like the diamond which tho clothd
In rugged covering in the mine, is open all within
And in his hallowd center holds the heavens of bright eternity
Ozoth here builds walls of rocks against the surging sea
And timbers crampt with iron cramps bar in the joys of life
From fell destruction in the Spectrous cunning or rage. He Creates
The speckled Newt, the Spider & Beetle, the Rat & Mouse,
The Badger & Fox: they worship before his feet in trembling fear.

But others of the Sons of Los build Moments & Minutes & Hours
And Days & Months & Years & Ages & Periods; wondrous buildings
And every Moment has a Couch of gold for soft repose,
(A Moment equals a pulsation of the artery)
And between every two Moments stands a Daughter of Beulah
To feed the Sleepers on their Couches with maternal care.
And every Minute has an azure Tent with silken Veils.
And every Hour has a bright golden Gate carved with skill.
And every Day & Night, has Walls of brass & Gates of adamant,
Shining like precious stones & ornamented with appropriate signs:
And every Month, a silver paved Terrace builded high:
And every Year, invulnerable Barriers with high Towers.
And every Age is Moated deep with Bridges of silver & gold.
And every Seven Ages is Incircled with a Flaming Fire.
Now Seven Ages is amounting to Two Hundred Years
Each has its Guard, each Moment Minute Hour Day Month & Year.
All are the work of Fairy hands of the Four Elements
The Guard are Angels of Providence on duty evermore
Every Time less than a pulsation of the artery
Is equal in its period & value to Six Thousand Years.

For

For in this Period the Poets Work is Done; and all the Great
Events of Time start forth & are conceiv'd in such a Period
Within a Moment: a Pulsation of the Artery.

5 The Sky is an immortal Tent built by the Sons of Los
And every Space that a Man views around his dwelling-place
Standing on his own roof, or in his garden on a mount
Of twenty-five cubits in height. such Space is his Universe:
And on its verge the Sun rises & sets. the Clouds bow
10 To meet the flat Earth & the Sea in such an orderd Space:
The Starry heavens reach no further but here bend and set
On all sides & the two Poles turn on their valves of gold:
And if he move his dwelling-place, his heavens also move.
Where'er he goes & all his neighbourhood bewail his loss:
15 Such are the Spaces called Earth & such its dimension:
As to that false appearance which appears to the reasoner,
As of a Globe rolling thro Voidness, it is a delusion of Ulro
The Microscope knows not of this nor the Telescope. they alter
The ratio of the Spectators Organs but leave Objects untouchd
20 For every Space larger than a red Globule of Mans blood.
Is visionary: and is created by the Hammer of Los
And every Space smaller than a Globule of Mans blood opens
Into Eternity of which this vegetable Earth is but a shadow:
The red Globule is the unwearied Sun by Los created
25 To measure Time and Space to mortal Men. every morning.
Bowlahoola & Allamanda are placed on each side
Of that Pulsation & that Globule. terrible their power.

But Rintrah & Palamabron govern over Day & Night
In Allamanda & Entuthon Benython where Souls wail:
30 Where Orc incessant howls burning in fires of Eternal Youth,
Within the vegetated mortal Nerves; for every Man born is joined
Within into One mighty Polypus, and this Polypus is Orc.

But in the Optic vegetative Nerves Sleep was transformed
To Death in old time by Satan the father of Sin & Death
35 And Satan is the Spectre of Orc & Orc is the generate Luvah
But in the Nerves of the Nostrils, Accident being formed
Into Substance & Principle, by the cruelties of Demonstration
It became Opake & Indefinite; but the Divine Saviour,
Formed it into a Solid by Los's Mathematic power.
40 He named the Opake Satan: he named the Solid Adam

And in the Nerves of the Ear, (for the Nerves of the Tongue are closed)
On Albions Rock Los stands creating the glorious Sun each morning
And when unwearied in the evening he creates the Moon
Death to delude, who all in terror at their splendor leaves.
45 His prey while Los appoints, & Rintrah & Palamabron guide
The Souls clear from the Rock of Death, that Death himself may wake
In his appointed season when the ends of heaven meet.

Then Los conducts the Spirits to be Vegetated, into
Great Golgonooza, free from the four iron pillars of Satans Throne
50 Temperance. Prudence. Justice. Fortitude. the four pillars of tyranny.
That Satans Watch-Fiends touch them not before they Vegetate.

But Enitharmon and her Daughters take the pleasant charge.
To give them to their lovely heavens till the Great Judgment Day
Such is their lovely charge. But Rahab & Tirzah pervert
55 Their mild influences. therefore the Seven Eyes of God walk round
The Three Heavens of Ulro. where Tirzah & her Sisters
Weave the black Woof of Death upon Entuthon Benython
In the Vale of Surrey where Hereford terminates in Rephaim.
The stamping feet of Zelophehads Daughters are covered with Human gore
60 Upon the treadles of the Loom. they sing to the winged shuttle:
The River rises above his banks to wash the Woof:
He takes it in his arms: he pulses it in strength thro his current
The veil of human miseries is woven over the Ocean.
From the Atlantic to the Great South Sea. the Erythrean.

65 Such is the World of Los the labour of six thousand years.
Thus Nature is a Vision of the Science of the Elohim.

End of the First Book

How wide the Gulf & Unpassable! between Simplicity & Insipidity

Milton.

Contraries are Positives
A Negation is not a Contrary

Book the Second.

There is a place where Contrarieties are equally True
This place is called Beulah. It is a pleasant lovely Shadow
Where no dispute can come. Because of those who Sleep
Into this place the Sons & Daughters of Ololon descended
With solemn mourning into Beulahs moony shades & hills
Weeping for Milton: mute wonder held the Daughters of Beulah
Entraptured with affection sweet and mild benevolence

Beulah is evermore Created around Eternity: appearing
To the Inhabitants of Eden, around them on all sides.
But Beulah to its Inhabitants appears within each district.
As the beloved infant in his mothers bosom round incircled
With arms of love & pity & sweet compassion. But to
The Sons of Eden, the moony habitations of Beulah,
Are from Great Eternity a mild & pleasant Rest.
And it is thus Created. Lo the Eternal Great Humanity
To whom be Glory & Dominion Evermore Amen
Walks among all his awful Family seen in every face
As the breath of the Almighty such are the words of man to man
In the great Wars of Eternity, in fury of Poetic Inspiration
To build the Universe stupendous: Mental forms Creating

But the Emanations trembled exceedingly, nor could they
Live, because the Life of Man was too exceeding unbounded
His joy became terrible to them they trembled & wept
Crying with one voice. Give us a habitation & a place
In which we may be hidden under the shadow of wings
For if we who are but for a time, & who pass away in winter
Behold these wonders of Eternity we shall consume
But you O our Fathers & Brothers, remain in Eternity
But grant us a Temporal Habitation, do you speak
To us; we will obey your words as you obey Jesus
The Eternal who is blessed for ever & ever. Amen

So spoke the lovely Emanations; & there appeard a pleasant
Mild Shadow above; beneath; & on all sides round, Into

Into this pleasant Shadow all the weak & weary
Like Women & Children were taken away as on wings
Of dovelike softness, & shadowy habitations prepared for them
But every Man returnd & went still going forward thro'
The Bosom of the Father in Eternity on Eternity
Neither did any lack or fall into Error without
A Shadow to repose in all the Days of happy Eternity

Into this pleasant Shadow Beulah, all Ololon descended
And when the Daughters of Beulah heard the lamentation
All Beulah wept, for they saw the Lord coming in the Clouds
And the Shadows of Beulah terminate in rocky Albion.

And all Nations wept in affliction Family by Family
Germany wept towards France & Italy: England wept & trembled
Towards America: India rose up from his golden bed:
As one awakend in the night: they saw the Lord coming
In the Clouds of Ololon with Power & Great Glory!
And all the Living Creatures of the Four Elements, waild
With bitter wailing: these in the aggregate are named Satan
And Rahab: they know not of Regeneration, but only of Generation
The Fairies, Nymphs, Gnomes & Genii of the Four Elements
Unforgiving & unalterable: these cannot be Regenerated
But must be Created, for they know only of Generation
These are the Gods of the Kingdoms of the Earth: in contrarious
And cruel opposition: Element against Element, opposed in War
Not Mental, as the Wars of Eternity, but a Corporeal Strife
In Loss Halls continual labouring in the Furnaces of Golgonooza
Ore howls on the Atlantic: Enitharmon trembles: All Beulah weeps

Thou hearest the Nightingale begin the Song of Spring;
The Lark sitting upon his earthy bed: just as the morn
Appears; listens silent; then springing from the waving Corn-field! loud
He leads the Choir of Day! trill, trill, trill, trill,
Mounting upon the wings of light into the Great Expanse:
Reechoing against the lovely blue & shining heavenly Shell:
His little throat labours with inspiration; every feather
On throat & breast & wings vibrates with the effluence Divine
All Nature listens silent to him & the awful Sun
Stands still upon the Mountain looking on this little Bird
With eyes of soft humility, & wonder love & awe.
Then loud from their green covert all the Birds begin their Song
The Thrush, the Linnet & the Goldfinch, Robin & the Wren
Awake the Sun from his sweet reverie upon the Mountain:
The Nightingale again assays his song & thro the day,
And thro the night warbles luxuriant; every Bird of Song
Attending his loud harmony with admiration & love.
This is a Vision of the lamentation of Beulah over Ololon

Thou perceivest the Flowers put forth their precious Odours!
And none can tell how from so small a center comes such sweet
Forgetting that within that Center Eternity expands
Its ever during doors, that Og & Anak fiercely guard
First eer the morning breaks joy opens in the flowery bosoms
Joy even to tears, which the Sun rising dries: first the Wild Thyme
And Meadow-sweet downy & soft waving among the reeds
Light springing on the air lead the sweet Dance: they wake
The Honeysuckle sleeping on the Oak: the flaunting beauty
Revels along upon the wind: the White-thorn lovely May
Opens her many lovely eyes: listening the Rose still sleeps
None dare to wake her, soon she bursts her crimson curtaind bed
And comes forth in the majesty of beauty; every Flower:
The Pink, the Jessamine, the Wall-flower, the Carnation
The Jonquil, the mild Lilly opes her heavens; every Tree,
And Flower & Herb soon fill the air with an innumerable Dance
Yet all in order sweet & lovely, Men are sick with Love!
Such is a Vision of the lamentation of Beulah over Ololon

And

And the Divine Voice was heard in the Songs of Beulah. Say

When I first Married you, I gave you all my whole Soul
I thought that you would love my loves & joy in my delights
Seeking for pleasures in my pleasures O Daughter of Babylon
Then thou wast lovely, mild & gentle, now thou art terrible
In jealousy & unlovely in my sight, because thou hast cruelly
Cut off my loves in fury till I have no love left for thee
Thy love depends on him thou lovest & on his dear loves
Depend thy pleasures which thou hast cut off by jealousy
Therefore I shew my Jealousy & set before you Death.
Behold Milton descended to Redeem the Female Shade
From Death Eternal; such your lot, to be continually Redeem'd
By death & misery of those you love & by Annihilation
When the Sixfold Female perceives that Milton annihilates
Himself: that seeing all his loves by her cut off: he leaves
Her also: entirely abstracting himself from Female loves
She shall relent in fear of death; She shall begin to give
Her maidens to her husband: delighting in his delight
And then & then alone begins the happy Female joy
As it is done in Beulah, & thou O Virgin Babylon Mother of Whoredoms
Shalt bring Jerusalem in thine arms in the night watches; and
No longer turning her a wandering Harlot in the streets
Shalt give her into the arms of God your Lord & Husband.

Such are the Songs of Beulah, in the Lamentations of Ololon

And all the Songs of Beulah sounded comfortable notes
To comfort Ololons lamentation, for they said
Are you the Fiery Circle that late drove in fury & fire
The Eight Immortal Starry-ones down into Ulro dark
Rending the Heavens of Beulah with your thunders & lightnings
And can you thus lament & can you pity & forgive?
Is terror changd to pity, O wonder of Eternity:

And the Four States of Humanity in its Repose,
Were shewed them. First of Beulah a most pleasant Sleep
On Couches soft, with mild music, tended by Flowers of Beulah
Sweet Female forms, winged or floating in the air spontaneous
The Second State is Alla & the third State Al-Ulro:
But the Fourth State is dreadful; it is named Or-Ulro:
The First State is in the Head, the Second is in the Heart:
The Third in the Loins & Seminal Vessels & the Fourth
In the Stomach & Intestines terrible, deadly, unutterable
And he whose Gates are opend in those Regions of his Body
Can from those Gates view all these wondrous Imaginations

But Ololon sought the Or-Ulro & its fiery Gates
And the Couches of the Martyrs: & many Daughters of Beulah
Accompany them down to the Ulro with soft melodious tears
A long journey & dark thro Chaos in the track of Miltons course
To where the Contraries of Beulah War beneath Negations Banner

Then viewd from Miltons Track they see the Ulro: a vast Polypus
Of living fibres down into the Sea of Time & Space growing
A self-devouring monstrous Human Death Twenty seven fold
Within it sit Five Females & the nameless Shadowy Mother
Spinning it from their bowels with songs of amorous delight
And melting cadences that lure the Sleepers of Beulah down
The River Storge (which is Arnon) into the Dead Sea
Around this Polypus Los continual builds the Mundane Shell
Four Universes round the Universe of Los remain Chaotic
Four intersecting Globes, & the Egg formd World of Los
In midst; stretching from Zenith to Nadir, in midst of Chaos
One of these Ruind Universes is to the North named Urthona
One in the South this was the glorious World of Urizen
One to the East, of Luvah: One to the West: of Tharmas
But when Luvah assumed the World of Urizen in the South,
All fell towards the Center sinking downward in dire Ruin

Here, in these Chaoses the Sons of Ololon took their abode
In Chasms of the Mundane Shell which open on all sides round
Southward & by the East within the Breach of Miltons descent
To watch the time, pitying & gentle to awaken Urizen
They stood in a dark land of death, of fiery corroding waters
Where lie in evil death the Four Immortals pale and cold
And the Eternal Man even Albion upon the Rock of Ages
Seeing Miltons Shadow, some Daughters of Beulah trembling
Returnd, but Ololon remaind before the Gates of the Dead

And Ololon looked down into the Heavens of Ulro in fear
They said. How are the Wars of Man which in Great Eternity
Appear around, in the External Spheres of Visionary Life
Here renderd Deadly within the Life & Interior Vision
How are the Beasts & Birds & Fishes, & Plants & Minerals
Here fixd into a frozen bulk subject to decay & death
Those Visions of Human Life & Shadows of Wisdom & Knowledge

Are here frozen to unexpansive deadly destroying terrors.
And War & Hunting: the Two Fountains of the River of Life
Are become Fountains of bitter Death & of corroding Hell
5. Till Brotherhood is changed into a Curse & a Flattery
By Differences between Ideas, that Ideas themselves, (which are
The Divine Members) may be slain in offerings for sin
O dreadful Loom of Death! O piteous Female forms compelld
To weave the Woof of Death, On Camberwell Tirzahs Courts
10. Malahs on Blackheath, Rahab & Noah, dwell on Windsors heights
Where once the Cherubs of Jerusalem spread to Lambeths Vale
Milcahs Pillars shine from Harrow to Hampstead where Hoglah
On Highgates heights magnificent Weaves over trembling Thames
To Shooters Hill and thence to Blackheath the dark Woof! Loud
15. Loud roll the Weights & Spindles over the whole Earth let down
On all sides round to the Four Quarters of the World, eastward on
Europe to Euphrates & Hindu, to Nile & back in Clouds
Of Death across the Atlantic to America North & South

So spoke Ololon in reminiscence astonishd, but they
20. Could not behold Golgonooza without passing the Polypus
A wondrous journey not passable by Immortal feet, & none
But the Divine Saviour can pass it without annihilation.
For Golgonooza cannot be seen till having passd the Polypus
It is viewed on all sides round by a Four-fold Vision
25. Or till you become Mortal & Vegetable in Sexuality
Then you behold its mighty Spires & Domes of ivory & gold

And Ololon examined all the Couches of the Dead.
Even of Los & Enitharmon & all the Sons of Albion
And his Four Zoas terrified & on the verge of Death
30. In midst of these was Miltons Couch, & when they saw Eight
Immortal Starry-Ones, guarding the Couch in flaming fires
They thunderous utterd all a universal groan falling down
Prostrate before the Starry Eight asking with tears forgiveness
Confessing their crime with humiliation and sorrow.

35. O how the Starry Eight rejoic'd to see Ololon descended:
And now that a wide road was open to Eternity,
By Ololons descent thro Beulah to Los & Enitharmon.
For mighty were the multitudes of Ololon, vast the extent
Of their great sway, reaching from Ulro to Eternity
40. Surrounding the Mundane Shell outside in its Caverns
And through Beulah, and all silent forbore to contend
With Ololon for they saw the Lord in the Clouds of Ololon

There is a Moment in each Day that Satan cannot find
Nor can his Watch Fiends find it, but the Industrious find
45. This Moment & it multiply, & when it once is found
It renovates every Moment of the Day if rightly placed
In this Moment Ololon descended to Los & Enitharmon
Unseen beyond the Mundane Shell Southward in Miltons track

Just in this Moment when the morning odours rise abroad
50. And first from the Wild Thyme, stands a Fountain in a rock
Of crystal flowing into two Streams, one flows thro Golgonooza
And thro Beulah to Eden beneath Los's western Wall
The other flows thro the Aerial Void & all the Churches
Meeting again in Golgonooza beyond Satans Seat

55. The Wild Thyme is Los's Messenger to Eden, a mighty Demon
Terrible deadly & poisonous his presence in Ulro dark
Therefore he appears only a small Root creeping in grass
Covering over the Rock of Odours his bright purple mantle
Beside the Fount above the Larks Nest in Golgonooza
60. Luvah slept here in death & here is Luvahs empty Tomb
Ololon sat beside this Fountain on the Rock of Odours.

Just at the place to where the Lark mounts, is a Crystal Gate
It is the enterance of the First Heaven named Luther: for
The Lark is Los's Messenger thro the Twenty seven Churches
65. That the Seven Eyes of God who walk even to Satans Seat
Thro all the Twenty seven Heavens may not slumber nor sleep
But the Larks Nest is at the Gate of Los, at the eastern
Gate of wide Golgonooza & the Lark is Los's Messenger

When on the highest lift of his light pinions he arrives
At that bright Gate. another Lark meets him & back to back
They touch their pinions tip tip: and each descend
To their respective Earths & there all night consult with Angels
Of Providence & with the Eyes of God all night in slumbers
Inspired: & at the dawn of day send out another Lark
Into another Heaven to carry news upon his wings
Thus are the Messengers dispatchd till they reach the Earth again
In the East Gate of Golgonooza, & the Twenty-eighth bright
Lark. met the Female Ololon descending into my Garden
Thus it appears to Mortal eyes & those of the Ulro Heavens
But not thus to Immortals, the Lark is a mighty Angel.

For Ololon step'd into the Polypus within the Mundane Shell
They could not step into Vegetable Worlds without becoming
The enemies of Humanity except in a Female Form
And as One Female, Ololon and all its mighty Hosts
Appear'd: a Virgin of twelve years nor time nor space was
To the perception of the Virgin Ololon but as the
Flash of lightning but more quick the Virgin in my Garden
Before my Cottage stood for the Satanic Space is delusion

For when Los joind with me he took me in his fiery whirlwind
My Vegetated portion was hurried from Lambeths shades
He set me down in Felphams Vale & prepard a beautiful
Cottage for me that in three years I might write all these
Visions
To display Natures cruel holiness: the deceits of Natural
Religion
Walking in my Cottage Garden. sudden I beheld
The Virgin Ololon & addressd her as a Daughter of Beulah

Virgin of Providence fear not to enter into my Cottage
What is thy message to thy friend: what am I now to do
Is it again to plunge into deeper affliction? behold me
Ready to obey, but pity thou my Shadow of Delight
Enter my Cottage, comfort her, for she is sick with fatigue

Blakes Cottage
at Felpham

And the Forty-eight Starry Regions are Cities of the Levites
The Heads of the Great Polypus. Four-fold twelve enormity
In mighty & mysterious commingling enemy with enemy.
Woven by Urizen into Sexes from his mantle of years.
And Milton collecting all his fibres into impregnable strength
Descended down a Paved work of all kinds of precious stones
Out from the eastern sky. descending down into my Cottage
Garden; clothed in black severe & silent he descended.

The Spectre of Satan stood upon the roaring sea & beheld
Milton within his sleeping Humanity; trembling & shuddring
He stood upon the waves a Twenty-seven-fold mighty Demon
Gorgeous & beautiful: loud roll his thunders against Milton
Loud Satan thunderd, loud & dark upon mild Felpham shore
Not daring to touch one fibre he howld round upon the Sea.

I also stood in Satans bosom & beheld its desolations:
A rocky Man; a ruind building of God not made with hands;
Its plains of burning sand, its mountains of marble terrible;
Its pits & declivities flowing with molten ore & fountains
Of pitch & nitre; its ruind palaces & cities & mighty works;
Its furnaces of affliction in which his Angels & Emanations
Labour with blackend visages among its stupendous ruins
Arches & pyramids & porches colonades & domes:
In which dwells Mystery Babylon, here is her secret place
From hence she comes forth on the Churches in delight
Here is her Cup filld with its poisons, in those horrid vales
And here her scarlet Veil, woven in pestilence & war:
Here is Jerusalem bound in chains, in the Dens of Babylon

In the Eastern porch of Satans Universe Milton stood & said

Satan! my Spectre! I know my power thee to annihilate
And be a greater in thy place, & be thy Tabernacle
A covering for thee to do thy will, till one greater comes
And smites me as I smote thee & becomes my covering
Such are the Laws of thy false Heavns! but Laws of Eternity
Are not such: know thou: I come to Self Annihilation
Such are the Laws of Eternity that each shall mutually
Annihilate himself for others good, as I for thee
Thy purpose & the purpose of thy Priests & of thy Churches
Is to impress on men the fear of death; to teach
Trembling & fear, terror, constriction; abject selfishness
Mine is to teach Men to despise death & to go on
In fearless majesty annihilating Self, laughing to scorn
Thy Laws & terrors, shaking down thy Synagogues as webs
I come to discover before Heavn & Hell the Self righteousness
In all its Hypocritic turpitude, opening to every eye
These wonders of Satans holiness shewing to the Earth
The Idol Virtues of the Natural Heart, & Satans Seat
Explore in all its Selfish Natural Virtue & put off
In Self annihilation all that is not of God alone:
To put off Self & all I have ever & ever Amen.

Satan heard! Coming in a cloud, with trumpets & flaming fire
Saying I am God the judge of all, the living & the dead
Fall therefore down & worship me, submit thy supreme
Dictate, to my eternal Will & to my dictate bow
I hold the Balances of Right & Just & mine the Sword
Seven Angels bear my Name & in those Seven I appear
But I alone am God & I alone in Heavn & Earth
Of all that live dare utter this, others tremble & bow

Till All Things became One Great Satan in Holiness
Oppos'd to Mercy. and the Divine Delusion Jesus be no more

Suddenly around Milton on my Path, the Starry Seven
Burnd terrible: my Path became a solid fire, as bright
As the clear Sun & Milton silent came down on my Path.
And there went forth from the Starry limbs of the Seven: Forms
Human; with Trumpets innumerable, sounding articulate
As the Seven spake; and they stood in a mighty Column of Fire
Surrounding Felphams Vale, reaching to the Mundane Shell, Saying

Awake Albion awake! reclaim thy Reasoning Spectre. Subdue
Him to the Divine Mercy, Cast him down into the Lake
Of Los, that ever burneth with fire, ever & ever Amen!
Let the Four Zoa's awake from Slumbers of Six Thousand Years

Then loud the Furnaces of Los were heard! & seen as Seven Heavens
Stretching from south to north over the mountains of Albion

Satan heard; trembling round his Body, he incircled it
He trembled with exceeding great trembling & astonishment
Howling in his Spectre round his Body hungring to devour
But fearing for the pain for if he touches a Vital,
His torment is unendurable: therefore he cannot devour:
But howls round it as a lion round his prey continually
Loud Satan thunderd, loud & dark upon mild Felphams Shore
Coming in a Cloud with Trumpets & with Fiery Flame
An awful Form eastward from midst of a bright Paved-work
Of precious stones by Cherubim surrounded: so permitted
(Lest he should fall apart in his Eternal Death) to imitate
The Eternal Great Humanity Divine surrounded by
His Cherubim & Seraphim in ever happy Eternity
Beneath sat Chaos; Sin on his right hand Death on his left
And Ancient Night spread over all the heavn his Mantle of Laws
He trembled with exceeding great trembling & astonishment

Then Albion rose up in the Night of Beulah on his Couch
Of dread repose, seen by the visionary eye; his face is toward
The east, toward Jerusalems Gates; groaning he sat above
His rocks. London & Bath & Legions & Edinburgh
Are the four pillars of his Throne; his left foot near London
Covers the shades of Tyburn; his instep from Windsor
To Primrose Hill stretching to Highgate & Holloway
London is between his knees; its basements fourfold,
His right foot stretches to the sea on Dover cliffs; his heel
On Canterburys ruins; his right hand covers lofty Wales
His left Scotland; his bosom girt with gold involves
York, Edinburgh, Durham & Carlisle & on the front
Bath, Oxford, Cambridge Norwich; his right elbow
Leans on the Rocks of Erins Land. Ireland ancient nation
His head bends over London: he sees his embodied Spectre
Trembling before him with exceeding great trembling & fear
He views Jerusalem & Babylon, his tears flow down
He movd his right foot to Cornwall, his left to the Rocks of Bognor
He strove to rise to walk into the Deep, but strength failing
Forbad & down with dreadful groans he sunk upon his Couch
In moony Beulah. Los his strong Guard walks round beneath the Moon

Urizen faints in terror striving among the Brooks of Arnon
With Miltons Spirit: as the Plowman or Artificer or Shepherd
While in the labours of his calling sends his Thought abroad
To labour in the ocean or in the starry heaven. So Milton
Labourd in Chasms of the Mundane Shell, tho here before
My Cottage midst the Starry Seven, where the Virgin Ololon
Stood trembling in the Porch: loud Satan thunderd on the stormy Sea
Circling Albions Cliffs in which the Four-fold World resides
Tho seen in fallacy outside: a fallacy of Satans Churches

Before Ololon Milton stood & perceivd the Eternal Form
Of that mild Vision; wondrous were their acts by me unknown
Except remotely; and I heard Ololon say to Milton

I see thee strive upon the Brooks of Arnon. there a dread
And awful Man I see, oercoverd with the mantle of years,
I behold Los & Urizen. I behold Orc & Tharmas;
The Four Zoa's of Albion & thy Spirit with them striving
In Self annihilation giving thy life to thy enemies
Are those who contemn Religion & seek to annihilate it
Become in their Feminine portions the causes & promoters
Of these Religions, how is this thing; this Newtonian Phantasy
This Voltaire & Rousseau: this Hume & Gibbon & Bolingbroke
This Natural Religion! this impossible absurdity
Is Ololon the cause of this! O where shall I hide my face
These tears fall for the little-ones: the Children of Jerusalem
Lest they be annihilated in thy annihilation.

No sooner she had spoke but Rahab Babylon appeard
Eastward upon the Paved work across Europe & Asia
Glorious, as the midday Sun in Satans bosom glowing;
A Female hidden in a Male, Religion hidden in War
Namd Moral Virtue; cruel two-fold Monster shining bright
A Dragon red & hidden Harlot which John in Patmos saw

And all beneath the Nations innumerable of Ulro
Appeard, the Seven Kingdoms of Canaan & Five Baalim
Of Philistea, into Twelve divided, called after the Names
Of Israel: as they are in Eden. Mountain River & Plain
City & sandy Desart intermingled beyond mortal ken

But turning toward Ololon in terrible majesty Milton
Replied. Obey thou the Words of the Inspired Man
All that can be annihilated must be annihilated
That the Children of Jerusalem may be saved from slavery
There is a Negation, & there is a Contrary
The Negation must be destroyd to redeem the Contraries
The Negation is the Spectre; the Reasoning Power in Man
This is a false Body: an Incrustation over my Immortal
Spirit; a Selfhood, which must be put off & annihilated alway
To cleanse the Face of my Spirit by Self-examination.

To bathe in the waters of Life: to wash off the Not Human
I come in Self-annihilation & the grandeur of Inspiration
To cast off Rational Demonstration by Faith in the Saviour
To cast off the rotten rags of Memory by Inspiration
To cast off Bacon, Locke & Newton from Albions covering
To take off his filthy garments, & clothe him with Imagination
To cast aside from Poetry, all that is not Inspiration
That it no longer shall dare to mock with the aspersion of Madness
Cast on the Inspired, by the tame high finisher of paltry Blots,
Indefinite, or paltry Rhymes; or paltry Harmonies.
Who creeps into State Government like a caterpiller to destroy
To cast off the idiot Questioner who is always questioning,
But never capable of answering: who sits with a sly grin
Silent plotting when to question, like a thief in a cave;
Who publishes doubt & calls it knowledge: whose Science is Despair
Whose pretence to knowledge is Envy: whose whole Science is
To destroy the wisdom of ages to gratify ravenous Envy;
That rages round him like a Wolf day & night without rest
He smiles with condescension; he talks of Benevolence & Virtue
And those who act with Benevolence & Virtue, they murder time on time
These are the destroyers of Jerusalem, these are the murderers
Of Jesus, who deny the Faith & mock at Eternal Life:
Who pretend to Poetry that they may destroy Imagination;
By imitation of Natures Images drawn from Remembrance
These are the Sexual Garments, the Abomination of Desolation
Hiding the Human Lineaments as with an Ark & Curtains
Which Jesus rent: & now shall wholly purge away with Fire
Till Generation is swallowd up in Regeneration.

Then trembled the Virgin Ololon & replyd in clouds of despair
Is this our Feminine Portion the Six-fold Miltonic Female
Terribly this Portion trembles before thee O awful Man
Altho' our Human Power can sustain the severe contentions
Of Friendship, our Sexual cannot: but flies into the Ulro.
Hence arose all our terrors in Eternity! & now remembrance
Returns upon us! are we Contraries O Milton, Thou & I
O Immortal! how were we led to War the Wars of Death
Is this the Void Outside of Existence, which if enterd into

Becomes a Womb! & is this the Death Couch of Albion
Thou goest to Eternal Death & all must go with thee!

So saying, the Virgin divided Six-fold & with a shriek
Dolorous that ran thro' all Creation a Double Six-fold Wonder!
Away from Ololon she divided & fled into the depths
Of Miltons Shadow as a Dove upon the stormy Sea.

Then as a Moony Ark Ololon descended to Felphams Vale
In clouds of blood, in streams of gore, with dreadful thunderings
Into the Fires of Intellect that rejoic'd in Felphams Vale
Around the Starry Eight: with one accord the Starry Eight became
One Man Jesus the Saviour. wonderful! round his limbs
The Clouds of Ololon folded as a Garment dipped in blood
Written within & without in woven letters: & the Writing
Is the Divine Revelation in the Literal expression:
A Garment of War. I heard it namd the Woof of Six Thousand Years

And I beheld the Twenty-four Cities of Albion
Arise upon their Thrones to Judge the Nations of the Earth
And the Immortal Four in whom the Twenty-four appear Four-fold
Arose around Albions body: Jesus wept & walked forth
From Felphams Vale clothed in Clouds of blood, to enter into
Albions Bosom, the bosom of death & the Four surrounded him
In the Column of Fire in Felphams Vale; then to their mouths the Four
Applied their Four Trumpets' & then sounded to the Four winds

Terror struck in the Vale I stood at that immortal sound
My bones trembled. I fell outstretchd upon the path
A moment. & my Soul returnd into its mortal state
To Resurrection & Judgment in the Vegetable Body
And my sweet Shadow of Delight stood trembling by my side

Immediately the Lark mounted with a loud trill from Felphams Vale
And the Wild Thyme from Wimbletons green & impurpled Hills
And Los & Enitharmon rose over the Hills of Surrey
Their clouds roll over London with a south wind, soft Oothoon
Pants in the Vales of Lambeth weeping oer her Human Harvest
Los listens to the Cry of the Poor Man: his Cloud
Over London in volume terrific, low bended in anger.

Rintrah & Palamabron view the Human Harvest beneath
Their Wine-presses & Barns stand open; the Ovens are prepar'd
The Waggons ready: terrific Lions & Tygers sport & play
All Animals upon the Earth, are prepard in all their strength

To go forth to the Great Harvest & Vintage of the Nations

Finis

Beneath the Plow of Rintrah & the Harrow of the Almighty
In the hands of Palamabron. Where the Starry Mills of Satan
Are built beneath the Earth & Waters of the Mundane Shell
Here the Three Classes of Men take their Sexual texture Woven
5   The Sexual is Threefold: the Human is Fourfold

If you account it Wisdom when you are angry to be silent, and
Not to shew it: I do not account that Wisdom but Folly.
Every Mans Wisdom is peculiar to his own Individuality
O Satan my youngest born, art thou not Prince of the Starry Hosts
10   And of the Wheels of Heaven. to turn the Mills day & night
Art thou not Newtons Pantocrator weaving the Woof of Locke
To Mortals thy Mills seem every thing & the Harrow of Shaddai
A scheme of Human conduct invisible & incomprehensible
Get to thy Labours at the Mills & leave me to my wrath

15   Satan was going to reply. but Los rolld his loud thunders.

Anger me not! thou canst not drive the Harrow in pitys paths.
Thy Work is Eternal Death with Mills & Ovens & Cauldrons.
Trouble me no more. thou canst not have Eternal Life

So Los spoke! Satan trembling obeyd weeping along the way.
20   Mark well my words, they are of your eternal Salvation

Between South Molton Street & Stratford Place: Calvarys foot
Where the Victims were preparing for Sacrifice their Cherubim
Around their loins pourd forth their arrows & their bosoms beam
With all colours of precious stones, & their inmost palaces
25   Resounded with preparation of animals wild & tame
(Mark well my words. Corporeal Friends
        are Spiritual Enemies)
Mocking Druidical Mathematical
Proportion of Length Bredth Highth
Displaying Naked Beauty: with Flute &
Harp & Song

Then Los & Enitharmon knew that Satan is Urizen
Drawn down by Orc & the Shadowy Female into Generation
Of Enitharmon enterd weeping into the Space there appearing
An aged Woman raving along the Streets (the Space is named
Canaan) then she returned to Los weary frighted as from dreams
The nature of a Female Space is this: it shrinks the Organs
Of Life till they become Finite & Itself seems Infinite

And Satan vibrated in the immensity of the Space: Limited
To those without but Infinite to those within: it fell down and
Became Canaan: closing Los from Eternity in Albions Cliffs
A mighty Fiend against the Divine Humanity mustring to War
Satan. Ah me! is gone to his own place, said Los, their God
I will not worship in their Churches, nor King in their Theatres
Elynittria! whence is this Jealousy running along the mountains
British Women were not Jealous when Greek & Roman were Jealous
Every thing in Eternity shines by its own Internal light: but thou
Darkenest every Internal light with the arrows of thy quiver
Bound up in the horns of Jealousy to a deadly fading Moon
And Ocalythron binds the Sun into a Jealous Globe
That every thing is fixd Opake without Internal light
So Los lamented over Satan, who triumphant
divided the Nations

And Tharmas Demon of the Waters. & Orc. who is Luvah
The Shadowy Female seeing Milton. howld in her lamentation
Over the Deeps. outstretching her Twenty seven Heavens over Albion
And thus the Shadowy Female howls in articulate howlings.

5 I will lament over Milton in the lamentations of the afflicted
My Garments shall be woven of sighs & heart broken lamentations
The misery of unhappy Families shall be drawn out into its border
Wrought with the needle with dire sufferings poverty pain & woe
Along the rocky Island & thence throughout the whole Earth
10 There shall be the sick Father & his starving Family. there
The Prisoner in the stone Dungeon & the Slave at the Mill
I will have Writings written all over it in Human Words
That every Infant that is born upon the Earth shall read
And get by rote as a hard task of a life of sixty years
15 I will have Kings inwoven upon it. & Councellors & Mighty Men
The Famine shall clasp it together with buckles & Clasps
And the Pestilence shall be its fringe & the War its girdle
To divide into Rahab & Tirzah that Milton may come to our tents
For I will put on the Human Form & take the Image of God
20 Even Pity & Humanity but my Clothing shall be Cruelty
And I will put on Holiness as a breastplate & as a helmet
And all my ornaments shall be of the gold of broken hearts
And the precious stones of anxiety & care & desperation & death
And repentance for sin & sorrow & punishment & fear
25 To defend me from thy terrors O Orc! my only beloved!

Orc answerd. Take not the Human Form O loveliest. Take not
Terror upon thee! Behold how I am & tremble lest thou also
Consume in my Consummation: but thou maist take a Form
Female & lovely, that cannot consume in Mans consummation
30 Wherefore dost thou Create & weave this Satan for a Covering
When thou attemptest to put on the Human Form. my wrath
Burns to the top of heaven against thee in Jealousy & Fear.
Then I rend thee asunder. then I howl over thy clay & ashes
When wilt thou put on the Female Form as in times of old
35 With a Garment of Pity & Compassion like the Garment of God
His garments are long sufferings for the Children of Men
Jerusalem is his Garment & not thy Covering Cherub O lovely
Shadow of my delight who wanderest seeking for the prey.

So spoke Orc when Oothoon & Leutha hoverd over his Couch
40 Of fire in interchange of Beauty & Perfection in the darkness

Opening interiorly into Jerusalem & Babylon shining glorious
In the Shadowy Females bosom Jealous her darkness grew
Howlings filld all the desolate places in accusations of Sin
In Female beauty shining in the unformd void & Orc in vain
45 Stretchd out his hands of fire. & wooed: they triumph in his pain

Thus darkend the Shadowy Female tenfold & Orc tenfold
Glowd on his rocky Couch against the darkness: loud thunders
Told of the enormous conflict Earthquake beneath: around:
Rent the Immortal Females, limb from limb & joint from joint
50 And moved the fast foundations of the Earth to wake the Dead
Urizen emerged from his Rocky Form & from his Snows

And Milton oft sat up on the Couch of Death & oft conversed
In vision & dream beatific with the Seven Angels of the Presence

I have turned my back upon these Heavens builded on cruelty
My Spectre still wandering thro' them follows my Emanation
He hunts her footsteps thro' the snow & the wintry hail & rain
The idiot Reasoner laughs at the Man of Imagination
And from laughter proceeds to murder by undervaluing calumny

Then Hillel who is Lucifer replied over the Couch of Death
And thus the Seven Angels instructed him & thus they converse.

We are not Individuals but States: Combinations of Individuals
We were Angels of the Divine Presence: & were Druids in Annandale
Compelld to combine into Form by Satan, the Spectre of Albion.
Who made himself a God & destroyed the Human Form Divine.
But the Divine Humanity & Mercy gave us a Human Form
Because we were combind in Freedom & holy Brotherhood
While those combind by Satans Tyranny first in the blood of War
And Sacrifice & next in Chains of imprisonment: are Shapeless Rocks
Retaining only Satans Mathematic Holiness, Length: Bredth & Highth
Calling the Human Imagination: which is the Divine Vision & Fruition
In which Man liveth eternally: madness & blasphemy, against
Its own Qualities, which are Servants of Humanity, not Gods or Lords
Distinguish therefore States from Individuals in those States.
States change: but Individual Identities never change nor cease:
You cannot go to Eternal Death in that which can never Die.
Satan & Adam are States Created into Twenty-seven Churches
And thou O Milton art a State about to be Created
Called Eternal Annihilation that none but the Living shall
Dare to enter: & they shall enter triumphant over Death
And Hell & the Grave: States that are not. but ah! Seem to be.

Judge then of thy Own Self: thy Eternal Lineaments explore
What is Eternal & what Changeable? & what Annihilable!
The Imagination is not a State: it is the Human Existence itself
Affection or Love becomes a State when divided from Imagination
The Memory is a State always, & the Reason is a State
Created to be Annihilated & a new Ratio Created
Whatever can be Created can be Annihilated Forms cannot
The Oak is cut down by the Ax, the Lamb falls by the Knife
But their Forms Eternal Exist. For-ever. Amen Halleluyah

Thus they converse with the Dead watching round the Couch of Death
For God himself enters Deaths Door always with those that enter
And lays down in the Grave with them, in Visions of Eternity
Till they awake & see Jesus & the Linen Clothes lying
That the Females had Woven for them, & the Gates of their Fathers House

2

In Eden, in the auricular Nerves of Human life
Which is the Earth of Eden, he his Emanations propagated
Like & one & Daughters, Daughters of Beulah Sing
His fall into Division & his Resurrection to Unity —
Begun with Tharmas Parent power, darkning in the West

Lost! Lost! Lost! are my Emanations. Enion awoke off of her Prison
We are become a Victim to the living. We hide in secret
I have hidden Jerusalem in Silent Contrition O Pity Me
...

Enion said — Thy fear has made me tremble thy terrors have surrounded me
All Love is lost Terror succeeds & Hatred instead of Love
And stern demands of Right & Duty instead of Liberty
Once thou wast to the Lovely son of heaven — But now
Forget thou Terrible and art become my Tormentor
...
Unless some way can be found that I in weak hands take upon me this load
...
In secret of soft wings in mazes of delusive beauty

Vala incircle round the furnaces where Luvah was closd
In joy she heard his howlings, & forgot he was her Luvah
With whom She walkd in bliss, in times of innocence & youth

Hear ye the voice of Luvah from the furnaces of Urizen

If I indeed am Valas King & ye O sons of Men
The workmanship of Luvahs hands. in times of Everlasting
When I calld forth the Earthworm from the cold & dark obscure
I nurturd her I fed her with my rains & dews. She grew
A scaled Serpent, yet I fed her tho She hated me
Day after day she fed upon the mountains in Luvahs sight
I brought her thro the Wilderness, a dry & thirsty land
And I commanded springs to rise for her in the black desart
Till she became a Dragon winged bright & poisonous
I opend all the floodgates of the heavens to quench her thirst

And I commanded the Great deep to hide her in his hand

Till she became a little weeping Infant a span long

I carried her in my bosom as a man carries a lamb

I loved her I gave her all my ... my delight

... her ... ... & ... ...

Weaving ... ... the ... Paradise

... ... Sons & daughters

And then hid ... ... & hid ... from my sight

They ... surrounded me with ... ... of light, & raised

... ...

... ... that ... all ... ...

... our ... ...

... ... at ...

Because & ... ... I ... ... I ... ...

... ...

the hand ... ...

... ...

... ...

... ... of the ... form, & ... ...

... my ... I weep for this ... ...

... ... When will ... return, & ...

In maybe dreams gone . . . . nor inhibits fear
For man to found eternal death & uttermost extinction.
He builded Golgonooza on the Lake of Udan Adan
Upon the Limit of Translucence, then he builded Los Law
Thames laid the Foundation & his fourfold at . . clothing woe

But when fourteen summers & winters had revolved over
Their solemn habitation. Los beheld the ruddy boy
Embracing his bright mother & beheld malignant fires
In his young eyes discerning plain that Orc plotted his death
Grief rose upon his ruddy brows. a tightening girdle . . . . .
Around his bosom like a bloody cord . in twist . . .
He burst it, but next morn another girdle succeeds,
Burned his bosom. Every day he trod the fiery youth
With silent fear & his immortal cheeks grew deadly pale
Till many a morn & many a night passed over in dire woe
Forming a girdle in the day & burning it at . . . . .
The girdle was formed by day by night was burst in twain
Falling down on the rock an iron chain link by link locks

Enitharmon beheld the bloody chain of nights & days
Depending from the bosom of Los & hung with dismal pain
He went each morning to his labours with the spectre dark
Called it the chain of jealousy. Now Los began to speak
His woes aloud to Enitharmon . since he could not hide
His uncouth plague. He sees the boy in his immortal visits . . .
While Enitharmon petition'd times weeping on the dismal wire
Up to the iron mountains top & there the raging chain
. . . him his bosom, on the mountain. The Spectre dark
Held the raging boy as caused . . . . . . finding around . . chain
. . . deadly chain I have begot Enitharmon . . . . . one]
. . . her . . . . . . & nor bound down her . . . is it

Lay buried in the darkness, nor saw Heaven with a glance of fire
Lashing his abysmal journey thro the sightless worlds of doubt
Wasting in solar flames & groans in orbs of iron & ice
Th enormous wonders of the Abysses over his trophied joy [...]
Poured at the sound of [...] river [...] had risen to [...]
They wandered Messing in their flesh & him a gloomy mirror
[...] Orisions of fiery constellations in their dream
[...] battle of enmity were borne [...] first & [...] their loins
[...] or spirit of delight or broody [...] of periwinkle [...]
[...] to the dark Urizen not silent [...]
[...] on the expanse of the space more [...] his dark empire
[...] foundation Systems [...] & one head returns the party
[...] thought he did then the mountains on [...] wore

I burn of red hot iron & living with rivers of [...]
With molten [...] round their bones, some lying on beds of sulphur
On racks & wheels he railed [...] moaning over burning valleys
Refresh on bands of [...] & of [...] a [...] sometimes with
Lightnings shook they [...] after them upon their [...] to their march
In [...] rattles with loud thunder [...] king of [...]
Over the [...] deserts [...] [...] [...]
Of smoke with myriads [...] in the [...] regions, [...]
[...] the river his [...] his [...] [...]
And [...] [...] [...] in wonders [...] [...]
Fly on the [...] mountains & in rocks [...] their [...]
Ten came he among fiery [...] & [...] [...] [...]
[...] to inhale the fumes of typhon of [...] [...] [...]
Many a serpents & [...] [...] [...] enormous length
[...] the fallen [...] [...] [...] [...] [...]
[...] [...] [...] wrap [...] [...]
& had [...] monsters on arms in iron [...] & shell of brass
Or with a glittering [...] [...] in [...] [...] [...]
Some & [...] [...] of fire & of [...] [...] [...] a [...] [...]
[...] [...] [...] [...] [...] [...] [...] in [...] [...] for [...]
[...] [...] [...] [...] [...] [...] [...] for their [...]
[...] [...] of [...] & their eyes & [...] [...]
[...] [...] a [...] [...] [...] in words
[...] [...] as an [...] were one wrapt up
[...] [...] worlds regardless of this world, nor [...]
[...] [...] [...] the old age of [...]
[...] knew they were his children [...] in an equal world
[...] he had time enough to repent of his [...]

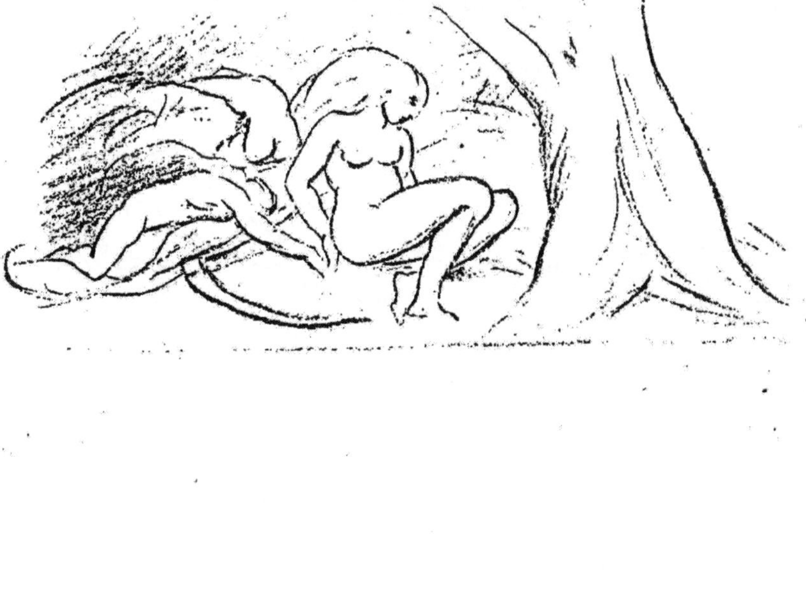

[illegible] in a little silken veil [illegible] in all a family [illegible]
My children that gave light that [illegible] the [illegible] [illegible]
And in the false family [illegible] & no one [illegible] them [illegible]
All things begin & end in [illegible] enjoy the delights of beauty
Once how I sang & calld the beasts & birds to their delights
Nor knew that I alone exempted from the joys of love
Must war with secret monsters of the animating worlds
O that I had not seen the day then blasts of [illegible] rage
Nor felt the stingings of desire nor longings after life
For life is sweet to Los the wretched to his winged woes
Is given a swarming joy that they may sit at night on barren rocks
And whet their beaks & snuff the air & watch the opening dawn
And shriek till at the smells of blood they stretch their boney wings
And cut the winds like arrows shot by troops of Destiny

Thus Los lamented in the night unheard by Enitharmon
For the Shadow of Enitharmon descended down the tree of Mystery
The Spectre saw the Shade Shivering over his gloomy rocks
Beneath the tree of Mystery which in the dismal Abyss
Began to blossom in fierce pain shooting its writhing buds
In throes of birth & now the blossoms falling shining fruit
Appeard of many colours & of various poisonous qualities
Of Plagues hidden in shining globes that grew on the living tree

The Spectre of Urthona saw the Shadow of Enitharmon
Beneath the Tree of Mystery among the leaves & fruit
Reddning the Demon strong prepard the poison of sweet Love
He turnd from side to side in tears he wept & he embracd
The fleeting image & in whispers mild wood the faint shade

Loveliest delight of Men. Enitharmon shady hiding
In secret places where no eye can trace thy watry way
Have I found thee have I found thee tremblest thou in fear
Because of Orc because he rent his discordant way
From thy sweet loins of bliss. red flowd thy blood
Pale grew thy face lightnings playd around thee thunders hoverd
Over thee, & the terrible Orc rent his discordant way
But the next joy of thine shall be in sweet delusion
And its birth in fainting & sleep & sweet delusions of Vala

The Shadow of Enitharmon answerd Art thou terrible Shade
Set over this sweet boy of mine to guard him lest he rend

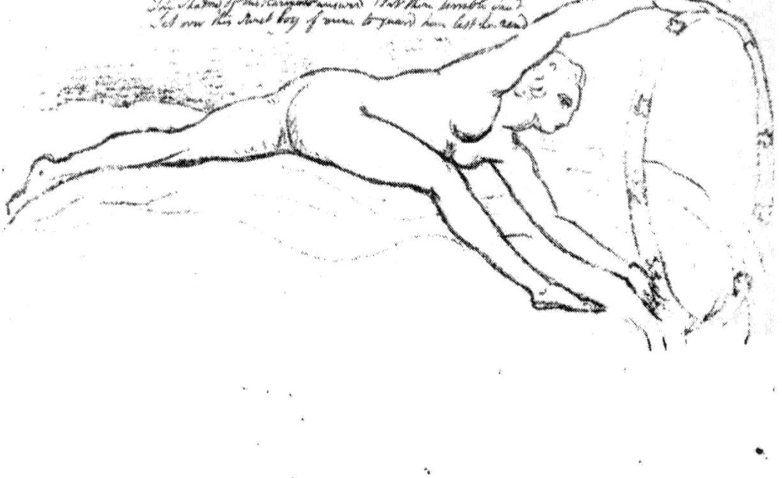

And must not I obey the God thou Shadow of Jealousy
I cry the watchman searcheth not Ahania may rein in sorrows
Vala trembles & shrinks & thinks & darkness & darkness covers my aching sight
Lift up Lift up O Los awake my watchman for he sleepeth
Lift up Lift up Urizen O Los it watchdman thy light is out
O Los unless thou rise my sons the Watchman will be slain

So Enitharmon cried upon her terrible earthy bed
While the broad Oak wreath'd his roots round her form & the dark ivy   20
Their tombs of death into vegetation The dreadful consummations
Terrific into the sinewy heavens The loud ones roaming
Stood their immortal energies in wisdom regenerated
Rending the heavens & earths & drinking blood on the Red battle
To feed their feast to gratify their hidden wars & slaughter
That far within the close recesses of their secret passions
Down the rast war & poys willing to vegetate
Into the Wonder of Enitharmon loud the roaring wrath
Beneath wrath silently lowd send, the Couch sullen the aching heap
Walks thro the battle Dashd & fierce the small his rage
Propagates thro the warring Earth & his limbs raging in flames
Say Ypygon reanimating nature The Serpent of the wood
End of the waters & the weapon of the desert combate
With anguish sings wrong heavy souls The Mortal Serpent stung
Along the snakes crying destdin to the Priest of God & warriors
Thy Couch upon my head to place in armies of Everlasting
And said Go forth & guide my battle take the peoples spears
Of them I knew than when I Plotted Man from life & light
Take him the same Division of Man More than for thing to come
In their homes no secret places that I will tell thee of
To be my priest & sacrificd enemy at thine own appointed   27

The Prophet despair ceast the War song wounded loud & strong
There all the heaven Hungry Wet returnd sounds on sounds

He finished
For silence Then on the lamme of the beam at or we laws is now in the beginning
of Night the seventh

End of The Seventh Night

In [illegible] confusion but the bitter pangs those that remain
Return in pangs & horrible convulsions to their habitual state
Of the monsters of the Elements Lions or Tygers or Wolves
Sound loud the howling music Inspird by [illegible] Sounding soon terrific men
They seem to one another laughing terrible among the banners
And when the revolution of their day of battles over
Relapsing in dire torment they return to forms of woe
To moping visages returning inanimate tho furious
No more erect tho strong drawn out in length they ravin
For senseless gratification & their visages thrust forth
Flatten above & beneath & stretch out into bestial length
Weakend they stretch beyond their power in dire droves till war begins
Or secret religion in their temples before secret shrines
And Urizen gave life & sense by his immortal power
To all his Engines of deceit that linked chains might run
Thro ranks of war spontaneous & that hooks & boring screws
Might act according to their forms by innate cruelty
He formed also harsh instruments of sound
To grate the soul into destruction or to inflame with fury
The spirits of life to pervert all the faculties of sense
Into their own destruction if perhaps he might avert
His own despair even at the cost of every thing that breathes
Thus in the temple of the Sun his books of iron & brass
And silver & gold he consecrated reading incessantly
To myriads of perturbed spirits thro the universe
They propagated the deadly words the Shadowy Female absorbing
The enormous Sciences of Urizen ages after ages exploring
The fell destruction. And she said O Urizen Prince of Light
What words of Dread pierce my faint Ear what falling snows around
My feeble limbs infold my destined misery
I alone dare the lash abide to sit beneath the blast
Unhurt & dare the inclement forehead of the King of Light
From dark abysses of the times remote fated to be

And distance woe ... in ... ... the holy
Divides ... ... the land of God within Jerusalems Veil
The ... Divine seen ... the ... ...
O fair Jerusalem ... me in a ... brain ...
... Sang the Sons of Eden ... ... of God & Lamb
Glory Glory Glory to the holy ... ...
... ... Jerusalem to put off the ... Satan ...
Now we behold redemption Now we know that life Eternal
Depends, alone upon ... ...
... ... ? endure ... ... again
... now ... in Lineb of ... & ... now ...
... ... of put off ...
... the ... ... body in the ... ...
... ... is ... ...
Thy poly is ... the foundation of the ... & thy ...
... ... in ... Come here ... of ... God
Come now ... Come ...
So sang they in ... ...
... was ... ... Gate ... ... a ...
Seen in the aggregate a Vast Hermaphroditic form
... ... Heard like an Earthquake ... with ... ...
Intolerable at length an awful wonder ...
From the Hermaphroditic bosom Satan he was named
Son of Perdition ... his form ... ...
A male without a female ... a howling ...
... ... a ... is the forms ...
Although ... ...

Being multitudes of tyrant Men in union blasphemous,
Against the Divine image ... ... 135.

... the Lamb of God ... his ... ...
To put off ... ... as a Man
To ... on ... So was in born of ... Jerusalem
... ... worn mantle & in the ... of ...
... ... an ... ... to ... in up ... Eden   200
... fallen ... ...
... ...
To be cut off & separated ... the ... ... may to ...

Trickles the essence of joy & all arose up from the deep

And Urizen arose up with them walking & were flowing

To their own world coming to perform what ever service fits them

Subdue to the Lord imparting song & there to mite in Consummation

together … Thousand Lands went into one Consummation

Then up go the Sons of Urizen in Plow & … they prolong it

From rising of ages till his ornaments, of Gold & Iron & brass,

Disdaine across the firm summer anon all the nations

Darken like solitude on the & divided fellows where he went

Trumpets on the own destruction hear with down his harvest

From the silent walls of heaven silence prophesy communicated

Whose beautiful and in silence of empires in & were morning of Demon,

Where silence a hill in remission sob … an sports of glory

In noise of awful work resounded like the founting of heaven,

A horse neigh from the battle thro the vault, while from the shelter waste

The tygers from the forests — the lions … from the sandy deserts

They … sick over the summits of harmony they read away

To shew the how the game the mutton they level the fortifications

They bear the weir empires of distruction into crosses

They give them to the harvest song singing the hammers drew

In sons of death to forge thunder & the mattock & the axe

The harrow wheels to break the clods & jo … over the mountains

The Sons of Urizen shout their fathers rose The Eternal Song

Resoundeth thus said to Urizen the harrow … at their call

The sons of Urizen there with ardor … from the …

The … … … He laid his hand on the Plow

age Eternal Embrace thence the Plow of ages drew over cities

And all their Villages over Mountains — all their Valleys

Over the graves & caverns of the dead Over the Planets

And over the vast spaces over … moon & star & constellation

Then Urizen commanded & the sons … kindled & blew

The brimstone sulphur' till the flame & … over Urizen

Weak wailing in the trembling air did wait or work & heat

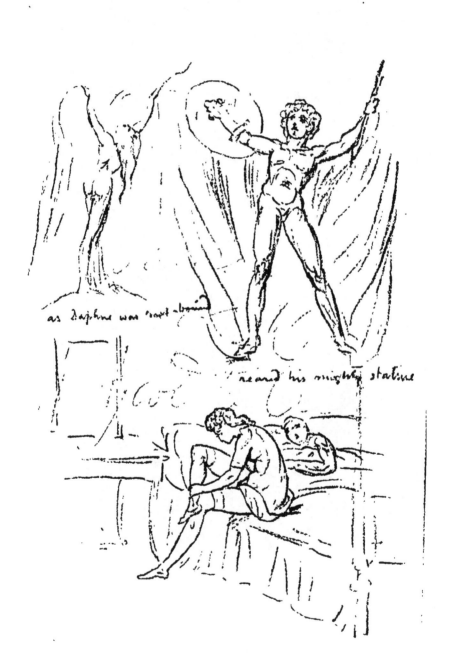

as daphne was root-bound

reard his mighty stature

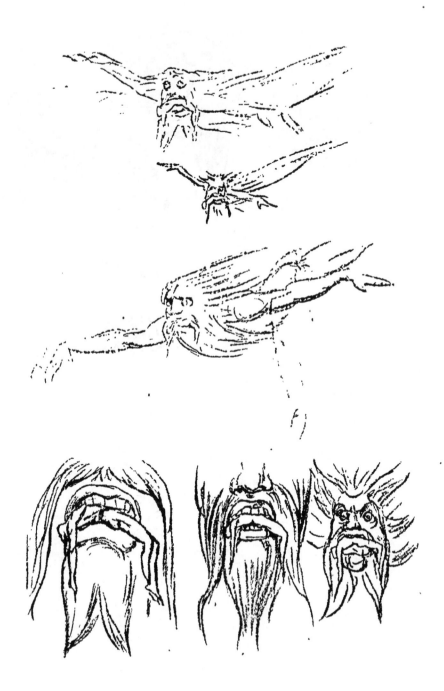

THE SOUL HOVERING OVER THE BODY.

LIBRARY
OF THE
UNIVERSITY
OF
CALIFORNIA.

THE SOUL EXPLORING THE RECESSES OF THE GRAVE.

REUNION OF THE SOUL AND BODY.

LIBRARY
OF THE
UNIVERSITY
OF
CALIFORNIA.

DEATH OF THE STRONG, WICKED MAN.

LIBRARY
OF THE
UNIVERSITY
OF
CALIFORNIA.

THE LAST JUDGMENT.

LIBRARY
OF THE
UNIVERSITY
OF
CALIFORNIA.

VALA.

VALA.

Night the First.

The song of the aged mother which shook the heavens with wrath,
Hearing the march of the long-resounding, long-heroic verse
Marshalled in order for the day of Intellectual battle.
The heavens quaked, the earth was moved and shuddered and the
    mountains
5 With all their woods and streams and valleys wailed in dismal fear.

Four Mighty Ones are in every Man. A perfect Unity
Cannot exist but from the Universal brotherhood of Eden
The Universal Man, to whom be glory, evermore; Amen,
Which on the nature of the Lamb's creation the Lamb's Father only,
10 No Individual knoweth, nor can know in all Eternity.

Los was the fourth immortal starry one, and in the Earth
Of a bright Universe, Empery attended day and night,—
Days and nights of revolving joy,—Urthona was his name.

In Eden, in the Auricular Nerves of Human Life,
15 Which is the Earth of Eden, he his emanations propagated
Like sons and daughters. Daughters of Beulah, sing
His fall into Division and his resurrection into Unity.
His fall into the generation of decay and death and his
Regeneration by resurrection from the dead.
20 Begin with Tharmas, Parent power, darkening in the West.

1

Lost, lost, lost are my Emanations! Enion, O Enion,
We are become a victim to the living,—we hide in secret.
I have hidden thee, Enion in a jealous despair, O pity me,
I will build thee a labyrinth where we may dwell for ever alone
25 Why wilt thou take Jerusalem from my inmost Tir(i)el?
Let her lay secret in the soft recesses of darkness and silence
It is not love I bear to Enitharmon, it is Pity;
She hath taken refuge in my bosom and I cannot cast her out.

Enion said: Thy fears have made me tremble, thy terrors have
   surrounded me.
30 All love is lost, Terror succeeds, and hatred instead of love,
And stern demands of Right and Duty, instead of Liberty.
Once thou wast to me the loveliest son of heaven, but now
Why art thou terrible? Yet I love thee in thy terror still.
I am almost extinct, and soon shall be a shadow in Albion,
35 Unless some way can be found that I can look upon thee and live.
Hide me in some shadowy semblance, secret, whispering in my ear
In secret of soft wings, in mazes of delusive beauty.
I have looked into the secret soul of him I love,
And in the dark recesses have found sin, and cannot return.

40 Trembling and pale sat Tharmas, weeping into his cloud

Sometimes I think thou art a flower expanding,
Sometimes I think thou art a fruit, breaking from its bud
In dreadful dolour and pain; and I am like an atom,—
A nothing, left in darkness; yet I am an identity.
45 I wish, and feel, and weep, and moan! Ah, terrible! terrible!
Why wilt thou examine every little fibre of my soul,
Spreading them out before the sun like stalks of flax to dry?

The Infant Joy is beautiful, but his anatomy
Horrible, ghast, and deadly. Nought shalt thou find in it
50 But dark despair and ever-brooding melancholy.
Thou wilt go mad with horror if thou examine thus
Every moment of my secret hours. Yea, I know

That I have sinned, and that my emanations are become harlots.
I am already distracted at their deeds, and if I look
55 Upon them more, Despair will try self-murder on my soul.
O Enion, thou art thyself a lost power in hell,
Though Heavenly beautiful to draw me to destruction.

She drew the Spectre forth from Tharmas in her shining loom
Of Vegetation, weeping in wayward infancy and sullen youth,
60 Listening to her soft lamentations. Soon his tongue began
To lisp out words, and soon in masculine strength augmenting he
Reared up a form of gold and stood upon the glittering rock
A shadowy human form winged, and in his depths
The dazzling gems shone clear. Rapturous in fury,
65 Glorying in his own eyes, exalted in terrific pride,
Searching for glory, wishing that the heavens had eyes to see,
And wishing that the earth could ope her eyelids and behold
Such wondrous beauty opening in the midst of all his glory,
That might but Enion could be found to praise, admire, and love.

70 Three days in self-admiring raptures on the rock he flamed,
And three dark nights repined the solitude, but the third morn
Astonished he found Enion hidden in the darksome cave.

She spoke : What am I? Wherefore was I put forth on these rocks,
Among the clouds, to tremble in the wind, in solitude?
75 Where is the voice that lately woke the desert? Where the face
That wept among the clouds, and where the voice that shall reply?
No other living thing is here, the sea, the earth, the heaven,
And Enion, desolate? Where art thou, Tharmas? O return.

Three days she wailed, and three dark nights sitting among the rocks,
80 While the bright spectre hid himself among the darkening clouds.
Then sleep fell on her eyelids in a chasm of the valley.
The seventh morn the spectre stood before her manifest.

The spectre thus spoke : Who art thou, diminutive husk and shell
Broke from my bonds? I scorn thy prison, I scorn, yet I love.

1 *

85   Art thou my slave? and shalt thou dare
    To smite me with my tongue? Beware lest I sting also thee.
    If thou hast sinned and art polluted, know that I am pure
    And unpolluted, and will bring to rigid strict account
    All thy past deeds. Hear what I tell thee, mark it well, remember.
90   This world is thine in which thou dwellest. That within thy soul,
    That dark and dismal infinite where thought rolls up and down,
    Is mine, and there thou goest when with one sting of my tongue
    Envenomed thou rollest inward to the place whence I emerged.

    She, trembling, answered· Wherefore was I born, and what am I?
95   A sorrow, a fear, a living torment, and a naked victim.
    I thought to weave a covering for my sins from wrath of Tharmas:
    Examining the sins of Tharmas, I soon found my own.
    O slay me not! Thou art his wrath embodied with deceit.

    In Eden, females sleep the winter in soft silken veils
100   Woven by their own hands to hide them in the darksome grave.
    But Males immortal live renewed by Female deaths. In soft
    Delight they die, and they revive in spring with music and songs
    Enion said: Farewell, I die, I hide from thy searching eyes.

    So saying, from her bosom weaving soft in sinewy threads
105   A tabernacle of delight she sat among the Rocks
    Singing her Lamentation Tharmas groaned among his clouds,
    Weeping; then, bending from his clouds he stooped his innocent head
    And stretching out his holy hand on the vast deep, sublime,
    Turned round the circle of Destiny with tears and bitter sighs
110   And said: Return, O wanderer, when the day of clouds is o'er.

    So saying, he sunk down in the sea, a pale white corpse.
    In torment he sunk down and flow'd among her filmy woof,
    His spectre issuing from his feet in flames of fire,
    In gnawing pain drawn out by her fair fingers. Every nerve
115   She counted, every vein and lacteal, threading them among
    Her woof of terror, terrified, and drinking tears of woe:

Shuddering she wove nine days and nights, sleepless; her food was
    tears.
But the tenth trembling morn, the circle of Destiny complete
Rolled round the sea, englobing, in a mighty globe self-balanced.
120 A frowning continent appeared, where Enion in the desert
Terrified in her own creation, viewing her woven shadow,
Sat in a dread intoxication of Repentance and contrition.

What have I done, said Enion, accursed wretch—what deed?
Is this a deed of love? I know what I have done, I know
125 Too late now to repent. Love is changed to deadly hate,
And life is blotted out, and I remain possessed with tears.
I see the shadow of the deed within my soul wandering,
In darkness and solitude, forming seas of doubt and rocks of repen-
    tance.
Already are my eyes reverted. All that I behold
130 Within my soul has lost its splendour, and a brooding fear
Shadows me o'er and drives me outward to a world of woe.
I thought Tharmas a sinner, I withstood his emanation,
His secret loves and graces. Wretched me! what have I done?
For now I find those emanations were my children's souls,
135 And I have murdered them with cruelty above atonement.
Those that remain have fled from my cruelty into the desert,
And thou the delusive tempter to these deeds sitt'st before me.
And art thou Tharmas? All thy soft delusive beauty cannot
Tempt me to murder my own soul. I wipe my tears and smile
140 In this thy world, not mine: though dark I feel thy world within.

The Spectre said: Thou sinful woman, was it thy desire
That I should hide thee with my power and delight with beauty?
And now thou darkenest in my presence. Never from my sight
Shalt thou depart to weep in secret. In my jealous wings
145 I evermore hold thee when thou goest out or comest in,
'Tis thou hast darkened all my world, oh woman, lovely bane

Thus they contended all the day among the caves of Tharmas,

Twisting in fearful forms and howling,—howling harsh, and shrieking,
Howling harsh, shrieking—mingling their bodies join in burning
   anguish.

150 |Mingling his brightness with her tender limbs, then high she soared,·
Half woman and half spectre. All his lovely changing colours mix
ᵕWith her fair crystal clearness. In her lips and cheeks his poisons rose
In blushes like the morning, and his scaly armour softening,
A monster lovely in the heavens or wandering in the earth,
155 With spectre voice incessant wailing in incessant thirst,
ᵢBeauty all blushing with desire, mocking her fell despair,
Wandering desolate, a wonder abhorr'd by gods and men,
Till, with fierce pain, she brought forth on the rocks her sorrow and
·   woe,—
ᵕBehold two little infants wept upon the desolate wind.

160 The first state weeping they began, and helpless as a wave
Beaten along its sightless way, growing in its motion
To its utmost goal, till strength from Enion like rich summer shining
Raised the bright, fierce boy and girl with glories from their heads
   out-beaming,
Drawing forth drooping mother's pity, drooping mother's sorrow.

165 But those in great Eternity met in the council of God
As one Man, hovering over Gilead and Hermon.
He is the good Shepherd, He is the Lord and Master
To create man morning by morning,—to give gifts at noonday.

Enion brooded over the rocks. The rough rocks groaning vegetate.
170 Such sorrow was given to the solitary wanderer.
The barked oak, the long-limned beech, the chestnut-tree, the pine,
The pear-tree mild, the frowning walnut, the sharp crab, apple sweet,
The rough bark opens, twittering peep forth little beaks and wings,
The nightingale, the goldfinch, robin, lark, linnet and thrush.
175 The goat leaped from the craggy cliff, the sheep awoke from the mould,
ᵢUpon its green stalk rose the corn, waving innumerable,
Infolding the bright infants from the desolating winds—

They sulk upon her breast, her hair became like snow on mountains,
Weaker and weaker, weeping, woeful, wearier and wearier,
180 Faded, and her bright eyes decay'd with pity and love.
And then they wandered far away, she sought for them in vain.
In weeping blindness, stumbling, she followed them o'er rocks and
    mountains.
Ingrate they wandered, scorning, drawing in her spectrous life,
Repelling her away, away, by a dread repulsive power .
185 Into Non-Entity, revolving round in dark despair
And drawing in her spectrous life in pride and haughty joy.

Till Eno, a daughter of Beulah, took a moment of time
And drew it out to seven thousand years with much care and affliction,
And many tears, and in evening years made windows into Eden.
190 She also took an atom of space, and opened its center out
Into infinitude, and ornamented it with wondrous care.
Astonished sat her sisters of Beulah to see her soft affection
To Enion and her children, and they pondered these things wondering,
And they alternate kept their watch over the youthful terrors.
195 They saw not yet the Hand Divine, for it was not revealed,
But they went on in silent hope and feminine repose.

There is from Great Eternity a mild and pleasant rest
Named Beulah, a soft moony universe, feminine, lovely,
Pure, mild and gentle, given in Mercy to all those who sleep,
200 Eternally created by the Lamb of God around
On all sides, within and without the Universal Man.
The Daughters of Beulah follow after sleepers in their dreams,
Creating spaces, lest they fall into Eternal Death.
The circle of Destiny complete, they gave to it a space,
205 Named the space Ulro, brooded over it in care and love.
They said: The Spectre is in every man insane, and most
Deformed. Through the three Heavens descending in fury and fire
We meet it with our songs and loving blandishments, and give
To it a form of Vegetation. But this Spectre of Tharmas
210 Is Eternal Death. What shall we do? O God, pity and help!

So spoke they, and closed the gate of the tongue in trembling fear.

But Los and Enitharmon delighted in the moony spaces of Eno,
Nine times they lived among the forests, feeding on sweet fruits,
And nine bright spaces wandered, weaving mazes of delight,
215 Snaring the wild goats for their milk.   We eat the flesh of Lambs,
A male and female, naked and ruddy as the pride of summer.

Alternate love and hate his breast, hers scorn and jealousy,
In embryon passions fill, they kissed not nor embraced for shame.
He could control the times and seasons and the days and years.
220 She could control the spaces, regions, desert, flood and forest,
But had no power to weave the veil of covering for her sins.
Females she drove away from Los, Los drove the males away.
They wandered long, till they sat down upon the margined sea

Conversing in the visions of Beulah in dark slumbrous bliss.
225 But the two youthful wonders wandered in the world of Tharmas;
Thy name is Enitharmon, said the fierce prophetic boy.
While thy mild voice fills all these caverns with sweet harmony,
O how our parents sit and mourn in their silent secret bowers!
But Enitharmon answered with a dropping tear and frowning
230 Dark as a dewy morning when the crimson light appears,—
We hear the warlike clarions, we view the burning spears,
Yet thou in indolence reposest, holding me in bonds.
To make us happy let them weary their immortal powers,
While we draw in their sweet delights, while we return them scorn
235 On scorn to feed our discontent, for if we grateful prove
They will withhold sweet love whose food is scorn and bitter roots.
Hear, I will sing a song of death : it is a song of Vala:—

The Fallen Man takes his repose, Urizen slept in the porch,
Luvah and Vala wake and fly up from the Human Heart
240 Into the Brain.   From thence upon the pillow Vala slumbered,
And Luvah seized the Horses of Light and rose into the Chariot of Day
Sweet laughter seized me in my sleep, silent and close I laughed,—

For in the visions of Vala I walked with the Mighty Fallen One—
I heard his voice among the branches and among sweet flowers,
245 Why is the light of Enitharmon darkened in the dewy morn?
Why is the silence of Enitharmon a cloud and her smile a whirlwind?
Uttering this darkness in my halls in the pillars of my Holy Ones,
Why dost thou weep as Vala and wet thy veil with dewy tears
In slumbers of my night repose infusing a false morning?
250 Dividing the female-emanations all away from Los,
And wilt thou slay with death him who devotes himself to thee,
For the sport and amusement of Man now born to drink up all his
    powers?
I heard the sounding sea, I heard the voice weaker and weaker,
The voice came and went like a dream : I awoke in my sweet bliss.

255 Then Los smote her upon the earth; 'twas long ere she revived.
He answered, darkening now with indignation hid in smiles :—

I die not, Enitharmon, though thou singest thy song of Death,
Nor shalt thou me torment, for I behold the Fallen Man
Seeking to comfort Vala : she will not be comforted.
260 She rises from his throne and seeks the shadows of her garden
Weeping for Luvah, lost in bloody beams of your false morning.
Sickening lies the Fallen Man, his head sick, his heart faint,
Refusing to behold the Divine Image which all behold
And live thereby, he is sunk down into a deadly sleep.
265 But we, immortal in our own strength, survive by stern debate
Till we have drawn the Lamb of God into a mortal form.
And that he must be born is certain, for One must be All,
And comprehend within himself all things, both small and great.
We therefore for whose sake all things aspire to be and live
270 Will so receive the Divine Image that among the Reprobate
He may be devoted to destruction from his mother's womb.
Mighty achievement of your power! Beware the punishment.
I see the invisible knife descend into the gardens of Vala
Luvah walking upon the winds! I see the invisible knife.
275 I see the showers of blood, I see the swords and spears of futurity.

Though in the Brain of Man we live and in his circling Nerves
Though this bright world of all our joy is in the Human Brain
Where Urizen and all his hosts hang their immortal lamps,
Thou never shalt leave this cold expanse where watery Tharmas mourns.

280 So spoke Los. Scorn and indignation rose upon Enitharmon.

Then Enitharmon reddening fierce stretched her immortal hands :—
Descend, O Urizen, descend with horse and chariot,—
Threaten me not, O Visionary, these the punishment,—
The Human Nature shall no more remain nor Human acts
285 Form the rebellious spirits of Heaven, but war and princedom, victory
      and blood.

Night darkened as she spoke, a shuddering ran from East to West.
A groan was heard on high. The warlike clarion ceased, the spirits
Of Luvah and Vala shuddered in their orb, an orb of blood.
Eternity groaned and was troubled at the Image of Eternal Death.

290 The Wandering Man bow'd his faint head and Urizen descended
      And the one must have murdered the Man if he had not descended.
      Indignant, muttering low thunders Urizen descended,
      Gloomy, sounding :—Now I am God from Eternity to Eternity.

Sullen sat Los plotting revenge. Silent he eyed the Prince
295 Of Light. Silent the Prince of Light viewed Los. At length a smile
      Broke from Urizen, for Enitharmon brightened more.
      Sullen he lowered on Enitharmon, but he smiled on Los,
      Saying :—Thou art the Lord of Luvah. Into thy hands I give
      The Prince of Love, the murderer ; his soul is in these hands.
300 Pity not Vala, for she pitied not the Eternal Man,
      Nor pity thou the cries of Luvah. Lo, these starry hosts,
      They are thy servants if thou wilt obey my awful law.

So spoke the Prince of Light and sat beside the seat of Los.
Upon the sandy shore rested his chariot of fire.

305 Los answered :—Art thou one of those who when complaisant most
    Mean mischief most? If you are such, lo! I am also such.
    One must be Master. Try thy arts. I also will try mine,
    For I perceive thou hast abundance which I claim as mine.
    Urizen startled stood, but not long. Soon he cried :—

310 Obey my voice, young Demon; I am God from Eternity to Eternity,—
    Thus Urizen spoke collected in himself in awful pride,—
    Lo I am God, the terrible Destroyer, and not the Saviour.
    Why should the Divine Vision control the sons of men
    To forbid each his free delight, to war against his spectre?
315 The Spectre is the Man. The rest is only delusion and fancy.

    Ten thousand thousand were his hosts of spirits on the wind,
    Ten thousand thousand glittering chariots shining in the sky.
    They pour upon the golden shore beside the silent ocean,
    Till Earth spread forth her table wide. The Night, a silver cup
320 Filled with the wine of anguish,—waited at the golden feast.
    But the bright sun was not as yet. He, filling all the expanse,
    Slept as a bird in the blue shell that soon shall burst away.

    Los saw the wound of his blow: he saw, he pitied, he wept.
    Los now repented that he had smitten Enitharmon. He felt love
325 Arise in all his veins. He threw his arms around her loins
    To heal the wound of his smiting.

    They eat the fleshly bread, they drank the nervous wine;
    They listened to the elemental harps and sphery song :
    They viewed the dancing hours quick sporting through the sky,
330 With winged radiance scattering joy through the ever-changing light.
    But Luvah and Vala standing in the bloody sky
    On high remained alone, forsaken in fierce jealousy—
    They stood above the heavens, forsaken, desolate, suspended in blood.
    Descend they could not, nor from one another avert their eyes.
335 Eternity appeared above them as One Man infolded
    In Luvah's robes of blood, and having all his afflictions,
    As the sun shines down on the misty earth : such was the Vision.

But purple night, and crimson morning, and golden day descending
Through the clear changing atmosphere displayed green fields among
340   The varying clouds like paradises stretched in the expanse,
With towns and villages and temples, tents, sheepfolds and pastures,
Where dwell the children of the elemental worlds in harmony.

Not long in harmony they dwell. Their life is drawn away
And wintry woes succeed,—successive driven into the Void
345   Where Enion craves,—successive driven into the golden feast.

And Los and Enitharmon sat in discontent and scorn.
The Nuptial song arose from all the thousand thousand spirits
Over the joyful earth and sea and ascended into the heaven,
For elemental gods their thunderous organs blew creating
350   Delicious viands. Demons of waves their watery echoes woke.
Bright souls of vegetative life budding and blossoming
Stretch their immortal hands to smite the gold and silver strings,
With doubling voices, and loud horns, wound round and round, re-
     sounding.
Cavernous dwellers filled the enormous revelry, responsing,
355   And spirits of flaming fire on high governed the mighty song.

And this is the song sung at the feast of Los and Enitharmon.
The Mountain called out to the Mountain, Awake, oh Brother Mountain.
Let us refuse the Plough and Spade, the heavy Roller and
Spiked Harrow Burn these cornfields all, throw all these fences down.
360   Fattened on blood and drunk with wine of life is better far
Than all these labours of harvest and vintage. See the river
Red with the blood of Men swells lustful round my rocky knees,
My clouds are not the clouds of verdant fields and groves of fruit,
But Clouds of Human Souls : my nostrils drink the Lives of Men.
365   The Villages lament, they faint, outstretched upon the plain.
Wailing runs round the Valleys from the Mill and from the Barn.
But most the polished Palaces, dark, silent, bow with dread,
Hiding their books and pictures underneath the dens of Earth.
The Cities send to one another saying :—My sons are mad

370 With wine of cruelty. Let us plat a scourge, on sister city.
Children are nourished for the slaughter. Once the child was fed
With milk, but wherefore now are children fed with wine and blood ?

Enion, blind and age-bent, wept upon the desolate wind.
Why does the Raven cry aloud and no eye pities her ?
375 Why fall the Sparrow and the Robin in the foodless winter ?
Faint, shivering, they sit on leafless bush or frozen stone
Wearied with seeking food across the snowy waste, the little
Heart cold, the little tongue consumed that once in thoughtless joy
Gave songs of gratitude to waving cornfields round their nest.
380 Why howl the lion and the wolf ? Why do they roam abroad ?
Deluded by the summer's heat they sport in enormous love,
And cast their young out to the hungry winds and desert sands.
Why is the sheep given to the knife ? The lamb plays in the sun.
He starts: he hears the foot of Man ! He says: Take thou my wool
385 But spare my life : but he knows not that winter cometh fast.
The spider sits in his laboured net, eager, watching for the fly.
Presently comes a famished bird and takes away the spider.
His web is left all desolate that his little anxious heart
So careful wove and spread it out with sighs and weariness.

390 This was the lamentation of Enion round the golden tent.
Eternity groaned and was troubled at the image of Eternal Death,
Without the body of Man, exuded from his sickening limbs.

Now Man was come to the Palm Tree, and to the Oak of Weeping
Which stand upon the edge of Beulah, and there he sank down
395 From the supporting arms of the Eternal Saviour who disposed
The pale limbs of his Eternal Individuality
'Upon the Rock of Ages, watching over him with love and care.

Jerusalem, his Emanation is become a ruin,
Her little ones are slain upon the top of every street,
400 And she herself led captive and scattered into the indefinite.
Gird on thy sword, O thou most mighty in glory and majesty.
Destroy these oppressors of Jerusalem and those that ruin Shiloh.

So spoke the Messengers of Beulah. Silently removing
The Family Divine drew up the universal tent
405 Above Mount Gilead and closed the messengers in clouds around
Till the time of the End. Then they elected Seven, called the Seven
Eyes of God, and the Seven Lamps of the Almighty.
The seven are one within the other. The seventh is named Jesus,
The Lamb of God blessed for ever. He followed the Man
410 Who wandered in Mount Ephraim seeking a Sepulchre,
His inward eyes closing from the Divine Vision, and all

His children wandering from his bosom outside fleeing away.
The Daughters of Beulah beheld the Emanation; they pitied, they
        wept.
They wept before the inner gates of Enitharmon's bosom,
415 And of her fine-wrought brain, and of her bowels within her loins.
These gates within, glorious, bright, open into Beulah
From Enitharmon's inward parts. But the bright female terror
Refused to open the bright gates. She closed and barred them fast
Lest Los should enter into Beulah through her beautiful gates.

420 The Emanation stood before the gates of Enitharmon,
Weeping. The Daughters of Beulah silent in the Porches
Spread her a couch unknown to Enitharmon. Here reposed
Jerusalem in slumbers soft, lull'd into silent rest.

Terrific raged the Eternal wheels of Intellect, and raged
425 The Living Creatures in the wheels, in the Wars of Eternal life.
But perverse rolled the wheels of Urizen and Luvah, back revolved
Downwards and outwards, consuming in the Wars of Eternal Death.

Then those in Great Eternity met in the councils of God
As One Man, for, contracting their exalted senses
430 They behold Multitude, or expanding they behold as one,
As One Man all the Universal Family, and that One Man
They call Jesus the Christ, and they in him, and he in them,
Live in perfect harmony, in Eden, the land of life,

Consulting as one Man above Mount Gilead sublime.

435   For messengers from Beulah came in tears and darkening clouds
Saying Shiloh is in ruins, our brother Albion is sick. He,
He whom thou lovest is sick. He wanders from his house of Eternity.
The Daughters of Beulah, terrified, have closed the gate of the tongue.
Luvah and Urizen contend in war around the holy tent.

440   So spoke the Ambassadors from Beulah with solemn mourning sound;
They were introduced to the Divine Presence and they kneeled down
In Beth Peor thus recounting the wars of Eternal Death:—

The Eternal Man wept in the holy tent. Our Brother in Eternity,
Even Albion whom thou lovest, wept in pain. His family
445   Slept round on hills and valleys in the region of his love.
But Urizen awoke, and Luvah awoke, and they conferred, thus.

Thou Luvah, said the Prince of Light, behold our sons and daughters
Repose on beds. Let them sleep on, do thou alone depart
Into thy wished kingdom, where in Majesty and Power
450   We may create a throne. Deep in the North I place my lot,
Thou in the South. Listen attentive. In silence of this night
I will infold the universal tent in clouds opaque, while thou
Seizest the chariots of the morning. Go; outfleeting ride
Afar into the Zenith high, bending thy furious course
455   Southward, with half the tents of men inclosed in clouds
Of Tharmas and Urthona. I in porches of the brain
Will lay my sceptre on Jerusalem, the Emanation,
On all her sons, and on thy sons, O Luvah, and on mine
Till dawn was wont to wake them, then my trumpet sounding loud,
460   Ravished away in night. My strong command shall be obeyed,
For I have placed my sentinels in stations. Each tenth man
Is bought and sold, and in dim night my word shall be their law.

Luvah replied: Dictate thou to thy equals, am not I
The Prince of all the hosts of men, nor equal know in Heaven?

465 If I arise into the Zenith, leaving thee to watch
    The Emanation and her sons, the Satan and the Anak
    Sihon and Og, wilt thou not, rebel to my laws, remain
    In darkness, building thy strong throne, and in my ancient night
    Daring my power wilt arm my sons against me in the deep,
470 My deep, my night, which thou assuming hast assumed my crown.
    I will remain as well as thou, and here with hands of blood
    Smite this dark sleeper in his tent, then try my strength with thee.

    While thus he spoke his fury reddened o'er the holy tent.
    Urizen cast deep darkness round him, silent, brooding death,
475 Eternal death to Luvah. Raging, Luvah poured
    The lances of Urizen from chariots round the holy tent.
    Discord began and yells and cries shook the wide firmament.

    Beside his Anvil stood Urthona dark, a mass of iron
    Glow'd furious on the anvil prepared for spades and coulters.
480 His sons fled from his side to join the conflict   Pale he heard
    The Eternal voice. He stood. The sweat chilled on his mighty limbs.
    He dropped his hammer. Dividing from his aching bosom fled
    A portion of his life. Shrieking upon the wind she fled,
    And Tharmas took her in, pitying.   Then Enion in jealous fear
485 Murdered her, and hid her in her bosom, embalming her, for fear
    She should arise again to life. Embalmed in Enion's bosom
    Enitharmon remains. Such thing was never known before
    In Eden, that one died a death never to be revived.

    Urthona stood in terror, but not long. His spectre fled
490 To Enion, and his body fell. Tharmas beheld him fall
    Endlong, a raging serpent, rolling round the holy tent.
    The sons of War astonished at the glittering monster drove
    Him far into the world of Tharmas, into a caverned rock.

    But Urizen with darkness overspreading all the armies
495 Sent round his heralds secretly commanding to depart
    Into the North. Sudden with thunder's sound his multitudes

Retreat from the fierce fight, all sons of Urizen at once
Mustering together in thick clouds, leaving the rage of Luvah
To pour its fury on himself, and on the Eternal Man.

500 Sudden, down fell they all together into an unknown space,
Deep, horrible, without end, from Beulah separate, far beneath.
The Man's exteriors are become indefinite, opened to pain,
503 In a fierce hungry void, and none can visit his regions.

END OF THE FIRST NIGHT.

2

Night the Second.

Reclining upon his couch of death Albion beheld his sons.
Turning his eyes outward to self, losing the Divine Vision,
Albion called Urizen and said :—Behold these sickening spheres,—
Whence is this voice of Enion that soundeth in my ears?
5 Take thou possession. Take this sceptre. Go forth in my might,
For I am weary and must sleep in the dark sleep of death.
Thy brother Luvah hath smitten me, but pity thou his youth,
Though thou hast not pitied my age, oh Urizen, Prince of Light.

Urizen rose from the bright feast like a star through the evening sky.
10 Exulting at the voice that called him from the feast of envy
First he beheld the body of Man, pale, cold. The horrors of death
Beneath his feet shot through him as he stood in the human brain.
No more exulting, for he saw Eternal Death beneath,
Where Enion, blind and age-bent, wept in direful hunger craving,
15 All ravening like the hungry worm and like the silent grave.
Mighty was the draught of voidness to draw existence in.

Terrific Urizen strode above in fear and pale dismay.
He saw the indefinite space beneath and his soul shrunk with horror,
His feet upon the verge of non-existence. His voice went forth,
20 Luvah and Vala trembling and shrinking beheld the great Work
    Master
And heard his word :—Divide ye bands influence by influence.
Build me a bower for Heavens, darting in the grizzly deep,
Build me the Mundane Shell around the rock of Albion.

The Bands of Heaven flew through the air singing and shouting to
    Urizen.

25   Some fixed the anvil, some the loom erected, some the plough
    And harrow formed and framed the harness of silver and ivory,
    The golden compasses, the quadrant, and the rule and balance.
    They erected the furnaces, they formed the anvils of gold in mills
    Where winter beats incessant, fixing them firm on their base,
30   The bellows began to blow, and the lions of Urizen stood round the
       anvil,
    And the leopards covered with skins of beasts tended the roaring fires,
    Sublime, distinct in their lineaments of human beauty, stood,
    Petrifying all the Human Imagination into rock and sand.
    Groans ran along Tyburn's brook and along the river of Oxford
35   Among the Druid Temples. Albion groaned on Tyburn's brook.
    Albion gave his loud death-groan. The Atlantic mountains trembled.
    Aloft the moon fled with a cry: the sun with streams of blood.
    From Albion's Loins fled all peoples, and nations of the Earth
    Fled, with the noise of slaughter, and the stars of Heaven fled.
40   Jerusalem came down in a dire ruin over all the Earth,
    She fell cold from Lambeth's vale in groans and dewy death,
    The dew of anxious souls, the death sweat of the dying,
    In every pillared hall and arched roof of Albion's skies.

    The brother and the brother bathe in blood upon the Severn,
45   The maiden weeping by, the father and mother with
    The maiden's father and her mother fainting over the body,
    And the young man the murderer fleeing over the mountains.

    Reuben slept on Penmaenmawr, and Levi slept on Snowdon,
    Their eyes, their ears, their nostrils and tongues roll outward, they
       behold
50   What is within now seen without; they rave to the hungry wind.
    They become Natures far remote in a little dark land.

    The daughters of Albion girded around their garments of needlework
    Stripping Jerusalem's curtains from mild demons of the hills
    Across Europe and Asia to China and Japan like lightnings
55   They go forth and return to Albion on his rocky couch.

                                      2 *

Guendolen, Ragan, Sabrina, Gonoril, Mehetabel, Cordella,
Boadicea, Conwenna, Estrild, Guinifred, Ignoze, Cambel,
Binding Jerusalem's children in the dungeons of Babylon.
They play before the Armies, before the hounds of Nimrod,
60 While the Prince of Light on Salisbury Plain covers the Druid
    Thrones.

The Tigers of wrath called the horses of instruction from their mangers,
They unloosed them and put on the harness of gold, silver and ivory,
In human forms distinct they stood round Urizen, Prince of Light.
Rattling, the adamantine chains heave up the ore
65 In mountainous masses plunged in furnaces they shut and sealed
The furnaces a time and times.   All the while blew the North
His cloudy bellows, and the South and East and dismal West,
And all the while the plough of iron cut the dreadful furrows
In Ulro, beneath Beulah, where the dead wail night and day.

70 Luvah was cast into the furnaces of affliction and sealed,
And Vala fed in cruel delight the furnaces with fire.
Stern Urizen beheld, urged by necessity to keep
The evil day afar, and if perchance with iron power
He might avert his own despair.   In woe and fear he saw
75 Vala incircle round the furnace, where Luvah was closed.
In joy she heard his howlings and forgot he was her Luvah
With whom she walked in bliss in times of innocence and youth.

Hear ye the voice of Luvah from the furnaces of Urizen:
If I indeed am Vala's King, and ye, oh Sons of Men,
80 The workmanship of Luvah's hands in times of everlasting.
When I called forth the earthworm from the cold and dark obscure
And nurtured her, I fed her with my rains and dews, she grew
A scaled serpent, yet I fed her though she hated me,
Day after day she fed upon the mountains in Luvah's sight,
85 I brought her through the wilderness, a dry and thirsty land,
And I commanded springs to rise for her in the dark desert,

Till she became a dragon, winged, bright, and poisonous.
I opened all the floodgates of the heavens to quench her thirst
Till she became a little weeping infant a span long.
90 I carried her in my bosom as a man carries a lamb,
I loved her, I gave her all my soul and my delight,
I hid her in soft gardens and in secret bowers of summer
Inextricable labyrinths. She bore me sons and daughters
And they have taken her away and hid her from my sight.
95 They have surrounded me with walls of iron and brass. Oh Lamb
Of God clothed in Luvah's garments! little knowest thou
Of Death Eternal,—that we all go to Eternal Death
To our primœval chaos in fortuitous concourse of incoherent
Discordant principles of Love and Hate. I suffer affliction
100 Because I love, for I was Love, but hatred awakes in me,
And Urizen who was Faith and certainty is changed to Doubt,
The Hand of Urizen is upon me because I blotted out
That Human Delusion to deliver all the Sons of God
From bondage of the Human Form. Oh first-born Son of Light,
105 Oh Urizen, my enemy, I weep for thy stern ambition,

But weep in vain. Oh, when will you return, Vala the Wanderer?
These were the words of Luvah, patient in afflictions,
Reasoning from the Loins in the unreal forms of Ulro's night.
And when Luvah, age after age, was quite melted with woe,
110 The fires of Vala faded like a shadow cold and pale,
An evanescent shadow. Last she fell, a heap of ashes
Beneath the furnaces, a woeful heap in living death.

Then were the furnaces unsealed with spades and pickaxes,
Roaring let out the fluid. The molten metal ran in channels
115 Cut by the plough of ages, held in Urizen's strong hand
In many a valley. For the bulls of Luvah dragged the plough.
With trembling horror, pale, aghast, the children of Man
Stood on the infinite earth and saw these visions in the air,
In waters, and in earth beneath. They cried to one another

120 ' What, are we terrors to one another? Come, oh brethren, wherefore
      Was this wide earth spread all abroad? Not for wild beasts to roam.
      But many stood silent, and busied in their families.
      And many said, We see no visions in the darkened air,
      Measure the course of that sulphur orb that lights the darksome day.
125   Set stations on the breeding earth and let us buy and sell.
      Others arose, and schools erected forming instruments
      To measure out the course of heaven. Stern Urizen beheld
      In woe his brethren and his sons in darkening woe lamenting
      Upon the winds in clouds involved. Uttering his voice in thunder
130   Commanding all the work with care and power and severity.

      Then seized the lions of Urizen their work and heated in the forge,
      Roar the bright masses. Thundering beat the hammers. Many a
          pyramid
      Is formed and thrown down thundering into the deeps of nonentity,
      Heated red-hot they, hissing, rend their way down many a league
135   Till resting each his centre finds. Suspended there they stand
      Casting their sparkles dire abroad into the dismal deep.
      For, measured out in ordered spaces, the sons of Urizen
      With compasses divide the deep. They the strong scales erect
      That Luvah rent from the faint heart of the Fallen Man,
140   And weigh the massy cubes, then fix them in their awful stations.

      And all the time in caverns shut the golden looms erected,
      First span, then wove the atmospheres. Then the spider and worm
      Plied the winged shuttle, piping shrill through all the listening threads,
      Beneath the caverns roll the weights of lead and spindles of iron,
145   The enormous warp and woof rage direful on the affrighted deep.

      While far into the vast unknown the strong-winged eagles bend
      Their venturous flight in human forms distinct through darkness deep.
      Their bear the woven draperies. On golden hooks they hang abroad
      The universal curtains, and spread out from sun to sun
150   The vehicles of light. They separate the furious particles
      Into mild currents as the water mingles with the wine

While thus the spirits of strongest wing enlighten the dark deep
The threads are spun and the cords twisted and drawn out. Then
   the weak
Begin their work and many a net is netted, many a net
155 Spread, and many a spirit caught : innumerable the nets,
Innumerable the gins and traps, and many a soothing flute
Is formed, and many a corded lyre outspread over the immense.
In cruel delight they trap the listeners, and in cruel delight
Bind them, condensing the strong energies into little compass.
160 Some became seed of every plant that shall be planted. Some
The bulbous roots thrown up together into barns and garners.

  Then rose the builders. First the Architect divine his plan
Unfolds, and the wondrous scaffold reared all round the infinite
Quadrangular the building rose, the heavens squared by a line,
165 Trigons and cubes divide the elements in finite bonds.
Multitudes without number work incessant, the hewn stone
Is placed in beds of mortar mingled with the ashes of Vala.
Severe the labour. Female slaves the mortar trod oppressed.

Twelve halls after the names of his twelve sons composed
170 The wondrous building, and three central domes after the names
Of his three daughters were encompassed by the twelve bright halls.
Every hall surrounded by a bright paradise of delight,
In which were towns and cities, nations, seas, mountains and rivers.
Each dome opened towards four halls, and the three domes encompassed
175 The Golden Hall of Urizen, whose western side glow'd bright
With ever streaming fires beaming from his awful limbs.
His Shadowy Feminine Semblance here reposed on a white couch,
Or hovered over his starry head, and when he smiled she brightened
Like a bright cloud in harvest ; but when Urizen frowned she wept
180 In mists over his carved throne. And when he turned his back
Upon his golden hall and sought the labyrinthine porches
  Of his wide heaven. Trembling, cold, in palsy fears she sat
A shadow of despair. Therefore toward the west Urizen formed

A recess in the wall for fires to glow upon the pale
185 Females, lonely in his absence, and her daughters oft upon
A golden altar burned perfumes with art celestial formed
Foursquare, sculptured and sweetly engraved to please their shadowy
      mother.
Ascending into her misty garments the blue smoke rolled to revive
Her cold limbs in the absence of her lord. Also her sons
190 With lives of victims sacrificed upon an altar of brass,
On the East side revived her soul with lives of beasts and birds
Slain on the altar, up ascending into her cloudy bosom :—
Of terrible workmanship the altar, labour of ten thousand slaves,
One thousand men of wondrous power spent their lives in its formation.
195 It stood on twelve steps named after her twelve sons,
And was erected at the chief entrance of Urizen's hall.

When Urizen returned from his immense labours and travels,
Descending she reposed beside him, folding him around
In her bright skirts. Astonished and confounded he beheld
200 Her shadowy form now separate. He shuddered and was silent.
Till her caresses and her tears revived him to life and joy.
Two wills they had, two intellects, and not as in time of old,
This Urizon perceived, and silent brooded in darkening clouds,
To him his labour was but sorrow and his kingdom was repentance,
205 He drove the male spirits all away from Ahania,
And she drove all the females from him away.

Los joyed, and Enitharmon laughed, saying, Let us go down
And see their labour and sorrow. They went down to see the woes
Of Vala, and the woes of Luvah, to draw in their delights,
210 And Vala like a shadow oft appeared to Urizen.
The King of Night beheld her moving among the brick-kilns compelled
To labour night and day among the fires, her lamenting voice
Is heard when silent night returns and labourers take their rest.

O Lord, wilt thou not look upon our sore afflictions

215 Among these flames incessant labouring?   Our hard masters laugh
At all our sorrow.   We are made to turn the wheel for water,
To carry the heavy basket on our scorched shoulders, to sift
The sand and ashes, to mix the clay with tears and repentance.
The times are now returned upon us.   We have given ourselves
220 To scorn, and now are scorned by the slaves of our enemies.
Our beauty is covered over with clay and ashes, and our backs
Furrow'd with whips, and our flesh bruised with the heavy basket.
Forgive us, Oh, thou piteous one whom we have offended !   Forgive
The weak remaining shadow of Vala that returns in sorrow to thee.
225 I cannot see Luvah as of old, I only see his feet
Like pillars of fire travelling through darkness and nonentity,
Thus she lamented day and night compelled to labour and sorrow.
Luvah in vain her lamentations heard : in vain his love
Brought him in various forms before her, still she knew him not,
230 Still she despised him, calling on his name and knowing him not,
Still hating, still professing love, still labouring in the smoke.

But infinitely beautiful the wondrous work arose
In sorrow and care, a golden world whose porches round the heaven,
And pillar'd halls and rooms received the eternal wandering stars.
235 A wondrous golden building, many a window, many a door,
And many a division let in and out the vast unknown.
Circled in infinite wall immovable, within its walls and recesses
The heavens were closed, and spirits mourned their bondage night
   and day,
And the Divine Vision appeared in Luvah's robes of blood.

240 There was the Mundane shell builded by Urizen's strong power.
Sorrowing went the planters forth to plant, the sower to sow,
They dry the channels for the rivers, they poured abroad the seas,
The seas and lakes. They reared the mountains and the rocks and hills
In beauteous order.   Thence arose soft clouds and exhalations
245 Wandering even to the sunny orbs of light and heat,
For many a window ornamented with sweet ornaments

Looked out into the world of Tharmas, where in ceaseless torrents
His billows roll where monsters wander in the foamy paths.

On clouds the sons of Urizen beheld heaven walled round
250 They weighed and ordered all, and Urizen comforted saw
The wondrous work flow forth like visible out of the invisible,
For the Divine Lamb, even Jesus who is the Divine Vision,
Permitted all lest Man should fall into Eternal Death,
For when Luvah sunk down himself put on the robes of blood
255 Lest the state called Luvah should cease, and the Divine Vision
Walked in robes of blood till he who slept should awake.

Thus were the stars of heaven created like a golden chain
To bind the Body of Man to heaven from falling into the abyss.
Each took his station and his course began with sorrow and care.
260 In sevens and tens and fifties, hundreds, thousands, numbered all
According to their various powers subordinate to Urizen.
And to his sons in their degrees, and to his beauteous daughters
Travelling in silent majesty along their ordered ways
In right lined paths outmeasured by proportion, number, weight,
265 And measure, mathematic motion wondrous along the deep
In fiery pyramid or cube, or on ornamented pillars square
Of fire, far shining, travelling along even to its destined end,
Then falling down a terrible space, recovering in winter dire
Its wasted strength it back returns upon a nether course,
270 Till fired with ardour, fresh recruited in its humble spring
It rises up on high all summer, till its wearied course
Turns into autumn. Such the periods of many worlds.
Others triangular, right-angled course maintain. Others obtuse,
Acute, travel in simple paths. But others move
275 In intricate ways, biquadrate, trapeziums, rhombs, rhomboids,
Parallelograms triple and quadruple, polygons
In their amazing hard subdued course in the dark deep.

And Los and Enitharmon were driven down by their desires,
Descending sweet upon the wind among soft harps and voices

280 To plant divisions in the soul of Urizen and Ahania,
    To conduct the voice of Enion to Ahania's midnight pillow.

    Urizen saw and envied, and his imagination was filled ;
    Repining he contemplated the past in his bright sphere,
    Terrified with his heart and spirit at the visions of futurity
285 That his dread fancy formed before him in the unformed void.

    For Los and Enitharmon walked forth on the dewy earth,
    Contracting or expanding all their flexible senses
    At will to murmur in the flowers small as the honey-bee,
    At will to stretch across the heavens and step from star to star,
290 Or standing on the earth erect, or on the stormy seas,
    Driving the storms before them or delighting in sunny beams,
    While round their heads the elemental gods kept harmony.

    And Los said : Lo, the lily pale and the rose reddening fierce
    Reproach thee, and the beamy garden sickens at thy beauty,
295 I grasp thy vest in my strong hands in vain.   Like water springs
    In the bright sands of Los evading my embrace.   Thus I alone
    Wander among the virgins of the summer.   Look, they cry,
    The poor forsaken Los mocked by the worm, the shelly snail,
    The emmet and the beetle, hark ! they laugh and mock at Los.

300 Secure now from the smitings of thy power, Demon of Fury,
    Enitharmon answered.   If the god enraptured me infold
    In clouds of sweet obscurity my beauteous form dissolving,
    Howl thou over the body of death. 'Tis thine.   But if among the visions
    Of summer I have seen thee sleep and turn thy cheek delighted
305 Upon the rose or lily pale, or on a bank where sleep
    The beamy daughters of the light, starting, they rise, they flee
    From thy fierce love, for though I am dissolved in the bright god
    My spirit still pursues thy false love over rocks and valleys.

    Los answered : Therefore fade I thus dissolved in raptured trance,
310 Thou canst repose on clouds of secrecy, while o'er my limbs

Cold dews and hoary frost creep, though I lie on banks of summer
Among the branches of the world. Cold and repining Los
Still dies for Enitharmon, nor a spirit springs from my dead corse,
Then I am dead till thou revivest me with thy sweet song.
315 Now taking on Ahania's form and now the form of Enion
I know thee not as once I knew thee in those blessed fields
Where Memory wishes to repose among the flocks of Tharmas.

Enitharmon answered,—Wherefore dost thou throw thine arms around
Ahania's image? I deceived thee and will still deceive.
320 Urizen saw thy sin and hid his beams in darkening clouds.
I still keep watch although I tremble and wither across the heavens
In strong vibrations of fierce jealousy, for thou art mine,
Created for my will, my slave, though strong, though I am weak.
Farewell, the God calls me away, I depart in my sweet bliss.

325 She fled, vanishing upon the wind and left a dead cold corse
In Los's arms. Howlings began over the body of death.

Los spoke. Thy God in vain shall call thee if by my strong power
I can infuse my dear revenge into his glowing breast.
There jealousy shall shadow all his mountains and Ahania
330 Curse thee, thou plague of woeful Los, and seek revenge on thee.

So saying in deep sobs he languished till dead; he also fell.
Night passed, and Enitharmon ere the dawn returned in bliss.
She sang over Los reviving him to life: his groans were terrible,
And thus she sang,—
335   I seize the sphery harp, awake the strings!

At the first sound the golden Sun arises from the deep
. And shakes his awful hair,
The echo wakes the moon again to unbind her silver locks,
The golden Sun bears on my song,
340 And nine bright spheres of harmony rise round the fiery king.

The joy of woman is the death even of her most beloved,
Who dies for love of her
  In torments of fierce jealousy and pangs of adoration.
The lovers' night bears on my song
345 And the nine spheres rejoice beneath my powerful control.

They sing unwearied to the notes of my immortal hand.
The solemn silent moon
Reverberates the long harmony sounding upon my limbs,
The birds and beasts rejoice and play,
350 And every one seeks for his mate to prove his inmost joy.

Furious and terrible they sport and rend the nether deep,
The deep lifts up his rugged head
And lost in infinite hovering wings vanishes with a cry.
The fading cry is ever dying,
355 The living voice is ever living in its inmost joy.

Arise, you little glancing wings and sing your infant joy,
Arise and drink your bliss,
For everything that lives is holy, for the source of life
Descends to be a weeping babe;
360 For the earthworm renews the moisture of the sandy plain.

Now my left hand I stretch abroad, even to Earth beneath,
And strike the terrible string.
I wake sweet joy in dews of sorrow and I plant a smile
In forests of affliction,
365 And wake the bubbling springs of life in regions of dark death.

O, I am weary. Lay thy hand upon me or I faint,
I faint beneath these beams of thine,
For thou hast touched my fine senses and they answered thee.
Now I am nothing, and I sink
370 And fall on the bed of solemn sleep till thou awakenest me,

Thus sang the lonely one in rapturous delusive trance.
Los heard, reviving. He seized her in his arms, delusive hope
Kindling she led him into shadows, and thence fled outstretched
Upon the immense like a bright rainbow, weeping, smiling, fading.

375 Thus lived Los, driving Enion far into the deathful infinite,
That he may also draw Ahania's spirit into her vortex.
Ah, happy blindness which sees not the terrors of the uncertain!
And thus she wails on the dark deep; the golden heavens tremble.

I am made to sow the thistle for wheat, the nettle for a nourishing
  dainty.
380 I have planted a false oath on the earth. It has brought forth a
  poison tree.
I have chosen the serpent for a councillor, and the dog
For a schoolmaster to my children.
I have blotted out from light and living the dove and the nightingale.
I have caused the earthworm to beg from door to door.
385 I have taught the thief a secret path into the house of the just.
I have taught pale artifice to spread his nets upon the morning.
My heavens are brass, my earth is iron, my moon a clod of clay,
My sun a pestilence burning at noon, a vapour of death in the night.
What is the price of experience? Do men buy it for a song?
390 Or wisdom for a dance in the street? No, it is bought with the price
Of all that a man hath,—his wife, his house, his children.
Wisdom is sold in the desolate market where none come to buy,
And in the withered fields where the farmer ploughs for bread in vain.
It is an easy thing to triumph in the summer's sun,
395 And in the harvest to sing on the waggon loaded with corn.
It is an easy thing to talk of patience to the afflicted,
To speak the laws of prudence to the houseless wanderer,
To listen to the hungry raven's cry in the winter season,
When the red blood is filled with wine and with the marrow of lambs.
400 It is an easy thing to laugh at wrathful elements,

To hear the dog howl at the wintry door, the ox in the slaughter-house moan;

‹To see a god on every wind and a blessing on every blast;

To hear sounds of love in the thunderstorm that destroys our enemy's house;

To rejoice in the blight that covers his field, in the sickness that cuts off his children.

405 While our olive and wine sing and laugh round our door, and our children bring fruits and flowers,

Then the groan and the dolor are quite forgotten, and the slave grinding at the mill,

And the captive in chains, and the poor in the prison, and the soldier in the fields

When the shattered bone hath laid him groaning among the happier dead.

It is an easy thing to rejoice in the tents of prosperity;—

410 Thus could I sing and thus rejoice: but it is not so with me.

Ahania heard the lamentation, and a swift vibration
Spread through her golden frame. She rose up e'er the dawn of day
When Urizen slept on his couch. Drawn through unbounded space
On to the margin of Non-Entity the bright female came.

415 There she beheld the terrible form of Enion in the void,
And never from that moment could she rest upon her pillow.

END OF THE SECOND NIGHT.

Night the Third.

———✦———

Now sat the King of Light again upon his starry throne
And bright Ahania bow'd herself before his splendid feet.
O Urizen, look on thy wife, that like a mournful stream
Embraces round thy knees and wets her bright hair with her tears.
5 Why sighs my lord? Are not the morning stars obedient sons?
Do they not bow their bright heads at thy voice, at thy command
Do they not fly into their stations and return their light to thee?
The immortal Atmospheres are thine. There thou art seen in glory
Surrounded by the ever-changing daughters of the light.
10 Thou sits in harmony, for God hath set thee over all.
Why wilt thou look upon futurity darkening present joy?

She ceased. The Prince of Light obscured the splendour of his crown,
Infolded in thick clouds from which his mighty voice went forth.
O bright Ahania, a boy is born of the dark ocean |
15 Whom Urizen doth serve with light replenishing his darkness.
I am set here a king of trouble, commanded here to serve
And do my ministry to those who eat of my wide Table.
All this is mine, yet I must serve, and that Prophetic boy
Must grow up to command his prince, and all his kingly power.
20 But Vala shall become a worm in Enitharmon's womb
Laying her seed upon the fibres, soon to issue forth,
And Luvah in the Loins of Los a dark and furious death.
Alas for me! What will become of me at that dread time?

Ahania bowed her head and wept seven days before the King.
25 And on the eighth day when his clouds unfolded from his throne
She raised her bright head sweet perfumed, and with heavenly voice,

O Prince, the Eternal One hath set thee leader of his works,

Raise then thy radiant eyes to him, raise thy obedient hands,
And comfort shall descend from heaven into thy darkening clouds.
30   Leave all futurity to him.   Resume thy fields of light.
Why didst thou listen to the voice of Luvah that dread morn
To give the immortal steeds of light to his deceitful hands?
No longer now obedient to thy will, thou art compelled
To forge the curbs of iron and brass, to build them iron mangers.
35   To feed them with intoxication from the wine-press of Luvah.
Till the Divine Vision and Fruition is quite obliterated.
They call thy lions to the field of blood.   They rouse thy tigers
Out of the halls of justice, till their dens thy windows framed
Golden and beautiful, but unlike those sweet fields of bliss
40   Where liberty was justice, and eternal science was mercy.
Then, oh my dear lord, listen to Ahania, hear this vision,
The vision of Ahania in the slumbers of Urizen
When Urizen slept in the porch and the Ancient Man was smitten.

The darkening Man walked on the steps of fire before his halls
45   And Vala walked with him in dreams of soft deluding slumber.
He looked up and saw the Prince of Light with splendour faded,
But saw not Los nor Enitharmon; Luvah hid them in shadow
Of a soft cloud outstretched across, and Luvah dwelt in this cloud.

The Man ascended mourning into the splendour of his palace,
50   Above him rose a shadow from his wearied intellect
Of living gold, pure, perfect, holy; in white linen pure it hovered,
A sweet entrancing self-delusion, a watery vision of Man,
Soft, exulting in existence, all the Man absorbing.
Man fell upon his face prostrate before the watery shadow
55   Saying, oh Lord, whence is this change? Thou knowest I am nothing.
And Vala trembled and covered her face and her locks were spread
       on the pavement.
I heard—astonished at the vision, and my heart trembled within me—
I heard the voice of the slumberous man, and thus he spoke
Idolatrous to his own shadow, words of eternity uttering,—

60   Oh, I am nothing if I enter into judgment with thee.
     If thou withdraw thy breath I die, and vanish into Hades;
     If thou dost lay thy hand upon me, behold I am silent;
     If thou withhold thy hand I perish like a fallen leaf;
     Or I am nothing, and to nothing must return again.
65   If thou withdraw thy breath, behold I am oblivion.

     The shadowy voice was silent, but the cloud hung o'er their heads
     In golden wreathes, the sorrow of Man, and the balmy drops fell down
     And lo! that Son of Man, that shadowy spirit of the Fallen One,
     Luvah, descended from the cloud. In terror Man arose.
70   Indignant rose the Awful Man and turned his back on Vala.

     We heard the voice of the Fallen One starting from his sleep.
     Whence is this voice crying Enion that soundeth in my ears?
     Oh, cruel pity. Oh, dark deceit, can love seek for dominion?
     Why roll thy clouds in sickening mists. I can no longer hide
75   The dismal vision of mine eyes. Oh, love! Oh, life! Oh, light!
     Prophetic dreads urge me to speak. Eternity is before me.
     Like a dark lamp. Eternal death haunts all my expectations.
     Rent from Eternal Brotherhood we die and are no more.

     And Luvah strove to gain dominion over the Ancient Man.
80   They strove together over the body where Vala was enclosed.
     And the dark body of Man left prostrate on the crystal pavement
     Covered with boils from head to foot, the terrible smitings of Luvah.
     Then frowned the Fallen Man and put forth Luvah from his presence.
     I heard him;—frown not, Urizen, but listen to my vision—
85   Saying,—Go die the death of Man for Vala the sweet Wanderer.
     I will turn the volutions of your ears outward, and bend your nostrils
     Downward, and your fluxile eyes englobed roll round in fear,
     Your writhing lips and tongue shrink up into a narrow circle
     Till into narrow forms you creep. Go take your fiery way
90   And learn what it is to absorb the Man, you spirits of pity and love.

     Oh, Urizen,—why art thou pale at the visions of Albion?
     Listen to her who loves thee, lest we also are driven away.

They heard the voice and flew, swift as the winter setting sun
And now the Human Blood flow'd high. I saw that Luvah and Vala
95 Went down the Human Heart where Paradise and its joys abound,
In jealous fears and rage, and flames rolled round their fervid feet,
And the vast form of Nature like a serpent played before them,
And as they went in folding fires and thunders of the deep
Vala shrunk in like the dark sea that leaves its slimy banks,
100 And from her bosom Luvah fell far as the East and West
And the vast form of Nature, like a serpent, rolled between.
Whether this is Jerusalem or Babylon we know not.
All is confusion, all is tumult, and we alone are escaped.

Albion closed the western gate, and shut America out
105 By the Atlantic, for a curse, and for a hidden horror,
And for an altar of victims offered to Sin and Repentance.

Am I not God, said Urizen ? Who is equal to me ?
Do I not stretch the heavens abroad, and fold them up like a garment ?
He spoke, mustering his heavy clouds around him, black, opaque.
110 Then thunders rolled around, and lightnings darted to and fro ;
His visage changed to darkness, and his strong right hand came forth
To cast Ahania to the earth. He seized her by the hair,
And threw her from the steps of ice that froze around his throne,
Saying, Art thou also become like Vala ? Thus I cast thee out.

115 Shall the feminine indolent bliss, the indulgent self of weariness,
The passive idle sleep, the enormous night and darkness and death,
Set herself up to give her laws to this active masculine virtue ?
Thou little diminutive portion that darest be a counterpart,
Thy passivity, thy laws of obedience and insincerity,
120 Are my abhorrence. Wherefore hast thou taken this fair form ?
Whence is this power given thee ? Once thou was in my breast
A sluggish current of dim waters, on whose verdant margin
A cavern shagged with horrid shades, dark, cool and deadly, where
I laid my head in the hot noon, after the broken clods
125 Had wearied me. There I laid my plough, and there my horses fed :

3 *

And thou hast risen with thy moist locks into a watery image,
Reflecting all my indolence, my weakness and my death,
To weigh me down beneath the grave into Non-Entity,
Where Luvah strives, scorned by Vala, age after age wandering,
130 Shrinking and shrinking from her Lord and calling him the Tempter.
And art thou also become like Vala? Thus I cast thee out.

So loud in thunder spoke the King, folded in dark despair,
And threw Ahania from his bosom obdurate. She fell like lightning.
Then fled the sons of Urizen from his thund'rous throne, petrified;
135 They fled to East and West and left the North and South of Heaven.

A crash ran through the universe; the bounds of Destiny were broken.
The bounds of Destiny crashed direful, and the swelling sea
Burst from its bonds in whirlpools fierce, and roaring with human voice,
Triumphing even to the stars at bright Ahania's fall.
140 Down from the dismal North the Prince of thunders and thick clouds,
As when the thunder-bolt downfalleth on the appointed place,
Fell down rushing, ruining, thundering, shuddering,
Into the caverns of the grave and places of human seed,
Where the impressions of despair and hope enroot for ever
145 A world of darkness,—Ahania fell far into nonentity.   !
She continued falling. Loud the crash continued, loud and hoarse.
From the crash roared a blue sulphurous fire, and from the flame
A dolorous groan that struck with dumbness all confusion,
Swallowing up the horrible din in agony on agony.
150 Through the confusion, like a crack across from immense to immense,
Loud, strong, a universal groan of death louder was heard
Than all the elements, deafened and rendered worse
Than Urizen and all his hosts in curst despair down rushing.
But from the dolorous groan on high a shadow of smoke appeared,
155 And human bones rattling together in the smoke and stamping
The nether abyss, and gnashing in fierce despair, and panting in sobs,
Thick, short, incessant, bursting, sobbing, deep despairing, stamping,
Struggling to utter the voice of man, to take features of man,
To take the limbs of man. At length, emerging from the smoke

160 Of Urizen dashed in pieces from his precipitate fall,
Tharmas reared up his hands and stood on the affrighted ocean,
The dead reared up his voice and stood on the resounding shore,

Crying: Fury in my limbs! Destruction in my bone and marrow!
My skull riven into filaments, my ears into sea-jellies,
165 Floating upon the tide, wander bubbling and bubbling,
Uttering lamentations and begetting little monsters
Who sit mocking upon the little pebbles of the tide
In all my rivers, and on my dried shells that now the fish
Have quite forsaken. Oh, fool! fool! to lose my sweetest bliss.
170 Where art thou, Enion? Ah, too near thou seemest, too far off,
And yet too near, dashed down I send thee into distant darkness
Far as my strength can hurl thee; wander there, and laugh and play,
Scream and fall off and laugh at Tharmas, lovely summer beauty,
Till winds rend thee into shivers as thou hast rended me.

175 So Tharmas bellowed on the ocean, thund'ring, sobbing, bursting.
The bounds of Destiny were broken, and hatred now began
Instead of love to Enion. Enion, blind and age-bent,
Plunged into the cold billows, living a life in midst of waters.
In terrors she withered away to Entuthon Benython,
180 A world of deep darkness where all things in horror are rooted.

These are the words of Enion, heard from the cold wave of despair:
Oh, Tharmas, I had lost thee when I hoped that I had found thee;
Oh, Tharmas, do not thou destroy me quite, but let
A little shadow, but a little showery form of Enion,
185 Be near the lovéd terror. Let me still remain. Do thou
Thy righteous doom upon me; only let me hear thy voice.
Driven by thy rage I wander like a cloud into the deep
Where never yet existence came; there losing all my life,
I back return, weaker and weaker. Consume me not away
190 In thy great wrath, though I have sinnéd, though I have rebelled.
Make me not as the things forgotten,—as they had not been.

Tharmas replied, riding on storms, his voice in thunder rolled :
Image of grief, thy fading lineaments make my eyelids fail.
What have I done? Both rage and mercy are alike to me ;
195 Looking upon thee, image of faint waters, I recoíl
From my fierce rage into thy semblance. Enion, return.
Why does thy piteous face evanish like a rainy cloud
Melting, a shower of falling tears, nothing but tears ! Enion !
Substanceless, voiceless, weeping, vanished, nothing but tears, Enion !
200 Art thou for ever vanished from the watery eyes of Tharmas.
Rage, rage shall never from my bosom. Winds and waters of woe
Consuming,—all to the end consuming ! Love and hope are ended.

For now no more remained of Enion in the distant air,
Only a voice eternal wailing in the elements.
205 Where Enion, blind and age-bent, wandered, Ahania wanders now.
She wanders in eternal fear of falling into the indefinite ;
For her bright eyes behold the abyss. Sometimes a little sleep
Weighs down her eyelids. Then she falls ; then, starting back in fear,
200 Sleepless to wander round, repelled on the margin of nonentity.

END OF THE THIRD NIGHT.

Night the Fourth.

But Tharmas rode on the dark abyss. The voice of Tharmas rolled
Over the heavy deluge. He saw Los and Enitharmon emerge
In strength and brightness from the abyss. His bowels yearned over
    them.
They rose in strength above the heaving deluge, in mighty scorn,
5 Red as the sun in the bright morning of the bloody day,
Tharmas beheld them, and his bowels yearnéd over them.

He said : Ah, Enion, wherefore do I feel such love and pity ?
How is this ? All my hope is gone ! Enion for ever fled !
Like a famished eagle, eyeless, raging in the vast expanse.
10 Incessant tears are now my food, incessant tears and rage.
Deathless for ever now I wander, seeking oblivion—
In torrents of despair—in vain. For if I plunge beneath,
Stifling I live. If dashed to pieces from a rocky height,
I re-unite in endless torment. Would I had never risen
15 From death's cold sleep beneath the bottom of the raging ocean.
And cannot those who once have loved ever forget their love ?
Are love and rage the same passion ? They are the same in me.
Are those who love like those who died, risen again from death,
Immortal in immortal torment never to be delivered ?
20 Is it not possible that one risen again from death
Can die ? When dark despair comes over, can I not then
Flow down into the sea and slumber in oblivion ?
Deformed I see these lineaments of ungratified desire.
The all-powerful curse of an honest man be upon Urizen and Luvah.
25 But thou, my son, glorious in brightness, comforter of Tharmas,
Go forth, rebuild this universe beneath my indignant power,
An universe of Death and Decay ! Let Enitharmon's hands

LIBRARY OF THE UNIVERSITY OF CALIFORNIA.

Weave soft delusive forms of man above my watery world,
Renew these ruined souls of men through Earth, Sea, Air and Fire,
30 To waste in endless corruption, renew those I will destroy.
Perhaps Enion may resume some little semblance yet
To ease my pangs of heart and to restore some peace to Tharmas.

Los answered in his furious pride, sparks issuing from his hair,
Hitherto shalt thou come, no further; here thy proud waves cease.
35 We have drunk up the Eternal Man by our unbounded power.
Beware lest we also drink up thee, rough Demon of the Waters.
Our God is Urizen, the King, King of the Heavenly hosts.
We have no other god but him, thou father of worms and clay.
And he is fallen into the deep, rough Demon of the waters,
40 And Los remains God over all, weak father of worms and clay.
I know I was Urthona, keeper of the gates of Heaven,
But now I am all-powerful Los, and Urthona is but my shadow.

Doubting stood Tharmas in the solemn darkness. His dim eyes
Swam in red tears. He reared his waves above the head of Los
45 In wrath; but pitying, back withdrew again with many a sigh.
Now he resolved to destroy Los, and now his tears rolled down.

In scorn stood Los, red sparks of blighting from his furious head
Flew o'er the waves of Tharmas. Pitying, Tharmas stayed his waves,
For Enitharmon shrieked amain, crying:—Oh, my sweet world,
50 Built by the Architect divine, whose love to Los and Enitharmon,
Thou rash abhorred Demon in thy fury hast o'erthrown!
What Sovereign Architect, said Tharmas, dare my will control?
For, if I will, I urge these waters: if I will, they sleep
In peace beneath my awful frown. My will shall be my law.

55 So saying, in a wave he raped bright Enitharmon far
Away from Los, but covered her with softest brooding care
On a broad wave in the far west, balming her bleeding wound.
Oh, how Los howled at the rending asunder! All the fibres rent
Where Enitharmon joined to his left side, in grinding pain.

60 He, falling on the rocks, bellowed his dolour, till the blood
Stanched. Then in ululation wailed his woes upon the wind.

But Tharmas called to the Dark Spectre, who upon the shores
With dislocated limbs had fallen. The spectre rose in pain,—
A shadow blue, obscure and dismal, like a statue of lead
65 Bent by its fall from a high tower, the dolorous shadow rose.
Go forth, said Tharmas, works of joy are thine: obey and live.
So shall the spongy marrow issuing from thy splintered bones
Bonify, and thou shalt have rest, when this thy labour is done.
Go forth, bear Enitharmon back to the Eternal Prophet,
70 Build her a bower in the midst of all my dashing waves;
Make first a resting place for Los and Enitharmon, then
Thou shalt have rest. If thou refusest, dashed abroad on all
My waves thy limbs shall separate in rottenness, and thou
Become a prey to all my demons of despair and hope.
75 The Spectre of Urthona, seeing Enitharmon, writhed
His cloudy form in jealous fears, and muttering thunders hoarse
And casting round thick glooms, his fierce pangs of heart thus uttered:

Tharmas, I know thee—how are we altered, our beauty decayed!
But still I know thee, though in this horrible ruin whelmed.
80 Thou, once the mildest son of heaven, art now a Rage become,
A terror to all living things. Think not I am ignorant
That thou art risen from the dead, or that, my power forgot,
I slumber here in weak repose. I remember the day,
The day of terror and abhorrence . . . . . .
85 When fleeing from the battle, thou fleeting, and, like the raven
Of dawn, outstretching an expanse where no expanse had been,
Drewest all the sons of Beulah into thy dread vortex, following
The eddying spirit down the hills of Beulah. All my sons
Stood round me at the anvil, where, new-heated, the red wedge
90 Of iron glowed furious, prepared for spades and mattocks hard.
Hearing the symphonies of war loud sounding, all my sons
Fled from my side. Then pangs smote me unknown before   I felt
My loins begin to break forth into veiny pipes and writhe

Before me in the wind, englobing, trembling with vibrations,
95 The bloody mass began to animate.   I, bending over,
Wept bitter tears incessant, still beholding how the form
Dividing and dividing from my loins, a weak and piteous
Soft cloud of snow, a female pale   I saw, and soft embraced
My counterpart, and called it love.   I named her Enitharmon.
100 But found myself and her together issuing down the tide
Which now our rivers were become, delving through caverns huge
Of gory blood, struggling to be delivered from our bonds.
She strove in vain.   Not so Urthona strove, for, breaking forth,
A shadow blue, obscure and dismal, from the breathing nostrils
105 Of Enion I issued to air, divided from Enitharmon.
I howled in sorrow.   I beheld thee rotting upon the rocks.
I, pitying, hovered over thee; I protected thy ghastly corse
From vultures of the deep; then wherefore shouldst thou rage as now
Against me who thee guarded in the night of death from harm?

110 Tharmas replied,—Art thou Urthona, my friend, my old companion,
With whom I lived in happiness before that deadly night
When Urizen gave the horses of light into the hands of Luvah?
Thou knowest not what Tharmas knows.   Oh! I could tell thee tales
That would enrap thee as it has enrapped me, even
115 From death in wrath and fury.   But now, come, arise, bear back
The lovéd Enitharmon   Thou hast her here before thine eyes.
But my sweet Enion is vanished, and I never more
Shall see her, unless thou, O Shadow, will protect this son
Of Enion, and him assist to bind the fallen king,
120 Lest he should rise again from death in all his dreary furor.
Bind him.   Take Enitharmon for thy sweet reward, while I
In vain am driven on false hope, the sister of despair.

Groaning the Terror rose, and drave his solid rocks before
Upon the tide, till underneath the feet of Los a world,
125 Dark, dreadful rose, and Enitharmon lay at Los's feet.
The dolorous shadow joyed.   Weak hope appeared around his head
Tharmas before Los stood, and thus the voice of Tharmas rolled.

Now all comes into the power of Tharmas. Urizen is fallen,
And Luvah hidden in the elemental forms of life and death.
130 Urthona is my son. Oh, Los, thou art Urthona, and Tharmas
Is God. The Eternal Man is sealed, never to be delivered.
I roll my floods over his body. My billows and waves pass over him,
The sea encompasses him and monsters of the deep are his companions,
Dreamer of furious oceans, cold sleeper of weeds and shells ˙
135 Thy eternal form shall never renew. My uncertain prevails against
    thee,
Yet though I rage, God over all, a portion of my life
That in eternal fields in comfort wandered with my flocks
At noon, and laid her head upon my wearied bosom at night ;—
She is divided. She is vanished, even like Luvah and Vala.
140 Oh, why did foul ambition seize thee, Urizen, Prince of Light ?
And thou, oh Luvah, Prince of Love, till Tharmas was divided ?
And I,—what can I now behold but an Eternal Death ?
Before my eyes, and an Eternal weary work to strive
Against the monstrous forms to breed among my silent waves,
145 Is this to be a God ? For rather would I be a Man,
To know sweet science, and to do with simple companions
Sitting beneath a tent and viewing sheepfolds and soft pastures.
Take thou the hammer of Urthona. Rebuild these furnaces.
Dost thou refuse ? Mind I the sparks that issue from thy hair ?
150 I will compel thee to rebuild by these my furious waves
Death choose or life. Thou strugglest in my waters now. Choose life,
And all the elements shall serve thee to their soothing flutes.
Their sweet inspiring lyres thy labour shall administer,
And they to thee only resist not. Faint not thou, my son,
155 Now thou dost know what 'tis to strive against the god of waters.

So saying, Tharmas on his furious chariots of the deep
Departed far into the unknown and left a wondrous void
Round Los. Afar his waters bore on all sides round with noise
Of wheels and horses' hoofs, and trumpets, horns and clarions.
160 Terrified, Los beheld the ruins of Urizen beneath

A horrible chaos to his eyes, a formless immeasurable death
Whirling up broken rocks on high into the dismal air,
And fluctuating all beneath in eddies of molten fluid.

Then Los with terrible hands seized on the Round Furnaces
165   Of Urizen : enormous work ; he builded them anew,
Labour of ages in the darkness and the wars of Tharmas
And Los formed anvils of hard iron petrific, for his blows
Petrify with incessant heating many a rock, a planet,
But Urizen slept in a stony stupor in the nether abyss,
170   A dreamful, horrible state in tossings on his icy bed
Freezing to solid all beneath.   His grey oblivious form
Stretched over the immense heaves in strong shudders silent
In brooding contemplations stretching out from north to south
In mighty power.   Round him always Los rolled furious,
175   His thund'rous wheels from furnace to furnace tending diligent
The contemplative Terror, frightened in his sorrowing sphere.
Frightened with cold infectious madness. In his hands the thundering
Hammer of Urthona, forming under his heavy hand,
The days and years in chains of iron round the limbs of Urizen,
180   Linked hour to hour, and day to night, night to day, year to year,
In periods of pulsative furor.   Mills he formed and works
Of many wheels resistless in the power of dark Urthona.

But Enitharmon wrapped in clouds wailed loud, for as Los beat
The anvils of Urthona link by link the chain of sorrow
185   Warping upon the winds and whirling round in the dark deep,
Lashed on the limbs of Enitharmon, and the sulphur fires
Belched from the furnaces wreathed round her chained in ceaseless fire.
The lovely female howled, and Urizen beneath deep groaned
Deadly, beneath the hammers beating, grateful to the ears
190   Of Los absorbed in dire revenge.   He drank with joy the cries
Of Enitharmon, and the groans of Urizen, fuel for wrath,
And for his pity secret, feeding on thoughts of cruelty.

The Spectre wept at his dire labours when from ladles huge
He poured the molten iron round the limbs of Enitharmon.

¹⁹⁵ But when he poured it round the bones of Urizen, he laughed
Hollow upon the hollow wind, his shadowy form obeying
The voice of Los, compelled he laboured round the furnaces.

And thus began the binding of Urizen, day and night in fear
Circling round the Demon, dark with howlings and dismay,
²⁰⁰ The prophet of Eternity beat on iron links and brass,
And as he beat, the hurtling Demon terrified at the shape
Enslaved humanity put on, became what he beheld
Raging against Tharmas, his god, and uttering aloud
Ambiguous words, blasphemous, filled with envy, firm resolved
²⁰⁵ On hate eternal in his vast disdain he laboured beating
The links of fate, link after link, an endless chain of sorrow.
The Eternal Mind bounded, began to roll. Eddies of wrath
Round and round, and the sulphurous foam now surging thick,
Settled, a bright and shining lake, as clear and white as snow.

²¹⁰ Forgetfulness, dumbness, necessity, in chains of the mind locked up,
In fetters of iron shrinking, disorganized, rent from Eternity,
Los beat on his fetters and heated his furnaces,

And poured iron solder and solder of brass.
Restless, the immortal, enchained, heaving dolorous,
²¹⁵ Anguished, unbearable, till a roof, shaggy, wild, enclosed
In an orb his fountain of thought.
In a horrible, dreamful slumber like the linked chain,
A vast spine writhed in torment upon the wind,
Shooting out pained roots like a bending cavern,
²²⁰ And bones of solidness froze over all his nerves of joy.
And a first age passed over and a state of dismal woe.

From the curves of his pointed spine down sunk with fright,
A red round globe hot burning, deep down into the abyss
Panting, conglobing, trembling, shooting out ten thousand branches

²²⁵ Around his solid bones, and a second age passed over him.
In harrowing fear rolling his nervous brain shot branches

Round the branches of his heart, ...
On high into two little orbs hiding in two little caves,
Hiding carefully from the wind.   His eyes beheld the deep,
230   And a third age passed over and a state of dismal woo.

The pangs of hope began, a heavy pain striving and struggling,
Two ears in close volutions from beneath his orbs of vision
Shot spiring out and petrified,
And a fourth age passed over and a state of dismal woe.

235   In ghastly torment sick, hanging upon the wind,
Two nostrils bent down to the deeps .   .   .   .
And a fifth age passed over, and a state of dismal woe

In ghastly torment sick, within his ribs bloated round
A craving hungry cavern; thence arose his channelled throat,
240   Like a red flame a tongue of hunger and of thirst appeared,
And a sixth age passed over and a state of dismal woe.

Enraged and stifled with torment, he threw his right arm to the north,
His left arm to the south, shooting out in anguish deep,
And his feet stamped the nether abyss in trembling and dismay,
245   And a seventh age passed over and a state of dismal woe.

The Council of God on high watching the Body
Of Man clothed in Luvah's robes of blood, beheld, and wept,
Descending over Beulah's mild moon-covered regions,
The daughters of Beulah saw the Divine Vision comforted.
250   And as a double female form, loveliness and perfection
They bowed their head and worshipped, and with mild voice spoke
        these words :

Lord Saviour, if Thou hadst been here our brother had not died,
And now we know that whatsoever thou wilt ask of God
He will give it Thee, for we are weak women and dare not lift
255   Our eyes to thy Divine pavilion, therefore in mercy thou
Appearest clothed in Luvah's garments that we may behold

And live. Behold Eternal Death is in Beulah; behold
We perish and shall not be found unless thou grant a place
In which may be hidden, under the shadow of wings.
200 If we who are but for a time and who pass away in winter
Behold these wonders of Eternity we shall consume.

Such were the words of Beulah, of the feminine emanations.
The Empyrean groaned throughout. All Eden was darkened.
The corse of Man lay on the rock. The Sea of Time and Space
205 Beat round the rocks in mighty waves, and as a polypus
That vegetates beneath the sea, the limbs of man vegetated
In monstrous forms of death, a human polypus of death.

The Saviour mild and gentle bent over the corse of death,
Saying,—If ye will but believe your brother shall rise again.
270 And first he found the limit of opacity and named it Satan
In Albion's bosom, for in every human bosom these limits stand.
And next he found the limit of contraction, and named it Adam,
While yet those beings were not born nor knew of good or evil.

Then wondrously the deeps beneath felt the Divine hand. Limit
275 Was put to Eternal Death. Los felt the limit and saw
The finger of God go forth and touch the seventh furnace in terror.
And Los beheld the hand of God over his furnaces
Beneath the deeps in dismal darkness beneath immensity.

In terror Los shrank from his task. His great hammer
280 Fell from his hand, his fires hid their mighty limbs in smoke.
For with noises ruinous, hurtling and clashing and groans,
The immortal endured, though bound in a deadly sleep.
Pale terror seized the eyes of Los as labouring he beat round.
The hurtling demon terrified as he beheld the shape
285 Enslaved Humanity put on: he became what he beheld;
He became what he was doing and he was himself transformed.
Spasms seized his muscular fibres writhing from his lips
Unwilling moved as Urizen howled, his loins wave like the sea,

At Enitharmon's shrieks his knees each other smote as he looked
200 With stony eyes on Urizen, and then swift writhed his neck
Involuntary to the couch where Enitharmon lay.
The bones of Urizen hurtle in the wind.   The bones of Los and his
    iron sinews bend like lead and fold
203 Into unusual forms, dancing, and howling, stamping the abyss.

END OF THE FOURTH NIGHT.

Night the Fifth.

——❦——

Infected, mad, he danced on his mountains high and dark as heaven,
Now fixed into one steadfast bulk his features stonify.
From his mouth curses, from his eyes issuing sparks of blighting,
Beside the anvil cold he danced with the hammer of Urthona.
5 Terrific, pale, Enitharmon stretched on the dreary earth,
Felt her immortal limbs freeze, stiffening, pale, inflexible.
His feet shrunk withering, from the deeps shrinking and withering,
And Enitharmon shrunk up, all their fibres withering
As plants withered by winter, leaves, stems, and roots decaying
10 Melt into thin air, while the seed, driven by the furious wind,
Rests on the distant mountain tops, so Los and Enitharmon
Shrunk into fixed space stood trembling on a rocky cliff,
Yet beauty, majesty, and bulk remained, but unexpansive.
As far as highest Zenith from the lowest Nadir they shrunk,
15 Los from the furnaces a space immense, and left the cold
Prince of Light bound in chains of intellect among the furnaces.
But all the furnaces were out and the bellows had ceased to blow.
He stood trembling and Enitharmon clung around his knees,
Their senses unexpansive in one steadfast bulk remained.
20 The night blew cold, and Enitharmon shrieked on the dismal wind.
Her pale hands cling around her husband, and over her weak head
Shadows of Eternal Death sit in the leaden air.

But the soft pipe, the flute and viol, organ, harp and cymbal,
And the sweet sound of silver voices calm the weary couch
25 Of Enitharmon, but her groans drown the immortal harps.
Loud and more loud the living music floats upon the air,
Faint and more faint the daylight waxes; wheels of turning darkness
Began in solemn revolutions. Earth convulsed with pangs
Rocked to and fro and cried out sore at the groans of Enitharmon.

4

30 Still the faint harps and silver voices calm the weary couch,
But from the caves of deepest night, ascending in clouds of mist,·
The winter spreads his wide black wings across from pole to pole,
Grim frost beneath, and terrible snow linked in a marriage chain
Began a dismal dance.   The winds around on pointed rocks .
35 Settled like bats innumerable, ready to fly abroad.
The groans of Enitharmon shake the skies, the labouring earth,
Till from her heart, rending his way, a terrible child sprang forth
In thunder, smoke, and sullen flames, and howlings, fury and blood.

Soon as his burning eyes were opened, looking on the abyss,
40 The horrible trumpets of the deep bellowed with bitter blasts,
The enormous demons woke and howled around the new-born king,
Crying Luvah, King of Love, thou art the king of rage and death.

Urizen cast deep darkness round him, raging, Luvah poured .
The spears of Urizen from chariots round the eternal tent.
45 Discord began, and yells and cries shook the wide firmament—

Where is sweet Vala, gloomy prophet?   Where the lovely form
That drew the body of Man from heaven into this dark abyss?
Soft tears and sighs, where are you?   Come forth!   Shout on bloody
        fields.
Show thy soul, Vala! show thy bow and quiver of secret fires.
50 Draw thy bow, Vala, from the depth of Hell, thy black bow draw,
And twang the bowstring to our Hautbois; let thine arrows black
Sing in the sky as once they sang upon the hills of light
When dark Urthona wept in torment of the secret pain,
He wept and he divided and he laid his gloomy head
55 Down on the rock of Eternity in darkness of the deep,
Torn by black storms and ceaseless torrents of consuming.fire.
Within his breast his fiery sons chained down and filled with cursing,
And breathing terrible blood and vengeance, gnashing his teeth with
        pain,
Let loose the Enormous Spirit on the darkness of the deep,

60 And his dark wife, that once fair crystal form divinely clear,
Within his ribs producing serpents whose souls are flames of fire.
But now the times return upon thee. Enitharmon's womb
Now holds thee, soon to issue forth. Sound, clarion of war,
Call Vala from her close recess in all her dark deceit,
65 Then rage on rage shall fierce redound out of her crystal quiver.

So sang the demons round red Orc, and round faint Enitharmon.
Sweat and blood stood on the limbs of Los. In globes his fiery eyelids
Faded. He roused, he seized the wonder in his hand, and went
Shuddering and weeping through the gloom and down into the deeps.

70 And Enitharmon nursed his fiery child in the dark deeps
Sitting in darkness: over her Los mourned in anguish fierce.
Covered with gloom this fiery boy grew, feeding on the milk
Of Enitharmon. Los around her builded pillars of iron,
And brass, and silver, and gold, fourfold, in dark prophetic fear,
75 For now he feared Eternal Death and uttermost extinction:
He builded Golgonooza on the lake of Udan Adan.
Upon the limit of translucence then he builded Laban.
Tharmas laid the foundation stone; Los finished it in howling woe.

But when fourteen summers, and winters, had revolvéd over
80 This solemn habitation, Los beheld the ruddy boy
Embracing his bright mother, and beheld malignant fires
In his young eyes, discerning plain that Orc plotted his death.

Grief rose upon his ruddy brows. A tightening girdle grew
Around his bosom like a bloody cord. In secret sobs
85 He burst it, but next morn another girdle soon succeeds
Around his bosom. Every day he viewed the fiery youth,
With silent fear, and his immortal cheeks drew deadly pale.
Till many a morn and many a night passed over in dire woe.
Forming a girdle in the day, and bursting it at night—
90 The girdle was always formed by day: but night 'twas burst in twain,
Falling down on the rock, an iron chain link by link locked.

4 *

Enitharmon beheld the bloody chain made of the nights and days,
Depending from the bosom of Los,—and how with grinding pain
He went each morning to his labours with the spectre dark,—
95 Called it the chain of jealousy. Now Los began to speak
His woes aloud to Enitharmon ; since he could not hide
His uncouth plague he seized the boy in his immortal hands,
While Enitharmon followed him, weeping in dismal woe,
Up to the iron mountain top, and there the jealous chain
100 Fell from his bosom on the mountain, and the spectre dark
Held the fierce boy. Los nailed him down, binding over his limbs
The accursed chain. O how bright Enitharmon howled and cried
Over her son. Obdurate, Los bound down his lovéd joy.

The hammer of Urthona smote the rivets in terror—of brass
105 Tenfold. The Demon's rage flamed forth tenfold with rending fires,
Roaring, resounding, loud, loud, louder, ever louder, fired,—
The darkness, warring with waves of Tharmas, and snows of Urizen,—
Crackling the flames went up with fury from the immortal Demon
Surrounded with flames the Demon grew, loud howling in his fires
110 Los folded Enitharmon in a cold white cloud, in fear
Then led her down into the deeps, and into his labyrinth,
Giving the spectre eternal charge over the howling fiend
Concentred into love of Parent, storgeous appetite, craving.

His limbs bound down mock at his chains, for over them a flame
115 Of circling fire unceasing plays to feed them with life, and bring
The virtues of the Eternal Worlds. Ten thousand thousand spirits
Of life lament around the Demon, going forth and returning.
At his enormous call they flee into the heavens of heavens,
And back return with wine and food, or dive into the deeps
120 To bring the thrilling joys of sense to quell his ceaseless rage.
His eyes, the lights of his large soul, contract, or else expand.
Contracted they behold the secrets of the infinite mountains,
The veins of gold and silver, and the hidden things of Vala,
Whatever grows from its pure bud, or wreathes a fragrant soul.
125 Expanded they behold the terrors of the Sun and Moon,

The elemental planets, and the orbs of eccentric fire.
His nostrils breathe a fiery flame, his locks are like the forests
Of wild beasts, there the lion glares, the tiger and wolf howl there,
And there the eagle hides her young in cliffs and precipices
130 His bosom is like the starry heavens expanded. All the stars
Sing round. There waves the harvest; the vintage rejoices there.
The springs flow into rivers of delight. Spontaneous flowers
Drink, laugh and sing; the grasshopper, the emmet and the fly,
The golden moth builds there a house and spreads her silken bed.
135 His loins inwove with silken fires are like a furnace fierce,
As the strong bull in summer time when bees sing round the heath,
When the herds low after the shadow and after the water-spring.
The murmurous flocks cover the mountains and shine along the valley,
His knees are rocks of adamant, ruby, and emerald,
140 Spirits of strength in palaces rejoice in golden armour
Armed with the spear and shield they drink and rejoice over the slain,
Such is the Demon, such his terror on the nether deep.

But when returned to Golgonooza Los and Enitharmon
Felt all the sorrow parents feel, they wept toward one another.
145 And Los repented that he had chained Orc upon the mountain.
And Enitharmon's tears prevailed. Parental love returned.
Though terrible his dread of that infernal chain, they rose
At midnight hasting to their much beloved care.
Nine days they travelled through the gloom of Entuthon Benython.
150 Los taking Enitharmon by the hand led her along
The dismal vales and up to the iron mountain tops where Orc
Howled in the furious wind. He thought to give to Enitharmon
Her son in tenfold joy, and to compensate for her tears
Even if his own death resulted, so much pity him pained.

155 But when they came to the dark rock and to the spectrous cave,
Lo, the young limbs had strucken root into the rock, and strong
Fibres had from the chain of jealousy inwove themselves
In a bright vegetation round the rock and round the cave,
And over the immortal limbs of the terrible fiery boy.

160 In vain they strove now to unchain, in vain with bitter tears
    To melt the chain of jealousy.   Not Enitharmon's death,
    Nor the consummating of Los could ever melt the chain.
    Nor could unroot the infernal fibres from their rocky bed.
    Nor all Urthona's strength, nor all the power of Luvah's bulls,
165 Though they each morning drag the unwilling sun out of the deep,
    Could uproot the infernal chain, for it had strucken root.
    Into the iron rock, and grew a chain beneath the earth,
    Even to the centre, wrapping round the centre and the limbs
    Of Orc, with fibres become one with him, a living chain
170 Sustained by the Demon's life.   Despair, terror, and woe and rage
    Enwrap the parents in cold clouds as they bend howling o'er
    The terrible boy, till fainting by his side, the parents fell.

    Not long they lay, Urthona's spectre found herbs of the pit.
    Rubbing their temples he revived them.   All their lamentations
175 I write not here, but all their after life was lamentation. ·

    When satiated with grief they returned back to Golgonooza,
    Enitharmon on the road of Dranthon felt the inmost gate
    Of her bright heart burst open and again close with a deadly pain.
    Within her heart Vala began to re-animate in bursting sobs,
180 And when this gate was open she beheld that dreary deep
    Where bright Ahania wept.   She also saw the infernal roots
    Of the chain of jealousy and felt rendings of howling Orc
    Rending the caverns like a mighty wind pent in the earth,
    Though wide apart as furthest north is from the furthest south.
185 Urizen trembled where he lay to hear the howling terror.
    The rocks shook, the eternal bars tugged to and fro were rifted.
    Outstretched upon the stones of ice the ruins of his throne
    Urizen shuddering heard, his trembling limbs shook the strong caves.

    The woes of Urizen shut up in the deep dens of Urthona.

190 Ah! how shall Urizen the king submit to this dark mansion?
    Ah! how is this? Once on the heights I stretched my throne sublime.

The mountains, once of silver, where the sons of wisdom dwelt,
And on whose tops the virgins sang, are rocks of desolation.

My fountains, once the haunt of swans, now breed the scaly tortoise,
195 The houses of my harpers are become a haunt of crows,
The gardens of wisdom are become a field of horrid graves,
And on the bones I drop my tears and water them in vain.

Once how I from my palace walked in gardens of delight,
The sons of wisdom stood around, the harpers came with harps,
200 Nine virgins clothed in light made songs to their immortal voices,
And at my banquet of new wine my head was crowned with joy.

Then in my ivory palaces I slumbered in the noon
And walkéd in the silent night among sweet-smelling flowers
Till on my silver bed I slept and sweet dreams hovered round,
205 But now my land is darkened and my wise men are departed.

My songs are turnéd into cries of lamentation
Heard on my mountains, and deep sighs under my palace roofs,
Because the steeds of Urizen, once swifter than the light,
Were kept back from my lord and from his chariot of mercies.

210 Oh, did I keep the horses of the day in silver pastures?
Oh, I refused the Lord of Day the horses of his Prince!
Oh, did I close my treasuries with roofs of solid stone
And darkened all my palace walls with envying and hate?

Oh, fool! to think that I could hide from his all-piercing eye
215 The gold and silver and costly stones, his holy workmanship!
Oh, fool! Could I forget the light that filled my bright spheres
Was a reflection of his face who called me from the deep.

I well remember, for I heard the mild and holy voice
Saying, Light spring up and shine, and lo, I sprang up from the deep.
220 He gave to me a silver sceptre, crowned with a golden crown,
And said, Go forth and guide my son who wanders on the ocean.

I went not forth, I hid myself on black clouds of my wrath,
I called the stars around my feet in the night of council dark,
The stars threw down their spears of light and fled naked away.
225   We fell.   I seized thee, dark Urthona, in my left hand falling.

I seized thee, beauteous Luvah; thou art faded like a flower
And like a lily thy wife Vala, withered by the winds.
When thou didst bear the golden cup at the immortal tables
Thy children smote their fiery wings, crowned with the gold of heaven.

230   Thy pure feet stept on steps divine, too pure for other feet,
And thy fair locks shadowed thine eyes from this divine effulgence,
And thou didst keep with strong Urthona the living gates of heaven,
But now thou art bowed down with him, even to the gates of hell.

Because thou gavest Urizen the wine of the Almighty
235   For steeds that they might run in the golden chariot of pride
I gave to thee the steeds of light, I poured the stolen wine,
And drunken with the immortal draught fell from my throne sublime.

I will arise, explore these dens, and find that deep pulsation
That shakes my cavern with strong shudders.   This may be the night
240   Of prophecy, and Luvah hath burst his way from Enitharmon
When thought is closed in caverns, love shows roots in deepest hell.

END OF THE FIFTH NIGHT.

Night the Sixth.

So Urizen arose and leaning on his spear explored his dens.
He threw his flight through the dark air to where a river flowed,
And taking off his silver helmet filled it and drank;
But when, his thirst being sated, he assayed to gather more,
5 Lo, three terrific women at the verge of the bright flood,
Who would not suffer him to approach but drove him back with storm.

Urizen knew them not, and thus addressed the spirits of darkness:
Who art thou, eldest woman, sitting wrapped in these thy clouds?
What is that name written upon thy forehead?   What art thou?
10 And wherefore dost thou pour this water forth in sighs and care?
She answered not, but filled her urn and poured it forth abroad.

Answerest thou not? said Urizen.   Then thou must answer me,
Thou terrible woman clad in blue, whose strong attractive power
Draws all into a fountain at the rock of thy attraction,
15 With frowning brow thou sittest, mistress of these mighty waters.
She answered not, but stretched her arms and threw her limbs abroad.

Or wilt thou answer, youngest woman clad in shining green?
With labour and care thou dost divide the current into four.
Queen of these dreadful rivers, speak, and let me hear thy voice.

20 Then Urizen raised his spear, but they reared up a wall of rock.
They gave a scream—they knew their father: Urizen knew his
      daughters.
They shrank into their channels dry,—the strand beneath his feet,—
Hiding themselves in rocky forms from the eyes of Urizen.
Then Urizen wept, and thus his lamentations poured forth:

23 Oh, horrible! Oh, dreadful state! Those whom I lovéd best,
On whom I poured the branches of my light, adorning them
With jewels and jealous ornament laboured with art divine,
Vests of the radiant colours of heaven and crowns of golden fire,—
I gave sweet lilies to their breasts and roses to their hair,
30 I taught them songs of sweet delight, I gave them tender voices
Into the blue expanse, and I made, with laborious art,
Sweet instruments of sound. In pride encompassing my knees
They poured their radiance above all. The Daughters of Luvah envied
At their exceeding brightness, and eternity sent gifts.
35 Now will I pour my fury on them, and I will reverse
The precious benediction. For their hues of loveliness
I will give blackness; frost for jewels; ill form for ornament;
For crowns, wreathed serpents; for sweet smell, corruptibility;
For voices of delight, hoarse croaking, inarticulate;
40 For laboured flattery, care and sweet instruction. I will give
Chains of dark ignorance and cords of twisted self-conceit
And whips of stern repentance, and the food of obstinacy,
That they may curse Tharmas, their god, and Los, his adopted son;
That they may curse and worship the dark demon of destruction;
45 That they may worship terrors and obey the violent.
Go forth, sons of my curse. Go forth, daughters of my abhorrence.

Then Tharmas heard the deadly scream across his watery world,
And Urizen's loud-sounding voice lamenting on the wind,
And he came riding in his fury. Frozen were his waves,
50 Silent in ridges he beheld them stand round Urizen,
A dreary waste of solid waters. For the king of light
Darkened his brows with his cold helmet, and his gloomy spear
Darkened before him. Silent on the ridgy waves he took
His gloomy way. Before him Tharmas fled, and flying fought,

55 Crying: What and who art thou, cold demon? Art thou Urizen?
Art thou, like me, risen again from death? or art thou deathless?
If thou art he, my desperate purpose hear, and give me death,

For death to me is better far than life,—death, my desire,
That I in vain by various paths have sought, but still I live.
60 The body of man is given to me. I seek in vain to destroy,
For still it surges forth in fish and monsters of the deeps,
And in these monstrous forms I live in an Eternal woe,
And thou, oh Urizen, art fallen, never to be delivered.
Withhold thy light from me for ever, and I will withhold
65 From thee thy food, so shall we cease to be, and all our sorrows
End, and the Eternal Man no more renew beneath our power.
If thou refusest, in eternal fight thy beams in vain
Shall pursue Tharmas, and in vain shall crave for food. I will
Pour down my flight through dark immensity Eternal, falling.
70 Thou shalt pursue me, but in vain, till starved upon the void
Thou hangest, a dried skin, shrunk up, weak, wailing in the wind.

So Tharmas spoke, but Urizen replied not, on his way
He took, high sounding over hills and deserts, floods and chasms.
Infinite was his labour, without end his travel. He strove
75 In vain, for hideous monsters of the deep annoyed him sore,—
Scaled and finned with iron and brass, devoured the path before him
Incessant with the conflict. On he bent his weary steps,
Making a path toward the dark world of Urthona. He rose
With pain upon the weary mountains, and with pain went down
80 And saw their grizzly fears, and his eyes sickened at the sight,
The howlings, gnashings, groanings, shriekings, shudderings, sobbings,
    burstings,
Mingled together, to create a world for Los. In delight
Los brooded on the darkness, nor saw Urizen's globe of fire
Lighting his dismal journey through the pathless world of death,
85 Writing in bitter tears and groans in books of iron and brass
The enormous wonders of the Abysses, once his brightest joy.

For Urizen saw the terrors of the Abyss wandering among
The ruined spirits once his children, and the children of Luvah
Scared at the sound of their sigh that seemed to shake immensity.

90   They wander moping, in their heart a sun and weary moon,
An universe of fiery constellations in their brain,
An earth of wintry woe beneath their feet, and round their loins
Waters or winds, or clouds, lightnings and pestilential plagues
Beyond the bounds of their own self their senses cannot reach.
95   As the tree knoweth not what is outside its leaves and bark,
And yet it drinks the summer joy and fears the winter sorrow,
So in the regions of the grave none knows his dark compeer
Though he partakes of his dire woes, though he returns the pang,
The throb, the dolor, the convulsion, in soul-sickening woes.
100   The horrid shapes and sights of torment in burning dungeons and
Fetters of red-hot iron, some with serpent crowns and some
With monsters girding round their bosoms. Some in sulphur beds,
On racks and wheels. He beheld women march in burning wastes
Of sand in bands of hundreds, fifties, thousands, stricken with
105   Lightnings which blazéd after on their shoulders in their march,
Successive volleys, with loud thunder. Swift flew the king of light
Over the burning deserts. Then the deserts passed in clouds
Of smoke, with myriads moping in the stifling vapours. Swift
Still flew the king, though flagged his powers, labouring, till over rocks
110   And mountains weary wandered he where multitudes were shut
Up in the solid mountains and in rocks their torment heaved.
Then came he among fiery cities, castles of fiery steel,
There beheld forms of Tigers, Lions, dishumanized men,
Many in serpents and in worms stretched out enormous length
115   Over the solid mould, and slimy tracks obstruct his way
Drawn out from deep to deep. Woven and ribbed
And scaléd monsters armed in iron shell, or shell of brass
Or gold, a glittering torment hissing in eternal pain,—
Columns of fire, or of water, sometimes stretched in height,
120   Sometimes in length, sometimes englobing, wandering in vain for ease
His voice to them was inarticulate thunder, for their ears
Were dull and heavy and their eyes and nostrils coséd up.
Oft he stood by a howling victim, questioning in words
Soothing or furious. No one answered, everyone wrapped up

125 In his own sorrow howled regardless of his voice, nor words
    Or sweet response could he obtain though oft assayed with tears.
    Oft would he stand and question a fierce scorpion glowing with gold
    In vain; the terror heard not.   Then a lion he would seize
    By the fierce mane, staying his howling course ; in vain the voice
130 Of Urizen, in vain the eloquent tongue.   Rock, mountain, cloud
    Were now not vocal as in climes of happy eternity.
    Where the lamb replies to the infant's voice and the lion to the wail
        of ewes,
    Giving them sweet instructions, when the cloud, or furrow'd field
    Talk with the husbandman and shepherd. But these attacked him sore,
135 Seizing upon his feet, rending the sinews, that in caves
    He had to revive his obstructed power with rest and oblivion.

    When he had passed the Southern terrors he approached the East,
    Void, pathless, beaten with eternal sleet, and eternal hail and rain.
    No form was there, no living thing, and yet his way lay through
140 This dismal world.   He stood awhile and looked back over his
    Terrific voyages—hills and dales of torment and despair—
    Sighing, and weeping a fresh tear.   Then turning round he threw
    Himself into the dismal void.   Falling he fell and fell,
    Whirling in unresistible revolutions down and down
145 In the horrid bottomless vacuity, falling, falling,
    Into the Eastern vacuity, the empty world of Luvah.

    The Ever-pitying One who seeth all things, saw his fall
    And in the dark vacuity created a bosom of clay.
    When wearied—dead—he fell, his limbs reposed in the bosom of slime.
150 As the seed falls from the sower's hand so Urizen fell, and death
    Shut up his powers in oblivion.   Then as the seed shoots forth
    In pain and sorrow, so the slimy bed his limbs renewed.
    At first an infant-weakness period passed.   He gathered strength,
    But still in solitude he sat.   Then rising threw his flight
155 Onward, though falling, through the waste of night ending in death
    And in another resurrection to sorrow and weary travail.
    But still his books he bore in his strong hands, and his iron pen,

For when he died they lay beside his grave, and when he rose
He seized them with a gloomy smile, for wrapped in his death-clothes
160 He hid them when he slept in death.   When he revived the clothes
Were rolléd by the winds ; the clothes remained still unconsumed
Still to be written and interleaved with brass and iron and gold,
Time after time, for such a journey none but iron pens
Can write, and adamantine leaves receive, nor can who goes
165 The journey obstinate refuse to write, time after time.
Endless had been his travail, but the Hand Divine him led
For infinite the distance and obscured by combustion dire.
By rocky masses flourishing in the abyss revolving erratic,
Round lakes of fire in this dark deep, the ruins of Urizen's world.

170 Oft would he sit in a dark rift and regulate his books
Or sleep such sleep as spirits eternal wearied in the dark
Tearful and sorrowful state, then arise, look out and ponder
His dismal voyage, eyeing the next sphere though far remote,
Then darting into the abyss of night his venturous limbs
175 Through lightnings, thunders, earthquakes and confusion, fires and
          floods,
Stemming his downward fate, labouring up against futurity.
Creating many a vortex, many a science in the deep,
And thence throwing his venturous limbs into the vast unknown.
Swift, swift from chaos to chaos, from void to void a road immense.
180 For when he came to where a vortex ceased to operate
Nor down nor up remained.   Then if he turned and lookéd back
From whence he came, 'twas upward all, and if he turned and viewed
The unpassed void upward was still his mighty wandering.
The midst between an equilibrium grey of air serene,
185 Where he might live in peace and where his life might meet repose.

But Urizen said, Can I not leave this world of cumbrous wheels
Circle over circle, nor on high attain a void
Where self-sustaining I may view all things beneath my feet
Or sinking through those elemental wonders, swift to fall,

190 I thought perhaps to find an end, a world beneath of voidness,
Whence I might travel round the outside of this dark confusion.
When I bend downward, bending my head down into the deep,
'Tis upward all which way soever I my course begin,
But when a vortex formed on high with labour, sorrow and care,
195 And weariness begins on all my limbs, then sleep revives
My wearied spirits. Waking then 'tis downward all which way
Soever I my spirits turn, no way I find of all.
Oh, what a world is here, and how unlike those climes of bliss
Where my sons gather round my knees! Oh, thou poor ruined world,
200 Thou horrible ruin! Once, like me, thou wast all glorious,
And now, like me, partaking desolate thy master's lot.
Art thou, oh ruin, the once glorious heaven on these thy rocks
Where joy sang on the trees and pleasure sported in the rivers,
And laughter sat beneath the oaks, and innocence sported round,
205 Upon the green plains, and sweet friendship met in palaces,
And books and instruments of song and pictures of delight?
Where are they? Whelmed beneath these ruins, in horrible destruction.
And if, eternal-falling, _ repose on the dark bosom
Of winds and waters, or thence fall into the void where air
210 Is not, downfalling through immensity ever and ever,
How my powers weakened every revolution, till a death
Shuts up my powers; then in womb of darkness as a seed
I dwell in dim oblivion. Over me, the enormous worlds
Reorganize in shooting forth, in bones and flesh and blood.
215 I am regenerate, to fall, or rise, at will, or remain
A labourer, a dire discontent, a living awe
Wandering in vain. Here will I fix my foot and here re-build.
These mountains of brass promise riches in their deepest bosom.

So saying he began to form of gold, silver and iron
220 And brass, vast instruments to measure out the immense and fix
The whole into another world better, and made to obey
His will, where none should dare oppose his will, himself being king.
Of all, and all futurity he bound in his vast chain

And the sciences were fixed and the vortexes began to work

225 On all the sons of men, and every human soul terrified
At the living wheels of heaven shrunk inward, withering away.
Gaining a new dominion over all his sons and daughters,
And over the sons and daughters of Luvah in the horrible abyss.
For Urizen made over them a selfish lamentation

230 Till a white woof his cold limbs covered o'er from head to feet,
Hair white as snow now covered him in flakey locks terrific,
Overspreading his limbs.　In pride he wandered weeping on,
Clothed in an aged venerableness, obstinately resolved,
Travelling through darkness, and wherever he travelled a dire web

235 Followed behind him, as the web of a spider dusky and cold,
Shivering across the vortexes, drawn from his mantle of years,
A living mantle joined to his life and growing from his soul,
And the web of Urizen stretched, direful, shivering, as clouds
And uttering such woes, and bursting with such thunderings.

240 The eyelids expansive as morning and the ears
As a golden ascent winding round to the heaven of heavens—
Within the dark horror of the abyss, lions or tigers, or scorpions.
For everyone opened into Eternity at will,
But they refused, because their outstretched forms were in the abyss

245 And the wing-like tent of the universe, beautiful, surrounding all,
Or drawn up or let down again at will of the immortal man,
Vibrated in such anguish as the eyelids quivered, weak,
That weaker their expansive orbs began again to shrink,
Pangs smote through all the brain and then a universal shriek.

250 Torment on torment through the abysses ran, rending the web.

Thus Urizen in sorrows wandered many a weary way
Warring with monsters of the deep in hideous pilgrimage
Till his bright hair scattered in snows, his skin barked o'er with
    wrinkles,
Four caverns rolling downwards, their foundations thrusting forth

255 The metal, rock, and stone in painful throes of vegetation.
The cave of Orc stood in the south, a furnace of dire flames,

Quenchless, unceasing. In the west the cave of Urizen ;—

For Urizen fell, as midday sun falls down, into the west.
North stood Urthona's steadfast throne, a world of solid dark,
260 Obstruction stifling, shut up, rooted in dumb despair.
The East was void. But Tharmas rolled his waves in ceaseless eddies
All through the caverns of fire, air, and earth, seeking in vain
For Enion's limbs, nought finding but black sea and sickening slime
Flying away from Urizen that he might not give him food,
265 Above, beneath, on all sides round, in the deep of immensity,
That he might starve the sons and daughters of Urizen on the wind,
Making between horrible chasms with the vast unknown.
All these around the world of Los cast forth their monstrous births.

But in Eternal times the seat of Urizen in the south,
270 Urthona in the north, Luvah in east, Tharmas in west.

And now he came into the abhorred world of dark Urthona,
By Providence Divine conducted, not bent by his own will
Lest Death Eternal be the result,—for the will cannot be violated,—
Into the doleful vales where no tree grew or ruin flowed,
275 No man nor beast nor creeping thing, nor sun nor cloud nor star,
Till with his globe of fire immense, held in his venturous hand,
He bore on through the affrighted vales, ascending and descending,
And wearied in his cumbrous flight he ventured o'er dark rifts,
Or down dark precipices, or with pain and labour climbed,
280 Till from Urthona's peaked rock he saw the world of Los,
And heard the howling of red Orc distincter and distincter.

Redoubling his immortal effort, through the narrow vales
With difficulty down descending, guided by his ear
And by his globe of fire, he went down through Urthona's vale
285 Between the enormous iron walls built by the Spectre, dark,
Dark grew his globe reddening with mists, and full before his path,
Standing across the narrow vale the shadow of Urthona
A spectre vast appeared, whose legs and feet, with iron scaled,

. 5

Stamped the hard rocks expectant of the unknown wanderer
290 Whom he had seen wandering his nether world when distant far,
And watched his swift approach.   Collected, dark, the spectre stood.
Beside him Tharmas stayed his flight and stood with stern defiance,
Communing with the spectre who rejoiced along the vale.
Around his loins a girdle glowed with many coloured fires,
295 And in his hand a knotted club whose knots like mountains frowned,
Desert among the stars there withering with its ridges cold.
Black scales of iron arm the dread image.   Iron spikes instead
Of hair shoot from his orbéd skull, the while his glowing eyes
Burned like two furnaces   He called with voice of thunder loud.

300 Four winged heralds mount the furious blast and blow their trumps
Gold, silver, brass, and iron clangours, clamouring, rend the shore.
Like white clouds rising from the vales, his armies fifty-two
Around the spectre, glowing, from Urthona's four cliffs rise.
Four sons of Urizen the squadrons of Urthona led, in arms
305 Of gold and silver, brass and iron: he knew his mighty sons.

Then Urizen arose upon the wind, back many a mile,
Returning into his dire web, scattering fleecy snows
As he ascended howling.   Loud the net vibrated strong.
From heaven to heaven and globe to globe its vast eccentric paths,
310 Compulsive rolled the comets at his dread command their way,
Falling with wheel impetuous down among Urthona's vales
And round red Orc, to Urizen returning, gorged with blood.
Slow roll the massy globes at his command, and slow o'erwheel,
The dismal squadrons of Urthona weaving the dire web
315 In this progression, and preparing Urthona's path before him.

END OF THE SIXTH NIGHT.

Night the Seventh.

———◆◆———

Then Urizen arose. The spectre fled, and Tharmas fled ;
The darkening spectre of Urthona hid beneath a rock.
Tharmas threw his impetuous flight through the deeps of immensity
Revolving round in whirlpools fierce all round the caverned worlds.

5   But Urizen went silent, down to caves of Orc, and saw
A caverned universe of fire. The horses of Urizen
Here bound to fiery mangers, furious dash their golden hoofs,
Striking fierce sparkles from their golden fetters. Fierce his lions
Howl in the burning dens ; his tigers roam on redounding smoke
10 In forests of affliction. The adamantine scales of justice
Consuming in the raging lamps of mercy poured in rivers.
The holy oil rages through all the caverned rocks. Fierce flames
Dance on the rivers and the rocks, howling and drunk with fury.
The plough of ages and the golden harrow wade through fields
15 Of gory blood. The immortal seed is nourished for the slaughter.
The bulls of Luvah, breathing fire, bellow on burning pastures
Round howling Orc, whose awful limbs cast forth red smoke and fire,
That Urizen approached not near but took his seat on a rock
And ranged his books around him, brooding envious over Orc.

20 Howling and rending his dark caves the awful demon lay :
Pulse after pulse beat on his fetters, pulse after pulse his spirit
Dashed and dashed higher and higher to the shrine of Enitharmon,
As when the thunder folds himself in robe of thickest clouds,
The watery nations couch and hide in the profoundest deeps,
25 Then bursting from his head, with dreadful face and flaming hair,
His swift-winged daughters sweep across the vast blue ocean.

5 *

Los felt the envy in his limbs, like to a blighted tree ;
For Urizen fixed in envy sat brooding and covered with snow,
His book of iron on his knees. He traced the dreadful letters
30 While his snows fell and his storms beat to cool the flames of Orc,
Age after age, till underneath his heel a deadly root
Struck through the rock,—the root of Mystery, accursed, shooting up
Branches into the heaven of Los, then pipe-formed bending down
Take root again where'er they touch, and, again branching forth
35 In intricate labyrinths overspreading many a grizzly deep.

Amazéd started Urizen, finding him compassed round
And high roofed over with the trees. He arose, but now the stems
Stood so thick, he with difficulty and with great pain brought
The books out of the dismal shade,—all but the book of iron.

40 Again he took his seat, again he ranged his books around
On a rock of iron frowning over the foaming fires of Orc.
And Urizen hung over Orc and viewed his terrible wrath,
Sitting upon an iron crag. At length his words broke forth :

Image of dread, whence art thou ? Whence is thy most woeful place ?
45 Whence these fierce fires, but from thyself ? No other living thing
In all the chasm I behold. No other living thing
Dare my most terrible wrath abide, bound here to waste in pain.
Thy vital substance in these fires that issue new and new
Around thee. Sometimes like a flood, and sometimes like a rock
50 Of living pangs, thy horrible bed glowing with ceaseless fires
Beneath thee and around. Above, a shower of fire now beats
Moulded to globes and arrowed wedges, rending thy bleeding limbs.
And now a whirling pillar of burning sand to overwhelm thee,
Steeping thy wounds in salts infernal and in bitter anguish.
55 And now a rock moves on the surface of this lake of fire
To bear thee down beneath the waves in stifling despair.
Pity for thee moved me to break my dark and long repose,
And to reveal myself before thee in a form of wisdom.
Yet thou dost laugh at all these tortures, and this horrible place,

60 Yet throwest these fires abroad, that back return upon thee now,
While thou reposest, throwing rage on rage, feeding thyself
With visions of sweet bliss far other than this burning clime.
Sure thou art bathed in rivers of delight on verdant fields,
Walking in joy in bright expanses, sleeping on bright clouds,
65 With visions of delight so lovely that they urge thy rage
Tenfold with fierce desire to rend thy chains and howl in fury,
And dire oblivion of all woe and desperate repose,—
Or is thy joy founded on torment that others bear for thee?

Orc answered: Curse thy hoary brows, what dost thou in this deep?
70 Thy pity I contemn. Go forth, scatter thy snows elsewhere.
I rage in the deep, my feet and hands are nailed to the burning rock,
Yet my fierce fires are better than thy snows. Shuddering thou sitt'st.
Thou art not chained. Why should'st thou sit, cold, grovelling demon
    of woe,
In torture of dire coldness? Now a lake of water deep
75 Sweeps over thee, freezing to solid. Still thou sitt'st, closed up
In that transparent rock as if in joy of thy bright prison,
Till, overburdened with its weight, down through immensity,
With a crash breaking clear across, the horrid mass comes down,
Thundering, and hail and frozen iron hailed from the element,
80 Rend thy white hair. Yet thou dost, fixéd, obdurate, brooding, sit
Writing thy books. Anon a cloud, filled with a waste of snow,
Covers thee. Obdurate still, resolved still, and writing still,
Though rocks roll o'er thee, though floods pour, though winds black
    as the sea
Cut thee in gashes, though the blood pour down around thy ancles,
85 Freezing thy feet to the hard rock. Still thy pen obdurate
Traces the wonders of Futurity in horrible fear of the future.
I rage here furious in the deep: my feet and hands are nailed
To the hard rock, or thou should'st feel my enmity and hate
In all diseases falling on thy grey accursed front.

90 Urizen answered: Read my books, explore my constellations,

Enquire of my sons and they shall teach thee how to war.
Enquire of my daughters, who, accursed in the dark deeps,
Knead bread of sorrow by my stern command, for I am god
Of all this ruin.   Rise, oh daughters, at my stern command.

95 Rending the rocks, Eleth and Uvith rose, and Ona rose,
Terrific with their iron vessels, driving them across
In the dim air.   They locked the book of iron, and placed above
On clouds of death, and sang their songs, kneading the bread of Orc.

Orc listened to the song, compelled, hungering on the cold wind
100 That swaggéd heavy with the accursed dough.   The hoar frost raged
Through Ona's sieve.   The torrent rain poured from the iron pail
Of Eleth, and the icy hands of Uvith kneaded bread.

The heavens bow with terror underneath these iron hands,
Singing at their dire work the words of Urizen's book of iron,
105 While the enormous scrolls rolled dreadful in the heavens above;
And still the burden of their song in tears was pouréd forth.
The bread is kneaded, let us rest, oh cruel father of children !

But Urizen remitted not their labours on his rock,
And Urizen read on his book of brass in sounding tones :
110 Listen, oh daughters, to my voice ; listen to the words of wisdom.
To bring the shadow of Enitharmon beneath our wondrous tree,
That Los evaporate away like smoke, and be no more.
Draw Enitharmon down unto the spectre of Urthona,
And let him have dominion over Los, the terrible shade.

115 Compel the poor to live upon a crust with soft mild arts,
So shall you govern over all.   Let duty tune your tongue,
And be your hearts far harder than the nether milestone is.
Smile when they frown, frown when they smile, and when a man
          looks pale
With labour and abstinence, then say healthy and glad he seems,
120 And when his children sicken let them die.   There are enough

Born, even too many, and our earth will soon be overrun
Without these arts. If you would make the poor with temper live,
With pomp give every crust of bread you give; by gracious cunning
Magnify gifts; reduce the man to want, then give with pomp.
125 Say, if you hear him sigh, he smiles; if pale, say he is ruddy.
Preach temperance: say that he is overgorged, and drowns his wit
In strong drink, though you know that bread and water must be all
He can afford. Flatter his wife, pity his children, till
We can reduce all to our will, like spaniels taught with art.

130 Lo! how the heart and brain are forméd in the breeding womb
Of Enitharmon. How it breeds with life and forms the bones,
The little heart, the liver, the red blood in labyrinths,
By gratified desire, devouring appetite, she fills
Los with ambitious fury that his race shall all devour.

135 Then Orc cried: Curse thy cold hypocrisy! Around thy tree
In scales that shine with gold and rubies, thou beginn'st to weaken
My divided spirit. Like a worm I rise in peace, unbound
From wrath. Now when I rage my fetters bind me more.
Oh, torment! oh, torment! A worm compelled! Am I a worm?
140 Is it in strong deceit that man is born? In strong deceit
Thou dost restrain my fury that the worm may bind the tree.
Avaunt, cold hypocrite! Thou could'st not use me thus unchained.
The Man shall rage, bound with this chain, the worm in silence creep.
Thou wilt not cease from rage. Grey demon, silence all thy storms,
145 Give me example of thy mildness. King of furious hail,
Art thou the cold, attractive power that holds me in this chain?
I well remember how I stole thy light and it became fire,
Consuming. Now thou knowest me, Urizen, Prince of Light,
And I know thee. Is this the triumph? This the golden state
150 That lies beyond the bounds of science on the grey obscure?

Terrified Urizen heard Orc, now certain that he was Luvah.
And creeping Orc began to organize a serpent-body,

Despising Urizen's light and turning it to flaming fire,
Receiving as a poisoned cup receives the heavenly wine,
155 And turning affliction into fury, thought into abstraction,—
A self-consuming, dark devourer, raging into the heavens.

Urizen, envying, brooding, sat and saw the secret terror
Flame high in pride and laugh to scorn the source of his deceit,
Nor knew the source of his own, but thought himself the author sole
160 Of all his wandering experiments on the horrible abyss.
He knew that weakness stretches out in length and breadth, and knew
That wisdom reaches high and deep; and therefore he made Orc
In serpent form compelled to stretch out and up the mysterious tree.
He suffered him to climb that he might draw all human forms
165 Unto submission to his will, nor knew the dread result.

Los sat in showers of Urizen watching cold Enitharmon.
His broodings rush down to his feet, producing eggs that hatching
Burst forth upon the winds above the tree of Mystery.
Enitharmon lay on his knees. Urizen traced his verses.
170 In the dark deep the dark tree grew. Her shadow was drawn down,
Down to the roots; it wept o'er Orc,—the shadow of Enitharmon.

Los saw her stretched, the image of death, upon his withered valleys;
Her shadow went forth and returned. Now she was pale as snow,
When the mountains and hills are covered, and the paths of men
     shut up.
175 But when her spirit returned, as ruddy as morning when
The ripe fruit blushes into joy in heaven's eternal halls,
Sorrow shot through him from his feet and shot up to his head,
Like a cold night that nips the roots and scatters all the leaves.
Silent he stood o'er Enitharmon, watching her pale face.
180 He spoke not, he was silent, till he felt the cold disease.
Then Los mourned on the dismal wind in his jealous lamentation.

Why cannot I enjoy thy beauty, lovely Enitharmon?
When I return from clouds of grief in the wandering elements,

When thou in thrilling joy, in beaming summer loveliness,
185 Delectable reposest, ruddy in my absence, flaming with beauty,
Cold, pale in sorrow at my approach, trembling at my terrific
Forehead and eyes thy lips decay like roses in the spring.
How art thou shrunk! Thy grapes that burst in summer's ripe excess
Shut up in little purple covering faintly bud and die.
190 Thy olive-trees that poured down oil upon a thousand hills
Sickly look forth and scarcely stretch their branches to the plain.
Thy roses that expanded in the face of glowing morn
Hid in a little silken veil scarce breathe and faintly shine.
Thy lilies that gave light what time the morning lookéd forth
195 Hid in the vales, faintly lament, and no one hears their voice.
All things beside the woeful Los enjoy delights of beauty!
Once how I sang and called the beasts and birds to their delight,
Nor knew that I alone, exempted from the joys of love,
Must war with secret monsters of the animating worlds.
200 Oh, that I had not seen the day! Then should I be at rest!
Nor felt the strivings of desire, nor longings after life,
For life is sweet to Los the wretched. To his winged woes
Is given a craving cry: they sit at night on barren rocks,
And whet their beaks and snuff the air, and watch the opening dawn,
205 And shriek till at the smell of blood they stretch their bony wings,
And cut the winds like arrows shot by troops of destiny.

Thus Los lamented in the night, unheard by Enitharmon.
Her shadow descended down the tree of mystery.
The spectre saw the shadow shivering o'er his gloomy rocks
210 Beneath the tree of mystery, which in the dismal abyss
Began to blossom in fierce pain, shooting its writhing buds
In throes of birth, and now, the blossoms falling, shining fruit
Appeared, of many colours and of poisonous qualities.
Of plagues, hidden in shining globes that grew on the living tree,

215 The spectre of Urthona saw the shadow of Enitharmon
Beneath the tree of Mystery among the leaves and fruit,

Reddening the demon strong prepared the poison of sweet love,
He turned from side to side in tears. He wept and he embraced
The fleeting image, and in whispers mild woo'd the faint shade.

220 Loveliest delight of men; oh ! Enitharmon, shady, hiding
In secret places where no eye can trace thy watery way,
Have I found thee ?   Have I found thee ?   Tremblest thou in fear ?
Because of Orc ?   Because he rent his loud discordant way
From thy sweet loins of bliss ?   Red flow'd thy blood on that dread
       day,
225 Pale grew thy face. Around the thundering horror lightnings played
Over thee, and the terrible Orc, and rent his discordant way,
But the next joy of thine shall be in sweet delusion,   .
Its birth in faintings and in sleep, delusions sweet of Vala.

The shadow of Enitharmon answered, Art thou, terrible shade,
230 Set over this sweet boy of mine to guard him lest he rend
His mother to the winds of heaven, intoxicated with fruit
Of this delightful tree? Behold, I cannot flee away
From thy embrace, else be assured so horrible a form
Should never in my arms repose. Now listen, I will tell |
235 The secrets of Eternity which ne'er before unlocked
My golden lips, nor took the bar from Enitharmon's breast;
Among the flowers of Beulah walked th' Eternal Man, and saw
Vala, the lily of the desert. Melting in high noon
Upon her bosom in sweet bliss he fainted. Wonder seized
240 All heaven, for they saw him dark. They built a golden wall
Round Beulah. There he revelled in delight among the flowers.
Vala was pregnant and brought forth Urizen, Prince of Light,
First-born of generation. Then a wonder to the eyes
Of the now fallen man, a double form Vala appeared, a male
245 And female shuddering. Pale at sight the fallen man recoiled,
And calling the Enormity, Luvah and Vala, turned
Down vales to find his way back into heaven, but found none.
For his frail eyes were faded, and his ears heavy and dull.

Urizen grew up in the plains of Beulah. Many sons
250 And many daughters flourished round the holy tent of man
Till he forgot Eternity, delighted in his sweet joy,
Among his family, his flocks and herds, and tents and fields.

But Luvah close conferred with Urizen in darksome night
To bind the father and enslave the brethren. Nought he knew
255 Of sweet Eternity. The blood flow'd round the holy tent and river;
All Beulah from its hinges fell, uttering its final groan
In dark confusion. Meantime Los was born and Enitharmon,
But how, I know not. Then forgetfulness quite wrapped me up
A period, nor do I more remember, till I stood
260 Beside Los in the cave, enslaved to vegetative forms
According to the will of Luvah, who assumed the place
Of the Eternal Man and smote him. But thou, Spectre dark,
Must find a way to punish Vala in the fiery south,
To bring her down subjected to the rage of my fierce boy.

265 The Spectre said, Thou lovely vision, this delightful tree
Is given us for a shelter from the storms of void and solid,
Till once again the morn of ages shall renew on us,
To re-unite in those mild fields of happy Eternity,
Where thou and I in undivided essence walked abroad
270 Imbodied,—thou my garden of delight, and I the spirit
Mutual dwelt in one another, mutual joy revolving.
Eternal days with Tharmas mild and Luvah sweet, melodious,
Upon our waters; thou rememberest, Sisters, I will tell
What thou forgetest. They in us and we in them have lived,
275 Drinking the joys of Universal Mankind. One dread morn—
Listen, oh Vision of Delight,—one morn of gory blood
The Manhood was divided. Gentle passions making way
Through th' infinite labyrinth of the heart and nostrils issuing,
In odorous stupefaction, stood before the eyes of Man
280 A female bright. I stood beside my anvil dark, a mass

Of iron glow'd bright prepared for spade and plough-share, sudden
    down
I sunk with cries of blood, issuing downward in the veins
Which now my rivers were become, rolling in tube-like forms
Shut up within themselves descending down. I sunk along
285 The gory tide even to the place of seed. Divided there
I was in darkness and oblivion. Thou an infant woe,
And I an infant terror in the womb of Enion.
My masculine spirit scorning the frail body issued forth
From Enion's brain, in this deformed form, leaving thee there
290 Till times passed over thee, my spirit still returning hovered
And formed a male, to be a counterpart to thee, oh love,
Darkened and lost ! In due time issuing forth from Enion's womb
Thou and that demon Los were born. Ah, jealousy and woe!
Ah, poor divided dark Urthona, now a Spectre wandering,
295 In deeps of Los, the slave of that creation I created.
I labour night and day for Los, but listen thou my vision,
I view futurity with thee. I will bring down soft Vala
To the embraces of this terror, and I will destroy
The body I created ; then shall we unite in bliss.
300 For till these terrors planted round the gates of Eternal life
Are driven away, annihilated, we cannot repass the gates.
Thou knowest that the Spectre is in every man, insane, brutish,
Brutish, deformed, that I am thus a ravening lust continually
Craving, devouring ; but my eyes are upon thee, oh lovely
305 Delusion, and I cannot crave except for thee : not so
The Spectres of the dead : I am the Spectre of the living.

Although filléd with tears, the spirit of Enitharmon beheld
And heard the Spectre. Bitterly she wept, embracing fervent
Her once loved Lord, now but a shade, herself also a shade,
310 Conferring times on times among the branches of that tree.
Thus they conferred among th' intoxicating fumes of Mystery
Till Enitharmon's shadow, pregnant in the deeps beneath,
Brought forth a wonder horrible, while Enitharmon shrieked

And trembled through the worlds above, and Los wept, terrified
315 At the shrieks of Enitharmon and her tossings, nor perceived
The cause of her dire anguish, for she lay the image of death,
Moved by strong shudders till her shadow was delivered, then
Raving ran through the upper elements in maddening fury.

She burst the gates of Enitharmon's heart with direful crash,
320 Nor could they e'er be closed again, the golden hinges were broke,
And the gates broken in sunder, and their ornaments defaced
. Beneath the tree of Mystery, for the immortal shade
Brought forth this wonder horrible. A cloud she grew and grew
Till many of the dead burst through the bottoms of their tombs
325 In male forms without female counterparts or emanations,
Cruel and ravening with envy, hatred, and with war,
In dreams of Ulro, dark, delusive, drawn by the lovely shade.

The Spectre, terrified, gave her charge over the howling Orc,
Men took the tree of Mystery cast in the world of Los.
330 Its top boughs shoot a fibre beneath Enitharmon's couch,
The double-rooted labyrinth soon waved around their heads.

The Spectre entered Los's bosom. Every sigh and groan
Of Enitharmon bore Urthona's Spectre on its wings,
Obdurate Los felt pity; Enitharmon told the tale
335 Of Urthona. Los embraced the Spectre as a brother first,
Then as another self, astonished, humanizing in tears
In self-abasement giving up his domineering lust.

Thou never canst embrace sweet Enitharmon. Demon dread,
Thou art united with thy Spectre, to consume by pains
340 That mortal body, and by self-annihilation come
Back to Eternal Life to be assured I am thy self,
Though thus divided from thee and the slave of every passion
Of thy fierce soul. Unbar the gates of memory: look on me
Not as another, but as thy real self. I am thy Spectre,

345 Though horrible and ghastly to thine eyes, buried beneath
The ruins of the universe. Hear what, inspired, I speak;
If we unite in one another bitter worlds will be
Opened within your heart and in your loins and wondrous brain
Threefold, as in Eternity, and this fourth universe
350 Will be renewéd by the three, consumed in mental fires.
Thou didst subdue me in old times by thy immortal power
When I was ravening hungry, thirsting cruel, murder and lust,
But if thou dost refuse another body will be prepared
For me, and thou annihilate, vanish and be no more.
355 For thou art but a form and organ of life, and of thyself
Art nought, by Mercy and Love Divine continually created.

Los answered, Spectre horrible, thy words astound my ear
With irresistible conviction. I feel I am not of those
Who, when convinced, persist, though furious, controllable
360 By Reason's power. I already feel a world within
Opening its gates, and in it all the real substances
Of which these in the outer world are shadows which pass away.
Come then into my bosom, in thy shadowy arms, with thee
Bring lovely Enitharmon. I will quell my fury and teach
365 Peace to the soul of dark revenge, and repentance to cruelty.

So spoke Los, and embracing Enitharmon and the Spectre,
Clouds would have folded round in love and extacy uniting,
But Enitharmon trembling, fled and hid beneath Urizen's tree,
But mingling together with his spectre, the Spectre of Urthona
370 Wondering, beheld the centre opened. By Divine Mercy inspired,
He in his bosom gave tasks to Los, enormous, to destroy
That body he created, but in vain, though Los performed wonders of
    labour. . . .
They builded Golgonooza, Los builded the pillars high,
And domes terrific in the nether heavens, for beneath
375 Was opened a new heaven, a new earth beneath within,
Threefold within the brain, within the heart, within the loins

A threefold atmosphere continuous from Urthona's world,
But yet having a limit twofold named Satan and Adam,
But Los stood on the limit of translucence weeping, trembling,
380 Filled with doubts in self-accusation beheld the fruit
Of Urizen's mysterious tree, for Enitharmon spake.

When in the deeps beneath I gathered of this ruddy fruit,
It was by that I knew that I had sinnéd, and I knew
That, without ransom, I could not be saved from Eternal death.
385 That life lives upon death, and by devouring appetite
All things subsist on one another. Thenceforth in despair
I spend my glowing times, but thou art strong, and mighty thou
To bear this self-contrition. Take, then, eat thou also of
The fruit, and give me proof of life eternal or I die.

390 Then Los pluckéd the fruit and eat and sat down in despair,
And must have surely given himself to death eternal, but
Urthona's spectre ministering within him comforted,
As medium between him and Enitharmon, but this union
Was not to be effected without cares and sorrows and troubles,
395 Six thousand years of self-denial and of bitter contrition.

Urthona's Spectre, terrified, saw the spectres of the dead,
Each male without a counterpart, without a concentering vision,
The Spectre wept before Los, saying, Behold I am the cause
That this dim state commences. I begin the dreadful state
400 Of separation, and on my dark head the punishment
Must fall unless a way be found to ransom and redeem.
But I have this, my counterpart,—given miraculous.
These spectres have no counterparts, therefore they raven thus
Without the food of life. Let us create them counterparts.
405 The Spectre is Eternal Death, without a created body.
Los trembling, answered : Now I feel the weight of stern repentance,
Tremble not so, my Enitharmon, at the awful gates
Of thy poor broken heart. I see thee like a shadow withering

As on the outside of existence.   But behold, take comfort,
410 Turn inwardly thine eyes, and there behold the Lamb of God
Clothéd in Luvah's robes of blood descending to redeem.
Oh, Spectre of Urthona, take comfort!   Enitharmon,
Could'st thou but cease from terror, and from trembling and affright,
When I appear before thee in forgiveness of injuries,
415 Why should'st thou remember to be afraid ?
Often enough thy jealousy and terror convince.   I have died in pain.
Come hither ; patient be ; let us converse together, for
I also tremble at myself and all my former life.

Enitharmon answered : I behold the Lamb of God descending
420 To meet the spectres of the dead.   I therefore fear that he
Will give us to Eternal death for punishment, for such
Hideous offenders' last extinction is eternal pain.
An ever-dying life of stifling and obstruction, shut
Out of existence to be a sign, and terror to who see.
425 Lest any in futurity should do as we in heaven,
Such is our state, nor will the Son redeem us, but destroy,

So Enitharmon spoke trembling, and in torrents of tears
Los sat in Golgonooza at the gate of Laban, where
He had created porches where branched the mysterious tree.
430 Where the spectrous dead wail ; sighing thus he spoke to Enitharmon.

Lovely delight of men, Enitharmon, shady refuge from war,
Thy bosom translucent is a soft repose for weeping souls
Of piteous victims of battle, where they sleep, happy, obscure.
They feed upon our life.   We are their victims.   Stern desire
435 I feel to make embodied semblances in which the dead
May live in our palaces and in our gardens of labour,
Which now, opened within the centre, we behold spread round
To form a world of sacrifice of brothers, sons, and daughters,
To comfort Orc in his dire sufferings.   Look, my fires afresh
440 Before my face assembling with delight as in old times !
Enitharmon spread her beamy locks upon the wind, and said—

Oh ! wonder of Eternity, Los, my defence and guide,
Thy works are all my joy and in thy fires my soul delights,
If mild they burn in just proportion and in secret night
445 And silence.   Build their day in shadow of soft clouds and dens.
I can sigh forth on the winds of Golgonooza piteous forms
That vanish again in my bosom ; but if thou, my Los,
Wilt in sweet moderate fury fabricate these forms sublime,
Such as the piteous spectres may assimilate them with,
450 They shall be ransoms for our souls, that we through them may live.

So Enitharmon spoke, and Los, his hands inspired, began
To moderate his fires, studious, the loud roaring flames
He vanquished with the strength of art, bending their iron points,
And drawing them forth deflected on the winds of Golgonooza.
455 From out the ranks of Urizen's war, and from the fiery lake
Of Orc, bending down as the binder of the sheaves follows
The reaper, embracing in both arms the furious raging flames,
Los drew them forth out of the deeps, planting his right foot firm
On the iron crag of Urizen, thence springing up aloft
460 Into the heavens of Enitharmon in a mighty circle.

And first he drew a line upon the walls of shining heaven,
And Enitharmon tinctured it with beams of blushing love
It remained permanent, a lovely form, inspired, divine, human.
Dividing into just proportion, Los unwearied laboured
465 The immortal lines upon the heavens, till, with sighs of love,
Sweet Enitharmon mild, entranced, breathed forth upon the wind
The spectrous dead, weeping. The Spectre viewed the immortal work
Of Los, assimilating to those forms Embodied. Lovely
In youth and beauty, in the arms of Enitharmon mild.

470 First Rintrah, and then Palamabron, drawn from ranks of war,
In infant innocence reposed on Enitharmon's bosom.
Orc was comforted in the deeps; his soul revived in them ;
As the elder brother is the father's image, so Orc became

G

As Los, a father to his brethren, and forged in the dark lake,
475 Then bound with chains of jealousy and scales of iron and brass.

Los loved them, and refused to sacrifice their infant limbs,
And Enitharmon's smiles and tears prevailed o'er self-protection.
They rather chose to meet Eternal Death than to destroy
The offspring of their care and pity. Urthona's spectre was comforted,
480 But Tharmas most rejoiced in hope of Enion's return,
For he beheld new female forms borne forth upon the air,
Who wore soft silken veils of covering in sweet raptured trance,
Mortal, and not as Enitharmon, without a covering veil.
First his immortal spirit drew Urizen's spectre away
485 From out the ranks of war, separating him in sunder,
Leaving his spectrous form, which could not so be drawn away.
Then he divided Tiriel, the eldest of Urizen's sons.
Urizen became Rintrah, Tiriel became Palamabron :
Thus divided the power of every warrior.
490 Startled was Los—he found his enemy Urizen now
In his hands. Much he wondered that he felt love and not hate,
His whole soul lovéd him. He as an infant him beheld,
Lovely, from Enitharmon breathed. He trembled in himself.

But in the deeps beneath the breasts of Mystery in night
495 Where Urizen sat on his rock, behold, the shadow brooded.
Urizen saw and triumphed, and he cried to his warriors :—
The Time of Prophecy is now revolved at last, and all
The universal ornament is mine, and in my hand
The ends of heaven. Like a garment I will fold them round,
500 Consuming what must be consumed. In power and majesty
I will walk forth through these wide fields of endless Eternity,
A God and not a Man, a conqueror in triumphant glory,
And all the sons of mortality shall bow down at my feet.

First trades and commerce, ships and armed vessels he builded
     laborious
505 To swim the deep; and on the land children are sold to trades

Of dire necessity, still labouring day and night, till, all
Their life extinct, they take the spectre form in dark despair,
And slaves in myriads, in shiploads, burden the sounding deep.

And Urizen laid the first stone, and all his myriads
510   Builded a temple in the image of the human heart.
And in the inner part of the temple, wondrous workmanship,
They formed the secret place, reviving all the altars of delight,—
That whomsoever entered into the temple might not be sold
The hidden, wondrous allegories of the generations—
515   Of secret lust, when hid in chambers dark the mighty harlot
Plays at disguise in whispered hymn and mumbling prayer. The
      Priests
He ordained, Presbyters, and clothed in disguises bestial,
Inspiring secrets. They bore lamps. Intoxicating fumes
Roll round the temple. And they took the Sun that glowed o'er Los
520   And with immense machines, down-rolling, the terrific orb
Compelled. The sun, reddening, like a lion in his chains,
Descended to the sound of instruments that drowned the noise
Of the hoarse wheels and the terrific howling of wild beasts
That dragged the wheels of the sun's chariot. And they put the sun
525   Into the temple of Urizen, to give light to the Abyss,
To light the war by day, to hide his secret braves by night—
The day for war, the night for secret religion in his temple.

Los reared his mighty stature : on earth stood his feet, above
The moon his furious forehead, circled with black bursting thunders,
530   The naked limbs glittering upon the dark blue sky, his knees
Bathéd in bloody clouds, his loins in fires of war where spears
And swords rage, where the eagles cry and the vultures laugh, saying :

Now comes the night of carnage, and the flesh of kings and princes
Pampered in palaces for our food, the blood of captains nurtured
535   With lust and murder for our drink. The drunken raven shall wander
All night among the slain and mock the wounded that groan in the
      field.

6 *

Tharmas laughed, furious among the banners clothed with blood,
Crying: As I will I rend the nations all asunder, rending
The people. Vain their combinations, I will scatter them.
540 But thou, oh ! Son, whom I have crownéd and enthroned the strong,
I will preserve thee. Enemies rise round thee numberless.
I will command my winds and they shall scatter them, or call
My waters like a flood around thee. Fear not, trust in me,
And I will give thee all the orbs of heaven for thy possession.
545 In war shalt thou bear rule, in blood shalt thou triumph for me,
Because in times of everlasting I was rent in sunder,
And what I loved, divided was among my enemies.
My little daughters were made captives, and I saw them beaten
With whips along the sultry roads. I heard those whom I loved
550 Crying in secret tents at night, and in the morn compelled
To labour; and, behold, my heart sunk down beneath in sighs,
In sobbings, until all divided I divided was
In twain, and, lo, my crystal form that in my bosom lived,
Followed her daughters to the field of blood: they left me naked,
555 Alone, and they refused to return from the fields of the mighty.
Therefore I will reward them as they have rewarded me;
I will divide them in my anger, and thou, oh! my king,
Shalt gather them from out their graves, and put thy fetters on,
And bind them to thee, that my crystal form may come to me.

560 So cried the Demon of the Waters in the clouds of Los.
Outstretched upon the hills lay Enitharmon. Clouds and tempests
Beat round her head all night: all day she riots in excess.
But night and day Los follows war. The moon rolls over her,
That, when Los waned upon the south, reflected the fierce fires
565 Of his immortal head in north, upon faint Enitharmon.
Red rage the furies of fierce Orc. Black thunders roll round Los,
Flaming: his head like the sun seen through mist that magnifies
The disk into a terrible vision to th' eyes of dreaming mortals.

And Enitharmon, trembling in fear, uttered these words :—

570 I put not any trust in thee, nor in thy glittering scales;
Thy eyelids are a terror, and the flaming of thy crest;
The rustling of thy scales confounds me, thy hoarse rustling scales.
And if that Los had not built me a bower upon a rock,
I must have died in the dark desert among noxious worms.
575 How shall I flee? How shall I flee into the bower of Los?
My feet are turnéd backwards and my footsteps slide in clay,
And clouds are closéd round my towers. My arms labour in vain.
Does not the God of Waters in the rocking elements
Love those who hate, rewarding with his hate the living soul?
580 And must I not obey the God, thou shadow of jealousy?
I cry; the watchman heareth not. I pour my voice in roarings:
Watchman! the night is thick, and darkness chokes my rayie sight.
Lift up! lift up! oh, Los! awake my watchman, for he sleepeth.
Lift up! lift up! Shine forth, oh, Light! Watchman, thy light is out.
585 Oh, Los! unless thou keep my tower the watchman will be slain.

So Enitharmon cried upon her terrible earthy bed,
While the broad oak wreathed his roots round her, forcing his dark
    way
Through caves of death into existence. The beech, long-limbed,
    advanced
Terrific into the pained heavens. The fruit-trees humanizing,
590 Showed their immortal energies in warlike desperation,
Rending the heavens and earths, and drinking blood in the hot battle
To feed their fruit, to gratify their hidden sons and daughters,
That far in close recesses of their secret palaces
Viewed the vast war and joy'd therein writhing to vegetate
595 Into the worlds of Enitharmon. Loud the roaring winds
Burdened with clouds howl round the couch. Sullen the woolly sheep
Walks through the battle. Dark and fierce the strong bull in his rage
Propagates through the warring earth. The lions raging in flames,
The tiger in redounding smoke, the serpent of the woods,—
600 With harsh songs every living soul. The prester serpent runs
Along the ranks, crying, Listen to the priest of God, ye warriors,

This cowl upon my head he placed in times of everlasting
And said, Go forth and guide my battles. Like the pointed spears
Of Man I made thee when I blotted Man from life and light.
605 Take thou the seven diseases of Man. Store them for time to come,
In store-houses, in secret places I will tell thee of,
. To be my great and awful curses at the appointed time.
The prester serpent ceased. The war song sounded loud and strong
Through all the heavens. Urizen wet, vibrated torrent on torrent.

610 Now in the caverns of the grave and places of human seed
The nameless shadowy vortex stood before the face of Orc.
The shadow raised her dismal head over the flaming youth
With sighs and howlings and deep sobs, that he might lose his rage,
And with it lose himself in meekness. She embraced his fire,
615 As when the Earthquake rises from his den, his shoulders huge
Appear above the crumbling mountains, silence waits round him
A moment. Then astounding horror belches from the centre,
The fiery dogs arise again, the shoulders huge appear;
So Orc rolled round his clouds upon the deeps of dark Urthona.
620 Knowing the arts of Urizen were pity and affection,
And by these arts the serpent form exuded from his limbs |
Silent as is despairing love, and strong as jealousy,
Jealousy that she was Vala, now become Urizen's harlot.
And the harlot and the deluded harlot of the kings of the earth
625 His soul was gnawn asunder . . . .
The hairy shoulders rend the links, free are the wrists of fire,
Red rage resounds, he roused his lions from his forests dark,
They howl around the flaming youth, rending the nameless shadow,
And running their immortal course through solid darkness borne.

630 Loud sounds the war-song round red Orc in his resistless fury,
And round the nameless shadowy female in her howling terror,
When all the elemental gods joined in the wondrous song.
Sound the war-trumpet terrific, souls clad in attractive steel!
Sound the shrill fife, serpents of war! I hear the northern drum

635 Awake! I hear the flapping of the folding banners . . . . .
The dragons of the north put on their armour . . . . .
Upon the eastern sea . . . . they take their course . . . .
The glittering of their horses and trappings stains the vault of night
Stop we the rising of the glorious king,—spur, spur your steeds,
640 Oh, northern drum! awake—oh, hand of iron, sound
The northern drum. Now give the charge! Bravely obscured
With deaths of wintry hail. Again the black bow draw :
Again the elemental strings to your right breasts draw,
And let the shadowy drum speed on the arrows black.

645 The arrows flew from cloudy bow all day till blood,
From east to west, flowed like the human victims in rivers
Of life upon the plains of death and valleys of despair.
Now sound the clarions of victory, now strip
The slain, now clothe yourselves in golden arms, brothers of war,
650 They sound the clarions strong, they chain the howling captives,
They cast the lots into the helmet, they give the oath of blood,
They vote the death of Luvah and they nailed him to a tree
To die a death of six thousand years bound round with desolation.
The sun was black and the moon rolled, a useless globe through
    heaven.

655 Then left the sons of Urizen the plough and harrow and loom,
The hammer and the chisel and the rule and compasses.
They forged the sword, the chariot of war, the battle axe,
The trumpet fitted to the battle, and the flute of summer,
And all the arts of life they changed into the arts of death
660 The hour-glass contemned because its simple workmanship
Was as the workmanship of the ploughman and the waterwheel
That raises water into cisterns broken and burned with fire,
Because its workmanship was like the workmanship of the shepherd,
And in their stead intricate wheels, involved, wheel within wheel,
665 To perplex youth in their outgoings, to bind the labourers
Of day and night, the myriads of eternity, that they might file

And polish brass and iron hour after hour, laborious work,
Kept ignorant of the use; that they might spend the days of wisdom
In sorrowful drudgery to obtain a scanty pittance of bread,
670   In ignorance to view a small portion and think that All,
And call it demonstration, blind to the simple rules of life.

And now the battle rages round thy tender limbs, oh! Vala.
Now smile among thy bitter tears, now put on all thy beauty.
Is not the wound of the sword sweet and the broken bone delightful?
675   Wilt thou now smile among the slain when the wounded groan in the
          fields?
Lift up thy blue eyes, Vala, and put on thy sapphire shoes,—
On melancholy Magdalen, behold the morning breaks.
Gird in thy flaming loins, descend into the sepulchre,
Scatter the blood from thy golden bow and tears from thy silver locks,
680   Shake off the water from thy wings, dust from thy white garments.
Remember all thy feigned terrors on the secret couch
When the sun rose in glowing morn with arms of mighty hosts
Marching to battle, who was wont to rise with Urizen's harps
Girt as a sower with his seed to scatter life abroad.
685   Arise, oh! Vala, bring the bow of Urizen, bring the swift arrows of
          light,
How raged the golden horses of Urizen, bound to the chariot of love,
Compelled to leave the plough to the ox, to snuff up desolation,
To tramp cornfields in boastful neighings. This is no gentle harp,
This is no warbling brook, nor shadow of a myrtle-tree,
690   But blood and wounds and dismal cries and clarions of war,
And hearts laid open to the light by the broad grizzly sword,
And bowels hid in hammered steel ripped out upon the ground,—
Call forth thy smiles of soft deceit,—call forth thy cloudy tears,
We hear thy sighs in trumpets shrill when morn shall blood renew.

695   So sang the demons of the deep. The clarions of war blew loud.
Orc rent her, and his human form consumed in his own fires
Mingléd with her dolorous members, strewn through the abyss.
She joyed in conflict, gratified and drinking tears of woe.

No more remained of Orc but the serpent round the tree of mystery.
700 The form of Orc was gone.   He reared his serpent bulk among
The stars of Urizen in furor, rending the form of life
Into a formless indefinite and strewing her on the abyss
Like clouds upon a winter sky, broken with wind and thunders.
This was, to her, supreme delight. The warriors mourned disappointed.
705 They go to war with many shouts and with loud clarions.
Oh, pity! They return with lamentations, mourning, weeping.
Invisible or visible, drawn out in length or breadth,
The shadowy female varied in the war in her delight.
Howling in discontent, black, heavy uttering harsh sounds
710 Wandering through fires and slimy weeds and making lamentations
To deliver Tharmas in his rage, to soothe his furious soul,
To stay his flight that Urizen might live although in pain.
He said: Art thou bright Enion? is the shadow of hope returned?

And she said · Tharmas, I am Vala, bless thy innocent face!
715 Doth Enion avoid the sight of thy blue watery eyes?
Be not persuaded that the air knows this, or the falling dew.

Tharmas replied: Oh! Vala, once I lived in a garden of delight;
I watered Enion in the morning and she lived always
Among the apple-trees; and all the garden of delight
720 Swam like a dream before my eyes. I went to seek the steps
Of Enion in the garden and the shadow compassed me
And closed me in a watery world of woe where Enion stood
Trembling before me like a shadow, like a mist, like air.
And she is gone, and here alone I war with darkness and death
725 I hear thy voice, but not thy form see. Thou and all delight
And life appear and vanish,—mocking me with shadows of false hope.
Hast thou forgot that the air listens through all its districts telling
The subtlest thoughts shut up from light in chambers of the moon?

Tharmas, the moon has chambers where the babes of love lie hid,
730 And whence they never can be brought in all Eternity
Unless exposed by their vain parents   Lo, he whom I love

Is hidden from me, and I never in all Eternity
Shall see him. Enitharmon and Ahania, combined with Enion,
Hid him in that outrageous form of Orc, which torments me for sin
735 For all my secret faults which he brings forth upon the light
Of day in jealousy and blood. My children are led to Urizen's war
Before my eyes, and for every one of these I am condemned
To eternal torment in these flames, for though I have the power
To rise on high, yet love here binds me down, and never, never
740 Will I arise till him I love is loosed from this dark chain.

Tharmas replied : Vala, thy sins have lost us heaven and bliss,
Thou art our curse, and till I can bring love into the light
I never will depart from my great wrath . . . . .

So Tharmas wailed.   Dreadful they rode upon the stormy deep,
745 Cursing the voice that mocked them with false hope in furious mood.
Then she returned, swift as a blight upon the infant bred,
Howling in all the notes of woe to stay his furious rage,
Stamping the hills, wandering, swimming, flying furious, falling,
Or like an earthquake rumbling in the bowels of the earth,
750 Or like a cloud beneath, or like a fire flaming on high,
Walking with pleasure on the hills or running in the dales |
Like to a rushing torrent beneath and a falling rock above,
A thunder-cloud in the south and a chilling voice heard in the north.

And she went forth and saw the forms of life and of delight
755 Walking on mountains or flying in the open expanse of heaven.
She heard sweet voices in the winds and in the voices of birds
That rose from waters, for the waters were as the voice of Luvah,
Not seen to her like waters or like this dark world of death,
Though all those fair perfections which men know only by name
760 In beautiful substantial forms appeared and served her
As food or drink or ornament or in delightful works
To build her bowers, for the elements brought forth abundantly
The living soul in glorious forms, and everyone came forth
Walking before her shadowy face and bowing at her feet.

765 But in vain delights were poured forth on the howling melancholy.
For her delight the horse his proud neck bowed, and his whole mane,
And the strong lion deigned in his mouth to wear the golden bit,
While the far-beaming peacock walkéd on the fragrant wind
To bring her fruits of sweet delight from trees of richest wonder,
770 And the strong eagle bore the fire of heaven in the night.
Woo'd and subdued into eternal death the demon lay,
In rage against the dark despair, the howling melancholy.
For far and wide she stretched through all the worlds of Urizen's
    journey,
And was adjoined to Beulah as the polypus to the rock.
775 Mourning, the daughters of Beulah saw, nor could they have sustained
The horrid sight of death and torment.   But the Eternal promise
They wrote on all their tombs and pillars and on every urn,
These words,—If ye will believe your brother shall rise again,—
In golden letters ornamented with sweet labours of love,
780 Waiting in patience for the fulfilment of the promise Divine.

And all the songs of Beulah sounded comfortable notes,
Not suffering doubt to rise up from the clouds of the shadowy female.
The myriads of the dead burst through the bottoms of their tombs,
Descending on the shadowy female's clouds in spectrous terror,
785 Beyond the limit of translucence on the lake of Udan Adan.
These they named Satans, and in the aggregate they named them
    Satan.

END OF THE SEVENTH NIGHT.

Night the Eighth.

Then all in great Eternity, which is called the counsel of God,
Met as one Man, even Jesus, upon Gilead and Hermon,
Upon the limit of contraction to awake the fallen Man.
The fallen Man stretched like a corse upon the oosy rock,
5 Washed with the tide, pale, overgrown with the waves,
Just moved with horrible dreams, and waving high over his head
Two winged immortal shapes were seen, one standing at his feet
Toward the east, one standing at his head toward the west,
Their wings joined in the Zenith overhead; but other wings
10 They had that clothed their bodies like a garment of soft down,
Silvery, bright, shining upon the dark blue sky in silver.
These wings touchéd the heavens. Their fair feet hovered above
The swelling tides; they bent over the dead corse like an arch,
Pointed at the top in highest heaven of precious stones and pearl.
15 Such is a vision of all Beulah hovering over the sleeper.

The limit of contraction was now fixed, and Man began
To wake upon the couch of death. He sneezed seven times,
A tear of blood dropped from either eye. Again he reposed
In the Saviour's arms, in the arms of tender mercy and loving kindness.

20 Then Los said: I behold the Divine Vision through the broken gates
Of thy poor broken heart, astonished, melted into compassion and love.

Enitharmon said: I see the Lamb of God upon Mount Zion.

Wondering with love and awe they felt the Divine Hand upon them;
For nothing could restrain the dead in Beulah from dissolving
25 Unto Ulro's night, tempted by the shadowy females, sweet
Delusive cruelty. They descend away from the daughters of Beulah

And enter Urizen's temple, Enitharmon pitying, and her heart—
Gates broken down.   They descend through the gate of Pity—
The broken heart-gate of Enitharmon.   She sighs them forth upon the
    wind
30 Of Golgonooza.   Los stood at the gate receiving them—
For Los could enter into Enitharmon's bosom and explore
Its intricate labyrinths now the obdurate heart was broken—
From out the war of Urizen and Tharmas receiving them
Into his hands.   Then Enitharmon erected looms in Laban's gate,
35 And called the looms Cathedron.   In these looms she wove the Spectres
Bodies of vegetation.   Singing lulling cadences to drive away
Despair from the poor wandering spectres ; and Los lovéd them
With a parental love, for the Divine hand was upon him
And upon Enitharmon, and the Divine countenance shone
40 In Golgonooza.   Looking down, the daughters of Beulah saw,
With joy, the bright light, and in it a human form,
And knew he was the Saviour, even Jesus : and they worshipped,
Astonished, comforted, delighted, in notes of rapturous ecstacy.

All Beulah stood astonished, looking down to Eternal Death.
45 They saw the Saviour beyond the pit of Death and of Destruction
For whether they looked upward they saw the Divine Vision,
Or whether they looked downward still they saw the Divine Vision,
Surrounding them on all sides beyond sin and death and hell.

And Enitharmon, now in tears, singing songs of lamentation
50 And pitying comfort, as she sighs forth on the wind the Spectre,
Also the vegetated bodies which Enitharmon wove,
Opened within their hearts, and in their loins, and in their brain,
To Beulah ; and the dead in Ulro descended from the war
Of Urizen and Tharmas, and from the shadowy female's clouds.
55 And some were woven single, and some twofold, and some threefold,
In head or heart or reins, according to the fittest order
Of most merciful pity and compassion to the spectrous dead

When Urizen saw the Lamb of God clothed in Luvah's robes,

Perplexed and terrified he stood, though well he knew that Orc
60 Was Luvah. But he now beheld a new Luvah, or Orc,
Who assumed Luvah's form and stood before him opposite.

But he saw Orc, a serpent form, augmenting times on times
In the fierce battle ; and he saw the Lamb of God and the world of Los ·
Surrounded by his dark machine, for Orc augmented swift
65 In fury, a serpent wondrous amongst the constellations of Urizen.
A crest of fire rose on his forehead, red as a carbuncle,
Beneath, down to his eyelids, scales of pearl, then gold and silver
Inmingled with the ruby, overspread his visage down
His furious neck ; writhing, contorted in dire budding pains,
70 The scaly armour shot out. Stubborn down his back and bosom
The emerald, orange, sulphur, jasper, beryl, amethyst,
Stood, in terrific emulation which should gain a place
Upon the mighty fiend—the fruit of the mysterious tree
Kneaded in Uvith's kneading trough. Still Orc devoured the food
75 In raging hunger. Still the pestilential food, in gems and gold,
Exuded round his awful limbs, stretching to serpent length
His human bulk. While the dark shadowy female, brooding o'er,
Measured his food morning and evening in cups and baskets of iron.
With tears of sorrow incessant she laboured the food of Orc,
80 Compelled by the iron-hearted sisters, daughters of Urizen.
Gathering the fruit of that mysterious tree, circling its root,
She spread herself through all the branches in the form of Orc.

Thus Urizen, in soft deceit, his warlike preparations fabricated.
And when all things were finished, sudden waved among the stars
85 His hurtling hand gave the dire signal. Thund'rous clarions blow.
And all the hollow deep re-bellowed with the thund'rous war.
But Urizen his mighty rage let loose in the mid-deep.
Sparkles of dire afflictions issued round his frozen limbs.
Horrible hooks and nets he formed, twisting the cords of iron
90 And brass and molten metals, cast in hollow globes and bored
Tubes in petrific steel, and rammed combustibles, and wheels

And chains and pulleys, fabricated all round the heavens of Los,
Communing with the serpent Orc in dark dissimulation,
And with the Synagogue of Satan in dark Sanhedrin,
95 To undermine the world of Los, to tear bright Enitharmon
To the four winds, hopeless of future.   All futurity
Seems teeming with endless destruction never to be expelled;
Desperate remorse swallows the present in a quenchless rage.

The battle howls, the terrors fired rage in the work of death;
100 Enormous work.   Los contemplated, inspired by the holy Spirit.
Los builds the walls of Golgonooza against the stirring battle,
That only through the gates of death they can enter to Enitharmon.
Raging they take the human visage and the human form,
Feeling the hand of Los in Golgonooza, and the force
105 Attractive of his hammers beating, and the silver looms
Of Enitharmon singing lulling cadences on the wind.
They humanize in the fierce battle, where in direful pain,
Terrified and astonished, Urizen beheld the battle take a form
Which he intended not, a shadowy hermaphrodite, black and opaque,
110 The soldiers named it Satan, but he was as yet unformed and vast.
Hermaphroditic it at length became, hiding the male
Within as in a tabernacle, abominable, deadly.
Troop by troop the bestial drove rend one another, sounding loud
The instruments of sound; and troop by troop, in human forms, they
  urge
115 The dire confusion till the battle faints.   Those that remain
Return in pangs and horrible convulsions to their bestial state;
For the monsters of the elements, lions or tigers or wolves
Sound loud the howls, music inspired by Los and Enitharmon
  sounding loud and terrific.   Men
They seem to one another, laughing terrible among the banners.
120 And when the revolution of the day of battles was o'er,
Relapsing in dire torment, they return to forms of woe,
To moping visages, retiring, inanimate, furious.
No more erect, though strong, drawn out in length they ravin

For senseless gratification, and their visages thrust forth,
125   Flatten above and beneath and stretch out into bestial length.
Weakened they stretch beyond their power in dire droves till war
    begins,
Or secret religion in their temples before secret shrines.

And Urizen gave life and sense by his immortal power
To all his engines of deceit, that linked chains might run
130   Through ranks of war, spontaneous : that hooks and boring screws
Might act according to their forms by innate cruelty.
He formed also harsh instruments of sound . . . . .
To grate the soul into destruction, or to inflame with fury
The spirits of life, to pervert all the faculties of sense
135   Into their own destruction, if perhaps he might avert
His own despair even at the cost of everything that breathes.

Thus in the temple of the sun his books of iron and brass
And silver and gold he consecrated, reading incessantly
To myriads of perturbed spirits : through the universe
140   They propagated the deadly words, the shadowy female absorbing
The enormous science of Urizen, age after age exploring
The fell destruction, and she said : Oh ! Urizen, Prince of Light,
What words of dread pierce my faint ear ? What falling snows around
My feeble limbs enfold my destined misery ?
145   I alone dare the last abide to sit beneath the blast
Unhurt, and dare the inclement forehead of the King of Light,
From dark abysses of the times remote, fated to be.
The Sorrower of Eternity in love with tears, submiss I rear
My eyes to thy Pavilions   Hear my prayer for Luvah's sake.
150   I see the murderer of my Luvah clothed in robes of blood,
He who assumed my Luvah's robes in times of Everlasting
Where hast thou hid him whom I love ; in what remote abyss
Resides that God of my delight?   Oh ! might my eyes behold
My Luvah, then would I deliver all the Sons of God
155   From bondage of these terrors, and with influences sweet,

As once in those eternal fields of brotherhood and love,
United we should live in bliss as those who sinnéd not.
The Eternal Man is sealed by thee, never to be delivered.
We are all servants to thy will.   Oh! King of Light, relent
160 Thy furious power; be our father and our lovéd king.
But if my Luvah is no more, if thou hast smitten him
And laid him in the sepulchre, or if thou wilt revenge
His murder on another, silent I bow with dread.
But happiness can never come to thee, oh! King, nor me,
165 For he was the source of every joy that this mysterious tree
Unfolds in allegoric fruit.   When shall the dead revive?
Can that which has existed cease?   Can love and life expire?

Urizen heard the voice, and saw the shadow underneath
His woven darkness, and in laws and deceitful religions,
170 Beginning at the tree of Mystery, circling its roost,
He spread himself through all the branches in the power of Orc,
A shapeless and indefinite cloud, in tears of sorrow incessant.
Steeping the direful web of religion, swagging, heavy, it fell
From heaven to earth, through all its meshes, altering the vortexes,
175 Misplacing every centre.   Hungry desire and lust began
Gathering the fruit of that mysterious tree, till Urizen,
Sitting within his temple, furious, felt the ruining stupor,
Himself caught in his own net, in sorrow, lust, repentance.

Enitharmon wove in tears, singing songs of lamentations,
180 And pitying comfort as she sigh'd forth on the wind the spectres,
And wove them bodies, calling them her beloved sons and daughters,
Employing the daughters in her looms, and Los employed the sons
In Golgonooza's furnaces among the anvils of time and space.
Thus forming a vast family, wondrous in beauty and love,
185 And they appeared a Universal female form created
From those who were dead in Ulro, from the spectres of the dead.

And Enitharmon named the female Jerusalem the Holy.
Wondering, she saw the Lamb of God within Jerusalem's veil;

7

The Divine Vision seen within the inmost deep recess
190   Of fair Jerusalem's bosom in a gently beaming fire.

Then sang the sons of Eden round the Lamb of God, and said,—
Glory, Glory—Glory to the Holy Lamb of God,—
Who now beginneth to put off the dark Satanic body.
Now we behold redemption.   Now we know that life eternal
195   Depends alone upon the Universal hand, and not in us
Is aught but death   In individual weakness, sorrow and pain,
We behold with wonder Enitharmon's looms and Los's forges,
And the spindles of Tirzah and Rahab, and the mills of Satan and
      Beelzebub.
In Golgonooza Los's anvils stand and his furnaces rage,—
200   The hard dentant hammers lulled by the flutes' lula-lula—
The bellowing furnaces blaze by the long resounding clarions,
Ten thousand demons labour at the forges creating continually
The times and spaces of Mortal life, the Sun, the Moon, the Stars,
In periods of pulsative furor, breaking into wedges and bars,
205   Then drawing into wires the terrific Passions and Affections
Of Spectrous Dead, thence to the looms of Cathedron conveyed.
The daughters of Enitharmon weave the ovarium and integument
In soft silk, drawn from their own bowels in lascivious delight,
With songs of sweetest cadence to the turning spindle and reel,
210   Lulling the weeping spectres of the dead, clothing their limbs
With gifts and gold of Eden.   Astonished, stupefied with delight,
The terrors put on their sweet clothing on the banks of Arnon,
Whence they plunge into the river of space for a period, until
The dread sleep of Ulro is passed.   But Satan, Og, and Sihon
215   Build mills of resistless wheels to unwind the soft threads and reveal
Naked of their clothing the poor spectres before the accusing heavens,
While Rahab and Tirzah far different mantles prepare, webs of torture,
Mantles of despair, girdles of bitter compunction, shoes of indolence,
Veils of ignorance, covering from head to foot with a cold web.
220   We look down into Ulro, and we behold the wonders of the grave.
Eastward of Golgonooza stands the lake of Udan Adan, in

Entuthon Benython, a lake not of waters but of spaces,
Perturbed, black, and deadly. On its strands and its margins,
The mills of Satan and Beelzebub stand round the roots of Urizen's
    tree,
225 For this lake is formed of the tears and sighs and death-sweat of the
    victims
Of Urizen's laws, to irrigate the roots of the tree of Mystery.
They unweave the soft threads, then they weave them anew in forms
Of dark death and despair, and none from Eternity to Eternity could
    escape.
But thou Universal Humanity, who is One Man, blessed for ever,
230 Receivest the integuments woven. Rahab beholds the Lamb of God.
She smites with her knife of flint. She destroys her own work
Times upon times, thinking to destroy the Lamb, blessed for ever.
He puts off the clothing of blood,—he redeems spectres from their
    bonds.
He awakes sleepers in Ulro. The daughters of Beulah praise him,
235 They anoint his feet with ointment, they wipe them with the hairs of
    their head.
We now behold the ends of Beulah, and we now behold,—
Where death eternal is put off eternally. Oh! Lamb,
Assume the dark Satanic body in the Virgin's womb.
Oh! Lamb Divine, it cannot thee annoy! Oh! pitying one,
240 Thy pity is from the foundation of the world, and thy Redemption
Begins already in Eternity. Come, then, oh! Lamb of God,
Come, Lord Jesus, quickly.

So saying in Eternity, looking down into Beulah,
The war roared round Jerusalem's gates. It took a hideous form
245 Seen in the aggregate, a vast Hermaphroditic form,
Heaved like an earthquake, labouring with convulsive groans
Intolerable. At length an awful wonder burst
From the Hermaphroditic bosom. Satan, he was named
Son of Perdition, terrible his form, dishumanized, monstrous,
250 A male without a female counterpart, a howling fiend

7 *

Forlorn of Eden, and repugnant to the forms of life—
Yet hiding the shadowy female Vala, as in an ark and curtains—
Abhorred, accursed, ever dying an eternal death.
Being multitudes of tyrant men in union blasphemous
255   Against the Divine Image, congregated assemblies of wicked men.

Pitying, the Lamb of God descended through Jerusalem's gates
To put off the Mystery, time after time, and as a Man
Is born on earth, so was he born of fair Jerusalem
In Mystery's woven mantle, and in the robes of Luvah.
260   He stood in fair Jerusalem to awake up into Eden
The fallen Man,—but first to give his vegetated body
To be cut off that the Spiritual body may be revealed.

The Lamb of God stood before Satan opposite,
In Entuthon Benython, in the shadows of torment and woe,
265   Upon the heights of Amalek, taking refuge in his arms.
The victims fled from punishment, for all his words were peace.
Urizen called together the synagogue of Satan in dark Sanhedrin,
To Judge the Lamb of God to death as a murderer and a robber,
As it is written he was numbered among the transgressors.
270   Cold, dark, opaque, the assembly met twelvefold in Amalek,
Twelve rocky unshaped forms, terrific forms of torture and woe,
Such seemed the synagogue to distant view, amidst them beamed
A false female counterpart of Lovely Delusive Beauty,
Dividing and uniting at will in cruelties of holiness,—
275   Vala,—drawn down into a vegetative body, now triumphant,
The synagogue of Satan clothed her with scarlet robes and gems,
And on her forehead was her name, written in blood,—"Mystery."
When viewed remote she is One, when viewed near she divides
To multitudes, as it is in Eden, so permitted because
280   It was the best possible in the state called Satan to save
From Death Eternal, and to put off Satan continually.
The synagogue created her from fruit of Urizen's tree,
By Devilish arts, abominable, unlawful, unutterable,

Perpetually vegetating in detestable birth
285 Of female forms, beautiful through poisons hidden in secret,
Which give attraction to false beauty. Then was hidden within
The bosom of Satan the False Female, as in an ark and veil,
Which Christ must rend and her reveal. Her daughters are called
Tirzah. She is named Rahab. Their various divisions are called
290 The daughters of Amalek, Canaan, and Moab, binding on the stones
Their victims, and with knives wounding them, singing with tears
Over their victims. Hear ye the song of the females of Amalek.

Oh, thou poor human form! Oh, thou poor child of woe!
Why dost thou wander away from Tirzah; why we compel to bind
thee?
295 If thou dost go away from me, I shall consume upon the rocks
These fibres of thine eyes that used to wander in distant heavens
Away from me. I have bound down with a hot iron chain
These nostrils that expanded with delight in morning skies,
I have bent downward with lead molten in my furnaces.
300 My soul is seven furnaces, incessant roar the bellows,
Upon my terribly flaming heart the molten metal runs
In channels through my fiery limbs. Oh, Love! Oh, Pity! Oh, Pain!
Oh, the pangs, the bitter pangs of love forsaken!
Ephraim was a wilderness of joy where all my wild beasts ran.
305 The River Kanah wandered by my sweet Manasseh's side.
Go, Noah, fetch the girdle of strong brass, heat it red hot,
Press it around the loins of this expanding cruelty.
Shriek not so, my only love.
Bind him down, sisters, bind him down on Ebal, mount of cursing.
310 Malah, come forth from Lebanon, and Hoglah from Mount Sinai—
Come, circumscribe this tongue of sweets, and with a screw of iron
Fasten this ear into the rock. Milcah, the task is thine.
Weep not so, sisters, weep not so; our life depends on this.
Or Mercy and Truth are fled away from Shechem and Mount Gilead,
315 Unless my beloved is bound down on the stems of Vegetation.

Such are the songs of Tirzah, such the loves of Amalek.
The Lamb of God descended through the nether portions of Luvah,
Bearing his sorrows and receiving all his cruel wounds.

Thus was the Lamb of God condemned to death.
820 They nailed him upon the tree of Mystery, weeping over him,
And then mocking, and then worshipping, calling him Lord and King.
Sometimes as twelve daughters lovely, sometimes as five,
They stood in beaming beauty.   Sometimes as one, even Rahab,
Who is Mystery, Babylon the great, mother of Harlots.

325 Jerusalem saw the body dead upon the Cross   She fled away,
Saying :—Is this Eternal death ?   Where shall I hide from death ?
Pity me, Los ! Pity me, Urizen !—and let us build
A Sepulchre, and worship Death in fear while yet we live—
Death !   God of all !   From whom we rise, to whom we all return,—
330 And let all nations of the Earth worship at the Sepulchre
With gifts and spices, and with lamps embossed, jewels and gold.

Los took the body from the Cross, Jerusalem weeping over,
They bore it to the Sepulchre, which Los had hewn in the rock
Of Eternity for himself : he heard it despairing of Life Eternal.
335 But when Rahab had cut off the Mantle of Luvah from
The Lamb of God, it rolled apart, revealing to all in heaven
And all in earth, the Temple, the Synagogue of Satan, and Mystery,
Even Rahab in all her turpitude.   Rahab divided herself—
She stood before Los in her pride among the Furnaces,
340 Dividing and uniting in delusive feminine powers, questioning him.
He answered her with tenderness and love, not uninspired.

Los sat upon his anvil stock.   They sat beside the forge.
Los wiped the sweat from his red brow, and thus began
To the delusive female forms shining among his furnaces :

345 I am that shadowy prophet who, six thousand years ago,
Fell from my station in the Eternal bosom.   I divided

To multitude and my multitudes are children of care and labour.
Oh! Rahab, I behold thee. I was once like thee, a son
Of Pride, and I have pierced the Lamb of God in pride and wrath.
850 Hear me repeat my generations that thou may'st also repent.
And these are the generations of Los and Enitharmon, Rintrah,
 Palamabron,
Theotormon, Bromion, Antamon, Ananton, Ozoth, Ohana,
Sotha, Mydon, Ellayol, Natha, Gon, Hurlath, Satan,
Har, Ochim, Ijim, Adam, Reuben, Simeon, Levi, Judah, Dan, Naphali,
855 Gad, Asher, Issachar, Zebulun, Joseph, Benjamin, David, Solomon,
Paul, Constantine, Charlemagne, Luther, Milton.
These are our daughters: Ocalythron, Elynitria, Oothoon, Leutha,
Elythiria, Enanto, Manatha Varcyon, Ethinthus, Moab, Midian,
Aah, Tullah, Caina, Naamah, Tamar, Rahab, Tirzah, Mary.
860 And myriads more of sons and daughters to whom our loves increased,
To each according to the multiplication of their multitudes.
But Satan accused Palamabron before his brethren, also he maddened
The horses of Palamabron's harrow, wherefore Rintrah and Palamabron
Cut him off from Golgonooza. But Enitharmon, in tears,
865 Wept over him, and created him a space with a tender moon,
As he rolled down beneath the fires of Orc, a globe immense
Crested with snow in a dim void. Here, by the arts of Urizen,
He tempted many of the sons and daughters of Los to flee
Away from them. First Reuben fled, then Simeon, then Levi, then
 Judah,
870 Then Dan, then Naphali, then Gad, then Asher, then Issachar,
Then Zebulun, then Joseph, then Benjamin,—twelve sons of Los.
And this is the manner in which Satan became the tempter.
There is a state named Satan. Learn distinct to know, oh! Rahab
The difference between states and individuals of those states.
875 The state named Satan never can be redeemed to all Eternity.
But when Luvah in Orc became a Serpent, he descended into—
That state called Satan. Enitharmon breathed forth on the winds
Of Golgonooza her well beloved, knowing he was Orc's human remains.
She tenderly loved him above all his brethren. He grew up

380 In mother's tenderness. The enormous worlds rolling in Urizen's power

Must have given Satan, by these mild arts, dominion over all,

Wherefore Palamabron being accused by Satan to Los,

Called down a great solemn assembly   Rintrah, in fury and fear,

Defended Palamabron, and rage filled the universal tent.

385 Because Palamabron was good-natured, Satan supposed he feared him,

And Satan not having the science of wrath, but only of pity,

Was soon condemned, and wrath was left to wrath, and pity to pity.

Rintrah and Palamabron, cut sheer off from Golgonooza,

Enitharmon's moony space, and in it, Satan and his companions.

390 They rolled down a dim world, crushed with snow, deadly and dark.

Jerusalem, pitying them, wove them mantles of life and death,

Times after times, and those in Eden set Lucifer for their guard.

Lucifer refused to die for Satan. In pride he forsook his charge.

They sent Molech. Molech was impatient. They sent—

395 Molech impatient—they sent Elohim, who created Adam,

To die for Satan   Adam refused, but was compelled to die

By Satan's arts. Then the eternals sent Shaddai.

Shaddai was angry. Pahad descended. Pahad was terrified

And then they sent Jehovah, who, leprous, stretched his hand to Eternity.

400 Then Jesus came, and died willing beneath Tirzah and Rahab.

Thou art that Rahab. To the tomb. What can we purpose more?

To Enitharmon, terrible and beautiful in eternal youth,

Bow down before her, you, her children. Set Jerusalem free.

Rahab, burning with pride and revenge, departed from Los.

405 Los dropped a tear at her departure, but he wiped it away in hope.

She went to Urizen in pride. The Prince of Light beheld

Revealed before the face of heaven his secret holiness.

Darkness and sorrow covered all flesh. Eternity was darkened.

Urizen sitting in his web of deceitful religion

410 Felt the female death,—a dull and numbing stupor, such as never

Before assaulted the bright human form.   He felt his pores
Drink in the deadly dull delusion.   Terrors of Eternal Death
Shot through him.   Urizen sat stonied upon his rock.
Forgetful of his own laws, petrifying he began to embrace
The shadowy female.   Since life cannot be quenched, life exuded,
His eyes shot forward, then his breathing nostrils drawn forth.
Scales covered over a cold forehead and a neck outstretched
Into the deep to seize the shadow.   Scales his neck and bosom
Covered ; scales his hands and feet.   Upon his belly falling
Outstretched through the immense ; his mouth wide open, tongueless,
His teeth a triple row, he strove to seize the shadow in vain,
And his immense tail lashed the abyss.   His human form a stone.
A form of senseless stone remained in terrors on the rock,
Abominable to the eyes of mortals who explore his books.
His wisdom still remained, and all his memory stored with woe.
And still his stony form remained in the abyss immense,
Like the pale visage in its sheet of lead that cannot follow.
Incessant stern disdain his scaly form gnaws inwardly,
With deep repentance for the loss of that fair form of Man.
With envy he saw Los, with envy Tharmas and Urthona,
With envy and in vain he swam around his stony form.
No longer now erect, the king of light, outstretched in fury,
Lashes his tail in the wide deep.   His eyelids, like the sun
Arising in his pride, enlightens all the grizzly deeps,
His scales transparent give forth light like windows of the morning,
His neck flames with wrath and majesty.   He lashes the deeps,
Beating the deserts and the rocks ; the deserts feel his power.
They shake their slumbers off, they wave in awful fear,
Calling the lion and the tiger, the horse and the wild stag,
The elephant, the wolf and bear, the llama and the satyr.
His eyelids give their light around.   His foaming tail aspires
Among the stars.   The earth and all the abysses feel his fury.
When, as the snow covers the mountains, oft petrific hardness
Covers the deeps at his vast fury, moving in his rock,
Hardens the lion and the bear, writhing in the solid mountain.

They view the light and wonder, crying out in terrible existence.
Up-bound the wild stag and the horse, behold the king of pride.
Oft doth his eye emerge from the abyss into the realms
Of his eternal day, and memory strives to augment his ruthfulness.

450 Then weeping he descends in wrath, drawing all things in his fury
Into obedience to his will, and now he finds in vain
That not of his own power he bore the human form erect,
Nor of his own will gave his laws in times of everlasting.

For now fierce Orc in wrath and fury risen into the heavens,
455 A king of wrath and fury, a dark enraged horror,
And Urizen, repentant, forgets his wisdom in the abyss
In forms of priesthood, in the dark delusions of repentance,
Repining in his heart and spirit that Orc reigned over all,
And that his wisdom served but to augment the indefinite lust.

460 Then Tharmas and Urthona felt the stony stupor rise
Into their limits   Urthona shot forth a vast fibrous form.
Tharmas like a pillar of sand rolled round by the whirlwind,
An animated pillar rolling round in incessant rage.

Los felt the stony stupor and his head rolled down beneath
465 Into the abysses of his bosom   The vessels of his blood
Dart forth upon the wind in pipes, writhing about in the abyss,
And Enitharmon, pale and cold, in milky juices flowed
Into a form of vegetation, living, having a voice,
Moving in root-like fibres, breathing in fear upon the earth.

470 And Tharmas gave his power to Los, Urithona gave his strength
Into the youthful prophet for the love of Enitharmon
And of the nameless shadowy female, into the nether deep,
And for the dread of the dark terror of Orc and Urizen.

Thus in a living death the nameless shadow all things bound,
475 All mortal things made permanent that they may be put off

Time after time by the Divine Lamb who died for all,
And all in him died and he put off all mortality.

Tharmas on high rode furious through the afflicted worlds,
Pursuing the vain shadow of hope, fleeing from identity
480 In abstract false essences that he may not hear the voice:
The voice incessant calls on all the children of Men,
For she spoke of all in heaven and all upon the earth,—
Saw not yet the Divine Vision. Her eyes are toward Urizen,
And thus Ahania cries aloud to the caverns of the grave :

485 Will you keep a flock of wolves and lead them? Will you take the
    wintry blast
For a covering to your limbs or the summer pestilence for a tent to
    abide in?
Will you erect a lasting habitation in the mouldering churchyard;
Or a pillar and palace of Eternity in the jaws of the hungry grave?
Will you scent pleasure from the festering wound, or marry for a wife
490 The ancient leprosy that the king and priest may feast on your decay?
And the grave mock and laugh at the ploughed field saying,—
I am the nourisher, thou the destroyer; in my bosom is milk and wine,
And a fountain from my breasts. To me come all multitudes
To my breasts. They obey, they worship me. I am goddess and queen.
495 But listen to Ahania, oh! ye sons of the murdered one,
Listen to her whose memory beholds your ancient days,
Listen to her whose eye beholds the dark body of corruptible death
Looking for Urizen in vain. In vain I seek for morning.
The Eternal Man sleeps in the earth, nor feels the glorious sun
500 Nor silent moon, nor all the hosts of heaven move in his body.
His fiery halls are dark, and round his limbs the serpent Orc
Fold without fold encompasses him, and his corrupting members
Do vomit out the scaly monsters of the restless deep.
They come up in the rivers and among the nether parts
505 Of Man who lays upon the shore, leaning his faded head
Upon the oozy rock enwrapt with the weeds of death.

His eyes sink hollow in his head.   His flesh covered with slime
And shrunk up to the bones.   Alas! that Man should come to this!
His strong bones beat with snows and hid within the caves of night,
510   Marrowless, bloodless, falling into dust, driven by the winds.
Oh! how the horrors of Eternal Death take hold on Man.
His faint groans shake the caves and issue through the desolate rocks,
And the strong eagle now with numbing cold, blighted of feathers,
Once like the pride of the sun now flagging on cold night,
515   Hovers with blasted wings aloft, watching with eagle eye
Till Man shall leave a corruptible body.   He, famished, hears him
       groan,
And now he fixes his strong talons in the pointed rock,
And now he beats the heavy air with his enormous wings.
Beside him lies the lion dead, and in his belly worms
520   Feast on his death till universal death devours all,
And the pale horse seeks for the pool to lie him down and die,
But finds the pool filled with serpents devouring one another.
He droops his head and trembling stands, and his bright eyes decay.
These are the visions of my eyes, the visions of Ahania.

525   Thus cries Ahania   Enion replies from the caverns of the grave:
Fear not, oh poor forsaken one.   Oh land of grass and thorns,
Where once the olive flourished and the cedar spread his wings.
Once I wailed desolate like thee; my fallow fields in fear
Cried to the churchyards and the earthworm came in dismal state.
530   I found him in my bosom, and I said the time of love
Appears upon the rocks and hills in silent shades, but soon
A voice came in the night, a midnight cry upon the mountains:
Awake! The Bridegroom cometh!   I awoke to sleep no more.
But an eternal consummation is dark Enion.
535   The watery grave.   Oh! thou cornfield.   Oh! thou vegetative happy.
More happy is the dark consumer.   Hope drowns all my torment,
For I am now surrounded by a shadowy vortex drawing
The spectre quite away from Enion that I die a death
Of bitter hope, although I consume in these raging waters,

540 The furrowed field replies to the grave, I hear her reply to me,—
Behold the time approaches fast that thou shalt be as a thing
Forgotten. When one speaks of thee he will not be believed.
When the man gently fades away in his immortality.
When the mortal disappears in improved knowledge, cast away
545 The former things; so shall the mortal gently fade away,
And so become invisible to those who still remain.
Listen. I will tell thee what is done in the caverns of the grave.
The Lamb of God has rent the veil of mystery, soon to return
In clouds and fires around the rock, and thy mysterious tree.
550 And as the seed waits eagerly watching for its flower and fruit,
Anxious its little soul looks out into the clear expanse
To see if hungry winds are abroad with their invisible array.
So Man looks out in tree, and herb, and fish, and bird, and beast,
Collecting up the scattered portions of his immortal body
555 Into the elemental forms of everything that grows.
He tries the sullen north wind, riding on its angry furrows,
The sultry south when the sun rises, and the angry east
When the sun sets and the clods harden and the cattle stand
Drooping, and the birds hide in their silent nests. He stores his
      thoughts
560 As in store-houses in his memory. He regulates the forms
Of all beneath and all above, and in the gentle west
Reposes where the sun's heat dwells. He rises to the sun
And to the planets of the night, and to the stars that gild
The Zodiacs, and the stars that sullen stand to north and south
565 He touches the remotest pole, and in the centre weeps
That Man should labour and sorrow, and learn and forget and return
To the dark valley whence he came, and begin his labours anew.
In pain he sighs, in pain he labours, and his universe
Sorrowing in birds over the deep, or howling in the wolf
570 Over the slain, and moaning in the cattle, and in the winds,
And weeping over Orc and Urizen in clouds and dismal fires,
And in the cries of birth and in the groans of death his voice
Is heard throughout the universe. Wherever a grass grows

Or a leaf buds, the Eternal Man is seen, is heard, is felt,
575 And all his sorrows, till he re-assumes his ancient bliss.

Such are the words of Ahania and Enion, and Los hears and weeps. ·
And Los and Enitharmon took the body of the Lamb
Down from the cross, and placed it in a sepulchre he had hewn
For himself in the rock of Eternity, trembling and in despair.
580 Jerusalem wept over the sepulchre two thousand years.

END OF THE EIGHTH NIGHT.

Night the Ninth

BEING

THE LAST JUDGMENT.

And Los and Enitharmon builded Jerusalem, weeping
Over the sepulchre and over the crucified body,
Which, to their phantom eyes, appeared still in the sepulchre.
But Jesus stood beside them in the spirit, separating
5 Their spirit from their body.   Terrified at Non-Existence—
For such they deemed the death of the body—Los his vegetable hands
Outstretched, his right hand branching out in fibrous strength,
Seized the sun.   His left hand, like dark roots, covered the moon,
And tore them down, cracking the heavens across from immense to
    immense.
10 Then fell the fires of eternity with loud and shrill
Sound of loud trumpet thundering along from heaven to heaven.
A mighty sound articulate: Awake, ye dead, and come
To Judgment from the four winds; awake and come away.
Folding like scrolls of the enormous volume of heaven and earth,
15 With thund'rous noise and dreadful shakings, rocking to and fro,
The heavens are shaken, and the earth removéd from its place,
The foundations of the eternal hills are all discoveréd,
The thrones of kings are shaken, they have lost their robes and crowns,
The poor smite their oppressors, they awake up to the harvest,—
20 The naked warriors rush together down to the sea-shore
Trembling before the multitude of slaves now set at liberty.
They become like wintry flocks, like forests stripped of leaves.
The oppressed pursue like the wind.   There is no room for escape.

The spectre of Enitharmon let loose upon the troubled deep,
25 Wailed shrill in the confusion, and the spectre of Urthona
Received her in the darkening south.   Their bodies lost, they stood
Trembling and weak, and faint embrace, a fierce desire as when
Two shadows mingle on a wall   They wail, and shadowy tears
Fell down, and shadowy forms of joy mixed with despair and grief—
30 Their bodies buried in the ruins of the universe,
Mingled with the confusion   Who shall call them from their graves?
Rahab and Tirzah wail aloud in the wild flames.   They give up them-
    selves to consummation.
The books of Urizen unroll with dreadful noise.   The folding serpent
Of Orc began to consume in fierce raving fire.   His fierce flame
35 Issued on all sides, gathering strength in animating volumes.
Roaming abroad on all the winds, raging intent, reddening
Into restless pillars of fire, rolling round and round, gathering
Strength from the earth's consumed, and heavens, and all hidden
    abysses,
Wherever the Eagle has explored, or Lion or Tiger trod,
40 Or where the comets of the night, or stars of asterial day
Have shot their arrows or long-beamed spears in wrath or fury.

And all the while the trumpet sounds,—Awake, ye dead, and come
To Judgment.   From the clotted gore, and from the hollow den,
Start forth the trembling millions into flames of mental fire,
45 Bathing their limbs in the bright visions of Eternity.
Then, like the doves from pillars of smoke, the trembling families
Of women and children throughout every nation under heaven
Cling round the men in bands of twenties and of fifties, pale
As snow that falls around a leafless tree upon the green.
50 Their oppressors have fallen, they have stricken, they awake to life,
Yet pale.   The just man stands erect, and looking up to heaven,
Trembling and stricken by the universal stroke.   The trees uproot,
The rocks groan horrible and run about.   The mountains and
The rivers cry with a dismal cry.   The cattle gather together;
55 Lowing they kneel before the heavens.   The wild beasts of the forests

Tremble. The Lion, shuddering, asks the Leopard : " Feelest thou
The dread I feel, unknown before ? My voice refuses to roar,
And in weak moans I speak to thee. . . . . This night,
Before the morning's dawn, the Eagle calléd to the Vulture,
60 The Raven calléd to the Hawk,—I heard from my forests black—
Saying : Let us go up, for soon I smell, upon the wind,
A terror coming from the south. The Eagle and Hawk fled away
At dawn, and ere the sun arose, the Raven and Vulture followed.
Let us flee also to the north." They fled. The Sons of Men
65 Saw them depart in dismal droves. The trumpets sounded loud,
And all the Sons of Eternity descended into Beulah.

In the fierce flames the limbs of Mystery lay consuming, with howling
And deep despair. Rattling go up the flames around the synagogue
Of Satan. Loud the serpent Orc raged through his writhing folds.
70 The tree of Mystery burned up in folding flames.
Blood issued out in rushing volumes, pouring in whirlpools fierce,
From out the flood-gates of the tree. The gates are burst, downpouring
The torrents black upon the earth. The blood pours down incessant.
Kings in their palaces lie drowned. Shepherds, their flocks and tents,
75 Roll down the mountains in black torrents. Cities, villages,
High spires and castles drowned in the black deluge ; shoal on shoal
Float the dead carcases of men and beasts, driven to and fro on flames
Of foaming blood beneath the black incessant sky, till all
Mystery's tyrants are cut off, and not one left on earth.

80 And when all tyranny was cut off from the face of the earth,
    Around the dragon form of Urizen, and round his strong form,
The flames rolling intense abroad through the wide universe,
Began to enter the Holy City. Entering the dismal clouds,
The furious lightnings break their way. The wild flames rushing up,
85 The bloody deluge,—living flames, wingéd with intellect
And reason. Round the earth they march in order, flame by flame.
Issuing from the clotted gore, and from the hollow den,
Start forth the trembling millions into flames of mental fire,
Bathing their limbs in the bright visions of Eternity.

8

90   Beyond this universal confusion, beyond the remotest pole,
     Where their vortexes began to operate, there stands
     A horrible rock far in the north.   It was forsaken when
     Urizen gave the horses of light into the hands of Luvah.
     On this rock lay the faded head of the Eternal Man,
95   Enwrapt round with weeds of death, pale, cold in sorrow and woe,
     He lifts the blue lamps of his eyes, and cries with heavenly voice.
     Bowing his head over the consuming universe, he cries:

     Oh, weakness !   Oh, weariness !   Oh, war within my members !
     My sons exiled from my breast, pass to and fro before me.
100 My birds are silent in my hills, flocks die beneath my branches.
     My tents are fallen, my trumpets and the sweet sound of my harps
     Is silent on my clouded hills that belch forth storms and fires.
     My milk of cows, and honey of bees, and fruit of golden harvest
     Are gathered in the scorching heat and in the driving rain.
105 My robe is turned to confusion, and my bright gold to stone.
     Where once I sat, I weary walk in misery and pain,
     For from within my withered breast grown narrow with my woes
     The corn is turned to thistles and the apples into poison;
     The birds of song to murderous crows, my joys to bitter groans;
110 The voices of children in my tents to cries of helpless infants,
     And all exiled from the face of light and shine of morning,
     In this dark world, a narrow house, I wander up and down.
     I hear Mystery breathing in the flames of consummation.
     When shall the man of future times become as in days of old ?
115 Oh, weary life!   Why sit I here and give up all my powers
     To indolence, to the night of death, when indolence and mourning
     Sit hovering over my dark threshold ?   Though I arise, look out
     And scorn the war within my members, yet my heart is weak
     And my head faint.   Yet I will look again into the morning.
120 Whence is this sound of rage of men drinking each other's blood;
     Drunk with the smoking gore, and red, but not with nourishing wine ?

     The Eternal Man sat on the rock and cried with awful voice:

Oh, Prince of Light, where art thou? I behold thee not as once
In these eternal fields, in clouds of morning stepping forth
125 With harps and songs, when bright Ahania sang before thy face,
And all thy sons and daughters gathered round thy ample table.
See you not all this racking furious confusion?
Come forth from the slumbers of thy cold abstraction. Come forth,
Arise into eternal births. Shake off thy cold repose,—
130 Schoolmaster of our souls,—great opposer of change, arise,
That the eternal worlds may see thy face in peace and joy,
That thou, dread form of certainty, may'st sit in town and village,
While little children play around thy feet in gentle awe,
Fearing thy frown, loving thy smile. Oh! Urizen, Prince of Light,

135 He called. The deep buried his voice, and answer none returned.
Then wrath burst round. The Eternal Man was wrath again. He
cried:

Arise, oh! thou strong form of Death, oh! Dragon of the deeps,
Lie down before my feet, oh! Dragon, let Urizen arise.
Oh! how could'st thou deform those beautiful proportions
140 Of life and person; for as the person, so is his life proportioned.
Let Luvah rage in the dark deep, even to consummation,
For if thou feedest not his rage it will subdue in peace.
But if thou darest, obstinate, refuse my stern behest,
Thy crown and sceptre I will seize, and regulate all thy members
145 In stern severity, and cast thee out into the indefinite
Where nothing lives, there to wander, and if thou returnest weary,
Weeping, at the threshold of existence, I will steel my heart
Against thee to Eternity, and never receive thee more.
Thy self-destroying, beast-formed science shall be thy eternal lot.
150 My anger against thee is greater than against this Luvah,
For war is energy enslaved, but thy religion,
First author of this war, and the destruction of honest mind
Into confused perturbation, and strife, and horror, and pride,
In a deceit so detestable, that I will cast thee out

8 *

¹⁵⁵ If thou repentest not, and leave thee as a rotten branch to burn,
With Mystery the harlot, and with Satan for over and ever.
Error can never be redeemed in all Eternity—
But sin, even Rahab, is redeemed in blood and fury, and jealousy,
That line of blood that stretches across the windows of the morning,
¹⁶⁰ Redeemed from Error's power,—wake, thou Dragon of the Deep.

Urizen wept in the dark deep, anxious his scaly form
To re-assume the Human—and he wept in the dark deep,
Saying —Oh ! that I had never drank the wine or eat the bread
Of dark mortality, or cast my eyes into futurity, nor turned
¹⁶⁵ My back, darkening the present, clouding with a cloud,
And building arches high, and cities, turrets, towers and domes,
Whose smoke destroyed the pleasant garden, and whose running kennels
Choked the bright rivers; burdening with my ships the angry deep;
Through chaos seeking for delight, and in spaces remote
¹⁷⁰ Seeking the eternal, which is always present to the wise ;
Seeking for pleasure, which, unsought, falls round the infant's path,
And on the fleeces of mild flocks who neither care nor labour ;
But I, the labourer of ages, whose unwearied hands
Are thus deformed with hardness, with the sword and with the spear,
¹⁷⁵ And with the chisel and the mallet—I, whose labours vast
Order the nations, separating family by family,
Alone enjoying not. I alone in misery supreme,
Ungratified, give all my joy unto this Luvah and Vala,
Then go to dark Futurity I will cast thee out from these
¹⁸⁰ Heavens of my brain, nor will I look on dark futurity more.
I cast futurity away, and turn my back upon that void,
Which I have made, for, lo ! Futurity is in this moment.
Let Orc consume, let Tharmas rage, let dark Urthona give
All strength to Los and Enitharmon, and let Los's self, enraged,
¹⁸⁵ Rend down this fabric, as a wall ruined, a family extinct.
Rage, Orc ! rage, Tharmas ! Urizen no longer curbs your rage.

So Urizen spoke, and shook his snows from off his shoulders, and arose

As on a pyramid of mist, his white robes scattering
The fleecy white renewed.   He shook his aged mantle off
190 Into the fires, then, glorious, bright, exulting in his joy,
He sounding rose into the heavens in naked majesty,
In radiant youth, when, lo ! like garlands in the eastern sky
When vocal May comes dancing from the East, Ahania came,
Exulting in her flight.   As when a bubble rises up
195 On to the surface of a lake, Ahania rose in joy.
Excess of joy is worse than grief.   Her heart beat high ; her blood
Burst its bright vessels : she fell down dead at the feet of Urizen,
Outstretched, a smiling corse.   They buried her in a silent cave.
Urizen dropped a tear.   The Eternal Man darkened with sorrow.

200 The three daughters of Urizen guard Ahania's death-couch ;
Raging from the confusion, in tears and howling and despair,
Calling upon their father's name, upon their father dark.

And the Eternal man said,—Hear my words, O Prince of Light
Behold Jerusalem, in whose bosom the Lamb of God
205 Is seen ; though slain before her gates, he self-renewed remains
Eternal, and I through him awake from death's dark vale.
The times revolve.   The time is coming when all these delights
Shall be renewed, and all these elements that now consume
Shall re-flourish.   Then bright Ahania shall awake from death,
210 A glorious vision to thine eyes, a self-renewing vision,—
The spring—the summer—to be thine.   Then sleep the wintry days
In silken garments, spun by her own hands against her funeral.
The winter thou shalt plough and lay thy stores into thy barns,
Expecting to receive Ahania in the spring with joy.
215 Immortal thou, regenerate she, and all the lovely sex
From her shall learn obedience and prepare a wintry grave,
That spring may see them rise in tenfold joy and sweet delight.
Thus shall the female also live the life of Eternity
Because the Lamb of God creates himself a bride and wife,
220 That we his children evermore may live in Jerusalem,

Which now descendeth out of heaven, a city, yet a woman.
Mother of myriads redeemed and born in her spiritual palaces
By a new spiritual birth regenerated from death.
Urizen said : I have erred and my error remains with me.
225 What chain encompasses ? In what rock is the river of light confined
That issues forth in the morning by measure and in the evening by
    carefulness ?
Where shall we take our stand to view the infinite and unbounded ?
And where our human feet, for, lo ! our eyes are in the heavens.

He ceased, for, riven link from link, the bursting universe exploding,
230 All things revived flew from their centres, rattling bones
To bones join, shaking, convulsed, the shivering clay breathes.
Each speck of dust, to the Earth's centre, nestles round and round
In pangs of an Eternal Birth, in torment, awe, and fear.
All spirits deceased, let loose from reptile prisons, come in shoals.
235 Wild furies from the Tiger's brain and from the Lion's eyes,
And from the Ox and Ass come moping terrors   From the Eagle
And Raven, numerous as the leaves of autumn,—every species
Flock to the trumpet, fluttering over the sides of the grave and crying
In the fierce wind round the heavy rocks and mountains filled with
    groans.
240 On rifted rocks, suspended in the air by inward fires,
Many a woeful company ; and many on clouds and waters,
Fathers, friends, and mothers, infants, kings, and warriors,
Priests and chained captives meet together in horrible fear,
And every one of the dead appears as he had lived before ;
245 And all the marks remain of the slave's scourge and tyrant's crown,
And of the priest's overgorged abdomen, and of the merchant's thin
Sinewy deceptions, and of the warrior's all-braving thoughtlessness,
In lineaments too extended and in bones too straight and long.
They show their wounds · they accuse : they seize the oppressor ;
    howlings began
250 On the golden Palace ;—songs of joy on the desert. The cold babe
Stands in the furious air ; he cries. The children of six thousand years

Who died in infancy rage furious,—a mighty multitude rage furious,
Naked and pale. Standing in the expecting air to be delivered,
Rend limb from limb the warrior, the tyrant, reuniting in pain.
255 The furious wind still rends around. They listen not to entreaty,
They view the flames red rolling on through the wide universe
From the dark jaws of death beneath and desolate shores remote,
These covering vaults of heaven and these breathing globes of earth.
One planet calls to another and one star inquires of another:
260 What flames are these, coming from the south? What noise, what
dreadful rout
As of a battle in the heavens! Hark! Heard you not the trumpet
As of fierce battle? While they spoke, the flames come intense roaring.
They see him whom they have pierced, they wail because of him,
They magnify themselves no more against Jerusalem, nor
265 Against her little ones. The innocent accused before the judges
Shines with immortal glory. Trembling, the judge springs from his
throne,
Hiding his face in the dust beneath the prisoner's feet and saying:
Brother of Jesus, what have I done? Entreat thy Lord for me:
Perhaps I may be forgiven. While he speaks the flames roll on
270 And after the flames appears the cloud of the Son of Man
Descending from Jerusalem with power and great glory.
All nations look up to the cloud and behold Him who was crucified.
The prisoner answers: You scourged my father to death before my face
When I stood bound with cords and heavy chains. Your hypocrisy
275 Shall now avail you nought. So saying he dashed him with his foot.

The cloud is Blood, dazzling upon the heavens, and in the cloud
Above, upon its volumes, is beheld a throne, as a pavement
Of precious stones, surrounded by twenty-four venerable patriarchs,
And these again surrounded by four Wonders of the Almighty
280 Incomprehensible, pervading all, within and round about
Fourfold, each in the other reflected. They are named Lifes in
Eternity
Four starry universes, going forward from Eternity to Eternity.
And the Fallen Man who was arisen upon the Rock of Ages,

And Urizen, arose with him, walking through all the flames
285 To meet the Lord, coming to Judgment, but the flames repelled them.
Still to the Rock, in vain, they strove to enter the consummation
Together, for the redeemed Man could not enter the consummation.

Then seized the sons of Urizen the plough. They polished it
From rust of ages   All its ornaments of gold, silver and ivory,
290 Re-shone across the field immense when all the nations
Darkened, like mould, in the divided furrows where the weed
Triumphs in its own destruction. They took down the harness
From the blue walls of heaven, starry, jingling, ornamented
With beautiful art,—the study of Angels, the workmanship of
    Demons,—
295 When Heaven and Hell in emulation strove in the spirits of glory.
The noise of rural works resounded through the heavens of heavens,
The horse neighs from the battle, the wild bulls from the sultry waste,
The tigers from the forests, the lions from the sandy deserts.
They sing; they seize the instruments of harmony; they throw away
300 The spear, the bow, the gun, the mortar. They level the fortifications.
They beat the iron engines of destruction into wedges.
They give them to Urthona's sons. Ringing the hammers sound
In dens of death to forge the spade, the mattock, and the axe,
The heavy roller to break the clods,—to pass over the nations.

305 The Sons of Urizen shout: their father rose. The Eternal horses
Harnessed, they call to Urizen. The heavens move at their call.
The limbs of Urizen shone with ardour. He laid his hand on the
    plough,
Through dismal darkness drove the plough of ages over cities
And all their villages; over mountains, and all their valleys;
310 Over caves and caverns of the dead, over the planets,
And over the void spaces; over sun and moon, and star and con-
    stellation.

Then Urizen commanded and they brought the seed of Men.
The trembling souls of all the dead stood before Urizen,

Weak, wailing in the troubled air, East, West, and North and South.
315 He turned the horses loose and laid the plough in the northern corner
Of the wide universal field, then stepped forth into the immense.
Then he began to sow the seed. He girded round his loins
With a bright girdle, and his skirt, filled with immortal souls.
Howling and wailing fly the souls from Urizen's strong hand,
20 For from the hand of Urizen the myriads fall like stars
Into their own appointed places, driven back by the winds.
The naked warriors rush together down to the sea-shore.
They are become like wintry flocks, like forests stripped of leaves,
The kings and princes of the earth cry with a feeble cry,
325 Driven on the unproducing sands, and on the hardened rocks.

And all the while the flames of Orc follow the venturous feet
Of Urizen, and all the while the trump of Tharmas sounds.
Weeping and wailing fly the souls from Urizen's strong hands.
The daughters of Urizen stand with cups and measures of strong wine
330 Immense upon the heavens with bread and delicate repasts.
Then follows the golden harrow in the midst of mental fires,
To ravishing melody of flutes, and harps, and softest voice.
The seed is harrowed in while flames heal the black mould and cause
The human harvest to begin.   Toward the south first sprang
335 The myriads, and in silent fear they look out of their graves.

Then Urizen sits down to rest, and all his wearied sons
Take their repose on beds. They drink, they sing, they view the
    flames
Of Orc. In joy they view the human harvest springing up.
A time they give to sweet repose, till all the harvest is ripe.

340 And lo ! like harvest moon, Ahania cast off her dark clothes—
She folded them up in care, in silence, and her brightening limbs
Bathed in the clear spring of the rock. Then from her darksome cave
Issued in majesty divine. Urizen rose from his couch
On wings of tenfold joy, clapping his hands, his radiant wings

345 In the immense.   As when the sun dances upon the mountains
    A shout of jubilee in lovely notes responds from daughter to daughter,
    From son to son, as if the stars beaming innumerable
    Through night, should sing soft warbling, filling the earth and heaven,
    And bright Ahania took her seat by Urizen in songs and joy.

350 The Eternal Man also sat down upon the couches of Beulah,
    Sorrowful that he could not put off his newly risen body
    In mental flames. The flames refused, they drove him back to Beulah.
    His body was redeemed to be permanent through mercy Divine.

    And now fierce Orc had quite consumed himself in mental flames,
355 Expending all his energy against the fuel of fire.
    The Regenerate Man stooped his holy head over the universe, and in
    His holy hands received the flaming demon and dimness of smoke
    And gave him to Urizen's hands.   The immortal frowned, saying,
    Luvah and Vala, henceforth you are servants; obey and live.
360 You shall forget your former state.   Return and love in peace,
    Into your place, the place of seed, not in the brain or heart.
    If Gods combine against Man setting their dominion above
    The Human Form Divine, thrown down from their high station
    In the eternal heavens of Human Imagination, buried beneath
365 In dark oblivion, with incessant pangs, ages on ages,
    In enmity and war first weakened, then in stern repentance
    They must renew their brightness, and their disorganized functions
    Again reorganize till they resume the image of the human,
    Co-operating in the bliss of Man, obeying his will,
370 Servants to the infinite and eternal of the human form

    Luvah and Vala descended and entered the gate of dark Urthona
    And walked from the hands of Urizen in the shadow of Vala's garden,
    Where the impressions of despair and hope for ever vegetate
    In flowers and fruits, fishes and birds, and beasts and clouds and waters.
375 The land of doubts and shadows, sweet delusions, unformed hopes,
    They saw no more, the terrible confusions of the wracking universe
    They heard not, saw not, felt not the horrible confusion,

For in their orbed senses within closed up they wandered at will.
And those upon the couches viewed them in the dreams of Beulah,
380 As they reposed from the terrible wide universal harvest.
Invisible Luvah in bright clouds hovered over Vala's head,
And thus their ancient golden age renewed, for Luvah spoke
With voice mild from his golden cloud upon the breath of morning.

Come forth, oh! Vala, from the grass and from the silent dew;
385 Rise from the dews of death, for the Eternal Man is risen.

She rises among flowers and looks toward the eastern clearness,
She walks, yea runs, her feet are winged on the top of the bending grass,
Her garments rejoice in the vocal winds, and her hair glistens with dew.

She answers thus: Whose voice is this, the voice of the nourishing air
390 In the spirit of the morning, awaking the soul from its grassy bed?
Where dost thou dwell? For thee I seek, and were it not but for thee
I must have slept eternally, nor felt the dews of the morning.
Look how the opening dawn advances with local harmony.
Look how the beams foreshow the rising of the glorious power.
395 The sun is thine. He goeth forth in his majestic brightness.
Oh, thou awaking voice that callest! And who shall answer thee?
Where dost thou flee, oh! fair one? Where dost thou seek thy happy
place
To yonder brightness? There I haste, for since I came from thence
I must have slept eternally nor have felt the dew of morning.

400 Eternally thou must have slept nor have felt the morning dew.
But for yon nourishing sun, 'tis that by which thou art arisen.
The birds adore the sun: the beasts rise up and play in his beams,
And every flower and every leaf rejoices in his light,
Then, oh! thou fair one, sit thee down, for thou art as the grass,
405 Thou risest in the dew of morning and at night art folded up.

Alas! I am but as a flower; then will I sit me down,
Then will I weep, then I'll complain, and sigh for immortality,

And chide my maker,—thee, oh! sun, that raisedst me to fall.
So saying she sat down and wept beneath the apple-trees.

410 Oh! be thou blotted out, oh! sun, that raisedst me to trouble,
That gavest me a heart to crave, that raisedst me, thy phantom,
To feel thy heart, and see thy light, and wander here alone,
Hopeless, if I am like the grass, and so shall pass away.

Rise, sluggish soul.   Why sit'st thou here?   Why dost thou sit and
    weep?
415 Yon sun shall wax old and decay, but thou shalt ever flourish.
The fruit shall ripen and fall down, the flowers consume away,
But thou shalt still survive.   Arise and dry thy dewy tears.

Ah, shall I still survive?   Whence came that sweet and comforting
    voice?
And whence that voice of sorrow? Oh! sun, thou'rt nothing now to me.
420 Go on thy course rejoicing and let us both rejoice together.
I walk among his flocks and hear the bleeting of his lambs.
Oh! that I could behold his face and follow his pure feet.
I walk by the footsteps of his flocks.   Come hither, tender flocks.
Can you converse with a pure soul that seeketh for her maker?
425 You answer not.   Then am I set your mistress in the garden.
I'll watch you and attend your footsteps.   You are not like the birds
That sing and fly in the bright air . but you do lick my feet
And let me touch your woolly backs and follow me as I sing.
For in my bosom a new song arises to the Lord,
430 Rise up, oh! sun, most glorious minister of light and day.
Flow on, ye gentle airs, and bear the voice of my rejoicing.
Wave freshly yon clear water flowers around the tender grass.
Follow me, oh! my flocks, and hear me sing my rapturous song.
I will cause my voice to be heard on the clouds that gather in the sun.
435 I will call; and who shall answer me? I will sing; who shall reply?
For from my pleasant hills behold the living, living spring,
Running among my green pastures, delighting among my trees.

I am not here alone: my flocks, you are my brethren.
And you, oh! birds that sing and adorn the sky, you are my sisters.
440 I sing and you reply to my song; I rejoice, and you are glad.
Follow me, oh! my flocks; we will now descend into the valley.
Oh, how delicious are the grapes, flourishing in the sun!
How clear the spring of the rock, running among the golden sand!
How cool the breezes of the valley, and the arms of the branching trees!
445 Cover us from the sun. Come near and let us sit in the shade.
My Luvah here hath placed me in a green and pleasant land
And given me fruits and pleasant waters, and warm hills, and cool
valleys.
Here will I build myself a house, and here call on his name.
Then I'll return when I am weary and take my pleasant rest.

450 So spoke the sinless soul and laid her head in the snowy fleece
Of a curled ram, who stretched himself, laid down in sleep beside,
And soft sleep fell upon her eyelids in the silent noon of day.

Then Luvah passéd by, and looked, and saw the sinless soul,
And said: Let a pleasant house arise to be a dwelling-place
455 Of this immortal spirit growing in lower Paradise.
He spoke, and pillars were builded, and walls, as white as ivory.
The grass she slept upon was paved with pavement as of pearl.
Beneath her rose a downy bed, and a ceiling covered all.

Vala awoke. When in the pleasant gates of sleep I entered
460 I saw my Luvah like a spirit stand in the bright air.
Around him stood spirits like me, who reared me a bright house,
And here I see the house remain in my most pleasant world.
My Luvah smiled. I kneeléd down. He laid his hand on my head,
And when he laid his hand upon me from the gates of sleep I came
465 Into this bodily house to tend my flocks in my pleasant garden.

So saying, she arose and walked around her beautiful house,
And then from her white door she looked to see her bleating lambs,
But her flocks were gone up from beneath the trees into the hills.
I see the hand that leadeth me doth also lead my flocks,

470 She went to her flocks, and turnéd oft to see her shining house.
　　She stooped to drink of the clear spring, and eat the grapes and apples.
　　She bore the fruits in her lap.   She gathered flowers for her bosom.
　　She calléd to her flocks, saying often, Follow me, oh! my Flocks.
　　They followed her to the silent valley beneath the spreading trees,
475 And on the river's margin she ungirded her golden girdle.
　　She stood in the river and viewed herself within the wavy glass,
　　And her bright hair was met with waters   She rose from the river,
　　And as she rose her eyes were opened to the world of waters,
　　And saw Tharmas sitting upon the rocks beside the weary sea.

480 He stroked the water from his beard and mourned through the summer
　　　valley.
　　And Vala stood on the rocks of Tharmas and heard the mournful voice:
　　Oh! Enion, my weary head is in the bed of death,
　　For weeds of death have wrapped around my limbs in the hoary deeps.
　　I sit in the place of shells and mourn, and thou art closed in clouds.
485 When will the time of clouds be past, and the dismal night of Tharmas?
　　Arise, oh! Enion, arise and smile upon my head,
　　As thou dost smile upon the barren mountains, and they rejoice.
　　When wilt thou smile on Tharmas, oh! thou bringer of golden day?
　　Arise, oh! Enion, arise, for lo! I have calmed my seas.

490 So saying, his faint head he laid upon the oozy rock,
　　And darkness covered all the deep.   The light of Enion faded,
　　Like a faint flame quivering upon the surface of the darkness.

　　Then Vala lifted up her hands to heaven to call on Enion
　　She called, but none could answer her, and the echoes her voice returned.
495 Where is the voice of God that called me from the silent dew?
　　Where is the Lord of Vala?   Dost thou hide in clefts of the rock?
　　Why should'st thou hide thyself from Vala, from the soul that wanders
　　　desolate?

　　She ceased, and light beamed round her like the glory of the morning.
　　And she arose out of the river and girded her golden girdle.

500 And now her feet step on the grassy bosom of the ground
Among her flocks. She turned her eyes toward her pleasant house.
She saw in the doorway beneath the trees two little children playing.
She drew near to her house, and her flocks followed in her footsteps.
The children clung around her knees. She embraced them and wept.

505 Thou, little boy, art Tharmas, and thou, bright girl, Enion.
How are ye thus renewed and brought into the garden of Vala ?
She embraced them in tears, till the sun descended the western hills,
And then she entered her bright house, leading her mighty children.
And when night came, her flocks laid round the house beneath the trees.

510 She laid the children on the beds which she saw prepared in the house,
Then last, herself, laid down, and closed her eyelids in soft slumbers.
And in the morning, when the sun arose in the crystal sky,
Vala awoke, and called her children from their gentle slumbers:
Awake, oh ! Enion, awake, and let thine immortal eyes
515 Enlighten all the crystal house of Vala ! Awake ! awake !
Awake, Tharmas ! Awake, awake, thou child of many tears.
Open the orbs of thy blue eyes and smile upon my gardens.

The children awoke and smiled on Vala. She kneeled by the golden
     couch.
She pressed them to her bosom, and her pearly tears dropped down.
520 Oh, my sweet children ! Enion, let Tharmas kiss thy cheek.
Why dost thou turn thyself away from his sweet watery eyes ?
Tharmas, henceforth in Vala's bosom thou shalt find sweet peace.
Oh, bless the lovely eyes of Tharmas and the eyes of Enion !

They rose; they went out wandering, sometimes together, sometimes
     alone.
525 Why weep'st thou, Tharmas, child of tears, in the bright house of joy ?
Doth Enion avoid the sight of thy blue heavenly eyes ?
And dost thou wander with my lambs, and wet their innocent faces
With thy bright tears, because the steps of Enion are in the gardens ?
Arise, sweet boy, and let us follow the path of Enion,

530 So saying, they went down into the garden among the fruits,
And Enion sang among the flowers that grew among the fruits,
And Vala said : Go, Tharmas ; weep not,—go to Enion.

And he said : Oh ! Vala, I am sick. All this garden of pleasure
Swims like a dream before my eyes. But the sweet smiling fruit
535 Revives me to new death. I fade, even as a water-lily
In the sun's heat, till in the night, on the couch of Enion,
I drink new life, and feel the breath of sleeping Enion.
But in the morning she arises to avoid my eyes,
Then my loins fade, and in the house I sit me down and weep.

540 Cheer up thy countenance, bright boy, and go to Enion.
Tell her that Vala waits her in the shadows of her garden.
He went with timid steps, and Enion, like the ruddy morn
When infant spring appears in swelling buds and opening flowers,
Behind her veil withdraws ; so Enion turned her modest head.

545 But Tharmas spoke. Vala seeks thee, sweet Enion, in the shades.
Follow the steps of Tharmas, oh ! though brightness of the garden.
He took her hand reluctant. She followed in infant doubts.
There in eternal childhood, straying among Vala's flocks,
In infant sorrow and joy alternate, Enion and Tharmas play'd
550 Round Vala, in the garden of Vala, and by her river's margin.
They are the shadows of Tharmas and Enion in Vala's world.

And the sleepers who rested from their harvest work beheld these
     visions.
Then were the sleepers entertained upon the couches of Beulah,
When Luvah and Vala were closed up in their world of shadowy forms.
555 Darkness was all beneath the heaven : only a little light,
Such as glows out from sleeping spirits, awoke in the deeps beneath.
As when a wind sweeps over a cornfield the noise of souls
Through all the immense, borne down by clouds swagging in autumnal
     heat,
Muttering along from heaven to heaven, hoarse roll the human forms

⁵⁶⁰ Beneath thick clouds, the dreadful lightnings burst and thunders roll,
Down pour the torrent floods from heaven on all the human harvest.

Then Urizen, sitting at his repose on beds in the bright south,
Cried, "Times are ended." He exulted, he arose in joy.
He poured his light, and all his sons and daughters poured their light
⁵⁶⁵ To exhale the spirits of Luvah and Vala through the atmosphere.
And Luvah and Vala saw the light. Their spirits soon exhaled
In all their ancient innocence. The floods depart, the clouds
Dissipate, or sink into the sea of Tharmas. Luvah sat
Alone on the bright heavens in peace. The spirits of men beneath
⁵⁷⁰ Cried out to be delivered, and the spirit of Luvah wept
Over the human harvest, and over Vala, the sweet wanderer.
In pain the human harvest waved in horrible groans of woe.
The universal groan went up, the Eternal Man was darkened.

Then Urizen arose and took his sickle in his hand.
⁵⁷⁵ There is a brazen sickle, and a sceptre of iron hid
Deep in the south, guarded by a few solitary stars.
This sickle Urizen took; the scythe his sons embraced,
And went forth and began to reap, and all his joyful sons
Reaped the wide universe, and bound in sheaves a wondrous harvest.
⁵⁸⁰ They took them into the wide barn with loud rejoicings, and triumphs
Of flute and harp and drum and trumpet, horn and clarion.
The feast was spread in the bright south; and the Regenerated Man
Sat at the feast rejoicing, and the wine of Eternity
Was served round by the flames of Luvah all day and all the night.

⁵⁸⁵ And when morning began to dawn upon the distant hills,
A whirlwind rose up in the centre, and in the whirlwind a shriek.
And in the shriek a rattling of bones, and in the rattling of bones
A dolorous groan, and from the dolorous groan in tears,
Rose Enion like a gentle light, and Enion spoke, saying:

⁵⁹⁰ Oh! Dream of Death, the human form dissolving, compassèd
By beasts and worms and creeping things, and darkness and despair.

9

The clouds fall off from my wet brow, the dust from my cold limbs,
Into the sea of Tharmas.   Soon renewed, a golden Moth
I shall cast off my death-clothes and embrace Tharmas again.

595 For, lo! the winter melted away upon the distant hills,
And all the black mould sings. She spoke to her infant race; her milk
Descends down on the land, the thirsty land drinks and rejoices.
Wondering to behold the emmet, the grasshopper, the jointed worm.
The roots shoot thick through solid rock, bursting their fibrous way.

600 They cry out in the joys of existence, and the broad tree stems
Rear on the mountains stem by stem.   The scaly newt creeps forth
From the stone, and from the rocky crevice springs the armed fly,
The spider and the bat burst from the hardenéd slime, crying
To one another: What are we ?   And whence is our delight ?

605 Lo ! the little moss begins to spring, and lo ! the tender weed
Creeps round about our secret nest. Flocks brighten on the hills,
Herds throng up through the valley, and the wild beasts fill the woods.

Joy thrilled through all the furious forms of Tharmas, humanizing.
Mild he embraced her whom he sought.   He raised her through the
    heavens,
610 Sounding his trumpet to awake the dead.   On high he soared
O'er ruined worlds, the misty tomb of the Eternal Prophet.

Then the Eternal Man arose.   He welcomed them to the feast.
The feast was spread in the bright south; and the Eternal Man
Sat at the feast rejoicing, and the wine of Eternity

615 Was served round by the flames of Luvah all day and all the night.
And many Eternal Men sat at the golden feast to see
The female form now separate.   They shuddered at the horrible thing
Born for the sport and amusement of Man, soon to drink up his
    powers.
They wept to see the shadow.   They said to one another: This is sin.

620 This is the vegetative world.   They remember the days of old.
And one of the Eternals spoke; all was silent at the feast.

Man is a worm renewed with joy, he seeks the caves of sleep

Among the flowers of Beulah in his selfish cold repose,
Forsaking brotherhood and universal love in selfish clay,
625 Folding the pure wings of his mind, seeking the places dark,
Abstracted from the roots of Nature then enclosed anew
In walls of gold. We cast him like a seed into the earth
Till times and spaces have passed over him. Duly every morn
We visit him, covering with a veil the immortal seed.
630 With windows from the inclement sky we cover him, and with walls
And hearths protect the selfish terror, till divided all
In families we see our shadows born, and thence we know
That Man subsists by brotherhood and universal love.
We fall on one another's necks, more closely we embrace,
635 Not for ourselves, but for the Eternal Family we live.
Man liveth not by self alone, but in his brother's face
Each shall behold the Eternal Father and love and joy abound.

So spoke the Eternal at the Feast. They embraced the new-born Man,
Calling him Brother, image of the Eternal Father. They sat down
640 At the immortal tables, sounding loud their instruments of joy,
Calling the Morning into Beulah. The Eternal Man rejoiced.
When Morning dawned the Eternals rose to labour in the vintage
Beneath they saw their children, wondering inconceivably
At the dark myriads in shadows in the worlds beneath.

645 The Morning dawned. Urizen rose, and in his hand the flail
Sounds on the floor, heard terrible by all beneath the heavens.
Dismal, loud, redounding, the nether floor shakes with the sound,
And all the Nations were threshed out, and the stars threshed from
 their husks.

Then Tharmas took the winnowing fan. The winnowing wind furious
650 Above, veered round by violent whirlwind driven west and south,
Tossèd the Nations like chaff into the sea of Tharmas.

Oh! Mystery, fierce Tharmas cried, behold thy end is come!
Art thou she that made the Nations drunk with the cup of Religion?

9*

Go down, ye kings and counsellors and giant warriors,
655 Go down into the depths, go down and hide yourselves beneath.
Go down with horse and chariots and trumpets of hoarse war.
Lo! how the pomp of Mystery goes down into the caves.
Her great men howl and throw the dust, and rend their hoary hair.
Her delicate women and children shriek upon the bitter wind,
660 Spoiled of their beauty, their hair rent, their skin shrivelled up.
Lo! darkness covers the long pomp of banners on the wind,
And black horses, and armed men, and miserable bound captives.
Where shall the graves receive them all, and where shall be their
    place?
And who shall mourn for Mystery, who never loosed her captives?
665 Let the slave, grinding at the mill, run out into the field;
Let him look up into the heavens and laugh in the bright air.
Let the enchained soul shut up in darkness and in sighing,
Whose face has never seen a smile in thirty weary years.
Rise and look out; his chains are loose, his dungeon doors are open.
670 And let his wife and children return from the oppressor's scourge.
They look behind at every step and believe it is a dream.
Are these the slaves that groan along the streets of Mystery?
Where are your bonds and task-masters? Are these the prisoners?
Where are your chains? Where are your tears? Why do you look
    around?
675 If you are thirsty, there is the river; go, bathe your parched limbs,
And the good of all the land is before you, for Mystery is no more.

Then all the slaves from every earth in the wide Universe
Sing a new song, drowning confusion in its happy notes,
While the flail of Urizen sounded loud, and the winnowing wind of
    Tharmas
680 So loud and clear in the wide heavens, and the song that they sang,
    was this,
Composed by an African Black from the little earth of Sotha:—

Aha! Aha! How came I here, in my sweet native land?
How came I here? Methinks I am as I was in my youth,

When in my father's house, in joy, I heard his cheering voice.
685 Methinks I see his flocks and herds and feel my limbs renewed,
And lo ! my brethren in their tents, and their little ones around them !

The song arose to the golden feast. The Eternal Man rejoiced.
The Eternal Man said : Luvah, the vintage is ripe. Arise !
The sons of Urizen shall gather the vintage with sharp hooks,
690 And all thy sons, oh ! Luvah, bear away the families of earth.
I hear the flail of Urizen. His barns are full. No room
Remains, and in the vineyards stand the abounding sheaves beneath
The falling grapes that odorous burst upon the winds   Arise !
My flocks and herds trample the corn, my cattle browse upon
695 The ripe clusters. The shepherds shout for Luvah, Prince of Love.
Let the Bulls of Luvah tread the corn and draw the loaded waggon
Into the barn while children glean the ears around the door.
Then shall they lift their innocent hands and stroke his furious nose,
And he shall lick the little girl's white neck, and on her head
700 Scatter the perfumes of his breath, while from his mountains high
The lion of terror shall come down, and bending his bright mane,
And crouching at her side shall eat from the curly boy's white lap
His golden food, and in the evening sleep before the door.

Attempting to be more than man we become less, said Luvah,
705 As he arose from the bright feast, drunk with the wine of ages.
His crown of thorns fell from his head, he hung his living lyre
Behind the seat of the Eternal Man, and took his way,
Sounding the song of Los, descending to the vineyards bright.
His sons, arising from the feast with golden baskets, follow,
710 A fiery train, as when the Sun sings in the ripe vineyards

Then Luvah stood before the wine-press. All his fiery sons
Brought up the loaded waggons with shoutings · ramping tigers play
In the jingling traces ; furious lions sound the song of joy
To the golden wheels circling upon the pavement of heaven, and all
715 The villages of Luvah rising ; the golden tiles of the villages

Reply to violins and tabors, to the pipe, flute, lyre, and cymbal.
These fill the legions of Mystery with maddening confusion.
Down, down, through the immense, with outcry, fury, and despair,
Into the wine-presses of Luvah, howling, fall the clusters
720 Of human families through the deep.   The wine-presses are filled,
The blood of life flowed plentiful ; odours of life arose
All round the heavenly arches, and the odours sang this song:

Terrible wine-presses of Luvah ! Oh, caverns of the grave !
How lovely the delights of those risen again from death !
725 Oh, trembling joy! Excess of joy is like excess of grief.

So sang the human odours round the wine-presses of Luvah.
But in the wine-presses is wailing, terror and despair.
Forsaken of their elements they vanish and are no more—
No more but a desire of being, a ravening desire,
730 Desiring like the hungry worm, and like the gaping grave.
They plunge into the elements.   The elements cast them forth,
Or else consume their shadowy semblance; but they, obstinate, •
Though framéd for destruction, cry—Oh, let us exist! for
This dreadful non-existence is worse than the pains of eternal birth :
735 Eternal death who can endure ?   Let us consume in fires,
In waters stifling, or in air corroding, or in earth shut up :
The pangs of eternal birth are better than the pangs of eternal death.

How red the sons and daughters of Luvah ! How they tread the grapes,
Laughing and shouting, drunk with odours ! Many fall overwearied :
740 Drowned in the wine is many a youth and maiden. Those around
Lay them on skins of tigers, or the leopard or wild ass,
Till they revive, or bury in cool grots with lamentation.
But in the wine-presses the human grapes sing not nor dance,
They howl and writhe in shoals of torment and fierce flames consuming,
745 In chains of iron and in dungeons circled with ceaseless fires,
In pits and dens and shades of death, and shapes of torment and woe;
The plates and the screws, and wracks, and saws, and cords, and fires,
     and floods ;

The cruel joy of Luvah's daughters, lacerating with knives
And whips their victims, and the deadly sport of Luvah's sons.
750 Timbrels and violins sport round the wine-presses. The little seed,
The sportive root, the earthworm, the snake-beetle, the wise emmet,
Dance round the wine-presses of Luvah. The centipede is there,
The ground spider with many eyes, the mole clothed with velvet,
The earwig armed, the tender maggot, emblem of immortality;
755 The slow slug, the grasshopper that sings and laughs and drinks:
The winter comes; he folds his slender bones without a murmur.
There is the nettle, that can sting with her soft down; and there
The indignant thistle, whose bitterness is bred in his milk, who lives
On the contempt of his neighbours. There are all the idle weeds
760 That creep about the obscure places, showing their various limbs
Naked in all their beauty, dancing round the wine-presses.
They dance around the dying, and they drink the howls and groans;
They catch the shrieks in cups of gold; they hand them to one another.
These are the sports of love, the sweet delights of amorous play:
765 Tears of the grape, the death-sweat of the cluster, the last sigh
Of the mild youth who listens to the luring songs of Luvah.

The Eternal Man darkened with sorrow, and a wintry mantle
Covered the hills. He said—Oh, Tharmas, rise! and oh, Urthona!
Then Tharmas and Urthona rose from the golden feast, satiated
770 With mirth and joy: Urthona, limping from his fall, on Tharmas leaned,
In his right hand his hammer. Tharmas held his shepherd's crook
Beset with gold, the ornaments formed by sons of Urizen.

Then Enion, and Ahania, and Vala, and the wife of dark Urthona,
Rose from the feast, with joy ascending to their golden looms.
775 Then the winged shuttle sang, the spindle, the distaff and reel
Rang sweet the praise of industry through all the golden room.
Heaven rang with winged exultation. All beneath howled loud,
With tenfold rout and desolation roared the caverns beneath
When the wide woof flowed down and when the Nations were gathered
    together.

780 Tharmas went down to the wine-presses, and beheld the sons and
    daughters
Of Luvah quite exhausted with the labour and quite filled
With new wine, that they began to torment one another and tread
The weak. Luvah and Vala slept on the floor, o'erwearied.

Urthona called his sons around when Tharmas called his sons
785 Numerous. They took the wine, they separated the lees,
And Luvah was put for dying on the ground by the sons of Tharmas
    and Urthona.
They formed the heaven of sweetest wood, of gold and silver and ivory,
Of glass and precious stones. They loaded all the waggons of heaven
And took away the wine of ages, with solemn songs and joy.

790 Luvah and Vala awoke, and all the sons and daughters of Luvah
Awoke. They wept to one another. They re-ascended
To the Eternal Man. In woe he cast them wailing into
The world of shadows, through the air, till winter is come and gone.
But the human wine stood wondering in all these delightful expanses,
795 The elements subsided, the heavens rolled on with vocal harmony.

Then Los, who is Urthona, rose in all his regenerate power.
The sea that rolled and foamed with darkness and the shadow of death
Vomited out and gave up all. The floods lift up their hands,
Singing and shrieking to the Man. They bow their hoary heads,
800 And murmuring in their channels flow and circle round his feet.

Then dark Urthona took the corn out of the stores of Urizen;
He ground it in his rumbling mills,—terrible the distress
Of all the Nations of the Earth, ground in the mills of Urthona.

In his hand Tharmas takes the storms: he turns the whirlwinds loose
805 Upon the wheels. The starry seas roar at his dread command,
And, eddying fierce, rejoice in the fierce agitation of the wheels
Of dark Urthona. Thundering earthquakes, fierce water-floods,
Rejoice to one another. Loud their voices shake the abyss,

Their dread forms tending the dire mills. The grey hoar-frost was
  there,
810 And his pale wife the aged snow. They watch over the fires,
They build the ovens of Urthona. Nature in darkness groans,
And Men are bound to sullen contemplation all the night.
Restless they turn on beds of sorrow, in their inmost brain
Feeling the crushing wheels: they rise, they write the bitter words
815 Of stern Philosophy, and knead the bread of Knowledge with tears
  and groans.

Such are the works of dark Urthona. Tharmas sifts the corn.
Urthona made the bread of ages, and he placed it
In golden and in silver baskets, in heavens of precious stone,
And then took his repose in winter, in the night of time.

820 The sun has left his blackness and has found a fresher morning,
And the mild moon rejoices in the clear and cloudless night,
And Man walks forth from midst of fires: the evil is all consumed.
His eyes behold the angelic spheres among the night and day;
The stars consumed, like a lamp blown out, and in their stead, behold !
825 One earth—one sea beneath ; nor erring globes wander, but stars
Of fire rise up nightly from the ocean ; and one sun
Each morning, like a new-born May, issues with songs of joy,
Calling the ploughman to his labour, the shepherd to his rest.
He wakes upon the eternal mountains, raising his heavenly voice
830 Conversing with the animal forms of wisdom night and day,
That, risen from the sea of fire, renewed walk over the earth ;
For Tharmas brought his flocks upon the hills, and in the vales
Around the Eternal Man's bright tent the little children play
Among the woolly flocks. The hammer of Urthona sounds
835 In the deep caves beneath, his limbs renewed ; the lions roar
Around the furnaces, and in evening sport upon the plains.
They raise their faces from the earth, conversing with the Man :

How is it we have walked through fire and yet are not consumed ?

How is it that all things are changed, even as in ancient times ?
840 The sun arises from his dewy bed, and the fresh airs
      Play in his smiling beams, giving the seeds of life to grow,
      And the fresh earth beams forth ten thousand thousand springs of life.

      Urthona is arisen in his strength: no longer now
      Divided from Enitharmon—no longer the Spectre of Los.
845 Where is the Spectre of prophecy? where is the deluded phantom?
      Departed: and Urthona issues from the ruinous walls,
      In all his ancient strength, to form the golden armour of science
      For intellectual war—the war of swords departed now,
849 In dark religions are departed—and sweet science reigns.

                    END OF THE DREAM.

ERRATA AND ADDENDA.

At the head of the addenda to "Vala" we must place the following lines, which were omitted from the text by error. They occur between lines 7 and 8, and lines 8 and 9, of Night II. The sentence should read thus :—

The horrors of death

Beneath his feet shot through him as he stood in the human brain, ·

No more exulting, for he saw eternal death beneath.

Pale, he beheld futurity ; pale, he beheld the abyss

Where Enion blind, and age-bent, wept in direful hunger craving,

All ravening like the hungry worm, and like the silent grave.

The next omission occurs between lines 88 and 89. The sentence should read :—

I opened all the floodgates of the heavens to quench her thirst,

And I commanded the great deep to hide her in his hand,

Till she became a little weeping infant, a span long.

In Night III. the following line is missing after line 103 :—

She ended ; from his wrathful throne burst forth the black-haired storms.

The next omission is between lines 126 and 127 of Night VI. The line is a sentence in itself :—

He knew they were his children, ruined in his ruined world.

After line 136, the following should be added :—

Then he had time enough to repent of his rashly-threatened curse.
He saw them accursed beyond his curse; his soul melted with fear.
He could not take their fetters off, for they grew to the soul,
Nor could he quench the fires, for they flamed out from the heart
Nor could he calm the elements, because himself was subject.
So he threw his flight in terror, in pain, and in repentant tears.

Other omissions occur in Night IX. Lines 454 and 455 conceal
the loss of a line. They should read thus :—

The furious wind still rends around. They flee in sluggish effort.
They beg, they entreat in vain now; they listened not to entreaty.

Between lines 283 and 284 a line is lost. The sentence should
read :—

And the fallen Man, who was arisen upon the Rock of Ages,
Beheld the visions of God, and he arose up from the Rock,
And Urizen rose with him, &c.

The restoration of these lines would alter the numbers of all the
references to such parts of each Night as follow them. This would
involve reprinting most of the first volume as well as of the poem,
and would delay the issue of the book to another season. The
omissions were discovered too late to be corrected in the press. The
original MS. was copied out twice; once before it was thoroughly
read and its order understood, and once after. These lines were lost
partly through the complexity of the MS., and partly through the
re-copying and the interpretation having been carried on at the same
time. The reader is begged to accept apologies.

The oversight of sending an un-read revise of the printed pages to
press has caused the following minor errors to be left in it :—

Night I —The new paragraph should begin at line 224, not 225.
Night II.—Line 8, for *though* read *thou*.
    „   108, for *right* read *night*.
    „   395, not numbered
New paragraphs should begin at lines 257 and 278, not at 255 and 276.
Night VI.—Line 274, for *ruin* read *river*.
Night VII.—Line 302, omit the last word *brutish*.
    „   307, omit the last word *conferred*.
    „   406, begin a new paragraph.

Night VII.—Line 420, misnumbered 20.

,, 426, end with a full stop.

,, 428, for *Luban* read *Laban.*

,, 564, for *waned* read *warned.*

,, 672, should begin, *Now, now, the battle*, &c.

Night VIII.—Line 1, for *counsel* read *council*

,, 23, for *Wand* read *Hand.*

,, 170, last word, for *roost* read *roots*

,, 240, numbered 40 erroneously

,, 402, for the first word *To*, read *Lo.*

,, 430, for *Urithona* read *Urthona.*

Night IX.—Line 130, before *great*, read *oh*

,, 224, begin a new paragraph.

,, 229, omit the word *bursting.*

,, 230, and 231, should read thus :—

All things revived, flew from their centres Rattling bones to bones,
Trembling and shaking, join : the shivering clay breathes.

,, 432, for *yon*, read *you.*

,, 546, for *though* read *thou.*

FRAGMENTS.

The following fragments discovered among the pages of the MS. of "Vala" are interesting. Some were used in the poem with variations. They give a useful glimpse into the growth of the ideas.

The following bears two illustrations—the first representing Urizen; the second, Ahania, not seeing Luvah as of old, but only his feet. The whole passage was as carefully copied out by Blake as the Nights I. and II., and seems to have been intended for Night II. But there is no place where it could come in. We must suppose it to have been rejected. Some lines will be recognized as afterwards used later in the poem.

> The horse is of more value than the Man, the Tiger fierce
> Laughs at the Human form. The Lion mocks and thirsts for blood.
> They cry, O Spider, spread thy web! Enlarge thy bones, and fill'd
> With marrow, sinews, and flesh, exalt thyself, attain a voice.
> 5 Call to thy dark armed hosts, for all 'the sons of Men muster
> together,
> To desolate their cities! Man shall be no more! Awake, O Hosts,
> The Bowstring sang upon the hills. Luvah and Vala rode
> Triumphant in the bloody sky. The Human form is no more.
>
> The listening stars heard. The first beam of the morning started
> back.
> 10 He cried out to his father—Depart! Depart! But sudden seized,
> And clad in steel, and his horse proudly neighed. He smelt the
> battle
> Afar off. Rushing back, reddening with rage, the Mighty Father
> Seized his bright sheep-hook, studded with gems and gold. He
> swung it round

His head, shrill sounding in the sky. Down rushed the sun with
    noise

15   Of war. The mountains fled away; they sought a place beneath.
Vala remained in deserts of dark solitude, nor sun nor moon
By night nor day to comfort her. She laboured in thick smoke.
Tharmas endured not; he fled howling. Then a barren waste sunk
    down,
Conglobing in the dark confusion. Meantime, Los was born ;

20   Thou, O Enitharmon. Hark! I hear the hammer of Los.
They melt the bones of Vala and the bones of Luvah in wedges ;
The innumerable sons and daughters of Luvah, closed in furnaces,
Melt into furrows. Winter blows his bellows. Ice and snow
Tend his dire anvils. Mountains moan, and rivers faint and fail

25   There is no city, nor cornfield, nor orchard ; all is rock and sand.
There is no sun, nor moon, nor stars, but ragged wintry rocks
Jostling together in the void: suspended by inward fires.

Impatience now no longer can endure. Distracted Luvah,
Bursting forth from the loins of Enitharmon, thou fierce terror,

30   Go, howl in vain. Smite, smite his fetters; smite, O wintry
    hammers ;
Smite, Spectre of Urthona ; mock the fiend who drew us down
From heavens of joy into their deep. Now rage, but rage in vain

Thus sang the demons of the deep   The clarion of war blew loud.
The feast redounds, and crowned with roses and the circling vine

35   The enormous Bride and Bridegroom sat. Beside them Urizen,
With faded radiance, sigh'd : forgetful of the flowing wine,
And of Ahania, his pure Bride ; but she was distant far.

But Los and Enitharmon sat in discontent and scorn,
Craving the more the more enjoying, drawing out sweet bliss

40   From all the turning wheels of heaven and the chariots of the slain,
At distance—far in night repelled, in direful hunger craving,

⁴² Summer and winter round revolving in the mighty deeps—
Enion ——

And so the fragment ends Though it was carefully re-copied
by Blake, the metre and music were never sufficiently considered.
Line 33 will be recognized as line 695 of "Vala," Night VII. The
Demons of the deep there sing the song attributed to the Spectre Sons
of Albion in "Jerusalem," p 65 The feast of which we have heard
is part of the Sun-myth of Urizen. Line 38, as will be noticed, is
line 646 of "Vala," Night II. It was for this portion of the book that
the page was destined, as is shown by its similarity in paper, style of
sketch, and handwriting to the whole of Night II. as much as by the
subject.

Here is another fragment—

. . . . Rahab triumphs over all. She took Jerusalem
Captive, a willing captive by delusive arts impelled
To worship Urizen's dragon form, to offer his own children
Upon the bloody altars. John saw these things revealed in heaven
5 On Patmos Isle, and heard the soul cry out to be delivered.
He saw the harlot of the Kings of Earth, and saw her cup
Of fornication, food of Orc and Satan, pressed from the fruit of
    Mystery.
But when she saw the form of Ahania weeping on the void,
And heard Enion's voice sound from the caverns of the grave,
10 No more spirit remained in her. She secretly left the synagogue;
She communed with Orc in secret; she hid him with the flax
That Enitharmon had numbered away from the heavens.
She gathered it together to consume her Harlot Robes
In bitterest contrition; sometimes self-condemning, repentant,
15 And sometimes kissing her robe of jewels and weeping over them;
Sometimes returning to the synagogue of Satan in pride,
And sometimes weeping before it in humility and trembling.
The synagogue of Satan uniting against mystery,—
Satan divided against Satan,—resolved in open Sanhedrin
20 To burn Mystery with fire, and form another from her ashes.
For God put it into their heart to fulfil all His will.

The ashes of Mystery began to animate; they called it Deism
And Natural Religion.   As of old, so now anew began
24   Babylon again in infancy, called Natural Religion.

In this fragment lines 4 and 5 repeat what is told in "Milton,"
p. 42, l. 22, and show, along with many other examples, that the
symbolic sense in which Blake read the Bible was the sense in which
he wrote his own poems.

The last lines show the same idea as that contained in the accounts
of the Twenty-seven Heavens—"Where Luther ends Adam begins
again in eternal circle."—"Jerusalem," p. 75, line 24.

Another fragment.   This time we have evidently a sketch of a
portion of Night I.   The symbol is *Virgo-Scorpio* in an early mental
form.   The next fragment will show it more matured.

Beneath the veil of Vala rose Tharmas from dewy tears.
The Eternal Man bow'd his bright head, and Urizen, Prince of Light,
Awakened Vala.   Ariston ran forth with bright Ahana, (*sic*)
And dark Urthona roused his shady bride from her deep den.
Pitying, they viewed the new-born demon, for they could not love
Male-formed the demon mild, athletic force his shoulders spread,
And his bright feet firm as a brazen altar; but the parts
To love devoted female.   All astonished stood the hosts
Of heaven, whilst Tharmas with winged speed flew to the sandy shore,
He rested on the desert wild, and on the raging sea
He stood and stretched his wings and——

With printless feet, scouring the corners of the joyful sky,
Female her form, bright on the summer, but the parts of love
Male, and her bow (? brow), radiant as day, darted a lovely scorn.
Tharmas beheld from his rock——

On the back of the paper bearing these fragments the following is
written in pencil:—

The ocean calm, the clouds fold round.   The fiery flame of love
Inwraps the immortal limbs, struggling in terrific joy

10

Not long. Thunders and lightnings swift, rendings and blushing
    winds
Sweep o'er the struggling copulation in fell writhing pangs.
They lie in twisting agonies beneath the covering heavens.

———

The womb impressed, Enion fled and hid in verdant mountains,
Yet her heavenly orbs——

———

From Enion pours the seed of life, and death in all her limbs
Froze. In the womb of Tharmas rush the rivers of Enion's pain.
Trembling he lay, swelled with the deluge in the anguish——

———

Here a fragment from Night I., hardly altered when incorporated
with the poem. Yet here, as elsewhere, some hint of the essential
idea escapes, and reveals itself in the first improvisation, though the
thought is less obvious when the sustained myth is produed.

Mingling his horrible brightness with her tender limbs, then high
    she soared,
Shrieking above the ocean, a bright wonder that Nature shuddered
    at—
Half woman and half serpent. All his lovely changing colours
    mix
With her fair crystal clearness. In her lips and cheeks his poisons
    rose
In blushes like the morning, and his scaly armour softening,
A monster, lonely in the heavens or wandering on the earth,
With female voice warbling upon the hills and hollow vales,
Beauty all blushing with desire, a self-enjoying wonder.
For Enion brooded, groaning loud; the rough sea vegetates
    golden rocks,
And thus her voice ;—Glory! Delight! O sweet enjoyment born
To mild eternity, shut in a three-fold shape delightful,
To wander in sweet solitude, enraptured at every wind.

Then across the ocean Enion brooded groaning. The golden rocks
    vegetated,
Infolding the bright woman from the desolating winds.

The last two lines are erased. The idea grew with contemplation. In the poem we no longer have merely the *virgo-scorpio*, the woman-serpent, the mixture of beauty and desire. The two attributes come forth and reveal themselves as twin children, who draw her life into themselves—or absorb her attributes—till she vanishes, and they appear as Time and Space in their first innocence.

In the above lines a few verbal alterations were made, not without significance. In the first line *brightness* was crossed out and *darkness* substituted. In the third *serpent* was struck out and replaced by *cherub*. In the fifth, *scaly armour* is made to give place to *rocky features*. The meaning is obvious The brightness of the serpent's gems (or the rainbow's colours), being food of the five senses, *is* darkness to the spirit. The cherub of mortal love *is* the serpent (compare second illustration to "Vala"), and the rocky features of the flesh or of literal scripture, or of morality are the same as the scales of Satan's natural armour.

On the other side in pencil is a mere scrap, also from Night I.

That I should hide thee with my power and d——

And now thou darkenest in thy presence; never from my sight——

There is no more here. A sketch beside it shows the back of a woman who is seated in the coils of a serpent, whose body seems to have grown from her thighs like the fishy half of a mermaid.

Another fragment begins with the passage in Night VIII., line 263.

The Lamb of God stood before Satan opposite.

The first ten lines are the same, but at the tenth and after we have the following :—

Such seemed the synagogue to distant view; around them stood
The daughters of Canaan and Moab, binding on the stones
Their victims, and with knives tormenting them, singing with tears
Over their victims. Thus was the Lamb of God condemned to death. ·
They nailed him upon the tree of Mystery, and weeping over him,

10 *

And mocking, then worshipping, calling him lord and king,
Sometimes as twelve daughters lovely, and sometimes as five
They stood in beaming beauty, and sometimes as one, even Rahab
Who is Mystery, Babylon the Great, Mother of Harlots,

The following continues the passage, but has all been struck out :—

And Rahab stripped off Luvah's robe from off the limbs of God,
Then first she saw his glory, and her harlot form appeared
In all its turpitude beneath the divine light——
She made herself a mantle of Luvah's robes,
Also the vegetative bodies which Enitharmon wove in her loins
Opened within the heart, and in the loins, and in the brain
To Beulah, and the dead in Beulah descended through their
    gates.
And some were woven one-fold, some two-fold, and some three-
    fold.
In head and heart and reins, according to their fittest order,

Of most mournful pity and compassion to the spectrous dead.
Darkness and sorrow covered all flesh; eternity was darkened.
Urizen sitting in his web of deceitful religion was tormented.
He felt the female death,—a dull and numbing stupor——

This brings us to line 262 of the same Night.

Such are the fragments found among the pages of the MS. of
" Vala."

TEXT OF "VALA."

AUTHOR'S AND EDITORS' VERBAL EMENDATIONS.

All alterations not marked as Blake's are by the Editors.

———◦◦◦◦———

NIGHT THE FIRST.

Line 23, after *Enion* Blake has inserted later reading, for the line
is, *I have hidden thee Jerusalem in silent contention.*

„ 93, Blake's other reading to *whence I emerged* is *of death and
hell;* it is struck out.

„ 104, later the words *For Jerusalem* were inserted after *a
tabernacle.*

„ 117, the word *on* after *But* omitted for metre.

„ 126, after *I, alone* before *remain* omitted.

„ 129, *are* transposed from after *eyes* to before *my.*

„ 132, *and* after *sinner* omitted.

„ 133, originally *Ah me! Wretched! What have I done?*

„ 133, the words *that all* after *find* omitted.

„ 142, *thee with* after *delight* omitted.

„ 145, *will* after *evermore* omitted.

„ 148, *and* inserted before *shrieking.*

„ 151, *all his lovely changing colours mix* altered later to *his scaly
armour softening* by Blake.

„ 161, The word *enormous* after *growing* omitted. The word *and*
before *growing* omitted by mistake.

„ 162, *richest* altered to *rich.*

Line 183, *in* after *drawing* inserted, an alteration required for metre, and suggested by *line* 185.

After line 186, a line not printed here, which read :—

> *Thus Enion gave them all her spectrous life in dark despair,*
> but *spectrous life* is erased, and there is no substituted expression.

Line 189, altered from *gave visions and sent heaven,* into *made windows into Eden,* by Blake.

„ 190, the last word, *out,* inserted.

„ 194, *their* after *kept* inserted.

„ 199, *all* after *Mercy, to* inserted.

„ 202, *after* before *sleepers* inserted ; *all* before *their* omitted.

„ 205, *and* before *named,* also *and* before *brooded* omitted.

„ 218, *fill* after *passions* inserted, *and fear* after *shame* omitted.

„ 222, stood thus : *She drove the females away from Los ; Los drove the males from her away.*

„ 254, stood : *First born for the sport and amusement of man now born to drink up all his powers.*

„ 274, *upon* for *on.*

„ 259 and 296, stood thus :

> *Of Light.   Silent the Prince of Light viewed Los, At length a*
> *- brooded*
> *Smile broke from Urizen, for Enitharmon brightened more and more.*

„ 305, stood thus : *Los answered furious, art thou one of those who when most complaisant—*

„ 353, ended thus : *wound round, sounding.*

„ 356, later alternative reading of Blake, *Ephraim called out to Tiriel ; Awake, oh brother Mountain!*

„ 358, 359, 360 and 361, stood thus :

> *Let us refuse the Plough and Spade, the heavy Roller, and spiked*
> *Harrow.   Burn all these cornfields.   Throw down all these fences*

Fattened on Human blood and drunk with wine of life is better far
Than all these labours of the harvest and the vintage. See this river.

Line 372, *wine, and* before *blood* inserted as belonging both to metre and to the correspondence with line 359.

,, 382, last words, *sandy deserts*, altered to *desert sands.*

,, 392, *an exudation* altered to *exuded*

,, 394, *there* before *he sank* inserted.

,, 399, *on* altered to *upon.*

,, 424, at the end of the line, *terrific raged* altered to *and raged.*

,, 434, *Snowdon* offered as a later and alternative reading for *Gilead* by Blake.

,, 434, last word, *sound*, inserted.

,, 442, *Beth Peor* altered later to *Conway Vale* by Blake.

,, 446, last word, *thus*, inserted.

,, 456, after *I, remaining* omitted.

,, 463, after *dictate, thou* inserted

,, 468, for *the deep,* Blake gives later, *the Atlantic.*

,, 487, last word, *before,* inserted.

,, 497, *conflict* altered to *fight, the* after *all* omitted.

,, 501, stood : *Deep, trouble, without end, separated from Beulah, far beneath.*

NIGHT THE SECOND.

Line 3, *Man* altered later to *Albion* by Blake.

,, 4, *Porches* later for *Ears* by Blake.

,, 28, after *gold, beaten* omitted.

,, 32, last word, *stood,* inserted.

,, 103, *Human Terror* altered to *Human Delusion* by Blake

,, 132, *globe* altered to *Pyramid* by Blake

,, 135, *centre* altered to *basement,* and both erased by Blake

,, 140, *Globe* altered to *Cube* by Blake.

,, 245, *orbs* altered later to *cubes* by Blake.

,, 270, *spring* altered later to *season* by Blake.

Line 338, *again* inserted.

„ 341, *even* inserted.

„ 348, *sounding* inserted.

„ 361, *abroad, even* inserted.

„ 394, *vintage* altered into *harvest*. The words are usually coupled together. In the present line the waggon of corn points out that *harvest* was the figure intended.

„ 415, *terrible* afterwards altered to *spectrous* by Blake.

NIGHT THE THIRD.

Line 1, *again* inserted.

„ 5, after *stars, thy* omitted.

„ 14, *Ahania* altered later to *shadow* by Blake.

„ 39, after *but, oh, how* omitted.

„ 41, after *Ahania, Listen to* altered to *hear*

„ 66, *He ceased* before *The shadowy* omitted; *hovered* altered to *hung*.

„ 68, *Fallen one* altered later to *Albion* by Blake.

„ 69, *Man arose* altered later to *Albion rose* by Blake.

„ 71, *Fallen one* altered later to *Albion* by Blake.

„ 79, *Ancient Man* altered later to *Albion* by Blake.

„ 81, *Man* altered later to *Albion* by Blake.

„ 83, *Fallen Man* altered later to *Albion* by Blake.

„ 91 to line 103 is written later, and belongs to the time when *Albion* became substituted for *Man*.

„ 104, 105, 106, were written also at this time. On the margin of the MS. they stood thus:

Albion closed the western gate and shut America out
By the Atlantic, for a curse and hidden horror.
And an altar of victims to sin and repentance.

Line 107. The rest of the poem is all first draught in Blake's handwriting. The previous part had been copied in a school-child text hand, probably by Blake and corrected here and there for mystical, but never for metrical reasons. A considerable time seems to have passed between the writing of the copied part, and the making of the corrections and the writing of all the rest. Judged by the ink and look of the hand, all from here onwards belongs to one period, and was written very rapidly, in sections of over fifty, or over a hundred lines at a time.

Line 147, before *blue, flame of* omitted.

„ 151, after *louder, was heard* inserted.

„ 157, the last word of the line, *struggling,* omitted, as repeated next.

„ 168, after *on, my ;* and after *that, now* inserted.

„ 182, after *hoped, that* inserted.

„ 185, after *remain, and then* omitted.

NIGHT THE FOURTH.

Line 21, last word, *then,* inserted.

„ 31, last word, *yet,* inserted.

„ 38, *he* altered to *him*

„ 45, *again* inserted.

„ 73, after *separate in, stench and* omitted.

„ 81, after *not, that* omitted.

„ 83, before *remember, well* omitted.

„ 85, after *fleeting, and* inserted.

„ 89, before *wedge, red* inserted.

„ 90, last word, *hard,* inserted.

„ 94, before *vibrations, strong* omitted.

„ 96, before last word, *form, piteous* omitted.

„ 98, before *soft embraced, saw and* inserted.

„ 105, *into the,* before *air,* altered to *to.*

„ 108, last words after *rage, as now,* inserted.

„ 116, after *Enitharmon, for* omitted.

„ 122, after *hope, the* inserted.

„ 167, before *iron, hard* inserted.

„ 168, after *rock, many* omitted.

„ 172, after *silent, his voice* omitted

Line 174, before *Los, always* inserted.

„ 180, after *to-night, and,* and after *day, and* omitted.

„ 191, before *wrath, his* omitted.

„ 199 to 204, stood thus:

> *Circling round the dark demon with howlings, dismay, and*
> *sharp blightings,*
> *The Prophet of Eternity beat on his iron links and links of brass*
> *And as he beat round the hurtling demon, terrified at the shape*
> *Enslaved humanity put on, he became what he beheld,*
> *Raging against Tharmas, his god, and uttering*

„ 207, before *wrath, ceaseless* omitted.

„ 208, before *surging, now* inserted.

„ 209, stood thus:

> *Settled, a lake, bright and shining, and clear, white as the snow.*

„ 219, after *shooting, out* inserted.

„ 221, first word, *and,* also after *passed over, and* inserted.

„ 223, after *deep, deep* omitted.

„ 225, last word, *him,* inserted.

„ 230, after *passed, over and* inserted.

„ 234, after *over, and* inserted.

„ 237, after *passed, over* inserted.

„ 240, first word, *then,* omitted; *of* before *thirst* inserted.

„ 241, after *passed, over and a state* inserted.

„ 244, before *dismay, howling* omitted.

„ 247, *saw,* altered to *beheld.*

„ 249, before *comforted, they were* omitted.

„ 253, *whatever,* altered to *whatsoever.*

„ 256, last word, *Thee,* omitted.

„ 264, for *Man, Albion,* by Blake.

„ 269, after *will, but* inserted.

„ 274, for *deeps beneath, starry wheels* by Blake.

„ 276, after *God, go forth and* inserted.

„ 280, *strong* altered to *mighty.*

„ 283, after *as, labouring* inserted.

Line 284, after *terrified, at* altered to *as he beheld.*

  ,, 286, after *doing, and* inserted.

After this line is a pencil note by Blake :—

    " *Bring in here the globe of blood, as in book of ' Urizen.'* "

NIGHT THE FIFTH.

Line   3, after *curses, and.* omitted.

  ,,   9, after *leaves, and* omitted.

  ,, 13 and 14, stood :

      Yet mighty bulk, and majesty, and beauty remained, but
        unexpansive,

      As far as highest Zenith from lowest Nadir, so far they shrunk.

  ,, 27, after *waxes, the* omitted.

  ,, 28, after *with, rending* omitted.

  ,, 29, after *cried, out* inserted.

  ,, 38, after *howlings, of* omitted.

  ,, 39, after *opened, looking* inserted.

  ,, 70, first word, *And,* inserted.

  ,, 71, after *darkness, and* omitted.

  ,, 72, *fed by* altered to *feeding on.*

  ,, 78, before *Los, and* omitted.

  ,, 85, before *succeeds, soon* inserted.

  ,, 90, before *formed, always* inserted.

  ,, 92, after *chain, of* altered to *made of the.*

  ,, 100, after *mountain, and* inserted.

  ,, 105, stood : *Tenfold. The demon's rage flamed tenfold forth, rending.*

  ,, 106, after *louder, and* altered to *ever.*

  ,, 107, before *waves, the* omitted.

  ,, 131, 132 stood :

      There waves the harvest and the vintage rejoices. *The springs*
      Flow into rivers of delight. *There the spontaneous flowers.*

  ,, 163, after *Nor, could* inserted.

  ,, 169, after *Orc, entering* omitted.

Line 170, after *Despair, and* omitted.

„   182, after *felt, the* omitted ; before *howling, fierce* omitted.

„   192, after *mountains, of Urizen* omitted.

„   198, *from my palace* transposed to precede *walked.*

„   199, after *Harpers, followed* altered to *came.*

„   200, after *light, composed* altered to *made.*

„   204, *round me hovered,* altered to *hovered round.*

„   219, before *I, lo* inserted.

„   220, after *sceptre, and ;* and after *vrown, me* omitted.

„   224, after *spears, of light* inserted.

„   227, after *lily, is* omitted.

„   236, after *steeds, of light* transposed from after *steeds* in line 235.

„   239, *perhaps this is* altered to *this may be.*

„   241, stood : *When thought is closed in caverns, love shall show its roots in deepest hell.*

NIGHT THE SIXTH.

Line   1, after *arose, and* inserted.

„   4, *unsated his thirst* altered to *his thirst being sated.*

„   8, after *sitting, wrapped,* and after *in, these* inserted.

„   9, *on* altered to *upon.*

„   12, first word, *answer,* altered to *answerest.*

„   31, *invited* altered to *made.*

„   34, after *and, the sons of,* and after *sent, them* omitted.

„   36, *colours* altered to *hues.*

„   37, stood thus : " *I will blackness ; for jewelry, hoary frost ; for ornament, deformity.*

„   38, after *sweet odours, stinking* altered to *smell.*

„   39, after *inarticulate, through frost* omitted.

„   42, after *and, the* inserted ; before *obstinacy, stubborn* omitted.

„   44, *obscure,* altered to *dark.*

„   47, first word, *then,* inserted.

„   49, *froze to solid* altered to *frozen.*

Line 73, before *chasms, horrible* omitted.

„ 76, after *brass, they* omitted.

„ 79, last word *descended,* altered to *went down.*

„ 82, *cruel* before *delight* omitted.

„ 83, *Urizen with* altered to *Urizen's.*

„ 87, *beheld* altered to *saw.*

„ 89, *The immense* altered to *immensity.*

„ 93, before *lightenings, or brooding* omitted.

„ 94, last word *penetrate* altered to *reach.*

„ 98, after *woes, and mutual* altered to *though he.*

„ 100, last word, *in,* omitted.

„ 101, *crowns of serpents* altered to *serpent crowns.*

„ 102, *lying in beds of sulphur* altered to *in sulphur beds.*

„ 103, *marching* altered to *march.*

„ 104, after *hundreds, and of;* and after *fifties, and of* omitted.

„ 105, before *their shoulders, them upon* altered to *on.*

„ 106, first word *in* omitted.

„ 109, first word *still* inserted.

„ 110, before *weary, faint* omitted, *he* transposed after *wandered.*

„ 111, *heaved with their torment,* altered to *their torment heaved.*

„ 112, before *castles, and* omitted; after *castles, built* omitted.

„ 113, after *There, he;* after *beheld, the;* after *tigers, and of* omitted.

„ 117, after *monsters, or* omitted.

„ 118, after *torment, shining and* omitted.

„ 119, before *columns, some;* after *stretched, out* omitted.

„ 120, *seeking ease* altered to *for ease.*

„ 121, before *inarticulate, but an* omitted.

„ 123, *heavy and dull,* altered to *dull and heavy.*

„ 130, *A rock, a cloud, a mountain* altered to *rock, mountain, cloud.*

„ 133, *The furrows and the field* altered to *or furrow'd field.*

„ 135, after *feet, and* omitted.

„ 140, last word, *former,* omitted.

„ 145, a third repetition of *falling* omitted by mistake,

„ 155, before *ending, and* omitted.

„ 164, before *who goes, the man* omitted.

Line 166, *Divine Hand* altered to *Hand Divine,* as elsewhere written
  ,, 172, *rise* altered to *arise.*
  ,, 175, after *earthquakes, and* omitted.
  ,, 177, after *vortex, fixing* omitted.
  ,, 192, after *head, downward* altered to *down.*
  ,, 194, after *labour, and* omitted.
  ,, 212, stood· *Shut up my powers.   Then a seed in the vast womb of*
        darkness.
  ,, 213, after *oblivion, brooding* omitted.
  ,, 215, before *remain, to* omitted.
  ., 216, after *labourer, of ages* omitted. ·
  ,, 218, after *promise, much* omitted.
  ,, 224, last word, *operate* altered to *work.*
  ,, 226 before *inward, away* omitted.
  ,, 329, 230 stood :
        For Urizen lamented over them in a selfish lamentation.
        Till a white woof covered his limbs from head to foot.
  ,, 231, after *snow, now* inserted.
  ,, 232, last word, *on,* inserted.
  ,, 236, from *vortex to vortex* altered to *the vortexes ;* after *drawn,*
        out omitted.
  ,, 237, *adjoined* altered to *joined.*
  ,, 239, after *bursting, with* inserted.
  ,, 246, after *down, again* inserted.
  ,, 247, after *anguish, as* inserted.
  ,, 248, first words *weaker and* altered to *that;* last word, *shrinking,*
        altered to *again to shrink.*
  ,, 249, after *Through, all ;* after *and, then* inserted.
  ,, 250 stood : *Ran through the abysses, rending the web, torment on*
        torment.
  ,, 252, before *hideous, his most* omitted.
  ,, 255, before *painful, ever* omitted.
  ,, 258, before *midday, the* omitted.
  ,, 259, last word, *darkness,* altered to *dark.*
  ,, 260, first words transposed from *shut up in stifling obstruction.*

Line 262, last words, *in vain*, inserted.

„ 263, before *black, the ;* and after *sea, around* omitted.

„ 265, before *deep, vast* omitted.

„ 276, after *Till, he* omitted.

„ 277, first word, *he*, inserted.

„ 278, *O'er wearied and in,* altered to *and wearied in his.*

„ 279, *climbed* transposed from before *with* to after *labour ;* the last word, *high,* being omitted.

„ 280 stood : *Till he beheld the world of Los from the peaked rock of Urthona.*

„ 283, *down the Vale of Urthona* altered to *down through Urthona's Vale.*

„ 298, after *skull, the while* inserted.

„ 299, last word, *loud,* inserted.

„ 302, *armies* transposed from after *fifty-two.*

„ 303 stood: *From the four cliffs of Urthona rise glowing around the Spectre.*

„ 310, *the dreary* altered to *their.*

„ 312, *returning back to Urizen* altered to *to Urizen returning.*

NIGHT THE SEVENTH.

Line 1, *rose* altered to *arose.*

„ 5, *Urizen silent descended to the caves* altered to *Urizen went silent down to caves.*

„ 6, before *fire, flaming* omitted.

„ 9, before *redounding, the* omitted.

„ 17, *Around* altered to *round.*

„ 23, before *thickest, robe of* inserted.

„ 25, stood: *Then bursting from his troubled head with terrible visages and flaming hair.*

„ 34, *Wherever* altered to *where'er ;* after *touch, and* inserted,

„ 36, *when he found himself* altered to *finding him.*

Line   40, after *seat, again* inserted.

  ,,   60, *throw* altered to *throwest;* last word, *now,* inserted.

  ,,   70, *Go forth* inserted.

  ,,   71, after *deep, for lo* omitted.

  ,,   77, before *weight, own* omitted.

  ,,   78, before *across, clear* inserted ; *horrible* altered to *horrid.*

  ,,   82, *still* transposed from before *obdurate* to after *resolved.*

  ,,   87, before *furious, here* inserted ; after *deep, for lo* omitted.

  ,,   89, before *diseases, the,* before *falling, of man,* omitted ; *upon*
            altered to *on.*

  ,,   94, before *ruin, dreadful* omitted.

  ,,   102, before *bread, the* omitted.

  ,,   108, *upon* altered to *on.*

  ,,   112, after *evaporate, away* inserted.

  ,,   113, *down* transposed from before to after *Enitharmon ; to* altered
            to *unto.*

  ,,   115, after *crust, of bread* omitted.

  ,,   117, after *hearts, far ;* after *milstone, is,* inserted.

  ,,   119, stood : *With labour and with abstinence, say he looks healthy*
            and happy

  ,,   121, after *will, soon* inserted.

  ,,   122, *with temper* transposed from after *live.*

  ,,   123, before *gracious, by* inserted.

  ,,   124, before *gifts, small* omitted ; after *want, a gift* omitted.

  ,,   125, *he smiles* transposed from before *if you hear.*

  ,,   127, after *water, are* altered to *must be.*

  ,,   128, last words *we can* omitted.

  ,,   129, first words, *we can,* inserted ; after *spaniels, that are* omitted.

  ,,   132, before *labyrinth, its* omitted.

  ,,   133, before *devouring, by strong* omitted.

  ,,   135, after *hypocrisy, already* omitted.

  ,,   142, stood : *Avaunt cold hypocrite ; I am chained, or thou could'st*
            not use me thus.

  ,,   145, last word *storms* omitted.

  ,,   148, *now* transposed from after *me ;* before *Urizen, oh* omitted.

Line 152, *Orc* transposed from before *creeping;* before *began,* *he* omitted. Blake partly corrected this line. He drew his pen through *creeping,* but offered no substitute, and left *he* as well as *Orc.*

,, 155, Blake altered *wisdom* into *affliction.*

,, 159, ended *thought himself sole author.*

,, 171, *over* altered to *o'er.*

,, 179, the same change.

,, 203, before *they, that ;* after *they, may,* omitted.

,, 208, stood : *For the shadow of Enitharmon descended,* &c.

,, 209, *shade* altered to *shadow, over* to *o'er.*

,, 213, before *poisonous, various* omitted.

,, 220, before *Enitharmon, Oh* inserted.

,, 223, before *discordant, loud* inserted.

,, 224, *on that dread day* inserted.

,, 225, *lightnings play'd* transposed from before *around.*

,, 228, stood : *And its birth in faintings and sleep, and sweet delusions of Vala.*

,, 231, before *print, the* omitted.

,, 232, before *I, behold* inserted.

,, 240, after *heaven, for* inserted.

,, 243, after *then, behold* omitted.

,, 245, after *pale, at sight* inserted.

,, 246, 247, stood :

From the enormity, and called them Luvah and Vala, turning down

The vales to find, &c.

,, 252, last word, *pastures,* altered to *fields.*

,, 256, stood : *Then from its hinges, uttering its final groan, all Beulah fell.*

,, 260, *cavern dark* altered to *cave.*

,, 266, *tempests* altered to *storms.*

,, 267, *upon* altered to *on.*

,, 270, after *spirit, in the garden* omitted.

,, 271, before *dwelt, there* omitted ; before *joy, mutual* inserted.

11

Line 273, after *waters, this* omitted.

   " 274, after *them, alternate* altered to *have.*

   " 276, before *morn, dread* omitted.

   " 277, after *divided, for the* omitted.

   " 285, *and there divided* altered to *divided there.*

   " 286, after *I was, divided* omitted.

   " 290, *but still my spirit* altered to *my spirit still.*

   " 299, after *unite, again* omitted.

   " 301, before *annihilated, and* omitted ; *never can* altered to *cannot.*

   " 302, last word, *brutish,* should be omitted.

   " 303, first word, *brutish,* inserted ; after *ravening, and devouring*
                   omitted.

   " 304, after *eyes are, always* omitted.

   " 305, *for anything but,* altered into *except for.*

   " 306, after *dead, for* omitted.

   " 311, after *thus they, conferred* omitted.

   " 314, ended : *Los wept, and his fierce soul was terrified.*

   " 315, ended : *nor could his eyes perceive.*

   " 317, last words, *she ran,* omitted.

   " 318, after *raving, about* altered to *ran through.*

   " 320, last word, *broken,* omitted.

   " 321, after *gates, broke* altered to *broken.*

   " 322, *shadow shuddering* altered to *shade.*

   " 326, before *war, with* inserted.

   " 327, last word, *shadow,* altered to *shade.*

   " 330, *topmost* altered to *top ; shooting* to *shoot.*

   " 332, first words, *But then,* omitted.

   " 335, *first* transposed from after *spectre* to after *brother.*

   " 338, *terrible Demon* altered to *Demon dread.*

   " 339, *consummating by pains and labours* altered to *to consume by*
                   pains.

   " 340, *back returning* altered to *come.*

   " 341, *To life Eternal* altered to *back to Eternal life ;* before *self*
                   real omitted.

   " 343, last word but one *upon* altered to *on.*

Line 345, before *buried, though* omitted.

„ 346, last words, after *speak, and be silent* omitted.

„ 348, after *heart and, in* inserted.

„ 349, before *in Eternity, it was* omitted.

„ 350, *and consummated* altered to *consumed.*

„ 352, stood, *When I was a ravening, and hungry thirsting cruel lust and murder.*

„ 354, *evaporate* altered to *vanish.*

„ 356, stood : *Art nothing, being created continually by Mercy and love divine.*

„ 357, after *Los, furious* omitted.

„ 359, after *convinced, can still* omitted.

„ 360, after *power, even* omitted.

„ 373, after *Los, labouring* omitted ; after *builded, the* inserted.

„ 375, after *heaven,* and after *beneath, and* omitted.

„ 377, after *atmosphere, sublime* omitted.

„ 379, after *creeping, and* omitted.

„ 381, before *spake, thus* omitted.

„ 383, before last word, *knew, I* inserted.

„ 384, before *ransom, a* omitted.

„ 387, last word *thou* inserted.

„ 391, before *given, surely* inserted.

„ 392, after *spectre, in part* omitted ; last word *him* omitted.

„ 393, first words, *being a,* altered to *as.*

„ 395, first word *of* omitted.

„ 396, *beheld* altered to *saw.*

„ 398, after *spectre, of Urthona* omitted ; before *I am, Behold* inserted.

„ 400, before *punishment, curse and* omitted.

„ 403, last word, *thus,* inserted.

„ 405, first word, *for,* omitted ; *without a created body* transposed.

„ 409, before *behold, look* omitted.

„ 413, before *trembling, from* inserted.

„ 414, before *injuries, ancient* omitted.

„ 415, before *have, surely* omitted,

11 *

Line 416, stood: *Often enough to commence thy jealousy in fear and terror.*

" 417, *be* transposed from before *patient; because* altered to *for.*

" 422, *uttermost* altered to *last.*

" 423, last word, *out,* omitted.

" 424, first word, *out,* inserted; *all who behold* altered to *who see.*

" 425, *should* transposed from before *in futurity;* before *in heavens, have done* omitted.

" 429, after *created, many* omitted.

" 430, before *sighing, and* omitted.

" 431, before *war, furious* omitted.

" 432, before *weeping, the* omitted.

" 433, before *piteous, those* omitted; before *happy, in* omitted; *obscure* for *obscurity.*

" 435, *fabricate* altered to *make.*

" 438, before *sons, and* omitted.

" 440, *Ancient* altered to *old*

" 442, before *Wonder, lovely terrible Los* omitted; after *eternity, oh* omitted.

" 446, first words, *and then,* omitted.

" 448, after *fabricate, these* inserted.

" 449, *themselves* altered to *them.*

" 450, before *may live, through them* inserted.

" 451, before *inspired, divine* omitted.

" 454, *upon* altered to *on.*

" 469, last word, *reposing,* omitted

" 470, before *ranks, out the* omitted.

" 474, before *forged, he* omitted.

" 475, before *scales, in* omitted.

" 476, before *Los, but,* and before *refused, he,* omitted.

" 486, after *could not, so* inserted.

" 491, after *hands, much* inserted.

" 492, ended: *He beheld him as an infant.*

" 493, *breathed* transposed from before *from; within* altered to *in.*

" 494, before *night, darkest* omitted.

Line 495, after *rock, behold* inserted.

  ,,   497, after *revolved, at last* inserted.

  ,,   499, last word, *me*, omitted.

  ,,   508, before *sounding, hoarse* omitted.

  ,,   518, *secrecy*, altered to *secrets; they bore* transposed from after
           lamps.

  ,,   521, before *lion, furious* omitted.

  ,,   541, *arise* altered to *rise.*

  ,,   547, *was* transposed from before *divided.*

  ,,   551, last words, *in sighs*, inserted.

  ,,   552, first words, *in sighs*, omitted; the line continued, *and
           sobbings, till all divided I was divided.*

  ,,   553, *lived* transposed from before *in my bosom.*

  ,,   558, last word, *them*, omitted.

  ,,   563, before *moon, distant* omitted.

  ,,   565, *into the* altered to *in.*

  ,,   567, before *sun, bright* ; before *mist, a,* omitted.

  ,,   571, after *terror, to me* omitted.

  ,,   579, before *hate, his* inserted.

  ,,   593, *within the* altered to *in.*

  ,,   594, before *writing, therein* inserted.

  ,,   597, before *bull, strong* inserted.

  ,,   606, after *places, that* omitted.

  ,,   607, *appointed* transposed from after *time.*

  ,,   616, *around* altered to *round.*

  ,,   618, after *arise, again* inserted.

  ,,   622, before *despairing, is* inserted.

  ,,   640, last word, *steeds,* altered after to *clouds* by Blake.

  ,,   648, last words, *the slain*, transferred to first of 649.

  ,,   668, last word, *workmanship*, altered to *work.*

  ,,   672, before *the, all* omitted.

  ,,   734, the words *of Orc* added later by Blake.

  ,,   748, before *swimming*, and again before *falling, or* omitted.

  ,,   770, before *eagle, pinioned ;* and after *night, season*, omitted.

NIGHT THE EIGHTH.

Line   7, after *shapes, were seen* added.

  ,,   22, first word, *and,* omitted.

  ,,   155, *the human form* altered later to *these terrors* by Blake.

  ,,   164, after *never, come* inserted.

  ,,   430, *Urthona* altered later to *the spectre* by Blake.

  ,,   503, first word *do* inserted.

NIGHT THE NINTH.

Line   17, after *hills, are all* inserted.

  ,,   59, after *called, to* inserted.

  ,,   60, after *heard, them* omitted.

  ,,   69, last word, *freds,* transposed from first of next line.

  ,,   82, after *intense, abroad* inserted.

  ,,   87, first word, *issuing,* inserted.

  ,,   129, after *arise, to* altered to *into.*

  ,,   130, before *souls, of* inserted; before *great, oh !* is wanted.

  ,,   137, before *strong, thou* inserted.

  ,,   155, last words, *to be burned,* altered to *to burn.*

  ,,   218, after *female, also* inserted.

  ,,   229, before *universe, bursting* should have been omitted.

  ,,   230, 231, lines untouched, but should have been printed thus :—

> All things revived flew from their centres : then the rattling bones
>
> To bones join, shaking and convulsed : the shivering clay breathes.

  ,,   262, before *intense, on* omitted.

  ,,   284, before *flames, all* inserted.

  ,,   285, omitted in error.

  ,,   344, after *Urizen rose, up* omitted.

  ,,   344, after *hands, his feet* omitted.

  ,,   348, before *earth, the* inserted.

Line 391, last words, *but for thee,* altered to *were it not for thee.*

„ 432, after *freshly, you* inserted, and misprinted *yon.*

„ 439, before *birds, oh* inserted.

„ 445, after *come, near* inserted.

„ 451, after *himself, laid down* inserted.

„ 456, *and saw* altered to *and looked and saw.*

„ 461, first word, *round,* altered to *around.*

„ 470, after *went, up* omitted.

„ 473, before *follow, often* inserted.

„ 480, after *mourned, faint* omitted.

„ 504, *round* altered to *around ;* last words, *over them,* omitted.

„ 560, before *dreadful, the* inserted.

„ 563, last words repeating *he exulted* omitted.

„ 599, before *solid, the* omitted, before *way, fibrous* inserted.

„ 600, before *joys, the ;* after *existence, and ;* before *stems, tree,* inserted.

„ 601, and 602, stood :

> *Rear on the mountains stem after stem. The scaly newt creeps*
> *From the stone, and the armed fly springs from the rocky crevice.*

„ 603, after *spider, and* inserted.

„ 604, before *delight, joy and* omitted,

„ 605, before *the tender, lo* inserted.

„ 606, after *round, about ;* after *brighten, on,* inserted ; last word *mountains* altered to *hills.*

„ 607, after *throng up, through ;* after *valley, and the* inserted ; last word, *forests,* altered to *woods.*

„ 611, stood : *over the ruined worlds,* &c.

„ 612, first word, *then,* inserted.

„ 615, before *night, all the,* omitted.

„ 618, stood : *not born for the sport and amusement of Man but soon to drink up all his powers.*

Compare Night I., line 254, also in this list.

„ 626, *nature* corrected later to *science* by Blake.

„ 643, stood : *Beneath they saw their sons and daughters wondrous inconceivable.*

Line 682, after *here, so soon* omitted.

„   684, after *house, in joy* inserted.

„   722, *rose singing,* altered to *sang.*

„   729, before *ravening, distracted* omitted.

„   741, before *leopard, spotted* omitted.

„   743, after *bury them,* omitted ; *making* after *grots* altered to
          with.

„   759, first words, *who lives,* transferred to end of line above.

„   760, *show* altered to *showing.*

„   764, after *love, and these* omitted.

„   768, after *he said, he said,* repetition, omitted.

„   772, after *gold, gold were* omitted.

DESCRIPTIVE NOTES TO "VALA."

The following notes assist the comprehension of the growth of the idea:—

The early pages of "Vala," up to Night III., line 106, were probably written in 1797, all but the opening lines which occupy space when a complete erasure has been made.

Lines 9 and 10 are even more recent, and are in pencil. So is line 18. In the margin occur two lines that seem to have no place in the text but rather to be an author's note of visionary experience. They are written side ways—

> The men have received their death-wounds and their emanations are fled
> To me for refuge, and I cannot turn them out for pity's sake.

Lines 38, 39, and 40 are later than the rest.

Lines 41 to 45 (inclusive) in pencil opposite the serpent's mouth in design, seem to be intended for the words that Tharmas wept into his cloud.

Lines 46 to 57 inclusive, sideways on margin, later than text.

Lines 66 to 98 inclusive, marked later by Blake for erasure.

Lines 99 to 122 inclusive, left to stand as the story of the incident.

Lines 123 to 131 inclusive, obliterated. The following added to them and separately obliterated.

> So wailed she, trembling before her own created phantasm,
> Which animating times on times by the force of her sweet song,
> Reared . . . . . .

The last altered before erasure to—

> But standing on the rocks her woven shadow glowing bright,
> Reared . . . . . .

Instead of these, namely 99 onwards, the lines 197 to 211 inclusive, were to have been inserted there. They are of later date.

Lines 132 to 154 inclusive, left to stand as the story.

Lines 155 to 157 inclusive, crossed out in pencil by Blake.

Lines 158 to 164, to stand.

Lines 165 to 168, later. See fragment No. I.

Lines 169 to 177, not to stand.

Lines 178 to 186, not to stand.

Lines 187 to 196, later.

Lines 197 to 211 should perhaps have been placed as already indicated, before 132. But they have no real position here at all, being a late paragraph written separately

Lines 212 to 224, to stand.   Then an erased lines—

Nine years they view the glowing spheres reading the visions of Beulah.

Then comes a note that the next line, that numbered 225, is to be the beginning of Night II. If this division had remained as final, Night I. would, after all erasures, have been disproportionately brief.

Lines 225 to 262, to stand

Lines 263 to 270 afterwards erased by Blake

No long erasures restored after this, all to stand.

Lines 305 to 315, later.

Lines 331 to 337, later

Line 348 erased in pencil

After line 397 the words—

End of the First Night,

are written This is the second place marked for the end of the First Night.

Lines 398 to 427 is a much later fragment, written on two sides of a piece of paper. At the end of line 413 we read for the third time—

End of the First Night.

Lines 428 to end of Night I are much later than the former pages, and are written on another kind of paper Of these lines, 488 is an addition to the rest, made later in pencil

Attributing these lines to Night I. at all is conjectural. They have no other place. They were written later than the pages of Night II., which follow, but belong to the date of the lines 398, &c , which are marked as belonging to this Night.

By comparing the fragments of MS. given above on the Hermaphrodites, and the woman-serpent, with the passages marked for erasure by Blake, in the early pages of Night I., three stages of symbolic idea are seen like successive growths in the poet's mind. Beauty, the female, and Desire, the male—called Enion and Tharmas —are the hero and heroine of the story. They are *Virgo* and *Scorpio;* they mingle, and are seen as Hermaphrodite. They mingle more simply and are seen as marriage. Finally, they separate into Feeling and Change, and appear as Enitharmon and Los, the infants afterwards "known to mortals" (note the *to mortals*) as Time and Space Blake is seen here still groping among his visions for the best expression of what his reflections told him must be their true meaning.

NIGHT THE SECOND.

Night II was headed Night the First, and the word *First* erased. It is early in date except a few insertions

Line 4 is later. So is line 8. So are lines 23 and 32, added in pencil. Lines 33 to 60 are also of later date. At 61 the MS , as originally copied out in fair hand, continues. Line 69 is later, in pencil. Line 95, last words, and 96, 97, and 98 are later, and so is 101. The first MS. read thus—

> She bore me sons and daughters,
> And they have taken her away and hid her from my sight.
> They have surrounded me with walls of iron and brass,—
> Discordant principles of love and hate. I suffer affliction
> Because I love, for I was lone, and hatred awakens in me.

The speaker is Luvah in the furnaces, whose walls of iron and brass are thus explained clearly.

Line 108 is later. Lines 117 to 130 are later. The MS. continued originally so that 116 preceded 131. Lines 164 and 165 are later.

Lines 169 to 206 form also a passage written later.

Lines 239 and 240, later; line 240 in pencil.

Lines 252 to 256, later.

Lines 260 to 277, later. Line 280, later.

Lines 293 to 374, all later. Line 376, also later.

According to Blake's counting at an early period—not known when—line 150 as printed was marked as 100, and line 283 as 200.

NIGHT THE THIRD.

Here lines 28 and 29 were erased and line 30 inserted in the later period of the MS.

Lines 91 and 92 are later. The word *Albion* was perhaps *Ahania*.

Lines 104 to 106, about closing the Western Gate, are later, in pencil.

At "'Am I not God,' said Urizen," &c., begins the portion of the MS. not copied out, but from now to the end apparently of a date *nearly* that of the insertions. Though another change, probably at their exact date, occurs in Night VI.

Line 130 and 131, later.

NIGHT THE FOURTH.

The lines of the seventh age, 242, 245, are later, but seemingly by oversight. The lines 246 to 278 are apparently later. Of these, the line 271 is later still, in pencil, thus dating the pencil insertions as belonging to a third period, the pen insertions of the early books being probably made at Felpham, or when the MS. was resumed. This would account for its being in itself a sort of compound of all Blake's other books, except "Milton" and "Jerusalem," which are enriched by scraps taken from "Vala," but are not summarised in it, except in so far as the myth of Satan and Palamabron is concerned, an episode in the earlier part of "Milton" designed when "Milton" was still intended to be a poem in twelve books   "One thing of real consequence I have accomplished by coming into the country, which is to me consolation enough," writes Blake in January, 1802, " I have re-collected all my scattered thoughts on art." " Vala," in its corrected and enlarged form, seems to have been the noting-place of this re-collection.

Here and there, pages written after the Felpham time seem to have been added to the later nights.

NIGHT THE FIFTH.

This is practically of one date.

NIGHT THE SIXTH.

Also practically of one date   Some lines omitted, in arranging for press the various insertions, will be found among the *errata*

The word Southern in line 137 is confusing. They were his children, and so southern, yet they were in the North with him. Compare line 78.

Lines 218, 227 and 228 are late   Line 237 is in pencil.

After line 250 a later handwriting than that used since Night III. Line 107 characterizes the rest of the MS   It resembles that of the alterations, such as the change of " Man " to " Albion," &c.

In this Night, on facsimile No. 7, a hint of faint words may, perhaps, be detected on the right-hand margin. They are a little couplet in pencil, of which one word, illegible in the original, looks like nothing but an impossible term, and causes the couplet to read as follows.—

> Till thou dost (?)injure the distrest
> Thou shalt never have peace within thy breast.

After fruitless efforts, we reluctantly leave the deciphering of the word that cannot be *injure* to future editors. It would have biographical interest.

NIGHT THE SEVENTH.

This, like Night I., was written in fragments, and their order indicated by Blake ·in a series of contradictory directions. It has been arranged for press conjecturally, and the beginning taken according to Blake's last idea. The first lines bear the number of the Night at their head, and are the third commencement destined for it

The lines 115 o 134 are later, a concrete illustration of the preceding abstractions. Line 135 succeeded 114 originally.

In line 287, "From Enion's brain," is later.

Lines 300 to 306 are later.   Here the MS. is resumed after a pause, but all at about the same date.

Lines 325 to 327 are later.

Line 494 begins a fresh portion of MS. It is called line 153 of Blake's first draught of this Night, and is another commencement.

Line 609 ends a page. The MS. calls it 272, and directs that one of the beginnings shall be brought here, and used as the remainder of the Night.

In what follows, lines 620, 621 and 623 are later, and also lines 676 and 677.

Line 692 is later, also lines 698, 704 and 708.

Beside the passage that ends with line 694 a pencil note, that has no place in the poem, occurs on the margin :—

> Unorganised innocence an impossibility :
> Innocence dwells with Wisdom, but never with Ignorance.

The passage 729 to 743 is later.

Line 786 is the only possible end of Night VII.

NIGHT THE EIGHTH.

In this Night the line 4 is later, and in defiance of the lack of a full stop, lines 10 to 15 were to be erased, but are restored, as they were never re-written.

Line 100 is later. Lines 104 to 106 are later. Lines 108 to 112 are an insertion, apparently later.

Lines 197 to 235 is a later fragment on other papers, but its place for insertion marked here. See facsimile No. 15, where line 255 bears the early numbering, as 195.

Line 252 is later. Line 261, containing the four Zoas by name, erased, as these are united, not cut off when the spiritual body is revealed.

Lines 263 to 409 is an enlargement of a late fragment. See addenda. Of this enlargement the line 273 is still later, and lines 275 to 290 are later. Lines 325 to 334 are later.

The passage " But when Rahab," &c., line 335, was written three leaves earlier. The MS. directs us to take it from there and place it here, to line 408. This terminates the enlargement of the fragment. The original MS. had, when sketched, the line 609 as next after 263. It continues without a break to end of Night VIII.

NIGHT THE NINTH.

The heading of this Night suggests that it was conceived at the time when the title of the poem was to have been (writing be a guide) The Death and Judgment of the Ancient Man. The name " Albion" not being used in the MS. here.

In this Night, line 32 is later, also line 50. Lines 113 and 127 are later. They seem utterances produced by the realization of the subject of the poem in the mind of the poet as he sat reading his own manuscript. The same may be said of lines 139 and 140, also insertions.

The lines 200 to 202 are also insertions. In the next line it is noteworthy that The Eternal Man is the phrase employed. " Albion " is not used after Night IV.

Line 256 is later, and also lines 354 to 256.

Lines 328 and 329, later; also lines 378, 379 and 383.

Lines 487 to 490 are also later. Line 584 is later, also line 617, repeated from an earlier page.

No other changes of the MS., other than the corrections of separate words given in the notes on the texts above, have been found in Blake's hand as contemporary with the writing itself.

FATE IN ARCADIA :· AND OTHER POEMS   BY EDWIN J.
ELLIS.

Illustrated by the Author. A Large Paper Edition, limited to 100
copies, which contains nine additional Illustrations, printed by the
Author at his own press, 33 Illustrations in all. Impl. 8vo. Price 21s.
    An Edition in crown 8vo.   Price 7s 6d.

The Academy says :—" His poetry is distinctly a criticism upon life, often tantalizing
by the fantastic subtlety of its thought, but just as often fascinating by the beauty
of its poetic form. There is indeed enough of the stuff of thought in this volume
to furnish forth many of our contemporary poets."

The Artist says :—" The ' Eros ' is a virile conception, strongly handled, and the
groups facing the 63rd and 123rd pages show considerable sense of composition.
. . . ' The Shepherd ' is a distinct success, and the Christ-subject, if not treated
to our satisfaction, is at least handled with dignity."

St. James's Gazette.—" Mr. Ellis is able to express himself much better with
pencil than with pen."

Daily Chronicle :—" Though his designs have a certain quaint prettiness, his
poems show, we think, the greater promise."

The Bookseller :—" It might seem a reflection upon Mr. Ellis's poetry to praise
the designs with which he accompanies them, but such is not the case ; the
illustrations are worthy of the verse, and that is saying much, for the verse is far
above the average."

The Speaker :—" A work likely to attract much attention. It is embellished with
twenty-four full-page illustrations by the author, which seem to be real embellish-
ments, the product of a very unusual gift."

The New Review :—" Mr. Ellis has already learnt to feel for himself . . . . and he
is able not only to feel, but to think for himself—which is a rare accomplishment."

OTHER WORKS BY W. B. YEATS.

THE WANDERINGS OF OISIN. Ballads, Lyrics, and Dramatic
    Sketches. (*T. Fisher Unwin.*)
    " At once the words begin to murmur and sing, and skim before the breath of
poetic inspiration ; again the common is made uncommon, the old miracle is
wrought anew ; you are carried away into rainbow-coloured lands of fantasy, there
is a blowing of magic horns, a lovely enchantress is speaking in silken phrases, the
swords of heroes are ringing in onsets, and the work-a-day world is for a time
forgot."—*Scots Observer.*

JOHN SHERMAN AND DHOYA. (Pseudonym Library. *T. Fisher Unwin.*)

"Clever as John Sherman is, cleverness seems almost an odious quality to ascribe to pathos so unassertive, humour so delicate, and observation so penetrative. . . . . *Dhoya* is not a story, and is far slighter. It is an Irish legend, or apologue, of the days when there were giants in the land, and fairies, and magical influences. If there are any admirers of *Ossian* that yet remain among us we would ask them to read *Dhoya*, and purpend thereon."—*Saturday Review.*

THE COUNTESS KATHLEEN, and Various Legends and Lyrics. (*T. Fisher Unwin.*)

"In these poems the immediate charm is their haunting music, which depends not upon any wealth of words, but upon a subtle strain of music in their whole quality of thoughts and images, some incommunicable beauty, felt in the simplest words and verses. Collins, Blake, Coleridge, had the secret of such music; Mr. Yeats sings somewhat in their various ways, but with a certain instinct of his own, definitely Irish. The verse is stately and solemn, without any elaboration; the thought falls into a lofty rythm. Or the verse is wistful and melancholy, an aërial murmur of sad things without any affectation. . . . . . In all the poems, even the most mystical in thought, there is a deep tone of sympathy with the world's fortunes or with the natures of living things; a curious tender gladness at the thought of it all. The poet finds:

"In all poor foolish things that live a day,
Eternal Beauty wandering on her way."

"His ballads are full of this natural sentiment, shown rather in their simple mention of facts and things, as an old poet might mention them, than in any artificial simplicity. There is humour in his verse: a sense of the human soul in all things, a fearless treatment of facts, a gentleness towards life, because it is all wonderful and nothing is despicable. And through the poems there pierces that spiritual cry, which is too rare and fine to reach ears satisfied with the gross richness of a material muse."—*Academy.*

G. NORMAN AND SON, PRINTERS, HART STREET, COVENT GARDEN, LONDON.

LIBRARY OF THE UNIVERSITY OF CALIFORNIA

NN 447
B6 E4
v. 3

Lightning Source UK Ltd.
Milton Keynes UK
UKHW022250110722
405715UK00003B/70